A HISTORY OF THE DEMOCRATIC SOCIALIST PARTY AND RESISTANCE

VOLUME 2: 1972-92

AGAINST THE STREAM

JOHN PERCY

Published in 2017 by Interventions

Interventions is a not-for-profit, independent left wing book
publisher. For further information:

    www.interventions.org.au
    admin@interventions.org.au
    Trades Hall Suite 68
    54 Victoria Street
    Carlton VIC 3053

Printed and bound in Australia by ImpactDigital

National Library of Australia Cataloguing-in-Publication entry

    Creator: Percy, John (John Knowles), 1946-2015 author.

    Title: Against the stream : the socialist workers party, 1972-92 /
    John Percy ; Allen Myers, editor.

    ISBN: 9780994537836 (paperback)

    Series: History of the Democratic Socialist Party and Resistance ;
    Volume 2.

    Subjects: Democratic Socialist Party (Australia)--History.
    Socialist parties--Australia--History.
    Political parties--Australia.

    Other Creators/Contributors:
    Myers, Allen, 1942- editor.

CONTENTS

FOREWORD

John Percy died in August 2015, before he had completed this book.

I had helped with the editing of the first volume of his planned three volumes on the history of the Democratic Socialist Party and Resistance, and had agreed to edit this volume.

John had written different parts of the work at different times and as he was able to make time to do so, based on all the constraints faced by most writers of non-fiction, as well as the demands on his time for his political activity, which continued until his final hospitalisation. Some parts of the book were basically finished and ready for publication; others were not much more than a note on the topics to be covered; and there was everything between those two extremes.

However, by far, the majority of uncompleted sections of the book contained shorter or longer statements of the points that John intended to make and references to documents – usually *Direct Action* articles – that explained or illustrated those points. The most time-consuming part of my task has been to read those articles and then decide how to summarise or quote from them appropriately.

This is still, as much as it could be in the circumstances, John's personal history. Where John cites things from memory, I have usually left the text that way, rather than trying to hunt out documents that might confirm or contradict his memory; to do otherwise would have delayed publication for too long. In a very few places where reliable sources of information were easily accessible, I have provided a short summary in the text; these are enclosed in curly brackets: {}. My insertions of endnotes are marked with my initials.

Even within those limitations, this volume is not as complete as John intended it to be. There are many places in the text where he left himself a reminder to introduce or expand on this or that point, but without indicating a documentary source, if there was one. In such situations, I have regretfully had to leave the reminder unheeded. One of the biggest such areas concerns what other left groups were doing at any point. That is referred to in many parts of this volume, but John clearly intended to write more on this subject, particularly to compare how different strategies and tactics pursued by different groups succeeded or failed relative to our successes and failures.

This was because John's primary concern in writing history was to contribute ideas and experiences that might help today's and tomorrow's political activists to conduct their struggles. As the convinced Marxist that he was, John believed that we have the capacity, and the need, to learn from history.

Most of what John wrote for this volume – and what he intended to write – was well documented by numerous endnotes – well over 700 of them. But, as he wrote at the beginning of the notes, they were intended primarily for editors' checking, and should be removed before publication because this is a book for activists, not for pure academics. Accordingly, references to articles in *Direct Action* or other publicly available publications have mostly been incorporated into the text, where I hope they will be a helpful reminder of the dates of events being discussed rather than an annoying interruption. Citations of SWP/DSP internal publications have mostly been dropped as of no practical use to the great majority of readers, who would not have access to those documents.

Readers will soon discover that in both the SWP/DSP and SYA/Resistance, pseudonyms were used frequently. There were a number of reasons for this: to avoid the risk of sacking or discrimination in members' jobs, to protect their membership in the ALP (which eventually banned us from membership), so that comrades could write about themselves (for instance, if reporting on a talk they had given to a conference) or sometimes simply to prevent the same name from appearing on too many articles in that issue.

When the text refers to a publication with a signed article, that name is cited; if the name is a known pseudonym, the real name is given in parentheses. John had prepared a list of the real name behind many pseudonyms, and some others I was able to find by inquiring of people who were members of the SWP or Resistance during the relevant period. But there remain more than a few names that are or may be pseudonyms and for which the real name is not known.

Finally, a word on acknowledgments: Not having finished this volume, John did not leave a list of those who had assisted. But I am certain that John's most heartfelt appreciations would have been, among the living, to his long-time partner Eva To, and among those no longer with us, to his brother Jim. I know there are many others that John would have named, but I cannot know them all, and to name those I do know would be an injustice to those omitted. Since I have been involved in the project, numerous former members of the DSP, current members of Socialist Alternative and comrades associated with Interventions have made further valuable contributions; for the same reason, they are not listed here by name. You know who you are, and I hope you understand how much your contributions are appreciated.

Allen Myers

INTRODUCTION

Volume 1 of this history, focusing on our tendency's origins and the early years of Resistance and the founding of our party, was published in early 2005,[1] and I had already drafted the outlines and taken some notes for Volumes 2 and 3. But shortly after publication, a major political struggle broke out in the Democratic Socialist Party. This is not the place to recount that struggle and its aftermath, except to mention that those of us in the minority in that struggle were expelled from the DSP and, in 2013, united with Socialist Alternative just before the opening of its Marxism conference in Melbourne.

Reclaiming, reviving and benefiting from the positive traditions of the DSP and Resistance is certainly a task for Socialist Alternative. Younger revolutionaries being spurred into action today by the horrors and inequities of capitalism can learn from the experiences of those of us who struggled in previous decades – avoiding our mistakes, not having to learn the lessons all over again and being inspired by the successes and struggles we went through.

A political history like this of course will have to maintain a balance between the history of the party, and the main lessons and themes from that history, and the political developments in Australia and the world, and the struggles and campaigns and issues. My main focus is on building the party, and not a general history of those years.

Nevertheless, while concentrating on our party history and party building, I hope the book gives readers a feeling for the main political events and developments, the ups and downs in the class struggle.

And even though I was centrally involved in the organisation and direction of the party in this period, I also acknowledge the story is going to be distorted because of the particular sources I had access to. The documents, talks and reports will inevitably skew the balance in my direction, as well as my memory favouring particularly interesting stories and anecdotes. Also, I was based in Melbourne from 1982 to 1991, and not directly involved in the weekly national leadership meetings, although I received news of any important developments and participated in all the National Committee meetings and conferences and in some of our international work.

But I hope the story will be interesting and the lessons useful to a wider readership, not just those of us who have been engaged at some time in this narrative, or those who are committed activists today. I hope the history of this struggle will inspire new young comrades to take up the banner.

The story so far

To make the second volume comprehensible to readers who haven't read Volume 1, or haven't read it recently, I'll briefly sketch out the main events of our development in 1965-1972 in very condensed form.

The first chapter of Volume 1 describes the revolutionary traditions we drew on, from the Industrial Workers of the World, the early Communist Party and the old Trotskyist movement.

All these traditions were important, but to build an organisation able to respond to the needs of the times, a new start was necessary: the old Trotskyist group was tiny and divided, unable to relate to the changing political conditions and the worldwide radicalisation of youth, and never very good at party building.

Around the world, but especially in countries like the USA and Australia, young people were in revolt against the stifling social, cultural and political mores of the older generation. Capitalist universities were changing; students were demanding their right to a decent education and defending the rights of others; in the US, the civil rights movement exploded in defence of the rights of Black people; and the protests against the war in Vietnam were spurred on by the heroic resistance of the Vietnamese people against the military might of the US and allied invaders. The '60s and '70s were a special period of radicalisation of young people.[2]

The old Trotskyist group in Australia was unable to recruit and build a revolutionary Marxist party. For that, a democratically functioning organisation was necessary, and an ability to relate to the new layers and new political issues, especially conscription and the Vietnam War and the escalating protests against it.

Some of us who had joined the Sydney University Labor Club, traditionally controlled by the Communist Party of Australia, generally sons and daughters of CPA members, were recruited and won to Trotskyism in 1965 by some comrades from the old Fourth International section. We were influenced by Bob Gould, who had set up the Vietnam Action Committee and organised protests against the war and provided us with overseas magazines and books, and by Ian MacDougall, who helped give classes on Marxism. Although we were won to a Trotskyist perspective, there was not really a group that we could join, just a loose association of former members of the old Trotskyist group, the minority remaining after the majority led by Nick Origlass had split from the Fourth International in 1965.

In 1966 we won leadership of the Sydney University Labor Club, and started republishing the club's magazine, *Left Forum*, which I edited. My brother Jim, who was still in high school in 1965, also got involved and played an increasingly central role. From early on, we were pushing those who recruited us to Trotskyism to establish a proper party group. It was an increasingly hectic political pace, with Vietnam demonstrations and protests on many other issues – a real political awakening for us. The main narrative of those early years was our efforts to build a revolutionary Marxist organisation, learning from Lenin and the Bolsheviks, against the reluctance, foot-dragging, cynicism, scepticism and sometimes downright opposition from that older generation of Trotskyists. *Socialist Perspective* was produced as a very irregular roneoed magazine (six issues between October1966 and June 1969), largely under our prodding, giving the views of the Fourth International in Australia.

Our efforts to build a party arose out of and in opposition to the CPA, which was still very dominant on the left, although declining. An early effort to intervene was the pamphlet "30 Questions and Answers on the History of the Soviet Union", by Ernest Germaine (Ernest Mandel). It had no authorisation or contact address, only an enigmatic "fi" logo. It was printed for us by Southwood Press, set up by some of the other former members of the old Trotskyist group, who thought that the way forward was to organise a printing business and produce a social democratic magazine, called *Comment*.[3]

Resistance

In mid-1967 we set up Resistance. The radicals recruited to revolutionary Marxism recognised the need for an off-campus youth organisation, to relate to the radicalising youth, high school students and young workers, as well as to campus students. We rented an old disused shop downtown in Goulburn Street, opposite the Trades Hall, and initially called ourselves SCREW – the Society for the Cultivation of Rebellion Every Where; or the alternative acronym, the Sydney Committee for Revolution and the Emancipation of the Working class, for the more serious, taking our lead from an organisation once led by Lenin. After a few months we changed our name to Resistance, after a fight with some anarchists in the group, who were *much* too attached to the name SCREW.

In the front of the building we set up the Third World Bookshop. Some of the main activists lived upstairs. In the back we held our meetings and forums, social events, film nights and folk-singing nights. After a while we expanded to the building next door and knocked a hole in the wall, so had a double shop front, more comrades living upstairs and a permanent silk-screening workshop. We organised protests and demonstrations from there on Vietnam and many other issues. We organised High School Students Against the War in Vietnam, and produced and distributed huge numbers of our school newssheet *Student Underground* as well as individual school newssheets. It was a busy, exciting youth political and cultural activist centre.

Resistance was run by "Gould and the Percy brothers", as others on the left described us, but the description was true – we *did* have problems of democracy and organisation, and waged a long struggle to overcome this. We had a fierce faction fight with Gould in 1969-70, for a democratically functioning party and youth organisation. We had the majority in Resistance, and broke with our initial mentor and collaborator. We left him the bookshop; we got the political organisation.

Meanwhile, we had also formed the Socialist Review Group, as a "party group", uniting for a while with some of the other former comrades from the old Trotskyist group who supported the Fourth International and who had set up the printing business, Southwood Press – Roger Barnes, Sylvia Hale, Tony Kelly. With them we published the magazine *Socialist Review*.

Having broken with Gould and his mixed bag of anarchistic supporters, we held our founding national conference of Resistance on August 29-30, 1970, mostly with Sydney comrades, plus a few from Adelaide and Canberra, and started publishing *Direct Action* in September as a monthly socialist newspaper. It certainly made a splash! It was a big challenge to the CPA's drab weekly, *Tribune*. We also changed our name to Socialist Youth Alliance (switching back to Resistance at the end of the decade).

Resistance came first. We had no party, so Resistance activists had to found and build the party, the Socialist Workers League, which eventually became the Democratic Socialist Party. The young comrades still had to lead it, even though we'd recruited some of the earlier generation from the old Trotskyist group. Over the decades Resistance continued to renew the party, and continued to build it. New generations of leaders were recruited and trained in Resistance. Trotskyism began as the fight against Stalinism, in Australia as well as internationally. In the '30s, '40s and '50s, it was very hard going building the old section of the FI. In the '60s and '70s, it was also difficult, starting from nothing much, but with the youth radicalisation we made progress against a declining CPA. We built in opposition to the CPA and their youth group, the Eureka Youth League. (We won over some of the sons and daughters, at one stage having a "faction" of 10 in the EYL.)

Early on, our ideological identification with the Trotskyist movement was still fairly nebulous.

As we consolidated the party organisationally and politically, we also formalised our ties with the international Trotskyist movement. We were especially impressed and influenced by the US Socialist Workers Party, for its leading role in the antiwar movement in the US. Within the Fourth International, they were in a minority, having opposed the "guerrilla warfare" line adopted by the majority at the 1969 FI World Congress. We avidly followed their activities and used their publications. Trotskyism was slower to develop in other cities. In Melbourne, it was initially the Maoists, especially at Monash University, who benefited from the '60s youth and student radicalisation. In Adelaide and Brisbane, it was more semi-anarchist groups modelled on the US Students for a Democratic Society.

In late 1970, we heard of another Trotskyist group that had started, in Brisbane, the Labor Action Group, led by John McCarthy. They were supporters of the majority current in the FI, and had been influenced by the International Marxist Group in Britain. We initially thought: great, let's unite our forces. But they backed off for a year, until agreeing at the end of 1971 to get together and attend our founding conference.

Socialist Workers League

The Socialist Review Group organised our founding national conference in Sydney on January 1-3, 1972, attended by just over 100 members and supporters. We adopted the name Socialist Workers League, adopted a program, constitution and documents on the international situation and Australian perspectives. We took a big leap in our level of organisation and political clarity. We fused with the Labor Action Group immediately after the conference, and applied to become a section of the Fourth International.

But soon afterwards we suffered two splits. In February 1972 a group of 11 comrades around Roger Barnes and Sylvia Hale from the old FI group resigned. They were not willing to be part of a disciplined party, and still adhered to the old Trotskyist line of "deep entry" into the Australian Labor Party.

Our youth organisation was still carrying the weight of our activity and recruiting. We held the SYA third national conference in Melbourne, March 31-April 3, 1972, attended by 170 people. *DA* went fortnightly immediately after the conference.

But we were headed for a major split, roughly along the lines of the division in the FI. The Communist League was formed in August 1972 as a third of the membership split along with John McCarthy and supporters who sided with the FI majority, the European leadership. The CL split was aided by some forces in the FI; we learned that internationalism was a two-edged sword.

But we were pleased to receive a letter from the FI United Secretariat signed by Belgian FI leader Ernest Mandel and Jack Barnes of the US SWP (representing both tendencies in the FI), condemning the split as unjustified, and refusing to make the CL a sympathising organisation of the FI.[4]

We had established our "party", the SWL, and Resistance/SYA was still healthy. Most of us had been aroused to acute political awareness by major international events, so we were very conscious of breaking out into the wider world politically. We formed our new party just in time in a sense. The radicalisation period was ending. In 1972 Vietnam was not yet liberated, but most thought the war over.

CHAPTER 1

THE WHITLAM LABOR GOVERNMENT

On December 2, 1972, the Whitlam ALP government was elected, swept to office on a wave of popular protest against the Vietnam War and conscription. There were high expectations among workers after 23 years of outright conservative federal government, with Robert Menzies ("Pig Iron Bob") as prime minister from 1949 to 1966. "It's Time" was Labor's campaign slogan and its theme song. It struck a chord. Many people had hopes and illusions that Australian society was in for a fundamental change.

Conscription and Vietnam were still the key issues in the lead-up to the elections, although the big demonstrations had declined after the three massive Moratorium marches against the war around the country in May 1970, September 1970 and June 1971. (Coalition PM Billy McMahon had decided to withdraw most of the troops on July 26, 1971, before Labor got in.) There was also rising unemployment, and increased militancy of workers' struggles, pushing for a change.

The election was also shaped by events in the ALP. The ALP had last been in office in 1949, when the Chifley government had been defeated by Menzies after the government used troops to smash the coal miners' strike, and the bourgeoisie mobilised against Chifley after an attempt to nationalise the banks. The party was still affected by the Democratic Labor Party split in the mid-1950s engineered by the right-wing Catholic-controlled National Civic Council, especially in Victoria, where most of the ALP right had split away, leaving militant unionists dominant in the Victorian ALP.

The ALP was at low ebb in the Cold War period of the '50s. It sank even lower after the DLP split in 1955. In some states, e.g. NSW, the NCC types largely remained in the party. In Victoria, the left was in control, with the Socialist Left in the majority. In NSW the Steering Committee, the body that had been formed to fight the NCC, was a minority.

Gough Whitlam, a new image for the ALP, defeated Arthur Calwell as leader in 1967. Calwell was an old guard Catholic, against the NCC, but right wing, especially on social issues. In 1966, however, Calwell strongly campaigned against the Vietnam War, leading big demonstrations against the visit of South Vietnam dictator Marshal Nguyen Cao Ky. Whitlam defeated Calwell for the leadership, and also succeeded in watering down Labor's policy on Vietnam: "withdraw the troops" became "withdraw to holding areas". (This policy direction was also supported by the Communist Party of Australia.)

But the momentum against the war and conscription grew, culminating in the huge Moratorium demonstrations. The protests were biggest in Melbourne, with turnouts of 100,000, 60,000 and 80,000.

Black rights and anti-racism were also important issues. Anti-apartheid sentiment against the South African regime and its racially segregated sporting teams was high, leading to very militant demonstrations and disruption of the 1971 Springboks tour. Militant Aboriginals were starting to agitate more strongly for their rights, partly encouraged by the growing Black Power movement in the US; the Aboriginal embassy was established on the lawns of Parliament House in Canberra in January 1972, and Black Moratorium demonstrations were held in July 1972 in Sydney, Darwin, Adelaide, Melbourne, Canberra, Brisbane and NSW regional centres. The notorious White Australia policy was in the process of being ditched, or at least toned down. Australian cities were becoming more multicultural.

University students were still radicalising in the early 1970s, contributing to the impetus for change and the election of the ALP. We were also involved in leading a secondary student strike on September 20, 1972 (reported by Greg Adamson in *DA* 27).

Union struggles were sharpening, such as the Builders Labourers Federation militant green bans from 1970 on many issues and areas in Sydney – preserving local bushland, preserving historic buildings, preventing mad destruction of communities.

These were the main forces behind Labor's election victory in December 1972 – the mass movement against the Vietnam War, the radicalisation and mobilisation of workers and young people.

The second aspect was the effort by ALP leaders to convince the capitalists that they were responsible, "fit to govern". The first step had been replacing Calwell with Whitlam, and watering down policy on Vietnam. The second step was posing as responsible in the industrial arena. Important here were the infamous Clyde Cameron proposals of fines for individual strikers. There was an outcry, but it was adopted in modified form.

This was in the context of growing unemployment and inflation. The ALP was the bosses' second option; rather than using the big stick, they could employ the soft sell, through a wage freeze, wage restraint or social contract. We saw that again a decade later with Hawke Labor's Prices and Incomes Accord in 1983.

So a section of the capitalists backed Whitlam, especially Rupert Murdoch.

The News Limited papers campaigned strongly for Whitlam. They hoped that Labor would be able to modernise some aspects of Australian capitalism and open up trade possibilities with China and the Soviet Union, which the Liberals were too set in their ways to adjust to.

We campaigned strongly for a Labor victory, with the slogan "Labor to Power! Fight for Socialist Policies!" on the cover of our October 27 *Direct Action*. We campaigned with *DA* covers on: unemployment (*DA* 27); social questions (28) "What will Labor do about: Abortion, Pollution, Homosexuality, Education"; and Vietnam (30) "End Australian Complicity in Vietnam". We produced our own manifesto as a four-page lift-out in *DA* 29, and proposed our socialist program in *DA* 31.

The elections had been an issue in the split from the SWL by the Communist League. They opposed our National Committee decision in mid-1972 to call for a vote for Labor. (They changed their views on this later, as did the SWL majority in our characterisation of the ALP.)

Massive rallies

There were massive enthusiastic ALP rallies in the lead-up to the elections, and we sold huge numbers of *DA*s at these meetings. We printed 46,000 copies of our special election broadsheet to hand out, and 4,000 posters to stick up.

I was editing *DA*, and produced circulars about copy, subscriptions and sales that we sent to all SYA and SWL branch organisers, *DA* copy directors and sales directors. The October 30 circular reported on our increased print run during the election campaign, and raised branch quotas by about 50 percent, motivating this by the higher sales rate generally and the big sales at ALP election rallies. These rallies were quite exciting, reflecting the mobilisations by working people angry at 23 years of conservative rule (and the high hopes in Labor). Some examples:

- Melbourne branch sold 500 copies between receiving the paper at midday to 10pm; Sol Salby sold 160 copies in two lunch hours on the UNSW campus; Chris Graham sold 300 plus copies in three nights around the pubs in Sydney.
- *DA* sold well at ALP rallies, but also at rallies for the Australia Party (the precursor to the), and in the last week of the campaign we cottoned on to the fact that there were more Labor supporters than Liberal supporters at Liberal leader Billy MacMahon's meetings, to heckle him, so we sold there as well!

Our November 9 circular pointed out that *DA* is "something we can be really proud of. In comparison with other left papers in Australia, and even with other papers of the Fourth International, we come out very favourably." The sales rate was excellent – Melbourne branch reported that during a recent power strike, "120 *DA*s were sold at a meeting of less than 400 workers".

In a November 13 letter to Jim Percy, who had left for Europe to attend the FI's International Executive Committee meeting in December, I reported that five of us went to Whitlam's Sydney meeting and sold more than 200 *DA*s and distributed more than 1,000 broadsheets, and not a single member of the Socialist Labour League or CL, our main potential rivals on the far left, was there. A later letter reported of further rallies that the "Healyites [SLL] seem to have given up on them". Another letter to Jim from Steve Painter reported that Whitlam's "campaign meetings were enormous … We murdered the Healyites with our intervention. They didn't even turn up during the second half of the campaign." We sold 400 at the St Kilda Town Hall ALP meeting in Melbourne.

When the Whitlam government was elected on December 2, the reaction was quite euphoric, and the feelings of optimism continued for several months. We saluted Labor's victory and gave our assessment in *DA* 32 with a front page article by Jim McIlroy (who had been on *DA* staff for most of this period): "What we can expect from a Labor Government":

> Labor's victory in the Federal election has thrown up a whole series of questions about what the ALP will do in the coming months. The broad majority of Australian working people of all ages have turned to Labor to provide political solutions to the social crises of our time. Labor has ridden to power on an extremely powerful current of popular frustration with the big business government and all its machinations. Workers, youth, women, blacks and homosexuals. All seek a government which *really* seeks to tackle the widespread exploitation and oppression which they suffer under this society.
>
> To those who believe that this Labor administration has the answers a big disappointment is in store. To those who see this tremendous Labor victory as one important stage in a long process of building a movement to replace capitalism, the first signs of the Whitlam leadership's intentions are already quite apparent. And the need for the continual fight to place alternative solutions before the majority of Australians is also clear.
>
> A process of backtracking on key election promises has already begun …
>
> Again and again, Labor policy is couched in terms which reflect the

enormous antiwar sentiment which has swept the nation in the last few years. Labor's policies, here as elsewhere, demonstrate the nature of the party as the mass party of the working class, responsive to movements among the working people. At the same time, ALP leaders continually strive to harness and divert anticapitalist feeling into harmless channels.

This process can be seen once again with Labor's policy on industrial relations. The new Minister for Labor, Clyde Cameron stated during the campaign that "There will be fewer strikes under Labor because we will remove the cause of industrial unrest. We would attempt to get over the problem of both parties failing to talk to one another by a system of mediation – which operates in other parts of the world." In other words, the bludgeon of the arbitration system would be replaced by an emphasis on conciliation …

But as for removing "the causes of industrial unrest" – this can only come about when a socialist economy based on workers' control is established. Present Labor official policies are aimed at alleviating unrest by integrating trade unions with the state machinery and calling on labour solidarity with their party in government! … It is the *balance of forces* within the party which is the key factor in the long run. A strong left wing such as the Victorian Socialist Left can defeat the right wing leadership, and in the process educate large numbers of working people in class politics. The challenge of the present crop of Labor fakers remains …

On a whole series of other issues we see the ambiguous character of Labor policy – as a response to broad pressures, and as an attempt to absorb those pressures. The broad movement of women for their rights finds its reflection in Labor policy with a commitment to support equal pay and build child care centres. Yet Whitlam and other Labor leaders fall over themselves to declare that the right to abortion was *not* an issue in the election and that the ALP has *no* policy on this question. What sort of approach is this to the struggle of women for democratic rights and freedom from sexual oppression?

An article in the same issue by Sol Salby (also on staff) explained why large sections of the bourgeoisie backed Labor. In order to improve their international competitiveness, they felt they needed three things: "a) the setting back or taming down of any working class upsurge in response to the employers' offensive on the workers living standards. b) a more dynamic intervention by the state in the economy, including 'indicative planning' and 'incomes policies'. c) a larger trade with the workers states, in particular the Soviet Union and China".

The employers believed "that because of the working class's allegiance to the ALP, the Labor leadership will be able to restrain and perhaps even turn back the working class movement. They know that an attempt by a Liberal government to send the army to scab on strikers, as was contemplated during the recent oil strike, will result in complete solidarity action by the whole class and will result in failure. On the other hand they can foresee the natural advantages which will enable an ALP Government to undertake precisely such a course."

Nevertheless, there was a raft of dramatic reforms by Labor in the first few weeks:

- conscription was ended, and the Vietnam draft resisters were freed;
- Australian Communist journalist Wilfred Burchett's passport was returned;
- the Australian government recognised the People's Republic of China;
- the government intervened in the equal pay case so that a new submission could be made to the Arbitration Commission;
- Medibank as a universal health scheme was proposed to be fully implemented in one and a half years;
- the sales tax on contraceptives as "luxury" goods was dropped, and they were placed on the pharmaceutical benefits list;
- racially selected South African sporting teams were banned from the country;
- steps were taken to preserve Aboriginal culture and land rights;
- a decision was made to restrict wage gains to those who are members of unions.

Labor in power

Soon Whitlam was getting down to the real business, the reason he was supported by the bourgeoisie: proposing a wage freeze – "wage restraint" – as his solution to inflation and unemployment. But workers' expectations were unleashed by the Labor victory. Whitlam's death at 98 in October 2014 let loose an outpouring of adulation from the myth makers, Labor and Liberals even, as though it was all about him, not the mass upsurge that pushed the Labor Party over the line in December 1972 and pushed the many overdue reforms in the first months of the ALP government. Almost like a beatification! Any attempt at a balanced assessment of Whitlam's legacy was treated as heresy.

Early on, in March 1973, we had an indication of the impossible situation for reformists faced with a hostile state apparatus. The raid by Attorney-General Lionel Murphy on the Australian Security Intelligence Organisation (ASIO)'s headquarters in Canberra, trying to gather evidence on Croatian fascists, just got a mouthful of feathers. Our *DA* 38 cover had a headline "Who runs Australia? The Labor Government or the Capitalist State?"

In May *DA* 40 and 41 carried a two-part series by Sol Salby, "Labor in Power": "No matter how much effort the Labor Government puts into running capitalism more efficiently and no matter what different factors give it more leeway, Labor will still face certain difficulties. They are: the problems of the hostile attitudes of the state apparatus and the contradiction between carrying a radical reform for change pressed from below and good relations with Australian capitalism. While the first set of problems have already been encountered they have been relatively minor compared to the latter ones." Labor lost the May 19 Victorian election, and we ran an editorial in *DA* 41, "Labor must fight!"

Workers themselves proved more than willing to fight – the big eight-week Ford Broadmeadows strike showed the militancy. Our June 28 *DA* cover proclaimed "Workers Fight Back" and editorialised on "The Strike Wave". Andrew Jamieson reported "Struggle erupts at Ford" with very graphic pictures and articles.

A feature article by Sol Salby on "The Labor Govt and the Union Movement" in *DA* 45 pointed out that many unions had previously "held back on claiming their just demands in case it would jeopardise Labor's electoral chances. Now that Labor is in office they have started raising their demands again." In the previous few months, a "whole new wave of militant strikes have been launched in all industries and States". As well as Ford, there were strikes in the power industry, building industry, Comalco, BHP and others.

A month later, *DA* 47 carried an article by Sol Salby, which stated, "The Labor Government is retreating right across the board ... The promises which Labor made last year are all but forgotten. The radical actions taken on its assumption of office are nine months old. On nearly every plane and in every sphere Labor is backtracking not only on its election promises but even on its actions of the last few months."

Given the issues, the mass enthusiastic rallies and the Labor victory on December 2, we resolved we had better get involved more actively in the Labor Party. We already had an "entrist" policy, requesting our members to join and do political work in the ALP, which we had inherited from the old Trotskyist movement.

On December 6, 1972, the SWL Political Committee and SYA National

Executive issued a joint statement to our members on "Our immediate tasks in the Labor Party". Our task was to create a "class-struggle left wing", and the precondition for that was to "Get in fully now", join the Labor Party if we hadn't already done so, without admitting our membership in the SWL or SYA. The thrust of the resolution was not that ALP or Labor youth work were at all times and in all situations our most important work, but it revved up its importance for us. We set up a national Labor Party fraction, with Sol Salby elected as fraction director.

We also began a very educational 10-part series in *Direct Action* by Peter Conrick on "The History of the Labor Party". It ran from December 21, 1972, to June 14, 1973. We later issued the series as a pamphlet.

SWL second conference

The second national conference of the Socialist Workers League was held January 27-29, 1973, in Sydney (at the Buffalo Hall again, near Central Railway Station). We decorated the venue with our very imposing 10ft x 5ft red and black canvas portraits of Marx, Engels, Lenin, Trotsky, Rosa Luxemburg and James P. Cannon, which we had painted in both Sydney and Melbourne and used to great effect at the May Day marches as well as at SYA and SWL events.

The main topics of political discussion were how to act in the new situation created by the Labor election victory, and responding to Nixon's escalation of the bombing of Vietnam. But it was especially a conference where we were getting better organised about our finances and more serious about building a party. Jim Percy became a full-timer for SWL just before the conference; before that he'd been in effect a full-timer for SYA.

The conference heard an international report by Jim McIlroy and a world movement report by Jim Percy on the discussion under way in the world Trotskyist movement in preparation for the World Congress of the Fourth International, expected to be held later that year. The political report was given by Dave Holmes, with sub-reports on antiwar by Greg Adamson, women's liberation by Jenny Ferguson, the Black movement by Steve Painter, youth by Nita Keig, the ALP by Sol Salby and unions by Col Maynard. The organisation report was also given by Dave Holmes (setting a drive for 500 new *DA* subs, and launching regular forums in Sydney and Melbourne) with sub-reports on *Direct Action* by John Percy and on the CL split by Steve Painter.

The conference also reinforced our orientation to the Fourth International. This was partly responding to the split by the CL, with both organisations jostling for formal FI recognition. We had become a sympathising organisation of the FI after our founding conference. We'd solicited and received greetings to the conference from other FI groups – the Socialist Action League from New Zealand; the League for Socialist Action/Ligue Socialiste Ouvrière from Canada; the Socialist Workers Party in the US; the Japan Revolutionary Communist League; the Israeli Socialist Organisation (Marxist); the Partido Revolutionario de los Trabajadores (Revolutionary Workers Party) of Uruguay; and the Partido Revolutionario de los Trabajadores of Argentina.

Registration was down from our founding conference a year before, 82 comrades being registered, reflecting the splits we had suffered. But in many ways we were stronger. Delegates and observers were extremely youthful. Forty-four were SWL members, with an average age of 22 years, and 38 were observers, whose average age was 19 years, mostly from SYA.

The conference elected an SWL National Committee of 15 full members: Greg Adamson, Gordon Adler, Peter Conrick, Jamie Doughney, Jenny Ferguson, Dave Holmes, Nita Keig, Col Maynard, Jim McIlroy, Jim Percy, John Percy, Steve Painter, Geoff Payne, Sol Salby and Allen Westwood. Three alternate members were elected: Dorothy Tumney, Doug Lorimer and Dave Riley.

The National Committee meeting immediately after the conference elected a Political Committee consisting of all full NC members in Sydney. All SWL full-timers, including those on *DA*, were constituted as an Administrative Committee subordinate to the PC. Dave Holmes was elected national secretary, Jim Percy national organiser and John Percy editor of *DA*.

The NC heard a personnel report, in which various comrades were just assigned to SWL, no longer in SYA, and withdrew Brisbane branch's charter since it had fallen below the minimum size. It also opened written discussions on the CPA and the Black movement, and took a decision to send Col Maynard to "study in the US" – i.e., to work on *Intercontinental Press* in New York – "subject to finance".

We were developing even closer collaboration with the US SWP. Our first direct contact had been the visit of Barry Sheppard in August 1969, when we were fighting with Bob Gould about building a party, and we tried – unsuccessfully – to appeal for direct political guidance.[5] Then, at the end of 1969, as part of a round the world tour for the US Student Mobilization Committee to End the War in Vietnam, SWP member Allen Myers visited Sydney for four days to speak at the December 15 Vietnam demonstration we organised,[6] and I was selected to go to the Young Socialist Alliance convention in Minneapolis.[7] We'd hosted speaking tours by SWP leaders Andrew Pulley in 1970 and Patti Iiyama in1971. SWP leader John Benson made an internal visit in August 1972 on the way back from a tour of Japan.[8] Jim Percy travelled to the FI IEC meeting in

Europe in December 1972, returning via Canada and New York, where he had extensive meetings with SWP leaders.

In April and May 1973, we organised ambitious speaking tours of SWP leaders and Marxist scholars Evelyn Reed and George Novack in Sydney, Brisbane, Canberra, Adelaide and Melbourne. Reed was an anthropologist and the author of *Problems of Women's Liberation* and *Woman's Evolution;* Novack wrote many books on Marxist philosophy, including *The Origins of Materialism, An Introduction to the Logic of Marxism, Empiricism and its Evolution* and *Democracy and Revolution.*

SYA fourth national conference

The SYA fourth national conference, held April 20-23, 1973, in Sydney, was reported in *DA* 40. The conference opened with a rally addressed by Evelyn Reed and Peter Rotherham from the NZ Socialist Action League.

The international report was probably given by Jamie Doughney, and the perspectives report, "SYA and the challenge of the Youth Radicalisation", by Nita Keig. There was also a secondary students report, a campus report, a report on Labor and youth, a world movement report and an organisational report.

Jamie Doughney was appointed SYA national secretary and was transferred to Sydney for the SYA NO. Alban Johnson was appointed SYA national organiser. Steve Painter had been working in Sydney as SYA national organiser, and was transferred back to Melbourne in February.

From April 20, 1973, we announced that *DA* was expanding from 16 to 24 pages, with the cover price rising to 20 cents. The fund drive launched at the SYA conference set a target of $300, and quickly reached $544, so we set an extra four-week drive for $400 in June.

Even though we'd pulled back from having a formal branch in Brisbane, the CL wasn't doing much better – Ian Walters, one of the comrades we'd sent up there, wrote to Jim Percy on January 31 that the "CL seem to have died in Brisbane".

In May we decided to divide Sydney SYA into three branches, focusing on the three main campuses we were involved in – Ryde, for Macquarie University; eastern suburbs, for UNSW; Sydney central for Sydney University. I don't recall how long it lasted, but it wouldn't have been for long – it was premature.

Our 1973 May Day contingents looked very impressive, in marches that were larger than usual. In Melbourne we had more than 80 in our SWL/SYA contingent. The Maoists, formerly dominant, were not organised and were in disarray. We had 130 in our contingent in Sydney. *DA* 40 reported on a big but dull march livened up a bit by the platform being occupied by women's liberation and gay liberation activists, protesting against the concept of having a "May Day Queen".

A month after the SYA conference, we held an SWL NC meeting, on May 25-26. The perspectives report was given by Jim Percy, the youth report by Jamie Doughney, the ALP/Young Labor Association report by Jim McIlroy, the women's liberation report by Nita Keig, the trade union report by Allen Westwood. Branch reports were given from Sydney by Allen Westwood, from Melbourne by Steve Painter and from Adelaide by Doug Lorimer. The organisation report was given by Dave Holmes. Nita Keig, Margaret McHugh, Alan Dalton and Doug Lorimer were graduated out of the SYA leadership, to further strengthen the party.

The student movement

This was a busy and hectic period of political activity for us even though the radicalisation had receded quite a lot, the Vietnam protests had dwindled and widespread illusions existed about the Labor government. There were many issues.

The student movement was still a significant arena for us. The Australian Union of Students was moving leftward, with SYA leading the push – a *DA* 47 article by Peter Conrick reported that AUS was taking "radical steps". Its August council reaffirmed its opposition to Zionism and its support for the Palestinian cause, and continued to stress its opposition to the apartheid regime in South Africa. Council unanimously protested against the French government's ban on the Ligue Communiste. Frans Timmerman was elected editor of AUS's paper, *National U* (produced with the assistance of Andrew Jamieson), and the only socialist organisation at AUS August council was SYA, represented by Frans Timmerman from UNSW, Jeff Hayler, Macquarie University chair of the students council, Barry Simpson from Monash and Peter Conrick from Melbourne University.

Macquarie University was the scene of some important struggles. A gay student, Jeremy Fisher (who may have been an SYA member), led some important campaigns against discrimination and victimisation. An outrageous homophobic attack in the pages of the student newspaper *Arena* from the editor, CPA member Mark Aarons (one of the sons of CPA national secretary Laurie Aarons), led to a mass campaign of outrage, reported in *DA* 38, that forced Aarons to resign. SWL member Rod Webb was working as an administrative officer at Macquarie, and was also the target of Aarons' attacks. A few months later, Jeff Hayler was re-elected chair of the students council, and Rod Webb was elected editor of *Arena* (*DA* 47).

The free university movement in 1973 was an attempt to set up an alternative "university" close to campus that broke with the conservative teaching methods and had a radical syllabus. The movement got its impetus and inspiration from similar efforts in the US that arose from the campus radicalisation of the '60s. In Sydney the Free Uni functioned for a while, using the Settlement building as a base, but the concept was utopian and took the heat out of actual struggles, rather than complementing them. It also ran counter to the various left efforts (like ours) to build organisations that carried out agitation and organisation as well as education in Marxism.

We were also conscious of the important political role high school students could play. *DA* 42 carried the SYA conference document, "A Socialist Strategy for the Secondary Student Revolt".

Political economy struggle

From May 1973, there had been an ongoing struggle in the economics department at the University of Sydney over the methods of teaching and course content. Some of the staff supported the majority of students, who were agitating for a "political economy" perspective (*DA* 82).

The struggle was also spurred on by a revolt in the philosophy department, with a campaign to teach women's studies (*DA* 49).

In 1975, a new department of political economy was formed.[9] In July 1976 Helen Jarvis reported in *DA* 126 that Sydney University students were on strike for the political economy course. Jon West covered it in the following *DA* and in *Young Socialist* No. 9, writing that a meeting of 700 voted almost unanimously to strike. "For almost seven years students and staff at Sydney University have been struggling for political economy." Peter Annear wrote in the following *YS* (No. 10, September): "Supported by 5000 students and 75 members of staff, the week long strike at the University of Sydney in July marked a real step forward for the political economy movement there".

The initial mass student support for the political economy struggle can be gauged by the size of the conferences they held – 1,400 in June 1976 and 800 in August 1977, as reported in *DA* 174.

Political campaigns

Palestine was an important issue for us, because of the just struggle of the Palestinian people against their dispossession by the Zionist colonisers, but also partly because we were looking for an international issue to replace Vietnam as a focus for our campaigning. This led to big fights in the Australian Union of Students, where our comrades Sol Salby and Frans Timmerman played an important leading role on this issue.

The November 29, 1974, issue of *DA* had an article by Sol on "The PLO and the self-determination struggle", warning of the imperialist "drive to impose a settlement in the Arab East that would preserve the colonial settler-state of Israel and compromise the right of the Palestinian people to self-determination".

In January 1975, a planned tour of Australia by a delegation from the Palestine Liberation Organisation had to be cancelled when the federal Labor government went back on its word and refused visas for the delegation. *DA* 78 carried an article by Sol Salby, "Labor leaders head anti-PLO campaign", and another by Jamie Doughney, "Demonstrations set to protest PLO ban". Six hundred Arabs attended a protest meeting in Redfern, Sydney, at which we sold 180 *DA*s and ran out! The campaign eventually won enough support to force a backdown by the government: Eddi Zananiri and Samir Cheikh from the General Union of Palestine Students were granted visas and toured in May 1975.

In *DA* 79, Dave Deutschmann reported some good news: "On the first day of the annual council of the Australian Union of Students, a motion was unanimously passed condemning the government ban on the visit of representatives of the PLO". Later, the AUS also passed a motion calling for the creation of a democratic secular state in Palestine, which was the position we advocated.

Gay liberation campaigns developed in Australia in the early '70s, following the Stonewall demonstrations in New York in 1969. About 60 gay liberationists demonstrated outside the ABC offices in Elizabeth Street, Sydney, on July 11, 1972, protesting the cancellation of a *This Day Tonight* report on gay liberation. *DA* 43 carried a feature on gay liberation based on a talk by Jeff Hayler to a Sydney *DA* forum. This noted two aspects of the developing gay liberation movement: on the one hand, a personal overcoming of the social and psychological effects of oppression, and on the other an attempt to combat the root social and political causes of gay oppression. A big step forward was Gay Pride Week actions in Sydney (300), Brisbane, Melbourne (200) and Adelaide (150), September 8-16, 1973 (*DA* 48). A campaign defended trainee teacher Penny Short against losing her teacher scholarship after she published a lesbian poem.

The May 1973 SWL NC opened a written discussion on gay liberation. The regular Gay and Lesbian Mardi Gras demonstrations began in 1978, with much more radical and directed demands than the commercialised and tamed parades of today.

Women's liberation issues were mobilising increasing numbers of women, young and old, and raising consciousness. After Labor's 1972 election victory, we sent a circular to all SWL and SYA executives about women's liberation perspectives for 1973. We proposed to go along with the idea for a March 10-11 "Women's Commission/Tribunal", a consciousness-raising activity, but our main concern was to organise activities that would involve women in mass action. Thus we helped to establish WAAC, the Women's Abortion Action Campaign, and promoted militant demonstrations for March 8, International Women's Day (a contrast to the elitist bureaucrat breakfasts that IWD is now celebrated with).

In April we sent out a circular about our perspectives for the abortion campaign, projecting demonstrations for June 30 to repeal the abortion laws. Four hundred marched. WAAC decided to produce its own paper, *Right to Choose*, which appeared in September and was reviewed in *DA* 49. May 1974 abortion actions attracted 500 in Sydney and 1,500 in Melbourne.

In 1973 there was a strong campaign for a women's course at Sydney University, including a four-week strike, with up to 2,500 students and staff involved. In *DA* 44, Debby Payne reported on the victory of the struggle.

The first Sydney Women's Liberation House was established at 67 Glebe Point Road in 1971, seamlessly taking over from the Sydney University Labor Club, which first rented the building in 1969. Then it moved to Alberta Street in the city, just off Goulburn Street near Hyde Park in an old building – since demolished and buried under big residential towers – and later moved to a building in Regent Street. For a time, the Glebe building became a headquarters for Gay Liberation.

Workers' struggles were on the rise again after a short breathing space following Whitlam's victory. The June 28 *DA* front page proclaimed: "Workers Fight Back! Ford, BHP SEC ..." Andrew Jamieson reported, "Struggle erupts at Ford: Rank-and-file workers expose union bureaucrats". AMWU official and CPA leader Laurie Carmichael had his coat torn by workers at a mass meeting when he tried to persuade them to return to work after their six-week strike. Graphic pictures illustrated the "most militant demonstrations for many years". "Workers of many nationalities gave vent to their anger against Ford by pushing down brick walls, breaking windows, and pelting down the growing number of strike-breaking police with fruit and vegetables." A back page interview with some of the workers illustrated their militancy. Eventually they were defeated after nine weeks on strike.

A major article, "The Labor Government and the Union Movement", by Sol Salby, in the *DA* of August 9, 1973, warned that the ALP government's strategy was to divert and coopt workers' struggles into the mechanisms of the Arbitration Commission.

We campaigned strongly against Labor's prices and incomes referendum, one of the main reasons sections of the bosses had initially supported the election of the Whitlam government, expecting it to control worker militancy more successfully than the Liberals. We produced posters and leaflets and covered it thoroughly in *DA*. The editorial in our September 27 issue urged "Vote No on both Counts" of Whitlam's referendum . We organised public meetings on "The Fraud of Price Control and the Struggle against the Wage Freeze". We organised on university campuses in Sydney, Melbourne, Adelaide, Canberra and Geelong, and organised public meetings in Sydney at the Trades Hall, and in Melbourne at the Lower Town Hall. In December 1973, the referendum was massively defeated.

We campaigned energetically for a "no" vote on both questions, with meetings, posters and paint-ups. (Our slogans around Glebe stayed up for quite a few years.) The CPA campaigned with an equivocal "yes-no" position. But the fact is, under capitalism you can't control prices; the whole would have been a cover for a wage freeze. The Stalinists and ALP lefts didn't see that (making the same mistake as they did with the Accord in the early '80s).

We also sided firmly with the NSW BLF, which was under attack over its green bans by bosses, the state government and sections of the labour movement. In *DA* of November 8, 1973, Bernie Murphy reported "Builders Labourers Locked Out", describing police attacks on a BLF occupation of a building site to prevent the use of scab labour. I wrote an accompanying article, pointing out that the bosses' attacks on the NSW BLF were being supported not only by John Ducker, the right-wing leader of the NSW Labor Council but also by Pat Clancy, federal secretary of the Building Workers Industrial Union and a leader of the Socialist Party of Australia, and Norm Gallagher, federal secretary of the BLF and vice-president of the Communist Party of Australia (Marxist Leninist).

Building a leadership team

There was a constant dialectic between our involvement in and building the range of political campaigns, and building our party organisation. We knew we were too small to make a really significant impact, so it was imperative that we recruited, trained cadres and grew. But we also had to be involved in the different political campaigns to give leadership where we could and to recruit from them; otherwise we'd degenerate into an irrelevant sect. This dilemma for most small revolutionary groups was a constant challenge throughout our history.

At the formation of the SWL in January 1972, we had 50 members. By the end of 1973, we had grown to 90-100 members, despite the splits of the Roger Barnes grouping and the Communist League. We had certainly consolidated and organised well, and continued to develop politically.

The June 6, 1973, PC set up an administration committee of Jim Percy, John Percy, Dave Holmes and Jamie Doughney.

The SWL NC met June 9-10, 1973, with the following reports: world movement; youth; national organisation, with branch reports from Sydney, Melbourne, Adelaide and Brisbane; women's liberation; gay liberation; Labor; Socialist Left; antiwar movement; finance and literature; *Direct Action;* and other tendencies.

The NE chartered two separate branches in Melbourne: central and northern suburbs.

The SYA NC met in Melbourne July 7-8, discussing an international report; a political and organisational report plus branch reports; a women's liberation report; a YLA report; a campus report; a secondary students; a gay liberation report; a finance and administration report; and a *Direct Action* report .

We organised an SWL cadre school for Sydney, Brisbane and Canberra comrades on July 21-22, with the talks: Jim Percy: Building a Revolutionary Leadership; John Percy: Democratic Centralism; Jamie Doughney: Organising our Branches; Jamie Doughney: Presenting our Public Face; John Percy: What it Means to Be a Revolutionary Today.

The SWL PC on September 16 elected John Percy as Sydney organiser, Nita Keig as *DA* editor, Jim Percy as SWL national secretary, Dave Holmes as national organisation secretary. Nita replaced John on the administration committee; Deb Shnookal was transferred to Melbourne.

On September 22-23, 1973, the SWL NC met and heard reports: world movement, by Jim Percy (following which most, or maybe all, NC members joined the Leninist Trotskyist Faction of the FI); draft political resolution; wage freeze; women's liberation; CPA; Communist League; personnel and assignments; organisation; *Direct Action*; and branches: Sydney, Melbourne and Adelaide.

Battling the CPA

Our main political opponent and obstacle on the left was still the CPA. For a while, the CPA's "left" feint made it harder for revolutionary Marxists to grow. In 1968, led by the Aarons wing, the CPA had opposed the Soviet invasion of Czechoslovakia. Some people had been conned that this was a real break with Stalinism (including some from the old FI group.) *Intercontinental Press* editor Joe Hansen, in politely editing out unclear formulations in an article sent to the FI magazine in New York by Ian MacDougall, explained: "What is not clear is the exact reason for the CP's turn. It appears to be a tactical adjustment aimed at snaring support among the radicalising youth …

"The joyful reaction of the New Left is cause for concern. They can be in for a very bitter disappointment."

Joe was absolutely right. A prime example was Denis Freney, an ex-Trotskyist who had joined Nick Origlass' group from the CPA in 1956. He responded to the Aarons line and formally rejoined the CPA in 1970. He'd been Michel Pablo's secretary in Algeria for a year, and was thoroughly implementing Pablo's line of looking for solutions in the CPs.[10]

The CPA tried to adapt to the youth radicalisation a bit, when they realised they were being bypassed, especially by us. Freney had set up Liberation, at Manly on the northern beaches, in 1969, trying to imitate our successful Resistance model. Other efforts were Foco (copying a Brisbane effort by Brian Laver) and Barricades in Sydney (which got out of their control and gave rise to some SLL members, including Jim Mulgrew, who ran the group for the next decade). ASIO later revealed the CP's worries about us, from tapping their phones.

In the early '70s a Left Tendency was formed in the CPA, after the 1971 split of the hard-line pro-Soviet wing to form the Socialist Party of Australia (which later grabbed back the name "CPA" after the final dissolution of the CPA). It won back one or two academics in Melbourne initially attracted to us and recruited the leaders of the ex-SDS Adelaide Revolutionary Marxists (from memory: Rob Durbridge, Pat Ranald, Winton Higgins).

In the 1974 *Socialist Register*, Winton Higgins wrote a long article, "Reconstructing Australian Communism", analysing the SPA split and arguing that "the CPA is now demonstrating the potential to lead a viable communist movement in Australia".

In February 1970, Jim Percy wrote to Barry Sheppard after the first phase of our split with Gould: "As to the CP itself. On paper Aarons is 'progressive.' In action it's business as usual and the Moratorium campaign is a good example." (They were bureaucratically trying to exclude us.) "Our approach should be to continually throw up revolutionary positions to them and to see if their rhetoric is matched by deeds. So far it isn't and Freney is alone (even among the Pabs [supporters of Pablo]) in deluding himself that it will be."

The CPA soon showed more of its true colours, supporting the Whitlam government's efforts to rein in the militant unions, and in the 1980s initiating and supporting the Accord, re-emphasising the essence of its popular front politics – the main thrust of its line since the mid-1930s.

In the early '70s we carried many feature articles in *DA* analysing the CPA and trying to explain to our radical left readers its real nature. Dave Holmes in 1973 wrote a four-part series (*DA*s 43, 44, 48 and 53) on the historical record of Stalinism and the CPA: "Tribune's 50 Years – What Is the Real Record?", "The

Internationalism of the CPA", "Chile: Where the Communist Party Goes Wrong" and "Where Is the Communist Party Headed?". Gordon Adler had joined us from the CPA and had been elected to our NC at the second SWL conference.[11] In 1973 he was excluded from the CPA Sydney district conference, where he was planning to move a motion on the rightward direction of the CPA and Stalinism.[12] He wrote an article for *DA* 39 on "The Record of Australian Stalinism", pointing out, "Its [CPA's] analysis of Stalinism was superficial, and limited to a rejection of only the most glaring and repulsive manifestations of repression in the workers states".

The CPA organised a Workers Control Conference at Easter, April 21-22, which Jim McIlroy analysed in *DA* 41. Because capitalist control of particular factories is today closely bound up with capitalist control of the whole economy, Jim argued, "the demand for workers' control, to be made meaningful, immediately raises the question of workers' control of society as a whole – socialism". At the conference, the CPA counterposed workers' control to the demand for nationalisation of particular industries. The sectarian Socialist Labour League did the opposite. But the two demands go together, Jim wrote:

"Workers' control under nationalisation distinguishes workers' control under socialism from workers' control under capitalism. The demand for nationalisation thus provides workers' control with its revolutionary thrust. It provides the bridge from workers' control as a transitional step to socialism where the workers actually *do* control. Neither the CPA nor the SLL saw this."

On September 27, 1974, in Sydney we organised a debate on Chile at Trades Hall between the CPA and the SWL. Sixty were present (and Bob Gould excluded, much to his chagrin). We obviously thought we'd won the debate, and the ASIO agent reporting also agreed it was "obviously won hands down by the Trotskyists". We also covered the issue in *DA* 69: "CPA, SPA sectarianism in Chile defence".

As the revolution in Portugal developed, we also castigated the CPA for its line on that: "CPA covers for betrayal in Portugal" (*DA* 68), by Dave Holmes, pointed out that the CPA was backing the course of the Portuguese Communist Party, which was trying to keep everything "within the bounds of capitalist property relations": "They played the principal role in breaking the massive post-coup strike wave. The PCP has also supported the Government's manoeuvres to preserve Portuguese capitalism in the African colonies." The CPA's *Tribune* blamed the government's reactionary moves on its head, General António de Spinola, without pointing out that Spinola "is only able to carry out his plans because of the firm support he enjoys from the SP [Socialist Party] and PCP".

We also consistently analysed the CPA's line on women's liberation with many articles, for example, a feature in *DA* 75 by Nita Keig on "The CPA and feminism: Confusion and Opportunism".

Other left currents

As we were consolidating and expanding in our first few years, other currents were starting out or in decline. The Maoists had been the biggest beneficiary from the '60s youth radicalisation, especially in Melbourne and Adelaide, but continued to wane in the '70s.

In the 1970s other Trotskyist currents rose and fell. Our main rivals in the '70s were the mad sectarians of the Healyite Socialist Labour League (SLL). (Ironically, some of Gould's supporters, and eventually Gould as well for a while, flipped right over to being Healyites.) It was a terrible example of an international sect, led by one group, in this case one person, Gerry Healy. It gave Trotskyism a bad name. They suffered a total collapse in 1985 in Britain, and similarly here. Their hallmark became violence against others on the left. *DA* 43 reported an SYA member bashed by an SLLer in Canberra; they carried out a violent attack on SYA *DA* sellers outside one of their meetings at Sydney Trades Hall; they disrupted the Sydney Trades Hall SWP meeting for Willie Mae Reid.

The International Socialist tradition developed a few years later than the SWL/DSP, in Melbourne. Dave Nadel and Tess Lee Ack from the Monash Labor Club in the '60s went on to form the Marxist Workers Group in December 1971 and, with Tom O'Lincoln and Janey Stone, who had returned from Berkeley in the US in 1972, the Socialist Workers Action Group – the "SWAGgies". They produced the *Battler*, which had a halting start, with two issues numbered 1, two years apart, in 1972 and 1974. (Tom O'Lincoln points to the front page of the first one, which from a distance read as though it was calling for the downfall of the ALP in the 1972 election, as indicating it was probably premature for them to produce a paper.) A Socialist Alternative leader, Mick Armstrong, describes their early days in Melbourne: "[I]n 1970 the far left split between the Maoists and Dave Nadel's Independent Communist Caucus. By 1971 the influence of the Maoists had waned. Over the next few years a small Trotskyist current – the Revolutionary Communist Club led by Nadel – eclipsed the Maoists as the leading radical force at Monash. A key turning point was a 1973 public debate between the Maoists and the Revolutionary Communists (by now linked to the recently formed Socialist Workers Action Group) over the issue of nationalism. Most of the several hundred radicals that attended the debate backed the Revolutionary Communists' internationalist position against the Maoists' increasingly strident Australian nationalism."[13]

In the SWL we had a head start on other left groups from the radicalisation, but only just.

Getting fully into the Fourth International

After the Communist League split in August 1972, taking a third of our membership, we felt we had better get more thoroughly involved in the international Trotskyist movement (to make sure we knew what was going on, to ensure that our back was protected and to look for allies). At our October 1972 NC plenum, we adopted our first report on the world movement differences. Jim Percy attended the FI International Executive Committee on December 2-6, 1972, our first international FI meeting. Jim also attended the meeting of the Leninist Trotskyist Tendency in Toronto, August 14-15, 1973, that converted the tendency into a faction.

Shortly after returning from North America, Jim left on an Asian trip on October 1, 1973, on behalf of the LTF, which included Japan, Sri Lanka and Hong Kong. A November 21, 1973, letter from Jim to Mary-Alice Waters of the US SWP in New York gave a report of the trip. He wrote that he had addressed the Colombo membership of the Lanka Sama Samaja Party (Revolutionary) and "was sympathetically received on the European and Latin American questions". The whole trip seemed to go well and registered our increased authority in the FI.

I travelled to the USA via Honolulu, departing December 23, 1973, attending the US SWP Special World Congress Convention, on the way to the FI World Congress in Europe. In a December 26, 1973, letter to Jim from Chicago, I reported on the gossip regarding the intentions of the Internationalist Tendency minority in the SWP; the international guests who were attending the convention; and the LTF meeting we held.

I also attended the YSA convention in Chicago, December 28, 1973-January 1, 1974, which 900 attended. The leadership was debating with the Internationalist Tendency, a small current supporting the FI majority. Malik Miah debated them on the Black struggle. Proportional representation was given to the IT, which received two full and two alternate spots on the NC. I wrote back that I planned to spend 10 days in New York, then fly to England and then to the World Congress.

The debate in the FI

We weren't seriously involved in the Fourth International when we started organising in the 1960s and barely knew what was happening, although we sort of considered ourselves supporters. We were aware only that Barry Sheppard, a leader of the US SWP, was returning from the 1969 World Congress via Australia to see what might exist in the way of Trotskyist supporters here. That was our first contact. Guerrilla warfare in Latin America was the key issue on which there was argument at the 1969 World Congress, but the debate had expanded to many other questions. By 1973 it was fierce and quite factional. The FI was divided sharply into two sides (although there were also some efforts to establish an "in-between" tendency).

All involved may have felt the faction fight was a threat to the FI, and limiting our possibilities for useful activity, and some would have seen it as not worth the trouble, but the debate itself was extremely educational all round. More bulletins were written than in any previous FI debate. Valuable books of the discussion were a lasting legacy, for example *The Leninist Strategy of Party Building: The Debate on Guerrilla Warfare in Latin America* by Joseph Hansen.[14] New recruits to revolutionary Marxism were assured of a thorough grounding in theory.

The Leninist Trotskyist Tendency was called to defend the minority positions after the December IEC meeting, and formed in March 1973 at a meeting in Chile. The International Majority Tendency was also formed following the IEC meeting in 1972, but there were already indications that it existed and was functioning as a secret faction before that. The LTT was converted into the Leninist Trotskyist Faction in August 1973, in response to the increasingly factional situation. The aim was to prevent a split in the FI, against the secret faction of the leadership, which was revealed mainly in the US SWP.[15]

The Communist League

The split by the Communist League was certainly a consequence of the factional situation in the FI. I described it in Volume 1, and we published all the documents in two bulletins.[16] We organised SWL-CL debates on the main international issues in dispute, and cooperated on some solidarity issues.

On June 28, 1973, French President Georges Pompidou and his government outlawed the Ligue Communiste, the French FI section, arresting prominent leaders Alain Krivine and Pierre Rousset and hunting down others. We collaborated well with the Communist League in organising a broad defence campaign around Australia. We picketed the French consulate in Sydney on July 3, and organised broad protest meetings in the main cities. Tariq Ali from the British International Marxist Group was touring for the CL at the time, so he was a key speaker at some of the meetings. (His visit had originally been planned for the previous year. His separate public meetings drew 200 in Sydney and 250 in

Melbourne, according to *DA* 45.)

The August 1 public meeting at Sydney Trades Hall calling to "Lift the ban on the Ligue Communiste – Free Krivine and Rousset" was attended by more than 200 and had a broad platform of speakers: Tariq Ali; John Bechara from the Palestinian community; Bill Brown, SPA; Joan Evatt, Young Labor Council; Denis Freney, CPA; Hall Greenland from the International group; Dave Holmes, SWL; Jim Mulgrew, SLL; George Petersen, Member of the Legislative Assembly; Di Zetlin, CL; with Nita Keig chairing.

A similar broad meeting was held in Melbourne with 150 attending, according to *DA* 46. At the Presbyterian Church hall, Peter Conrick chaired. (It was disrupted by the Maoists complaining that we weren't also defending *their* comrades in France!)

There was an outpouring of protest around the world. A protest meeting of 10-15,000 people was held in Paris. *DA* 47 reported that Krivine and Rousset had been freed following strong protests in France and internationally.

The second conference of the Communist League was held January 26-28, 1974, and we were able to send an observer. Dave Holmes reported on January 30 that it was attended by 20-25 CLers and sympathisers, and about 10 observers. John McCarthy gave all the reports. There was very little discussion. The observers were: from John Scott's group – Tony Dewberry, Tony Kelly, Megan Sharpe; Dave Holmes; Lynda Boland and Lee Walkington; Chris Gafffney; Peter McGregor; Chris White and a woman from Adelaide.

"Compared to ourselves these people seem to have stood still since the split eighteen months ago", Dave wrote. Especially, there were differences with the CL's Melbourne branch. (These centred on the branch's view that CL "practice was often sectarian; that the newspaper had an abstract propagandist tone, which was not very interesting or accessible to militant workers; and that the CL's economic and political analysis was often copied from Fourth International resolutions, without adequately analysing the specific features of the Australian situation"; following the 1975 CL conference, the entire Melbourne branch left the organisation.[17]) Dave referred further to "… the fact, admitted by everyone and expressed explicitly in their documents, that the CL has been a complete failure since it was formed". "In summary: the CL is in crisis and sees itself as in crisis. The membership is confused and demoralised."

Shortly after this conference, in early 1974, we persuaded Lynda Boland and Lee Walkington, who had been in the UK when the split occurred and supported the International Majority Tendency, to resign peacefully from the SWL and join the CL (with whom they were clearly collaborating politically anyway). An important joint solidarity campaign was the Brisbane Three defence in 1975.

Trying to clamp down on the developing Black movement, the Brisbane police staged a frame-up, charging John Garcia from the CL and Dennis Walker, son of Black poet Oodgeroo Noonuccal (Kath Walker), and Lionel Fogarty with "attempting to obtain money with menaces" and "conspiracy". *DA* 92 reported joint CL-SWL meetings with John Garcia in Sydney, Adelaide, Melbourne and Brisbane. In a victory for the Black rights movement, the Brisbane Three case was dismissed at the end of the year.

Third SWL conference

Our third conference registered significant growth and our serious attitude to building the party. Dave Holmes stated in his organisation report, as quoted in *DA* 54, "1973 has been a very good year for the SWL. We have definitely grown into a solidly-structured, well-functioning nucleus". The conference was held near Sydney, December 29, 1973-January 1, 1974, very much as preparation for the FI World Congress. Ninety-three attendees registered, including 69 members, 20 observers and three international guests, including Harry Ring from the US SWP and Matt Robson from the NZ SAL. The draft political resolution for the congress had been adopted by the NC on September 22, 1973.

Reports for the PC and counter-reports for the IEC Majority Tendency were given on the international political situation, Europe, Latin America and world movement. Other reports were on the political resolution, youth and organisation.

The NC elected was: Jim Percy, Jamie Doughney, Greg Adamson, Geoff Payne, John Percy, Sol Salby, Nita Keig, Allen Westwood, Steve Painter, Gordon Adler, Jim McIlroy, Peter Conrick, Dave Holmes, Andrew Jamieson and Doug Lorimer. Alternate NC members in order were: Col Maynard, Dave Deutschmann, Bernie Murphy, Jenny Ferguson, Jane Beckman and Deb Shnookal. (At that time we were *very* weak in the representation of women in our leadership.)

We followed up with a Socialist Summer Educational Camp, January 26-28 in Victoria (at Stieglitz), with talks by Harry Ring, Nita Keig, Jamie Doughney and Sol Salby.

Membership had increased by 60 percent since our last conference, with a very low turnover. Two big branches in Sydney and Melbourne had developed, and the branch in Adelaide and an SYA group in Canberra, although we had closed down the Brisbane branch. Dave Holmes in his conference organisation report pointed out we were getting "away from an exclusively youth image which can be a barrier to recruiting many of the people we meet in the women's liberation movement, the Labor Party, etc." We had projected a regular forum series at the previous national conference, "and now Sydney and Melbourne and lately Adelaide have well-established forums fortnightly".

"Every SWL branch should aim to set up a regular program of educational classes" over and above any classes on our basic political positions on current issues, to provide a grounding in basic Marxism, the report said. This could be on two levels: one for newer comrades and concentrating on more elementary questions, and another one for more advanced comrades (e.g. on Trotsky's *History of the Russian Revolution*) using a syllabus from the US SWP Education Department.

"For some time the most important educational activity we've been engaged in has been the international discussion in preparation for the coming world congress of the Fourth International [February 1974]. While the object of this discussion is to lead to the adoption by the organisation of a position on the disputed issues, it has been a tremendously important educational experience, one which has partly compensated for our failings on the regular classes. I think it's no exaggeration to say that despite everything our membership has never been so well grounded in the ideas of revolutionary Marxist politics."

The report also noted: "We need cadre and we need money if we're to be able to implement our program. Firstly, locally and nationally we've made a number of definite advances financially in 1973. The NO now receives a substantial and regular income from the branches (even if we haven't met our per capita sustainer target of $2 per week) … Some months ago the NO projected an almost 75% increase in expenditure and income in early 1974 … We need to give *DA* a regular and large subsidy; allocate substantial amounts for international collaboration, overseas trips; put on more full-time staff, and have them visit all centres regularly."

Literature distribution was running at 160 percent of 1972 figures. The legal incorporation of Pathfinder Press (Australia) was shortly to be finalised. "One key task in 1974 is to professionalise the local bookstalls", Holmes said, while building up *Intercontinental Press* circulation was another priority. Overall circulation of *IP* in Australia was now 130.

He reported that we had two comrades full time for SWL and three on *DA*, and we would aim to strengthen staff during the year. (We also had two in the Melbourne branch, one in the Sydney branch.) In the early years, comrades would be stretching out their student status, taking advantage of commonwealth scholarships, or on the dole. As we got more serious, we were able to raise money to keep comrades on as full-timers, with a small sustainer, just enough to live on.

Direct Action was our single most important weapon. The paper was "the organiser of our tendency", putting out a clear political line on all the issues that concerned us here and abroad. During the year, we had increased the size to 24 pages. "Compared to the Communist Party's paper *Tribune, Direct Action* is just so obviously superior. Also,

we know that our circulation is comparable to theirs. And even on subs we have at times equalled theirs." Boosting *DA* circulation was set as a major task in 1974, which should involve the whole membership, with:
1. a renewal drive on subs, visiting subscribers;
2. a drive for 500 new subs;
3. an ongoing effort throughout the year to meet our sales quotas regularly, to raise them and to get the street sales up substantially.

We also projected a public fund drive for *DA* of $3,000, over 10 weeks.

The 1974 FI World Congress

We'd been preparing for the 10th World Congress of the Fourth International in February 1974 through reading the extensive international discussion bulletins, holding some organised debates with the CL, organising educational series and using our third SWL conference. Jim Percy and I attended the World Congress, held in Rimini, Italy, for the SWL. We also attended a pre-World Congress LTF meeting in Brussels. I had also attended the US SWP Special World Congress Convention and the YSA convention beforehand.

The World Congress was attended by 250 comrades from 41 countries. It adopted a nine-point "Agreement on Measures to Help Maintain Unity of the Fourth International", which had been unanimously adopted on February 14 by the presiding committee. The congress recognised both the SWL and CL as sympathising organisations.

The World Congress was a victory for the LTF and the FI as a whole; it was a hollow victory for the IMT in maintaining their mechanical majority. The LTF achieved its main goal and prevented a split, blocking the exclusion of our forces; all were inside the FI for the next stage of political struggle. It was not a conclusive World Congress; there was only limited discussion on many issues.[18]

I returned to Sydney on March 14, 1974, via India and Hong Kong.

Indian visit

In India I had a very inspiring experience visiting Gujarat state, Baroda and Surat. The comrades there were only a small group, in relation to the enormous population and in comparison with the large Stalinist parties, but the FI group, the Communist League of India, had recently recruited Magan Desai, a former Gujarat state leader of the CPI (M), the largest of the Communist parties (in office in West Bengal at the time). Magan had been in prison, where he studied the works of Trotsky and Mandel. The Gujarat group was growing, and they had recruited some very dynamic young people. Magan and the Gujarat comrades generally supported the politics of the LTF.

I sent a letter to SWP leader Gus Horowitz in New York in March, reporting on my India trip: "I found the whole experience inspiring and enjoyable. This was despite some fear and uncertainty before I got there, caused partly I think by your stories about the food, water and so on. As it turned out, I adapted very quickly to the Indian environment … At the end of the week I found that I'd fallen in love with the country, in spite of, or perhaps because of, the incredible poverty and contradictions of the society."

I arrived in Bombay on March 6, and spoke to a meeting of the comrades, giving an overall report on the World Congress and the role of the LTF in preventing a split. I also gave a brief report on the development and the activities of the SWL in Australia. "The following evening I left by train for Baroda. I met Magan Desai … in the afternoon I addressed some of the comrades on the World Congress. About 15 were there, all LTF members or supporters. (The Bombay group was sloppily organised, they hadn't informed Magan Desai about my arrival details.) I again reported to about 9 LTF members the following day.

"In the evening, the Study and Struggle Alliance (their youth group) had organised a meeting for me at their headquarters … At a day's notice they had assembled about 45 students … and I spoke on the student revolt around the world … They seem to have a lot of new, eager young people around them."

The next day I left for Surat, and reported to the comrades there on the World Congress, and noted the contrast between "the proclamation style of politics which seems to be the norm in Bombay and the actual party-building work that Magan is carrying out in Gujarat". There seemed to be jealousy from Bombay directed at the youth advances in Gujarat. In Surat the group "was in the student movement as leaders of that movement. (At one stage Bhagirath was arrested as a leader of a demonstration, and thousands of men and women students sat down and blockaded the police station where he was being held, forcing his release.) A lot of comrades were very insistent that I stay longer or at least come back soon … I was given an extremely hospitable welcome."

Working on *Intercontinental Press*

I had been asked to work full time on *Intercontinental Press*, the Marxist international news magazine based in New York that the US SWP produced for the FI. The understanding was also that I'd be an Australian comrade participating in the international leadership of the LTF. Initially the assignment had been projected for a period of six months, but eventually I was persuaded to stay for 18 months. On arrival back in Australia from the India trip after the World Congress, I found myself faced with a very large backlog of work, so I had to delay my intended departure for New York until immediately after the SYA national conference, June 15-17, 1974. On June 18, I left Sydney for New York via San Francisco. Joe Hansen, the SWP leader and theoretician, and bodyguard to Trotsky at Coyoacán in the late 1930s, was the founding editor of *IP* in 1963, and still editing it through the '70s. Joe and Reba Hansen had initially gone to Europe to establish the magazine and edit it there, as a result of the 1963 FI reunification. They had to return to New York and publish it from there after Joe became ill in Europe. Allen Myers was managing editor of *IP* in the early '70s, but soon after I started there in 1974, he and Helen Jarvis moved to Australia for good. That meant a loss for *IP*, but very real gains for us – we gained a very capable and well-trained Marxist editor. Contributing editors from the FI were listed as Pierre Frank, Livio Maitan, Ernest Mandel and George Novack. Also on staff at the time I arrived were Mike Baumann, Gerry Foley, Judy White, Ernest Harsch, Dick Fidler (from the Canadian group LSA/LSO) and Cristina Rivas (from the Mexican FI group). Others who worked there at different times while I was there were Caroline Lund, Dave Frankel and a comrade from the Argentine PST. Steven Warshell was assistant business manager to Reba Hansen, and Mary Roche was copy editor.

My life in New York was a big shock for the first month, but then I acclimatised, seeming to adjust better than US comrades from outside New York, who hated the place. I was fascinated at the raw life, the contrasts, the extremes of wealth and poverty, the life on the streets. I was living six floors above the corner of 6th Avenue and 11th Street, in Greenwich Village. New York building regulations stipulated that for any buildings over six floors, the landlord had to install an elevator, so whole blocks of slummy cheap six floor buildings mushroomed, and of course the cheapest apartments were on the sixth floor, where you had to trudge up and down six flights! These were the cheapest apartments at the time, and close to our office, but I'm told that today the area has skyrocketed in value, and it would be very expensive to live there now.

The area had constant noisy traffic throughout the night, and due to my jetlag after a long flight, and adjusting to very new surroundings and my new assignment, I didn't get much sleep in that first month. I was sharing the flat first with Lew Jones, then with Barry Sheppard, then with Wendy Reissner. Initially I had hoped to get a small apartment for myself, but after searching around lower Manhattan and inspecting some terrible dumps and some flats at inflated prices, I eventually ended up sharing the same place throughout my stay.

New York was a fascinating, but also dangerous, place. Muggings and street crime and burglaries were common. I led a charmed life the whole time I was there, but many of the other comrades working on *IP* or in the SWP National Office at 410 West Street were not so lucky. Judy White seemed to have the record for muggings, followed by Gerry Foley, who seemed to be a natural victim. Gerry was a quiet, harmless looking guy, who spoke dozens of languages, and had the incredible talent to be able to master a new language in a few weeks if a revolutionary upsurge occurred in a new place, such as Czechoslovakia. In order to deter potential muggers, Barry Sheppard told me his tactic was sometimes to adopt the persona of a crazy guy staggering down the street. Allen Myers and Helen Jarvis had a particularly unhappy record with burglaries, including when, after they installed multiple locks and door bars on their door, the robbers just knocked a hole in their wall and cleaned them out! The deal they had worked out between themselves for alternately spending five years in New York in the US SWP, then five in Sydney in the Australian SWL, was abandoned some time after their 1974 move to Sydney, fortunately for us. They didn't fancy another five years in New York, so after that first five-year stint, they were members and leaders of our party for good.

The SWP national office and editing and printing operations were in a building on West Street, which ran along the Hudson River. It was a smart buy negotiated by Barry Sheppard, the national organisation secretary of the SWP. It was a four-storey old building on the waterfront, close to Greenwich Village, which had been an old ship chandler's building. The SWP comrades renovated it, built comfortable and modern air-conditioned offices, eventually with their own web offset printing press on the ground floor. It housed the SWP and YSA national offices, the *Militant* editorial, typesetting and layout, Pathfinder Press publishing, *Intercontinental Press* and a library and lunch area and deck on the top floor. It was a very impressive and efficient national office for a party that had been growing rapidly from its leading role in the movement against the Vietnam War.

Covering all the side wall of the building was a very impressive mural – depicting the revolutionary traditions and the revolutionary printing press churning out the publications of Marx, Lenin, Trotsky etc. The mural was painted by Mike Alewitz, with contributions from other revolutionary artists from different countries. Alewitz had been one of the leaders of the antiwar movement at Kent State University in Ohio, where four students were shot by the National Guard trying to intimidate an anti-Vietnam War demonstration on May 4, 1970. He is still working as a mural painter and teacher of mural painting. He survived the degeneration of the US SWP and was expelled prior to the project's conclusion and excluded from its opening ceremony. Jack Barnes attempted to amend the mural as his politics degenerated, and eventually had it erased.

The West Street building was sold for US$20 million in 2003, and Jack Barnes was sitting on the cash as the SWP's politics degenerated further and the membership was purged and dwindled, much to the chagrin of all those who were expelled or forced out after putting so much of their effort and money into it over the years. The building was demolished, and the site is now occupied by a high-rise building of very posh apartments. (When I visited New York to speak at Caroline Lund's memorial meeting in 2006, I strolled past it to inspect nostalgically what was there now.)

I adjusted to life in New York and my new assignment after a while. I invited the whole *IP* staff, including Joe and Reba Hansen, over for dinner one night, cooking an impressive Indian meal using Charmaine Solomon's shorter cookbook, which I had taken with me to New York. All the dishes turned out extremely well, impressing all the comrades that I was a very good cook, which I wasn't really. My reputation spread, reaching the ears of Jim, who was a bit peeved, hearing "your brother's a great cook". We both knew he was a *much* better cook than I was; the big meals he put on for comrades were legendary.

Writing as Peter Green

I had to overcome the "awe" of writing under the eye of Joe Hansen. Joe was totally political, and actually quite friendly and not aggressive, but his political reputation and knowledge and enormous experience were a bit scary for a young comrade coming from a new socialist party in Australia. My first efforts were stumbling, and not up to scratch, needing to be heavily edited. After a while I got more into the rhythm of it, and probably learned quite a bit about writing good articles for socialist papers. (I never felt very confident or fluent, although I had been editing or writing for *Direct Action* for nearly five years by then.)

Using the pen name Peter Green, the name of my smart black cat I'd left behind in Sydney, I contributed articles that covered Australia and other countries in the Asian region. That was my beat (and also arranging reprints covering Australia and some of the Asian developments). The articles I contributed covered a wide area, including:

"The Big-Character Posters on the Walls of China", August 5, 1974, also in *DA* 69, September 2, 1974, a lengthy piece;
"Dictator Park Steps Up Political Witch-Hunt", September 9, 1974;
"Two Million in Rallies Against Ford Visit to Japan," November 4, 1974;
"Behind the Diego Garcia Buildup", November 25, 1974;
"Palestinian Protests Sweep Occupied West Bank", December 2, 1974;

"Genoveva Forest Tortured by Franco's Police", December 9, 1974;

"American Intellectuals Protest Terror in Iran", December 16, 1974.

But by far the most exciting area to cover was Vietnam, chronicling the rapid and total collapse of the US puppet Thieu regime in the south. Some of the articles:

"Saigon: Will the Retreat Turn Into a Rout?", March 31, 1975;

"Swift Rise in Anti-American Sentiment in Saigon", April 7, 1975;

"The US Military Intervention Comes to an End", May 5, 1975;

"Saigon Cheers As Liberation Forces March In", May 12, 1975;

"Ford's Last 'Humanitarian' Mission Runs Into Flak", May 19, 1975;

"Calm in Saigon Punctures 'Bloodbath' Myth", June 2, 1975.

Fred Halstead's excellent book *Out Now!* on the history of the US movement against the war in Vietnam,[19] by probably the most important organiser of it, was squeezed out of Fred by Joe. He used the subterfuge of asking to view the first chapter, and then published it in *IP*, forcing Fred to write the rest to a regular schedule! It was published in *IP* during 1975 and then as a book.

While based in New York, I also attended the SWP confvention at Oberlin, Ohio, in August 1974 and 1975, and the YSA convention in Saint Louis in December 1974, and some other political events such as conferences and demonstrations, in Boston and Washington, DC. But mainly it was the weekly rhythm of helping on *IP* – researching, writing, proofreading, LTF meetings, following Australian politics and reporting back home.

On my weekly day off, I was able to explore New York a bit. A particularly memorable excursion was to the Cloisters, a beautiful old building on the northern tip of Manhattan, part of the Metropolitan Museum of Art, housing art treasures and tapestries from Europe (the beautiful "Unicorn Tapestries" from the late Middle Ages). The buildings had been transported stone by stone from European abbeys bought up by John D. Rockefeller. I also hiked across the George Washington Bridge to the Palisades, a park along the Hudson River where I was able to pick blackberries. I also wandered through Harlem (somewhat to the consternation of my US comrades a bit worried about my safety).

I subscribed to a cheap way to attend some classical music concerts, and expanded my knowledge and appreciation of music (I found new favourites – Janacek) and scoured second hand record shops for cheap vinyl records (which I eventually took with me back to Sydney).

Learning to stand on our own feet

Our experience in the FI in the '70s taught us the importance of building leaderships and parties that could stand on their own. It also dispelled many illusions we had about the FI in the early days – our naive view of a big, broad international movement that could provide the answers to all our problems of party building.

This lesson was also impressed on us theoretically through study of the lessons of the US SWP, with which we were aligned, especially the tradition of James P. Cannon. It was also practically impressed on us by the experience of the factional jungle in the FI. If you didn't have your own team, you'd be lost in the factional wrangling.

Through my experience in New York in 1974-75, we also started to realise the limits of our collaboration with the US SWP. The significance of this in the '70s was that we built our own leadership and our own political organisation. We did some things better than our mentors. We always did youth work better, and from early on we thought we were publishing a better revolutionary paper, and certainly distributing it more effectively. Nevertheless, I was able to send lots of information and reports on FI meetings, LTF meetings and SWP functioning, at the centre of things in New York:

- My June 24, 1974, letter to the SWL Political Committee enclosed extensive transcripts by me of a report to the LTF on the Internationalist Tendency by Jack Barnes; a report on Latin America by Ed Shaw; a world movement report to the SWP NC by Mary-Alice Waters and other reports to the SWP NC plenum.
- My July 11, 1974, letter to the SWL PC from New York reported on the YSA plenum, that it had a more confident tone than the SWP plenum, and that membership was now 1140. Ginny Hildebrand joked that their per capita sustainer had its most sudden leap in the YSA's history after the IT split. There was a good summary of the IT split. Thirty-nine percent of YSA members were in the SWP.
- My July 28, 1974, letter to comrades reported that Allen and Helen were coming back to Sydney – "the SWP leadership consider him probably the best journalist in the party". It also included an LTF bureau report by Anders Svedin on Sweden.
- My August 30, 1974, letter to the SWL PC from New York reported on the Oberlin SWP educational conference and that I'd sold 31 *DA* subs at the gathering. I gave details of the faction

meeting. I also reported the death of James P. Cannon.

• My September 5, 1974, letter to the SWL PC included a report to the LTF steering committee by Joe Hansen on the draft statement on the Argentine PST. I had extensive notes on the discussion from Jack Barnes, Peter Camejo, Joe Hansen and others.

• My September 12, 1974, letter to the SWL PC had a report on the recent FI United Secretariat meeting, plus an attached article from the Stalinist *Information Bulletin* attacking the CPA.

• My September 19, 1974, letter to the SWL PC included a report by Caroline Lund on Japan, noting that Yoichi Sakai, the leader of the Japanese Trotskyists of the Revolutionary Communist League, was increasingly following Pablo's theories.

• My October 10, 1974, letter to the SWL PC enclosed a report on the September 5 meeting of the steering committee: a report on the IEC by Mary-Alice Waters, a report on the World Congress by Joe Hansen, a report on the International Internal Discussion Bulletins by Gus Horowitz, a report on Argentina by Hugo (last name now unknown).

• My October 24, 1974, letter to the SWL PC enclosed a report by Joe Hansen on a meeting with the Lambertistes and information from Jack Barnes on the October United Secretariat meeting about the FI leadership wanting a top SWP member on the Bureau.

• My November 5, 1974, letter to the SWL PC included a report on Greece by Ed Shaw.

• My November 22, 1974, letter to the SWL PC had a report by Ed Shaw on the French LTF, a report on the United Secretariat meeting and a report on France by Mary-Alice Waters.

• My December 3, 1974, letter to the SWL PC enclosed a report by Mary-Alice Waters to the LTF after returning from Europe, on France, and the IEC meeting.

• My January 7, 1975, letter to the SWL PC from New York after attending the St. Louis YSA convention had lots of news and gossip – it mentioned the expulsion of Alan Thornett and 200 others from the Healyite Workers Revolutionary Party. (We benefited: WRP NC member Kate Blakeney fled to Australia, and we recruited her into our leadership for several years.) US Workers League leader Tim Wohlforth had been ousted by

Healy. I gave a very positive description of the YSA conference rally: "a glimpse of the future mass revolutionary party that the SWP will become"; it was "well-polished" and "professionally delivered".

A serious attitude to building the party

We had struggled for five years in the late '60s to get a Marxist party going. We were very serious about this goal. The first five years of the '70s were very much our early years, when we developed the skills and habits of party building.

Direct Action was our regular agitator, propagandist and educator and was central to our functioning. It was our main tool, and organised our forces, but we increasingly developed other weapons:

- publishing our own pamphlets and books;
- speaking tours by international comrades;
- educational conferences and camps.

Propaganda

We seriously sold and promoted all the books and pamphlets published by the US SWP and its publishing arm Pathfinder Press (and Monad Press). The SWP by this time was producing an impressive variety of Marxist literature. Its catalogue included a very extensive range of works by Leon Trotsky and the Left Opposition, Ernest Mandel and the Fourth International, James P. Cannon, Farrell Dobbs, Joe Hansen and George Novack and books on US labour movement history.

We also made good use of taped lectures that the SWP produced. A March 1973 circular listed the US SWP educational tapes that were available for hiring by branches.

Our earliest Resistance publications in the 1960s and early 1970s were roneoed reprints of pamphlets published by Pathfinder Press, or sometimes copies of interesting articles from *New Left Review*. We initially published our own pamphlets and distributed Pathfinder Press books under the label "Socialist Books". These early reprints were often pamphlets by Ernest Mandel, such as *An Introduction to Marxist Economic Theory; The Marxist Theory of the State; The Debate on Workers Control; Revolutionary Strategy in Imperialist Countries; Leon Trotsky – The Man and his Work; The Leninist Theory of Organisation;* or by Leon Trotsky: *I Stake My Life; The Death Agony of Capitalism and the Tasks of the Fourth International; Fascism – What It Is and How to Fight It.* We also reprinted *On the Revolutionary Potential of the Working Class,* by Mandel and Novack; and pamphlets by Evelyn Reed: *Women: Caste, class or oppressed sex?; Is Man an Aggressive Ape?; Problems of Women's Liberation.* We also reprinted *The Politics of Women's Liberation Today,* by Mary-Alice Waters, and *In Defence of the Women's Movement,* by Waters, Ruthann Miller and Reed. We reprinted *The Truth About Israel and Zionism,* by Nathan Weinstock and Jon Rothschild, and *Burning Issues of the Mid-East Crisis,* by Peter Buch.

In 1973 we decided to establish our book distribution on a more professional basis, so Socialist Books became Pathfinder Press (Australia) and we set ourselves up on a more legal basis. The books we published from 1977 on were under this imprint. Was New York a bit upset by us using the same name? I think so. We intended the copying as respectful, but even back then I think Jack Barnes was resentful of anything he didn't have complete control over.

We continued to reprint pamphlets. In the 1980s, when we acquired access to photocopy machines and a more sophisticated reproducing machine in the Sydney National Office and a small printing press in Melbourne, we embarked on even more extensive reprinting of pamphlets. The quality was a lot better now. We reproduced many short works by Trotsky and Mandel (works by Marx, Engels and Lenin were published cheaply by Moscow and Beijing, and available through CPA bookshops). We also reprinted Novack's *An Introduction to Dialectical Logic; The Bourgeois Revolutions: Their Achievements and Limitations; The First and Second Internationals* and *The Labour Theory of Human Origins.* A perennial reprint was Peter Camejo's *Liberalism, Ultraleftism or Mass Action,* Che Guevara's *Socialism and Man* and some works by James P. Cannon, such as his 1953 speech on *Internationalism and the SWP.* In Melbourne we reproduced pamphlets by Rosa Luxemburg, Gregory Zinoviev, Leo Huberman and Robin Blackburn as well as our standard texts.

In the mid-1980s an interesting current in the USA was moving away from its Maoist origins and producing a number of useful theoretical works. It published the journal *Line of March,* and we reprinted some of its most interesting articles as pamphlets: *Toward a Communist Analysis of Black Oppression and Black Liberation,* by Linda Burnham and Bob Wing; *The Labour Aristocracy* by Max Elbaum and Robert Seltzer; and *The Impossible Marriage* by Linda Burnham.

When Doug Lorimer was running the SWP full-time party school in the 1980s and afterwards, he reprinted a number of historical and theoretical works in the form of multiple pamphlets, initially for the comrades attending the school or other courses, but they were also available for sale in our bookshops and stalls. For example, Farrell Dobbs' *From the Communist Manifesto to the Communist International: A History of the Marxist Movement, 1848-1921,* was reproduced as four pamphlets. Doug abridged into five pamphlets the book *Fundamentals of Dialectical Materialism* (Progress Publishers, Moscow, 1967), which would have helped him write his own book, which we published in 1999, *Fundamentals of Historical Materialism. The Marxist View of History and Politics.*

International speaking tours

The tour we organised for US SWP member Jim Little – "Watergate: the view from the left" – gained wide coverage on national television, radio and in student and daily papers. The media were especially interested in the US SWP's US$27.3 million suit filed against the government for spying and harassment (its Cointelpro program). Campus meetings and *DA* forums were held in Sydney on May 31, 1974, Adelaide June 7, Melbourne June 13 and Canberra. A total of 800 attended the Melbourne campus meetings, according to *DA* 64.

Ironically, of course, we were being spied on too, and Jim Little especially was being spied on by ASIO, probably under instructions from Washington. They filmed everyone going into our 1974 SYA fifth national conference, held in Melbourne at the Greek Community Hall in Lonsdale Street on the corner of Russell Street, June 15-17. (The footage is a handy reminder for us about who were our members in those early days!)[20]

The international report was given by Jamie Doughney, the women's liberation report by Deb Shnookal. Geoff Payne presented the report on Europe. Doug Lorimer gave the report on Latin America. Peter Conrick reported on the political resolution, and Greg Adamson gave the organisation report.

The rally was addressed by Jim Little and Mike Tucker from the NZ Young Socialists, Tony Maron, the general secretary of Friends of Palestine, Jenny Neilson (Ferguson) a leader of the 32 socialists expelled from the Victorian YLA, Jim Percy and Deb Shnookal, the organiser of Melbourne SYA. The rally fund appeal raised $1,550 in cash and pledges.

I flew off to my *IP* assignment in New York the day after the conference. Mike Tucker gave talks to *DA* forums in Melbourne and Sydney, and US WONAAC (Women's National Abortion Action Campaign) speaker Jessica Star toured Australia in July-August, after her NZ tour.

The most successful speaking tour was that by Ernest Mandel, organised by the SWL and the CL in September 1974, speaking in Sydney, Brisbane, Adelaide and Melbourne on "Can Capitalism Survive?" He also spoke on the topic "What is the Soviet Union and Where is it Going?" on campuses. It was especially important for Mandel, breaking the ban that had been imposed on him by the previous Liberal government in 1970, and confronting the ban that still existed in a number of countries.

It was very useful for us. Thousands heard him speak. People were turned away at the doors. There were 900 at Assembly Hall, Melbourne, 1,100 at Melbourne University, 900 at the main Sydney meeting. We wrote in *DA* 70 that it was "the largest in terms of audiences, impact and press coverage of any tour by a left-wing figure for decades".

Education

We were also organising other successful educational activities, in branches and nationally, and taking our education program more seriously. On April 12-14, 1974, Sydney SYA organised a Socialist Education Conference, with speakers John Percy, Jamie Doughney, Jim Percy and Dave Holmes.

For the end of the year, December 28, 1974-January 1, 1975, we organised a summer education camp at Ocean Grove Camp in Victoria. We had a good turn-up, with 134 attending (*DA* 77). We reprinted some of the reports from the trade union panel at Ocean Grove in our internal information bulletin (No. 2 in 1975).

And we developed the rhythm of organising special national educational conferences every two years, in between our national decision-making conferences.

We also organised regular "Introduction to Socialism" series in the larger branches, to attract new people. The next stage after Introduction to Socialism classes was our "Introduction to Marxism" series for new members, to give comrades a grounding in basic Marxism. We also organised special class series on particular topics of current interest.

A serious attitude to finances

A serious attitude to finances, and being able to raise money, are essential for a serious socialist group. We were very impressed by the professionalism of the US SWP, and learned from them. We had many tiers of raising funds.

First, all members paid regular dues (quarterly), which were fairly nominal and not beyond the reach of any comrade. These went directly to the National Office.

Second, comrades were encouraged to pay a weekly pledge, according to their financial circumstances. This was voluntary, but comrades were politically motivated to pledge as much as they could afford. We held regular campaigns to encourage everyone in the branch to pay at least some sort of pledge, and to raise it when they could. This was organised in the branches, and was partly used to run the branch, while some was sent as a regular "sustainer" to the National Office, which we campaigned to raise.

Third, we organised fund drives, usually launched with rallies, at both our educational and decision-making conferences, at which comrades were encouraged to pledge a significant amount and pay it off over a year. These were a feature of our conferences, taken from the US SWP; comrades were inspired, and knew that we were stretching ourselves. We also organised special fund-raising events in the branches to contribute to the fund drive.

Sometimes we were able to encourage richer supporters to make a sizeable donation for special projects, such as new office equipment, or towards new buildings we wanted to buy. And we encouraged members and supporters to remember us in their wills.

As we grew and got more organised, we projected increasingly ambitious fund drives. Our fund drive from July 29 to mid-December 1972 raised $2,001, just over the quota we'd set. (Some of it was needed to pay for Jim's trip to the Fourth International IEC meeting.) The 1973 *DA* fund drive was set for $5,000; our 1975 fund drive had a target of $7,000 and raised $8,022. The 1976 drive raised $23,359. By 1981 our fund drive target was up to $58,000, reaching $57,119 by the last *DA* for the year, and probably going over.

Banquets and dinners became a regular part of branch life and our fund-raising activities. The first in Sydney we held in the first building we bought, at 139 St. John's Road in Glebe, on September 29, 1973. We promoted them usually as supporting and raising money for *DA,* and scheduled a few speeches, plus live music if we could get it. They became regular launches for our election campaigns and other political projects.

This first dinner had a fairly poor attendance, although we couldn't have fitted too many more supporters into the small downstairs room. But they gradually grew, until they were very popular, and filled local town halls that we hired. A Sydney banquet on December 14, 1974, to commemorate the life of James P. Cannon, had 110 people at Balmain Town Hall. In July 1975 the Sydney dinner had 120. We prided ourselves on serving good food, and had a number of good cooks, including Jim Percy and Peter Holloway.

As well as raising money and promoting our paper or election campaign, the dinners served other very useful purposes, consolidating our members and building our periphery of supporters. We built up dinner kits, acquiring good collections of cooking pots, crockery and cutlery and glasses, at auctions and special sales. This also saved money from hiring and avoided using less impressive paper plates and plastic utensils.

Another regular fundraising institution became our jumble sales. These required a fair bit of time and effort by comrades to solicit, collect and sort the donated goods, advertise the event and staff the stalls on the day. They often allowed newer or less confident comrades to make a contribution, and also had the spin-off of sometimes being able to advertise our local presence and activities.

The first jumble sales I remember were organised from our Glebe building and held across the road outside Glebe Town Hall. One on August 25, 1973, organised by Sydney central SYA branch, raised $137 (about a third of our national fund drive target). We collected unwanted goods, clothing, bric-a-brac not only from comrades and relatives, but by leafleting the surrounding houses.

An unfortunate incident happened at one Glebe jumble sale when our over-enthusiastic volunteers collected the bags of jumble stored in our headquarters across the road, and inadvertently also collected the bags of laundry from branch organiser Al Westwood, who was living in the building. Al was involved in frantic scenes trying to rescue his clothes from the jumble sale, at one stage having a tug of war with a potential buyer who fancied his jeans!

We also raised money by running serious raffles. We advertised a colour TV set as the first prize in a 1976 raffle, and second or third prizes could be a sub to *DA*, or a book voucher for our bookshop. Later raffle prizes were solicited from local businesses, which were happy to donate prizes in return for the advertising on the raffle tickets, and in the late '80s we organised very ambitious raffle prizes, including flights and holidays in Czechoslovakia and a return trip to the Soviet Union.

Starting to buy our own buildings

The serious attitude to finances paid off, with us ending up buying our own buildings, saving money on rent and eventually getting significant financial windfalls as the buildings increased in value.

We bought our first building in 1972, a three-storey terrace at 139 St. John's Road in Glebe.

It had previously been a hamburger shop, next to a newsagent, opposite Glebe Town Hall. It was just a block or two from Sydney University, and not too far from the city, many of our *DA* selling spots and most of the demos, so it served us well.

We bought the building for $28,000, with a $3,000 deposit and repayments of $80 per week. That was a fair bit in those days, and it stretched us, but it was much more logical than paying monthly rent to landlords. Eventually we owned the building, and it forced us to take the task of raising money, and accounting for it, more seriously.

We organised working bees to fix the place up – clean it up and clear out the junk, and build partitions and furniture that served our needs. We always had moved into dumps for our headquarters, but now all the hard work was being put into something we owned. We reaped the benefits when we sold.

And it ensured we continued to develop a serious and professional attitude to raising money for our political activities, gradually accumulating assets that assured our stability. We were also getting more professional in our national office. Dave Holmes played an important role in getting our finances in order (beyond our initial slapdash state, when they were mostly notes in Jim's shirt pocket). We were also well served in the finance office by Peter Holloway and Dot Tumney, who was a stalwart for many years in the '80s and '90s. (Dot joined SYA at age 18 in 1971, and attended the founding conference of the SWL. She remained a devoted member for the rest of her life, despite being diagnosed with multiple sclerosis in 1979. She died, from cancer, in December 2003.)

Raising our profile

Selling our press, putting on public meetings and forums, carrying large banners at rallies and building contingents for May Day marches or other demonstrations were all methods of raising our profile and competing with others on the left, especially the traditional left organisation, the CPA. *DA* 61, for example, reported that our 1974 May Day contingent was 145 in Sydney and 100 in Melbourne.

We were conscious of trying to break into the bourgeois media, which we had succeeded in doing during the '60s and the campaign against the war in Vietnam, but it was becoming harder in the '70s as the capitalists became more conscious that any publicity, even red-baiting, helped build us.

At the end of 1975, standing in elections for the first time was intended both to raise our profile and to raise the key issues. In the 1974 double dissolution election, we enjoyed big *DA* sales at Labor rallies.

Our political interventions

The perspectives document adopted by the SWL National Committee plenum, January 1-2, 1975, reported:

> The last year has been one of the most hectic years yet for our
> tendency. We participated in and helped to lead and organised a wider

range of activities than at any year since SYA was founded in 1970. Our range of activity included the following:

1. A campaign in the YLA in Victoria, supported by activity in other states, to win readmission after being expelled bureaucratically by the right-wing executive ... our success in winning reinstatement gained us prestige and respect as a serious and determined tendency.

2. We played a major role in the debate on campuses around the Palestine question. Almost alone of tendencies on the left we were able to build a campaign of support for the Palestinians.

3. In Melbourne we played a major role in building International Women's Day, the largest political march in that city this year.

4. We have led the campaign for the repeal of abortion laws. Activity has included demonstrations in May and a tour of WONAAC activist Jessica Star.

5. We have played an active role in the campaign against the repression in Chile. We were able to deal the Stalinists a big blow in Sydney by heading off an attempt to exclude us.

6. We have played an important role in many other campaigns from the defence of Black activist Dennis Walker to the protest against the visit of the Shah of Iran.

7. We have played a role in a key union, the Builders Labourers Federation through our activity in the rank-and-file group in Melbourne.

8. We made an important intervention in the Feminism and Socialism conference attended by 600 women in Melbourne.

Party-building steps

We also went through the important party-building steps we had taken in 1974:

(a) We have participated in the 10th World Congress of the Fourth International and made the views of our organisation known on the issues in dispute.

(b) We organised big contingents in May Day in Sydney and Melbourne – the second biggest contingent in Sydney and the biggest in Melbourne.

(c) We organised our biggest SYA conference ever, our open rally drawing 170 people.

(d) We organised a successful tour by YSAer Jim Little on Watergate.

(e) We organised the biggest public meetings on the left for years with the tour of Ernest Mandel which we jointly sponsored with the Communist League.

(f) We have run a regular series of forums in Sydney and Melbourne. We are alone on the left in our ability to do this.

(g) We have put out our now regular fortnightly newspaper – 23 issues have appeared this year.

(h) Our advances in party building have been significant. Our financial situation has steadily improved allowing us to have 12 comrades nationally on full-time political work. Melbourne and Sydney branches have stabilised and broadened their leaderships and Adelaide branch has begun to grow significantly. While we have lost some members, particularly in Sydney, our membership has gone over the 90 mark in the SWL. Without a doubt we have grown qualitatively much stronger during the year.

We projected running candidates in the next elections, outlining our reasons: "the primary reasons we did not run in 1972 or 1974 … were largely related to our own small size and apparatus. We also estimated that in 1972 it would not be quite so easy to expose Labor. We would be arguing too much on what they did in 1949, not the present.

"Both these factors have changed. We are much stronger and Labor stands exposed starkly on key questions. Moreover, while the Victorian YLA is important to us, we note a comparative limiting of ferment in the ALP ranks signalled by the decline of mass participation in the Victorian Socialist Left.

"The main danger is routinism and pessimism because of the lull in the youth radicalisation. We need to go on a permanent campaign footing: we want a conscious, vigorous propaganda campaign aimed at popularising our party and our ideas. Running candidates fits into this perspective precisely." (If we'd known at the time how long the lull would continue, there would probably have been even fewer of us who would last the distance!)

We also projected regular forums, expansion of sales of our press and Pathfinder titles, organising tours of international comrades and, in collaboration with SYA, organising a big series of social activities. We projected a fund drive of $7,000 for *DA*, a drive for 700 new subs, and a push to boost our sustainer to the NO to $3 per member per week. We stated, "A sustained and intensive educational campaign is central to our work in the months ahead".

We soberly assessed our opponents, especially the CPA. "We are gaining on our opponents and the CPA remains our biggest problem. We hurt them in a number of ways. Firstly through our press – its readership is bigger than theirs and they know it. Secondly on campus – we are stronger. Thirdly in the women's movement they regard us as their major opponent. We also dealt them a big blow over Chile."

We also produced *Samizdat*, a Marxist journal of the arts, initiated by comrade Gordon Adler. The first issue, in November 1974, was published as supplements in *Arena*, the publication of Macquarie University Students Council, and *Tharunka*, the publication of the University of New South Wales Students Union.

We participated in the big conference on feminism and socialism that took place in Melbourne October 5-6, with 600 in attendance. Our comrades presented five papers. We printed four of the papers as an eight-page lift-out in *DA* 72.

Expansion projections

In the first months of 1975, we made good progress on our projections. So the Political Committee on May 18, 1975, adopted a proposal to launch an Expansion Fund. It set a target of $17,000 to be raised in the next six months, aiming at getting nest eggs and big donations, on top of the normal dues, pledges and *DA* fund drive. We had already raised $5,000 of the $7,000 *DA* fund, and presented a list of equipment and special projects that we regarded as essential:

- for *DA* and *Young Socialist* we needed new typesetting equipment, an IBM Selectric composer to replace the old IBM electric typewriter;
- a photocopy machine;
- a sub-wrapping machine, as our subscription base grew;
- shelving for the National Office;
- a pamphlet publishing program;
- collaboration with the world Trotskyist movement, i.e. international travel;
- our election campaign;
- renovating the new Melbourne headquarters;
- moving back into Brisbane;
- moving the Sydney branches of SWL and SYA downtown.
- In March-April 1975 we organised a speaking tour for Black US SWP leader Nan Bailey.

In June SYA launched its own paper, *Young Socialist*.

The SWL NC on July 26-27, 1975, assessed our progress. It adopted a resolution on the Tasmanian Socialist Labour Club, with which we were in the process of uniting, and heard an optimistic tasks and perspectives report: "At our last NC we said that 1974 was our busiest year yet. But events this year have been at an even quicker tempo ... Other party-building tasks we achieved were:

"1. We held our summer educational camp – our biggest yet.

"2. We acquired and moved into new headquarters in Melbourne.

"3. Big contingents were built in the May Day demonstrations.

"4. Several successful dinner-dances were organised.

"5. We attended conferences of the SAL and NZ YS as well as the IEC.

"6. We achieved 852 subs in our drive in the first part of the year.

"7. We raised $8022, well over our fund drive target.

"8. We held the successful Nan Bailey tour and Easter educational conferences.

"9. We defended ourselves against red-baiting attacks and Maoist violence.

"10. We helped SYA launch its new *YS* paper."

ALP allegiances

The ACTU congress in September 1974 accepted the principle of wage reduction, and ACTU secretary Bob Hawke praised Labor's budget.

The Labor government continued to show who its real boss was by selling out the Leyland workers in Sydney. Sol Salby reported in *DA* 72: "In granting the Leyland Motor Corporation more than $25m for restructuring its operations in Australia the Labor Government has indicated its real priorities. It has shown its pro-business, anti-workers character by rushing to the aid of an ailing corporation while ignoring the plight of the workers being sacked." A mass meeting of the workers at the Zetland plant that was being closed down had voted that the "only solution they would accept was nationalisation".

But the ALP was still a long way from the lifeless hulk it was to become. One sign of this was our small victory, reported by Andrew Jamieson in *DA* 73: "Vic YLA socialists to be reinstated", as decided by the state ALP conference.

The background to this was that the October 1973 Victorian YLA state conference had defeated a motion to proscribe the SWL and SYA. Nevertheless, in February 1974, the newly elected YLA state executive at its first meeting summarily expelled 34 YLA members, including three members of the state executive, for "supporting Fourth International" and advocating "revolutionary ideas". Our campaign for reinstatement received motions of support from more than 15 YLA branches and more than 30 ALP branches. The petition was signed by more than 100 YLA and 500 ALP members. Prominent Labor figures including federal ministers Moss Cass and Kep Enderby gave support.

Another encouraging sign as the year ended was a result in the Victorian Tramways Union election, where SWL member Doug Jordan ran for vice-president and got a commendable result, just under 10 percent (*DA* 76).

Extending my New York assignment

For 18 months I was in New York, involved in and covering a lot of exciting political developments, but I missed an exciting 18 months of the development of our organisation back home. Jim Percy went to Europe in early 1975 for the FI IEC meeting. On February 6, Jim wrote to the PC from London, saying that LTF action had again prevented a split in the international. Jim had suggested to the LTF leadership and *IP* staff that I finish my *IP* assignment and head back to Australia quickly, but Joe and others disagreed – "John is one of the pillars of *IP*", he claimed. So it was agreed that I stay there until the end of the year.

So it was more *IP* writing (and I got to cover the final victory of the Vietnamese people), more immersion in the international, the debates and manoeuvring, and more missives back to Sydney. A few examples:
- My February 12, 1975, letter to the PC, discussing Nan Bailey's tour topics.
- My February 25, 1975, letter to the PC enclosed a report on Italy and the LTF by Art Young, and reports on India and Israel by Gus Horowitz; Japan and Hong Kong by Rich Finkel; and on Portugal by Ed Shaw.
- My March 12, 1975, letter to the PC. I was lining up a meeting with Doug Jenness to talk about election campaigns, which we were contemplating. I attached reports from Gus Horowitz on India; Gus on Israel; Rich Finkel on Japan and Hong Kong; Ed Shaw on Portugal.
- My June 5, 1975, letter to the PC. I enclosed a report by Mary-Alice Waters to the LTF meeting during the SWP NC plenum.
- My June 13, 1975, letter to the PC. Jack Barnes was strongly urging Jim to attend Oberlin. I attached a report on the FI United Secretariat meeting from Ed Shaw.
- My July 10, 1975, letter to the PC discussed the furore in the FI caused by the invitation to the French Lambertiste group to observe the SWP Oberlin conference.

- My July 22, 1975, letter from New York to the PC enclosed a report on the United Secretariat meeting that detailed Charles Michaloux's report on the IMT line on Portugal, and a debate about FI finances.
- My August 22, 1975, letter to the PC reported on the preparations for Oberlin. The main thing was Portugal, the "two sides of the barricades". It was "essential to reach [CL leader John] McCarthy on this".

Vietnam victory

Nixon had been re-elected on November 7, 1972. Peace negotiations were going on, and people had the feeling the war was over, but by November 18 the accord was still not signed. Small demos took place in the US, the largest, 2,000, in New York. They were also small in Australia: 1,000 in Melbourne, 500 in Sydney.

On December 18, Nixon resumed the bombing. The CPA and the Association for International Co-operation and Disarmament (AICD) were jolted. Several unions commendably placed bans on US commercial activities. For example, on December 29 the Seamen's Union black-banned US ships, with the support of other maritime unions.

An action was called for January 20, 1973, by the National Peace Action Coalition in the US, and taken up in Australia. But AICD and the CPA wouldn't be part of an all-in coalition, and there were all sorts of bureaucratic manoeuvres to try to make AICD *the* antiwar movement again.

In Washington on January 20, 1973, 100,000 turned up for the "counter-inaugural", but the actions were small in Australia: Sydney 600, Melbourne 700, Perth 350, Brisbane 200, Adelaide 200.

On January 23, Nixon announced that a cease-fire agreement had been reached. Bombing in the south continued until the signing on January 27. Bombing in Laos and Cambodia continued. But it was two more years before the real end of the war. The US rushed in enormous amounts of war supplies, "advisers" and technicians for its puppet regime. Fighters and B-52s were still stationed in Thai bases and on aircraft carriers off the coast.

The February 8, 1973, *DA* had as its cover story, "Why Vietnam Treaty Won't Bring Peace". The editorial concluded: "The struggle will continue in Vietnam against the Thieu regime's bloody dictatorship. Our struggle here will continue until the US is forced to withdraw entirely, and without imposing any conditions, from all of Southeast Asia. Only when that is done will the Vietnamese be able to determine their own future. Only then can there be peace in Indochina."

The final victory

With the US and Australian troops out, the antiwar movement went into recess, but the struggle in Vietnam continued against the Saigon puppet regime, until the final liberation of the country on April 30, 1975.

At the time I had the good fortune to be working on *Intercontinental Press*, and I had the pleasant task of chronicling the final collapse of the Lon Nol and Thieu regimes. Many of the important battles have been recorded in the memoirs of General Nguyen Van Rinh, who commanded the tank brigade that smashed through the gates of the Presidential Palace in Saigon.[21]

Beginning with the capture of the capital of Phuoc Long province on January 7, 1975, by the forces of the Provisional Revolutionary Government, the whole military position of the Saigon regime collapsed like a pack of cards. Its retreat from the central highlands and northern provinces of South Vietnam became a rout. Discipline evaporated in the puppet army, as soldiers and officers fought US "advisers" as well as civilians associated with the Thieu regime for places on planes and ships to flee.

In many places the PRG units could not keep up with the retreating Saigon army. In Cambodia the puppet regime there was collapsing at the same time – the Khmer Rouge troops entered Phnom Penh on April 17, after Lon Nol fled by air. In Vietnam, huge stockpiles of US-supplied weapons fell into PRG hands. Washington started making plans to reintroduce US troops into South Vietnam, but the Saigon regime melted away too fast for any such plans to be considered seriously.

A sustained propaganda campaign was mounted in the US and around the world about the impending "bloodbath". Part of the US propaganda effort to save face in this situation was its "Operation Babylift", a plan to airlift thousands of Vietnamese "orphans" to the US for adoption. Most Vietnamese reacted with disgust and anger, even including officials of the doomed Saigon regime, especially when it was revealed that some of the so-called orphans had living parents. The Provisional Revolutionary Government denounced the operation as "kidnapping on a vast scale", and it was internationally condemned. The operation itself was a disaster – the first plane carrying the so-called orphans crashed, killing 78 of them and about 50 adults. President Ford was left waiting in vain at the airport in the US to greet the plane's arrival.

The touted "bloodbath" didn't occur of course – the victorious National Liberation Front troops were joyously welcomed into Saigon by the majority of the population. What "bloodbath" occurred took place around the US embassy, as hangers-on of the imperialists fought with each other to get on the last helicopters lifting off from the roof of the building. Fantastic scenes followed as these evacuees were crowded onto the 40 US naval ships standing off the coast. People were crushed, some fell overboard and weren't picked up, and helicopters were ditched in the sea.

An Italian journalist, Tiziano Terzani, witnessed the final liberation of Saigon, and wrote a fascinating book – *Giai Phong* (Liberation).[22] He was with the first tanks that reached Thieu's palace and toured the city on the back of NLF tanks and jeeps.

"In working class neighbourhoods", he wrote, "the enthusiasm was overwhelming. A priest in a cassock runs up to a tank to climb aboard and embrace the soldiers.

"Near Chi Hoa Prison, a shouting crowd was tearing down propaganda banners, ripping flags of the republic, and hanging onto the trucks …

"In its midst I saw an old woman, with a typical conical peasant hat throw her arms around a young guerrilla. 'Peace, peace', she cried …

"Relatives who hadn't seen each other for years, decades, were reunited.

"Story after story of the joy, the relief, the jubilation that the decades long struggle was over, and victorious."

When Saigon was finally liberated on April 30, 1975, we immediately published a special eight-page Vietnam victory issue (No. 84). The cover proclaimed: "Saigon Liberated! A VICTORY FOR ALL HUMANITY". The issue included articles on "The real Vietnam bloodbath is over", by Sol Salby, "Liberation forces take Saigon", by Jim McIlroy, "War and Revolution in Vietnam – Lessons of the 30-year struggle", by Allen Myers[23] and an article on the history of the anti-Vietnam War movement in Australia, and its lessons, by Jim Percy. The editorial proudly stated:

"The fall of Saigon to the Vietnamese liberation forces is a decisive victory in the Vietnamese people's three-decades-long struggle for national self-determination …

"This stunning reversal for imperialism is a great victory for the Vietnamese masses who have died in the hundreds of thousands and suffered in their millions …

"But their victory is also a victory for all of oppressed humanity. The indomitable struggle of the Vietnamese people against the American war of intervention has inspired the oppressed throughout the whole world."

A victory for all humanity is what it was, not just for the Vietnamese. As I wrote 20 years later in *Green Left Weekly* 193:

The Vietnamese finally won their independence and freedom after decades of brave struggle. They showed that a people, united in its just aims, can withstand the military firepower of the most powerful imperialist force on earth.

They were assisted in no small measure by people in the US and Australia and around the world who raised their voices, organised, leafleted, put up posters, held teach-ins, resisted conscription, and demonstrated on the streets in their millions, demanding the end to the war, the withdrawal of the US and Australian troops.

It showed the power of a truly mass movement. The 'Vietnam Syndrome', that fierce opposition by ordinary Americans to the sending of troops abroad for imperialist adventures, though weakened, is still there.

Thousands of young people were radicalised, had their eyes opened to the nature of imperialism and the capitalist system, became implacable foes of that system, and joined or formed Marxist organisations.

And for that, those of us who were radicalised, have an extra special debt to the heroic Vietnamese people.

Moving ahead, slowly

Revolutionary upsurge in Portugal

On April 25, 1974, a military coup overthrew the dictatorship in Portugal that had been installed by fascism in 1928. The fundamental causes of the coup were the wars attempting to hold on to Portugal's colonies in Africa and the growing opposition they created in Portugal. The overthrow unleashed a prerevolutionary upsurge.

The objective of the military junta, called the Armed Forces Movement (MFA), led by General Spinola, was to replace direct control of the colonies with neo-colonialism. It also sought to modernise the economy stifled under the fascist regime by moving toward bourgeois democracy and joining the rest of Europe. But the explosion from below threatened to go much further. The Communist and Socialist parties grew rapidy as workers poured into them. A broader layer of workers joined the formerly illegal trade unions. Peasants in the south began to seize land from the landlords.

However, the leaders of both the SP and CP sought to keep the struggle limited to winning democracy within capitalism, while using militant and leftist rhetoric in appealing to the workers. The MFA sought the help of these parties in keeping things under control; it even formed a second provisional government with CP participation.[24]

Over the following months, leftists in Australia and around the world closely followed and debated the sometimes complicated twists and turns of the Portuguese class struggle. We were sharply critical of the competition between the Portuguese CP and SP to win the favour of the MFA, and of the CPA's apologies for that disastrous strategy.

In *DA* of May 29, 1975, Jim McIlroy reported on a "lively debate" in Sydney between Dave Holmes and Denis Freney of the CPA, attended by more than 100 people. The article summarised Dave Holmes' argument that the biggest obstacle to progress in Portugal was the PCP's attempt to form an alliance with "progressive" capitalists and army officers. We returned to this theme, *DA* of September 4, 1975, carrying a centrespread article by Dave Holmes, "Communist Party of Australia backs military dictatorship in Portugal".

Party consolidation

We held an SWL National Committee meeting on July 26-27, 1975, which registered the end of the first stage in building our party and planned for our consolidation in the next. I was still in New York working on *IP*. The reports presented were: tasks and perspectives; youth; Palestine work; women's liberation; trade union work; world movement; finance and administration; relations with the Communist League; relations with the Tasmanian Socialist Labour Club; and, our national conference. Most of the reports were published in the SWL Discussion Bulletin (Vol. 3, No. 1).

A Political Committee was elected consisting of all full NC members resident in Sydney, and a political Bureau consisting of Dave Holmes, Jim McIlroy, Jim Percy and Nita Keig. Jim Percy was elected national secretary, and Dave Holmes national organisation secretary.

Young Socialist

We had also decided to launch a separate paper for the Socialist Youth Alliance, called *Young Socialist*. We'd been campaigning against uranium mining for a long time, and against education cutbacks; these were key campaigns for SYA. *Direct Action* became just an SWL paper. So SYA members had two papers to sell.

Young Socialist No. 1, dated July 1975, consisted of 12 tabloid pages. The editorial board was: Greg Adamson, Peter Annear, Jamie Doughney, Jenny Eastwood, Nita Keig, Geoff Payne, Paul Petit, Dominica Whelan. Jamie Doughney, SYA national secretary, was quoted in an editorial introducing the paper:

"For some time now we have felt the need to produce a paper for revolution-ary-minded youth – a paper which could concentrate much more on issues of concern to students and young workers and introduce people to the ideas and activities of the SYA".

Young Socialist No. 2, August 1975, had articles by Nita Keig on "The mass upsurge in Portugal" and by Richard Wilson on "Fighting homosexual oppres-sion", with excerpts from a paper prepared for the AUS-sponsored National Homosexual Conference in Melbourne, August 16-17. John Lukevic reported "SYA candidates run successful campaign on Flinders University", with seven candidates for the SYA club. Dave Lovell and Jeff Richards won positions on the coordinating committee. Gayle Burmeister stood for AUS secretary, and Steve O'Brien for general secretary. We carried an ad for a Secondary Students Conference, August 29-31.

Young Socialist No. 3, September/October 1975, carried a complaint from the Healyites about the use of "their" name. It had an editorial on "Defend the Brisbane Three", and an article by Bruce Hannaford. Elizabeth Wheelahan reported on the "Successful secondary student conference" in Sydney, August 29-31, at which 150 registered, coming from most states. The issue carried two papers presented to the conference: Vivienne Archdale on "How to build a secondary student organisation" and Elizabeth Wheelahan on "Aims and objectives of a secondary student organisation".

Young Socialist No. 4, November/December 1975, now listed Nita Keig as editor, and no editorial board. Responding to the Kerr coup and the elections, the cover called "For mass labor demonstrations and a socialist campaign", and the editorial stated, "Labor must fight for socialist policies!"

The issue carried a report of the "Socialist Youth Alliance 6th National Conference", October 4-5, by Deborah Shnookal. Jamie Doughney, SYA's outgoing national secretary, reported on the draft political resolution; Greg Adamson gave a Palestine report; Jim Percy gave a guest talk on the key issues of the Portugal revolution. There was a panel on our women's liberation work, with Mary Merkenich, Dominica Whelan and Deb Shnookal, and a panel on the history of the labour movement in Australia, with Peter Conrick and Paul Petit. Geoff Payne wrote that the rally was the "highlight of conference" with Brett Trenery, Kay McVey from the NZ YS, Jim McIlroy, *DA* journalist, bringing greetings from the SWL, Alan Pinjen, Malaysian student, John Garcia from the Brisbane Three and Nita Keig (who was elected as the new SYA national secre-tary.) The issue carried Nita Keig's talk to the rally on "The lifelong profession of revolutionary politics".

Efforts to reunite our forces

A major goal for us was to heal the split in our forces (and in the supporters of the FI in Australia) caused by the split of the Communist League. Discussions on this occupied our leadership. But we were given an impetus and some training in how to unite by our fusion with a small group in Tasmania, the Socialist League, formerly the Socialist Labour Club at the University of Tasmania. (They included Alban Johnson, John Tully and Tony Forward.) John Tully had been an SLL leader, and in October was interviewed in *DA* 96 on "The dead end of sectarian politics".

The Tasmanians were also in contact with the developing International Socialist (state capitalist) current, and different political ideas were being debated. The Socialist Labour Club Internal Bulletin in August 1975 carried a debate over state capitalism and the nature of the Soviet Union between Alban Johnson and Rana Roy. By September factions had been formed, with six members supporting Rana, five supporting Alban and two undecided.

By October we had reached agreement with a majority of the Socialist League to fuse, and this was announced in *DA* 96. Our conference was postponed to consolidate the fusion.

Fusion with the CL wasn't going so well, however. In September Dave Holmes wrote to Jim Percy in Hong Kong about the dallying by John McCarthy and the CL on unity discussions, reflecting the differences in their leadership. He speculated that "if we don't do something else they might recover their balance and the wreckers like Boland et al will be able to cool the whole thing down and maybe halt any moves towards fusion".

The SWL held an NC meeting on October 6, 1975, and heard reports on "Fusion with the Socialist League" by Jim Percy, and also a perspectives report by Jim, a report on "Finance and *Direct Action*" by Dave Holmes and a youth report by Nita Keig.

Following the NC, Jim wrote to Mary-Alice Waters in New York that we had put off our congress for a month, until January 24-28, 1976, because of: 1. the looming elections; 2. the need to think out our labour movement perspectives for 1976; and 3. the CL discussions. He reported that John McCarthy had "declared himself very much in favour" of unity, and we were hoping to be able to fuse at our congress at the end of the year.

I wrote to the PC on October 28 about discussions I'd had in New York with Jack Barnes about our prospects for fusion with the CL and our positive hopes, writing that "Jack seemed to be fairly sceptical about our chances of successfully pulling it off". He considered it "a pretty hazardous prospect". My letter the following week elaborated on Barnes' reasons for opposing/being sceptical about our fusion possibilities, specifically on the organisational question, that it was likely to be more up front in the coming period. (We were having decent discussions with John McCarthy; then they went on their wild weekly *Militant* adventure.)

In a November 12 letter, I commented on the Hawkesbury Agricultural College venue for our coming 1976 conference: "The venue for our conference sounds very luxurious. For years we've had trouble getting a decent place. If this works out it might be a good idea to try and make it a regular booking like Oberlin [the usual site of US SWP conferences]. Making it an institution like that in comfortable surroundings, a regular time and place, something that every comrade looks forward to throughout the year – it does a lot to consolidate the party." That's what Hawkesbury became for us for the next three decades.

Paris, Lisbon and home

Finishing up on *IP* in New York, I packed my gear collected over 18 months, shipped my record collection and books back home, said goodbye to friends made in New York and farewelled my apartment six floors above Broadway. I returned via Paris, for an FI United Secretariat meeting, and Lisbon, to see first hand what was happening with the Portuguese revolution.

I wrote home that Jack Barnes gave a report to the LTF coordinating committee on November 25, summarising the results of the United Secretariat meeting on November 23. They passed motions on *IP* and the IEC. "Their motion prepares them to take the initiative for the biggest break with us since the reunification", Jack reported, and their concern was "to impose democratic centralism on an international scale".

"There was no split", I wrote, "although leading up to it and even during it, it seemed closer than ever before – but two time-bombs were set, the IEC date and the *IP* motions. I get the impression that the thinking of the SWP comrades is that the point of no return has been reached …" I also reported that the Argentinean PST was operating a secret faction within the LTF.

I visited Lisbon on the way home and tried to meet up with the two FI groups there. Was the revolution still happening, or had the bourgeoisie succeeded in throttling it? Lisbon was a bit like a ghost town, except that every bit of wall space was plastered with revolutionary posters. The revolutionary groups still had the buildings they'd occupied for their headquarters, but their future seemed uncertain.

I spent six days in Lisbon, and there was not very much opportunity for meeting with comrades. They were battening down the hatches and keeping their heads down. So I functioned more like a normal tourist, rather than a political tourist – seeing the sights, tasting the food. My memories are of excellent food, in inexpensive workers' restaurants. The revolution hadn't seemed to curtail the basic needs of workers!

Back home it was clear that the Labor government was heading towards a crisis, coming to the end of its time. The Kerr coup had turfed out the Whitlam government on November 11, elections were pending, and we were planning our first election campaign.

The Labor Party and entrism

Although I think our biggest acquisition in the 1970s was our developing understanding of the party question – the *need* to build a revolutionary party and *how* to go about it – there were obviously many other political and theoretical areas where we also made big advances. We became a lot more serious about Marxist theory as a whole after our youthful, "unbalanced" activism of the 1960s. As we grew and became better organised and more experienced, we were able to implement better educational programs in the party and Resistance – classes, study guides, forums, educational conferences. After we joined the Fourth International, some of our educational work was unbalanced from the point of view of our later positions. We paid some attention to the classics, but were lopsided towards Trotsky's writings rather than Lenin and Marx. But overall our educational work improved immensely. The debate in the FI, though factional and sometimes misguided, provided us with useful training as well, certainly honing our polemical skills, and forcing us to read and study in order to defend our positions.

A key question for Australian revolutionary Marxists was the ALP – how to analyse it, and what tactics to adopt towards it. The traditional attitude of the old Trotskyist movement in Australia, and the position of those who had initially recruited us to Marxism, was to work inside the ALP. This is how we started out, and over the course of our first decade or so through the experience of our overall political work, through our actual work in the ALP and through our increasing political reading and sophistication, we changed our analysis and our tactics.

In some places we had been quite successful with this entry work. In Victoria we came close to winning control of the Young Labor Association, which is why the YLA leadership reacted by expelling 34 of us.

The nature of the ALP

I won't detail the all too heinous crimes, betrayals and pro-capitalist actions of the ALP, their racist, pro-imperialist, pro-boss record, in government and out, although when they're out they sometimes have to put on a bit of an act. I'm sure readers today are all too familiar with this record. Groups like ours coming from the Trotskyist tradition were dragged down by some unfortunate consequences of a distorted view on the Labor Party. There are many proud and commendable aspects, but also some *false* inherited traditions, which have been hard to shake off.

None is more critical – and causes more disasters – than the inherited Trotskyist "wisdom" on the Labor Party (in Britain and Australia at least) that these parties are somehow workers parties, bourgeois workers parties, have a "dual nature", or are the "political expression of the trade unions" or some such formula. All these views are departures from or negations of the Marxist analysis that these parties are fundamentally *bourgeois* parties.

Such false analyses can have a long-term negative impact on a revolutionary Marxist party. Generally our revolutionary theory and analysis determine our general strategy, and within that framework we work out appropriate tactics, test them, adjust them, try other tactics where appropriate. We can be flexible in our tactics. With a wrong analysis, you can still sometimes produce the appropriate tactics for a time. The theory can be put on the shelf while the activists respond practically to the actual situation. But it's not a stable course – with your theory out of kilter, it can't last.

Bigger problems can result when wrong tactics are persisted in, not assessed and tested against experience. Or when tactics that might be OK for a particular situation or time are persisted in beyond their usefulness, and when the tactic is converted into a permanent strategy, and the theory is adjusted and facts covered up, to defend the elevation of the tactic to a strategy. This has happened all too frequently in the Trotskyist tradition. (In the FI, for example, in the late '60s and early '70s, the tactic of guerrilla warfare was elevated to a strategy, with disastrous consequences.)

It's important how we define the Labor Party, in Marxist, class terms, and thus how we *act*, and understand the complex and subtle interrelationship between our theory and practice.

Lenin on Australia and Britain

We don't take the word of the founders of our movement as holy writ –

sometimes they were wrong. But it is important to take the writings of someone like Lenin into account – he got so much right. And we should check it out, especially when some socialists *distort* what Lenin wrote.

On the Australian Labor Party, Lenin was clearest when he commented on Australia in a brief article in 1913 following a general election in which the ALP was defeated:[25]

"What sort of peculiar capitalist country is this, in which the workers' representatives predominate in the Upper House and, till recently, did so in the Lower House as well, and yet the capitalist system is in no danger? ...

"The Australian Labour Party does not even call itself a socialist party. Actually it is a liberal-bourgeois party, while the so-called Liberals in Australia are really Conservatives ...

"In Australia the Labour Party has done what in other countries was done by the Liberals, namely, introduced a uniform tariff for the whole country, a uniform educational law, a uniform land tax and uniform factory legislation ...

"Those Liberals in Europe and Russia who try to 'teach' the people that class struggle is unnecessary by citing the example of Australia, only deceive themselves and others. It is ridiculous to think of transplanting Australian conditions (an undeveloped, young colony, populated by liberal British workers) to countries where the state is long established and capitalism well developed."

Lenin was also very clear in relation to the British Labour Party. In 1920, at the Second Congress of the Communist International, Lenin contributed to the debate on the question of affiliation to the British Labour Party:

First of all, I should like to mention a slight inaccuracy on the part of Comrade McLaine, which cannot be agreed to. He called the Labour Party the political organisation of the trade union movement, and later repeated the statement when he said that the Labour Party is "the political expression of the workers organised in trade unions." I have met the same view several times in the paper of the British Socialist Party. It is erroneous, and is partly the cause of the opposition, fully justified in some measure, coming from the British revolutionary workers. Indeed, the concepts "political department of the trade unions" or "political expression" of the trade union movement, are erroneous. Of course, most of the Labour Party's members are workingmen. However, whether or not a party is really a political party of the workers does not depend solely upon a membership of workers but also upon the men that lead it, and the content of its actions and its political tactics. Only this latter determines whether we really have before us a political party of the proletariat. Regarded from this, the only correct point of view, the Labour Party is a thoroughly bourgeois party, because, although made up of workers, it is led by reactionaries, and the worst kind of reactionaries at that, who act in the spirit of the bourgeoisie. It is an organisation of the bourgeoisie, which exists to systematically dupe the workers with the aid of the British Noskes and Scheidemanns.[26]

So it's very clear what the view of Lenin and the Bolsheviks was.

The distorted view from the Trotskyist tradition

In the Australian Trotskyist movement in the early days, the tactic of entry into the ALP was converted into a permanent strategy, and the theory was changed to fit – the ALP was now characterised as a bourgeois workers party rather than a bourgeois party.

How and why did this distortion happen? I think it was the result of the terrible isolation of the early Trotskyist movement from the working class and its political life. Trotsky advocated the "French turn" in 1934-35 to try to remedy this. In some places it was effectively implemented. The US Trotskyists went into the US Socialist Party for one year, and came out twice the size. In the British Trotskyist movement there were fierce debates and splits over the issue during World War II and after.

In Australia, the small Trotskyist forces around Nick Origlass didn't decide to enter the ALP until 1942, and this was only after they had been banned by the government and didn't have much in the way of other choices. Another opposing group – Nick called them the "sectarian dingbats" – tried to maintain an open group for a few years. (John Kerr was briefly a member of this group.) The Balmain Trotskyists lost many of their group after the war – people like Laurie Short and Jim McClelland had found a comfortable home in the ALP and moved to the right.

In 1953 the entry strategy got cemented and extended and theorised by the Fourth International's secretary, Michel Pablo.

With the radicalisation in the 1960s and the escalating campaign against the Vietnam War, some young activists in Sydney were recruited to Trotskyism. That was the beginning of our party. There was no functioning party organisation following the1964-65 split in the small Trotskyist group, but those of us recruited to Trotskyism through the Vietnam Action Campaign, Resistance, Socialist Perspective and the International Marxist League inherited the accepted Trotskyist line on the ALP – it was a workers party, the *mass* party ("the big outfit", as Nick Origlass referred to it).

In August 1972 the SWL split, with the formation of the Communist League. The statement we issued ended on the main political question that was the framework for the split, the approach to the ALP. On this, the assessment from our later maturity and greater experience was that there was right and wrong on both sides. A stronger party, able to prevent the split, might have reached greater clarity on this issue earlier.

The CL statement charged that "the SWL defines the ALP as a 'working class party' on the basis of the ideological hold of social democracy over the working class. In understanding a political party one must consider many things besides its membership and following. In its program (which is an alternative administration of the capitalist system) and its role (which is to contain the working class within the capitalist system) it is a thoroughly bourgeois party. Support for the ALP is never a question of principle, but solely of tactics."[27]

On this they were absolutely right, and the reunited party in the 1980s came back to this Leninist approach to the ALP. On the actual tactical question of *what to do* in 1972, in the lead-up to the December election, they were wrong. The leadership of the CL came to this conclusion themselves a few years later.

The British Labour Party

The ALP had many similarities with the British Labour Party, so it's worth following the relevant debates there. In 1975 Tony Cliff from the IS current in Britain had this assessment of the nature of the British Labour Party:[28]

> The Labour Party of today is very different to what it was a generation or two ago. It has suffered a prolonged, irreversible decline in membership, and is now badly depopulated …
>
> Especially in the working-class areas, it has become a party of old people with longstanding membership …
>
> Constituency parties throughout the country are slowly dying. Delegates cannot be found for conferences …
>
> The party is dying, leaving unfettered power in the hands of its professional organisers and the tiny groups of middle-class people – professionals and white-collar workers – who see in the party little more than a prop for the "professionalised" and totally undemocratic cliques who run our large cities …
>
> One should not draw the conclusion that in the more working-class communities, where middle-class elements are weaker, the Labour Party

is stronger or healthier. Nothing of the sort …

Because the Labour Party is more and more divorced from real workers and real struggle, ward and General Management Committee meetings become increasingly empty and boring … The party is truly dying at its roots.

The changes in the social composition of the Labour Party have been reflected in the parliamentary group: … today not as many as 10 per cent [come from working class backgrounds] …

The Labour Party was not always so rotten. It was at one time deeply rooted in the working class …

Although it was better at one time than it is now, the Labour Party was never a *real socialist party*. Nor was it ever thought to be by the militants of the day at any stage in its history …

In office, the Labour Party has always ensured the continuity of the capitalist state and guarded its harshest, most anti-working-class plans:

The Labour Party can no longer be thought of as a party of reforms. It is a party of management of capitalism …

Both the Tories and Labour are committed to managing capitalism. They share a consensus about politics that has become more and more pronounced over the last 20 years and more appalling as its centre of gravity shifts to the right …

There is growing awareness among militants that politics is not something that can be left to the ballot box and the Tweedledum-Tweedledee Tory and Labour Parties.

So the clear lesson is: don't let your present particular tactical needs distort your theoretical analysis of what the Labor Party *is*.

ALP experience in running capitalism

In Australia all our experience with the ALP should have led us to similar conclusions just as early.

The brief whirlwind of reforms that immediately followed the election of the Whitlam government surprised many on the left. Sol Salby's analysis of the Labor government's first five months in *DA* 40 and 41, referred to earlier, pointed out that the one of the reasons the ALP government seemed so radical was simply that it was following on from 23 years of conservative government. The new government was reacting to the very real pressures from the mass radicalisation, particularly among youth. But the article of course put this in terms of our analysis at the time, that the ALP was a "bourgeois workers party": "The Labor Party is a very different type of party. Despite its brazen capitalist programme and pro-capitalist leadership it is a working class party. Its organisational links with the working class through the trade union movement mean that it is very much susceptible to mass pressure."

The major dilemma facing the Whitlam government, according to the article, was "the contradiction between carrying [out] a radical reform for change pressed for from below and good relations with Australian capitalism … Sooner or later the Whitlam leadership will have to show its true colors. Whitlam's attempt to wrest himself free of the trade union movement and even the ALP machinery can not be successful. So long as the ALP remains organisationally connected to the trade union movement, he will fail in his attempt."

Our perspective was to try to build a left wing in the ALP "to fight for socialist policies". Sol's concluding article argued that the next step in this direction would be to expand nationally the Victorian Socialist Left.

At the time the articles were written, Australian capitalism appeared to be emerging from the international recession of 1969-72, and we were not certain whether the Whitlam government would feel the need to proceed with its original plans to impose some form of wage freeze. But Labor concretised its plans through the prices and incomes referendum in December 1973. The whole referendum was defeated.

In May 1974 there was a double dissolution, mainly over the Medibank legislation, which the Liberals were blocking. Labor won and was returned to office. Again, we had big *DA* sales at ALP rallies.

After the defeat of the referendum, the next attempt to introduce a wage freeze was Cameron's fake indexation scheme. It was proposed in July 1974 and introduced in April 1975. It was only quarterly, and subject to court decision, with the "guidelines" being the government's fake index. It had the effect of reducing real wages. To enforce that, there were no actions or gains allowed outside of indexation. It was a form of incomes policy or social contract.

The way was paved by the September 1974 ACTU congress, which accepted wage reductions. Hawke praised the Labor government budget. The only opposition came from the Australian Manufacturing Workers Union's Laurie Carmichael. But he still preached "cooperation"; he just wanted a better deal (by the Accord!) Hawke's main condition was tax indexation.

A further indicator of Labor's role came in October 1974, when the Leyland car plant closed. Labor provided a $25 million handout for the company, but nothing for the workers. Three thousand jobs were lost. By February 1975, unemployment had risen to 5.2 percent, from 2 percent in 1972. Whitlam's solution was social spending cuts, scrapping the capital gains tax proposal, tariffs and his own form of social contract.

The final liberation of Vietnam by the Vietnamese people on April 30, 1975, also marked the beginning of the end for Whitlam. In the same issue of *DA* in which we announced "A Victory for all Humanity", we also reported on the introduction of indexation. From then, it was all downhill for the Labor government.

In spite of Medibank finally being introduced on July 1, 1975, the biggest gain of the Labor government (which we hailed in the *DA* 88 editorial, "Medibank a step forward, free health care a right for all"), crisis followed crisis:

- the Bass by-election, a devastating loss;
- the "loans affair" – (a manufactured crisis, as Jim McIlroy wrote in *DA* 90); Jim Cairns was sacked as deputy prime minister;
- the deepest economic crisis since the 1930s;
- the court tried to impose a wage freeze on metalworkers;
- Indonesia invaded East Timor, with Whitlam complicit in it;
- the September 1975 ACTU Congress again endorsed wage restraint;
- Rex Connor, the minister for minerals and energy, resigned.
- Jim McIlroy's *DA* article pointed out: "The whole affair has the characteristics of a set-up. The 'loans affair' has been manipulated by the capitalist establishment to bring pressure to bear on the Labor Government. In the view of business the present severe economic downturn now requires very strong measures. The coming Budget has to be extremely harsh according to every section of big business opinion. Two years ago, the loans affair would have hardly caused a ripple. Now it has caused tidal waves."

Obviously, there was an election looming. The SWL got in early and announced our first ever federal election campaign, proposing to run nine candidates for the Senate.

Sacking of Whitlam government

John Kerr, a rat of many years' standing (a double rat: he was briefly a member of one of the Trotskyist groups in the 1940s but deserted) who was appointed governor general by Whitlam, sacked the ALP government on November 11, 1975. When the Fraser-Kerr coup turfed Whitlam out of office, thousands of people mobilised to vent their anger. *DA* responded to the crisis by shifting from fortnightly to weekly publication. We called on Labor's supporters to fight back and urged them to follow a mass action approach, rather than "maintain their rage" in an election campaign, as advocated by Whitlam and his cronies.

The ALP's role as a party of capitalism had been well established, though its credentials as a party in some way threatening the status quo got a bit of a boost by the coup. But Labor's tactics when faced with ruling class hostility were very thoroughly exposed.

In the lead-up to the coup, after supply was blocked in the Senate, workers showed they were willing to fight. There were huge rallies, Jim McIlroy reporting in *DA* 98, "Mass mobilisations play key role" as "Liberal grab for power falters", with 20,000 demonstrating in Melbourne on October 20, and in Sydney 16,000 rallying in the rain in Hyde Park on October 24 (where we sold 659 *DA*s), and in Adelaide 4,000 on October 25 (where we sold 200 *DA*s).

Workers responded to the sacking with huge spontaneous strikes and demos, and then a few days later with more demos – 40,000 in Melbourne, 15,000 in Brisbane, 10,000 in Adelaide, according to *DA* 100.

Following the coup, *DA* 99's cover called for: "No 'restraint'! Fight back! LABOR SHOULD CALL FOR A GENERAL STRIKE". The same issue also presented "A socialist program for Labor" on how to defeat the Liberal offensive, since with this election we were standing our own candidates for the first time.

Explaining "Where Whitlam Government went wrong" in the same issue, Jim McIlroy recalled the similar sacking of NSW Premier Jack Lang in 1932. Both sackings "occurred at a time of catastrophic economic crisis", and both "were a result of a decision by the leading circles of the capitalist class that Labor had to be thrown out by any means possible, in order to bring in a government of the bosses' parties committed to an open assault on the democratic rights and living conditions of the majority".

A further parallel, the article continued, was "the fundamental failure of Labor Party governments and ALP leaderships generally to defend the interests of the working class in a crunch". The Whitlam government, like Lang's, put capitalist profits ahead of workers' needs, and now, again like Lang, it was refusing to mount a real fight back against its sacking.

In the 100th issue of the paper, Sol Salby optimistically reported "Mass rallies meet Fraser-Kerr coup", with 400,000 on strike in Melbourne. *DA* included an eight-page SWL election manifesto, with biographies of our nine candidates.

The following issue reported rallies opening Labor's campaign, with 30,000 in the Sydney Domain, 8,000 in Melbourne's Festival Hall, even 2,500 in Cairns. Jim McIlroy wrote "Socialist campaign makes impact", with big *DA* sales, 1,200 papers sold at the Melbourne Labor rally of 40,000, and 600 sold at Sydney's big

Domain rally. The huge protests and mass outrage showed a willingness to act, but Whitlam wanted to play by the rules, urging workers to cool it and trust in the ballot box. There was an all-out effort by the social democrats to demobilise the working class.

Similarly, the leaders of the unions and the ACTU established that they were "responsible" too, endorsing wage restraint and reduction at successive ACTU congresses.

Predictably, at the December 13 elections, Labor lost. The experiences of the betrayals of three years of a Labor government were bitter for workers, after the high hopes in the early days of the Whitlam government. With the onset of recession, there was massive unemployment and inflation. It was clearly a bosses' government. Inside the party, the Terrigal conference of the ALP in January 1975 had demonstrated the complete triumph of the right in the ALP, displacing Cairns and Cameron.

We benefited from our experience of working in the ALP. We sharpened our analysis of the ALP, but it was to be another decade before we fully came to grips with the animal.

CHAPTER 2

FROM LEAGUE TO SOCIALIST WORKERS PARTY

I returned home just before the election from my 18 months in New York, and after seeing the aftermath of revolutionary possibilities in Portugal. The end of 1975 marked the transition from the SWL to SWP, when we started standing in elections and changed our name from League to Party.

When the Whitlam government was thrown out of office, it concluded a three-year experiment in which the claims of Laborism were put to the test. The ALP had played by the rules and clearly supported the system. It didn't work; it was still turfed out.

Our experiences marking big steps forward were codified in the resolution for our fourth Socialist Workers League conference in January 1976. The conference changed our name to Socialist Workers Party, and also took the decision to produce *DA* as a regular weekly (it had gone weekly after November 11 and during the election campaign). During the upsurge after the sacking of Whitlam, *DA* was still listed on the masthead as "A socialist fortnightly", although it was coming out weekly.

We'd come of age, learned lessons at first hand about the role of a reformist government, social contracts, wage freezes under various bosses' disguises. We'd been active in many different movements – abortion, AUS, solidarity campaigns, gay liberation, Black defence, high school students – but we didn't have a base in the working class. That was an essential lesson for us, that the masses still looked to and had illusions in the ALP, e.g. over anti-uranium mining.

The experience of a Labor government trying to run a capitalist economy better than the capitalists helped dispel many myths about the ALP. The Hawke experience a decade later should have removed any remaining illusions.

Our first election campaign

We stood nine Senate candidates to pose ourselves as a socialist alternative. In *DA* 97 we published an eight-page special supplement, "Towards a Socialist Australia", the draft program of the SWL that we would adopt at our January 1976 conference, plus an Action Program: "How Labor can defeat the Liberals".

We initially announced eight candidates standing for the Senate: Helen Jarvis and Gordon Adler in NSW; Rod Quinn in the ACT; John Tully in Tasmania; Peter Conrick and Jenny Ferguson in Victoria; and Brett Trenery and Peter Abrahamson in SA. We later added Renfrey Clarke for Queensland, and in Victoria Di Ewin replaced Jenny Ferguson. We produced posters for each candidate and stuck them up ambitiously. We had very successful SWL campaign dinners: in Sydney attended by110, Melbourne 75, Adelaide 55.

We had a good experience with our election campaign. Our votes weren't big, but we got our ideas and program around; Helen Jarvis was interviewed by *Honi Soit*, the student newspaper at Sydney University, emphasising her views on women's liberation.

The working class had gone through experiences, and so had we. Sol Salby in *DA* 103 analysed the reasons for Labor's loss, explaining how the Whitlam government's pro-capitalist policies had caused it to lose working-class support.

Changing our name to Socialist Workers Party reflected our growth and our increasing intervention in the political process. (Occasionally we'd cheekily refer to Lenin's short 1913 article on Australia – "Naturally, when Australia is finally developed and consolidated as an independent capitalist state, the condition of the workers will change, as also will the *liberal* Labour Party, which will make way for a *socialist* workers party".[29]) We were standing in elections, and all the others who stood called themselves parties, so we thought we had better act serious and look like we deserved workers' votes.

The second half of the 1970s was very much a period of consolidation for our party. We were still following the political developments in the FI, perhaps even more closely, but it was increasingly the case of what we learned and established ourselves. We had become a much stronger party. We established *DA* as a regular weekly paper from the beginning of 1976. The SWP had grown, and the Communist League had also grown. We extended ourselves geographically, setting up branches in Perth, Wollongong, Newcastle, Canberra and Hobart as well as the traditional Sydney, Melbourne, Adelaide and Brisbane.

Fourth SWP conference, January 1976

The SWL fourth national conference was held January 24-28, 1976. It reflected our growth and increased confidence. We'd come a long way in the two years since our third conference in 1974. The party had grown, so that we had a total of 96 members, electing 32 delegates: Sydney had 45 members (15 delegates), Melbourne 29, Adelaide 13, Hobart 4, Brisbane 5. The conference was held at Hawkesbury Agricultural College, and we had negotiated with the college to make it easier for as many comrades as possible to live in for the whole conference.

This was the first of many conferences that we held at Hawkesbury. It was an excellent venue for our purposes: a semi-rural setting, with more than enough meeting rooms for plenary sessions, for our conference rally and for smaller educational sessions. It was live-in and fully catered, but only an hour's drive from Sydney, so some comrades travelled out each day, but most lived there, in single or double rooms in colleges. It had an Olympic size swimming pool, a bar (and playing fields and tennis courts, although we didn't have time to make much use of those).

We alternated a decision-making conference with an educational conference each year (probably copying the rhythm and model of the US SWP at Oberlin College in Ohio). It was a feature of our political activity for nearly three decades. Hawkesbury is now part of the University of Western Sydney. We were eventually forced out as governments tried to squeeze more out of their "assets": the costs for us were rising, and it also became harder for comrades to get five, six or seven days off work.

The conference rally on January 25, chaired by Kim Reynolds, had the theme: "Build the Weekly *Direct Action*". Keith Locke from the NZ Socialist Action League spoke on "Internationalism and the Revolutionary Press", Jim Percy on "The Role of the Press in Building our Party", Nita Keig on "Highlights from the Past of *DA*", I spoke on plans for the expansion of *DA*, and Allen Myers on "Financing the Revolutionary Press". The conference rally launched the fund drive for our weekly *DA*, pledging more than $14,000 towards the $25,000 needed for the weekly.

We seated two delegates from Brisbane and one delegate from Hobart. We also had Hugh Fyson and George Fyson as well as Keith Locke as international guests from the NZ SAL, and a comrade from their youth organisation, and invited two observers from the CL leadership (although no-one showed up).

I reported on the international situation (having just returned from 18 months in New York, attending the FI United Secretariat meeting in Europe and visiting Portugal). "Following the April 15, 1974 military coup that ousted the Salazar dictatorship", *DA* 108 quoted me as saying, "a mass upsurge developed that began to challenge capitalist rule. The great mass of working people and large sections of the petty bourgeoisie came to the conclusion that their aspirations for economic security and democratic freedoms – the opposite of the totalitarian oppression they had suffered for 48 years – could be realised only under socialism. Capitalism and capitalist ideology were thoroughly discredited. The Portuguese capitalist class found itself in a weak political position as the radicalisation among the masses deepened."

Dave Holmes reported on the political resolution; Nita Keig gave the tasks and perspectives report; Jamie Doughney reported on the party program; Leesa Wheelahan gave the youth report; and Jim Percy reported on the world movement. We increased the size of the NC to 19 full members and eight alternates.

We reported on the conference as heralding "A new stage for our party", *DA* 104 carrying a three-page article by Jim McIlroy stressing the weekly *DA*, the drive for 1,000 new subs and the name change to SWP.

Perspectives for growth

The conference tasks and perspectives report presented by Nita Keig was printed in the SWP internal bulletin. It projected a confident and optimistic perspective:

- continuing with a weekly *Direct Action*;
- setting a sub drive target of 1,000 new subs in four months;
- a fund drive target of $25,000;
- moving Sydney branch downtown (aware from the positive experiences of Melbourne branch);
- increasing our NO and *DA* staff;
- producing more pamphlets and our own books;
- planning more national and international travel;
- geographical expansion to new branches;
- helping SYA grow and recruit;
- running in further elections;
- expanding our union work and women's liberation work.

The Political Committee meeting on March 6, 1976, endorsed plans for an educational conference at Easter and established the category of provisional membership.

The June 12-14, 1976, SWP NC plenum met in an optimistic framework, hearing the following reports: international situation; Australian political situation; discipline (we lifted the suspensions of two comrades and readmitted them as members); tasks and perspectives; youth; women's liberation; other tendencies; world movement, which included a motion to send two observers, Jim Percy and Nita Keig, to the SWP's Oberlin conference; administration.

DA 123 printed Jim McIlroy's political report to the NC under the heading, "The Coming Confrontation with Fraser". The SWP information bulletin printed the text of the tasks and perspectives report by Jim Percy. It went through and followed up our results in the previous four and a half months, following the headings of Nita Keig's conference report.

In July, we conducted a tour by Willie Mae Reid from the US SWP, which helped us in Adelaide, 70 people attending the evening meeting at Adelaide University and 80 at Flinders University at lunchtime.

The US SWP conference at Oberlin, August 7-13, 1976, was big, with 1,650 attending, as reported in *DA* 137. We had a very large Australian contingent of 10: Jim Percy, Nita Keig, Allen Myers and Helen Jarvis were NC members who attended, as well as Ken Davis, Warren Harrison, Alan Dalton, Darryl Hillgrove, Ian Walters and Lynley Learmouth.

Palestine solidarity

When Israeli General Moshe Dayan visited Australia in July 1976, we collaborated with Nabil Kaddoumi of the United Palestinian Workers and other pro-Palestinian forces to organise protests. In *DA* 127, Sol Salby reported on a demonstration of 1,500 at Dayan's Sydney meeting, "possibly the largest pro-Palestinian demonstration to have ever taken place in Australia". On the same page of *DA*, David Nizoz (Sol Salby) reported "500 massacred by Lebanese rightists at Tel Al-Zaatar".

In *DA* 128, Peter Conrick reported on a demonstration of more than 500 against Dayan in Melbourne, despite the intimidating presence of more than 200 police. On the same page, Nabil Kaddoumi described some of the record of Israeli terrorism against Palestinian civilians, including by Unit 101, formerly headed by Dayan.

We set down our views on Palestine, Zionism and imperialism in a resolution, "The socialist revolution in the Arab East", submitted by the Political Committee to the SWP fifth national conference, held at the end of January 1977.

We also sought to defend East Timor and to denounce the collaboration of the Whitlam and then Fraser governments with the invading Indonesian dictatorship. For example, on the back cover of the March 25, 1976, *DA*, Jon West denounced "Australian complicity in Jakarta invasion" and reported on the East Timor Moratorium demonstrations: Melbourne 1,500; Sydney 850; Canberra 300; Adelaide 500; Brisbane 300; Hobart 100.

ASIO exposures

Capitalist states will always spy on working class and socialist organisations. We should assume they're always present, but we shouldn't allow ourselves to be paranoid. Their aim is to disrupt our work as much as to gather information, so an agent hunt can sometimes be more damaging than their actual presence.

We can get some idea about the extent of ASIO's activities after the fact. They have a 30-year disclosure rule, which allows you to apply for copies of your ASIO files through the National Archives. For the purposes of writing these books on Resistance and DSP history, I applied for all the available files on myself and Jim, and more recently for those of Doug Lorimer, since his will made me his heir and executor. (They're taking a while to comply.) ASIO vets the files and blacks out details of their agents' names, and they also deleted reports and facts that might help disclose the identities of their agents (sometimes all you get is a totally black page), but enough remains to give us an idea that they must have had an agent or two (sometimes three) present. But also sometimes the *lack* of ASIO reports on an important meeting probably indicates they *might not* have had anyone infiltrated at that time. For example, the final big split meetings with Gould in 1970 aren't covered in their reports.

The agents we expose are probably only the tip of the iceberg; no doubt the smarter ones slipped by, but we had a number of exposures of ASIO agents in the '70s. The first one who surfaced and who was definitely identified was Max Wechsler, in February 1975. He was a Czechoslovakian migrant, and had previously been in the CPA before he joined us. Wechsler sold his story as a big muckraking scandal to Maxwell Newton's *Sunday Observer*. Newton had edited the *Financial Review*, turning it into a daily, then edited Murdoch's *Australian* for the first two years before falling out with Rupert, then broadened out into comics and porn and built the *Sunday Observer* to a circulation of 200,000. Wechsler surfaced with a bang on the front page of the *Sunday Observer* with lurid headlines: "ASIO's top agent exposes our amazing world of Sex, Treachery and Terror", "Terror plot to ruin us", "ASIO's super agent exposes the treachery poised to ruin us".

He wasn't much of a "super agent". He probably had strange psychological motives, and ASIO had got themselves a loose cannon (as often seems to happen). We issued an SWL statement in *DA* 80 denouncing the *Sunday Observer* articles as an attempt at a "witch-hunt".

"Red-baiting the SWL: Greenwood gets in the act" wrote Dave Holmes in *DA* 81, reporting on a political attack on us in the Senate using the Wechsler "exposures". There were also attacks on the Women's Abortion Action Campaign and the Victorian Secondary Students Union. Jamie Doughney debated Senator Ivor Greenwood on Channel 9. Wechsler was subsequently arrested with a loaded rifle; who knows what he was planning.

We took Maxwell Newton to court over the sensationalist attacks on us, having Jamie Doughney as the complainant. Representing us was Clive Evatt QC. Evatt picked the jury of four well. The court case against Newton was successful, and a few years down the track, in 1978, we were awarded $15,000. "A jury of four awarded Doughney $15,000 damages after a hearing lasting only one and a half hours", *DA* 202 reported. Getting the dough from our court win against Newton was a little harder. As a result of the judgment and other big debts, Newton was declared bankrupt. We eventually collected only $6,700 of the $15,000, but that was still a fair bit for us back in those days.

The following year we actually won a political victory over ASIO. Lisa Walter was a young woman in Adelaide who had been recruited by ASIO with stories that she would be doing her patriotic duty in infiltrating and spying on the nasty terrorists in the SYA and SWP. But in early 1976, we succeeded in winning her over politically, convincing her that our goals were worth supporting, and were perfectly legal, and she revealed her secret to us.

We set a trap for her ASIO handler. She usually met him in an Adelaide car park, so we informed the *National Times*, and they arranged for journalist John Edwards to be on hand for the next meeting, along with Brett Trenery, the Adelaide SWP organiser, to take photographs and tape the confrontation. The agent tried to speed away in his car, but Brett was able to keep up with him for a while, and we got some good photographs of the embarrassed fleeing agent.

The subsequent extensive *National Times* coverage was very embarrassing for ASIO and excellent publicity for us. We made the most of it, with an "ASIO exposed" cover and a four-page feature in *DA* 118. *Young Socialist* for June 1976 played it up: "Ex-ASIO agent tells: 'Why I became a socialist …'" "As John Edwards reported in the May 24 *National Times:* She told the leadership of the SWP of her past activities and her desire to be part of the socialist movement.

"'From this time on Lisa became a double agent, reporting to ASIO and accepting their money and then reporting her conversations to the SWP and handing over the money to their funds …'" We held forums for Lisa Walter in Adelaide, Sydney and Melbourne. The media coverage of the exposure continued in the following weeks. We were able to campaign on the issue for a while, Jim Percy writing an article about "Further allegations on ASIO that have not been denied" for *DA*, and Anne Summers writing[30] about revelations of ASIO being used to monitor the Trotskyist left.

Tom Sheppard was a fairly incompetent and obvious ASIO agent whom we finally expelled in 1979. He had been a member for about five years, again someone we recruited from the CPA. (As we were growing, and the CPA declining, ASIO would have had to adjust its workforce.) I had written about Sheppard in a February 6, 1979, letter to Jim in Paris. "That guy is incredible. He must be the most inept 007 around, somebody is going to find it impossible to restrain themselves from saying something to his face one day. He wanted to know whether it might be possible for him to do some filing in Paris [at the Fourth International centre] ... Make sure he doesn't get anywhere near anything over in Paris. I wish we could think of some way of excluding him whenever he comes back here. We haven't been wording anyone up about him, but apparently about half the membership in Sydney has come to that conclusion about him independently ..."

Finally we acted, and asked the Control Commission to investigate. I was appointed the PC representative on the CC. The CC met during the SYA conference in Melbourne on June 17, and in the week beginning July 2. Many contradictions in his story were exposed in the CC report. He had very little political understanding, and there were multiple contradictions in the stories he told different people about his life, and about how he earned his living. Reading it, it's embarrassing that we put up with him for so long. Sheppard was expelled by the PC on July 8, on the grounds that he was a police agent. On July 9, 1979, we sent around a circular about the Control Commission report and the expulsion.

The report pointed out: "We are well aware of the dangers of conducting an agent hunt in our ranks – the damage to the party as a whole from such an investigation can sometimes be worse than any potential damage from a real agent. We know that it's a standard cop tactic for their agents to start up a witch-hunt for agents, partly to assist their own cover, but more importantly, because they know how disruptive such an atmosphere can be."

My report concluded: "... comrades should not assume that just because we have removed one agent from our ranks there are no others left. We should not become paranoid or obsessive about such matters, but it should serve as a salutary reminder to comrades to observe our security policy against the use of illegal drugs, for example, and not to broadcast around unnecessary details about where they work and so on. We should always assume that the forces of the bourgeois state have the physical and technical means of penetrating our party to a certain extent, and our best defence is our political program and organisational principles."

When I got my ASIO files 30 years later, they contained detailed (but not very political) minutes of our Sydney meetings in 1973-78. They were obviously taken by Sheppard, who always volunteered to take minutes, a task not relished by anyone else. Sheppard subsequently fell out with ASIO over workers' compensation claims – the stress became too much for him, and they refused to pay for his psychological counselling! The full story was told in an interview in *Overland*.[31] Sheppard was interviewed for the four-part *Persons of Interest* documentary on ASIO, and said he had been about 20 years with ASIO. Then he had his breakdown. We must have joined him from the CPA in about 1973-74.

He had joined the CPA sometime in the '60s. What was he doing after us? I can't imagine that he would have had any value to ASIO after being expelled by us for being an agent. The expulsion probably contributed to his mental breakdown and his dispute with ASIO over compensation.

Ian Gordon was another member who was exposed and admitted to working for ASIO, and was expelled. His case and motives were a bit more enigmatic. He had played a good role in Melbourne in the September 20, 1972, high school strike, and for quite a few years was an active member, even an SYA organiser for a time. But in mid-1977 an article in *DA* 163 by Jamie Doughney revealed that Gordon had admitted spying for ASIO, and had been on their payroll for four weeks. (There's even a story that he spent some of his ill-gotten gains on buying a megaphone for SYA!)

We didn't establish whether he had been spying and disloyal for a longer period before that. It's possible, but it's also possible that he was only trying to big note himself. He had that sort of character, arrogant and full of himself, and a range of political slights and events might have tipped him over the psychological edge.

There were definitely other ASIO agents in our ranks who escaped exposure, and some who indirectly revealed their presence. There were certainly several agents at our founding conference in 1972, both inside the conference hall and in a surveillance van parked outside. There was certainly one in Brisbane branch in February 1978 after the CL-SWP fusion. The agent took detailed notes of our tasks and perspectives meeting. There's also an ASIO report from Queensland responding to Val Edwards' report to the Brisbane branch executive on the Control Commission report on the expulsion of Tom Sheppard in 1979. (The agent inaccurately reported Jim Percy as being on the CC, not John Percy.)

Getting organised

Our policy on transfers was not as brutal as the US SWP's, which put a lot of pressure on comrades to move, and didn't really allow them to settle in and develop political roots in new cities before moving them on again. Nevertheless, some comrades, especially our organisers, were moved around frequently. Doug Lorimer may have organised in every branch in the country in the 1970s and '80s, coming from Adelaide to Sydney, then to Melbourne, to Brisbane, to Hobart; he may also have been in Perth and Wollongong.

After the 1976 conference, Daran Ward, Peter Annear, Doug Lorimer and Renfrey Clarke were transferred from Sydney to Brisbane. In December 1976 Sol Salby was transferred from Sydney to Melbourne, Andrew Jamieson from

Melbourne to Adelaide and Doug Jordan from Melbourne to Adelaide, and in February 1977 Steve Painter was transferred from Brisbane to Melbourne.

We chartered an SWP branch in Hobart in November 1976. By the end of the '70s we had set up branches in the major cities, expanding beyond our "traditional" branches of Sydney, Melbourne and Adelaide. And we had divided the largest branches, in Sydney and Melbourne, into smaller units.

In early 1976 we moved Sydney branch downtown, to the second floor at 215A Thomas Street, Haymarket. (For a while we still had the National Office and *DA* in Glebe, with the Sydney branch office at Thomas Street). It was an excellent location, just opposite Paddy's Market. We later rented the first floor as well as the second.

In late 1975 we obtained our headquarters at 361 Little Bourke Street, Melbourne. In July 1976 there was a fortunately unsuccessful arson attack on the office.

In *DA* of May 19, 1977, Geoff Payne reported that Brisbane SWP had opened new headquarters at 345 George Street in the city centre. The article promised regular fortnightly forums beginning in the first week of June, and "educational classes on the revolutionary movement throughout the world".

First books and bookshops

When we began with Resistance in 1967, our Third World Bookshop was an important part of our operations. We received our first books and magazines that began our Marxist education via Bob Gould, including one tattered copy of Cannon's *The Struggle for a Proletarian Party*. When we fell out with him and had to break in order to continue building a party, that served as a bit of a "manual" for waging a faction fight. In the split in 1970, we got the better deal – winning the majority of members – and we went on to launch Resistance as a national youth organisation, launch *Direct Action* and build the SWL. He hung on to the bookshop. So we naturally wanted eventually to develop our own political shopfront bookshops for our branches, as a more prominent part of our headquarters.

Initially our main focus was on distributing the growing range of Pathfinder Press books published by the US SWP. We organised to promote them and get them stocked in other bookshops. A National Office literature circular, January 31, 1976, announced that we had sold 145 subs to *Intercontinental Press* so far, and a February 14 circular instructed branches to appoint a Pathfinder Press sales representative. In August 1976 *DA* 128 carried a very comprehensive eight-page Pathfinder Press lift-out catalogue. The contribution of the US

SWP's Pathfinder Press in translating and printing the writings of Trotsky, and publishing the writings of Cannon and other US leaders, was invaluable. (Initially they were at reasonable prices, encouraging young activists to read them, but following the US SWP's sectarian degeneration in the '80s, they upped the prices, making their books very expensive.)

We made a number of subsequent efforts to build bookshops, more than just bookstalls in our headquarters, that stocked our main educational writings, especially in our Sydney and Melbourne offices. Melbourne set up our Pathfinder Bookshop at 82 Smith Street, Collingwood, in 1978.

We made a big step forward when we moved our Sydney offices from Thomas Street in 1979 and opened a street-front bookshop at 757 George Street, just down from Railway Square. (After the arson attack on our building in 1980, we had to move again several doors up to 761A, still on George Street, but on the first floor.) It was a prime location, and we made an effort to build it and stock it with a range of left books. Our core stock was what we received from Pathfinder US, especially the writings of Leon Trotsky, and any Marx, Engels and Lenin we could get from the local distributors of Moscow's Progress Publishers, and what we printed ourselves.

We also padded out the basic political stock of our new public bookshops with a range of more or less political remainders, a taste for which I'd acquired from Gould when we ran the Third World Bookshop. I would scour the remainder houses for any books that were even vaguely left and political. Some of the academic publications on Australian labour history were very useful additions to our shelves. They were permanently useful for us, although their life on the shelves of normal bookshops might have been no more than a year, so we were able to expand our range and make the shops a bit more interesting. These remainders were bought very cheaply, and still sold very cheaply, but allowed a bigger mark-up. But we were still not capitalised enough to make it a "normal" bookshop.

We also started publishing our own books. The first book the SWP published was *Towards a Socialist Australia, How the labor movement can fight back*, a collection of our documents, published in September 1977 by Pathfinder Press (Australia). It contained "Fraser's Offensive: How the Labor Movement Can Fight Back" (adopted at our fifth conference, January 1977); "The Labor Party and the Crisis of Australian Capitalism" (adopted at our fourth conference, January 1976); and "Towards a Socialist Australia," (the program adopted at our fourth conference).

The next book we produced was Allen Myers' *Is There Life on Earth? Evidence from the Lucky Country*, in October 1978. This consisted of a selection of Allen's

"Lucky Country" satirical columns that had appeared in *DA* for the previous three and a half years. Allen's many-sided journalistic drive is still going; from Phnom Penh, he's writing and subbing for *Red Flag* and *Marxist Left Review,* and also writing a satirical blog, "News from Somewhere". Allen also contributed another *DA* column in the late '70s, "Looking at the Left", which carried his sharp comments on the wayward tendencies of other left groups.

Then we published *Women's Liberation and the Socialist Revolution,* the resolution drafted for the Fourth International in the lead-up to the World Congress in 1979, with an introduction by Nita Keig. It was published simultaneously by Pathfinder Australia and Pathfinder New York, and printed by Southwood Press here. We sold 2,000 to FI sections in the US, Canada, England and New Zealand, and had 2,000 to sell ourselves.

Also in 1979 we published *Socialism or Nationalism? Which Road for the Australian Labor Movement?* It contained articles by Jon West, Dave Holmes and Gordon Adler. It was published in October 1979, and we organised a national speaking tour by Jon West to promote it.

Education

Over Easter, April 16-19, 1976, we held an SWP educational conference, attended by 60 people, at our new headquarters at 215A Thomas Street, Haymarket.

Educational camps were a useful tool for us. Jim Percy and Dave Deutschmann travelled to Adelaide and Melbourne for educational conferences, Melbourne holding an educational camp December 3-5, 1976, at Lake Eppalock.

We held Teamster educational weekends August 19-20, 1978, based on studying Farrell Dobbs' books on the US Teamsters Union in the 1930s, in Adelaide, Brisbane, Hobart, Melbourne and Sydney. David Lawrence (Ron Poulsen) reviewed the four Teamster books in *DA* 220.

At the end of the year, we held summer SYA educational camps in Melbourne, Adelaide and Sydney on "Capitalism, Socialism and the Environment".

Organisational principles

We developed the organisational principles of Resistance and the SWP from three sources:
- Lenin and the Bolsheviks, with their concept of democratic centralism, from whom we learned the general principles.
- The US SWP, concretising the Bolsheviks' practices for a

wealthy English-speaking country, with a wealth of experience from the 1930s to the 1960s. Initially we also had some links and got some ideas from the FI in Europe, e.g. the British IMG, but eventually we opted for the US tradition and practices, and learned from their experiences.

• Our own fight in Resistance to build the party, and our own practical experience, from which we learned a lot.

We adopted a constitution embodying our basic principles of democratic centralism at the founding conference of the SWL in January 1972, and refined and amended these at subsequent conferences. But we felt the need to get down in print a more thorough, explanatory exposition of our ideas and principles of functioning. So we set out to draft such an organisational principles resolution; Allen Myers wrote it and reported on it to our November 1976 NC and our 1977 SWP conference, where it was adopted.

But we didn't feel totally comfortable with our product, and we were in the process of fusing with the Communist League, so we kept the discussion on it open. We printed the document in the third issue of *Socialist Worker*, August-September 1977 (but cutting down the final section 8 on "Bolshevising the SWP", which we printed again in the bulletin before the conference).

Amendments and an alternative document were put forward in 1978 by some former members of the CL,[32] and this and the SWP document were debated in the pre-conference discussion. Doug Lorimer wrote "In defence of Leninism: Against the alternative organisational principles document".[33]

The report on the document was presented by Peter Annear to our 1979 conference and printed in Party Organiser Vol. 2, No. 4 (most of those opposing our organisational principles soon left the SWP).

In the '90s we produced a book, *Organisational Principles and Methods of the DSP*,[34] with articles by Reihana Mohideen, John Percy, Doug Lorimer, Pat Brewer and Chris Spindler, mostly based on talks to a Melbourne Resistance leadership training school in July 1992. Its topics included: the need for a revolutionary party; our understanding of how to build such a party; the selection of a national leadership team; the political and the personal; and criteria for joining new members.

DA sales

We produced bound volumes of the first 76 issues of *DA* for 1970-74. We bound 200 sets, as a special incentive for contributors to the fund drive. We also sold the bound volumes to individuals, to libraries and to other institutions.

An important result of going weekly was that sales more or less doubled. I told the June 26, 1976, Sydney banquet: "As many copies of the paper are now being sold each week as had last year been sold in a fortnight". We were averaging 1,750 sales per week. In May, *DA* 158 announced a drive for 1,000 subs, and a total of 964 subs were sold, with John Coleman the top seller. The NC set a target of 3,500 sales per week by the end of the year.

As one of the incentives to boost our *DA* sales, top sellers were listed in the weekly sales newsletter. For issues 131 to 134, Steve Painter, the organiser in Brisbane branch, stood out, with 167, 133, 144 and 146 sales, out of national totals of 1,515, 1,355, 1,293 and 1,525. For the next five issues, Steve was still the top seller, going over 100 each time.

Supporters

Through *DA* we were able to gather around us a large number of supporters who bought the paper fairly regularly or took out a subscription. We organised regular dinners, dinner dances or "banquets" to bring these supporters together. The dinners also raised money from our supporters, and could focus on our major political activities or launch our election campaigns. In Sydney and Melbourne we developed a tradition of serving good food (Jim Percy's role was initially important as a serious hands-on cook) and putting on good entertainment and some entertaining political speakers.

In Sydney the dinners grew. The banquet on September 25, 1976, at Balmain Town Hall was attended by 144 (*DA* 136). The next year we held a July banquet to launch our Leichhardt Council election campaign, and a *DA* banquet on December 3, 1977, at Heffron Hall in Surry Hills. In 1978 we held a Sydney *DA* banquet to celebrate 200 issues. One hundred and eighty attended, and speakers were Jim McIlroy and Pat Garcia (*DA* 202). *DA* dinners got up to as many as 300 attending.

The July 1, 1980, Sydney branch meeting heard a report on the recent banquet. Numbers were down on the previous time, but everything went smoothly, and we did well financially, raising $1,900. Some very good contacts were there. I explained "what the functions of our banquets are, and what the branch should expect to get out of them, and what individual comrades should expect from them.

"They're increasingly our main contacting and recruiting vehicle, and also a very important financial prop to our party.

"… we should view the whole evening politically, as a political assignment.

"Of course, the *aim* is to make them enjoyable affairs for comrades as well as our supporters. But we are doing party business that night, it's not just one possible type of entertainment for comrades that Friday night.

"So comrades should not take it on themselves to decide half-way through to head off for some alternative function. Even if it's not your favourite music (and we can't please all, although we're trying) and even if you feel you might enjoy yourself better elsewhere for that particular night, it's a political assignment, and comrades should stick around, and try to persuade contacts to stay as long as possible also."

Supporters contributed to the depth and spread of the party, and in some cases made significant financial contributions. One supporter in Perth, J.F. Crespin, initially donated $400 for a gestetner in 1978. In later years he made another sizeable contribution, which helped us to equip our National Office. We encouraged supporters to remember the party in their wills.

We never settled on a permanent structure for organising them, experimenting with supporters clubs, associate memberships and supporter subscriptions. We didn't want to dilute the cadre membership of the party.

Election campaigns

We got a good taste for running in elections with our first efforts in the December 1975 federal election. We appreciated the possibilities for reaching out with our political message to a much wider audience. We came across what Lenin had to say about running in elections, and took our cue from a good teacher: "Whilst you lack the strength to do away with bourgeois parliaments and every other type of reactionary institution, you *must* work within them because *it is there* that you will still find workers who are duped by the priests and stultified by the conditions of rural life; otherwise you risk turning into nothing but windbags".[35] In the second half of the 1970s we continued the tactic, running in:
- the March 1976 Victorian elections;
- the May 1976 NSW elections;
- the December 1976 Tasmanian elections;
- the September 1977 NSW local government elections;
- the September 1978 Werriwa by-election;
- the October 1978 NSW state elections;
- the 1978 Victorian elections;
- the 1979 Grayndler by-election.

We announced in *DA* 105 that we were running in the March 1976 Victorian state election, standing Andrew Jamieson for Richmond and Lou-anne Barker for Melbourne. *DA* published our four-page election manifesto. We gained 2.3 percent in Richmond, and 2.8 percent in Melbourne.

We followed up with a campaign for the May 1 NSW state election, again with a four-page election manifesto in *DA* 112. Nita Keig received 3.5 percent in Balmain, Geoff Payne 3.0 percent in Marrickville and Deb Shnookal 2.4 percent in Philip. We described it in *DA* 115 as a "Good vote for SWP in NSW elections", noting that it compared well with the votes for the CPA and SPA.

We also contested the December 11, 1976, Tasmanian elections, standing John Tully and Roseanne Fidler in Denison, again with a four-page election manifesto, in *DA* 144. According to *DA* 147, we received only 0.2 percent, but it was double our Denison vote in the 1975 federal election.

We ran a joint campaign of the SWP and CL for the September 17, 1977, Sydney municipal elections, leading up to our reuniting. We planned to letter-box all houses in all of the four wards we contested. Leichhardt Council was the base of the former Trotskyists Nick Origlass and Issy Wyner. They were elected to council again from the Balmain ward.[36] In the '60s we'd campaigned for them for the council elections as well as for the state elections, when they ran as the Balmain Labor Party after their expulsion from the ALP. (We discussed with Nick about where to stand.)

In this council election for Leichhardt, we stood two candidates in Annandale ward – Nita Keig from the SWP and Lynda Boland from the CL, and two in Glebe ward from the SWP, myself and Deb Shnookal. A banquet launched the Sydney election campaign, at which Ron Poulsen from the CL spoke in support. Our results in Glebe were very encouraging. Out of 5,349 votes, I received 706 (13 percent) and Deb 311 (6 percent), that is, 1,017 (19 percent) people in Glebe giving their first preference to Socialist Workers Party candidates. (We were the only opposition to the ALP in this ward.) In Annandale, Nita Keig got 179 votes and Lynda Boland 70, for a total of 249 (6.2 percent) (*DA* 180).

In South Sydney, Martin Tuck from the CL, standing in Redfern ward, received 233 votes (6.6 percent); we were the only opponent of the ALP in that ward. Paul Petit from the SWP in Newtown ward received 227 (7.2 percent) (*DA* 175).

For the Werriwa by-election on September 23, 1978, we stood John Garcia as our candidate for the (by then united) SWP. A big Sydney banquet on July 22 launched the socialist campaign, with 200 supporters packing into Glebe Town Hall (*DA* 217). *DA* published a run-on: "Vote 1. Socialist Workers 2. Labor in Werriwa".

SWP candidates polled well in the October 1978 NSW state election. Labor had a smashing win in the election, with a 9 percent swing. Liberal leader Peter Coleman lost his seat to Labor's Rod Cavalier. Our final vote totals were: Lynda

Boland, 7.4 percent in Balmain, getting our deposit back; Gordon Adler, 3.5 percent in Philip; Paul Petit 3.3 percent in Granville; Andrew Jamieson 2.2 percent in Wollongong. (The CPA and SPA results were similar or smaller.)

We also ran in the 1978 Victorian campaign, launched with a dinner dance attended by 140 supporters at Footscray Town Hall, with Peter Abrahamson for Melbourne, Ruth Egg for Footscray and John Tully for Dandenong. The fund appeal raised $698, *DA* 228 reported. The final results, not available until the following May, were reported in *DA* 252. A short article, which listed a different arrangement of candidates, said that Ruth Egg received 0.7 percent of the vote in Dandenong and Peter Abrahamson a bit more than 5 percent in Footscray. John Tully's vote was not mentioned in the report.

SYA campaigning on campuses

Along with the name change to SWP and *DA* becoming a weekly, we also managed to make many of our areas of work much more professional. But our main recruitment still was through our youth organisation. AUS annual council in January 1976 witnessed both "retreats and advances", Mark Carey reported in *Young Socialist* No. 5. SYA distributed "A fighting program for the AUS" leaflet to the council. Peter Holloway reported in *DA* 104 "AUS retreats on Palestine", with the CPA a leader of this retreat.

Young Socialist 7 (June 1976) carried "Eight years of high school struggles", by Elizabeth Wheelahan, the Melbourne organiser for SYA, based on her talk to a NZ Young Socialists national conference, and reported on our campaign to sell *YS* outside high schools. *Young Socialist* 8 reported that we'd formed an SYA branch at Flinders University, part of a push to set up more campus branches.

The SYA NC met on May 15-16, 1976, and heard a perspectives report from national secretary Nita Keig, and an organisation report from organisational secretary Dave Deutschmann.

In July there was a rally of 1,000 in Brisbane against education cuts (*DA* 128). Peter Annear reported in *Young Socialist* 9: "Qld students strike and 1000 demonstrate to demand No Cutbacks and a living income". Annear was then AUS international officer at Queensland University and was running for AUS secretary. Greg Adamson wrote in *Young Socialist* 10 (September 1976) that AUS was "weathering a storm of criticism from sections of the daily press and prominent cold-warriors" such as Frank Knopfelmacher. They wanted students to "go back to their studies" after the radicalism of the late '60s. But the 1973 referendum at Latrobe University had rejected secession from AUS by 84 percent to 16 percent. "Here is where the right-wing ideologues falter. They confuse a lull in the student movement with the predominance of conservative thinking." On a vote on the right of Palestinians to return, only 5 percent voted in 1974. In 1975 that had risen to 20 percent, and the Zionists were afraid of a real vote, so they were mobilising against the student union.

In the second half of the '70s, the student movement was declining, and in retreat. Defensive struggles predominated against the attacks from the Fraser government.

On August 23, 1976, Fraser was trapped by 2,000 students at Monash University. Elizabeth Wheelahan reported in *DA* 131 that Fraser, who apparently thought he was safe because the university was on holiday, "was most unpleasantly surprised to be confronted by a mass demonstration of students, Aboriginals, migrants, trade unionists, housewives and others suffering the effects of the [government's education and welfare] cutbacks".

A national student strike was planned for September 30, 1976, with rallies directed against Fraser. SYA played a key role in that strike, originally proposed by two SYA members at Macquarie University, according to *Young Socialist* 11. The cover of *Young Socialist* 10 exhorted: "All Out Sept 30! Support the national strike! Fight the education cutbacks!"

The strike was a big success, 18,000 taking part in demonstrations nationally, according to *DA* 137. It forced some gains, but the left was divided. Dave Deutschmann wrote in *DA* 138, under the heading "CPA fails challenge of September 30 student strike": "From the very beginning of the strike campaign it was obvious that *Tribune* was doing its best to downplay it". *Tribune*, he noted, had devoted fewer column inches to the strike than had Rupert Murdoch's *Australian* newspaper.

The student movement was also hampered by the reactionary antics of Maoist students. At the January 1977 annual council of AUS, Dave Deutschmann reported in *DA* 151, the Maoists devoted their efforts to red-baiting the SYA in alliance with right-wing students, and to promoting Australian nationalism.

In November 1976 Peter Annear was elected as AUS Queensland regional organiser.

Our political development in the 1970s

We learned from our varied experiences in the mass social movements in the 1970s – in the women's liberation movement, the gay liberation movement and our continuing international solidarity work with Vietnam, Chile and Palestine.

The second half of the '70s certainly slowed down politically. This was especially noticeable in the student movement, and in the relatively limited working-class response to Fraser's attacks.

But our party was growing, learning, developing, strengthening.

Women's liberation

When we started *Direct Action*, the modern women's liberation movement was also just getting off the ground in Australia, so our history is that history too. We covered the key discussions in the women's movement and campaigned strongly on the issues we judged most important.

In the 1970s our major campaign was in support of a woman's right to choose. This often featured on *DA*'s cover. We had full-timers for WAAC, the Women's Abortion Action Campaign, including Deb Shnookal.

Sectarian currents rejected the demands of women as women, e.g. on abortion, and extreme workerists (such as the Healyites) rejected women's liberation altogether. They didn't see it as an issue for all women, but only working-class women. The early CL also suffered from errors in this area.

Every year *DA* helped build the International Women's Day marches and activities. Our supporters were always there, and in later years were crucial in helping revive activities when others were flagging in their enthusiasm.

The 1975 IWD march in Sydney had 5,000 at it (and we sold 508 *DA*s); in Melbourne there were also 5,000 (where we sold 310 *DA*s); and Adelaide had 1,000 (*DA* 81). From the start, ALP women attempted to depoliticise IWD, and they thoroughly succeeded after a few years.

The 1977 SWP conference heard a report on "Women's Struggle and Socialist Revolution" by Mary Rabbone (*DA* 152). The document from Mary-Alice Waters prepared for the Fourth International discussion was reported on by Helen Jarvis.

The women's movement organised a range of interesting and well-attended conferences in the 1970s. Five hundred and fifty attended a women's trade union conference in 1976, *DA* 129 reported. On June 11-13, 1977, 350 attended a Marxism and Feminism Conference in Sydney. On August 12-14, 1977, 300 attended the Working Women's Charter Conference in Sydney (*DA* 174).

However, some elements in the women's movement didn't want the gatherings to be open, certainly not to the left. They focused their initial exclusion policies on women from the Spartacist League, an easier target. In April 1977 an attempt by Margo Moore, with CPA support, to ban the Spartacists from the Sydney Women's Liberation general meeting was initially defeated, by 100 to 88, with some 40 abstaining, according to *DA* 157. But Nita Keig reported in the following *DA* that there was a "New challenge to democracy in Sydney women's movement" with an attempt still to exclude the Spartacists despite the previous week's vote. Such political censorship was followed through at the 1978 Women and Labor Conference, attended by 2,000 women at Macquarie University, with a ban on the right to distribute the left press (*DA* 206).

Joan Shields from NZ's abortion campaign toured Australia August 12-26, 1978, speaking in Brisbane, Sydney, Wollongong, Newcastle, Adelaide, Hobart, Launceston and Melbourne. In return, Peta Stewart from the SWP toured NZ for the abortion campaign there in September 1978, speaking on the abortion campaign, and was able also to attend the SAL National Committee meeting, September 16-17 (*DA* 226). Rallies to defend the right to choose, in solidarity with the big march in NZ, were held in Brisbane, drawing 200, in Sydney 100, Melbourne 300-400 and Adelaide 200 (*DA* 225).

Workers' struggles

Soon after getting into office, Malcolm Fraser started trying to whittle away the main gain of the Labor government, Medibank. Sol Salby wrote in *DA* 123 "Why Medibank Levy must be rejected outright". The ACTU called a national 24-hour strike to defend Medibank on July 12, 1976. The Medibank strike was a success, and we argued in *DA* 125 that it needed to be followed up.

One year after the Fraser-Kerr coup, on November 11, 1976, thousands rallied against Fraser and Kerr in actions called by Citizens for Democracy. In Sydney there were 10-15,000, Melbourne 6,000, Adelaide 700 and Canberra 1,000, reported *DA* 143.

With unemployment rising, we helped launch the Right to Work campaign in Sydney and then in other cities. A February 10, 1977, circular by Jamie Doughney from the National Office promoted the campaign, and *DA* launched its "On the Picket Line" column. There were Right to Work contingents in the 1977 May Day marches (*DA* 159), and a May 10, 1977, Right to Work campaign circular from Nita Keig in the NO reported that the Sydney campaign now had an office in Trades Hall, and that relations with the CPA in it had calmed down after we out-argued them. Right To Work rallies were organised for August 1977. Four hundred turned up for the Sydney rally on August 11. The Adelaide rally was taken over by the Maoists (*DA* 174).

Also in August 1977, there was a "Living Standards Conference" in Adelaide, attended by 100, with speakers Tom Uren, Andrew Jamieson and Laurie Carmichael (*DA* 173). But on October 31, the CPA walked out of the Right to Work campaign.

In 1978 *DA* covered a growing number of workers' struggles resisting Fraser and the bosses' attacks, with little help from the ALP or union tops. In April

Doug Jordan wrote in *DA* 202, "Meatworkers face anti-union campaign", and the cover pointed out "Hawke betrays meatworkers". In May, Doug Jordan reported "The sackings begin at Chrysler", and Jim McIlroy reported "Metal strike challenges phony indexation", referring to Fraser's attempts at a wage price freeze fraud (*DA* 207).

In September there was a NSW teachers' strike, and DA 227 reported that 5,000 rallied at Wentworth Park. In November (*DA* 232) Sean Flood (John Tully) reported that Melbourne paper workers walked out, where he was working. And the following *DA* reported that brewery workers in Queensland had escalated their strike. That same issue, we launched the 20-page *DA*, with a four-page centre spread on unemployment.

The following issue, 234, reported industrial action by postal workers, SEC maintenance workers, an ABC strike, a 2,000-2,500 rally by ACT unionists, action at APM, by Victorian public servants and by Sydney ICI riggers, and that the Transport Workers Union had won a dispute with petrol companies.

Stepped-up campaigns for homosexual rights

The first National Homosexual Conference had been held in Melbourne in 1975. Ken Davis reported in *DA* 133 on the Second National Homosexual Conference in 1976, in Sydney, attended by 300, and Richard Wilson in *DA* 177 on the third conference in 1977, at the University of Adelaide, attended by more than 300.

The SWP NO sent a circular to organisers from Andrew Marshall (Max Pearce) on May 25, 1978, about the stepped-up possibilities for work in the homosexual movement, and the following month a call for a day of homosexual solidarity with Stonewall was received from San Francisco. A dance, demonstration, meeting and Mardi Gras were organised. This was the first Mardi Gras, which subsequently became a Sydney institution.

Terry Lemon [Ken Davis] wrote "Nine years after Stonewall riots" in *DA* 212, and the following issue reported a cop attack on the June 24 Sydney gay march of 600. Police grabbed the sound trucks, and 25 women and 28 men were arrested. Two thousand attended the Mardi Gras event in the evening. Liam Gash reported in the following month (*DA* 216) "Big march protests attack on gays".

In August *DA* 218 carried a review on homosexual history in Britain by Liz Ross from *Lesbian Newsletter.*

The Fourth National Homosexual Conference was the "most successful yet," reported *DA* 223, with 900-1,000 meeting at Paddington Town Hall August 25-27, 1978. *DA* produced a special supplement for it in issue 221. Members of the SWP or SYA also presented four papers to the conference: 1. The Socialist Movement and Homosexuals: The Record; 2. Demands for the Gay Liberation Movement; 3. The Way Forward for the Lesbian and Male Homosexual Movements; 4. How to Fight the Right – or One More Victory Like That and We'll Be Back in Paris.

DA reported that the conference endorsed the Greg Weir defence campaign as a high priority (Weir studied at Kelvin Grove in Queensland to become a teacher, but was denied employment after his graduation because he was openly gay). Also projected was a national campaign to oppose the Festival of Light, and a motion was passed holding Premier Neville Wran responsible for the recent actions of the NSW police. Another motion passed "called on homosexual organisations across Australia to hold activities each year at the end of June to commemorate the Stonewall riot".

"The concrete projections for the coming year and the new militancy of the homosexual community should mean that the fifth conference will be even more activist-oriented and successful than the fourth", *DA* noted hopefully.

Ken Davis reported in *DA* 226 on the failure of a rally by British anti-gay campaigner Mary Whitehouse in Sydney in September 1978, at which we got to see an early window into the mind of Tony Abbott. The Festival of Light supporters in Sydney Square were outnumbered not only by radicals, but also by uniformed and Special Branch police. After revivalist songs praising Jesus and attacking Buddha came "Tony Abbott, president-elect of Sydney University Students Representative Council".

"He mentioned neither God nor child abuse, but instead intoned a litany culled from the pages of Bob Santamaria's *News Weekly*. It seems a tiny Marxist conspiracy, funded by the government, has for many years been in control of all education and media in Australia."

Five hundred marched at a gay solidarity rally in Sydney on November 7 to protest the anti-gay Briggs initiative in California (*DA* 232).

Following the upsurge in the movement, we prepared a draft resolution on The Revolutionary Strategy for Gay Liberation for our January 1979 conference, where it was adopted.

Defending AUS in 1977

"AUS council sets campaigns for '77" at its Melbourne meeting January 13-21, wrote Jon West, in *Young Socialist* 12. An anti-cutbacks campaign was set as the union's first priority. A "no-policy motion" was passed on Palestine, but Jon reported that a debate would still take place. "Solidarity with South

African students" was another issue, with a decision to support and fund the
"No ties with apartheid" campaign. AUS council also resolved to defend the
women's department against attacks, to fund the Black student union, to support the anti-uranium campaign and to support an independent East Timor
Peter Annear (the Queensland regional organiser of AUS) in the same issue
defended the union against vicious right-wing attacks from the *Australian*. He
defended AUS's "support for progressive change", pointed optimistically to the
"continued radicalisation of the student movement" and projected 1977 as "a
year of self-defence". He debated with other currents on campus, arguing that
direct elections of AUS officers weren't a principle, and pointed out that the
"CPA rejects democracy".

Lou-anne Barker predicted an "Exciting year ahead for the SYA and the
student movement" at the SYA NC in Melbourne, January 9-10. The perspectives report by Dave Deutschmann, SYA national secretary, projected speaking
tours, by Goh Siong Hoe on "The recent upheavals in China: A socialist view" in
March-April, and a second tour in April with Peter Annear speaking on Australian imperialism in the Pacific. Peter had just returned from a fact-finding tour
that included Fiji, New Caledonia and the New Hebrides (now Vanuatu). We
were pushing to build campus branches of SYA.

Young Socialist carried a column, "Education is our right", by Mary
Merkenich and Jon West, and a regular column by Simon Marginson, "Life
wasn't meant to be easy". It carried an ad for campus meetings at Melbourne
University, Monash, Latrobe, Caulfield, Sydney University, UNSW, Macquarie,
Griffith, Queensland, Tasmania and Adelaide.

We pushed to organise another national mobilisation on education, on
April 28. "Students around Australia have voted overwhelmingly for the Aus-
tralian Union of Students National Education Mobilisation on April 28", wrote
Elizabeth Wheelahan in *Young Socialist*. "By a margin of about 3 to 1 nationally
students voted to strike." Campus delegates voted 154 for, 58 against, wrote Jon
West in *DA* 158.

But there were obstacles and sabotage. Mike Hansen wrote "'National U'
sabotages strike". Jefferson Lee, the Maoist editor of the AUS paper, had produced three issues so far that year, and there was no mention of the AUS vote
for action. "After the first issue, the AUS national executive moved to activate
the editorial board to meet prior to each issue and advise Lee on content."
They ordered him to print an article by Frans Timmermann replying to attacks
on AUS from the right-wing media. Lee "lost" the first and second copies of
an article on the strike campaign supplied by AUS president Peter O'Connor
(*Young Socialist* 13). Nevertheless, 8,000 students mobilised in the national

strike, Kathy Fowler (Mary Rabbone) reported in *DA* 159.

With Labor and Liberals pushing for direct elections, "Right wing attack on AUS fails", Deb Shnookal reported in *DA* 160, arguing that direct elections would be less democratic than the existing system of election by the delegates (themselves elected) to the AUS annual council, because direct elections would be "stacked in favor of those candidates with a large party machine behind them". The next week Dave Deutschmann reported, "AUS executive censures Maoist editor". *DA* carried a two-part interview in issues 164 and 165 with AUS president Peter O'Connor about the attacks.

SYA conference, May 1977

The SYA seventh conference was held May 21-23, 1977, at Queens College, on the Melbourne University campus, with 150 attending.

After the conference *Young Socialist* 14 had a campaigning cover, "Defend AUS!" and a new editor, Tony Forward, from Tasmania, and assistant editor Jon West. Lou-anne Barker reported on the conference: "Socialist youth say Fight Back!" Dave Deutschmann reported on "Youth and the crisis of capitalism – A strategy to fight back", and Deb Shnookal on "World Revolution Today – Palestine and South Africa". Elizabeth Wheelahan reported, "The growth of SYA in the last two years – in the three months before the conference alone the SYA membership had increased by 40 per cent – is reflected in the doubling of *Young Socialist* sales over that time". She noted, "… campus clubs exist on many Australian campuses, while on others SYA has been able to establish independent SYA branches". Tony Forward wrote "Students fight union bashers", reporting Peter Annear's presentation to the conference, and Peter Annear wrote on "Tasks of the Student Movement".

The August 1977 *Young Socialist* (No. 15) reported that *National U* had been "returned to AUS". Jefferson Lee had been sacked after a motion was passed on a majority of AUS's 74 campuses. Mark Carey wrote "Left and Labor students organise", and there was an ad for a conference in Sydney August 30-31, "For a movement to build a militant Australian Union of Students". It carried a half page of endorsements from activists around the country. Simon Marginson noted in his column, "A noticeable feature of the debates inside AUS this year has been the increasingly close and public collaboration between campus right wingers (Liberals, Danbyite Labor and the NCCers) and the campus Maoists. Both groups supported the AUS 'spill' motion to dismiss AUS officers and Executive members and they organised jointly at general meetings on several occasions, raising the same slogan—'smash the AUS bureaucrats.'"

SYA's September 3-4 NC meeting planned student and anti-uranium campaigns, Dave Deutschmann reporting on "Defending and Building AUS", Mike Hansen on "Tasks in the Student Movement", Deb Shnookal on "Tasks and Perspectives", Alan Pluejen on "The State of the Overseas Student Movement" and Leesa Wheelahan on "Progress of the Right to Work Groups" (*DA* 179). Dave Deutschmann wrote in *DA* 178, "Students call for end to travel service", reporting on the August 30-September 1 Left and Labor Students conference. *Young Socialist* 16 reported, "150 student activists and student leaders from all states met at Sydney University", also carrying a statement by David Spratt, Frans Timmerman and Simon Marginson on "AUS travel collapse: Contradictions of a service union".

The AUS council of 300 delegates met September 17-18 in Sydney, but as Deb Shnookal and Tony Forward reported in *DA* 180, failed to meet the challenge. Tony Forward analysed in *DA* 182 "Why AUS education mobilisation failed". The right wing attacks continued. In December *DA* 189 carried an interview with Peter Annear, Queensland regional organiser of AUS.

There was a right-wing shift at AUS annual council, Jon West reported in February 1978, with the backtracking supported by the CPA (*DA* 193). In the next issue he wrote "Left leaders retreat before right wing" at AUS council. Greg Adamson asked in *DA* 207 in May, "Are campuses becoming conservative?" They certainly were. Jon West went on a national speaking tour for SYA from July 13 to August 10 on the topic "Fraser Attacks Student Unions". Tony Abbott won the election for Sydney University SRC president, and cops had to be called to install him (*DA* 227)! Fraser introduced bills directly threatening student unions.

Anti-uranium movement

Opposition to uranium mining was widespread and often militant. Hiroshima Day demonstrations in August 1977 were reported in *DA* 173 under the headline, "Thousands say: 'Leave uranium in the ground'". The demonstrations drew 20,000 in Melbourne, 11,000 in Sydney, 7,000 in Adelaide, 700 in Hobart and 1,000 in Brisbane.

The cover story and centrespread feature of *DA* October 20, 1977, was "Issues facing the uranium movement", by Mary Rabbone. After cataloguing the dangers of both nuclear weapons and nuclear power, and warning of attempts by union misleaders like Bob Hawke to roll back the ALP's official policy of opposition to uranium mining, the article dealt with the movement's strategy. "The central task facing the anti-uranium movement in view of [Fraser government] attacks and the government's determination to go ahead with mining is to win the majority of the Australian people to a position of opposition to uranium mining."

The mass demonstrations had already had the effect of increasing public opposition to uranium, the article pointed out. "Only by building the opposition movement in this country into a decisive and powerful political force, such as the mass movement that was instrumental in bringing about an end to the Vietnam war, will it be possible to force Australian capitalism to retreat from the nuclear course, a retreat with implications for the whole of the capitalist world."

There were big anti-uranium rallies and/or marches April 1, 1978: Brisbane 3,000, Sydney 7,000, Melbourne 15,000, Perth 6,000, Adelaide 2,500, Hobart 250 (*DA* 201).

In February 1978, an ACTU special conference on uranium adopted a wishy-washy policy of opposition to new uranium mines but support for fulfilling existing export contracts. This provided a handy pretext for the pro-Moscow SPA, which couldn't support a blanket ban on nuclear power because of the Soviet bureaucracy's use of that dangerous source of energy. In *DA* 208, Jim McIlroy wrote in "SPA knifes anti-uranium movement" that the Brisbane SPA had produced and was distributing a leaflet which claimed: "Opposition to the mining and processing of uranium, and through it the production of nuclear power, is unrealistic and flying in the face of the facts". The leaflet encouraged readers "to mobilise total support for the February 10th decisions of the A.C.T.U. special conference on uranium".

There were further problems for the anti-uranium movement. In *DA* 210, Ian Walters, in "CICD sectarianism threatens Melbourne Hiroshima Day", wrote that the Campaign for International Cooperation and Disarmament was trying to give "the peace movement" – that is, itself – priority on the 1978 Hiroshima Day speakers platform over the ALP, which had shortly before adopted a strong anti-uranium stand at its Victorian state conference. Walters explained: "There is an obvious connection between uranium mining and nuclear weapons, but that does not mean that the call for disarmament should be taken up by, or identified with, the anti-uranium movement".

For one thing, there were quite different views within the movement about *how* to bring about disarmament. Furthermore, the movement "has a responsibility to do everything in its power to take the ALP up on its promise to support the Hiroshima Day mobilisation, drawing it as fully as possible into the campaign.

"Such a course will make it more difficult for the ALP's leaders to retreat on the question of uranium in the future."

There was at least a beginning of linking up of uranium with other struggles.

A Feminism and Uranium Conference was held in Melbourne in August 1978. Lou-anne Barker presented a paper there, which we reprinted as a centrespread in *DA* 224, "Women's oppression and nuclear power".

She began by taking issue with some of the advertising for the conference, which said that women's oppression and nuclear power were linked "historically through the common oppression of both women and nature".

"I think there are a few assumptions behind the idea that women and nature are both oppressed", Barker wrote. "First I think there is the 'mother-earth' idea: that women are biologically attuned to nature while men are not. Secondly, it assumes that women have nothing to do with humanity's control over nature. The third implication is that all technology is bad and anti-woman." She proceeded to challenge each of those false ideas.

However, more conservative elements in the anti-uranium movement didn't like the idea of regularly involving masses of ordinary people. In the *DA* of October 5, 1978, Paul Petit reported: "Sydney anti-uranium rally cancelled": "In an unprecedented move, the September 27 general meeting of the Movement Against Uranium Mining voted to cancel the October 28 mobilisation which had been called by the previous meeting". Opponents of the mobilisation counterposed small actions and a fundraising dance. The article noted: "The Communist Party of Australia, which claims to be a strong supporter of the movement, was one of the most vocal opponents of the demonstration proposal".

In *DA* of October 12, Greg Adamson reported that plans for an October 28 demonstration in Brisbane had been reversed at an "unconstitutional 'emergency general meeting'" of the Campaign Against Nuclear Power, of which only those CANP members opposed to the demonstration had been informed. The main argument used against the demo was that it had been proposed by the SWP. "The majority of people at the meeting were not active CANP members. Some had dropped out, others had never attended a meeting before. They were brought along on the promise of 'helping beat the radicals.'" The cancelling of the demonstration came in conjunction with a series of organisational proposals that would "kill CANP as a coalition of anti-uranium forces in Brisbane".

The March 28, 1979, partial meltdown of the Three Mile Island nuclear reactor near Harrisburg, Pennsylvania, did much to explode the nuclear "safety" myth, as the article in *DA* 248 by Richard Ingram (Allen Myers) pointed out. The issue was on the cover as a demand for "No more Harrisburgs".

DA 249 reported on the April 6-7 anti-uranium mobilisations: Sydney 20,000, Melbourne 20-25,000, Adelaide 3,000, Brisbane 1,000, Wollongong 1,000, plus smaller actions in Canberra, Newcastle, Perth and regional towns.

But the movement's conservatives continued their efforts to prevent mass actions, using undemocratic methods to do so. In the *DA* of May 24, Lou-anne Barker and Robert Johnson (Dave Sampson), under the heading "Can we stop uranium mining?", reported that a "National Uranium Moratorium Consultation" had met in Adelaide and voted, by 8 to 6, "that there be no national rally or mobilization on Hiroshima Day". The meeting had been kept deliberately small: Barker and Johnson noted that although it was held in Adelaide, anti-uranium groups there did not find out about it until it was over. Three of the eight people voting against a demonstration were supposedly representing the Sydney Movement Against Uranium Mining, which had already voted to organise a Hiroshima Day demonstration. "None of them had made any prior attempt to discuss their views with any of the bodies of the movement they were supposed to represent." The anti-demonstration bloc had largely relied on a paper prepared by CPA member Geoff Evans.

Hiroshima Day demonstrations did take place in many cities, and the *DA* distributed at the actions (263) carried a centrespread, "Socialists and the anti-nuclear struggle", explaining our views on the way forward for the movement and on issues raised within it, such as the arms race and nuclear disarmament.

The *DA* of August 9 cover was "Thousands march against uranium", and the article reported demonstrations in Sydney of 10,000, Adelaide 1,000, Newcastle 300, Wollongong 500-1,000 and Melbourne 5,000. Greg Harris (Greg Adamson) reported that the movement in Brisbane had won a permit for its march, despite the state government's ban on marches.

On September 14, 1979, the ACTU congress voted decisively against uranium mining. "The vote of 512 to 318 gives anti-uranium forces on the ACTU national executive and within the union movement a powerful mandate to enforce union bans against the mining and export of uranium", Dave Deutschmann wrote in *DA* 270. The vote came despite the fierce intervention of ACTU president Bob Hawke, who "pulled few punches in opposing the strong ant-uranium move". However, as the article also noted, some unions – chiefly the Miscellaneous Workers and the Australian Workers Union – had indicated their intention to ignore the ACTU resolution. Labor Party politicians were clearly feeling the heat on this issue. In *DA* 281, Jim McIlroy reported on a rally of 2,000 in Sydney Town Hall Square, organised by Labor Against Uranium. It was addressed by ALP federal leader Bill Hayden, NSW Premier Neville Wran and Paul Keating, at the time minerals and energy spokesperson for the ALP. This was "the first time that Wran and Keating have publicly spoken at an anti-uranium rally". The same article noted that Bob Hawke was continuing his efforts to undermine the ACTU's official position by organising a stacked meeting of unions connected with the uranium industry, which voted narrowly against considering industrial action to enforce the ACTU ban.

As the first anniversary of the Three Mile Island accident approached, plans were made in many countries to mark the date with anti-uranium demonstrations. "Harrisburg demo on April 19", reported Robert Johnson (Dave Sampson) in the February 6, 1980, *DA*. The article added: "… it is unfortunate that the leadership of the Movement Against Uranium Mining in Sydney has decided not to actively build the demonstration", instead "concentrat[ing] on rebuilding their organisation – which has suffered a serious decline over the last eighteen months".

The Harrisburg Day march and rally in Sydney drew at least 5,000 participants, Brian Jones reported in *DA* 296. The organising committee for the event had been composed of "activists from Labor Against Uranium, Greenpeace, the Total Environment Centre, and the Aboriginal Land Rights Trust". The march had "contingents from environmental organisations, the women's liberation movement, political parties, and trade unions". Thirty or more ALP branch banners were carried by their members.

Polemics with other tendencies

In addition to the column "Looking at the Left" in this period (1977-79), *DA* ran quite a few polemical articles exposing the politics of other tendencies (and also helping to sharpen up our own comrades' political understanding). Jim McIlroy wrote a nine-part series for *DA* in 1977 criticising the CPA's "People's Economic Program". We then published this as a pamphlet. In July 1977 we held joint CL and SWP forums on the People's Economic Program in Brisbane, Melbourne and Sydney.

Also in 1977, Allen Myers wrote a nine-part *DA* series exposing Australian Maoism. Some subjects were: "'Australian independence' – progressive or reactionary?"; "A wrecking operation in the student movement"; "Maoism's war on workers democracy"; "Maoism's search for a popular front".

But the Maoists were becoming increasingly irrelevant. Dave Deutschmann wrote in May 1978 (*DA* 208) about "The split in Melbourne's Maoists" after a year-long debate in the organisation. The issue was which faction of the Chinese CP the CPA (ML) should support: the party's industrial base plumped for Hua Guofeng, premier and chairperson of the CPC, while the student wing mostly went with the Gang of Four. The debate came to an end with the CPA (ML) paper *Vanguard* announcing that the supporters of the Gang of Four had "expelled themselves from the party". To add to the fragmentation, around the same time, a small pro-Albanian group split or was expelled.

In 1978 Dick Nichols wrote a three-part analysis (*DA* 196-198) of the CPA's "New Course" program. The CPA's *A New Course for Australia* was, he wrote, a retreat even from "classical left reformism". It reflected a common view in the CPA that Australia was a "conservative society", and there wasn't much that could be done to change that.

Dick wrote that the CPA documents blamed "multinationals" rather than the capitalist system for the economic crisis, and then put forward a series of proposals aimed at gradually introducing rationality and social responsibility into the capitalist order. "The scheme proposed is basically a repeat of the Jim Cairns-Rex Connor plan to 'buy back the farm' – the scheme the bosses succeeded so well in making fail dismally in 1974-75."

The final article of the series traced the reformism of the *New Course* to the CPA's desperation to retain its positions in the union movement, which led it to see everything in terms of a right-left division of the bureaucracy and thus to end up tailing the left bureaucrats.

We had started to recruit a few more members from the CPA, so our exposures were important and helpful. We ran an interview in *DA* 202 with one of those recruits, Debra Altorfer: "Feminist tells why she joined SWP". Some other articles in our ongoing exposure were: Allen Myers, "CPA defends tariffs. 'Protection' of industry: Who benefits?" (*DA* 177). Bernie Murphy, "Why CPA split from Right to Work Campaign" (*DA* 187). Alan Ramage (who had joined from the CPA), "The Communist Party today: No place for revolutionaries" (*DA* 194). Alan Ramage then responded to a letter from CPAer Greg Giles in *DA* 199 with "'Transitional' or reformist?" (We were to have a similar polemic within the DSP 30 years later.) Bill Clarke, "CPA finds attractions in Eurocommunism" (*DA* 235). Jim McIlroy wrote a two-part series in late 1978 on "Protectionism: How the left shapes up".

In 1979 Allen Myers wrote a seven-part *DA* series, "A criticism of the CPA draft program" (*DA* 248-254). The headings were: "The Marxist view of the state"; "Towards Chile in Australia?"; "A false formula for alliances"; "How can workers change society?"; "Reformism and the Labor Party"; "Internationalism and socialism"; "Politics and party structure".

SWP-CL fusions and consolidation

We carried out two fusions with the Communist League. In 1976-78 we were finally able to overcome the split that had occurred in 1972, and in several steps were able to reunite into the SWP.

The first, in 1976-77, was with the majority of their leadership. The second, in 1977-78, was with the rest of the CL. This was an important lesson and achievement for us, because it was against the tide in the rest of the FI, where splits weren't healed, and against the pessimistic predictions of the US SWP leadership. It showed our independence and ability to overcome the factionalism in the FI, and demonstrated once again our intention of building a non-exclusive team leadership.

DA 181 reported in October 1977 that the Canadian Trotskyists had united in a new party, and issue 183 on the fusion of the Mexican Trotskyists.

CL fusion, first phase

During mid-year 1975, Jim Percy had reached agreement with John McCarthy to attend the US SWP conference together. But the CL leadership said no. The excuse was that there was no money, despite McCarthy having a ticket in his pocket.

In 1976, after the defeat of the Whitlam Labor government, the CL had over-projected with a weekly *Militant*. They were trying to keep up with us, but it only served to exhaust thoroughly the leading comrades who were producing it. Differences within the CL arose in 1976, leading to a major split. In November, John McCarthy, Peter Robb and Marcia Langton, three leading comrades who were responsible for producing the weekly *Militant*, split from the CL to join the SWP (*DA* 144). John McCarthy[37] was the CL national secretary, Peter Robb[38] was the editor of *Militant*, and Marcia Langton was a well-known Black activist.

Our SWP National Committee meeting on November 20-21, 1976, as its first item of business voted to fuse with the three comrades and seated John McCarthy as a full member, Marcia Langton as an alternate and Peter Robb as a guest. (He was added to the *DA* editorial board.) The NC elected a Political Committee of seven: Dave Deutschmann, Dave Holmes, Nita Keig, John McCarthy, Jim McIlroy, Jim Percy and John Percy.

The NC also issued a conference call and discussed reports on our political resolution; tasks and perspectives; youth work; our women's liberation resolution and perspectives; the Arab revolution resolution; our organisational principles resolution; and the world movement.

Jim Percy explained the developments in a November 25, 1976, letter to Caroline Lund in New York:

> At our plenum last weekend we fused with John McCarthy and two other leaders of the CL.

They had resigned from the CL about two or three weeks before. At the last conference of the CL John had got a majority for his document and perspectives which I gather went somehow against a new mass vanguard approach.[39] Lynda Boland led the opposition to him. Part of their perspectives were for a weekly paper. When they tried to carry this out given the fact that it was a big over projection they got hounded by the Boland group who went on a sit down strike. Tensions built up. The paper failed. One or two NCers changed sides. John, a little exhausted, resigned.

When I heard I suggested a fusion. This process led him to do some rethinking. We had been going in to our annual round of fusion discussions and even before he resigned John had told us at these that the CL had been reckless in their relations with us in the past ...

We confidently expect over the next few weeks to take a majority of their full NC if not a majority of their ranks.

We have with these initial three substantial agreement on Australian questions while they remain in the IMT. Of course they will eventually have to understand that IMT politics led to their difficulties but we will be letting this develop naturally. We also have real agreement with John on international democratic centralism and most of the related organisational disputes. Everything looks really good for making this fusion work.

In December *DA* 147 reported that two more Communist League members, Dave Armstrong and Mike Keenan, had joined the SWP fusion. In January, PC meetings noted that Chris White and Tony Dewberry "have resigned from the CL and to accept them as part of the fusion with the group of ex-CL members", then Gaele S, then Wally Matters. A total of 12 CL members came across in this fusion (out of about 40 total in the whole CL, and 120 in the SWP at about this time). Jim Percy wrote in a January 9 letter to Caroline Lund in New York that the CL fusion was "going like a dream". He reported that now we had won five out of nine of the former CL's NC and one of three alternates. By then we had won eight in all, and expected that another six or seven would join. Sakai, an FI leader from Japan, was in Australia to try to counter John McCarthy. His letter was to be published in our discussion bulletin. Jim reported that the fused ex-CLers were much closer to us on all questions than to the rump CL, and they wouldn't be organised as a minority position at our conference.

SWP fifth conference, January 1977

The SWP fifth national conference was held January 27-31, 1977, at Hawkesbury, and had a very positive outlook marked by that first phase of the CL fusion. Jim McIlroy presented the political resolution: "The Fraser Offensive: How Labor Can Fight Back"; Jim Percy the tasks and perspectives report; Dave Deutschmann the youth report; Jim Percy on relations with the CL; Allen Myers on the organisational principles resolution; Helen Jarvis on women's liberation; Sol Salby on "Socialist Revolution in the Arab East". Nita Keig gave a world movement report for the SWP majority, and John McCarthy for the minority. John McCarthy gave a special talk on "The Struggle for Workers Democracy in Eastern Europe" and Dave Holmes on "Alliances and the Revolutionary Party". Workshops were held on the international situation, fundraising, distributing the socialist press, the Black movement, the New Zealand situation, the labour movement, producing *Direct Action*, recruiting and education, and work amongst Asian students.

There were 171 registrations, and the conference received greetings from the FI United Secretariat and FI groups in Colombia, France, the US, China, Greece, Britain, Vanuatu, India and Japan. At the fund drive rally, $30,750 was pledged, exceeding our target of $25,000. We had an expansion presentation, which I chaired. The conference rally was chaired by Peta Stewart, with speakers Jim Percy, Marcia Langton, John McCarthy, Lou-anne Barker, John Tully, Alan Pinjen and Allen Myers.

The NC at the end of the conference elected a PC of nine: Allen Myers, Dave Deutschmann, Dave Holmes, Jamie Doughney, Jim McIlroy, Jim Percy, John McCarthy, John Percy, Nita Keig. It elected Jim Percy as national secretary, Dave Holmes as organisation secretary, John Percy as *DA* editor and John McCarthy as *Socialist Worker* editor.

The report on relations with the Communist League was published in our Information Bulletin (No. 1 in 1977), and a letter from Lee Walkington to the United Secretariat, January 12, 1977. Further material on the split in the Communist League and the fusion of ex-CL members with the SWP was carried in Discussion Bulletin Vol. 4, No. 4, and an article "In reply to the Communist League's letter to members" by Jim Percy and John McCarthy in Discussion Bulletin Vol. 4, No. 5.

I was editing *DA*, and two of the former CL leaders were added to our editorial board, which now consisted of Diana Auburn, Di Ewin, Marcia Langton, Alec Martin (Peter Robb), Jim McIlroy, Allen Myers, John Percy and Mary Rabbone.

Shortly after the conference, we chartered a South Sydney branch, which opened its headquarters with a shopfront in a building at 163 Regent Street, Redfern. The Sydney tasks and perspectives meeting on February 20 elected the following:[40] Sydney regional executive: Nita Keig, Paul Keig, Paul Petit, Peter Karvounis, Peter Robb, Brett Trenery; Sydney branch executive: Peter Karvounis, Ian Gordon, Di Ewin, Brett Trenery, Gordon Adler; South Sydney branch executive: Marcia Langton, Paul Petit, Peter Robb, Dominica Whelan.

Socialist Worker

Direct Action was published continuously from 1970, first as a monthly, then a fortnightly and then as a weekly from late 1975. Our theoretical magazine was less consistent, but began again in March 1977 as *Socialist Worker*, with John McCarthy as editor. Four issues appeared in 1977-78. We had previously published a journal, *Socialist Review*, which ceased publication in mid-1972 after five issues.

The editorial in *SW* 1 introduced it as one of the "key decisions of the 5th National Conference" of the SWP. "*Socialist Worker* will promote Trotskyist theory and analysis in a situation where the realm of 'theory' has been left until now to the Stalinists of the Communist Party of Australia with their publication *Australian Left Review* and the neo-Stalinists and Althusserians of *Arena* and *Intervention*".

Socialist Worker No. 1, March 1977, listed the editorial board as Dave Holmes, Nita Keig, John McCarthy and Jim Percy. The cover focused on women's liberation, and the issue carried "The Crisis in Women's Liberation: the Need for a Socialist Perspective", by Nita Keig, and the document "Socialist Revolution and the Struggle for Women's Liberation". Dave Holmes wrote on "Alliances and the Revolutionary Party". We carried a section on "News of the Fourth International": a long report on the meeting in solidarity with Hansen and Novack in London, against Healy's slanders (with speakers Tim Wohlforth, Tariq Ali, Pierre Lambert, George Novack, Ernest Mandel and a message read from Michel Pablo), and a short report on the SWP fifth national conference.

Socialist Worker 2, May-June 1977, included "The Socialist Revolution in the Arab East" (adopted by the SWP conference in January 1977), and articles by Nita Keig on "Australian Nationalism: a Reactionary Ideology" and Dave Holmes on "Marxism and the National Question", plus a review by Fran Jelley of *Damned Whores and God's Police*.

Socialist Worker 3, August-September 1977, included our resolution on "Organisational Principles of the SWP", "Why Socialists Oppose Australian Nationalism" by Doug Lorimer, "Nationalism in Australian Literature" by Gordon

Adler and various reprints.

Socialist Worker 4, Winter 1978, had editorials on "Trotskyist Unification Shows Way Forward" and "Defend Democracy in the NSW ALP". It also carried the resolution "Fighting the Fraser Offensive" (adopted by the SWP sixth national conference in January 1978), the conference political report by Jim McIlroy and "The IWW and the Fight Against Imperialist War" by Gordon Adler. We also printed the resolution of the United Secretariat of the Fourth International, "Socialist Democracy and the Dictatorship of the Proletariat".

A new series of *Socialist Worker* was published, from October 1982 to 1983, and from 1988 to 1989, and it then became *Democratic Socialism*.

CL fusion, second stage

Jim Percy travelled to Hong Kong, India and the FI United Secretariat meeting in Europe in early 1977, and reported on our successful fusion with part of the CL. We soon proceeded to carry through further steps to complete the fusion.

The CL held its 1977 conference in Sydney, in early April, in the Latin American hut at Addison Road Community Centre. Jamie Doughney, Nita Keig and Peter Robb attended as observers for the SWP, Peter giving greetings. The conference had 22 members and candidate members attending, plus seven observers and the three SWP members.

Our May 29 PC heard a report on the world movement from Jim Percy on his return, and on May 30 the SWP sent a letter to the CL National Committee, signed by Jamie Doughney, with proposals "we wish to put to you as immediate steps towards the fusion of our two organisations. They were voted on at our Political Committee of May 29 and discussed with comrades Boland, Nichols, Poulsen, and Walkington that evening." The proposed steps were:

"1) The publication of a joint newspaper, weekly with four pages going to *Militant*.

"2) Systematic joint activities, particularly in the Right to Work campaign.

"3) Write joint documents – an action program, political resolution, and a tasks and perspectives resolution. These should not be seen as a precondition for fusion, however.

"4) Have the perspective of fusing in 3-4 months."

The SWP NC on July 2-3, 1977, was attended by three observers from the CL – Lynda Boland, Ron Poulsen and Lee Walkington – and heard a report on the process of fusion from Jim Percy, as well as the following reports: world movement;

political situation; tasks and perspectives; propaganda and education; finance and press; youth; national conference; and security. The NC elected a PC of 10 and established a subcommittee of the PC, the secretariat, consisting of Dave Holmes, Jamie Doughney, Jim Percy, John Percy and Nita Keig.

In July we organised joint SWP-CL forums around the country analysing the CPA-AMWU "People's Economic Program", and organised joint council election campaigns. In August and September, Ron Poulsen and Dave Holmes collaborated on a four-part series for *DA* on "How to make a socialist revolution?"

In August 1977 we published in DA 172 a joint statement by the PCs of the SWP and CL on our fusion plans.

Joint NC, October 1977

We held a joint SWP-CL National Committee meeting on October 15-16, 1977, at St. John's Road, where all meals were catered for, with a BBQ at Helen Jarvis and Allen Myers' house in Paddington after the last session. A good number of observers were invited, including our branch organisers, SYA NE members, full-timers in the NO and on *DA*, and Control Commission members, plus John Garcia and Diana Covell. Jim Percy gave a world movement report, and Jim and Lynda Boland each gave a separate report on fusion perspectives. Ron Poulsen reported on the Australian capitalism resolution we had drafted, Jim McIlroy reported on the Australian political situation, and Jamie Doughney reported on labour movement perspectives. Nita Keig reported on women's liberation, Lee Walkington on the anti-uranium movement and our perspectives and John Percy on organisation. We elected an SWP PC of 10 plus an SYA rep.

Before the NC, CL members were regularly being invited to SWP PC meetings, and after the NC we had joint PCs and joint NO circulars. I travelled to all branches in November, reporting on the fusion and the world movement, and following up on our organisational campaigns, and John Garcia travelled to Brisbane and Ron Poulsen to Melbourne.

In the lead-up to our fusion conference, we published 12 joint discussion bulletins, totalling 400 pages.

In the first, Discussion Bulletin Vol. 5, No. 1 (Joint CL/SWP Bulletin No. 1) we published the draft political resolution adopted by the joint CL-SWP National Committee meeting in October and the SWP organisational report from the NC.

In the second, we published the two fusion reports from the joint NC meeting. The third contained the NC labour movement report, the fourth the anti-uranium movement report. No. 5 contained the youth report, the women's liberation report and the world movement report to the joint NC. No. 6 contained "The crisis of Australian capitalism", the draft resolution for the fusion conference adopted by both Political Committees.

As preparation for unity, from October 20 we pioneered a two-in-one paper (a combined *Direct Action* and *Militant*). The *Militant* had four pages at the back of *Direct Action*. (The comrades from the Communist League saw it as *Direct Action* having 12 pages at the back of *Militant*.) The first combined "Two newspapers in one" had full colour rather than just spot colour on the cover.

We were able to present a similar position for the December 10, 1977, federal elections. The November 17 *Direct Action/ Militant* included as a centrespread our joint election manifesto "Vote Labor! Fight for Socialist Policies!" Both covers carried that slogan in December.

The December 15 issue reported that Labor had lost by about 50 seats. Jim McIlroy had an article on "Which way forward for Labor", and the "*DA/Militant* gets around" column reported that sales had doubled since the election announcement. We carried a joint statement: "For a massive campaign to win the right to march", and advertised "Come to the SWP-CL Conference. Build the socialist alternative." We printed the agenda for the six-day conference. Jim McIlroy wrote on the "Meaning of CL-SWP fusion", and *Militant* carried a "Statement of CL PC on Fusion and the Revolutionary Party".

January 1978 fusion conference

The fusion conference (the SWP's sixth national conference) was held January 8-15, 1978, at Hawkesbury. January 8 was taken up with separate conferences: the CL conference approved a report on fusion by Lynda Boland; the SWP conference voted for a report on fusion by Jim Percy, who had returned temporarily from Europe from his FI Bureau assignment.

I welcomed comrades to the united conference, noting that while our efforts to unite in 1975 had failed, finally we had succeeded, and we were still ahead of the overall trend in the FI.

Reports at the fusion conference were presented by: Nita Keig, on the international situation; Ron Poulsen, on the deepening crisis of Australian capitalism; Jim McIlroy, on the Australian political situation and labour movement; Jamie Doughney, on building a class struggle alternative in the labour movement; Lee Walkington, on the fight against uranium mining; John Percy, tasks and perspectives; Leesa Wheelahan, youth; Jim Percy, world movement.

We also had educational talks: "The Workers Upsurge in Spain and Europe" by John Garcia; "The Anti-Vietnam War Movement and the Struggle Against Uranium Mining" by Peter Conrick; "Building the Revolutionary Party: James

P. Cannon's Contribution" by Peta Stewart; and "Australo-Communism: the Continuing Stalinism of the CPA" by Doug Lorimer. We also had trade union fractions, workshops on our areas of work and our organisational tasks and a panel on the women's liberation movement. We screened all four parts of Ken Loach's film *Days of Hope*.

The conference rally was chaired by Pat Garcia, with speakers Jim Percy, Ron Poulsen, Pat Starkey (a guest from the NZ SAL), Leesa Wheelahan and Allen Myers.

Jim's world movement report was a very thorough description of the course of the factional struggle in the Fourth International, and the winding up of the factions and healing of most of the splits. It was adopted unanimously. We also adopted a motion sending Jim and Nita to work in the international centre.

By prior agreement, the new National Committee represented the two fusing organisations proportionally. The NC then elected a PC of Allen Myers, Dave Holmes, Tony Forward, Jamie Doughney, Jim McIlroy, Jim Percy, John Garcia, John Percy, Leesa Wheelahan, Nita Keig, Peta Stewart and Ron Poulsen. The PC elected a secretariat of Dave Holmes, Jamie Doughney, John Percy, Peta Stewart and Ron Poulsen. Jim Percy was elected national secretary, and John Percy was elected acting national secretary in his absence.

It had been a very thorough discussion leading up to the conference. Support for the fusion was not unanimous in the CL. There was opposition from Dave Fagan and Gwynyth Farr, and immediately after the conference, Garry MacLennan resigned.

The sectarian pests from the Spartacist League tried to intervene at the conference by anonymously renting a room on the campus so they could harass our comrades, so we got the college administration to cancel their booking.

We were able to trumpet in *DA:* "Socialists unite at fusion conference". The fund drive target was $15,000, with $6,000 pledged at the conference.

Our 200th member was signed up at the conference. After the fusion we had 15 teacher members. The conference decided to open a third branch in Sydney, in Parramatta. We also had plans for a branch in Geelong, constituted as part of a Melbourne region, and another in Tasmania.

Expansion projections

My tasks and perspectives report to the fusion conference described the conference as "a more ambitious one than any previous conference of the Trotskyist movement in Australia – not merely the fact of the fusion or the size of the conference or the impressive size of the fused organisation itself, but the length of this conference and the number of agenda items we've been able to squeeze in".

Before laying out our organisational perspectives for 1978, and how our major political tasks and perspectives fitted together, I put them in the perspective of what we had achieved in 1977:

> This year has been our busiest year ever.
>
> Firstly, of course, there is the fusion. This is the biggest single party building task we could have wished for …
>
> There's the offensive we've carried out against the Communist Party's class collaborationist People's Economic Program …
>
> There's the local government elections we contested in Sydney, for Leichhardt and South Sydney councils. Although we ran fairly limited campaigns, our candidates managed to get between 6 and 19 per cent of the vote, by far the most impressive results achieved by a Trotskyist campaign ever in Australia.
>
> There's the Barney Mokgatle[41] tour we organised jointly …
>
> There's also the joint Bala Tampoe[42] speaking tour …
>
> In addition to organising tours of overseas visitors, we've been able to send our own comrades to overseas political gatherings:
>
> - Jim Percy has been able … to attend conferences of other sections of the Fourth International.
>
> - Both Jim and Nita Keig were able to be present at the conference of the Socialist Action League in New Zealand at the end of last year.
>
> - Comrade Alan Pinjen was able to do a speaking tour of New Zealand on behalf of *Malaysian Socialist Review* last year.
>
> *Direct Action* was able to increase in size from 12 to 16 pages, and since the October plenum *Militant* has been weekly and we've published the joint newspaper.
>
> In most cities we've played a very important role in building the campaign against the mining of uranium.
>
> This year we've built Right to Work Campaigns in each city where we have branches …
>
> Our comrades in SYA have waged an important struggle in defence of AUS against right-wing and Maoist attacks, and built the left and labour students conference. CL comrades have played a key role in building the Working Women's Charter Campaign, and SWP comrades have built the abortion campaign in Sydney and Adelaide.
>
> Comrades in both organisations have been able to step up their union work in a modest way this year.

> We have been able to divide the SWP branches in Sydney and Melbourne and set up regional structures.
>
> We were able to raise a total of nearly $25,000 in our fund drive last year.
>
> Several issues of *Malaysian Socialist Review* were produced, we recruited quite a few Asian comrades to the movement; Goh [Siong Hoe] had a successful tour speaking on China.
>
> We produced three issues of a new magazine, *Socialist Worker*, giving us a theoretical journal of a standard way ahead of anyone else on the left.
>
> And we produced our first book, *Towards a Socialist Australia*.

We had set three campaigns at our October NC: on sales, finances and re-cruiting, and education, and result sheets were distributed. I projected that we continue with these campaigns, with goals of getting branch *DA* bundles up to 3,000, from the current total of 2,470, and increasing the percentage of branch members selling. SYA was not projecting the continued publication of *Young Socialist*, so *DA* campus sales were to be led by SYA, but with the SWP helping, and we decided to institute sales committees in all branches.

It was a perspective for expansion, building regional structures, going on a socialist propaganda offensive and "Bolshevising" the party.

Party Organiser

Following the successful fusion and a large and exciting conference, and with a larger membership, we felt the need to become even more organised. In February we began producing the bulletin Party Organiser, an A4 roneoed magazine that had a different purpose from our Discussion Bulletin (although its role overlapped somewhat with our Information Bulletin). The introduction in the first issue explained, "It will help fill the gap in circulation of ideas and information which is not easily or regularly covered by our current bulletins or by our press. In addition it will serve to extend the distribution of material in this category … to all comrades.

"The aim of the Party Organiser is to increase the awareness of comrades of all aspects of organising the Socialist Workers Party. In doing this its scope will be wide. There will be articles on our campaign work – in the anti-uranium movement, the unions, and the women's liberation movement, and so on. Material on organising *Direct Action* and *Socialist Worker* circulation and party finance campaigns will also figure prominently as will ideas for Pathfinder Press literature distribution."

The first Party Organiser contained reports from the Sydney regional conference: the regional organiser's report, the anti-uranium report and the trade union report; and reports from the Melbourne regional conference: the regional organiser's report and the anti-uranium report. It also carried a report to the PC on unemployment work perspectives.

The second Party Organiser, in May, covered the SWP 1978 financial campaigns, on sustainers, the fund drive and debts, with lots of tables and graphs. It also carried "How to give reports", from a US SWP document; a mobilisation to sell *Towards a Socialist Australia;* the special *DA* sales weeks; preparing copy for *Direct Action; DA* photos – what's needed; and a "Statement on childcare" adopted by the Political Committee.

The third Party Organiser, also in May, contained the educational classes on Farrell Dobbs' Teamster series. The fourth, in June, had reports on the *DA* sales mobilisation and the national metalworkers discussion. The fifth, in August, contained a report on "Building on the massive success of the special sales week" and my SWP greetings to the SYA national conference. No. 6, also in August, presented three reports to the July NC plenum: political situation, labour movement and tasks and perspectives, by John Percy. No. 7 carried other reports to the July NC plenum: youth, women's liberation, gay liberation and anti-uranium. Party Organiser 8, still in August, had an article exhorting "All out for the September 7-13 sales week!" and a Sydney regional labour report. No. 9, in November, had articles on the third special sales week and on branch meeting procedure.

The February and July 1979 issues (Vol. 2, Nos. 1 and 6) carried fairly thorough study guides for an Australian labour movement class series. Party Organiser, Vol. 2, No. 2 carried the organisation report to the seventh national conference. Vol. 2, No. 3 contained the perspectives report adopted by the National Committee on May 25. Vol. 2, No. 4 contained the report on our organisational principles document and the trade union report from the seventh national conference. No. 5 carried an article on the subscription drive and a report to the July 1 national steelworkers' fraction meeting. No. 7 focused on recruiting: "For a more active approach to winning members"; "Systematising our recruitment work"; "Some suggestions for Introduction to Socialism classes".

Some fallout from the fusion in Brisbane

A few comrades, mostly from the CL side, didn't adjust well to the fusion. Some of this related to differences over the Queensland right to march campaign, and a few resigned or dropped out, and a few were expelled for breaking discipline.

Brisbane had its first SWP meeting on January 28, 1978. Doug Lorimer was elected organiser, and Doug, Peter Annear, Barry Healy and Megan Martin were elected as a temporary executive until the branch tasks and perspectives meeting was held, on February 11. Doug Lorimer gave the organiser's report. Ron Poulsen and I had come up for the meeting, and I gave an NO report. There was a report on trade unions and the ALP by Greg Adamson, a Civil Liberties Coordinating Committee (CLCC) report by Peter Annear, which recommended against marching on March 4, an anti-uranium report by Barry Healy and a women's report by Megan Martin.

Peter Annear reported on the activity of some of the former CL members in the CLCC. Dave Atkinson and Peter Swann had volunteered to go on a speaking tour without seeking permission from the branch executive or branch organiser. Lesley Wenck, Sue McCarthy and Dave Atkinson had distributed a CLCC leaflet calling for a march, when the branch had voted the previous weekend (unanimously in this case) to oppose a march. Atkinson was charged, the report presented to the branch, and he was expelled (the other two were only recently in the SWP). Terry Farr counter-charged Healy, Annear and Lorimer.

Jim and Nita had left for their FI Bureau assignment in Paris after the conference, and I wrote to them on February 20 about the Brisbane trip: "The fusion hasn't taken well at all there, and a pretty serious situation has developed". The CLCC was "a degenerate rump that has degenerated about as far as it is possible to go. I went to last Thursday's meeting and they are really a bunch of p.b. arseholes. Kids playing at politics, and some of them middle aged kids who should know better. They represent nothing, no significant social forces. The forty or so attending were either individual dilettantes or members of one or other of the several semi-anarchist groups here – the Red and Black bookshop crowd, anarchist feminists, the Socialist Action conglomerate, which includes some of these groups plus some ISers, ex-CLers, and so on …"

The Brisbane branch executive elected was Peter Annear, Barry Healy, Megan Martin and Darren Ward. Doug Lorimer moved from Brisbane to Hobart.

At a Brisbane branch meeting in April, Greg Adamson presented a report that Sue McCarthy had broken discipline while on suspension over the CLCC march. A vote to expel her passed. Peter Annear gave the organiser's report, and proposed that Val Edwards be coopted to the executive; Peter Swann was also voted on to it.

At the Brisbane branch tasks and perspectives meeting on May 6, 1978, Greg Adamson gave a Labor report, pushing to get more members to join the ALP. The NSW ALP had banned members writing for or selling *DA;* Peter Annear claimed we had at least 40 comrades in the NSW ALP. The executive elected was Peter Annear, Barry Healy, Val Edwards, Megan Martin, Greg Adamson and Terry O'Neill.

The right to march struggle in Queensland

Queensland Premier Joh Bjelke-Petersen's dictatorially imposed ban on street marches caused deep debates and divisions on the left. On September 4, 1977, Bjelke-Petersen announced "The day of street marches is over", leading to a massive struggle for the right to march over the next few years.

Barry Healy reported in *DA* 180, soon after the ban was imposed, "Qld police attack civil liberties march", and a few weeks later, "Brisbane cops attack rally, arrest civil rights marchers" (*DA* 183).

The SWP took a pretty rigid position on tactics for the campaign, feeling a need to counter the ultra-left tactics of anarchist groups in Brisbane, and probably also of the ultra-left and sectarian tendencies of the comrades from the CL with whom we were in the process of uniting. We argued the need for mass action, rather than heroic civil disobedience leading to multiple arrests. Renfrey Clarke wrote in *DA* 187 in November, "What tactics in Queensland? Civil liberties and civil disobedience". In December he reported "Cops attack Brisbane civil liberties march", with 210 arrested (*DA* 190). In the same issue of the paper (the *Militant* part) Megan Martin replied to Renfrey with "How to win back the right to march". The debate continued in the campaign in the new year, with *DA* 196 and 197 articles by Renfrey "Qld civil liberties campaign at crossroad" and "Qld civil liberties campaign facing crisis". The SWP PC issued a statement at the end of February on "Qld: How to win the right to march".

Attempts to march, and arrests, continued. Renfrey reported in *DA* 198, "Police arrest 50 in Brisbane march", and Mark Carey wrote "Ultralefts sabotage Brisbane uranium rally" in *DA* 200.

The *DA* of April 13, 1978, carried a letter by Renfrey on the CPA's right to march tactics: while disagreeing with the tactic of small minority attempts to march, they wouldn't argue against them. Recently, one young CPA member had taken to proposing that the CLCC announce plans for a march, but then not carry them out.

In April *DA* 203 carried a centrespread by Renfrey on "Growing support for right to march in Queensland", and he reported in *DA* 204, "Queensland unionists rally for civil liberties" after a walk and picnic by 80 clergymen was stopped and 11 were arrested.

DA 206 carried a debate on Queensland tactics, with contributions from others on the left – Judy McVey, Carole Ferrier, John Minns and Graeme Grassie – and a reply by Renfrey Clarke, "Only mass action can win".

In October, Renfrey wrote "Qld ALP undermines civil liberties", arguing: "The continuing concentration on token attempts to march by self-sacrificing minorities has done nothing to attract broad working-class participation in the campaign. All that these ultraleft tantrums have accomplished has been to make it easier for the ALP and union leadership to withhold their support from the civil liberties struggle."

But some Labor lefts *were* getting involved. The next month, *DA* 231 reported that 300 people were arrested in a Brisbane march, including Senator George Georges and MP Tom Uren. This did prompt union action, Christine Beresford reporting in the next *DA* that Queensland unions went on strike over the arrests, and 500 from the combined maritime unions marched (on the footpath) to court.

Renfrey again discussed tactics in the November 16 *DA*, "Civil disobedience or mass action?" and reported two issues later that "TLC [Trades and Labour Council] backs Bris march". Were we too rigid in posing the mass action vs. civil disobedience dichotomy by this time?

In mid-December, Renfrey Clarke wrote in *DA* 237, "Civil Rights protests sweep Qld", with successful demonstrations in Collinsville, Gladstone, Rockhampton and other towns. In Brisbane 4,000 rallied, 1,500 marched; there were 1,300 cops and 346 arrests. He asked, "Can ALP lead civil rights struggle?" In answer, Mark Carey reported in *DA* 240, "Qld TLC marches to the rear"; it had refused to endorse the March 15 civil liberties march.

By August 1979, Paul Anderson (Peter Annear) wrote in *DA* 265, "5000 in Brisbane march against uranium" organised by the Campaign Against Nuclear Power on Nagasaki Day (but not Hiroshima Day!) It was an "important victory", since the ban had originally been introduced as a move to disrupt the anti-uranium movement in Brisbane. "The success of the rally and march confirms that the best way of building opposition to the mining and export of uranium and the policies of the State government in general, is by building demonstrations which draw in the largest number of people possible.

"Since the October 1977 demonstration of 5000 when 418 people were arrested, the anti-uranium and civil liberties movements have never realised their potential. In fact, no subsequent demonstration in Brisbane was as large until the Nagasaki Day rally and march on August 9.

"This was directly attributable to the tactic of confrontation with the police, which resulted in over 1800 arrests and a subsequent decline in the number of people attending demonstrations in King George Square."

In the *DA* of August 30, Renfrey wrote "The left and Qld civil liberties", debating with the CPA, which missed the significance of the August 9 march and didn't know what to do next, and with John Minns of the International Socialists, who refused to recognise how the minority action strategy had harmed the movement.

Party building experiences in the 1970s

Fourth International assignments

As we grew and became more politically experienced, we agreed to take on some responsibility for the Fourth International, assigning Jim Percy and Nita Keig to Paris to work in the FI Bureau from mid-1977, Jim for two years eventually, Nita for one year. Doug Lorimer replaced Jim in Paris in mid-1979 for a year.

At the SWP PC on July 21, 1977, Jim reported on the proposed division of labour in his absence. I was to take over the role of national secretary while he was away. Our ASIO spy reported: "John Percy recently left the *DA* editor position to become NSW regional organiser, he is likely to replace Jim as National Secretary". Allen Myers was taking over as *DA* editor.

Jim left for Paris after the July 23, 1977, *DA* banquet, going via the Canadian fusion conference of the League for Socialist Action/Ligue Socialiste Ouvrière, and then the SWP conference at Oberlin on August 6-13, 1977. There was a new team at the FI centre, with a common position about its role. In some ways it was like the successful fusion here. It was our contribution to the FI, assigning two of our leading comrades, and costing us $15,000 for the first year, but we also gained a lot from the experience. Responsibilities included helping run the Bureau, organising correspondence, travelling, especially communication with small sections and overseeing anti-nuclear work and women's liberation work.

Although it was isolated being away from their own comrades back in Australia, they were able to make a contribution, and we learned a lot from it. Barry Sheppard and Caroline Lund were in Paris at the same time as Jim and Nita, and became good friends and collaborators. And there were some social opportunities, as Nita wrote on January 1, 1978, as more comrades gathered for a United Secretariat meeting: "Jim cooked a spaghetti bolognese for 60 to feed comrades at the SWP's Brussels apartment. It was a great success with everyone."

Some tensions back home

While Jim was in Paris, I had a number of tussles with Jamie Doughney, feeling that he was trying to encroach on the national secretary's role. On February 20,

1978, I wrote to Jim and Nita about "a few areas of tension that have arisen with Jamie … encroaching on the national secretary's responsibilities and opposing ideas I put forward and supporting ideas I oppose. I'm not imagining this, Peta [Stewart]'s observed some of it too."

Jamie's assignment was finance and administration. There would have been "no problem if he stuck to his area of responsibility, but unfortunately he wants to be the one making all the decisions and taking the initiatives", I wrote. There were four of us in the National Office at the time – myself, Jamie, Dave Holmes and Ron Poulsen. "I know Jamie regarded me as a rival, and I recognised this would be one of my biggest problems when I took on this job."

The following week I wrote about more problems with Jamie in the NO. Tony Forward reported that Jamie's partner, Leesa Wheelahan, was dragging Jamie into the SYA NO to support her against him. A few months later, on May 27, I wrote on the question of the SYA national secretary. Leesa and Tony had been functioning jointly, but it was now getting sorted that it would be Tony.

In a letter I wrote to Jim on May 4, 1978, I was able to report that there was virtually "no vestige" of the old lines from the fusion in the party NO. But it wasn't all rosy – I felt the need to mention the ongoing leadership problems I faced from Jamie, "his need to be mover of motions and pacesetter, it leads him into bad decisions quite often". I also mentioned the differences over the question of child care that had developed with Helen Jarvis and Allen Myers.

I also informed him that long-time leader Peter Conrick had resigned from the party. Conrick hadn't developed any particular political differences with us, apart from the not so minor one that he no longer felt the need to build a revolutionary party. He had decided that he wanted to follow a hedonistic course, to enjoy his life as much as he could. (Ironically, the next time I saw him, his leg was in plaster: he'd pursued his pleasure-seeking course and had broken his leg while skiing!)

Malaysian Socialist Review

By 1976, the SWP had recruited three comrades of Malaysian background. An enthusiastic recruit, Alan Pinjen, initiated *Malaysian Socialist Review,* a magazine to reach out to the large number of Malaysian students in Australia. It started publishing in September 1976, with Alan Pinjen, in Sydney as editor, and listed Malaysian socialists in Melbourne, Goh Siong Hoe, and in Perth, Peter Boyle. Initially the editorial address was 139 St. John's Road, Glebe, the SWP office.

Its editorial statement in the first issue declared: "The Review is published by a group of Malaysian socialists who believe that the only solution to the social and economic problems which continue to plague our country thirteen years after 'Federation' is the establishment of a government of the vast majority, the workers and poor farmers, which will lead to the construction of a socialist society".

Clearly aiming at the Maoist dominance in the Malaysian student leadership, the editorial in the second issue stated, "We do not believe that Malaysians will be won over to the revolutionary cause if we hide behind the narrow mask of 'Nationalism' or 'Anti-imperialism'" and stated that the national bourgeoisie had no progressive role to play. *MSR* No. 2 appeared in November, printed by Media Press, which printed *DA* at the time.

The third issue, in April 1977, campaigned strongly in defence of Hishamuddin Rais, the former general secretary of the University of Malaya Students Union, demanding that the Australian government grant him political asylum. The fourth issue appeared in July and contained a picture of a rally in Melbourne calling for political asylum for Hishamuddin Rais. Its new address was the SWP's, at 215A Thomas Street, Haymarket.

The appearance of *MSR* precipitated fierce Maoist attacks and slanders against Alan Pinjen in *Salient* magazine in NZ as an agent of the Malaysian government, and a "Trotskyite" after a speaking tour of New Zealand for the NZ Young Socialists. In March 1977 Goh Siong Hoe went on a tour here, speaking on China; Peter Boyle wrote in *DA* 176, "Maoists set OSS on sectarian path".

We ran a petition ad against the Maoist sectarianism in *MSR* 4 signed by some of our comrades and supporters in AUS and elsewhere: Peter Annear, Queensland regional organiser of AUS; Laurie Bebbington, finance committee chairperson, AUS; Mark Carey, editor of *Arena*, Macquarie University; Dave Deutschmann, national secretary of SYA; G. Lum, Overseas Students Service director, Caulfield Institute of Technology; Max Pearce, president Young Labor Council, NSW; David Spratt, editorial collective member, Alternative News Service; S. Thomas, Victorian regional organiser, AUS; J. Nieuwenhuizen, president SRC, Melbourne University; Peter O'Connor, president AUS.

Towards the end of 1977, Alan Pinjen went into a crisis of some sort, and was out of action for a few months. In the new year, January 28, 1978, I wrote to Jim that he was back on deck. On March 4, I wrote to Jim and Nita, "Alan P gave a report to the PC on overseas student work, and like a yo-yo he's now for going flat out in it and pulling Peter B[oyle] out of party work for it. I'll have to try and talk to him and Peter about it informally, but it seemed to me that his report was a prime example of what we mean when we talk about the need for Asian recruits to be integrated totally into the work of the party. He has to work closer with us so he won't come up with bombshell reports, and his perspective is able to encompass all areas of party building. What we need is the sort of integration that Peter B's getting and the important education he's getting in learning how to head up an important unit of the party [the South Sydney branch]."

I followed it up in another letter on April 25: "Asian work. After listening to your last tape I became convinced of the defence bulletin perspective, and all PC members also agree. The problem, however, is thoroughly convincing Peter B and Alan P. I thought I had swung Alan around, but at the moment he's still sticking to the position that Asian Socialist Review[43] should be the priority, although he says he agrees with the other perspective and would like to do both. Then I had Peter B around to dinner, and convinced him of the defence bulletin perspective, but then he went away and spoke to Alan and got filled up with doubts again. So we've still got some work to do on this."

The perspective of the SWP leadership was to set up a defence committee for activists facing repression in the region – which eventually became the Committee Against Repression in the Pacific and Asia (CARPA). By May 17, I reported that our Asian work had now been sorted out, and that Dave Holmes, Gordon Adler and Helen Jarvis would be working with Alan and Peter on a defence committee initially. In a May 27-29 letter, I wrote that Asian defence work was well under way, and Alan, Peter, Dave and Gordon had visited supporter David Boyd, who donated $200 to start the kitty.

But the calm didn't last. On September 7, 1978, I had a discussion with Alan Pinjen and Peter Boyle about their mistaken perspective of building a Malaysian organisation, a rival party competing with the SWP for other Malaysian and Asian comrades. An ASIO telephone intercept on September 7 reported on a discussion between myself and Gayle Burmeister in Adelaide about a "bit of trouble here with Peter Boyle and Alan Pinjen", who wanted to resign from the party and set up separately. There was a danger that they might try to "line up Jeff Richards" (a comrade of Philippine background in Adelaide) and other Asian comrades.

On September 11, the SWP Secretariat had a follow-up discussion with Alan Pinjen and Peter Boyle, and a further discussion on September 16. On September 14, 1978, I wrote to Jim and Nita in Paris: "Alan Pinjen has scrambled his brains again, this time taking Peter Boyle with him". I reported that both had resigned from the SWP to set up shop outside and construct "the Malaysian section" of the Fourth International. Goh resisted. "It puts our Asian work back quite a bit, but we still want to press on with the CARPA perspective."

They went ahead and formed the Malaysian Socialist League. Their draft manifesto was published in *MSR* 5, October 1978. It was roneoed, with a separate

PO box in the Sydney University Union. *MSR* 6 appeared dated December 1978, featuring an article on "Self-determination for Sabah and Sarawak", based on a November 25, 1978, MSL forum on "Independence for Sarawak?"

A Political Committee meeting on October 18, 1978, adopted a statement on the resignation of Alan Pinjen and Peter Boyle, and a report by Dave Holmes, which were published in our Information Bulletin, along with an October 19, 1978, letter to the PC from Alan Pinjen and Peter Boyle, and a report on the inaugural meeting of the Malaysian Socialist League. After a year, Alan's project had folded and he rejoined us, although not lasting and not contributing to his potential. The PC rejoined Peter Boyle on October 11, 1981.

Committee Against Repression in the Pacific and Asia

It was a wrong tactic at the time by the Malaysian comrades in *MSR*, trying to establish a party group from Australia for a country facing repression in the region. It hindered the joining up of comrades and building the party *here* (actually drawing comrades away from us), which could in the future have assisted in the growth of a *real* party in that country.

Furthermore, there were so many countries in the region, and so many issues to take up. So we set up the Committee Against Repression in the Pacific and Asia as an organisation to fight on those issues, and to help organise the Asian comrades and supporters living in Australia. I wrote to Jim and Nita in Paris on June 10, 1978, about setting up CARPA.

CARPA Bulletin No. 1 was published in June 1978, with articles on Singapore, Sri Lanka, Indonesia, Thailand, New Zealand, the Philippines and the New Hebrides. Subsequent issues over the next six years also covered Malaysia, West Irian, South Korea, India, Pakistan, Cambodia, Vietnam and East Timor. The editor of the first issue was listed as Chuah Tze Min (Alan Pinjen). By No. 6 in September 1980, the publisher was listed as Goh Siong Hoe, and by No. 10 in May 1982 it was Helen Jarvis. Artist David Boyd played a useful role as the president of CARPA.

From the second issue, we campaigned to "Free Rendra", the Indonesian poet/actor muzzled by Suharto. By 1980 we had organised for Rendra to tour Australia, but he was denied an exit permit; we gathered an impressive list of signatories to petition against the refusal.

The third issue, in February 1979, launched a new campaign for freedom for Professor Syed Hussein Ali, detained without trial by the Malaysian government. By issue six we were able to announce he was out of detention, with a letter from him thanking CARPA. *CARPA Bulletin* No. 10 reported on the silencing of leading Indonesian novelist Pramoedya Ananta Toer. Gordon Adler reviewed Pramoedya's *This Earth of Mankind* in *DA* of August 31, 1982, describing it as "A work that frightens the Suharto regime". Max Lane, the Australian envoy recalled from the Jakarta embassy for translating Pramoedya's writings, subsequently joined the DSP and was on our NC for two decades, until being expelled with other comrades in 2008.

With issue No. 19 in March 1985, the name was changed to *Asia Pacific Solidarity*. Editors were Peter Boyle and Helen Jarvis (from the SWP) and Robin Osborne, plus a number of consulting editors, including Max Lane and Peta Stewart from the SWP. (It went to No. 21, September 1985.)

Organising the branches in 1978

On January 31, 1978, I reported to Jim that I was back in Sydney from Melbourne, where I'd attended the regional tasks and perspectives meeting. They were dividing into four branches from two, and Steve Painter, the organiser, had last minute hesitations. "In my opinion the chief consideration is the question of cadre, whether there are enough comrades as a whole in Melbourne to make up four branches [which would be Fitzroy-Collingwood (based at Smith Street), South-East Melbourne, Geelong and Western Suburbs], and whether there are enough comrades of executive calibre to make up four branch executives and a strong regional executive. Everyone agreed there was.

"The formula Steve had plumped for – a very unthought out organising committee for the Western Suburbs – had no merit at all in my opinion." I discussed it with Steve, and he agreed. I surmised that "Steve's barriers to communication gave rise to the problem, and his barriers also made it a little awkward to solve – the decision has to be changed without damaging the authority of the regional leadership".

On January 28, I reported that Peta Stewart was running the Sydney district. However, "Julie's done a bunk."[44] On February 3, my letter discussed the problems of a clique centred on Dominica Whelan.

I reported to Jim and Nita after the February 6 Sydney tasks and perspectives meeting, which had an extensive agenda of organiser's report, education and recruiting, sales, finance, anti-uranium campaign, women's liberation, the Right to Work Campaign, ALP and trade unions.

I wrote on March 28 that I'd come back from Melbourne educational camp, where I gave a talk on the revolutionary party, covering "Marxism in our Time".

I reported in early April that Adelaide branch now had 18 full members. We had exported three to other branches. Other possible recruits were on the way, so it could be up to 26. There were prospects for further inroads into the CP ranks after we joined Willie and Jeny, Debbie Altorfer and James Sinnamen.

A letter from Peta Stewart to Jim and Nita in Paris, April 12, 1978, reported on the Sydney banquet. There were160-180 at it, with lots of contacts, including ex-members like Al Westwood, Dot Tumney and Rod Quinn (some of whom would rejoin). Peta gave a run-down of the Sydney branches' internal and external work, the contacts, recruits etc.

In mid-April I wrote to Jim and Nita telling them we had made a booking for Hawkesbury. I suggested we should structure the conference differently, looking for an "enormous attendance for the Saturday and Sunday if we planned it right". On the first two days "we could present our most exciting, public type reports – political report, labor movement, international – and have the rally on the Sunday night, with slide show and cabaret on the Saturday night, then on the following days we could have the more esoteric reports, pre world congress discussion, perhaps a report on the CPA, then a world movement report, and in the last couple of days the youth report, the organisation report, election of NC and so on".

For the rally, perhaps "the biggest thing we'll be wanting to play up is a move to build two new party branches in two key industrial cities, Newcastle and Wollongong. We might have the teams already worked out for the moves, and make a big thing of the comrades who are transferring and making moves to get into industry."

I also reported that Adelaide was "really a cadre producing branch at the moment" and that recent banquets had been very good, with Sydney getting 180 and lots of contacts; about 42 in Adelaide, where "people liked my talk"; and Melbourne's also went well, with about 80.

My following week's letter (April 25) reported "a feeling I detect throughout the national office at the moment, which I suspect is somehow related to one of Parkinson's laws about work expanding to fill the available space, that there are so many things to be done and not enough time in the day to do them. I don't think this is really an indication that we're getting snowed under, but is in many ways a healthy sign, reflecting firstly a bigger and growing outfit, and secondly, a growing consciousness about nearly every single area of our work. For example, the NO is now trying to provide week to week guidance on all areas of our work, organisational and political, to a far greater extent than we ever did in the past."

We were holding regular Wednesday PC meetings, and discussed the attendance at SYA NC by PC members, having John Garcia and Ron Poulsen go rather than Jamie. We also discussed the Brisbane executive, and election perspectives, and planned for our Teamster educational weekends.

This report also discussed the question of Tony Forward vs. Leesa Wheelahan as SYA national secretary, and Leesa's illness at the time.

Before the Resistance conference, the SWP PC had passed a motion that we not have a debate on gay liberation in the youth before we'd sorted it out in the party. On May 15, I sent out a circular informing comrades: "To require party members in SYA to conduct discussion of homosexual oppression and gay liberation in the party IDB and not in the SYA pre-conference discussion.

"Although we don't currently operate as a fraction within SYA and do not intervene there by binding comrades to present the SWP line in the discussion, we felt that on the issue of gay liberation where we have not had the opportunity yet to have a thorough discussion on the question in the SWP itself, it would be wrong for party comrades to have that discussion in SYA before debating it properly in the party.

"Moreover, this year the Internal Discussion Bulletin is open for contributions throughout the year, not just in the three month pre-conference discussion period, and the first issues will be out shortly now that the typing backlog is starting to be cleared."

Resistance magazine

The SYA eighth national conference was held in Melbourne, June 3-5, 1978, for the first time at the comfortable, modern YWCA centre in Elizabeth Street. Registration was 160-170, and SYA membership was 101 (more than 100 for the first time since 1974). The average age of the membership there was just under 21.

DA 213 reported that Tony Forward presented the political resolution and report, which registered the downturn in the student movement, while Jon West gave a report on "The role of students in revolutionary struggle", Steve Robson reported on the anti-uranium mining movement, Dave Deutschmann gave a world movement report on the FI, and Deb Shnookal gave a feature talk on "France in May-June 1968". I presented greetings from the SWP, in large measure a reaffirmation by the party of the importance of youth work, which were well received, I reported to Jim.

I wrote to Jim in a June 10-12 letter that Dominica's clique had attached itself to the punk band led by Gavin Quinn. "However, they've got no politics of their own, so they've linked up with the remnants of the opposition in the CL, Fagan, White, Liam, and of course Gwynnyth Evans (Lesley Wenck is their Brisbane representative)."

We had printed the last *Young Socialist*, No. 17, March 1978, as a four-page insert in *DA* 200. At the conference, the magazine name was changed back to *Resistance*, a very wise move, and we ended up having big sales of the first issue of the new *Resistance* magazine. Two thousand five hundred copies were printed, and, after very successful sales at the Hiroshima Day demos, an extra 2,000 had to be printed. (In June 1980, the Socialist Youth Alliance Conference changed the organisation's name back to Resistance also.)

Resistance 1, Winter-Spring, 1978, was 16 pages, and included a centre lift-out poster, "Capitalism is a dead end".

Resistance 2, Summer 1978-79, went up to 20 pages, printed the "Secondary Students Bill of Rights", and the centre poster was Che, marking the "20th Anniversary Cuban Revolution". We started carrying a cartoon strip by Tony Dewberry on the adventures of the stranded alien Kzotz: "Close Encounters with an Outdated System".

Resistance 3, Autumn 1979, had a centre poster: "Leon Trotsky 1879-1940. 'Open the road to the youth'". Kzotz had an encounter with "Cults and society".

Resistance 4, Winter 1979, was now "published by Elizabeth Wheelahan", and carried an eight-page supplement, "Youth in Australia and the World Revolution", the draft political resolution for SYA's ninth national conference. Anthony Forward reviewed *National Student*, the fortnightly paper of AUS. It was the "first regular mass circulation publication put out by AUS since the editor of the old National U was sacked in 1977. But so far, National Student has failed to do its job as the union's organiser.

"The worst failing of the paper is its attitude to right-wing student moves to have campus unions leave AUS. At the date of publication 5 campuses have left the union. This includes three of the largest: Melbourne, Macquarie and NSW universities … But from the material printed in National Student you wouldn't know that the union that publishes it may go down the drain shortly."

The separate *Resistance* magazine generally appeared every two or three months, in tabloid format. In 1983 we produced a special A4 magazine format anti-nuke issue. The separate magazine was suspended in 1983. We restarted *Resistance* magazine in 1988, again appearing roughly every three months.

Fourth International 40th anniversary rallies

For September 1, 1978, we organised rallies to mark the 40th anniversary of the founding of the Fourth International. In Sydney 100 attended, 120 in Melbourne, 40 in Brisbane, 50 in Adelaide and 20 in Hobart.

The Melbourne rally was chaired by Liz Ross, and the highlight was a talk by Ted Tripp, one of the founders of the Australian Trotskyist movement in the 1930s, who had recently joined the SWP. Dave Deutschmann interviewed Tripp when he joined in 1978 for *DA* 230: "60 Years of Struggle for Socialism". We also ran a centrespread in *DA* 235 on Tripp's experiences at the Lenin School in Moscow.

Tripp had been a leader of the CPA, selected in the late 1920s to be its first student in an extensive one and a half years study and training course at the Lenin School in Moscow. After he returned, he was the leader of the Friends of the Soviet Union, but became convinced of Trotsky's perspectives and was removed and then expelled from the CPA in 1934. He joined the Workers Party, and later left it, to publish *Permanent Revolution*. After World War II he was associated with the Victorian Labor College, and was its secretary for more than 20 years.

After Ted died in Melbourne on September 21, 1979, aged 78, Dave Deutschmann wrote his obituary for *DA* 273, "Ted Tripp – Fighter for socialism", and we held a memorial meeting.

Written greetings read to the Fourth International anniversary rallies included one from David Boyd, artist and sponsor of the newly formed CARPA. Boyd acclaimed the founding of the Fourth International and looked forward to the time when humanity could live in harmony in a society free of repression. Lloyd Churchward, a reader in political science at Melbourne University and a long-time member of the CPA, sent the following message: "Congratulations on the fortieth anniversary of the founding of the Fourth International. This organisation has been of major importance in keeping alive the spirit of revolution and revolt and revitalising the socialist critique of the Soviet Union."

The rise and fall of the SLL

The Socialist Labour League was a group that claimed to be Trotskyist. It followed religiously the British Socialist Labour League (later Workers Revolutionary Party) founded and led by Gerry Healy. It got going in Sydney just a little after us, and for much of the 1970s was our main rival on the left. Its paper was our main competitor at many rallies and other political functions.

Its main leader was Jim Mulgrew, who had been around the CPA, building its youth centre "Barricades" in Glebe Point Road in opposition to Resistance, until a bitter struggle for control erupted there in mid-1970. Attempting to resist eviction by the Anglican Church landlords (with the CPA supporting the church), the centre in its final struggle lived up to its name – they barricaded themselves in.

Another leader was Phil Sandford, who had been around the Spartacist League in the US, and after being deported back to Australia, linked up with the SLL. Others came from the evolution of the Sydney Anti-Imperialist Caucus, and some who had been members of Resistance, supporting Gould in the fight in 1970, flipped over to becoming Healyites, although Gould wasn't allowed to join until a few years later! Terry Cook and a few from Brisbane had been part of John McCarthy's group, and Nick Beams from Hobart evolved from being a leader of SDS there. There were also a few who had come from Britain, influenced by the SLL there.

They were very much a sect, distinguished by their use of violence against their political opponents, and very hostile and sectarian towards anyone they disagreed with (which was everyone on the left). They organised dances for working-class youth in the suburbs, and recruited on a very minimal basis, with a very high turnover. They refused any joint political campaigns with other left groups, and for a while they grew.

They built profitable bookshops in Newcastle, Perth and Parramatta. They bought their own web offset press, and wanted to put out a daily paper, modelled on their mentor in Britain.

The British SLL had been part of the International Committee of the FI, which broke with the FI International Secretariat led by Michel Pablo and Ernest Mandel in 1953, but refused to participate in the 1963 reunification, refusing to recognise the reality of the Cuban Revolution. In 1975, conscious of the growth of the FI, especially in France, and also of the growth of the US SWP, Healy embarked on a mad campaign of slander against the US SWP, accusing SWP leaders Joe Hansen and George Novack of being GPU and FBI agents.

This wasn't just a casual statement, but became the overriding political campaign by Healy and all his satellite groups around the world, so after a while Joe Hansen answered the slanders. We carried his rebuttal, "On Healy's 'Investigation' – What the facts show" as a nine-page supplement to *DA* 106.

We followed it up with a polemic by Jim Percy in *DA* 117, "The political degeneration of a sect", pointing out that the actions of these so-called Trotskyists with their bashings and harassment of paper sellers from other groups, at May Day and elsewhere, allowed even the Stalinists to score points on workers democracy. "If you have constantly told everyone that you are *the* revolutionary party that will lead the working class and yet remain a small sideshow act then someone is conspiring (whether police or 'Pabloites') to prevent you from getting anywhere. So 35 years after the event you 'discover' that Hansen helped kill Trotsky and anyone that leaves you is a police agent, etc., etc. Since in spite of slanders political opponents prosper then the next step is physical disruption."Jim Percy followed it with another article, in *DA* 120, on "The dead-end logic of mindless sectarianism". In August we printed another eight-page supplement by Joseph Hansen, "Healy caught in the logic of the big lie".

In July 1976 we organised a speaking tour for US SWP Afro-American leader Willie Mae Reid, who was the SWP's vice-presidential candidate in that year's election, and the SLL did its utmost to disrupt her meetings. In Sydney they got in and tried to shout her down with a small demonstration (*DA* 126). There was disruption at the Canberra meeting, so we banned entry for known SLL members, and in Melbourne they tried to force their way in. In spite of this, the tour was very successful, 1,500 attending Reid's talks.

The SLL thuggery also made it into the media. Nita Keig reported in an April 20, 1977, letter to Jim: "Last night the first segment on 'A Current Affair' was devoted to Healyite violence. There was scandal around their YS conference over Easter. They roughed some kids from Melbourne up and then wouldn't give them a ride back on the bus. The cops stopped them ten miles from the camp and made them turn back and pick them up. They dumped them again halfway to Melbourne and made them hitchhike the rest of the way. Anyway the kids' parents got onto the press and they interviewed the kids, the parents, the bus driver and filmed a Healyite going into their Melbourne HQ with a newspaper over her head ... They strike us as in a crisis in more ways than one – pathetic interventions at events at YLC, not so cocky on the whole."

At the July 4, 1977, SWP Leichhardt branch meeting, Nita Keig gave a report on the developing chaos amongst the Healyites, that Bob Gould was forming a faction, total size about 50, which included former leaders Jim Mulgrew and Val Murphy. She reported also that Mick Costa and Peter Reid had now joined the CL. Other comrades who escaped included John Tully, in the early '70s.

A common response to members leaving, or even expressing doubts, was to bash them. *DA* 161 reported "SLL thugs threaten, assault ex-member" (Paul White). Grahame Adler was expelled on the spot for merely asking a question at their conference.

For a while the SLL had some support in sections of the Arab community. It was able to make use of the film *The Palestinian,* made by British SLL member Vanessa Redgrave. But after a while the SLL and the United Palestinian Workers had fallen out strongly over the cynical use of the film showings. Apparently Libyan leader Muammar Gaddafi had footed the whole bill, but the SLL had been making big appeals for cash. Allen Myers wrote a four-part series for *DA* in April 1978 exposing their line and practice on Palestine: "An answer to SLL slanders: Socialists and the defence of Palestine"; "How SLL opposed Arab national struggle"; "The SLL's slander campaign against PLO"; "How should revolutionaries support Arab struggle?"

For a while the SLL was able to turn out quite sizeable contingents for May Day, cordoning off their new members from other tendencies' paper sellers at the end of the marches. But on May 12, 1978, I reported to Jim and Nita in Paris that they were shrinking and had internal problems. I reported the following left contingents, which I made a habit of counting:

"SLL, 55; SWP and SYA, 120; CPA, 150; SPA, 60 + 30 YSL + 100 Arabs; Maoists, 55; IS, 25; Spartacists, 17; Anarchists, 35." I also had a detailed May Day listing of union and migrant group contingents and reported that in Melbourne the SWP/SYA contingent had 80.

I also reported an anecdote about the Healyites and how they were viewed by the printing workers at Media Press, which for a while printed our paper and theirs; the workers had put a sign on the phone: "This phone is bugged by the CIA, KGB, ASIO, Direct Action, and the Swiss Naval Intelligence". Kate Blakeney, a member of the British SLL's National Committee, whom Healy had sought to assault sexually, fled to Sydney with her family in 1978. We recruited her, and she was elected to our NC. Such scandalous antics by Healy were finally totally exposed, leading to his organisation's 1985 implosion in Britain.

Allen Myers wrote a further *DA* series on the SLL political degeneration, in five parts, in July 1979: "Workers solidarity under attack"; "National struggles and socialism"; "Revolution and reaction in Iran"; "A sect heads for the capitalist camp. Class struggle or class collaboration?"; "From ultraleftism to reaction".

Partly as a result of our approach, the educational polemics and their outrageous, apolitical behaviour, we won over some key members of the SLL, including some from the Resistance days. On April 25, 1978, I reported that Peter Voysey had joined from the Healyites, and Paul Brook was a possibility. We also recruited John Tully, Mick Costa, Jack Signorelli, Ray Allen and Tony Turnbull. This contributed to their demise (on top of the collapse of the WRP).

The central role of the revolutionary press

The original *Direct Action*

One of the traditions on which *Direct Action* built was that of the old Industrial Workers of the World, the Wobblies, who were the first publishers of a paper with this name in Australia, during World War I.

The IWW was formed in Chicago in 1905, and by the outbreak of the war was well established in Australia. The IWW set out to be an industrial union uniting all workers in struggle against the bosses. But it was also a revolutionary organisation based on a dedicated membership preaching the doctrines of all-out class struggle and the fight for a new social order.

In January 1914 in Sydney the IWW began publication of a weekly newspaper under the name *Direct Action*. The editorial in the first issue explained: "For the first time in the history of the working-class movement in Australia, a paper appears which stands for straight-out direct-actionist principles, unhampered by the plausible theories of the parliamentarians".

The IWW's revolutionary message was ceaselessly hammered home in *Direct Action*. The paper ridiculed the petty-bourgeois reformism of the Labor Party. It attacked the arbitration system, the pet creation of the ALP leadership. It attacked the nationalism, the white Australia racism and the imperialist jingoism of the ALP hierarchy – against which it counterposed the international solidarity of the working class in its struggle against international capitalism.

The IWW was the backbone of the struggle against the imperialist First World War and conscription in Australia. Against the war madness of the ruling class and its servants in the ALP leadership, *Direct Action* spread the ideals of international working-class solidarity. As the caption on the cover of the August 10, 1914, *Direct Action* said: *"War! What for? ... War is Hell! Send the capitalists to hell and wars are impossible."*

Our decision to adopt the name *Direct Action* was "deliberate", Roger Miles [Roger Markwick] wrote in an article on "The first 'Direct Action'" (*DA* 421). "It meant continuing today the best traditions of the old Wobblies, uncompromising internationalism and class struggle against the Australian ruling class."

Although the IWW lacked a well-rounded theory and was prone to sectarian mistakes, it waged an exemplary struggle and showed that revolutionary ideas are not alien to the Australian working class. The new *Direct Action* we founded in 1970 identified with these revolutionary pioneers of the labour movement, and carried on both the name and the tradition. And it revived the militant, campaigning tradition of selling the paper – in the factories, out on the streets, on the campuses – a tradition that had been increasingly neglected by the Communist Party of Australia as it declined in the 1950s, '60s, and '70s.

We were following in the tradition of the Communist International. At its Third Congress in 1921 the Comintern adopted theses on "The Organisational Structure of the Communist Parties, the Methods and Content of Their Work", which included a section on the party press. This was a 1980 Ink Links reprint, *Theses, Resolutions and Manifestos of the First Four Congresses of the Third International*, which we distributed in Australia, and used extensively at our full-time party school.

"The Communist paper must concern itself first and foremost with the interests of the exploited and militant workers. It must be our best propagandist and agitator, the leading advocate of the proletarian revolution …

"Each Communist should have close links with the paper for which he or she works and makes personal sacrifices. The paper is the Communist's daily weapon which has to be constantly steeled and sharpened in order to be effective ...

"The Communists must be more than just lively canvassers and agitators for the paper; they must be useful contributors."

The original *Militant*

The spark for the Australian Left Opposition when it got going in the 1930s was the *Militant*, first published in 1928 in New York by the US Trotskyist group led by James P. Cannon. Cannon elaborated on the sort of revolutionary "combination paper" needed when he was sentenced to 16 months in jail during World War II. He made use of his time and the limited communications allowed with the outside to set down his experience and many useful ideas in regular letters to comrades, which were later published as *Letters From Prison:*[45]

"*The Militant* must strive to be a *combination* paper; a paper which interests and serves the needs of the new reader who picks it up for the first time, the reader who is beginning to think of himself as a Trotskyist without yet thinking about the party, and the educated party militant – all at the same time ...

"We can only afford to publish one paper. And we must address ourselves to the politically educated as well as to the uninitiated."

"... we should deliberately plan it as a variegated combination paper which has something in it of special interest to all of its readers in all stages of their development; which conducts the new reader by stages from agitation on the burning issues of the day into all the more profound questions of the class and the party, and continue to interest him after he has assimilated them."

We drew on these positive traditions for publishing our paper in Australia, and certainly demonstrated it in a unique way when we published the combined *Direct Action/Militant* for three months during the final stages of fusing the SWP and the Communist League.

A paper for young people

Direct Action began as the paper of Resistance, and even when it was published jointly by the Socialist Workers Party and Resistance, and then just by the SWP/DSP, throughout its existence *DA* maintained its orientation to young people.

Young people are the most radical. They have an interest in overturning entrenched conservative traditions, so they are the natural readership and base of a socialist paper. *DA* had always been the paper with the best coverage of issues of special concern to young people – high school student actions; campaigns on university campuses; youth unemployment.

We were very much guided by the document from the FI 1969 World Congress, "The Worldwide Youth Radicalization and the Tasks of the Fourth International". This had been drafted by US SWP leader Caroline Lund:[46]

> While spreading the ideas of Trotskyism among the youth with whom they participate in united combat, the Fourth Internationalists must seek to construct a revolutionary-Marxist youth organization that will systematically educate its members and followers in the methods, doctrines and positions of the Trotskyist movement from its origins. All the results of activity among the youth can be jeopardized if the organizational requisite for this educational work is neglected.
>
> Work among the youth is not an end in itself. It reaches fruition in the impetus given to the construction or reinforcement of the revolutionary parties that will be capable of leading the working class to victory. The sections of the Fourth International are as yet too small to lead the masses in their own name and under their own banner in a decisive struggle for power. Their work has a preparatory and predominantly propagandistic character involving limited actions.
>
> Their task now is to win and educate decisive numbers of the radical youth in order to equip them for the greater task of winning leadership of the revolutionary elements among the working masses. To fulfil that function adequately, the youth recruits must thoroughly assimilate the organizational concepts of Bolshevism and its methods of constructing politically homogeneous and democratically centralized parties. The construction of such parties in the struggles that are erupting is the only means of overcoming the crisis of leadership which is the central contradiction of our epoch.
>
> Government authorities the world over, whether in the advanced capitalist powers, the workers states or the colonial world, are becoming increasingly concerned over the unrest among their youth, which is becoming more and more unmanageable. Their worries are justified. This rising generation has already manifested a tremendous potential for radical activity and a powerful will to change the status quo.
>
> Whoever succeeds in winning the allegiance of the most intelligent and devoted activists among the rebel youth holds the key to the future. For they will play a major role in making history and deciding the destiny of mankind for the rest of the twentieth century.

When Resistance members were in the forefront of the campaign against the war in Vietnam in the '70s or the campaign around the country against Labour's tertiary fees in the '80s, this was reflected in the pages of *DA*.

DA editors in the '70s

I edited the first *DA* in 1970, before transferring to Melbourne to build the branch there (and having a great time selling that first issue hand over fist at the second Melbourne Moratorium). Jim Percy then took over as editor. I returned to Sydney after the split with the CL in 1972, and edited the paper for most of 1973, handing over to Nita Keig, who edited it for the next few years. The editorial board was: Chris Graham, Tina Harsanyi, Dave Holmes, Nita Keig, Sol Salby, John Percy, Frans Timmermann and Al Westwood. Allen Myers was added in early 1975, and Dave replaced Nita as *DA* editor. I resumed as editor in 1976 after returning from 18 months working on *Intercontinental Press* in New York.

Shortly after the price rise to 30 cents on June 16, 1977, Allen Myers took over as editor with the July 21 issue. With the October 13, 1977, *DA*, the *DA* editor was listed as Allen Myers, with a new post added, labour editor, Jim McIlroy.

Direct Action production

From the April 20, 1973, issue, we raised the cover price for *DA* from 10 to 20 cents, and increased the size to 24 pages. We worried about it, had discussed it in branches from 1972, and weighed the possible impact.

We used various printers in the early days, in our search for the cheapest. Probably many of the smaller ones have since gone to the wall, or been gobbled up by bigger companies. Some of these printers were fairly dodgy. There were definitely some who couldn't print!

Often we used separate platemakers and printers, in search of the cheapest. We had some scary experiences with platemakers on the run, one step ahead of the cops, doing "foreign orders". One platemaker, before being carted off to the slammer when the cops arrived, was kind enough to tell us where our plates were! In the early years we suffered from "all-nighters", as we struggled to finish the editing and layout in time for the printing deadline. Often a couple of comrades would end up sleeping in the car by the Hawkesbury River, after doing an all-nighter and delivering the pages to the printer. When Allen Myers arrived from the US and joined the *DA* staff in 1975, he put an end to the all-nighters.

We managed huge technological changes in our equipment through the '70s and '80s (which mirrored huge changes in the whole printing business, before the revolutionary changes with computers and typesetting in the '80s and '90s.) We acquired new typesetting equipment in 1975, and in 1977 bought even improved new typesetting equipment.

We had regular columns: Jamie Doughney began On the Picket Line; Diana Auburn began Women in Revolt, also by Rose McCann and Mary Rabbone in the early years; Mary Rabbone wrote on the environment in Capitalism Fouls Things Up; Allen Myers wrote a humorous column, the Lucky Country; and Jim McIlroy did In Brief. We also had a column on Building the SWP, and one promoting the *Direct Action* fund drive.

Often branches would stick *DA* covers on their meeting room walls, proudly giving a very colourful and comprehensive display of the political issues we covered in those early years. After a while whole walls were totally covered, so it became impractical, and we started trying to spruce up our offices anyway.

As milestones were reached, we'd do a roundup article in *DA*: I wrote an article covering *DA*'s 200 issues; Renfrey Clarke covered the 250th issue.

We were always short of money, but often could call upon plentiful young volunteer labour. So we hit on a cheap way to produce posters and leaflets – print four- or eight-page inserts in the paper and gut them, and guillotine them where necessary. In September 1977, we printed a four-page insert that cut up into four three-fold election leaflets. Two *DA* issues in July 1978 produced a bounty of leaflets and posters for gutting and guillotining: for a series of eight classes based on the Farrell Dobbs' Teamster books, in Adelaide, Brisbane, Hobart, Melbourne and Sydney; and for the 40th anniversary of the Fourth International rallies on September 1 in Adelaide, Brisbane, Hobart, Melbourne and Sydney. In August 1979, issue 264 was a bonanza, providing six A5 Pathfinder Press Bookshop leaflets (for six different cities); three A5 "How to Stop Fraser" forum leaflets (for seven cities); one A5 ITS classes leaflet (for seven cities); one A2 Pathfinder Bookshop poster (for six cities); and one A4 "Labor must defend workers' interests" leaflet. (We must have printed the Sydney bookshop leaflet separately in larger numbers, advertising our prime spot at 755-757 George Street.)

Cartoons

Illustrations, and especially cartoons, were very important for making a socialist paper more attractive and readable. We always had a lot to say, and there was a temptation to fill every page with tight text. Good illustrations and cartoonists who could make a sharp political point were invaluable, and we often had to reprint cartoons from the left press or even capitalist papers from around the world.

We envied the talented cartoonists in the International Socialists. Even in their early years they had Mark Mattcott, who drew good political cartoons, and then David Pope, signing as Heinrich Hinze, now a regular cartoonist for the *Canberra Times*, with very sharp political commentary. Our cartoonists in the '70s were never up to this standard, and more often we'd rely on reprinting cartoons.

In 1978-79, for *Resistance* magazine, we did have a clever series of page cartoons by Tony Dewberry, on "Kzotz", a stranded alien, exposing the idiocies of life on Earth, and the need to join SYA to fight the contradictions.

When we switched to *Green Left Weekly* in 1991, it was a totally different matter, with excellent cartoons much more readily available, from talented (and sometimes commercially published) cartoonists. Often we had three good cartoons in an issue.

International solidarity coverage

DA had a lot to be proud of in its 20 years from 1970 to 1990, but probably our proudest achievement (recognised by most others on the left also) was our consistent coverage and solidarity with the struggles of the oppressed around the world. Of course, this was only natural, with our origins in the struggle against the war in Vietnam and our solidarity with the heroic and just struggle of the Vietnamese people for freedom and independence.

The year 1979 was momentous for oppressed people all around the world. In January and February, the Iranian workers and peasants succeeded in toppling the shah of Iran. *DA*'s coverage was exemplary. Also at the beginning of 1979, Pol Pot was overthrown, with the assistance of Vietnamese troops, and when China – with support from the US – invaded Vietnam, after an initial slowness to respond, *DA* campaigned strongly in defence of Vietnam. Then in July the Sandinista revolution toppled the hated Somoza dictatorship. We sent Ron Poulsen to Nicaragua to cover the new revolution and the tasks of reconstruction. He wrote articles from there, and came back and went on a national speaking tour in defence of the revolution.

Our August 23, 1979, issue had the cover "Nicaragua: On the Cuban Road", with a special supplement of coverage on Nicaragua making it a bumper 28-page issue. We also sent Renfrey Clarke there on the first anniversary of the revolution, and *DA* reporters travelled there regularly, as well as to Cuba and also to Grenada. Solidarity with the struggles of the people of Latin America and the Caribbean was a major concern of *DA* throughout its history. Before the coup in Chile, *DA* warned of the impending danger, and afterwards campaigned against Pinochet. Throughout the 1980s we had comprehensive coverage of the struggle by the people of El Salvador.

We also sent reporters to New Zealand to cover major developments. *DA* was the only paper in Australia to cover the growth of the New Labour Party in any thorough way.

Every time there was a major international development, we covered it well. We carried feature articles, and made a tremendous effort, given our limited resources, to get on-the-spot coverage. At the very least, we were able to draw on our co-thinkers in other countries, or the people in struggle themselves. These sources, which gave the real picture, were essential for understanding the world and breaking through the lies in the media of the press barons. Whether our positions were initially popular and well understood or not, many people were still wanting to read an alternative, so often big international events also meant a big rise in our circulation – for example, in the early months of the Soviet troops in Afghanistan, and our campaign against the Olympics boycott.

US imperialism has been waging war or engaging in gunboat diplomacy in the Middle East continuously since World War II, and *DA*'s coverage throughout its existence was excellent. The cover of issue number 2 featured "The Arab Revolution". *DA* debated and combated the Zionists from the beginning, campaigned against Israeli aggression in 1973; thoroughly covered the Iranian Revolution in 1979; opposed Australian troops in the Sinai in 1981; waged a strong campaign against Israel's invasion of Lebanon in 1982; denounced Washington's bombing of Libya.

The struggle for Irish freedom was also covered consistently by *DA*, with regular first-hand reports and interviews. Bernadette Devlin-McAliskey was a regular in our columns, first appearing in the early 1970s and also in our last issue. In the March 11, 1981, issue, we carried an interview with Michael McAliskey after the assassination attempt on himself and Bernadette. During 1981 we had on-the-spot reports during and after the hunger strikes by the H-Block prisoners, including an interview with Bernadette McAliskey. The April 14, 1982, issue also had an interview with McAliskey by two supporters of *DA* who were visiting Ireland. We were able to produce a book on the Irish freedom struggle – *Ireland Unfree,* edited by Martin Mulligan[47] (Martin Tuck) – based mainly on reports and essays that appeared in *Direct Action.*

DA also made use of coverage from like-minded socialists in other countries. In the 1970s, *Intercontinental Press* was invaluable. Later we made use of the US *Guardian.*

DA was the paper that covered the visits of socialists and left political activists from other countries. As a sampling, the following interviews or transcripts of speeches were carried in four consecutive issues in 1984: a speech by visiting Nicaraguan trade minister Alejandro Martinez (issue 471); an interview with a Tamil socialist activist from Sri Lanka (471); an on-the-spot report from Nicaragua (471); a speech by Vietnam's foreign minister Nguyen Co Thach, who was visiting Australia (472); a report from Cuba on its elections by a comrade who was part of a visiting Australian brigade (472); an interview with former CIA agent Phillip Agee, author of *Inside the Company* (473); an interview with Swedish socialist and car workers union leader Goete Kilden (473); an interview with Don Rojas, a leader of the Grenadian New Jewel Movement (473); an interview with Peruvian socialist and peasant leader Hugo Blanco (472, 473); an interview with Roman Bedor, director of the Belau Pacific Centre (474). Many of these were exclusive interviews, and certainly the material appeared nowhere else in any comprehensive form.

To maintain this excellent international coverage we frequently sent staff writers to different corners of the globe, sometimes as ongoing assignments, often for special events. We had two journalists based in Prague covering developments in Eastern and Western Europe, firstly Steve Painter and Tracy Sorensen, and then Peter Annear and Sally Low, and one comrade stationed in Moscow, Renfrey Clarke. As well there were comrades temporarily living in Germany and Greece sending back reports for *DA*, and several comrades were able to send articles from Ireland.

We had journalists based in the US at different times, and frequently in Europe. We sent a reporter to cover the rise of Solidarnosc in Poland, attending the first conference of the union in September 1981. We had supporters of the paper in Papua New Guinea who sent us regular coverage from there, and we sent comrades on regular trips to cover events in the Pacific – to Kanaky, the Philippines and Vanuatu. We rushed a Chinese-speaking comrade, Kristian Whittaker, to Beijing in 1989 to cover the pro-democracy movement, and he sent back interviews and reports before, during and after the Tiananmen Square massacre.

Workers' rights

As befits a paper carrying on the tradition of the original IWW paper, *Direct Action* built and supported any struggles by workers in defence of their rights and conditions. Where possible, *DA* encouraged workers to write for the paper, see it as their own and use it in their campaigns.

For example, in 1979 we carried comprehensive coverage of the Union Carbide sit-in at Altona, Melbourne. The petrochemical workers sat in for seven weeks in support of their demands for jobs and a 35-hour week, and *DA* campaigned vigorously in support, carrying interviews with strike leaders and their families, and building support outside. The articles and photos by Dave Deutschmann carried in *DA* were later produced as a booklet.

Throughout the 1980s, supporters of the paper working in both the Newcastle and Port Kembla steelworks provided regular coverage of all the major industrial campaigns there.

Our coverage of the vehicle industry was a feature, starting with the big 1973 strikes. In 1980 we produced a special supplement that also featured the SWP election campaign, when GM-H shut down its Pagewood plant, with the slogan: "Save Jobs: Nationalise GM-H Pagewood". Of course we reported on the sacking of our 10 comrades who'd recently gotten jobs, just before the announcement of closure! Already in early 1979, GM-H had sacked Robynne Murphy and several other militants at Pagewood. As Geoff Streeton (Renfrey Clarke) wrote in *DA* 248 at the time, economic conditions drove the company "to hunt down and throw out anyone in its plants who might lead the workers in fighting for their rights".

Also that year we had excellent coverage of the sit-in at AMI in Melbourne, provided by *DA* supporters working in the plant.

Our supporters were also involved in the big 1981 Ford strike in Melbourne. In fact, one comrade, Renfrey Clarke, was victimised and sacked two hours before the strike began. That strike went on for seven weeks, and *DA* was there all the time (camped on the picket line). The rank and file union members – mainly militant migrant workers – took charge of the campaign and gave a glimpse of what was needed.

When a big miners' strike developed at Rosebery on the west coast of Tasmania in 1983, our comrades in Hobart supported it, but we also sent Renfrey Clarke to cover it as a *DA* journalist. We later published his record of that struggle as a book, *The Picket,*[48] and covered the issues on the Tasmanian West Coast. We later asked Andrew Jamieson to move to Rosebery and get a job in the mines, and link up with a group of mineworkers who wanted to join the SWP and establish a branch.

Similarly, we defended the Builders Labourers Federation, from the green bans in Sydney in the 1970s, and throughout the 1980s – the deregistration, the raids, the slanders, the frame-up trial of Norm Gallagher. Our coverage of the historic Victorian nurses strike in 1986 was also a highlight, many of our members both helping lead the strike and reporting on it in *DA*.

Most importantly, we didn't just report strikes and workers' actions. *Direct Action* provided essential political analysis and direction for the labour movement. For example, our thorough analysis of the Accord, and the events leading up to it, was a model for a workers' paper. The September 23, 1981, issue carried an article by Allen Myers, "Should the left back an incomes policy?", and a policy statement from the SWP pointing out how it was a trap for workers. *DA* was the first on the left to warn of the looming dangers. Debate continued in the lead-up to the election of the Hawke Labor government in 1983. The November 4, 1981, issue began an ongoing polemic with the Communist Party of Australia, which supported the Accord and even helped draft it. And throughout 1982, *DA* ran thorough analyses on the looming social contract. In 1983 Hawke was elected, and implemented the Accord. The subsequent ongoing disaster for workers and the poor was recorded in the pages of *DA*.

Defending the environment

For two decades *DA* campaigned against the growing threat to the environment. The cover of issue number 3 featured the problem of pollution with the heading "Capitalism Fouls Things Up" and a double-page feature inside. In 1971 we carried articles like "The Shame of Westernport and "The Pollution Crisis: How can we save our environment?".

Over the years *DA* was an excellent source of information on environmental issues. Picking one year at random, here are some notable feature articles from 1984: February 8: "What have they done to our forests?" August 1: "Bulla; Victoria's Love Canal". August 29: "Behind the battle for Daintree". September 12: "The Baryulgil Disaster – Asbestos mining on the NSW N Coast". September 19: "The Problem with Roxby". October 10: "A radioactive car park and a nuclear iceblock" (on US nuclear reactors in Greenland and the Antarctic). November 7: "The Barren Hills of Mt Lyell". November 14: "Maralinga". We carried articles on the greenhouse effect, and the threat to the ozone layer, well before they became household words.

Throughout its two decades, *DA* was a consistent campaigner on all other important social issues as well. We defended Black rights, from the very first issue, through the 1972 Black Moratorium marches, the campaigns for land rights, and against Aboriginal deaths in custody. We campaigned in defence of gay rights, for the rights of migrants, in defence of democratic rights.

Selling the press

Throughout its existence, *Direct Action* depended on the dedication and enthusiasm of its young supporters to ensure both its production and successful circulation. Each week they were out on the streets, on campuses, outside high schools, doing pub runs, at factories, shopping centres or train stations, selling the socialist press. Without this army of sellers, *DA* wouldn't have lasted two issues, let alone two decades and 767 issues.

We soon learned the best sales techniques, and tried to generalise them where possible – be bold and confident, look potential buyers in the eye, look friendly. We discussed the virtues of yelling out, and agreed it helped. As well as attracting attention, it was a political statement of confidence in the politics of our paper. It was part of creating an alternative. It raised the flag.

We pioneered and experimented with new spots and learned to use different techniques for different situations. For city street corners, train stations, cinemas and shopping centres, it was important to be very visible, to stand up confidently and be noticed. For suburban spots, even if they were quiet, and not a very busy shopping centre, we realised they were still worth doing with the right technique. Become a regular on Saturday mornings, and you build up regular buyers; be approachable, look friendly, be ready to talk about politics.

Some comrades became very good at pub runs, especially if they were prepared to go through a lot of beers over a long run. The social nature of worker pubs has probably changed a lot and declined over the last few decades, but pub runs could still be useful in some areas.

Campus sales were best done in conjunction with a club stall, and contacts and possible buyers could be engaged in longer discussions about politics.

For sales at work or at factory gates, it was important to be regular and to get to know some of the workers.

For political meetings of all types, the mere fact of turning up and being visible was important. *DA* sellers became expected; *DA* became increasingly the main left paper. For rallies and demonstrations, we learned a number of principles and important techniques:

- It was important to swamp big rallies with our *DA* sellers – selling at the beginning, selling at the end, being the first and last there. As well as maximising sales, it demoralised the opposition sellers.
- We organised to have "outriders" around assembly points, so that *DA* was the first paper that people attending the demonstration saw.
- For big demos, we set up cordons of comrades selling across the street, so we missed as few potential buyers as possible.
- We organised to have *DA* sellers going alongside demos on the footpaths, selling to onlookers, shop workers, people drawn onto the street by the chants.

Especially it was important to boost comrades' confidence, to ensure they enjoyed selling the press. Standing up on a street corner is very far from what "society" encourages us to do: we're supposed to keep quiet, keep our heads down, not make a fuss. But comrades can be trained to ignore what's expected of them and concentrate on the actual gains of getting the paper into the hands of a new reader, of a potential new recruit to the movement. It can be positive and reinforcing, selling a few, or selling hundreds as I did at the second Moratorium demo in Melbourne, which ensured I continued as a very keen paper seller for decades.

Special sales weeks

Every now and then, a special effort was required to boost the circulation, and we scheduled a sales drive, or a special sales week, or a special sales month, when we devoted extra efforts to sales. I wrote to organisers on the proposal for our first special sales week. "… sales of *Direct Action* will be the top political priority for *all* branches and for *all* comrades. All branches should increase their bundle size for this week.

"We are not aiming for modest improvements with this special sales week, but a *spectacular* jump. Sales will naturally drop back the following week, but we hope not to their old level. There should be permanent gains from this special effort – new comrades who will have learned the habit of selling, new sales areas will have been opened up, and the morale of the branch will have been boosted by the knowledge that its usual sales quota is well within its capability each week."

I reported to Jim and Nita in Paris that the July 6-12, 1978, special sales week had been "a fantastic success". Confirmed sales stood at 5,200, with one and a half days to go. Brisbane sold out its bundle of 800 after two days. "The morale here is tremendous after such a success." "At the moment I'm the top seller with 208, but it's going to be a very close finish with John G[arcia] and Ron [Poulsen] just behind on 198 and 192 respectively. I think it will have very good effects on the membership for the national secretary, the national sales director, and the Sydney region sales director, to be the top sellers nationally. (John and Ron's enthusiasm is also an indicator of how well the fusion has gone, how absolutely complete it is.)" David Lawrence (Ron Poulsen) reported in *DA* 215 on the big success of the sales week: "On top of the established branches, a sales team in Wollongong made over 113 sales in two days, and another in Newcastle is within sight of its 100 goal". A Brisbane pub run sold 120 with two sellers. We had to send emergency bundles to both Brisbane and Adelaide after they sold out.

"The expanded sales testify to the increased effectiveness of the SWP since the fusion this year with the Communist League and the steady growth since. But it also testifies to the spreading interest in a militant socialist alternative."

The article added, "The swamping of the cities by sellers made *Direct Action* highly visible as *the* socialist paper.

"One passer-by queried if there was a glut of papers, as he had never seen so many sellers before. According to the supply and demand mechanism of the market, a glut is caused by oversupply in relation to demand. But our sellers found precisely the reverse – the more the paper was sold, the more it was in demand!"

"This wide interest in the socialist viewpoint gives the lie to the myth fostered by the media monopolies, the ALP leadership, and even the Communist Party that Australian workers are becoming more conservative.

"Moreover, many complimented *Direct Action* on its readability and its clear political direction. One CP supporter commented that the special issue *Direct Action* had 'far better industrial coverage than *Tribune.*'"

In the following issue, Ron analysed the reasons behind the success of the *DA* sales week. "The total circulation topped three times the sales in previous weeks, assuring the special issue by far the highest readership of any left paper in Australia.

"Thousands of new readers discovered *Direct Action* during the sales week, including in Perth, Wollongong, Newcastle and Albury, where teams sold for the first time.

"Hobart sellers braved snow-bound conditions to average more than 10 papers per hour.

"In Adelaide, 97 papers were sold among unemployed at dole offices …

"260 sales were made at Sydney University.

"Best industrial sales were made by the regular seller at the Fairfax newspaper plant, where 42 were sold in two hours! [This was Ron himself.]

"Three Sydney sellers cleared 200 sales for the week." Ron wrote up the success in a report for the Party Organiser, including the totals and the results branch by branch, results in different sales areas and the lessons to be gained from the experience. I wrote to Jim and Nita that for the next special sales week, we planned a print run of about 9,000. In November *DA* 235 reported that the sales drive had tripled sales. Probably the highlight was Adelaide selling 141 at one dole office.

In 1979 we opted for a special sales month in February. Rose McCann reported on the campaign for the Sydney region, pointing out that "Pub runs were as usual the most successful spots. The region now covers 12 different pub runs with these runs being done a total of 18 times in a one week period. Eleven suburban spots are covered regionally on 13 separate occasions. Six different industrial workplaces are covered, the most lucrative spots being Fairfax and GMH. There are 6 city spots covered 16 times during the week on a regular basis. The three campus[es] are covered at least one day and sometimes up to 3 times a week."

Subscription drives

We also organised regular drives to boost the subscription base of *DA*, setting targets of 300, 500, 1,000, once even 1,100 and ending up with 1,170 new subscribers. During these campaigns teams of young *DA* supporters organised sub-selling trips to far-flung places to reach people who normally didn't have access to *DA*. In 1980 a subscription selling team made a 3,000-kilometre car trip from Perth to the mining and port towns of the Pilbara, and sold 100 subs.

The September 1979 five-week sub drive target of 500 was easily passed, and extended to 800. Perth branch got excellent results from trips to country regions.

I sent out weekly Sub Drive Notes, the second featuring the excellent results achieved from doorknocking working-class suburbs in Sydney, Mt Druitt and Eastlakes. Of the 202 houses in Eastlakes that we visited, 108 were not home, at 28 we sold single copies, and at 10 we sold subs. "This gives the remarkable statistics of sales of single copies or subs to *forty percent* of houses that were home! If we could maintain that rate for all the working class suburbs in Sydney, imagine what our potential sub base could be. What these results show is that all we need to do to go way over our sub targets is put in sufficient hours doorknocking."

"Another very encouraging feature of the Sydney doorknocking was the large number of single copies sold in absolute terms. It was worthwhile just for those alone. But comrades should be careful when selling subs not to let on too early in the spiel that it is possible for people to buy a single issue. It should only be used as a last resort when they definitely refuse a sub."

In Sub Drive Notes No. 4, I reported on the excellent results from country trips: "On nearly every special trip that has been organised during this drive, comrades have had the same experience – there is almost unlimited potential for selling subs. People are much more open to us in these areas, the sales rate is higher than in the cities, and in many cases the only thing limiting our sales was that the teams ran out of Direct Actions."

Sub Drive Notes No. 5 reported that Melbourne was so far the only branch successfully selling in local industrial situations, with a total of 19 subs. But the response rate for industrial towns like Whyalla "was quite phenomenal", where two out of every three houses visited bought a paper, and one in every five bought a sub.

Sub Drive Notes No. 7 concluded that the drive was "A fantastic success!" with 828 subs sold in the five-week drive. "The drive has given a much needed boost to our subscription list, but perhaps more importantly, this success has boosted the morale of our party as a whole. It has given us all new confidence that when we set our minds on a task like this we can do it, and do it well." David Sampson of Sydney was the top seller, with 53 subs. The areas where subs were sold were: campus 135; at work 35; door to door 276; political events 93; street 39; pubs 23; mail-in 11; other 216. Now we needed a renewal drive.

Thirty per cent of the new subs came from doorknocking working-class areas of the major cities and from trips to regional industrial towns. However,

> Sales at comrades' workplaces were a neglected area … 25 of the 35 sold were in Melbourne, 7 at International Harvester, 7 at GMH Dandenong, and 9 at the Union Carbide picket. This shows what is possible. If all branches had worked at this area like Melbourne, it could have meant more than an extra 100 sales nationally.
>
> Another area that met with varied success from branch to branch was campus sales. The only branches that seemed to have put in a proper effort here were Perth and Wollongong, and to a lesser extent Sydney. Wollongong sold 30 subs on campus, and Perth at least 40. If all branches had paid the same attention to campus sales we would have had several hundred more subs.
>
> Street sales and pub sales contributed very little to the totals of any branch except Sydney, where 18 were sold on the street and 14 in pubs. What this shows is that comrades were neglecting to ask people to buy subs during their normal single copy sales spots. A persistent effort by all our paper sellers during their normal sales would have netted us several hundred more subs also.
>
> The real success story of the sub drive, however, was in the area of door-to-door sales, both in country industrial towns and in working class suburbs in the cities. This is an area that we have never exploited successfully in the past, and our experiences over the past month have opened it up as a whole new potential field for both sub sales and single copy sales.
>
> "Why did we succeed?" Because the drive was organised properly,

both at the national and local level. The organisation as a whole took it seriously. We gave it top priority among all our other tasks.

We took our sub drives seriously in the next few years also. The two-month drive for 1,000 new subs in February and March 1980 reached 1,053. (Seventy-eight were sold on a trip to Kalgoorlie, plus 250 single copies. On a later trip to the Pilbara, two comrades sold 100.) Our August 1980 sub drive, for 500, reached 592.

In April 1981 our sub drive for 1,100 reached 1,170. Trips to Whyalla sold 36, Broken Hill 40 and Kalgoorlie and Collie 52. Perth was exemplary. A team doorknocked the whole of town of Kwinana, selling a total of 30 subs and 250 individual copies. One supporter in Kalgoorlie sold 20 subs. A visit to Lithgow netted 12 subs and 150 single issues sold. A total of 14 subs were sold at the International Harvester and GM-H plants in Dandenong, and nine subs at the Union Carbide sit-in. A trip to Gladstone and Blackwater in Queensland netted 21 subs. A team to Whyalla in South Australia sold 18 subs and all of their 100 papers. A Broken Hill sub drive visit by comrades from different branches sold 40 subs and more than 160 individual copies.

In October 1981, *DA* 364 announced a sub drive for 750 in seven weeks, but a week or so later, it was decided to cancel this to focus attention on a developing financial crisis.

DA harassment

Comrades energetically and bravely were out on the streets distributing the paper, despite harassment at different times from the cops, the local councils, the ALP bureaucrats and even sectarians on the left such as the SLL or the Maoists. Officious cops didn't know the law, or just didn't like "commos" on the streets. Some councils tried to impose a legally dubious requirement for "permits" to sell papers.

In 1978 we had to organise a campaign against an ALP ban on selling *Direct Action*. We organised broad support for our right to sell. Prominent ALPers condemned the ban on *DA*, including MP Gordon Bryant, Bob Hogg and Senator Jean Melzer (*DA* 207). At the June 1978 ALP NSW state conference, SWP and ALP members wore hoods to sell *DA*. We circulated a petition, pointing out to the delegates the hypocrisy involved in banning *DA*, which supported all labour movement struggles, while it was OK to sell anti-Labor bourgeois papers. We took the debate to local branches where we could.

CHAPTER 3

THE TURN TO INDUSTRY

In 1978, following the initiative of the US SWP the previous year, we took the decision to make a big push to get the majority of our membership jobs as industrial workers, the "turn to industry". We threw ourselves into the turn wholeheartedly, carried it out thoroughly and tested it enthusiastically.

Some other left groups had earlier embarked on the colonisation of industry. It was premature for them, and would have been for us. Often their efforts were short-lived; some made a fetish of it, and it diverted them from some real political openings.

In an April 25, 1978, letter to Jim and Nita in Paris, discussing the process of our moving into Newcastle and Wollongong, I commented about

> … a concept I've been toying with that seems to me will govern the tempo of our proletarianisation and colonisation.
>
> With our present size and rate of growth it's not a realistic proposition to contemplate major colonisation immediately, even leaving aside all the arguments related to the necessity to thoroughly prepare our members for the step and to have more preliminary experience in order to do it properly and so on. What is really going to govern the tempo of the completion of our turn is when we are in the position to direct a significant section of our – *leading* – comrades into basic industry, as the American comrades seem to be starting to do now. It seems to me that because of the geographical situation in Australia and the relationship of forces vis a vis our opponents, we won't be able to seriously undertake this step until we have established branches in the ten real cities in Australia …
>
> It seems that as our cadre expands, the pressure is on to channel leading comrades into setting up new branches, where we can often expect to make quick short term gains and at least freeze out our opponents from picking up recruits they shouldn't get … Until we have branches in the major cities, it will be hard to spare leading comrades who could be organisers say, and send them into industry.

We did the turn in a sensible way, with the geographical expansion to Wollongong, Newcastle and Perth given stress, tying in with the turn. We gained valuable experience in trade union work, training our comrades, and carried out some excellent campaigns such as the Jobs for Women campaign in Wollongong.

The turn had some correct motivations. We, like most of the other groups in the FI that had grown or developed out of the '60s and '70s, had a membership that was primarily student in its origins. We recognised the crucial role of the industrial working class in making a socialist revolution in the advanced capitalist countries, and we recognised the need for revolutionary parties to develop a strong base among industrial workers. For a revolution to be successful in a country like Australia, we will need that base.

But the turn to industry was also based on some incorrect perspectives. It was predicated on rapidly looming class struggles. The turn was posed as an urgent necessity: we had to get into industry quickly in order to lead these struggles that were just around the corner. This prediction was false. There were some working-class struggles, some isolated actions that we often got involved in, but there was no fundamental, overwhelming trend in that direction.

The US SWP had initiated the turn, and undoubtedly some of their motivations were correct. But some were certainly not, such as "the looming class struggles" view, and some were possibly factional – an attempt to appear "more proletarian" than the Europeans in the FI.

A few FI groups just blindly followed New York. I wrote to Jim and Nita in June 1978 about worries I had about how they were carrying out the turn in New Zealand: "… unless the SAL is in tip top condition I have the feeling that they're moving too quickly, mechanically following the SWP's turn. I reckon they made that mistake in dividing their branches prematurely, just doing it because the SWP was doing it. And it seems that they have a few important tasks ahead of them before they can embark on a full scale colonisation – sorting out their leadership, shifting to Auckland, getting starts in Dunedin and Hamilton perhaps, strengthening their youth."

New branches

In June 1978 I wrote to Jim and Nita in Paris that we had sent an offer to the building owners of our offices in Sydney at 215A Thomas Street of $2/sq ft/ annum to rent the first floor, which had been vacant for so long, the same rent we were paying for our second floor offices. I pointed out it would be ideal for our NC meetings and forums, and ideal for the Leichhardt branch, our regional office and a bookshop. We eventually got the extra floor for $2.50/sq ft, but it would have been even better if we'd been able to buy the whole building at the time – it was on the market for $200-300,000 – in hindsight we should have stretched our resources.

We moved our NO and *DA* offices there as well, finally selling 139 Glebe Point Road (for $40,000) in 1978. Sydney branch took over the first floor, with a large space for meetings and a bookshop. The NO and *DA* were on the second floor.

We divided Sydney into new branches, reaching out into new areas. In March 1977, the South Sydney branch office opened, with a shopfront and offices at 163 Regent Street, Redfern. We next set up Parramatta branch with an office in Granville. And by the decision of Sydney regional conference in November 1978 we set up a new branch in Bankstown, with its own offices.

The Melbourne SWP opened new Fitzroy-Collingwood and South-Eastern Suburbs branches in October 1977. In early 1978 we set up two new branches, in Geelong and the Western Suburbs. Geelong branch was constituted as part of a Melbourne region. In June Melbourne set up our Pathfinder Bookshop at 82 Smith Street, Collingwood.

In mid-1978 we took the decision to establish a Wollongong branch, and one of the comrades we asked to move there to start it was Andrew Jamieson. I reported to Jim and Nita in Paris that he got into the steelworks in five days.

On August 7, I reported that Wollongong branch was established and that "Things are really popping in Wollongong. And it seems we're into the steel-works just in time. There's a big industrial confrontation brewing, over the use of scab labour by one of the companies that BHP uses … Andrew's already in the thick of it. There's a strike meeting tomorrow, but last week at the off shift meetings to discuss the strike he got up and spoke for an immediate strike, and won the vote, but this move lost on the other two shifts." Dave Andrews (Andrew Jamieson) reported on the struggle for *DA* 220: "Wgong steelworkers act against scabs."

On August 29 I wrote, "Andrew is again in the thick of it, he's really enjoying himself, and his morale is 200%. Last week he moved a motion at his off shift meeting for a 24 hour strike against the Budget, and it got carried, and becomes the official motion to be put to the other shift meetings! Did you imagine we'd be able to get into the thick of political activity in what is probably the biggest plant in the country so soon?"

In September (*DA* 224) we announced Andrew Jamieson as our Wollongong candidate in the October 1978 NSW state election, and in December (*DA* 237) he wrote that the Port Kembla steelworkers went on a week-long strike.

In 1978 we also expanded to Perth. In July I wrote to Paris that "our list for the Perth operation" already stood at 11. In September I wrote that Steve Painter was on his way to Perth (as organiser), plus Merrilyn Treasor, Peter Holloway and Judy Siddons. Barry Healy would be there in October, plus Graham Milner and Anthea Parker, so we'd have a Perth branch by October.

By November, Perth branch was established. *DA* 234 reported that we had a new socialist branch in Perth. A group of SWP members from Melbourne had moved over a month earlier, linked up with SYA members already there, and other members from Brisbane and Sydney arrived to assist. The branch was involved in *DA* sales, the Campaign Against Nuclear Energy and the Unemployed Workers Movement, and holding campus stalls at WAIT and UWA and a weekly socialist discussion class.

July 1978 SWP NC

We continued discussing and projecting the turn at our July 28-30, 1978, SWP National Committee meeting. This was a very comprehensive NC. Jim Percy presented a world movement report (he had just returned from the FI Bureau in Paris, and was to return just after the meeting, on August 2). Other reports were: Jim McIlroy, political situation; Jamie Doughney, labour movement; Tony Forward, youth; Leesa Wheelahan, women's liberation; Allen Myers, gay liberation; John Garcia, anti-uranium movement; John Percy, tasks and perspectives; Dave Holmes, the CPA; Peta Stewart, women's liberation document; Dave Deutschmann, the party-youth relations document; Ron Poulsen, the socialist democracy document.

We printed most of the NC reports in two issues of the Party Organiser. Jim McIlroy's political report began by emphasising: "The theme of this report (and of this plenum) ... is that we must set about from this plenum to *prepare the ground* for a push ahead to get a significant proportion of our party membership into basic industry. This preparatory period for the rest of this year is intended as a buildup to a more fundamental turn into industry to be taken at our national conference early next year."

My tasks and perspectives report had so much to cover, it went over time, for two hours, and took up 31 pages printed in the Organiser. It noted the "exciting and inspiring" plenum so far, and explained that the report would try to "explain *precisely* where the Political Committee thinks we are at, what *stage* in our turn to proletarianise our party". The report addressed *how* to make the turn happen, and the tempo, especially how to direct "a significant section of our *leading comrades* into industry". We aimed to get a third of our NC into industry by the conference.

"The second concept that we had to consider on the Political Committee is that we won't be able *seriously* to carry out the task of getting our *leading comrades* into industry until we have established branches, or the beginnings of branches, in the major industrial cities – Perth, Wollongong and Newcastle."

The third area I examined was the effects of the turn in preparing for our conference, having a thorough discussion on the international documents and our political document, getting a large number of contacts to it, especially the first two days, and launching the turn in a big way.

The fourth area I examined was our internal organisational tasks – our sales, finances, recruiting, education and publications.

Fifthly, I addressed how the turn would impact on the many areas of mass work that we saw before us, and continuing "the process of Bolshevisation" of the party.

World movement

In June 1978 Jim's tape to the PC arrived, and he reported that "a common line" had now emerged in the Bureau on all the key questions. "Our role was not central (that was played by Mandel, the two Charles [Charles Udry and Charles Michaloux], and Barry Sheppard)." But a northern trip he had made was "a big success", attending the Danish Central Committee meeting and the Swedish Political Bureau meeting. Jim came back just before the July NC, and returned to Paris straight after. Nita Keig was absent from the NC; she had already gone to Paris, and we could afford only Jim's fare.

Jim's world movement report to the July NC said: "In the nine months since the dissolution of the LTF and the IMT the Fourth International has taken some big steps in its internal functioning" and it was "on the threshold of a healthier period of growth and development".

There was a new majority developing in the international, a new political homogeneity that cut across the old lines entirely, Jim said. "I think we can be very proud that our party has been able to be an active part of the process of the last nine months."

Following the dissolution of the factions, there were three subsidiary decisions:

1. regarding IP and Inprecor, to consolidate the English language journals of the FI;
2. to give us more time, by postponing the World Congress, to have more discussion and write new political resolutions;
3. to build a united functioning centre of the FI.

Jim reported on Colombia, and the problems with Nahuel Moreno and the

Bolshevik Tendency, the crisis in Italy, where Udry and Caroline Lund visited together, Britain, Japan and Denmark. He reported that the last United Secretariat meeting had adopted the resolution, "The World Political Situation and the Tasks of the Fourth International".

October 1978 SWP NC

The decision on the turn to industry was formally taken at the October 21-22, 1978, SWP NC meeting in a report I presented. The turn was projected as a major tactical shift to get "a significant majority of our members into jobs in basic industry", based on an assessment that "the centre of world politics had shifted to the industrial working class". We'd been discussing it in the leadership all that year.

Reports presented to that NC were: Jim Percy, world movement; John Percy, political situation; Jamie Doughney, trade unions; Ron Poulsen, ALP; Leesa Wheelahan, youth; Peta Stewart, organisation. As well as full NC members (with Nita still in Europe) and alternates and Control Commission members, invitations were given to the SYA NE, organisers and NO staff, a total of 56.

The draft political resolution for the seventh national conference, "Building a revolutionary party of workers", was adopted unanimously by the NC and published in the Discussion Bulletin, as were my report on it and the organisation report. We published a total of 21 bulletins leading up to the conference.

My NC report was written up for *DA* 230 by John Compton (Jim McIlroy): "SWP plans major turn: 'Centre of politics' is industry":

> Percy presented a resolution to the meeting for discussion and adoption to go before the party membership leading up to the conference, calling it "*the most important political document* our party has produced in its history".
>
> "Our party has always had a proletarian orientation," the document explains.
>
> "We have always had the goal of building a truly Leninist party; a combat party based in the industrial working class. Over the last three years in particular our conference resolutions have increasingly oriented the party's attentions and activities towards the industrial proletariat, while at the same time we have been carrying out the essential party-building tasks that make it possible for the party to intervene effectively.
>
> "Our party has now reached the stage where it can and must make our proletarian orientation concrete. In other words, it is time to make

a major tactical step forward which will begin to make our strategic goal of a Leninist party into a reality. This tactical step is the colonisation of the majority of our comrades in basic industry …"

The document explains that in the face of a continuing world economic crisis which shows no sign of ending, the Australian ruling class, like its overseas counterparts, had launched a massive offensive aimed at rolling back the social gains won by the working class over the post-war period …

This means taking on in a direct confrontation the workers in basic industry – mining, transport, communications, manufacturing, construction, and so on …

Knowing that these big battles are looming, and that already "the centre of Australian politics has shifted to the industrial working class," the document concludes that the SWP must be there in order to experience and help lead a fight back by the ranks of the labour movement.

"If we don't change the composition of our party in a decisive way, we will place ourselves outside the arena where the big changes and developments in the class struggle are going to take place, and we won't be in touch with the rhythm of the class struggle," the document states.

"We are not at all changing the content or emphasis of the program we put forward. What is changing is the arena in which we fight for this program. We are taking advantage of the developing radicalisation of the working class and the maturity of our party to carry our program to the sector of society that will ultimately be decisive in the struggle for socialism: the industrial working class."

The document stresses that the radicalisation of youth, of students, of women, and of other oppressed sections of society is not being superseded by the growing radicalisation of workers.

Rather the two sectors reinforce one another …

The first of the preconditions for a successful fight back by the working class has already begun to appear, the document points out.

"A growing number of workers are disgusted and disillusioned with the leadership of the Labor Party and the trade union movement. More and more they are willing to engage in struggles, forcing the bureaucrats to respond at least in some measure to the bosses' offensive."

"But the other preconditions are not yet developed," the document explains. "A class struggle left wing is an indispensable instrument to fight the class-collaborationist policies of the reformist betrayers and lead the fight back." …

The final precondition for the successful conclusion of a fight back was "the drawing of these militants as they gain in political understanding into building a revolutionary party …."

In another report to the SWP National Committee meeting, Jim Percy outlined the argument that throughout the world, the working class in basic industry was now increasingly the centre of the political struggle. Both reports were endorsed unanimously.

January 1979 conference launches the turn

The turn was launched properly to our whole membership and the decision adopted at our seventh national conference, January 6-13, 1979, held at Hawkesbury Agricultural College. The reports were: world political resolution, Jim Percy; political resolution, John Percy; Socialist Revolution and the Struggle for Women's Liberation, Deb Shnookal; trade unions, Jamie Doughney; ALP, Ron Poulsen; Crisis in Capitalist Europe and the Tasks of Revolutionary Marxists, Nita Keig; Resolution on Latin America, John Garcia; Revolutionary Strategy for Gay Liberation, Brett Trenery; youth, Tony Forward; organisation, Peta Stewart; PC Statement on Childcare, Nita Keig; organisational principles document, Peter Annear.

International guests were Mary-Alice Waters from the US SWP (who gave talks on Cuba, women's liberation and the turn to industry), and Brigid Mulrennan and Russell Johnson from the NZ SAL. The conference rally participants donated and pledged $17,500 towards our $20,000 fund drive target.

It was a very buoyant and confident conference, with one bizarre interlude. During one session, Sue Phillips, a member from Melbourne branch, got up and hysterically attacked Mary-Alice Waters and the US SWP, exposing herself as a Healyite infiltrator. We convened our Control Commission, submitted a report to the conference, and she was expelled.

The credentials report presented by Dave Deutschmann reported that 206 members, 157 full, attended, with an average age of 26.2. Thirty-eight per cent were in SYA. Forty-eight non-members registered. Peta Stewart's organisation report could confidently announce that new branches had been established in Perth, Bankstown and Wollongong.

In my conference report on the political resolution, presenting the turn perspective, I said, "We are now at a point where we add together our traditional proletarian orientation, our Marxist program, and the gains, the cumulative progress we've made in the last three years, and we get a *qualitative change*".

We were making the turn in a changed objective situation: "With the international recession of 1974-75, the prolonged postwar boom came to an end … This recession hit all the imperialist economies simultaneously, and marked the beginning of a long-term downturn …" In this situation, capitalist classes were driven to try to inflict decisive defeats on the working class. "The reasoning for our turn flows logically from this … The capitalists' gains have been relatively minor so far compared to what they need to accomplish to find a way out of their economic difficulties at the expense of the working class."

Subsequent *DA*s carried reports on different conference sessions and the documents: Nita Keig's report on the draft document on capitalist Europe, and John Garcia's report on the resolution on Latin America, the beginning of the FI international discussion; Deb Shnookal's report on the FI women's liberation resolution; Brett Trenery's report on the Strategy for Homosexual Liberation; and the SYA report "A fighting program for the student movement". Peta Stewart's organisation report, Peter Annear's report on the organisational principles document and Jamie Doughney's trade union report were printed in Party Organiser.

Just after our conference, we received the news that Joe Hansen had died on January 18, 1979, aged 68. George Novack wrote: "Joe's reputation as a revolutionist remains spotless; the results of his 45 years of service are enduring. He was the trusted confidant of Leon Trotsky and James P. Cannon for good reasons."

Progress with the turn

I sent out a circular on January 19 reporting on our progress with the turn. Two PC members, Jamie Doughney and John Garcia, were released from their full-time assignments and were immediately successful in getting into GM-H at Pagewood. In the Sydney region, seven comrades had gotten jobs at Pagewood in the two days they had been hiring. Three more comrades were still trying there.

The vehicle industry was an early target for us in several branches, providing reasonable jobs in plants with large concentrations of workers. By February 1979, five comrades in Victoria were in the Vehicle Builders' Employees' Federation, two at International Harvester; six were in the VBEF in Brisbane; and Bernie Murphy was at GM-H Woodville in Adelaide. The VBEF national fraction had 22 members.

And we were very pleased when 11 of our comrades got jobs at GM-H Pagewood. But very soon *all* were chucked out in one go, and not much later the whole plant was shut down. Probably ASIO provided some assistance to the GM-H bosses ahead of their planned shutdown in helping identify the potential socialist troublemakers.

On February 6, I reported to Jim with a full breakdown of SWP and SYA membership by branches, and jobs: 187 SWP, 42 SYA, 28 full-timers. We were starting to get into the Newcastle steelworks, Geoff Payne being the first. On February 14 I reported to Jim projections for the fractions and the turn: 31 percent had got in, with a vehicle fraction of 26 so far. "I'm not at all complacent, but I reckon this is a pretty good start for our turn. The outline of our party as a party of industrial workers is starting to take shape."

"Our membership has remained at 187 in spite of the resignation of Alan R, Doug B following the expulsion of Gwynn[yth Evans], the resignation of Steve K, a provisional member from Melbourne who was in the tendency, and the lapsing of a few other inactive comrades … The overall quality of our membership has taken a decided turn upward recently. There are a couple more lapsings that might be necessary, but there are recruits in the pipeline that should replace these and start us growing again."

On February 20 I wrote to Jim that 31 comrades were now in the vehicle fraction and gave a breakdown of SWP and SYA membership almost identical to the one of two weeks earlier. Richard Lane, John Campbell, Joanne Turner and John Ebel had resigned, and Ian MacFarlane had lapsed. Apart from vehicle, some of our big concentrations in industry were: BHP, in Newcastle and Wollongong; the trams in Melbourne; the railways in Sydney. I reported on sales on the job, in Brisbane and in Melbourne on the trams.

Claims in later years from some of our critics, internal and external, that the turn lost us up to half our members were very wrong. For example, Graham Hastings in his book on the student movement claims we lost "nearly half" our members.[49] We lost some members – probably the ones our critics were inclined to speak to – but after a short while our trajectory was to grow again.

May 1979 SWP NC

The SWP NC meeting held on May 25-27, 1979, assessed our progress with the turn, prepared the party for the coming FI World Congress, and also called a special World Congress conference. Reports were given on: the Cuban Revolution, by Doug Lorimer; Indochina, by Ron Poulsen; counter-reports on Indochina, by Dick Nichols and John Tully; perspectives for the SWP, by Jim Percy; socialist election campaigns, by Nita Keig; youth work, by Leesa Wheelahan; trade union and organisation report, by John Percy; the world movement, by Jim Percy.

Jim's perspectives report was published in our Party Organiser.[50] While the report was optimistic about coming political opportunities in the industrial working class, it was also realistic in evaluating the very modest degree of fight back against the Fraser Liberal government by the unions, hampered as they were by the union bureaucracy and Labor Party politics.

The turn had been partly based on an overoptimistic view of the development of class struggle. But we maintained on this question, as on others, the attitude that we were testing our analysis and would change it if that was shown to be necessary. Jim's report emphasised this in its conclusion: "We have to be very careful about 'periods'. We say everything changed in '68, everything changed again in '74-75. When we analyse events, we seek to use 'periods' to allow us to understand more sharply and to understand qualitative changes from previous reality, but there's also an overlap. 'Periods' are only a rough guide, a crude approximation to reality."

Doug Lorimer's report on the Cuban Revolution noted that a "common view arrived at by the two factions" that the Fourth International had split into in the 1950s "on the historical significance of the victory of a non-Stalinist current in the Cuban revolution and of the stages the revolution went through, culminating in the establishment of a workers state in October 1960, played an important part in the reunification" of the FI. However, we still viewed the Cuban Revolution through the prism of the Trotskyist theory of permanent revolution, a view that we later corrected. Much of the report was devoted to refuting minorities in the FI and/or the US SWP who argued either that Cuba was now a state capitalist regime, or that the Castroist leadership was Stalinist. Probably engaging in this debate was a factor in helping us overcome the tendency to judge other political currents in terms of some preconceived schema rather than in terms of their real role. Certainly it was a lesson in the need to pay close attention to events; Lorimer's report noted, "Over the last seven or eight years we've let the fact that there does exist a revolutionary government on this planet slip from our press and our consciousness. This was the key factor in our slowness to recognise the revolutionary significance of the Cuban intervention in Africa."

Ron Poulsen's Indochina report set out our position on the overthrow of the Pol Pot regime in Cambodia by the Vietnamese army and Cambodian rebels against the Khmer Rouge, and the subsequent Chinese invasion of northern Vietnam. While we wholeheartedly supported the Vietnamese action, a majority of the FI United Secretariat – having little or no information on the horrors of the KR regime – initially called for the withdrawal of the Vietnamese forces.

In my trade union and organisation report, I reflected on a positive feature of NCs, which force us to lift our heads and take a long view of where the party is. I summarised some general lessons of our experiences with the turn since we'd launched it at our conference four and a half months earlier. Firstly, it was easier than we thought. Secondly, we now knew how to do it.

"Thirdly, we know from our Pagewood experiences that we have to be much more careful with security about comrades' jobs. For reasons related to our ALP work we're going to a system of pseudonyms in *DA* for all comrades in all states, except the recognised public spokespeople and candidates, and this is a wise precaution for our union work also."

I registered some shrinkage of the party due to the turn, noting that it was not unexpected. I commented on the two expulsions we'd had to make, which made "no difference to us, except better functioning. In fact, they made no difference to the two people concerned either; the party had very little meaning for them." A few of their sympathisers also left. They did not understand, or want to carry out, a) the turn or b) our organisational principles. It was no qualitative loss, I stated, but in fact a gain.

But I stressed that we needed to take steps to reverse this shrinkage, for the health of party finances, and for the health of the branches. "Our party is doing a lot of exciting things – election campaigns, the turn to industry itself – and we are now in a position to grow. We've got an excellent skeleton, our full-time apparatus, our national office, our equipment, and most of all our politics, and we now need to put some flesh on our bones …

"Recruiting has to be the responsibility of the *leading* comrades, the most experienced and most adept at putting across our ideas … It has to be *the* task of the party, not something secondary … We're not just paper sellers out there; we're socialist propagandists and recruiting agents for the party!

"By the same token, selling the paper is essential for the *integration* of new comrades, perhaps the most important aid to integration. If comrades are not selling, there's little chance of holding them … We also have to give the proper leadership attention to education. It's essential if we're going to grow."

I listed five levels on which we were conducting our educational activities: ITS (Introduction to Socialism) classes; consolidation classes (Introduction to Marxism – ITM); branch educationals; educational conferences; forums. All provisional members were to do the whole series of 10 ITM classes. I proposed we extend the period of provisional membership from three to six months.

I analysed our reasonably good election results, from 1975 to 1979. Our name was getting established, which was infuriating to the Stalinists. An SPA member thought we had 1,000 members; the CPA thought we got New York gold; B.A. Santamaria, the anti-communist fanatic behind the movement that had split the ALP, estimated we had 2,000 members!

We had a new Sydney headquarters, with a George Street frontage. Our first three books had almost sold out, and we'd made money on them. Now, we were about to publish Trotsky's book on the Balkan Wars,[51] and our nationalism book. At the conference, we had set ourselves the target of raising our national per capita sustainer to $6. Well, we were now at $5.99, I reported.

Sydney branch held its tasks and perspectives meeting in a confident mood on June 2. (Sixty-one were present, according to ASIO.) Reports were given on: the NC and perspectives, by Nita Keig; youth, Margo Condoleon; the turn and organisation, Rose McCann; election campaign, Kate Blakeney. *DA* 255 had announced Nita Keig as the SWP candidate for the Grayndler by-election in June, and 150 attended a banquet to launch the campaign, contributing $1,350 to the campaign (*DA* 256). There was a big swing against the Liberals in the by-election, and the SWP received a vote of 1.2 percent.

At the July 1982 NC meeting of the SWP, Jim Percy reported that some 80 percent of our members were in industry, were looking for jobs in industry or were on full time for the party.

International issues

While we were carrying out the turn to industry, there were tumultuous international issues we were watching, and were affected by, especially the Nicaraguan Revolution, but also the revolution in Iran, and events in Vietnam, China, Cambodia and East Timor.

Iranian revolution

We were enthusiastic about the rise of the mass movement in Iran that overthrew the shah, despite its religious garb. "Iran in Revolution" was the cover on *Direct Action,* November 23, 1978, and "Revolution in Iran" on the issue for February 15, 1979. The latter issue also carried an article "Iranian Trotskyists form new party", on the activities of Iranian supporters of the Fourth International, who were able to come out from underground in the new situation and form the Socialist Workers Party of Iran.

The following issue, 242, announced upcoming forums in March on "Revolution in Iran" in Sydney, Brisbane, Wollongong, Newcastle, Melbourne, Perth, and Adelaide. The same issue, under the heading "Fighting program for Iranian toilers", described a "Bill of Rights for the Workers and Toilers of Iran" being distributed by the Iranian Trotskyists. This document called for the rapid convening of a constituent assembly to "establish a government that can implement revolutionary measures".

Specific measures advocated included: confiscation of the land of big and absentee landlords, cancellation of peasants' debts to the state, easy long-term credit for peasants and the raising of agricultural workers' wages to the level of industrial workers' wages; "release of all the political prisoners, return of all the exiles, complete abolition of censorship, freedom to demonstrate and assemble, freedom of thought and expression, freedom for all political parties, freedom and equal rights for all religions, the right to bear arms, freedom for labor unions, full and equal political and civil rights for … immigrant workers"; the abolition of business secrets, nationalisation without compensation of the property of capitalists who had fled, automatic cost-of-living adjustments to wages, limiting of the workweek to 40 hours; the end of oppression and discrimination against minority nationalities; and the abolition of state repressive bodies.

The militancy and radical politics of the Iranian SWP soon made it a target for repression by the Khomeini government and its supporters. In June, Renfrey Clarke wrote in *DA* 256 on a major defence campaign for nine of the Iranian Trotskyists, who had been arrested by the regime's Revolutionary Islamic Committees because of their support of the national and democratic rights of the Arab residents of Khorramshahr city. The article reported that messages calling for the socialists' release had been sent to Iran by a number of ALP federal and NSW parliamentarians as well as union officials and academics.

Our opposition to the Khomeini government's attempts gradually to rein in the demands and activities of the Iranian masses was complemented by active campaigning against imperialist threats. After Iranian students seized the US embassy and held its employees hostage to back the demand that the shah be returned from the US to stand trial for his crimes, the US and Britain built up their naval forces and conducted "exercises" off the Iranian coast. In the November 22 *DA*, Renfrey Clarke denounced the Australian big business media's "strident campaign to win support for imperialism's planned invasion of Iran".

The editorial in the same issue warned that the US "has been seeking an opportunity to justify a military blow against the real enemy of imperialism, the heroic Iranian masses". It warned that Australian forces might also be involved in any US assault and called on the Australian labour movement to demand "hands off Iran" and no Australian involvement "in the plot against the Iranian revolution".

China attacks Vietnam

The Chinese military attack on northern Vietnam following the Vietnamese action in helping to rid Cambodia of the Khmer Rouge regime caused considerable disorientation on the left in Australia and internationally. How could it be that "socialist" countries were going to war with each other?

But once reliable reports began to emerge from Cambodia, it was clear that the Khmer Rouge had led a counter-revolution, not a revolution, and that their attacks on Vietnam had fitted neatly with imperialism's desire to continue attacking the Vietnamese Revolution. Our articles in *Direct Action* stressed that, in attacking Vietnam, the Chinese leaders were consciously assisting US imperialism in exchange for the promises of "detente". The main enemy was imperialism, not China.

DA 241 warned, "Peking threatens to 'punish' Vietnam". The cover of the following issue demanded "Hands off Vietnam!". "New Threats to Vietnam" was the cover headline of the March 1 issue, which carried a two-page feature by Allen Myers, "Background to attack on Vietnam: Imperialism, China and the USSR". Vietnam was on the cover again of the following issue, March 8: "Behind attack on Vietnamese revolution".

DA on March 15 carried a detailed statement by the SWP Political Committee, "The imperialist conspiracy against Vietnam". It also had ads for pickets outside US consulates in Sydney and Melbourne, and for SWP forums titled "Behind the Indochina Crisis – Imperialism's War Drive" in Adelaide, Brisbane, Melbourne and Sydney. "The Vietnamese revolution, which millions of people around the world rallied to defend in the 1960s and early 1970s, is still under attack", the PC statement began.

"At that time, the enemy, US imperialism and its allies, including the Australian ruling class, rained death and destruction on a massive scale on Vietnam and left the country devastated. Today, the enemy is the same, and the need to defend the Vietnamese revolution against this enemy is as pressing now as it was then."

The statement went on to point out that US imperialism had never accepted its 1975 defeat as final. It had reneged on its promised reconstruction aid and sought to encircle Vietnam militarily with right-wing guerrilla movements and especially by arming the Thai military dictatorship, which had taken power in 1976.

Because of what later was called "the Vietnam syndrome" – the widespread suspicion of government motives and hostility to new wars among the US population – "since 1975 Washington has tried to rely on substitutes for its own troops": South Africa to attack Angola, Somalia to attack Ethiopia, Israel and, until 1979, Iran to enforce its aims in the Middle East. The Chinese bureaucracy had demonstrated its willingness to betray Vietnam for the sake of "peaceful coexistence" with US imperialism as early as 1972, when it invited Nixon to Beijing even as the US was ferociously bombing Vietnam.

Prior to launching the invasion of Vietnamese territory, Chinese leader Deng Xiaoping visited Washington, where the details of the action were obviously worked out. "The moment the attack began, the imperialist governments immediately and unanimously called for a 'compromise' in which the Chinese troops would withdraw from Vietnam and Vietnamese troops from Kampuchea and floated such a motion in the United Nations. That is the aim which the Chinese bureaucracy is aiding: the attempt to force a Vietnamese withdrawal from Kampuchea so that imperialism will have a free hand to re-establish a neocolonial regime there."

The imperialist threat to Vietnam was a continued theme over the following months. For instance, the cover of *DA* 260 warned: "Imperialism threatens war on Vietnam". The following issue carried an article, "Imperialists step up war drive", and announced SWP forums on the topic in Adelaide, Brisbane, Melbourne, Newcastle, Perth, Sydney and Wollongong.

Jobs for Women campaign

The biggest women's rights issue throughout the 1980s – and the most heart-warming victory – was the Wollongong Jobs for Women campaign. This was a direct result of our turn to industry.

The April 30, 1980, issue of *Direct Action* announced the launching of the campaign. It was initiated by a group of women, including members of the Socialist Workers Party and supporters of *DA*, many of them migrant women, who demanded that BHP end its practice of sex discrimination and give them jobs in the steelworks. Many of the women had been knocked back time and again over many years. We set up a Jobs for Women Action Committee of the women seeking jobs.

The women filed a class action suit against BHP (Australian Iron and Steel). The *Illawarra Mercury* interviewed Robynne Murphy, Lou-anne Barker and others at the start of the campaign. A Wollongong leaflet launched the campaign from a seminar organised by the Working Women's Charter Campaign.

Early on, the women won the support of BHP workers, collected petitions signed by thousands of male steelworkers, set up a tent embassy, organised meetings and put pressure on BHP. Marion Hill (Robynne Murphy) reported in *DA* 303 in June: "W'gong unions back 'Jobs for Women' campaign". It was important to win the support of the Wollongong branch of the Federated Ironworkers Association. *DA* 307 reported that the South Coast Labor Council had agreed to support the campaign. *DA* 309 reported a Jobs for Women public meeting in Wollongong in which FIA secretary Nando Lelli endorsed the campaign, saying it would "not only assist the women but will assist the working class to create a more united working class, and one which will obviously be more difficult for the boss to exploit".

Also speaking at the meeting was Labor MLA George Petersen, who said that the problem of female unemployment in Wollongong was caused by "the greed of Australia's hungriest capitalist firm, BHP". Robynne Murphy, after explaining the legal aspects of the case to the meeting, added: "A purely legal campaign cannot be relied on to come down on the side of women and workers. That is why it is necessary to broaden our campaign throughout the whole community and the labor movement." Robynne Murphy and Lou-anne Barker appeared on John Singleton's Channel 10 show explaining their case, the *Daily Telegraph* carried an article, and *DA* 308 interviewed Lou-anne Barker, Robynne Murphy, Diana Covell, Louise Casson and Karen Myhre on the campaign winning growing support. *DA* led with campaigning covers, such as "Wollongong women take on BHP".

The case went to court later in the year. Eventually, as the case continued, the women were able to win legal aid.

The November 26, 1980, *DA* jubilantly announced on the cover: "Women Win Jobs From BHP". It was an anti-discrimination breakthrough. Cathy Rogers and Ann Lowder (Lou-anne Barker) wrote: "Women beat the 'Big Australian'". All the initial complainants, about 30, were offered jobs, and soon BHP was forced to employ about 150 women.

The discussion bulletin for our 1981 conference carried an article by one of the campaigners, Diana Covell, on "The significance of the Jobs for Women campaign". "Our party's turn to industry, which is still to be completed", she wrote, "surely needs no further justification than the experience and political development we have gained in the last year alone …

"Through the Jobs for Women campaign we have made a greater breakthrough for women's liberation than any other single campaign."

The December 3, 1980 issue of *DA* commented, "Knowing BHP, the fight's not over". But we wouldn't have predicted it would still be going on nine years down the track, and still extracting victories from the "Big Australian".

The initial victories won by the women had to be defended again and again, throughout the 1980s, by mass political campaigns and legal challenges. Most of the women who won jobs in 1980 were subsequently thrown out in a mass sacking in 1982-83. Thirty-six lodged a complaint with the NSW Equal Opportunities Board against BHP, on the basis that they lacked the seniority to avoid sacking only because of BHP's original discrimination. In 1986 the Equal Opportunity tribunal awarded more than $1 million in damages to the women. The legal challenges continued. The May 25, 1988, issue of *DA* reported the failure of BHP's appeal to the NSW Appeals Court. In May 1989, the company appealed sections of the decision in the High Court; in December of that year the appeal was dismissed.

BHP then dragged out the legal process of determining the amount of each woman's compensation, making use of a NSW law requiring that discrimination complaints be filed within a few months of the act of discrimination, to reduce the payment. Nevertheless, when the case formally concluded in March 1994, more than 700 women had received monetary compensation for BHP's discrimination against them.

For a record of this struggle, you need a file of *DA*. It had been a heroic battle, worthy of a book, providing inspiration not only to other women, but to everyone suffering injustice.

Steel and MAC campaign

We were also starting to get into the Newcastle steelworks, Geoff Payne succeeding, I wrote to Jim Percy in February 1979. Later Steve O'Brien also got in. In those pre-Accord days, it wasn't long before some of our members found themselves involved in industrial campaigns. In the May 17, 1979, *DA*, Andrew Jamieson, who was employed in the steelworks in Wollongong, wrote "Steelworkers step up bonus campaign". Delegates from the FIA, the Amalgamated Metal Workers and Shipwrights Union and other unions covered by the steel award had met to discuss tactics for a campaign to win a $40 over-award payment.

The article reported "misgivings about the amount of support that could be obtained from the State leadership of the FIA and over whether the NSW Trades and Labor Council would actively lead the campaign.

"It was felt at [an earlier] meeting that a strong move by the steel unions in Port Kembla would be needed to force a reaction from the conservative union bosses in Sydney."

A month later, *DA* 256 reported that a meeting of 2,000 steelworkers at the Wollongong Showgrounds had unanimously rejected an offer from BHP of only half the demanded over-award payment and unanimously passed a motion requiring regular reports on the progress of the campaign to be made to delegates' meetings. An accompanying article by Andrew Jamieson, "Why steelworkers are demanding $40", explained that workers were fed up with the existing production bonus scheme, which included many anomalies and tended to make workers compete against each other.

When the early 1980s international recession hit Australia, BHP responded with plans to make its workers pay. On May 7, 1982, BHP announced plans to eliminate 2,500 jobs in the Port Kembla steelworks. No-one really expected any serious resistance from the federal or state leadership of the FIA, which had been controlled for 30 years by bureaucrats close to B.A. Santamaria's National Civic Council. These officials' only real response to the lay-off threat was to call for tariff protection for the steel industry.

However, in elections between 1971 and 1974, militants organised in the Rank and File Committee won control of the Port Kembla branch. When SWP members got jobs in the steelworks, they worked with and through the R&FC to build a fight back against the company. Unfortunately, the leaders of the R&FC – mainly Graham Roberts and Nando Lelli – were not up to the task. Under pressure from the less favourable economic climate, they failed to offer any real leadership, instead falling in behind the right-wing "campaign" of the FIA state and federal leadership.

In these circumstances, we decided that it was necessary for our members in the FIA, who had been collaborating with other militants inside and outside the R&FC who were unhappy with the conservative course of the Roberts-Lelli leadership, to distinguish themselves clearly from the R&FC. They formally organised as the Militant Action Campaign, putting out leaflets and making proposals under that name for action to save jobs. In the November-December FIA elections, the MAC stood candidates against the federal leadership, against the Newcastle branch leaders, who were close to the federal leaders, and against the R&FC leaders in the Wollongong branch, where there was no right-wing ticket.

The candidates were: Robynne Murphy, a job delegate in the No. 2 machine shop in Port Kembla and one of the leaders of the Jobs for Women campaign, for national president; for national secretary, Kemal Pekin; for assistant national secretary, Ian Llewellyn; for full-time positions in Newcastle, Amanda Orr for branch president, Geoff Payne for branch secretary and Stephen O'Brien for assistant branch secretary; in Port Kembla, Andres Garin for secretary, Lou-anne Barker for assistant secretary and Phil Walker and Kevin Duff for organisers. The campaign also included a broad slate for the Port Kembla branch committee of management and other non-full-time positions.

The fight to save jobs was very much in the news, not just in the FIA elections. In response to BHP's announced plans to sack nearly 400 coal miners and more than 1,000 steelworkers and apprentices, 31 miners occupied the AI&S Kemira coal mine near Wollongong for more than two weeks, beginning on the morning of October 14. "Miners show the way" was the cover headline on the October 20 *DA*. Inside, that issue reprinted a MAC leaflet, "For united action to save jobs", and included a two-page feature on the election campaign.

While delegates and union officials were unanimous that industrial action was needed, the MAC leaflet argued that "lightning stoppages", proposed by the officials and endorsed by a delegates' meeting, would be insufficient. "Lightning stoppages, rolling strikes, or other such actions … can only *slow down* production in the steelworks and the mines. But BHP/AI&S *is already slowing down* production to meet their limited orders and they have stockpiles that will see them through." Given the situation in the industry, only an "all-out stoppage" could be effective, MAC said.

The feature included an interview with Bert Cant, a 30-year veteran of the steel industry and co-delegate who was standing on the MAC Port Kembla slate. Nationalisation of BHP was "the only way to solve the crisis", Cant said. "I've been a member of the Communist Party for 30 years and I'm very disappointed in their attitude toward nationalisation.

"They're going along with a soft line of not really doing much at all about it." Ian Llewellyn was quoted as saying that the national FIA officers had refused to mobilise the members to fight for jobs. "Instead they have meekly sought, cap in hand, to plead with BHP, the Fraser government, the Temporary Assistance Authority, and the NSW Industrial Commission to save jobs.

"This is a recipe for disaster for the FIA …"

The election result was reported in *DA* 420 under the heading "New militant current emerges among steelworkers". The vote for MAC candidates had varied from 15 to almost 21 percent. However, our hopes that this could form the basis for a militant current in the FIA were not met, as union politics were increasingly conservatised in the Accord years.

Union Carbide

The seven-week Union Carbide strike and sit-in in 1979, fighting for the 35-hour week, was covered thoroughly by Dave Deutschmann in *DA*. A sit-in by 52 workers "began on August 27, when Union Carbide responded to union overtime bans by calling in staff to operate the plant. The overtime bans had been imposed by several hundred workers at plants in the Altona chemical complex", Dave Deutschmann reported in *DA* 268. Union Carbide had often used staff in previous stoppages, but this time the workers spontaneously decided to stay in the plant to prevent staff scabbing.

The article reported that other companies in the chemical complex sought to provoke an all-out strike, which they thought they could defeat using staff labour. The other workers therefore decided to lift their overtime ban and focus on supporting the Union Carbide occupation.

The workers involved in the 35-hour campaign saw the shorter hours as both a benefit for themselves and a measure to reduce unemployment. *DA*

269 quoted a stood-down Union Carbide worker as saying it was "tragic" for "tens of thousands of young people to be unemployed, and our campaign here, especially the sit-in, is trying to overcome it". The same article pointed out that when the Altona Petrochemical Company – located just across the road from Union Carbide – was forced to concede a 35-hour week in 1974, the final result was a 25 percent increase in employment at the plant. Deutschmann wrote: "The Union Carbide sit-in has become the test case for the introduction of a 35-hour week. It is an action that must receive enthusiastic support from workers across the country. It is their fight as well."

To support the sit-in, *Direct Action* organised the screening of *With Babies and Banners,* a US film about the 1937 sit-in by striking workers at the General Motors car plant in Flint, Michigan, and especially the role of the Women's Emergency Brigade, made up of wives and family members of the strikers, in supporting the strikers – including by battling scabs and cops on the picket lines. The film was shown both at the gate and inside the plant, after a projector was lifted over the fence.

In the fourth week of the sit-in, Union Carbide, which was losing profits of $50,000 a day, announced that it would seek to have the occupiers "deregistered" from their unions, a move that was allowed under the Fraser government's anti-worker legislation. The article by Dave Deutschmann commented: "What is undoubtedly the longest sit-in in Australian labor history … promises shortly to become the national focus of the fight against Fraser's anti-union laws as well as of the campaign for the 35-hour week".

In *DA* October 4, Deutschmann reported an encouraging response from workers in other industries who were addressed by some of the stood-down Union Carbide workers, including substantial financial donations from Williamstown dockyard workers and metal trades workers. (Throughout the strike, donations from other workers made it possible for the 210 occupying and locked-out Union Carbide workers to receive strike pay of $75 a week. This was higher at the end of the occupation.) Of the occupiers' determination, he wrote, "Nothing has been able to get them out, not even the VFL Grand Final, for they were able to watch it inside" thanks to a TV handed in through a window.

After 51 days, the workers voted to end the sit-in. While the workers did not win their demand for a 35-hour week, we saw the sit-in strike as an important tactic to be popularised among workers. As Dave Deutschmann wrote in *DA* 275, "the Union Carbide workers discovered a tactic that is one of the most effective strike weapons … The occupation showed to the workers that they could actually halt production – that they could determine what did or did not happen in the plant."

Also important was the effect on the multiple unions whose members were involved. In *DA* 278, Deutschmann quoted the remarks of an electrician with 18 years' experience as a unionist: "There were six different unions on the site but there wasn't one inter union conflict the whole time of the sit-in. It definitely unites the unions. It unites workers, regardless whether they're unionists or not."

We also published many of Dave Deutschmann's articles as a pamphlet and held forums on the fight for the 35-hour week in Melbourne, Altona, Sydney and Wollongong with Deutschmann and a Union Carbide militant unionist, Vic Williams.

The Union Carbide sit-in had potential as an example to other unionists. On November 29, 1979, a mass meeting of 400 workers at the International Harvester truck plant in Melbourne, angered by the company's delay in backdating a pay rise to the previous July, voted to sit in in the company offices. IH summoned police immediately, who prevented the entire meeting from entering, but 60 workers sat on the floor, and in an hour the company had surrendered. *DA* 282 interviewed Mike Hansen, an SWP member and steward at International Harvester, who said the workers there explicitly identified their action with the occupation at Union Carbide. This was due, Dave Deutschmann wrote, to the fact that Hansen and others had kept them informed about what was happening in Altona. "Leaflets, posters, and clippings were displayed in the plant to explain to IH workers the meaning of the 35-hour struggle at the Union Carbide plant.

"Well over $100 was collected at the plant and sent to the Altona workers as part of a Vehicle Builders Union campaign to build support for the sit-in. The union itself donated $1000."

Wylies

We also gained some interesting experiences in the union movement at the result of a dispute at W.H. Wylie, where we had members. Wylie was an Adelaide car component manufacturer wholly owned by Chrysler Australia. Its workers were members of the Australasian Society of Engineers.

Unionists at Wylie tried to defend themselves and their fellow workers, but were constantly sabotaged by the state leadership of the ASE. A steward at Wylie was quoted in *DA* 265 as saying he had heard the company's managing director explain its preference for the ASE by saying: "Wylie will look after the interests of the ASE because the ASE will look after the interests of the company".

During a national wages campaign by the Metal Trades Federation in 1979, the ASE leaders openly threatened to pull out of the campaign, saying they would be content with "work value" cases in the Arbitration Commission, which were a device of the Fraser government to keep wage increases to a minimum.

As part of the campaign, at Wylie both production workers and tradesmen initially imposed overtime bans. The production workers later ended theirs, but the tradesmen voted to continue. The next day, the company sacked 10 of the most militant tradesmen. This resulted in an immediate strike by the whole shop floor. But they were sabotaged by the ASE. The shop stewards voted to replace the shop convener, who was loyal to the state union leadership and who was urging workers to cross the picket line. Then an ASE organiser walked through the picket line to speak to the company managing director, without stopping to speak to the sacked tradesmen.

The Wylie workers had had enough of the ASE, and a substantial majority of them soon joined the Amalgamated Metalworkers and Shipwrights Union. The AMWSU organised solidarity, such as banning the use of parts from Wylie that were smuggled out to the Chrysler car plant. The Waterside Workers Federation and the Transport Workers Union also refused to move Wylie parts. The company soon backed down, agreeing to allow the state industrial tribunal to decide on the reinstatement of the 10 sacked tradesmen. The only fly in the ointment was provided by the leaders of the Vehicle Builders Employees Federation, who had refused to support the strike, calling it a "demarcation dispute", but then tried to claim to represent the 10 tradesmen after the strike was over.

Other industrial experiences

The turn to industry changed the character or focus of many party activities. The weight of party organising activities shifted away from branch meetings in the direction of industrial fractions, especially, of course, in areas where we had a significant number of comrades working.

To finance party activities, we had long had a norm that comrades should make weekly pledges according to their means. This was not something enforced by rigid rules but rather a matter of developing members' political understanding of the necessity of a revolutionary party and a spirit of emulation in building it. The turn meant that many comrades' personal financial situation improved as they changed from being students or part-time workers to industrial workers, and that their ability to contribute financially also improved. Around this time, we set up what was called the "Over 30 Club". This had nothing to do with members' ages, and it was not really a club in the usual sense of the word – there were no separate meetings or privileges. One joined the "club" by making a weekly pledge to the party of $30 or more. This helped comrades in industry to remain aware of the need to devote some of their increased income to party finances. In Sydney, vehicle industry fraction decided to aim at a pledge of $40 per comrade.

In addition to the steelworks and vehicle industry, we had significant fractions in the transport industry – Melbourne trams and Brisbane buses.

In July and August we ran a series of three feature articles (*DA* 261, 263 and 264) by Jim McIlroy, titled "Union fight back under way: New stage in class struggle" "Rulers step up anti-union offensive" and "How Labor can defeat Fraser". We also held SWP forums in August in each branch with the title "How to stop Fraser – A fighting strategy for labor". The background was a revival of industrial action, which had declined in the early years of the Fraser government. A major impetus for this revival was the erosion of real wages by high inflation and a system of wage "indexation" that failed to keep pace.

The first article cited some examples of stepped-up industrial struggles: a seven-week strike at Hamersley Iron in the Pilbara, a wages campaign by NSW steelworkers, stoppages by public transport workers in Victoria and South Australia, an ongoing campaign by Kurnell oil workers in Sydney, a hard-fought strike by NSW railway maintenance workers and a "determined fight by members of the Australian Telecommunications Employees Association for a 20 per cent pay increase". McIlroy wrote that a turning point had been a national 24-hour work stoppage on June 21, called to protest against the arrest of two union officials in WA for "illegally" addressing a strike meeting – the state Police Act in effect at the time required prior police permission for anyone to address a public gathering. The June 21 strike demonstrated the potential power of the working class, and the capitalists were doing their best to obscure this, the article noted: "The aim of the employing class and its media mouthpieces is to undermine the growing self-confidence of the working class …

"Many trade union leaders did their part [to help the capitalists], first in attempting to limit the breadth of the June 21 action, and secondly, in going along with the false view that June 21 was unsuccessful."

The second article of the series said that, in response to the increasing fight back against the Fraser government, "the ruling class has launched the most vicious and hysterical campaign against unions and against strikes seen in Australia for decades". The campaign included things like a front-page editorial in Rupert Murdoch's *Australian* accusing unionists of "taking an axe to the nation" and an earlier editorial calling strikers "hijackers" and threatening violence against them: "They shoot real hijackers, given the opportunity. We are not suggesting that for the industrial hijackers – attractive as this might sometimes appear." McIlroy noted that the Fraser and state Coalition governments had been passing new laws to restrict union rights, but had so far pulled back from using them. "The anti-union propaganda offensive in the capitalist media is essential to weaken the unity of the labor movement prior to the next stage of the battle. Moves to break the strength of important unions in selected areas of the economy are vital to the ruling class's plans."

The final article pointed out that "the leaders of the labor movement have completely failed the challenge" of organising a massive fight back against the bosses. "It is because of the failure of the Labor and ACTU leadership that the Fraser government has been able to force cuts in wages, social services, and jobs on the working class over the past four years.

"At every turn, Hawke, Hayden and most of the others have organised a retreat in the face of Fraser's attacks."

Looking ahead to the upcoming congress of the ACTU in September, the article urged the adoption of a "fighting program" of transitional demands: automatic wage rises to match inflation, a 35-hour week with no loss of pay to fight unemployment, repeal of all anti-union laws, restoration of Medibank and other social services etc.

In August and September *DA* carried a seven-part series by Greg Adamson focusing on issues relating to the metal industry: "National metal award: Pacesetter for industrial workers", "Arbitration's effect on wage claims", "Penal powers—the mailed fist", "Future of the campaign".

Testing the Trotskyist perspective

In the 1970s we tested out the Trotskyist perspective to the fullest. As in everything we did, we went at it enthusiastically and wholeheartedly. For the first time in the history of the Trotskyist movement in Australia, we were actually integrated into the Fourth International. Both the SWL and the CL had been recognised as sympathising organisations, and when we carried out the fusion, we automatically became the official section of the FI.

We participated in all the debates in the FI, embraced the ideas of Trotskyism and the FI, but we were also partly responsible for developing them. We were one of the more successful groups in the FI, and one of the more independently thinking, which is why we passed the test in the 1980s when the period of renewal and rethinking came, and were able to take the overwhelming majority of our party with us.

We had Jim Percy, Nita Keig and Doug Lorimer working full time in the FI centre in Paris at different times from mid-1977 to mid-1980. In 1974-75 I was working on the FI's English language magazine *Intercontinental Press*, published by the US SWP from New York, and Col Maynard was there before me. Even back in the mid-1970s, from that experience in New York, we started to realise the limits of collaboration with the US SWP; we took a further step in understanding why we needed to build an independent party. We were lieutenants of the US SWP, but they didn't trust us or treat us as equals. And this realisation was thoroughly reinforced by our experiences working in Paris.

Foundations for the 1980s

The real significance of the 1970s was that we built our own leadership and our own political organisation. We did many things better than our mentors – our youth work and our newspaper, for example. Our experience in the FI taught us the importance of building leaderships and parties that could stand on their own. The political lessons and experiences of the 1970s laid the foundations for our development in the 1980s.

We had made steps towards a better understanding of the ALP, although our fuller, more rounded understanding wasn't reached until the mid-'80s. We gained a lot of experience in trade union and industrial work and experience in many areas of the mass movement. We began our election campaigns, helping towards an understanding of correct electoral tactics. And above all, we learned and understood well the need for a Leninist revolutionary party.

We became Trotskyists in the 1970s, participated in the FI enthusiastically and thoroughly. But we grew from it as we went through the experience. It wasn't an accidental, unconnected development, but laid the basis for our development in the 1980s.

Some casualties of the turn

It's always regrettable when you lose comrades. Especially at this early stage of the struggle to build a party, every contribution is valuable. During the turn to industry, we lost some comrades whom we might otherwise have retained.

As Jim Percy pointed out in his 1981 conference report, the party's turn had "been a difficult one". "We've lost comrades in the process. We even lost comrades who had gone into industry, who were quite willing to make the turn. There's a problem sometimes that any individual comrade can be faced with – the problem of narrowness of vision … We can begin to get comfortable as workers, to adopt their attitude and await developments."

The party occasionally suffered from the development of cliques: comrades who valued building their own little gossip and friendship circle above building the party; during a period like the turn to industry, they tended to get shaken loose. A classic clique builder during the late '70s was Dominica Whelan, at first in Sydney, and then in Melbourne. In May 1978, I wrote to Jim and Nita, "Without Dominica the Sydney clique has lost its oomph, although she's putting one together in Melbourne quick smart".

"The worst concentration of gripers and p.b. whingers is going to be in Sydney ...", I wrote to Jim on February 6, 1979. "But it's not really a very good climate at the moment for building a clique in our party." Eventually, Dominica was expelled, and five of her circle resigned. The Fitzroy Collingwood branch had to be dissolved.

One casualty of the turn was a group of comrades, mainly in Melbourne, mostly former CL members, who were critical of the turn and formed the "Proletarian Democracy Tendency". In Melbourne they had nine members and one sympathiser (Alan Ramage, Doug Broad, Joanne Turner, John Ebel, Gwynnyth Evans, Richard Lane, Chris Slee, Ian MacFarlane and John Campbell).[52] They held a national meeting in Melbourne, at which they referred to the Socialist Workers Party as "the SWamP".

My February 6 letter to Jim reported that charges were laid by Doug Lorimer, the regional organiser, against Gwynnyth Evans, and she was expelled, after a hearing commission report to Melbourne western suburbs branch, by a vote of 21-4. A few weeks later Richard Lane, John Campbell, Joanne Turner and John Ebel resigned, and Ian MacFarlane let his membership lapse.

The limitations of the youth radicalisation

The SYA National Committee met on March 10-11, 1979, at our 215A Thomas Street headquarters in Haymarket, Sydney. Tony Forward gave the perspectives report; Jon West presented the political resolution, Leesa Wheelahan the organisation report; Margo Condoleon reported on *Resistance* magazine and Steve Robson on the upcoming SYA conference.

The SYA conference was held June 16-18, 1979, at the YWCA Melbourne. Seven branches were represented, and the total attendance was 150. Tony Forward gave the main report, "Youth in Australia and the World Revolution". Greetings were presented from the NZ Socialist Action League by Patrick Mulrennan and a comrade leading the turn, and from the US SWP. Written greetings were read out from the United Secretariat of the FI, the YSA Netherlands and the Chinese Trotskyists. Anne Sabien (Peta Stewart) reported in *DA* 258: "Socialist youth in optimistic conference". *Resistance* magazine was going well and reflected that optimism. *Resistance* 5, Winter-Spring 1979, carried a report on the conference, and started carrying a centrespread lift-out poster, this one announcing: "Wanted: The Fraser Gang, for 500,000 unemployed". It also advertised bound copies of *Young Socialist/Resistance*.

Resistance 6, Spring 1979, campaigned for "A Labor government with socialist policies", by Anthony Forward. The centre poster was "Nicaragua on the Cuban road! Solidarity with Nicaragua! Nicaragua 1979 Cuba 1959".

Resistance 7, Summer 1979-80 urged "In the Federal elections: Campaign for socialism!", and Jon West wrote "Work hard, study hard, get ahead ... Unemployment". The centre poster was a Resistance 1980 calendar.

We certainly weren't in a pre-revolutionary situation; there were only the first stirrings of radicalisation. The key question was the role and weight of the working class, which was massively affected by racism, sexism etc. The composition of the working class was changing. But the majority of the working class in Australia was not struggling and mobilising (as a class) for its own overall economic and above all political objectives. That was even more apparent after the1974-75 recession. We had expected a fight back in 1976. There was the Medibank strike, for one day, and that was it. The hold of the union leaders and the ALP was total.

So in spite of the Fraser offensive (actually begun by Whitlam and Cairns at the Terrigal ALP federal conference in 1974), there was very little fight back. Unemployment soared to 10 percent, which was a big defeat for the working class. Then the defeats were institutionalised under the Accord.

Decline of the student movement

SYA sent out a circular on May 9, 1979, from Tony Forward about the AUS Emergency Council that had been called (for the same time as the SYA conference). In the next *DA*, 252, Tony wrote "AUS executive beats another retreat". Dave Deutschmann asked in a two-page *DA* 257 feature, "Can national student union be saved?" Already secession moves had "taken one third of the previous 275,000 affiliated membership out of AUS". "It is time to call a halt to this political stagnation and decay within AUS", Deutschmann wrote. "There must be no deals with the anti-AUS scabs and no compromise on the many progressive policies adopted by AUS in recent years." "Students, to win even the most elementary demands, must increasingly link up with the working class in these struggles."

On a motion moved by Tony Abbott, the president of the SRC, "Syd Uni votes to leave AUS" (*DA* 264). Such attacks continued. AUS lingered on for a few more years, unable to fight, and was finally wound up in 1984. Margo Condoleon reported, "ALP scuttles AUS", in an interview with Matthew Storey, AUS NSW organiser (*DA* October 17, 1984).

CPA's continuing decline

For most of its existence, the Communist Party was dominant on the Australian left. We built the DSP in opposition to the CPA, much of the time in its shadow, which we had to learn to grow out of.

Like many other parties that set out to work for socialist revolution under the influence of the Russian Revolution, the CPA was changed into something quite different by Stalinism. The general line, and even particular tactics, were dictated to national parties from Moscow. From the beginning of the 1930s until the mid-1960s, Moscow dictated CPA policies, often to terrible effect, and was also able to determine the leadership.

Stalin's Popular Front, which became Communist orthodoxy after the Seventh Congress of the Comintern in 1935, was intended as a cross-class alliance that would subordinate the working class and revolutionary struggle around the world to the narrow needs of Moscow. It reinforced the false views about the ALP common among socialists before the founding of the CPA, going along with the populist, nationalist tradition in the labour movement.

Under the influence of the split between the Chinese and Soviet CPs and the youth radicalisation, from the mid-1960s, the CPA leaders began trying to break with the party's Stalinist past. They concentrated on the question of independence from Moscow, and building an Australian party based on Australian traditions and conditions, and making its own decisions. This shift made it possible to recruit some of the radicalising youth of the 1960s, who in turn also contributed to something of a left turn of the party in the 1970s – particularly on issues such a feminism and environmentalism (Jack Mundey, the NSW BLF and green bans).

But the party did not carry through any fundamental re-evaluation of the class-collaborationist politics it had adopted and followed. In particular, it did not change its approach to the Labor Party. The ALP's policies were never socialist. It's a vital part of Australian capitalism's attempt to contain the political activity of workers and others struggling for social progress. The ALP attracts workers' support partly because of its links to the trade union bureaucracy and partly because its liberal policies seem fairer, so it can posture as the party of the working class. But its leadership is always dominated by political agents of the capitalist class.

The CPA was not clear about the nature and role of the ALP. Apart from the "Third Period" interlude in the early 1930s, when Comintern policy dictated a mad sectarianism to all social democratic or Labor parties, labelling them "social fascist", for most of the time the CPA treated the ALP as though it were a workers party. For the CPA's last 30-40 years, this meant tailing the Labor Party, and a framework of reform of the capitalist system, not fundamentally challenging it.

The CPA had many positive experiences in organising workers and leading them in struggle. CPA members were elected to leadership positions in many trade unions. Unemployed workers won to the CPA during the '30s Depression got jobs as the economy picked up and provided the base for the CPA winning control of key industrial unions. But other pressures also bore down on the party from the trade unionist milieu. In the 1950s, the political climate plus dwindling CPA membership at the base often led CPA union officials to adapt to the politics of their ALP counterparts. In later years the actions of Communist union officials were often indistinguishable from those of ALP trade union bureaucrats.

The "left turn" was largely associated with the Aarons grouping, which, among other things, publicly criticised the 1968 Soviet invasion of Czechoslovakia. This caused a split that formed the Socialist Party of Australia, taking a good share of the CPA's union activists and officials. The Aarons' course also aroused considerable opposition from sections of the CPA leadership associated with Bernie Taft and John Sendy, both of whom eventually left the CPA.

On May 1, 1978, I sent a circular to SWP organisers requesting information on the CPA for a report to be given to the the July 29-30 NC.[53] "Over the last six months we have been steadily recruiting CPA members or sympathisers and the process of demoralisation and disillusionment in the CP ranks is clearly accelerating."

Maoists

The other main Stalinist current was the Maoists of the Communist Party of Australia (Marxist Leninist). Their main strength was in Victoria. During the '60s radicalisation they had won the majority of the Monash University left-wing youth, and also had a base at Latrobe University. They also had some trade union leaders, mainly in the BLF. (BLF organiser John Cummins, at Latrobe studying English literature, from an English background, was rumoured to have practised in front of a mirror trying to lose his posh English accent to make the transition into the BLs.)

By the time we expanded to Melbourne, the CPA(ML) were already in decline. There was always a tension between their tactical and rhetorical ultra-leftism and their class-collaborationist support for "Australian independence". Their divisions were sharpened by divisions within the Maoist movement in China and in other countries (see chapter 2 for the 1978 split in the CPA[ML]).

Our party at the end of the 1970s

Towards the end of the 1970s our party had consolidated itself and felt quite self-confident. We were Trotskyists and had been recognised as a section of the Fourth International, the main grouping of Trotskyists around the world at the time (and the most sensible and least sectarian, to give it its due). We had successfully implemented the turn to industry, but the turn was based on an incorrect perspective of the Trotskyist movement, especially of the Leninist-Trotskyist Faction, the idea of the "long detour" of the world revolution. That is, the fact that all revolutions since 1917 had occurred in the colonial or semi-colonial countries was seen as an aberration, a "long detour" away from the supposed main course of the world revolution, which should be through the major advanced capitalist countries. The upsurge in France in 1968, and then the revolution in Portugal in 1974-75, were seen as key events presaging the end of the "long detour"; working-class revolution was again on the agenda in advanced capitalist countries. But this perspective for the revolutionary process was flawed, as we came to understand better in the 1980s.

By the time of the November 1979 World Congress of the FI, we were a growing party. We'd carried out the fusion of the SWP and the CL; we were enthusiastic about the turn to industry and were well on the way to carrying it out. We'd become the main lieutenants of the US SWP, a small but respected party in the FI. But we were also strong enough, and capable enough, of thinking for ourselves a lot more.

International solidarity

Given our origins as a political current in the campaign against the imperialist war against the people of Vietnam, it was very natural that international solidarity with oppressed peoples would be a continuing aspect of our political activity. It was logical for us, but not necessarily natural for all the political groups that had emerged from the '60s and '70s youth radicalisation. As a Marxist organisation in the Asia-Pacific, we had a special responsibility towards revolutionary struggles in our own region. Thus the formation of CARPA and our later development of close relations with revolutionary groups in the Philippines, our serious efforts to assist the development of revolutionary forces in Indonesia and support for the struggle in East Timor.

We also had an affinity with the real revolutionary struggles in Latin America. Following the Cuban Revolution, the level of struggle and of political consciousness was on a higher plane there than on other continents, so we looked to Latin America and organised solidarity with their struggles. But we still lacked a thorough appreciation of the revolutionary potential there.

The Nicaraguan Revolution and its impact

The Nicaraguan Revolution of July 1979 was decisive in shifting our orientation. The Sandinistas (FSLN) overthrew the Somoza dictatorship after a protracted military campaign. The FSLN successfully brought together in struggle all the main revolutionary organisations.

We hailed the revolution in *DA* 266 with the cover announcing "Nicaragua: On the Cuban road" and a special 12-page supplement, with articles by Pedro (Peter) Camejo, Sergio Rodriguez, Fred Murphy and Fidel Castro and an FI statement. It also included a report by John Garcia that the "Sydney festival for Nicaragua" had raised $1,500 for reconstruction, and a message from the SWP to the victorious revolution.

US imperialism feared the continued existence of the new upstart in its own backyard, and threatened to take action to overthrow the Sandinista government. *DA* 267 carried a statement by the US SWP Political Committee demanding "US hands off Nicaragua!", and in the following issue we carried an SWP statement, "Defend the Nicaraguan Revolution". That issue also reported on the stupid actions of the Moreno current in Latin America in sending a small band of armed members, the "Simon Bolivar Brigade", to cross the border into Nicaragua, supposedly to aid and help lead the Nicaraguan Revolution!

We sent NC member Ron Poulsen on a fact-finding tour of Nicaragua, and organised public meetings for him and Argentine comrade Mario Estrella around Australia in September on his return. There were 120 at the Melbourne forum, "the biggest left meeting for some time", *DA* 270 reported. A total of 1,300 heard Ron's eyewitness reports, plus many others through many radio and TV interviews. We publicised the meetings partly by printing eight pages in *DA* 267, which we gutted, producing 12 Ron Poulsen forum A5 leaflets (the front in English, the back in Spanish) and an A3 forum poster for each of seven cities.

DA regularly carried three or four pages of coverage of events in Nicaragua, reports on solidarity events, or analysis, often with covers demanding US: Hands Off Nicaragua!

A circular sent by Ron Poulsen on October 17, 1979, outlining a report adopted by the SWP PC on Nicaragua solidarity work, went through the importance of aid; the relationship of party work to the solidarity committees; national direction of the work and its coverage in *DA;* circulation of *Perspectiva*

Mundial (the Spanish version of *IP*); featuring Nicaragua in our election campaigns; using slide-shows and forums; and distributing the Sydney Nicaragua bulletin. Ron followed it up with another circular about organising delegations to Nicaragua from the ALP and ACTU.

SYA was of course also involved in this solidarity activity. A February 12, 1980, SWP-SYA joint circular on Nicaragua work was sent out by Ron Poulsen and Dave Adamson.

One year after the Nicaraguan Revolution, Renfrey Clarke reported from Managua in *DA* issues 311-313 with a three-part feature: "A government that doesn't lie", "We shall never stop marching" and "Literacy is liberation".

Our view that a workers and peasants government had been created in Nicaragua was contained in our "Theses on the Nicaraguan Revolution", which we submitted to the 1979 World Congress of the FI. The Theses were unanimously adopted by our National Committee on January 12, 1980, along with a report by Doug Lorimer.

From 1969, the fiercest debate in the FI had been over strategy for revolutionaries in Latin America, the role of armed struggle, how to assess guerrilla warfare. We followed this debate, participated in it and became "experts" on one side or the other in the 1970s. There were thousands of pages of discussion produced on this.

The key question was how to respond to the Latin American guerrilla movements inspired by the Cuban example. The International Majority Tendency, led by the main European Trotskyist figures, including Ernest Mandel, argued that Trotskyist groups should take their place along with the groups looking to follow the Cuban example. The Leninist Trotskyist Faction had a pessimistic view of the prospects for the Latin American revolution in the absence of mass Trotskyist parties. Although not ruling out guerrilla warfare as a tactic to be pursued in appropriate circumstances, it opposed elevating it into a general strategy, and didn't think it appropriate in the conditions in Latin America at that time.

In 1976 the IMT adopted a self-criticism. The LTF won the debate, but was proved wrong in practice. On July 19, 1979, the Sandinistas took power in Nicaragua, refuting in practice the LTF position. (One particular tragedy was that Fausto Amador, the brother of the founder of the FSLN, was won to Trotskyism, and the line he pushed, carried in articles in *IP* until the triumph of the revolution, was that the whole strategy of the FSLN was wrong, and that Cuba was a bureaucratised state.)

The Nicaraguan Revolution toppled our theory that socialist revolutions were one-stage affairs, and vindicated the two-stage theory of revolution developed by Lenin. We'd explained every revolution since 1917 as a rare exception, but the reality of Nicaragua's revolution unfolding in front of us couldn't be explained away with convoluted forulations. Nicaragua jolted us into a re-examination of our attltude to the Cuban Revolution as well. This shouldn't have been necessary – our current in the Trotskyist movement had initially distinguished itself by adopting a positive attitude to the Cuban Revolution. It was the event that helped unite the European and US tendencies in the Trotskyist movement, and was the event that demarcated the FI from diehard sectarians like the Healyite current. And in the early years of our movement in Australia, we totally identified with the Cuban revolutionaries and Cuba. Che Guevara and Fidel Castro were our heroes; we carried Cuban flags, wore Che badges, organised demonstrations in support of Cuba, read *Granma* and *Tricontinental* magazine avidly.

But during the 1970s, following the dynamic of the distorted debate on Latin America, we moved away from that early support, and were much more critical of the Cubans.

Following the 1979 Nicaraguan Revolution, both the US SWP and we changed our positions on Cuba. We became very partisan of the Castro leadership, and argued within the FI that the FI should characterise the Cuban CP as a revolutionary current, as genuine revolutionaries (as is rather obvious to anyone not blinded by sectarian Trotskyist blinkers).

In 1982 we wrote our major document on Cuba, *The Cuban Revolution and its Extension.* We amended and updated it in 1984, taking into account developments such as the tragic defeat of the Grenadian revolution, the consolidation of the Nicaraguan Revolution and the growth of the revolutionary struggle in El Salvador. We also incorporated into it our increased understanding of the Leninist theory of revolution in underdeveloped countries. We vigorously campaigned around the document in the FI, submitting it for a vote at the 1985 World Congress. This document is still essential reading.

Much of our solidarity work for Cuba, Nicaragua and other Western Hemisphere countries was done through the Committee in Solidarity with Central America and the Caribbean (CISCAC), whose name was later changed to Committee in Solidarity with Latin America and the Caribbean.

Organising elections

Our campaign for the 1980 federal elections was launched in October 1979, a full year before the elections occurred. The timing was mainly due to speculation in the capitalist media that Fraser would call an early election in late 1979 or early in the new year. Lynne Bryer was nominated for Gellibrand, Mark Carey for Griffith, Jamie Doughney for Blaxland, Therese Doyle for Hindmarsh,

Andrew Jamieson for Wollongong, Nita Keig for Sydney, Steve Painter for Perth and Geoff Payne for Newcastle. Sol Salby was added later for Wills.

The cover of *DA* 273 proclaimed: "Socialist Worker candidates launch call: THROW FRASER OUT!" Shortly before, a short (three-week) campaign in South Australia and the failure of the ALP to advocate progressive alternatives had resulted in the return of a Coalition government. Our launch was presented in this context, trying to spur leftists in the Labor Party to begin "immediately" "a fighting campaign to defeat the Liberals". The article criticised the Hayden leadership for focusing on government corruption while having "failed to provide any genuine solutions to the vital issues facing working people".

DA 275 announced banquets to launch the campaign in Adelaide, Brisbane, Melbourne, Newcastle, Perth, Sydney and Wollongong. *DA* 276 reported that the Sydney banquet attracted "well over 100" and heard candidate Jamie Doughney. "Bosses' governments are not simply guilty of failing to solve society's problems, Doughney pointed out. They *are* society's problem!

"'They're simply doing the job demanded of them by the ruling class they represent. Their job is to deepen unemployment and use inflation against the workers.'"

There were 70 at the Melbourne banquet to hear Lynne Bryer and 40 at the Brisbane launch, where Mark Carey spoke. Fifty people heard Therese Doyle at the Adelaide campaign launch, and 60 attended the WA launch banquet, where speakers were Steve Painter and Peter Holloway, our announced candidate in the upcoming state elections. The Wollongong election launch dinner heard Andrew Jamieson and donated $680 for the campaign, while 40 attended the Newcastle banquet, hearing candidate Geoff Payne and donating $360.

The last *DA* for the year, December 13, marked the 100th anniversary of the birth of Leon Trotsky with a special supplement containing articles by US SWP leaders Harry Ring and George Novack.

Preparing for the FI World Congress

Leading up to the FI World Congress, fundamental agreement had been reached by the two sides, and the majority caucus of the United Secretariat and Bureau, working together, adopted a statement (signed by 15 comrades from both former factions, including Jim Percy) to vote for the general line of four resolutions: "The World Political Situation and the Tasks of the Fourth International"; "Socialist Revolution and the Struggle for Women's Liberation"; "Resolution on Latin America"; "The Crisis in Capitalist Europe and the Present Tasks of the Fourth International". No decisive vote at this World Congress was proposed on the resolution "Socialist Democracy and the Dictatorship of the Proletariat".

"The key responsibility of this world congress", said the statement, "is to approve the following two aspects of the political line contained in these four resolutions: (a) the overall political orientation contained in them, and (b) the central political-organizational conclusion of this orientation, the proletarianization of our sections as outlined in these resolutions; the implementation of the general political line of these resolutions can be carried through only in combination with the turn to lead our sections to deeply root themselves in industry, with all the organizational consequences flowing from that".

On July 11, 1979, there was an FI circular, from Duret (Swiss comrade Charles-Andre Udry) and Stateman (Barry Sheppard), on behalf of the majority caucus of the United Secretariat and Bureau. Since there had been no IEC for three years, this reflected the reality at the centre.[54]

On September 29-30, 1979, we held a special SWP conference for election of delegates to the November 1979 FI World Congress. Reports were: political situation, women's liberation, Indochina and Nicaragua and Cuba.

The following day, October 1, we held a National Committee meeting. Reports were on assessment of the party turn and on organisation. We distributed charts of how far the turn had gone – the industrial fractions and their sizes, as well as the percentage of women comrades, and a list of full members dropped or expelled or who had left for overseas. Jim Percy's report on the turn noted that the proportion of our members in industry had risen from 16 percent in January to 34 percent in April. But since then it had remained virtually unchanged: it was now 35 percent. "Clearly we are a little bogged down", Jim said, proposing that the NC set a target of getting 50 percent of members into industry by the end of the year.

The report outlined how becoming a party of industrial workers would alter some of our organisational practices. This would occur mainly through the industrial fractions – the collective of comrades in a particular industry who met regularly to organise our activity in that industry. Jim stressed that the "basic unit" of the party would remain the branch. Industrial fractions would be "functioning units" that would "stand somewhere between the branch and campaign fractions".

Industrial fractions were different from campaign fractions, which organised our intervention in specific campaigns and therefore were concerned primarily with the particular demands and challenges of those campaigns. The industrial fractions were to "take far more of our politics and program into our central milieu", to organise "all-rounded political intervention in key industries". It would be a "test" whether we could "really centre our political work here".

As we developed our political work in industry, Jim said, we would be "pulling comrades in and out". Comrades shouldn't get "stuck" in one city, one job or one industry. We were still building a party of "footloose revolutionaries", of professional revolutionaries, and this should be particularly true of members of the National Committee.

FI 1979 World Congress

The 11th World Congress of the FI was held November 17-25, 1979. Five of us went as delegates (compared with two in 1974 to the 10th World Congress) – myself, Jim Percy, Nita Keig, Ron Poulsen and Leesa Wheelahan.

DA 282 reported "Fourth International Holds World Congress", "in Belgium the week of November 17-25". (It was actually held in Italy, where comrades were able to get a cheap deal for winter in some beach resort hotels in Rimini on the Adriatic that otherwise would have been shut down for the winter. We even had to endure a welcome speech by the local CP mayor to our cover organisation!) There were delegates from 48 countries. "The congress adopted by majority vote resolutions on the following points:

"1. The world political situation and the main overall tasks of the Fourth International.

"2. Building the Fourth International in capitalist Europe.

"3. Latin America.

"4. The international women's liberation movement.

"5. The revolution in Nicaragua."

"Indicative votes were taken on resolutions on the conflicts in Indochina and on the relation between socialist democracy and the dictatorship of the proletariat. Discussion on these points will continue and a definitive decision will be taken on them at a later time." The congress elected the International Executive Committee, which then elected the United Secretariat.

My notes for reporting to our NC stated: "Our intervention at the World Congress has been pleasing. We benefited from our large-size delegation. We intervened in discussion, talked to many different comrades. We learned a lot, saw more firsthand. We worked as a team, clearly one of the few *teams* yet built in the FI."

I added a bit more on the role of the British IMG at the World Congress and in the FI. How they performed was important for us, since as an English-speaking country we would be able to have various interchanges with them, and we had historical links. "So the failure of the turn in Britain was bad for us, and bad for the FI. Their role at the WC was to have the worst positions on nearly everything – Afghanistan, the turn, Nicaragua, the women's liberation document, Indochina … Thankfully, mostly the IMG positions were defeated."

Cuba

We were in some ways making up for lost time in resuming our interest in and enthusiasm for the Cuban Revolution. *DA* 215, July 13, 1978, included a three-page feature by Intercontinental Press editor Joe Hansen: "What the Cubans are doing in Africa".

The May 25-27, 1979, meeting of the National Committee heard and approved a report on the Cuban Revolution by Doug Lorimer.

In July 1980, we sent Renfrey Clarke to the Caribbean and Central America as a *Direct Action* correspondent. Issue 314 carried a three-page feature by Renfrey from Cuba. This included a report on the July 26 celebrations, which were held that year in the provincial town of Ciego de Avila. One of the speakers was Jaime Wheelock, a central leader of the Nicaraguan Sandinista National Liberation Front, who paid tribute to Cuba's assistance for their struggle:

"… when we were only a tiny group, we already enjoyed the help, the solidarity and the encouragement of Comandante Fidel Castro and the Cuban revolution.

"When for any reason, in the midst of our difficulties, we Sandinistas had differences … the help and advice of our brother Fidel was of great importance in bringing about the Sandinista unity which was the unity of the whole people and the guarantee of our revolution.

"And when our people were ready to struggle with stones and even with their own teeth to overthrow the dictatorship, we also had the concrete solidarity of the people of Cuba … Because we know you don't make revolutions with your teeth."

At the same event, Fidel Castro's speech included some comments on the course of the Nicaraguan struggle that must have contributed to our later decision to accept Lenin's strategy in preference to Trotsky's theory of permanent revolution. As quoted in the article, Fidel pointed out that a bourgeoisie still existed in Nicaragua. "Does this mean perhaps that there is a bourgeois revolution in Nicaragua?" he asked.

"No!", he answered, along with the crowd. "In Nicaragua there is a people's revolution whose fundamental power is based on the workers, the peasants, the students, and the middle layers of the population …

"The fundamental thing in a revolution – the basic thing which allows one to talk about a revolution and popular revolution – is to have the people and to have the arms."

The same issue carried an ad for a series of public forums by Renfrey Clarke on "Revolution in the Caribbean", held in Brisbane, Newcastle, Sydney, Wollongong, Melbourne, Adelaide and Perth.

The Cuban Communist Party held its Second Congress in December 1980. We were keenly interested in what happened there, but in those pre-internet days, it was not until the following March that we had enough of the resolutions and reports to write a considered analysis, which Doug Lorimer provided in *DA* 334-338.

This series, while not concealing where we disagreed with or had doubts about Cuban positions, was unmistakably written from the standpoint of supporters of the revolution and its leadership. For example, "Cuban Congress strengthens workers power" in *DA* 336 praised the organs of Peoples Power, saying that they "have increased the ability of the people to participate in running the country, and help make Cuba the most democratic country in the world today.

"Their development expresses the Cuban leadership's reliance on the conscious and mobilised support of the workers and peasants in order to defend and extend the revolution."

But the article also criticised the fact that Peoples Power candidates were elected solely as individuals and could not be part of a slate or endorsed by the Communist Party or any other organisation. This, the article said, could "de-emphasise the discussion of broader national issues and policies".

"In this respect the assemblies of Peoples Power in Cuba fall short of the democratic workers and peasants councils which existed in the USSR under Lenin and Trotsky."

While this criticism was correct in the abstract, we hadn't yet considered carefully enough the specifics of Cuba's situation. Elections based on competing slates of candidates would not have been real unless there was the opportunity for other political parties to organise and compete against the CCP. But that would inevitably have meant the "freedom" for counter-revolutionary parties funded and backed by imperialism to operate openly.

The last two articles in the series considered Cuba's foreign policy, contrasting it to the reactionary stance of Stalinism:

"... the Kremlin bureaucracy seeks not simply peaceful coexistence between states with different socio-economic systems, but peace between the conflicting social classes – between the imperialists on the one hand and the workers of the world on the other. Such a policy involves collaboration with the capitalists and can only be at the expense of the world struggle for socialism.

"In contrast, Cuba's foreign policy is based on subordinating its own national interests to those of the international struggle against imperialism. This was clearly demonstrated in 1975.

"The Cuban government sacrificed the possibility of having the criminal US economic blockade lifted as part of a general normalisation of its relations being discussed with the US at the time. It made this sacrifice in order to aid newly independent Angola to beat back a US-supported South African invasion."

The same article, however, noted that the Cubans appeared to have the "mistaken view" that the Stalinist regimes of the Soviet Union and Eastern Europe were capable of being "reformed and won to a revolutionary socialist course".

We got seriously involved in doing Cuba solidarity work. By 1982, we were leading the Australia-Cuba Friendship Society, and our comrade Greg Adamson was editing its magazine, *Cuba Today*. We drafted a resolution setting out our understanding of the Cuban Revolution and the revolutions in Nicaragua and Grenada, *The Cuban Revolution and its extension*. Allen Myers reported on this to our October 9-11, 1982, NC plenum, and Dave Holmes reported on it to the SWP ninth national conference, January 5-11, 1983, where it was adopted.

Grenada

Revolution began in Grenada on March 13, 1979, when the New Jewel Movement overthrew the dictatorship of Eric Gairy. We were alerted to the significance of what was happening there by the US SWP, which sent several of their comrades to the island and covered developments in the *Militant*.

We sent Jim Percy on a visit to Grenada in August 1981. When it was announced that Grenada's foreign minister, Unison Whiteman, would be attending the Commonwealth Heads of Government Meeting in Melbourne (September 30-October 7, 1981), we arranged for CISCAC to organise public meetings for him in both Melbourne and Sydney.

In 1982, we published a book on Grenada: *Forward Ever! Three years of the Grenadian Revolution. Speeches of Maurice Bishop*, with an introduction by Jim Percy (reviewed in *DA* of December 7). We saw Grenada, like Nicaragua, as an "extension" of the Cuban Revolution – not in the sense that Cuba interfered in any way in those countries, but as instances of the power of a revolutionary example. The Cuban Communists saw the two later revolutions as the beginning of a break in the net of hostility that imperialism was attempting to weave around them. *DA* 298 reported on Fidel Castro's 1980 May Day speech under the heading: "Grenada, Nicaragua, Cuba – 3 giants rising up".

US imperialism saw the same sorts of connections, from the other side of the class divide. The US immediately seized on the opportunity provided by the October 1983 coup against the Maurice Bishop government, invading and putting an end to the revolution.

CHAPTER 4

A TIME OF CHANGES IN THE '80S

In the 1980s our party went through major changes. We broke with our early mentors, the US SWP, before they headed totally onto the shoals of sectarianism and irrelevance. We left the Fourth International, although seeking to maintain comradely collaboration with it.

It was a decade when we thought many things through for ourselves, had our own full-time party school and drafted important documents – on Vietnam, on Cuba and a very thorough political program. We rethought our analysis of the Labor Party and our tactics towards it. We published many books and pamphlets in this period.

It was a decade of building big events, and unity attempts, both small and ambitious, and looking to take advantage of new openings. We made some mistakes, and had some false hopes. But we continued our efforts at building a revolutionary Marxist party.

1980 Socialist Education Conference

Our SWP gathering at Hawkesbury on January 5-9, 1980, was a Socialist Educational Conference. More than 200 attended, including an international guest, Peter Rotherham from the New Zealand SAL. Feature talks were given on: The Roots of the Capitalist World Crisis, by Jamie Doughney; The Turn in the Political Situation, from the '60s Radicalisation to the Fraser Offensive, by Nita Keig; Nicaragua, Cuba and the Permanent Revolution, by Ron Poulsen; Australian Trade Unions at the Crossroads, by John Garcia; The Labor Party and the Struggle for a Revolutionary Leadership, by Jim Percy; and Perspectives for SYA, by Margo Condoleon.

For this educational conference, we decided to invite comrades from the International Socialists to attend. Nita Keig explained our thinking in a December 3, 1979, circular to members: "We felt that our educational conference would be a good opportunity for us to open some discussions with this organisation about many of the main political question of the day. Unlike the SLL or the Spartacist League for example, the IS has been an organisation with whom it has been possible to work from time to time and with whom we consider political discussions to be worthwhile." Jim Percy sent them a letter. He referred to some precedents, for example in Britain, and the fact that representatives of the British SWP were observers at the recent FI World Congress.

The comprehensive and ambitious schedule of educational classes for the conference was advertised in the December 6, 1979, *DA*. Topics included Marxist economics, the Russian Revolution, Labor Party history, Indochina, the Aboriginal struggle, Australian capitalism, the history of Australian Trotskyism, the Chinese Revolution, the crisis of Stalinism, the Palestinian Struggle, trade unions, liberation struggles in Africa, migrants in Australia, Marxist philosophy, farmers in Australia, the origins of women's oppression, class struggle left wings, Latin America, the left and Australian literature, Iran, the feminist movement, the workers and farmers government, Australian imperialism.

January 1980 SWP NC

The SWP National Committee meeting held after the educational conference, on January 12-13, 1980, heard reports on the world political situation, Nicaragua, socialist democracy, world movement, tasks and perspectives.

At the time of the NC, we had 143 full members, 40 percent of whom were in industry, and 26 provisional members, 19 percent in industry.

In the conclusion to my tasks and perspectives report, I confidently noted: "At this NC I was struck, I think we all were, by the *political clarity* that is emerging, has emerged, in our party. More than ever, our party is characterised by political clarity on all the major questions of the class struggle. And at this plenum, absolute unanimity. Everything fits together, clarity on one question aids clarity on another – Indochina, Iran, Nicaragua, Afghanistan, socialist democracy … The reason? The turn! We're more and more in our right milieu, our home ground, the industrial working class. Everything falls into place, all our tasks fall into place. It's possible to see clearly how they are all interrelated, are all vital *political* tasks for us to complete.

"Elections; *DA*; our propaganda offensive; finance; education; recruiting; industrial fractions; the political issues we're taking up. All mesh together. It's clearer than ever before that this is so … We have an excellent year behind us. It's an even more challenging year ahead. With our clear perspectives, integrated by our revolutionary program, our working class orientation and our growing base in the industrial working class, we can take up this challenge!

"We can become a party of worker-Bolsheviks, able to lead and carry through the coming Australian revolution."

But we were much too optimistic. The radicalisation of the '60s and '70s was not going to be repeated. In fact, we were facing a long period of downturn and retreat in the workers' movement. They were difficult times for building revolutionary parties, although we fared a lot better than many others.

The '80s were a time of change, when we were able to grow modestly. Most importantly, they were a time when we thought things out for ourselves. We were very productive, writing many important resolutions and documents. And we tried many tactics, testing our perspectives and acting on them. We were ultimately held back by the defeats of the working class in Australia, and by a major international defeat at the end of the decade, the collapse of the Soviet Union.

Developing differences with the US SWP

From early on, we had been opposed to "international democratic central-ism"; we had no time for proconsuls being foisted on us. The US SWP was always a little suspicious of us. There were never equal relations between us. We at first put it down to the fact that we were a new party, just learning a lot of things. But even as we became a larger party, carried out useful interventions, produced successful publications and played an increasing role in the FI, they still treated us with less than 100 percent candour. They probably suspected our origins, coming very much out of the youth radicalisation, and were a bit hesitant about our initiatives and our independence. They were right. We weren't just follow-ers. One lesson we'd already learned by that time (strongly pushed, ironically, by former leaders of the SWP like James P. Cannon) was that you can't make a revolution if you don't develop an independent national leadership team.

When the US SWP made a sharp turn in 1976-78 to get the majority of its membership into industrial jobs, and argued this course for the whole interna-tional, we followed that course.

When the Nicaraguan Revolution broke out in 1978, we reacted enthusias-tically. It also prompted us to examine the experience of the Cuban revolution-aries more thoroughly, and then the Russian Revolution itself, coming to an understanding of some of the flaws in the Trotskyist position, especially on the question of "permanent revolution".[55]

At this time, the US SWP was heading in an increasingly sectarian direction. When they started factionalising in our party against our leadership, we were alarmed and eventually broke off relations with them. Their degeneration deepened, repudiating many of the positive lessons from their own history.[56]

We presented our views to the FI in the 1980s, submitting resolutions we had drafted: *The Struggle for Socialism in the Imperialist Epoch* and *The Cuban Revolution and its extension*.[57] We argued our case in the FI bulletins, and at the

FI 1985 World Congress. We didn't make much headway, and so decided that the best course would be to part company, at the same time proposing that we maintain comradely relations with the FI.[58]

We were one of the more successful groups in the FI, and one of the more independently thinking, which is why we passed the test in the 1980s when the period of renewal and rethinking came, and were able to take the overwhelming majority of our party with us.

The US SWP refused to support our resolution on Cuba, initially without any good reason at all, because they must have agreed with most of it, but just because it was written by us, and we were refusing to toe their line. Later they had an excuse in that it was also sponsored by Peter Camejo, one of their leaders whom they had expelled undemocratically, and who was now collaborating with us. Politically, the main difference that emerged between them and us on Cuba was that we clearly recognised that the Castroist current were conscious revolutionary Marxists even before taking power in Cuba, while the US SWP wouldn't come at that.

Afghanistan

Afghanistan was another world event that forced us to think things out more for ourselves. A few months after the Nicaraguan Revolution, in late 1979 Soviet troops went into Afghanistan to block a US-organised war to topple the radical regime in Kabul. Our reaction was prompt, to give strong support to the USSR and the regime in Kabul. (Our quick reaction allowed us to make amends, perhaps, for the abstentionist position we took initially when Vietnam overthrew the murderous Pol Pot regime.) Doug Lorimer gave a report to our January 12-13 NC, and we issued a strong statement. We had campaigning headlines on *DA* covers ("Soviet Troops Aid Afghan Revolution"), and our sales actually increased.

We were standing in the 1980 federal elections and campaigned on the issue, producing an SWP candidates statement, "Labor must defend Afghan revolution!". We had forums in seven cities on the theme "Afghan Revolution Versus Carter's War Drive", with 100 attending a Melbourne forum on Afghanistan with SWP candidates. In April, we printed 400,000 leaflets on Afghanistan for the election campaign, aiming to cover every letterbox in nine electorates.

The 1980 summer Olympic Games were due to be held in Moscow, but the United States, led by President Jimmy Carter, threatened a boycott if the Soviet Union refused to withdraw from Afghanistan. The US was supported by many Western governments, including Australia's, led by Malcolm Fraser.

We went on a campaign supporting the Moscow Olympics, against the attempt to boycott them over Afghanistan. *DA*'s January 24 editorial demanded: "Oppose Olympic Games boycott". Initially some sections of the labour movement also came out against the boycott. The Australian Young Labor conference, January 26-28, came out against the West's position. The NSW Trades and Labour Council condemned the boycott, as did the SA Labor Council, and the PLO hailed the Soviet aid to Afghanistan. But some of the Australian left found themselves on the same side as the right: Dave Deutschmann reported "'Leftists' join far right in anti-Soviet rally" (*DA* 284), Maoists and IS members gathering in the same demonstration as Nazis, the "Christian Mission to the Communist World" and the Baltic Council of Australia.

We continued to campaign over subsequent issues of *DA*, Renfrey Clarke writing "Olympic boycott campaign falters" (*DA* 285), Martin Mulligan (Martin Tuck) reporting "Growing opposition to Olympic boycott" (*DA* 286) and Nita Keig explaining "How bosses' media lies on Afghan war" (*DA* 293) and urging that we oppose Murdoch's crude Olympic boycott campaign. We continued to campaign with our covers, "No to Olympic boycott!" (*DA* 287)

We developed a united front with Australian sportspeople, as they also opposed the boycott, wanting to compete in Moscow. Martin Mulligan wrote in March "Aust. Athletes prepare for Moscow" as the worldwide Olympic boycott campaign fizzled. Champion swimmer Dawn Fraser spoke out and organised to go to Moscow. Even in February, Martin Mulligan was able to report that the Olympic boycott was "on the skids". *DA* covers continued to campaign: April 23 urging "Fight the Olympic Boycott". Peter Annear reported in May on "Olympics: anti-boycott protests", and athletes and politicians speaking out opposing the Olympic boycott. In June Martin Mulligan reported in *DA* 302 the desperation as "Fraser heats up boycott campaign" and Olympic athletes faced intimidation and even death threats. Nita Keig reported in August, as the Olympics went ahead, that it was "a big defeat for Fraser".

DA also carried many theoretical feature articles analysing the situation: Allen Myers on "Afghanistan and the right to national self-determination", Ernest Harsch "Afghanistan – the roots of revolution" (from the US SWP), and in *DA* 294, also from the US SWP, Fred Feldman asked, "Did US war drive gain from Soviet role in Afghanistan?", concluding: "Instead of strengthening Washington, the aftermath of the Soviet intervention in Afghanistan has further undermined Washington's capacity to use working people here or in Europe as cannon fodder against oppressed nations like Iran and Afghanistan". In July Allen Myers wrote a two-part series, "New openings for Afghan revolution" and "The Kremlin's role in Afghanistan".

We published a very good pamphlet, in large quantities, *The Truth about Afghanistan and the Crisis of Imperialist Domination.*[59] The articles, by Ernest Harsch, Steve Clark, Doug Jenness, Renfrey Clarke and Jim McIlroy, were reprinted from *Intercontinental Press,* the US *Militant* and *Direct Action.* In Sydney branch, we had a bundle of 600 to sell.

Initially the US SWP held a position similar to ours, that the Soviet intervention was a blow to US backed counter-revolution. But it didn't campaign on the issue, and then in August 1980 it suddenly did a 180-degree switch. Other sections of the FI aligned with the US SWP obediently followed suit. We politely disagreed, and put our reasons down in a 100-page document, "Debate on Afghanistan – Where the new line of the American SWP goes wrong". It was written by Allen Myers and adopted by our Political Committee in January 1981, firstly for the benefit and education of our own members, but also to argue our case with the US comrades. We shipped off 400 copies to New York for the benefit of US SWP comrades. It wasn't until quite a while later that we learned they were never distributed, but just sat in the boxes in their national office.

We later presented a draft resolution for the 12th World Congress of the Fourth International on "The civil war in Afghanistan", submitted by International Executive Committee members Pedro Camejo, Doug Lorimer and Jim Percy. Allen Myers wrote a six-part series for *DA* (April 22 – June 3, 1981) on Imperialism and the Afghan Revolution. Allen visited New Zealand in May to defend our line against that of the NZ SAL, which faithfully followed the US SWP, and we published all the documents in an August 1981 Discussion Bulletin.

Other political issues also developed into differences with the US SWP.

Solidarnosc

In response to the suppression of Solidarnosc by the Polish CP government, we had a disagreement over whether we should participate in and build demonstrations protesting the crackdown. The US SWP decided we shouldn't.

Initially it seemed we had the same perspective. In August 1980, *DA* came out with a cover "Support the Polish workers" and an article by Nita Keig. We followed it up in the next issue with articles by Nita – "Poland: Gain for socialism, all workers" (referring to Solidarnosc, not the government attacks on it) and "Polish strike: no joy for Fraser" – statements from the nine SWP candidates hailing the Polish struggle and an article reprinted from *IP* by David Frankel, "Massive strikes shake Polish regime". The September 17 *DA* printed a four-page feature, "Upsurge in Poland", with articles from *IP*; the following issue had two pages from *IP* from Gerry Foley, who was over there by then. *DA* 319 had more from Gerry Foley from *IP*.

At our July 11-12, 1981, National Committee meeting, Nita presented the report on Poland. But afterwards differences emerged. We sent Jim Percy to cover the rise of Solidarnosc in Poland, attending the first conference of the union in September 1981, and in January the PC issued a statement, "Defend the Polish Workers", and we organised SWP forums around the country on "The fight for socialist democracy in Poland" with Jim Percy and others speaking.

By the time of our SWP National Committee on April 24-26, 1982, the US SWP had hardened its line opposing actions in support of Solidarnosc that weren't organised by trade unions, which was supported by Nita Keig and a few others in our leadership. Allen Myers reported for the PC majority on Poland, Nita Keig for the PC minority. In the pre-conference discussion, Ron Poulsen and Nita Keig argued their case with "For class struggle solidarity with the Polish workers". At the January 5-11, 1983, SWP ninth national conference, Allen Myers reported on Poland for the majority, and Jamie Doughney for the minority.

Vietnam

On Vietnam, we made some fundamental reassessments of our past positions. Our party and Resistance had arisen in Australia out of the campaign against the Vietnam War, and had always had a positive attitude towards the Vietnamese revolutionaries. In addition to demanding the withdrawal of Australian troops from Vietnam, the ending of conscription and an end to US aggression, we also solidarised with the Vietnamese freedom fighters, produced National Liberation Front badges, flags and posters, carried Ho Chi Minh's portrait on demonstrations and chanted "Ho, Ho, Ho Chi Minh".

But as we consolidated our Trotskyist political positions, became integrated into the Fourth International and adopted more of its theory, we adopted some of the more bizarre, sectarian political positions. The US SWP in 1973-74 published two long attacks on the Vietnamese Communist Party as "Stalinist" and basically having misguided the Vietnamese revolution. We had followed this lead. It was a real contradiction: at the same time as defending and admiring the Vietnamese revolutionaries, we had to try to fit them into a Stalinist mould.

In the 1980s, we did a lot of rethinking on this as well, and in October 1984 we adopted a report by Allen Myers (printed as a pamphlet) that dumped our old characterisations. We pointed out that part of our errors flowed from the wrong schema, Trotsky's theory of permanent revolution, and once we developed a clearer understanding of Lenin's revolutionary strategy, we could make better sense of the revolutionary dynamic in Vietnam as well. We also recognised that we had developed very arbitrary revolutionary standards, trying to fit the Vietnamese revolution into them, and often were just ignorant of the facts. The US SWP also changed its positions on Vietnam, but was unable to make as honest a self-criticism as we were, and it publicly attacked our new positions.

In the early 1980s the organisational degeneration of the US SWP was becoming increasingly clear. It appeared more and more to be run as a clique, even a cult, around one man, Jack Barnes, the national secretary. While the overwhelming majority of our party had little difficulty in accepting that Trotsky's theory of permanent revolution was inferior to Lenin's two-stage theory, in the US there was considerable opposition and a major factional struggle. The leadership resolved it undemocratically, expelling a substantial proportion of the membership who still held to the traditional Trotskyist positions, and cancelling the party's 1983 convention. They had earlier expelled Peter Camejo, who'd developed similar views to ours, and forced out others who subsequently regrouped around Camejo in the North Star Network.

Agent Orange

One aspect of the imperialist war against Vietnam was the horrendous environmental destruction deliberately carried out by the US and its allies. This included the widespread use of chemical warfare, chiefly defoliants, whose effects are still being felt today. Particularly damaging was Agent Orange, which was contaminated with dioxin, a deadly by-product of its production.

This arose as an issue in Australia in April 1978, when it was revealed by NSW Attorney-General Frank Walker that the company Union Carbide had disposed of some 60kg of dioxin contained in industrial wastes in three Sydney rubbish tips in Menai, Homebush and Concord from 1949 to 1974. Reporting on the disclosure in *DA* 205, Mary Rabbone noted that the use of herbicides 2,4,5-T and 2,4-D in Victoria and Queensland had been associated with an increase in congenital deformities. (Agent Orange was a 50-50 mix of the two chemicals.) As well, in July 1976, an industrial accident led to the release of two kilograms of dioxin in a gas cloud over the town of Seveso in Italy, leading to an increase in congenital deformities and the deaths of numerous animals and plants.

Some of the Australian troops serving in Vietnam were exposed to Agent Orange and suffered the harmful consequences. *Direct Action* covered the attempt of some of these veterans to obtain compensation, beginning with the January 24, 1980, issue, in which Gordon Adler reported on a claim lodged with the Department of Veterans Affairs by 28 veterans. The article noted that Agent Orange had been used "not for the purpose of increasing crop yields ... but as part of a deliberate policy of devastation of the countryside …

"The Australian government should pay full compensation to the Australian victims of 'Agent Orange,' even though monetary payment cannot overcome the terrible consequences of major birth defects.

"What is even more important, however, is that Australia should compensate the people of Vietnam for the vastly greater numbers of birth defects, wounds, deaths and the effects of the defoliation of their countryside."

In less than a month after the first veterans lodged their claims, another 1,000 veterans had done so. The government rejected the claims. As Julie Campbell wrote in *DA* 287, the US and Australian governments, as well as the companies involved, denied the deadly effects of the chemicals in order to avoid paying compensation to the injured veterans, but even more so to evade their responsibility to "the people of Vietnam, Laos, and Kampuchea who were the *deliberate* targets of this chemical warfare".

The "government cover-up on Agent Orange" was the cover story of *DA* 294. Martin Mulligan (Martin Tuck) reported that 1,200 veterans had responded to a questionnaire of the Vietnam Veterans Action Association (VVAA), which represented some 2,000 veterans who were now seeking compensation. "[B]etween 350 and 400 children born to Vietnam veterans have birth defects – including missing fingers, missing limbs, club feet, cleft palates, and missing sex organs".

DA 300 carried an interview with Holt McMinn, the president of VVAA. He estimated that perhaps 15,000 of the 42,000 Australian veterans of Vietnam could have been affected, even if they were not close to areas that were sprayed – for example, by eating prawns, many of which had high levels of dioxin. "If you drank water from defoliated areas or that flowed through defoliated areas you could have been contaminated that way. The spray sometimes drifted up to tens of miles." And, McMinn pointed out, other defoliants used in addition to Agent Orange also had harmful effects on human beings.

Thirty-five years later, people are still campaigning for the victims of Agent Orange.[60]

Mexico conference on El Salvador

In March 1982 I travelled to Mexico on behalf of CISCAC to attend the World Conference in Solidarity with El Salvador, which was to set up the El Salvador World Front. The opening rally had 2,500 at it, and several hundred delegates at the conference itself. It had a broad participation. The conference adopted a declaration and an appeal, and heard reports from the FDR/FMLN on the political and military situation.

The World Front was set up with a permanent office in Mexico. It set a plan of action, for international solidarity demonstrations, for financial aid, to help refugees and to coordinate and strengthen international solidarity and disseminate information about the repression and the situation in El Salvador. Peter Camejo had also come to Mexico City to attend the conference, and called round to have discussions with George Novack, who was living there. I was billeted with George and his partner, and heard the strong arguments Camejo was making to Novack, who was mostly silent. (I surmised George probably agreed with a lot of Peter's arguments, but he was still financially dependent on New York, I think.)

We really had only an early glimpse of the degeneration of the US SWP. Did it have a demoralising or depressing effect on some of our comrades? Probably, especially those of us who had been around a while and knew them in their better days, and knew their strong traditions and history.

We held a national consultation of CISCAC in Melbourne after I returned, and heard reports from Rafael Gonzalez of the FMLN/FDR, whom we were touring, myself and other comrades who had seen first hand the situation in El Salvador, Nicaragua, Grenada and Cuba. We mapped out plans for an extensive range of actions.

Purges in US SWP

I attended the February 1982 US SWP National Committee plenum, on my way to the Mexico City conference. Peter Camejo had been undemocratically expelled from the SWP and was excluded from the plenum, but was trying to lobby the delegates from outside. He spoke to me as I was going in. I listened. Some of his tales seemed plausible, and seemed to fit in with some of the doubts and hesitations we'd been having about the SWP leadership – especially Jack Barnes – over the previous few years. I told him I was staying at Will and Wendy Reissner's place (across the Hudson River in New Jersey), so he phoned me later to give me his full story. I took extensive notes and reported back to the NO comrades in Sydney by telephone.

Twenty-seven motions were moved by the US SWP leadership against the Lovell-Breitman/Bloom and Weinstein-Henderson tendencies, with instructions to "cease and desist" – not to distribute written material, not to hold organised meetings, etc., etc. The meaning of motions like that was unmistakable: either stop thinking politically or be forced out.

There were probably earlier signs of Barnes' sectarian and cultish tendencies, but we can certainly note some signs of his degeneration from 1978. An

April 23, 1978, letter from Nita Keig in Paris reported that Barnes was moving to the US West Coast, and was out of contact with the national leadership. The following month a letter from Nita in Paris to myself and Peta Stewart reported she had chatted with US SWP leader Doug Jenness while they were in Switzerland. "Apparently they are getting a bit agitated about Jack at the moment – not seriously of course but sort of annoyed. It seems he is taking a protracted break/rest somewhere in the desert and can't be contacted except when he rings in." Barry Sheppard in Volume 2 of his history of the US SWP identifies some "disturbing developments" even earlier. When Mary-Alice Waters was in Paris in early 1978 and told Barry that she and Jack had broken up, they were able to have a frank discussion about how Jack had been acting. Barry wrote:

"My thinking at that point was that Jack was functioning in a way I had never seen before, since I first met him in the early 1960s. In fact, his behaviour was contrary to the way he had previously acted. He was 'turning the PC into a one-man band' was how I put it to Mary-Alice. I didn't use the word 'cult' because I thought Jack was making mistakes, not consciously furthering a cult of himself, and that it could be corrected. We talked late into the evening, and came to complete agreement."

Barry resolved that he'd raise the issue with Jack next time he saw him, which was in February in New York. When Barry had finished his "somewhat lengthy remarks, Jack's only response was to say, 'I can't imagine the SWP without you or Mary-Alice.' That was all. The meeting was over. I was stunned by this threat to expel us if we took our criticisms any further. From that point on, I knew I would be pushed out one way or another, and although I tried to suppress the knowledge back into my unconscious it bubbled to the surface in the next years." Barry and his partner Caroline Lund soldiered on in the US SWP until finally being forced out a decade later. Gus Horowitz was another central leader of the SWP in the 1970s who eased himself out at the beginning of the 1980s, probably aware by then of how things were going downhill. He later wrote of the development of the Jack Barnes cult in the SWP:

"So it was that from the late 1970s onward an unfortunate combination of circumstances worked like a cancer on the SWP: the decline of the radicalization; the party's small size and relative isolation from mass action; weaknesses and flaws in our traditions; unacknowledged political mistakes; the abnormal way of life in the group; and the human frailty of the leaders. None of these factors, taken alone, would have been sufficient to decimate the organization. But in combination, they were deadly."[61] Barry Sheppard's book points out that it was Jack's positive role in the previous period of growth of the US SWP during the radicalisation that earned his authority. "Gradually this authority was abused, until it turned into its opposite. From a positive force building the SWP, it became a negative and destructive force that wrecked the party ... One characteristic of this cult was that all political initiative had become the sole prerogative of Jack Barnes."

Were we all slow in recognising and facing up to the degeneration of the US SWP and the development of Barnes into a cult figure? Probably. Was I slow in 1982 because I still had so many personal and political friends in the US SWP, made during my 18 months in New York working on *IP*? Probably, although many of my friends were out already, having been expelled, or shunned or forced out anyway.

{At this point, the manuscript had only three notes indicating what John planned to cover here: "[1979 WC, preparing joint documents

Barnes forcing the issue on the turn

The 3 errors of G-war tactic]"

{In reply to my query, Barry Sheppard (email, October 16, 2015), suggested that John was intending to cover the events discussed in chapter 18 of volume 2 of Barry's history of the US SWP. The rest of the material within these brackets is summarised from that source.

{In preparation for the 1979 World Congress of the FI, in order to begin healing the factional divisions that had existed for a decade, leaders of the IMT and LTF collaborated to write a number of joint documents, including one rescinding the guerrilla warfare line, on socialist democracy, on Europe, on women's liberation and on the world political situation.

{There were two competing resolutions on Nicaragua even though "[t]here was broad agreement on supporting the revolution, the FSLN government, and the steps forward the Sandinistas had taken". The differences were over the US SWP's view that a workers and peasants government had been formed in Nicaragua – the European members of the FI mostly rejected the entire concept. But "Jack Barnes forced the issue in the SWP leadership" and hence at the World Congress, "a factional move that tended to fissure in the International along the lines of the old dispute".

{The world political resolution, drafted jointly by Barnes and Ernest Mandel, "contained a fundamentally flawed assertion that the working class in the capitalist countries worldwide, both imperialist and semi-colonial, was becoming radicalized", politically as well as in union struggles, and therefore all sections of the FI should make a turn to colonise their members into industry. Barry had the "impression that Ernest did not actually agree with this analysis or conclusion, but was brow beaten by Jack into accepting it under the threat of there being two resolutions".

{This perspective "repeated the methodological errors" of the 1969 guerrilla line in three ways. First, the generalisation about the objective political situation was not true; it was too broad and did not take account of the differences between countries and regions. Second, from that generalisation, it concluded that a single tactic could be elevated into a general strategy to be followed in every country. Third, it did not take any account of the differing realities of the various FI sections, some of which were minuscule compared to the US SWP or the French section.

{"As a strategy, [the turn to industry] failed. Jack then used this failure to divide some of the sections, into those who followed the SWP example and those who backed away from it. This factional move wrecked our attempts to rebuild the International."}

Cults and joining

The Barnes cult has dragged on for decades now, with a decreasing band of ageing followers, able to live off the assets accumulated by the US SWP in its healthier stage. It still publishes many of the Trotskyist classics, but sells them at very inflated prices, probably mainly to libraries, and fiercely calls in its lawyers to prevent any of its copyrighted works being published on the Marxist Internet Archive.

It's not the first socialist group to start off doing some useful work and ending up as an irrelevant or dangerous sect. Lynn Marcus was a former Trotskyist who set up his own cult, the National Caucus of Labor Committees, which made a habit of attacking other left groups and morphed into an extreme right-wing sect. The founder of Scientology, L. Ron Hubbard, a third-rate science fiction writer, was quite brazen about his scam. Some cult leaders obviously believe in their message; others are charlatans out to make a quid.

The Jonestown and other religious cults probably have something in common with *all* religions, and probably things in common with various political cults. They satisfy some needs of alienated individuals in an alienating world.

How close to this was the Healy group, which was a rival to us in the 1970s, and other left cults, such as the followers of Posadas, or Stalinism? It's not completely straightforward, being bound up with real forces, and with mixed motivations that will be different in different individuals. Many cult followers have genuine motives, are disinterested and committed, certainly when they start out. Pedro Camejo was a great speaker and recruiter. In one talk he addressed the "I'm not a joiner" argument, pointing out that we're all joiners, whether we like it or not. Capitalist society and its state don't give you a choice about joining them: following their laws and regulations is obligatory, even if you'd rather not. But at the same time, bourgeois society encourages non-joining: don't commit, don't be a "fanatic".

Some former socialist activists revert back to their religious past, or perhaps discover religion for the first time.[62] Some have exited via well-known cults such as the Hare Krishna. One of the members of the old Trotskyist group in Australia even went into Scientology.

One of the concepts we tried to encourage in our party was "party patriotism" or "party loyalty". Fundamentally, this meant loyalty to the politics for which the party stood: members were loyal to the party because it was the necessary means for implementing those politics. This is closely related to democratic centralism: discussion and debate, a democratic decision and a testing of the decision through the party's practice are the best way to advance the party's politics. Hence party loyalty necessarily involves a willingness to question the party's course and seek to improve or correct it if that appears warranted. Attaching one's loyalty to an individual or smaller group or a subset of the party's ideas rather than the party as a whole is a religious corruption of party loyalty, a substitution of faith for politics.

DSP and Resistance consolidation

The 1980s had two main sides for us. We established our organisational and political independence, stood on our own two feet, became stronger, in a time most of which was difficult for the workers and socialist movement. The Hawke Labor government and its Accord with the ACTU not only transferred wealth from the workers to the bosses, but also crippled the union movement's capacity to organise and resist.

It was also a time of thinking things out much more for ourselves. We experimented organisationally and took gambles that sometimes didn't succeed, but also had growth and successes, when others on the left found the going much harder and were in decline.

SWP NC May 1980

A plenum of the SWP National Committee was held May 10-11, 1980. It included a political report, ALP report, party tasks in industry, security policy, special education project, tasks and perspectives and world movement report.

The report on security concerned a reformulation of the party's policy on the use of illegal drugs. This was circulated by the National Office, on May 1, a week and a half before the NC plenum. We had previously banned any use of illegal drugs by our members and had treated any infraction as a matter requiring disciplinary action by the party. As the circular noted, "This policy is not based on moral considerations, but on the practical need to protect the party and its members from victimisation by the capitalist state".

While this threat of victimisation was real, it was not as severe as in a country like the United States. By 1980, we began to feel that it was necessary to treat the issue in a more political manner, while still protecting the party from any suggestion that it in any way encouraged the use of drugs. The circular noted: "Adherence to this policy is just as much an obligation of members as is adherence to such other norms as the obligation to sell Direct Action, to contribute to the party financially, to carry out majority decisions, etc.

"Violations of this policy – like any violation of party norms or discipline – should be dealt with according to the severity of the offense, the actual or potential harm it has caused to the party, the experience and understanding of the offender, etc. Obviously, violations such as selling illegal drugs, their use or possession on party premises or business, or their use/possession in circumstances that at all imply or suggest the party's condoning of such use (for example, in the presence of contacts or non-party SYAers, or at 'movement' social events) are sufficiently flagrant to require immediate disciplinary action by the appropriate party body. But in the case of the violation of using small quantities of marijuana in private, the party *may* decide that persuasion and explanation of the reasons for this policy are a more appropriate method than disciplinary action to put an end to the violation of party discipline. Such a decision would in no case, of course, imply that the party condones or overlooks the use of this illegal drug in particular circumstances, nor would it excuse other members committing a similar violation."

The political report was very optimistic: "… the imperialist system is in a state of deep crisis today. The relationship of class forces on a world scale has never been worse for the capitalist class. We are witnessing today an acceleration of the pace of the world revolution in the face of a continuing inability of imperialism, led by United States imperialism, to take measures which can stem and reverse this process."

While this underestimated the ability of imperialism to find ways around some of the dilemma it faced, the dilemma itself was real enough. As the report noted, in the aftermath of its defeat in Vietnam, US imperialism found it extremely difficult to police the world for capitalism in its traditional way. Examples included "the Cuban role in helping turn back the forces of colonialism in Angola; the Vietnamese intervention in Kampuchea; the civil war and ousting of Somoza in Nicaragua; and of course, the overthrow of the shah in Iran right through to the taking of the American hostages. In none of these instances did the United States feel in a position to intervene directly in its own interests."

(It is interesting to look back 35 years later and read in the report that capitalist propaganda intended to overcome the political limits on military intervention, while relying on traditional anticommunist arguments, was also beginning to warn of "Muslim 'fanaticism'".)

The report also focused on "the beginning of a stepped-up fight back" by Australian workers in response to inflation over 10 percent, 6 percent unemployment, 12 percent interest rates and "cuts in all areas of social spending". In 1980, there had been a number of successful industrial struggles, including by Philip Morris workers, wool storemen, NSW tanker drivers, Queensland power workers, government aircraft workers and Pilbara iron ore miners.

We saw the campaign for a shorter work week as "the most important focus for a broad campaign by the union movement". A 35-hour week campaign had been launched by the Amalgamated Metal Workers and Shipwrights Union, with the backing of the ACTU leadership. "While there is a big offensive being launched against it and there are moves to hold up the national wage case, it is still being discussed in terms of its inevitability."

What we didn't foresee was the success of the ALP and ACTU cutting across and blocking this rising militancy through the Prices and Incomes Accord, in the preparation of which the Communist Party played a crucial role.

On security, I gave a report to the June 10, 1980, Sydney branch meeting. We were prompted by a burglary of the Melbourne headquarters, which was an obvious cop job. Why now? ASIO legislation on June 1 had made such things legal. Also, there was the attempted Olympics boycott, and, our role in opposing it, and our increased impact in the unions.

The security involved making sure comrades were in the headquarters 24 hours a day, two comrades sleeping there overnight, one full-timer and one other comrade. It was not so much a defence guard – we were not expecting a violent attack. It was more a deterrent, against ASIO and the cops, who were less likely to attempt something if comrades were on the premises. No heroics were expected from comrades: if anything happened, they were to phone the cops and other comrades. Comrades were also asked to see this as a reason to be more conscious about security in the headquarters and in our political work in general.

We were still pretty sloppy, though. In September 1984 the Melbourne SWP office was burgled, and up to $2,000 in cash and equipment stolen.

Back to Resistance

Issue number 8 of *Resistance* magazine, March 1980, marked the new decade with a new masthead and an antiwar focus: "USSR aids Afghanistan" by Alan Lee (possibly Tony Forward) and a poster: "I WANT YOU! To go to war for my profits". Alan Lee also wrote "What Socialists Stand For".

The cover story of *Resistance* 9, in April, was "Nicaragua: Support the Revolution" by Jon Wright (Jon West). Other articles were "Unity is strength!" by Meg Connolly (Margo Condoleon), "Afghanistan: Fact and fiction" by Elizabeth Corrigan (Leesa Wheelahan) and "How I became a socialist" by Nita Keig. Tony Dewberry's "Kzotz" cartoon had an anti-uranium message. The poster was "Join us at the national conference of the Socialist Youth Alliance".

The national conference, June 14-16, 1980, held at the YWCA hall in Elizabeth Street in Melbourne, was attended by 180, mostly young, revolutionaries. The most important decision was to change the organisation's name back to Resistance (an overdue move in my opinion). Jim Percy gave a talk on the organisation's history. Resolutions were debated on Central America, the general political situation and organisational tasks for the coming year. Educational talks covered topics including Cuba, Nicaragua, Lenin, Trotsky, women's liberation and Afghanistan. There was a young workers panel. Barbara Burns from the NZ Young Socialists presented greetings.

The *Resistance* 10, July 1980, cover story was "Why schools are in revolt". Other articles included "A 35-hour week: How to fight unemployment", "The truth about Cuba" and a report on the Resistance national conference. Helen Pandazis wrote about Albert Park High School in Melbourne, where 40 copies of the previous issue had been sold and where school authorities were trying to prevent such things. Industrial coverage was provided by Meg Connolly (Margo Condoleon), "Doing 'men's' work" as a train driver, and by news of the Jobs for Women Campaign. The poster used Pink Floyd's "The Wall" verse: "Teacher – leave us kids alone", and in this issue "Kzotz" visited Cuba.

It appears that the issue 10 cover was popular with school students. *Resistance* 11, for September-October 1980, had a feature by Leesa Wheelahan, "Resistance hits schools" reporting that the Sydney Resistance branch had sold almost 300 copies in only one week at 13 schools. Wheelahan also described an *Illawarra Mercury* article that tried to create alarm over sales of *Resistance* on the NSW South Coast.

Also in that issue were "Revolution in Grenada!" by Jeff Richards, "Why Fraser must go" by Jon Wright, a "Resistance in action!" column and a "revolutionary portrait" of Karl Marx by Stephen Marks (Steve O'Brien). The poster declared: "Working people keep the country running. Working people should run the country." Kzotz was portrayed in trouble with the law.

In July we hosted a national speaking tour by Fatima Fellahi, a member of the Iranian Revolutionary Workers Party who had recently been freed from prison. She had toured the USA and New Zealand prior to her arrival in Australia. There were 220 people at her Sydney meeting and 100 at Sydney University. The subsequent Sydney branch meeting described it as the best tour we had had for years and reported that the Sydney public meeting had raised $540. There were 60 at the Brisbane meeting, 150 at her main Melbourne meeting, with a total of 700 in Melbourne, and about 200 in Perth.

At the Sydney University and Latrobe University meetings, the Spartacists did their best to disrupt both.

Launching our own school

The development of our own full-time party school played a very important role in our theoretical rethinking and the process of developing our own independent party.

The US SWP had set up their own leadership school, and invited us to send a comrade there for training. Jack Barnes was especially pressing in urging Jim Percy to attend. We, and especially Jim, were a little sceptical about it by that stage, fearing that Barnes might use the school as a way to inculcate acolytes, so we sent Dave Deutschmann, sort of as a guinea pig, since he was at a bit of a loose end, with no regular responsibilities in the leadership. The result confirmed our fears; he emerged as a "Jack says" factional agent for the US SWP.

So we set up our own live-in school in 1980, and it continued through to 1992, with our own building, four-month or one-month sessions for eight to 10 comrades at a time.

We had an initial discussion on cadre schools, and the possibility of setting up our own full-time school, possibly at an NC meeting in May, and at a Political Committee meeting on June 18, 1980. By July, we were starting to project our own school. We were very conscious at the time that we wanted a cadre school, in contrast to the US SWP's leadership school. The US school had little or no set syllabus, and it seemed primarily a venue for already established leaders to read and discuss among themselves, not a means of spreading knowledge of Marxism through the party, which is what we intended our school to do.

Our September 19, 1980, PC meeting had a more concrete discussion of plans for our school. We had come up with a possible list of students for the first session, comrades who both deserved it and could be freed from other assignments for four months: Peter Abrahamson, Brett Trenery, Catherine Brown, Eugene Sibelle, Diana Covell, Coral Wynter, with space for one or two more.

On October 15, Jim Percy reported to the PC on progress with our school, outlining the bad experiences of the US school, not wanting to be "under Jack's thumb". We'd worked out an outline of the sessions, which would have a different focus and emphasis than the US school, which concentrated on the writings of Marx. Ours was to concentrate very much on Lenin, his practice and his writings. It was arranged that all of our students would receive a full set of Lenin's *Collected Works*, all 45 volumes plus the index volumes. (Over the period of the school, throughout the 1980s and early 1990s, we probably distorted the distribution patterns of the English language edition of Lenin's *Collected Works* – more than 300 comrades went through the school, each getting a set, which was probably more than Moscow's Progress Publishers sold in the rest of the world.) Jim Percy and Dave Holmes worked on the initial syllabus, and both were involved in taking the classes. Other comrades were called in to give seminars on their areas of expertise. But it was Doug Lorimer who ended up running the schools, and living there permanently.

We were lucky in being able to get our own dedicated building. In the inner Sydney suburb of Dulwich Hill, it had been the home of the parents of comrades Coral Wynter and Geoff Channels, who inherited it when their parents died. They agreed to let the party have it for less than full compensation. It was a big four-bedroom house, with a garage, basement and large backyard. John Garcia was an architect and designed a six-bedroom, two-storey extension, and we hired a firm of reasonably cheap Vietnamese builders. So it ended up with a total of 10 bedrooms, a seminar room/library and a communal kitchen and dining room/common room.

There were many positive gains of this intensive educational process, but also some weaknesses. One question that later bothered me was why some (too many) of the school graduates later dropped away. Clearly, intensive study was not a guaranteed way of producing cadre.

After we were forced by financial pressures to sell the school building in 1992, we organised some one-month schools in our offices. The school building is now a boarding house. The tightening up of the hurdles that you have to jump through to remain on the dole would make it much harder to sustain such an ambitious full-time school today.

September 1980 SWP NC

We had an NC on September 20 or 21-22 with the agenda: the developing revolutions in the Caribbean; the world capitalist crisis and the coming Australian revolution; party development and cadre school; organisation; youth; security. The NC issued a call for the SWP eighth national conference. Jim Percy's report on the cadre school was later printed in the December 1982 issue of *Socialist Worker* under the title "Four Features of Our Revolutionary Party. Lessons from the SWP's first 10 years". The four features he described, which made the party school possible and necessary, were:

1. We were an inclusive party, based on a team leadership. This meant "a party of people who get satisfaction from the performance of the whole team, of the whole party. We're building a party of leaders who want to help other people become leaders." As a result of this approach, Jim said, we had made "substantial progress in the development of women leaders, more real progress than any other organisation in Australia".

2. We were an independent party. Here, Jim noted that, in our early contacts with the US SWP, the US comrades had helped us to learn this, by declining to offer the advice we sought. "The effect of that was to force us to become leaders ourselves." As well, the experience of the earlier factional struggle in the Fourth International, and the experience of having some of our comrades working in the FI centre, had also taught us that there was no substitute for building our own party, able to stand on its own two feet.

3. We were a Leninist party based on democratic centralism. Here, Jim considered our history and the question of why there had been "a comparatively high number of expulsions" in our early years. He said this was largely determined by our origins and by where we wanted to go. Our current grew out of a deliberately amorphous milieu and had either to win over or break with that milieu in order to build a party. Another factor was the 10-year faction fight in the FI and the 1972 split in our organisation. While these had been overcome, Jim said, they had left a residue: "People tended to be a little jumpy about political differences, which were seen as being factional by their very nature, as possibly leading to different parties or leading people to leave the movement. That's something we have to be very conscious [of] and attempt to overcome." Jim also looked at the loss of some members because of the industrial turn.

Could we have retained more of them?, he asked. "If we were stronger, better, smarter, if all our cadres were at a higher level, if all of us were more politically developed, we would have saved more; there's no doubt about that. But we did about the best we could, and took all the steps we had to take. Not to have acted decisively, to have compromised, would have jeopardised and demoralised the real cadre of the party as most of that cadre were going through decisive changes in their lives."

4.   We were an ambitious party. "Our ambition flows from the very nature of the task we've set ourselves, the overthrow of capitalism." The fact that we had always stretched ourselves had helped to maintain a healthy composition of the party even when most of our members were students rather than industrial workers.

The party cadre school was located in this context of an ambitious party. It would require an "enormous effort" from the entire party. It would also require changing priorities of some other party activities, Jim said. It would mean no longer assigning a leading comrade to the FI centre – something that we were already paying for "with money we didn't have". We would need a stronger national office, which would probably mean fewer full-timers in the branches. And it would mean a "partial stepping back" on the speed of getting leading comrades into industrial jobs (at the time of the plenum, 14 of 34 NC members were in industry, and 17 had industrial experience).

1981 political resolution

The draft political resolution for our January 1981 conference, adopted by the plenum, was a departure from our usual practice. "The world capitalist crisis and the coming Australian socialist revolution" was intended as a public document and printed in 20 tabloid pages (with a cover price of $1). In content, it was much broader than the usual conjunctural resolution. This was a broad summary of what we believed we had learned in a decade of party building about the strategic course toward socialist revolution. It contained both positions that we later rejected or modified and analyses that have held up well in the light of later events. The fundamental context of the resolution was: "The defeat of US imperialism in South Vietnam in April 1975 was a watershed in the struggle between imperialism and the tide of revolution in the semicolonial world ... This victory has inspired a rising tide of revolutionary struggles that threatens to overflow the imperialist defences."

The first of the resolution's five major sections, headed "The shift in the world relationship of class forces", discussed this shift and the state of the world class struggle in three contexts. The first was the rise of anti-imperialist struggles in Asia, Africa, the Middle East and Latin America.

The resolution then explained recent events in China, the Soviet Union and Eastern Europe in terms of the traditional Trotskyist analysis of Stalinism as a bureaucratic caste parasitically extracting material privileges from the workers states and seeking to maintain its position by seeking "peaceful coexistence" with imperialism. It looked hopefully to the then occurring creation of independent unions, raising "the possibility of the development of a conscious revolutionary current in Poland. Such a revolutionary current would dramatically transform the prospects for political revolution in Poland, the rest of Eastern Europe, and finally the Soviet Union itself."

The third part, headed "The crisis of imperialist domination", discussed the difficulty of US and allied imperialisms in intervening militarily to protect their interests because of the widespread opposition to war and distrust of imperialist governments.

All of these points were accurate as far as they went; even the optimism regarding Poland was called only a "possibility", not a certainty or even a better than 50-50 likelihood. But there was something missing from this "shift in the relationship of class forces": the relationship between the organised working class and the capitalists in the major imperialist countries. This was not because of a failure of analysis but because there had not been a significant shift in that relationship.

We of course realised that such a shift was necessary, but we mistakenly believed that it had already begun: the working class "was returning to centre stage", and "the long detour of the world revolution" was coming to an end. The resolution looked forward to a rapid intensification of the class struggle in Australia and other imperialist countries, spurred by a developing economic crisis:

"The [union] bureaucrats of both left and right either don't believe in the power of the organised working class, or they do believe in it – and fear it like the plague. In either case, their whole approach is to try to undermine the proletariat's confidence in its own strength and thus 'justify' their class-collaborationist manoeuvres.

"But it is becoming increasingly difficult for the bureaucrats to come up with credible justifications of their policies, because in the present period class collaboration not only doesn't work, but is also increasingly seen not to work …

"… the bureaucrats are less and less able to pose as people capable of delivering the goods unless they allow the ranks to take the kind of militant action that really can produce results."

We underestimated the ability of Stalinists, social democrats and union bureaucrats to prevent a concerted fight back against capital's attacks, and the ability of capitalists to grant short-term concessions when necessary to assist that project.

The resolution reaffirmed our existing strategy of trying to build a "class-struggle left wing" in the union movement. But our mistaken view of the ALP as a "bourgeois workers party", a party with "a dual class nature", caused the resolution to lay out what can now be seen as a quite mistaken perspective:

"… In the future we will see big battles in the Labor Party as radicalising workers seek to use it as a vehicle for their political needs. They will find it lacking, but because of the close organic links between the unions and the Labor Party, and because at this stage the political ideas of the working class are generally formulated through the Labor Party, motion towards the building of a class-struggle left wing will be reflected in the Labor Party as well as in the trade unions."

There was nothing inherently impossible in the idea of a party like the ALP developing a fighting left wing, even to the point of splitting the party – as later happened in New Zealand. But our mistaken view of the class character of the ALP led us to treat this not very likely possibility as a virtual certainty.

1980 federal elections

Federal elections were held on October 18, 1980. They came in the wake of the US and Australian ruling class scare campaign around the Soviet intervention in Afghanistan, and their failed attempt to boycott the Moscow Olympics. The SWP stood in nine House of Representatives seats. We produced and distributed 1 million pieces of literature, leaflets and posters, and had been campaigning in some way since the start of the year.

Our results were varied but creditable: Brisbane, Mark Carey in Griffith, 3.97 percent; Newcastle, Geoff Payne, 1.82 percent; Sydney, Jamie Doughney, Blaxland, 4.96 percent; Sydney, Nita Keig, Sydney, 2.50 percent; Wollongong, Andrew Jamieson, Cunningham, 1.67 percent; Melbourne, Sol Salby, Wills, 1.03 percent; Melbourne, Lynne Bryer, Gellibrand, 3.42 percent; Adelaide, Therese Doyle, Hindmarsh, 2.16 percent; Perth, Steve Painter, Swan, 1.21 percent.

We came out with a *DA* cover the issue before the elections (321) campaigning "For a Labor Government With Socialist Policies." Allen Myers wrote "Win or lose, the fight goes on", and "Fraser threatens another 1975". Martin

Mulligan (Martin Tuck) described it as the "Most ambitious SWP campaign yet". Peter Holloway reported, "SWP's Painter debates opponents" at Perth's Midlands markets: "'The capitalist system is responsible for the crisis, therefore the capitalists should bear the brunt of it …', said Painter.

"It was very obvious that of the four candidates, only Painter was able to draw any kind of enthusiastic response from the audience.

"He may have represented the smallest party, but his ideas certainly struck a chord with a large number of people in the audience."

Jim McIlroy reported in *DA* 324, "Fraser majority slashed in election", and Allen Myers analysed "Why Labor lost". Jamie Doughney described "What did SWP campaign achieve?" He also analysed the left campaigns, "Thousands seek left alternative to Labor", with the final votes of the SWP, CPA and SLL.

Arson attack in Sydney

We'd had a good year to that point in Resistance and the DSP, with our campaigns, party building steps and election campaign, but our stepped-up security precautions in the Sydney offices in June weren't enough to deter an arson attack on October 25. *DA* 323's cover protested the "Arson Attack On Socialist Offices". Jim McIlroy reported on it and announced that an Emergency Fire Fund Appeal had been launched.

In the next issue, Ray Fox (Jamie Doughney) reported "SWP calls for full inquiry into arson", following it with "SWP presses for fire investigation" (*DA* 325), and then "Pressure mounts for action on arson" (*DA* 326), reporting that the CPA and SPA had supported our call for action.

Luckily, we were insured and were able to make a fairly quick move just up the road in George Street, not on the ground floor, but in a reasonable office space, and we didn't lose financially. In the December 3 *DA* we were able to publicise our new offices and bookshop, at 761A George Street, with a grand opening and fire sale. The following issue announced that we had raised $4,161 in the emergency fire fund appeal so far. The February 3 *DA*, the first for the year, explained that it was delayed by the need to shift headquarters following the arson attack three months earlier. Almost $5,000 had been raised in the emergency fire appeal.

SWP eighth national conference, January 1981

The SWP eighth national conference was held January 4-9, 1981, at the Women's College, Sydney University. It was attended by 220, our largest conference so far. Reports presented were: The Developing Revolutions in the Caribbean; International Political Situation; The Capitalist Crisis and the Coming Australian Socialist Revolution; Program for a Socialist Australia (this reported on our draft program); Perspectives for Revolutionary Youth in the '80s; Building the SWP.

We had drafted a "Program for a socialist Australia," which was adopted by the SWP Political Committee on December 19, 1980. It was being presented, not for a vote at this conference, but as the basis for discussion leading up to the ninth national conference.

An indication of the progress we'd made with the turn is given by the statistics on the NC elected. Out of the full list of 25 comrades, 15 were on full time (three of these about to go into industry, or had been) and 10 were in industry. On the alternate list of 11, two were on full time, nine were in industry.

The congress rally, titled "The Struggle for Marxism in Australia", was promoted as the launch of our full-time cadre school. The first seven comrades for the school were introduced: Peter Abrahamson, Catherine Brown, Mario Estrella, Eugene Sibelle, Brett Trenery, Coral Wynter and Leesa Wheelahan. The school was scheduled to start in March.

There was a Spanish-language report and discussion of the political resolution, and special talks on Marx and Engels as revolutionary journalists, by Dave Deutschmann, and Propaganda, Agitation and Organisation – The Bolsheviks and the Revolutionary Press, by Jon West, and a special presentation on Winning Jobs for Women.

We had multiple orientation sessions for those attending their first SWP conference, and workshops on finances, *DA* circulation, Latin American work, ALP work and recruiting. We showed a range of radical political films: *Nicaragua '78*, *The Harder They Come*, *Frontline*, *Norma Rae*, *El Salvador – Revolution or Death* and *Harlan County, USA*.

At this time, Resistance had 133 members.

Organisational projections

My party-building report pointed out that we had basically completed the turn and were at a "post-turn stage, a stage when our milieu is the industrial working class". Fraction meetings were held during the conference, and improving our industrial fractions was projected as an important task; "talking socialism on the job" was our shorthand phrase for influencing fellow workers.

In this context, our main focus should be on "… a return to concentrating on the central institutions that are necessary to building the party today", chief among them *Direct Action*. "The most important party building task ahead of all of us … is to significantly increase the circulation of *DA*."

We needed a campaign to get full participation in *DA* sales. We'd had 62 percent participation nationally over the past year. Everyone was expected to sell a minimum of two hours per week. We were aiming for that 3,000 target again. We were projecting an industrial sales month from mid-February to mid-March, and blitzing campuses during O-weeks. We succeeded in 1980 with two very successful sub drives, I said, and planned to do that again this year.

We decided to persevere with supporters clubs, and also experiment with *DA* reader circles.

"In Sydney we've found it hard to fail on dinner dances. Whatever we do, we get 100-200 people there, and raise $1000-$2500."

"We survived the fire, and we survived each crisis, and at each step we were forced to respond in an ambitious way …

"We'd already projected the acquisition of a building for the party school, and major extension and reconstruction of it. The fire forced us not only into a more comfortable building for the NO, for Sydney branch, and a bigger bookshop and potential coffee shop. It also forced us to buy the Annandale building for *Direct Action* and the printshop … In the building in Annandale we'll have a better darkroom, much better typesetting facilities, and a proper printing operation."

We set a press and education fund drive target of $50,000.

I concluded by stressing how vital it was for us to grow. "We're a party with big goals, and we set our sights high. But in order to achieve those goals, we need to *recruit*."

At our PC meeting on January 10, 1981, Jim Percy was elected as national secretary, and we elected a secretariat of Allen Myers, John Garcia, John Percy and Peta Stewart.

We made the decision to set up supporters' clubs following a report by Jim to a PC meeting in early February.

The February 11 *DA* was the last with "incorporating Militant" on the masthead. The first forum in our new Sydney offices had 70 attending, with John Garcia speaking on El Salvador.

Jim reported to the PC on February18 on our Afghanistan reply to the US SWP. We decided to circulate it publicly, that having a public debate for the Fourth International would make it more attractive. Doug reported from overseas on April 6, 1981, that at the US SWP plenum, Jack seemed irritated by us, our tone, complaining about our "$4 public book" on Afghanistan.

A follow-up report from Doug on April 14 informed us that John Steele, a leader of the Canadian FI group, agreed with us on Afghanistan, and possibly a majority in the Canadian group did. He also informed us that a central US SWP leader, Gus Horowitz, was taking a computer job, an indication he was now out of the central leadership.

April 1981 Resistance conference

The April 18-20, 1981, Resistance 11th national conference was held at the YWCA in Melbourne. Impressive large banners decorated the hall. More than 200 attended. It was our largest conference yet, and we had 20 joiners from it. *DA* 341 reported: "More than half [of] those attending were young industrial workers, and almost one quarter were secondary students".

Resistance 14 reported on the conference, with pictures of the conference banners, and reporting greetings to the conference from the Young Socialists of Iran, the US YSA and the FI United Secretariat. The centre poster was Che Guevara, with his slogan, "To make a revolution, it takes revolutionaries".

Resistance 15, July-September 1981, had a Resistance in Action column, reporting on victimisation attempts by parents, teachers and cops at Tuart Hill High. The centre poster was "Solidarnosc", and Tony Forward wrote on "Poland: What is really happening". We started a column, Revolutionary Portraits, with Catherine Barker (Catherine Brown) writing a short history of James Connolly. It also carried an article on "NSW's only woman shunter", an interview with Christine Broi.

Our women comrades had played a key role in opening up other previously male-only jobs, for example engine drivers. In May 1980, *DA* 300 had reported on the "Breakthrough for Women in VicRail" and interviewed Margo Condoleon, who had succeeded in getting a job as an engine driver. A year later, *DA* March 4, 1981, had Margo on the cover and an article, "One year as a trainee engine driver".

In early 1981, the US stepped up its war on El Salvador, and we helped to organise rallies in solidarity with El Salvador through CISCAC in June. In preparation, *DA* of June 10 carried an El Salvador four-page lift-out, with articles by Ron Poulsen and Doug Lorimer and from the US SWP. A Melbourne *DA* dinner, with a keynote speech by John Garcia on El Salvador, raised $3,300. The rallies involved 500 in Melbourne and 150 in Perth.

Preparing for growth

I gave a report to the Melbourne branch meeting on June 14, 1981, as part of a tour to Brisbane, Melbourne and Perth, getting a feel for the state of the party in order to prepare the tasks and perspectives report for the upcoming July 11-12 NC, and to coordinate organisation of finances, sales, subs and recruiting.

In my report I noted that internationally the class struggle had heated up, e.g. in El Salvador, and we had responded with CISCAC actions. In Poland, the political revolution continued to unfold. In Ireland, there was a huge upsurge with hunger strikes and big demonstrations and Bobby Sands' election victory. There was a radicalisation in the unions in Britain and some other advanced capitalist countries. Fraser's attacks here had continued, but there had been some victories. This was not reflected yet in a major influx of workers into the ALP, but made it necessary for us to step up our work there. *Labor Militant* would be our big new initiative.

"Even campus students, politically quiescent for quite a few years, are starting to radicalise again." There was good response to our El Salvador film, and big meetings and rallies in response to cutbacks. "And we're increasingly in better shape to take advantage of these new openings and opportunities. Firstly, the successful turn is behind us. It's now the framework for all our work.

"A second feature to note is that, after suffering a loss of members while making the turn, this year we've turned the corner and have been starting to grow. Slowly, but it's been real growth." And that would be our key task in the period ahead.

"Thirdly, we're also in an excellent position to take advantage of this new period because of the strong apparatus and structure we've developed. *DA*, our NO, the school, our full-time staff. We're able to service an organisation many times our size, a skeleton waiting to put a lot of flesh on our bones.

"The more astute among our political opponents are able to recognise this. The CPA is our main opponent, and we know they fear us …

"One story gives an idea how some of their leadership see us. Jon West reported that John Kizzane, a CPA full-timer on *Intervention* and in the CPA NO, had remarked that 'the SWP had "come of age"'. He pointed to our school, a big project, but he knew we'd pull it off, because what we say, we do. Secondly, our differences with the US comrades on Afghanistan showed a political maturity. Thirdly, it was clear that we'd successfully completed the turn, we had established ourselves in industry. (These were interesting observations, contrasted with the inabilities of the CPA to complete comparable projects.)"

Marxist education

We had addressed the need for Marxist education much more seriously with our decision to set up our own school. But there was always a danger that it could make us feel satisfied that we were doing our bit and take attention away from the need for regular educational activity in the branches. Eventually, we established two series of classes, which were an ongoing feature of branch activity for several decades. "Introduction to Socialism" was aimed at party contacts to explain our basic ideas and, if possible, persuade them to join us. The "Introduction to Marxism" series was intended for new members, to give them a grounding in the basics of Marxism.

We had established a tradition of holding Resistance/SYA educational camps even before the SWL was established, and this continued even as we were establishing the party school. For example, *DA* in April 1980 announced SYA educational camps in Adelaide, Sydney, Melbourne, Brisbane and Perth over the Easter weekend. Over June 6-7, 1981, an SWP-Resistance educational camp was held at Camp Haveta in Minto, near Campbelltown, and drew around 50 people.

We also encouraged branches to conduct classes on particular topics; the National Office would generally circulate a list of readings and discussion questions. Special series organised around this time included a study of the four books on the US Teamsters Union in the 1930s by Farrell Dobbs of the US SWP; the party-building ideas of US Trotskyist James P. Cannon; and classes on women's liberation.

Labor Militant

A separate publication for our work in the ALP, *Labor Militant,* was planned at the Political Committee meeting on April 3, 1981. We projected it as a monthly. I gave an outline of the reasons to the Melbourne branch meeting on June 14, 1981, in a report from the National Office:

First, the international situation was encouraging. There was increasing politicisation and polarisation in the British Labour Party, with large numbers of new members flooding in. It seemed possible that the British example could encourage similar developments here.

Second, the official ALP lefts, the Steering Committee and the Socialist Left, had degenerated to the point that they could no longer contain and restrain people who were looking for serious solutions. This was reflected in a proliferation of papers, and although there was no big influx of workers, some young people were looking for socialist solutions and we wanted to reach them.

Third, we were in a position organisationally for such a move. With the turn behind us and a solid organisation, we needed to *implement* our ALP orientation. We'd never had a proper framework or vehicle. We'd been without a clear idea of how to implement our ALP orientation. *Labor Militant* provided a framework for the first time.

It would force us to write and talk with this milieu in mind. It would teach us *how* to get across our ideas, and enable us to draw in and organise our contacts in the ALP. It was also a possible recruiting vehicle. Our advantage over other tendencies in the ALP was that we had a national spread. That suited the type of paper we wanted, a national paper concentrating on important theoretical and political questions, rather than playing the ALP numbers game.

I reported on the reactions so far. There was a good impact at the NSW ALP state conference, and also a good response in Melbourne. There was an already existing group in Adelaide around John Scott and other of our ex-members that we would have to work with. *Labor Militant* began as a tabloid paper, and soon became an A4 magazine, aiming at monthly publication.

Optimistic SWP NC, July 1981

Our National Committee met on July 11-12, 1981, with reports: Poland, world movement, political situation and tasks, Resistance perspectives and youth, organisation, cadre school information.

The New Zealand SAL sent greetings. We reported that the tendency had grown to 230 total members, in the party and Resistance, with 39 comrades on full time. The second session of our cadre school would begin on August 16.

My organisational report declared:

> It's been a great year so far politically, the objective situation for revolutionaries has been very favourable. But just as importantly, so far this year it's been a good year for us *organisationally*.
>
> We've been able to build our party, the subjective factor, in conjunction with these Australian and international developments. It's a good sign of our correct political perspectives and our serious attitude to party building tasks.
>
> In fact, all the organisational campaigns we projected at our conference have been achieved or are on target. It's not often that you can say that at a plenum or conference. Our achievements are commendable:
> - We've been recruiting well and growing.
> - We went over our sub-drive target.
> - *DA* sales are way up; the bundles went from 1900 at the end of

last year to about 2700 now, and actual sales almost doubled.
- Our sustainer to the NO has risen steadily, and we should be able to go over the $12/member/week target before the end of the year. Our fund drive is nearly at $30,000, and we should be campaigning to go well over our $50,000 goal.

Not a bad half-year!

And these organisational successes allow us to carry out a bolder political intervention. Because our organisational campaigns are succeeding, we've been able to produce *Labor Militant;* we've been able to get involved in Irish work; we can plan to intervene in anti-cutback actions and so on.

But we have to always remember that any such interventions, stepped up political interventions, are contingent upon a continuing serious approach to the bedrock tasks of party building – *DA* sales, finances, recruiting.

Both sides of our party-building activity are interrelated, interdependent of course. But sometimes the objective situation or particular circumstances makes it hard to carry out one or the other.

What we have at the moment is a situation where both sides of our activity are going well, and we have to make sure we make the most of the current situation, because in times like these we can make big gains …

After suffering a slow loss of members while making the turn, this year we've turned the corner and have started to grow …

We have a huge number of contacts, in nearly all branches. And all branches are strong, homogeneous, politically clear, in a great situation to grow.

I concluded that there was no reason why, by the end of the year, we couldn't be around 200 full and provisional members. That should be the goal, set at this plenum.

Sales and finances the bedrock

Charts were distributed on party membership through 1981. We'd achieved modest growth over the first half of the year, in both Resistance and the party. The SWP had grown from 150 to 157, Resistance non-party comrades from 62 to 73. The total in industry grew from 70 to 91, so that comrades in industry plus full timers went from 69 percent to 83 percent of the total membership.

The national average sustainer went from $9.08 to $10.54. On sales, "Comparing this year and last year, it's like two different parties. There's been a qualitative turn around!" We presented an analysis of the past four subscription drives:

- August-September 1979, 828 (104 percent of target)
- March April 1080, 1,053 (103 percent)
- August-September 1980, 592 (118 percent)
- May-June 1981, 1,133 (103 percent)

And *DA* sales had risen from a weekly average of 1,482 in 1979 to 2,058 at present. We set an October 1981 sub drive for 750 (later cancelled).

Our 1981 fund drive target was $58,000, and the tally reported in the last *DA* reached $57,119, so the target was probably surpassed. In the next two years, we experienced further growth and consolidation, enabling us to buy two very large headquarters buildings, in Sydney and Melbourne.

International travel

Jamie Doughney and Jim Percy had gone to the United States and applied there for Polish visas in order to attend the Solidarnosc conference in September 1981. However, before they departed from New York, it was decided that Jim would go to Poland and Jamie would visit Ireland. From there, Jamie sent back reports, articles and interviews, including one with Bernadette McAliskey (*DA* October 7).

On his way back from Poland, Jim stopped in Sri Lanka to talk with the FI comrades there. In a phone conversation with him on September 17, I reported that our party membership was now 173, and combined party-Resistance total up to 250.

Problems

But there were some problems that slowed us down. The US SWP degeneration encouraged a small split in our ranks. The election of the Hawke ALP government and its Prices and Incomes Accord defused and diverted much of the increasing union militancy of the preceding period. So we didn't have the rapid growth we were anticipating for the rest of the decade, but we did experience other interesting developments, like the Nuclear Disarmament Party, and other experiences of attempting unity.

At our Political Committee meeting on October 11, 1981, we rejoined Peter Boyle to the party. Signs of political differences were developing with Nita Keig and Jamie Doughney (over Poland). Nita and Jamie were not on the secretariat for "non-technical reasons". And we had increasing worries about the direction in which the US SWP was heading.

A week later, the PC discussed a looming financial crisis, which made us decide to cancel the sub drive and step up our sustainer campaign. We reduced the number of full-timers, in Newcastle, Adelaide and Brisbane. Jamie gave a report on the New Zealand SAL, which was making a "wrong transposition of US experience to NZ" and following the US SWP not very thinkingly. They had written documents on Afghanistan and the Labour Party, and wanted to come to our conference and plenum to press their case.

Ford strike

Our members were involved in the big 1981 Ford strike in Melbourne. Renfrey Clarke, who was employed at Ford, was known as a militant and an author of articles in *Direct Action*. In August, a month before the strike began, Renfrey published a three-part series on "The crisis in the vehicle industry". This explained that the car industry globally was suffering a crisis of overproduction that was both increasing competition and forcing the car corporations to boost productivity, including by seeking to standardise car parts and models for the entire world market (the "world car"). The Australian car industry, which involved five different makers, had survived only thanks to tariffs and import quotas, and it was overdue for a shakeout. However, at that time, as a result of a "resources boom" – a flow of international capital into mining and minerals processing – the Australian car industry was doing well:

"With the car market in almost every other producing country in deep slump, the Australian industry finds itself in a paradoxical situation. New vehicle sales in the first half of 1981 were the highest since the record year 1976." Profits were booming. This situation must have given many Ford workers both a sense of urgency and some confidence about the possibility of winning a wage rise, and a further impetus for action had been provided by federal and state Coalition government budgets that had taken an average of $10-15 a week from working-class families.

In early September, the *Age* reported that Ford expected a profit of $100 million in 1981. On September 18, VBEF members at Ford's Broadmeadows plant voted for an indefinite strike in support of a $30 a week wage claim. As Geoff Streeton (Renfrey Clarke) pointed out in *DA* 362, Ford's planned profit for that year amounted to $20,000 per worker. Renfrey himself was sacked without explanation by the company less than two hours before the strike vote.

After a seven-week strike, a court-imposed secret ballot voted narrowly for a return to work. Geoff Streeton reported in *DA* 368: "Shop stewards at Ford, as well as the VBEF officials, had condemned the secret ballot as an undemocratic interference in the affairs of the union movement.

"In particular, the workers were expected to vote in the isolation of their own home, while subjected to a media anti-strike barrage, and without the benefit of arguments to continue the strike that would have been presented in a normal mass meeting." In addition, there were numerous irregularities in the ballot.

In the aftermath, workers from Ford Broadmeadows attended the November meeting of the VBEF Victorian branch and presented motions condemning the roles of VBEF federal secretary Len Townsend, the federal executive and the state executive – their failure to organise serious support for the strike or to take a principled stand against the court-imposed ballot. The meeting passed the motions overwhelmingly.

Other car plants in Victoria decided it would be wise to get rid of our comrades. Two days before Christmas, five of them were sacked: Bruce Hercus, Reihana Mohideen and Chris Slee from GM-H and Malcolm Johnson and Victor Moore from AMI-Toyota. The companies again gave no explanation aside from saying that they had the right to hire and fire as they pleased. But as *DA* 375 noted, all five had been active unionists in their plants and had also helped to organise solidarity with the Ford Broadmeadows strike.

January 1982 SWP NC

Before our SWP and Resistance educational conference in January 1982, we held an NC January 1-4, with a wide range of reports: The Crisis of Stalinism; The Fraser Offensive and the Party's Tasks in Industry; Developments in the ALP and the Party's Tasks; Party Organisation and Perspectives for 1982; Resistance Tasks and Perspectives for 1982; World Movement: The Differences within the FI on the Turn, Cuba, Poland and Iran; World Movement: The Labor Party Question in the USA, Britain, Canada and New Zealand; World Movement: Afghanistan, Report for the PC and counter-report.

Steve Painter's report on building the party noted that 1981 had been a good year for us. "For the first time since we made the turn, we grew." The total tendency grew by 16 percent. "We're more homogeneous, while other groups have problems."

We needed to grow further, to respond to the promising political situation, so we "want to prioritise our party-building activities", especially *DA* sales, which had to be a "top priority". We again projected the 3,000 sales goal we had set for ourselves a year earlier. We also needed properly organised industrial fractions, talking socialism through them, and taking our political campaigns onto the job. Youth work was also important.

"The most important united-front work that we've been doing and that we'll continue to do is around Central America and the Caribbean ... Even if we have to carry the CISCAC or CASC [Central America Support Committee] committees on our own, we want to keep up our work in this area." The work had to be given priority. There was a useful development in Sydney in breaking the stranglehold of the SPA over the Australia-Cuba Friendship Society. Two comrades were now on the executive. It was important to break down the massive ignorance over Cuba. And we wanted the labour movement to take more notice of the example of the Cuban Revolution. It was also an opportunity to start to forge links with the Castroist leadership.

"Another area of our international work that we want to pay some attention to is our CARPA work", around the dissident Indonesian author Pramoedya and East Timor. Also we wanted to "investigate stepping up solidarity work with the Vietnamese revolution".

On Polish solidarity, we had had six actions off the ground quickly in defence of Solidarnosc at the end of 1981. "Our quick response cut across the attempts of rightists to take up the issue"; they were labour movement protests in defence of Polish workers. The other area of international work we'd been involved in in 1981 had been Ireland, in particular solidarity with the H-Block prisoners.

"We're a small party that takes on big projects. We always have, and we've very rarely failed to pull them off. But the projects we take on – our international work, the school, the weekly – stretch us close to the limit", Steve said. So there was a necessity for recruiting; branches should be seen as recruiting machines. We needed regular forums, probably fortnightly in Sydney and Melbourne and monthly in the smaller branches, and regular social functions at our headquarters, plus regular Introduction to Socialism classes.

We had set a fundraising target of $50,000 in 1981 (having gone over $58,000 the previous year, when we had special expenses as a result of the fire, and moving to new headquarters), and projected a per capita sustainer rising to $13. This was needed for our international trips, our FI responsibilities and our Asian work, such as "our decision to aid their work by having some Asian comrades attend our school".

What didn't we achieve among our conference projections? "We dropped the experiment with supporters clubs; too much of our experience with these bodies was negative. The basic problem was that concentrating so many people who'd lost confidence in the party tended mainly to reinforce a lot of their cynicism. When *Labor Militant* appeared, we found that a number of the best of these people got interested in it, and that gave them something concrete to do."

The demands of the school forced us to expand our National Office from four full-timers to six. "The other area of our apparatus where we've registered major progress in 1981 has been our printshop … the gains that we've made there in terms of skill and productivity have enabled us over the year to churn out a constant steam of propaganda and educational material. The weekly *DA*, five issues of *Resistance*, four issues of *Labor Militant*, several bulletins, the Afghanistan document, and numerous posters and leaflets."

We had published four books – Trotsky on the Balkans War, on the Three Mile Island near meltdown, a Resistance book and on Ireland – and a book on Grenada was well advanced. In January we published *What Socialists Stand For, An introduction to Resistance*, by Jon West. In February, *Ireland Unfree*, edited by Martin Mulligan (Martin Tuck), was published.

Steve reported on our cadre school: why we were able to set it up, and why we needed it. Given the situation in the FI and the US SWP, "we had to develop ourselves as Marxists able to operate on our own account in our own framework". The turn made it necessary. In 1981 we put 17 cadres through the school; in 1982 we expected the figure to be at least 25.

The reports from the debate on Afghanistan at the NC were published in the SWP Discussion Bulletin.

SWP and Resistance Educational Conference, January 1982

We followed the NC with an SWP and Resistance Socialist Educational Conference, on January 6-10, 1982, at Hawkesbury Agricultural College. Two hundred and fifty members and contacts attended, our biggest gathering yet. By agreeing to a flat day rate – that is, no accommodation only and no meals only – we had been able to get a rate almost half of the college's normal conference accommodation cost.

Feature talks at the conference were: Imperialism's drive to war, by Peta Stewart; Six years of the Fraser offensive and the workers' fight back, Jon West; Revolutionary trade unionism, John Garcia; Poland, the developing political revolution, Nita Keig; and Ten years of building the revolutionary party, Jim Percy. (We also slotted in my NC report on the CPA as a conference talk.)

Special guests were Mac Warren from the US SWP, speaking on the US Black struggle; a comrade from Sri Lanka; and Russell Johnson from the NZ SAL (he presented the NZ SAL's views on Afghanistan and the Labour Party).

The conference rally marked our 10th anniversary. In the first *DA* after the education conference, Rose McCann reported it as our "largest conference yet" and quoted me as pointing to five aspects of the SWP today: "Firstly, our orientation to youth, our success in relating to young people and winning them to socialism. Secondly, our strong base in industry. Thirdly, our orientation to women workers, our success in fighting against women's oppression, waging the Jobs for Women campaign, and training women leaders. Fourthly, the inclusive nature of our party, our ability to weld together a team of people from different backgrounds and our ability to carry out successful fusions with other groups. And fifthly, our internationalism, both our internationalist program and our increasing international composition. More and more our party is reflecting the nature of the Australian working class."

A Political Committee meeting on February 2 assessed the educational conference. I gave a report on the talks, the features and the college facilities. We booked the next year for January 5-11, and discussed how to build it, expecting more than 300 to attend next time. We also discussed our growth:

1976	132
1977	171
1978	188
1979	205
1981	222
1982	266

The PC also assessed the NC Afghanistan discussion, Nita Keig claiming that the discussion had "put pressure" on people.

In March we launched a four-week drive to gain 500 subs to *Direct Action*. It was very successful, reaching a total of 576.

El Salvador solidarity

As US attacks on Nicaragua were stepped up and the civil war in El Salvador escalated, we devoted increasing attention. The March 24 *DA* reported plans for Rafael Gonzalez, a representative of the FDR/FMLN of El Salvador, to tour Australia. The cover of the March 31 issue declared: "Central America – the New Vietnam".

Public meetings for Gonzalez sponsored by CISCAC drew 600 at the main meeting in Sydney, 300 in Melbourne and 250 in Adelaide. He also addressed the national consultation of CISCAC in Melbourne and the rally of the Resistance national conference. In *DA* 387, Lynda Boland reported that in just 12 days, Gonzalez had "travelled 7000 kilometres, speaking at some 22 meetings and receptions, six press conferences, and 29 media interviews to explain the situation in El Salvador to thousands of people". The article emphasised the success of the tour in garnering public support from ALP politicians and trade union leaders.

DA 386 reported international solidarity actions with El Salvador: a march of 40,000 in Washington, DC, from *Intercontinental Press,* and demonstrations in Britain, Denmark, West Germany, the Netherlands and Canada.

I had attended the World Conference in Solidarity with the People of El Salvador in Mexico City from March 26 to 28, and I reported on this at the Gonzalez meetings in Sydney and Melbourne. My report to the meetings was carried in *DA* 389 under the heading "Nicaragua has won! El Salvador will win!":

"Solidarity committees from 42 countries were represented.

"There were more than 80 organisations present from outside Mexico (the largest contingent coming from the United States).

"More than 130 organisations and groups from Mexico itself were in attendance."

I concluded by saying that the next CISCAC national consultation would discuss a proposal to affiliate to the World Front in Solidarity with El Salvador, which had been established by the Mexico City conference. We would be organising educational materials about the struggle in El Salvador and solidarity actions with El Salvador, Nicaragua and Grenada.

On June 12 CISCAC rallies calling for "US Hands off El Salvador" drew 800 each in Melbourne and Sydney, 100 in Adelaide and 150 in Perth.

April 1982 Resistance Conference

In January, on the Australia Day weekend, 1,050 copies of *Resistance* were sold at a Melbourne rock concert.

The Resistance 12th national conference was held in Melbourne, April 10-12. More than 300 attended, and more than $1,300 was raised in the rally collection to help defray the costs of the FDR/FMLN tour of Rafael Gonzalez, who was a featured speaker. A huge mural that we'd painted in Sydney stretched the length of the hall: "The revolution advances". Sixty-five percent of participants were industrial workers, and 45 percent were women.

Resistance magazine number 19, May-June, included a lift-out on Central America. There was a poster supporting the FMLN, "An armed people will never be humiliated". Revolutionary Portraits was on Malcolm X.

Hardening of pro-US SWP opposition

At the SWP NC meeting held on April 24-26, 1982, the pro-US SWP opposition in our party became firmer. Jim Percy reported on Imperialism's Drive to

War and the Fight Against it, Doug Lorimer on The Political Situation and the Party's Tasks, Dave Holmes on Finance and Organisation; Allen Myers reported for the PC majority on Poland, and Nita Keig for the PC minority; and I gave a report on the world movement, following my trip to the US, Mexico and Europe for the FI United Secretariat meeting.

I reiterated that the two key issues in the FI were the turn and the orientation to the Cuban current. "The 'Cuban question' has been a vital one for the Trotskyist movement for 22 years. It has been the acid test for revolutionaries for over two decades and it still is. With the extension of the Cuban Revolution to Nicaragua and Grenada, and soon we hope El Salvador and Guatemala, it has become central to a correct revolutionary perspective." It was a pretty distorted report by me, not understanding how far the US SWP degeneration had already gone, despite some disturbing developments and the views I'd received from Peter Camejo in New York and Mexico City. Jim Percy's and Doug Lorimer's reports were printed in the May Party Organiser.

The Poland debate was thorough, and began with a PC statement carried in the February 10 *DA*, "Defend the Polish Workers". The majority and minority reports were printed in the Discussion Bulletin, as well as the PC statement and the PC minority counter-line amendments.

I made the point under Allen's report on Poland: "Even if we're wrong on Afghanistan, and on Poland, it's better we think it through and make our own mistakes than adopt a position because the US SWP says so, or because the Usec says so, or Havana Radio does". I had had this out with Mac Warren when I was in New York. I told him the fact that we might be wrong was less important than thinking it out for ourselves. "Don't appeal to authority, that it's 'not conceivable that the US SWP would make mistakes on such a fundamental question'. Imagine taking that argument to its conclusion; think it out. That's not the sort of party we need."

We raised a hypothetical question concerning the Poland debate. What if one of our Hong Kong comrades was arrested in China? Or 1,000 comrades were involved, and Chinese workers? Wouldn't we try to support them by raising similar demands to those we were raising regarding Poland? Or would we refuse to participate in protests unless they were organised by workers' organisations, as the minority wanted us to do in the case of the Polish workers?

SWP NC, July 1982. Organisational experimentation

In June 1982, we opened a new SWP and Resistance centre in Granville for our western Sydney branch. Peter Annear was the party organiser. The July 7

CLOCKWISE FROM TOP: Large portraits of revolutionary heroes featured in SWP May Day contingents; Martin Tuck; Rose McCann, November 1978; John Percy in early 1980s

CLOCKWISE FROM TOP: Peter Robb, Marcia Langton, John McCarthy; 23 Abercrombie St, Chippendale, shortly before it was purchased as SWP national office and Sydney headquarters; Dick Nichols

CLOCKWISE FROM TOP LEFT: Candidate picture of Steve Painter for 1983 SWP election campaign; candidate picture of Dot Tumney for the same year; Doug Jordan, April 1978; Will Wroth and Rob Miller, at October 1985 NSW and ACT Resistance conference; Dave Deutschmann at SWP fifth national conference

CLOCKWISE FROM TOP: Rally at 1982 Resistance conference. Bernie Brian (far left), Terry Townsend (speaking), Bernie Hocking (far right), Kerry Vernon (second from right); Sally Low speaking at SWP 12th national conference, 1988; Mike Hanson speaking to a Melbourne Direct Action forum on the 35-hour week, November 1980; Rafael Gonzalez of Salvadoran FMLN speaking to 1982 Resistance conference

CLOCKWISE FROM RIGHT: Putting up posters in the 1976 NSW state elections; SYA's 1977 national conference, held on Melbourne University campus; Greg Adamson selling *Direct Action*, 1976; Mary Merkenich at February 1979 Sydney rally defending right to abortion

CLOCKWISE FROM TOP: Helen
Jarvis speaking at Sydney
1975 election rally, with
Gordon Adler, Nita Keig and
Jim McIlroy (seated); Maree
Walk; Terry Townsend and
Steve Painter in *GLW* office;
Margaret Allan in DSP
national office

CLOCKWISE FROM RIGHT: James Balowski and Claudine Holt in DSP national office; Zanny Begg; Sean Moysey in Resistance national office, Jorge Jorquera, 1993

CLOCKWISE FROM OPPOSITE PAGE: Resistance contingent in antiwar demo; DSP and Resistance contingent in demo in support of East Timor; SWL contingent on day of sacking of Whitlam government; Peta Stewart; Resistance contingent in anti-nuclear demo

CLOCKWISE FROM TOP: 1983 SWP election posters; Peter Camejo speaking at Social Rights Conference, 1984; Nita Keig speaking at 1980 election rally; Dave Holmes speaking to SWL fourth conference with Di Ewen (seated)

CLOCKWISE FROM RIGHT: Therese Doyle at Hiroshima Day rally in Adelaide, 1980; Aftermath of arson attack on SWP national office in Sydney; CARPA contingent at East Timor demo; Blue Fisher

CLOCKWISE FROM TOP: Melbourne IWD demo, 1978; Reihana Mohideen, 1986; Melbourne May Day, 1973; Jim Percy speaking at 1982 SWP education conference rally

CLOCKWISE FROM TOP: *DA* production team in 1990 (l-r, f-b): Will Wroth, John Garcia, Steve Painter, Greg Adamson, Philippa Skinner, Peter Boyle, Scott Lewington, Dave Holmes; campaigning for Jobs for Women, 1980s. SWP members Robynne Murphy (above "S") and Diana Covell (above "M"); Janet Parker, Resistance national coordinator, 1980s

CLOCKWISE FROM TOP LEFT: Jock Ferguson speaking at a Hobart meeting in support of British miners' strike, September 1984; John Garcia selling Communist League paper Militant in October 1977; Jon West speaking at January 1982 educational conference; Ron Poulsen reporting at January 1978 SWP-CL fusion conference

CLOCKWISE FROM LEFT:
Nita Keig in 1976; Margo
Condoleon, engine driver,
1981; Lalitha Chelliah,
Victorian Royal Australian
Nursing Federation
organiser, 1980s

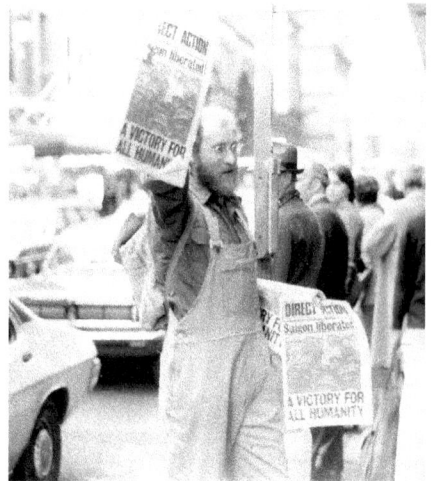

CLOCKWISE FROM TOP: Jim Percy
speaking at Karl Marx Centenary
Conference. Steve Painter (seated);
Renfrey Clark selling *DA* reporting
on Vietnam's 1975 victory;
Mary-Alice Waters from US SWP
speaking at SWP conference rally.
Allen Myers, Andrew Jamieson, Jim
Percy, Lynda Boland (seated)

CLOCKWISE FROM LEFT: Fourth SWP conference, January 1976. Allen Myers (speaking), Nita Keig, Jim Percy, John Percy; Nita Keig speaking at 1983 election rally; John McCarthy; Russell Johnson of NZ SAL speaking to January 1979 SWP conference

CLOCKWISE FROM TOP: Resistance camp, probably in 1981; Peter Abrahamson, 1979; Jure Lasich; John Tully and Rose Fidler, 1976

CLOCKWISE FROM LEFT: Val Edwards burns her ALP ticket in protest at party's abortion stance, 1986; Picket in defence of BLF, Wollongong, May 1986; Sydney May Day, 1972

CLOCKWISE FROM LEFT: Jamie Doughney at the SWL fourth national conference, January 1976; Doug Lorimer, early 1980s; rally at SWP fifth national conference

CLOCKWISE FROM TOP: 16th Resistance conference, 1987, marking 20 years of Resistance; Ernest Mandel speaking at the Karl Marx Centenary Conference in Melbourne, April 1983; John Percy addressing fourth SWP conference, January 1976

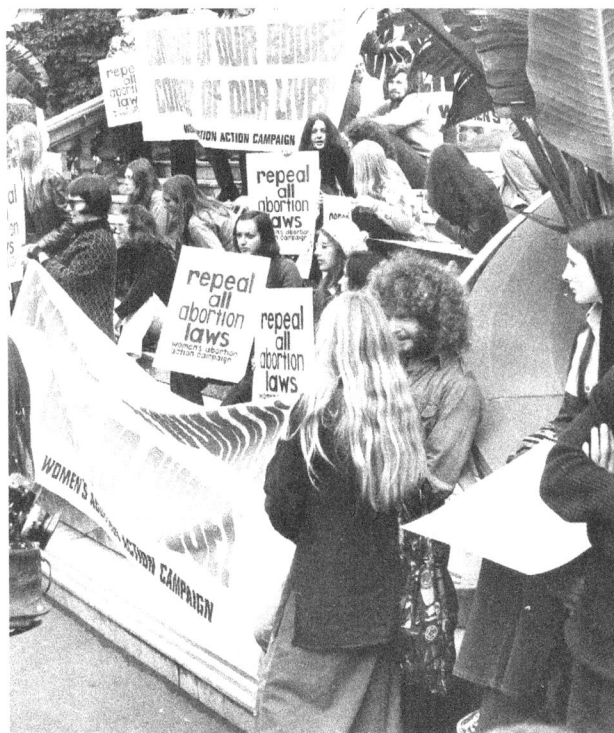

CLOCKWISE FROM TOP: Resistance and SWP educational conference, January 1984; Women's Abortion Action Campaign banners at June 30, 1973, demonstration in Sydney; Blue Fisher (left) at SWP solidarity demo for civil rights in Ireland, 1970s; Leesa Wheelahan, late 1970s; CISCAC banner at Palm Sunday march, 1986

CLOCKWISE FROM TOP: Jim Percy speaking to SWP-CL fusion conference; Paul Petit, 1976; Robynne Murphy (l) and other Jobs for Women activists by chance meet NSW Labor Premier Neville Wran outside a hearing of court case with the Anti-Discrimination Tribunal, August or September 1984; Alan Pinjen at SYA seventh national conference

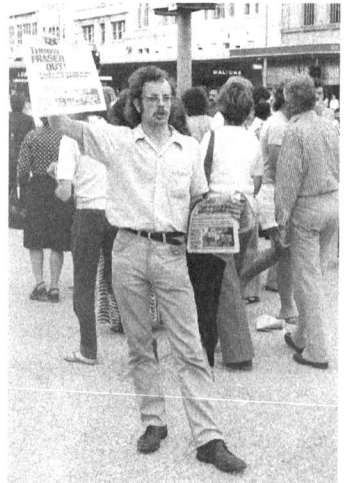

DA reported that there was a "packed hall" for the formal opening, at which speakers were Peter Annear and Elena Garcia, the Resistance organiser.

DA 396 reported the opening of a new bookshop by the Wollongong SWP, in Wentworth Street, Port Kembla.

An SWP NC was held on July 3. Jim Percy's report "Further Steps in Proletarianising the Party" initiated some tentative organisational changes, which we felt were made necessary by the industrial turn. "[W]e are always trying to improve our organisational forms", Jim said. "But completion of the turn makes it possible to experiment, and makes our discussion new in that we are dealing with a very changed party."

The question before us, the report stated, was "how to increase both democracy and centralism" in our party. Here there were two considerations. One was that, as we attracted workers, older workers, especially those who had families, sometimes found our hectic schedule of meetings and activities intimidating. The other was whether the democracy of our branch meetings sometimes descended into mere "formal democracy", comrades sometimes moving through the agenda of the meeting without much serious discussion. "The level of participation of comrades in meetings of the industrial fractions is much higher than in the party branches as a whole", Jim said, and this was probably the case in most other party fractions as well.

Based on these considerations, the Political Committee recommended, and the NC approved, shifting from weekly to monthly branch meetings. Much of the detail of particular political interventions would be worked out by fractions, under the overall supervision of the branch executive. The monthly branch meetings would take on some of the character of our tasks and perspectives meetings – analysing the political situation and setting out the main lines of what we wanted to achieve in the next month.

Jim's report and the plenum also discussed trying to organise party supporters more systematically. We had a growing periphery of people who shared our political outlook but would not become members for whatever reason. We had earlier tried to set up supporters' clubs, but these had not been a success. The report proposed, for a start, that we issue supporters' cards to sympathisers who were prepared to pay $5 a month, which would entitle them to a *DA* subscription and attendance at occasional meetings on such things as a report to branches on the latest NC meeting.

In August, we launched a five-week drive to gain 500 subscriptions to *Direct Action*. This was less successful than drives in the previous year, reaching a total of 414 subs.

Anti-nuclear, antiwar campaigns

At the start of the 1980s, the ALP had not yet abandoned its opposition to uranium mining, so Labor politicians could be persuaded to participate in major anti-uranium actions. *Direct Action* of August 13, 1980, reported on national Hiroshima Day marches: "As has been the case in all the major anti-uranium demonstrations in Sydney over the last two years, many ALP branches marched behind their own banners. There were also several contingents of unionists – including members of the Australian Railways Union and the Amalgamated Metal Workers and Shipwrights Union.

"The rally in Hyde Park was chaired by Federal Labor MP Tom Uren. Speakers included Stewart West, the Federal Labor opposition's spokesperson on Aboriginal affairs; Elizabeth Kirkby from the Australian Democrats; Pat Clancy, the Federal secretary of the Building Workers Industrial Union; and Cecil Patten from the Aboriginal Legal Service."

The article reported that 8,000 marched in Sydney, 200 in Newcastle, 1,000 in Brisbane, 400 in Adelaide and 350 in Perth, where a "proposal to allow US nuclear submarines to use the naval facilities at HMAS Stirling, Cockburn Sound, has brought the threat of nuclear contamination home to many people".

War and the threat of war were frequent subjects in *DA*. For instance, the cover of the April 14, 1982, issue hailed "Massive protests hit US war threat" and reported on Australian and international actions against the US threat to El Salvador.

When war erupted between Argentina and Britain over the Malvinas Islands, we had no hesitation in siding with Argentina against imperialism. "Why Argentina must be supported" was the cover of the April 21, 1982, issue. The article, by Rosemary McCann, explained that the claim of self-determination for the residents of the islands was a red herring:

"The current inhabitants of the islands are themselves a foreign population. They settled there after the original Argentine inhabitants were expelled when Britain militarily seized the islands from Argentina in 1833." The article noted that large offshore oil deposits had recently been discovered, and "the British capitalists have no right to plunder these resources".

The May 12 *DA* carried ads for pickets on the demand "Hands off Argentina" in Brisbane, Melbourne and Sydney, and for socialist forums on the Malvinas crisis in six cities.

Taking advantage of the world's preoccupation with war in the South Atlantic, in early June Israel launched an attack on Lebanon and the Palestinian refugees and exiles sheltering there. "Israeli terrorists invade Lebanon" by Peter

Boyle in the June 9 *DA* pointed out:

"'Terrorism' is the word for the Israeli methods – they bomb villages, refugee camps, and crowded towns …

"Israeli planes dropped leaflets on the town of Sidon threatening its residents, 'If you do not leave the city in two hours, we will shell and bomb everything.'"

The *DA* of August 11 reported "Thousands march to demand 'no more Hiroshimas'" in the annual march. The back page cover article by Jamie Doughney detailed the war against Lebanese and Palestinian civilians being waged by Israel. It quoted from a dispatch to the State Department by the US ambassador to Lebanon, which had been leaked to the London *Sunday Times*.

"Simply put, tonight's saturation shelling was as intense as anything we have seen", the ambassador wrote. "There was no 'pinpoint accuracy' against targets in 'open spaces'. It was not a response to Palestinian fire. This was a blitz against West Beirut."

Even after Yasser Arafat and the PLO withdrew from Lebanon, the Israeli attacks continued. Despite a supposed cease-fire, Israel ordered the Phalange – Lebanese fascists allied with the Israeli military – to invade Sabra and the adjacent Shatila refugee camp. For a day and a half in September, while Israeli troops surrounded the area to prevent anyone from fleeing and provided flares so that the Phalange could see what they were doing at night, the Phalangists carried out a horrific massacre of up to 3,500 men, women and children. In December, the UN General Assembly voted 123-0, with 22 abstentions, to condemn the massacre as an act of genocide.

Despite the international horror at Sabra-Shatila, Israel and the Lebanese army, backed by the multinational force of US, French and Italian troops, continued their "campaign of terror aimed at forcing the Palestinians out of Lebanon altogether", as Rosemary McCann wrote in the November 30, 1982, *DA*.

Opposition to war continued to be expressed around Hiroshima Day. The *DA* of August 9, 1983, reported, "Big antiwar rallies mark Hiroshima day". The Sydney march drew 15,000, Adelaide 5,000, Wollongong 2,000, Melbourne 1,000 and Brisbane 1,000, with smaller rallies in other cities.

Socialist Worker series 2

We restarted *Socialist Worker* in October 1982, with Allen Myers as the editor. We explained: "*Socialist Worker* now resumes publication not as a theoretical magazine but as a journal of politics and discussion of the Socialist Workers Party". Vol. 2 No. 1 contained resolutions for the SWP ninth national conference, January 5-11, 1983: "The capitalist recession and the fight for socialism" and "Revolutionary strategy and tactics in the trade unions".

The next issue, in November , contained two further resolutions for the conference: "The Cuban Revolution and its extension" and "The class-struggle road to peace", both of which had been adopted by the SWP National Committee plenum in October. *Socialist Worker* Vol. 2 No. 3, in December, was focused on what to do next as a small revolutionary party based in industry. It contained four articles. One was "The turn to industry and the tasks of the Fourth International", by US SWP leader Jack Barnes, from November 1979. The other three were talks by Jim Percy: "Four features of our revolutionary party", "Further steps in proletarianising the party" and "Preparing the party to meet the crisis". "Four features" and "Further steps" are described above. The third talk was given to the October 1982 NC. It set out an approach different from that which was becoming evident in the US SWP.

"What is the main way in which we will further the proletarianisation of our party?", Jim asked. He answered: "The main advance will come with winning more workers to our ranks". Our members, he said, couldn't become "more proletarian" as individuals; we didn't regard any area of industry as superior to another, "that if you go down the mines it would be better than working in steel". "Of course we still have a very great deal to learn and we are going to get a lot more experience in many different ways and jobs. But there is no turn within the turn: We can't spin faster and faster on the cadre that we have today."

Although not headlined as such, this was a clear difference with the US SWP, which was responding to the reality of the working class not being as radicalised as expected, not by adjusting its perspectives to the reality, but by "deepening the turn", which in practice meant pressuring members to become "more proletarian", usually by changing to more difficult or exploited industries. Barry Sheppard believes that the phrase "turn within the turn", as used by the US SWP, "referred to a rejection of the 1978 original turn, which projected that we wanted to get a majority of members in industrial unions, but that we would maintain our white collar fractions, e.g. the teachers". The changed position was that all members, except those who were too old to do so, had to become members of industrial unions. Those who couldn't do this would be demoted to the status of sympathisers.[63]

Earlier in the year, in another difference with the US party, we had dropped our ban on seeking leadership positions in unions, which we had adopted from the US SWP and which the latter still held to.

In this talk, Jim also discussed how the party handles internal differences. He warned against carrying over attitudes developed during the factional struggle in the Fourth International and during the splits that occurred in our early history. Debate was not something to be feared or avoided: "In a new period like this, with so many decisions to take and so much we need to understand, tactical debates are going to help. That is the sort of period we are entering. In that sort of period, we emphasise the thinking-out process. That won't break down our revolutionary discipline. That won't make us a weaker party at all; in my opinion, it will strengthen us."

In the same talk to the NC plenum, Jim presented the Political Committee's proposal that financial pressures made it necessary to cut *Direct Action* from 20 pages to 16: "That is a setback. There is no point beating around the bush; it is not what we want. We have to make the best of it. Making the best of it is to separate out some of the longer analytical articles … for *Socialist Worker*, put them in *Socialist Worker*, and try to lighten up *Direct Action*, make it more readable, have shorter articles."

We had originally projected that *Socialist Worker* would appear "approximately on a monthly basis", and we produced three issues between October and December 1982, but the next one was not published until June 1983. That issue carried "The Great Depression: its lessons for today", by Jonathan West; "Economic crisis and the class struggle today", by Jim Percy (a report adopted by SWP national conference in January); and a debate between NSW Labor left MLA George Petersen and Allen Myers about the Militant Action Campaign, which our members had helped to organise in the Federated Ironworkers Association. Petersen criticised the MAC for having stood candidates in FIA elections against the "Rank and File" officials who led the Wollongong branch. The Rank and File leaders had won office by opposing conservative officials from the left, and Petersen considered that the MAC had split the left in the union unnecessarily. Allen's reply argued that militants in the FIA had found the Rank and File leaders sorely lacking and ineffectual as jobs were being lost. The formerly left wing leadership was in retreat, and the MAC was the main force calling for a real fight back.

My move to Melbourne

In 1982, it was agreed that I would move to Melbourne, become Melbourne district secretary, and get a job in industry. This would send a message to comrades that we were serious about the turn, and that it was being led by the leadership. Other NC members had also gotten jobs in industry.

Also, this created a better balance of our national leadership between our two major branches and cities. I remained in Melbourne until 1991, when we learned that Jim was suffering from bowel cancer, misdiagnosed by his doctors, allowing it to spread to his liver, which was usually fatal. I returned to Sydney, and he proposed I take over as national secretary again, which I did in 1992.

The party was growing as a whole, after some initial casualties and attrition as a result of the turn, our over-optimism and the looming break with the US SWP. The branches were going well, warranting an expansion in Melbourne by buying our own offices. In 1982 we bought a huge building for our Melbourne HQ at 14 Anthony Street, a lane near Victoria Markets just up from Elizabeth Street. It was very run-down, very large, with three floors, and had not been occupied for a while. It cost us $170,000.

When we first moved in we were puzzled by the black paint covering the windows, the old cinema seats (which we made use of for years), the square of carpet in the middle of the top floor, and a rail dividing off the front of the hall. It must have been the Melbourne equivalent of Thommo's Two-Up School in Surry Hills, Sydney. This was indirectly confirmed to us later, when we were visited by two people from the Australian Tax Office, on the track of the previous operator.

It was run-down, like all our early headquarters, and we organised extensive working bees to clean it up, scrape the black paint off the windows and make it fit for our offices. A special effort was put in by Jure Lasic, a Croatian building worker who had joined us, and his friends, who helped build the partitions on the first floor to create separate rooms from the huge spaces.

We later used the building for Resistance conferences. We also used to let out the top floor for private functions, dance parties and such. We arranged to run the bar, but we didn't sell much grog, only lots of mineral water. We figured out later that the functions must have been for distributing designer drugs! To heat up the cavernous building during winter events, we had to hire big "jet engine" fan heaters. There was still a lot of work that needed to be done. For example, the dangerous back fire escape had rotting wooden stairs that we never succeeded in repairing.

We held a grand opening of the new Melbourne Resistance Bookshop and Resistance/Socialist Workers Party offices on May 1, 1983, as a May Day toast.

In later years we set up a wholefood shop on the ground floor, learning from the Hobart shop, selling bulk grains, nuts, dried fruit etc. Being close to Victoria Markets, it attracted some regular trade, but it was labour intensive for us, and never really made a lot of money.

More books, bookshops, publishing

Anthony Street was also not a bad spot for a public bookshop, and we tried with shops on both the first and ground floors. Over time, all of our branches of any size tried to establish bookshops, partly in the hope of making contact with people interested in left-wing books and partly in the hope of bringing in some money.

The Socialist Labour League built three very profitable bookshops, in Parramatta, Fremantle and Newcastle. These were more "mainstream" bookshops, with a minority section on left politics. (There were rumours that they had so much cash sloshing about that the Fremantle shop profits got transported back east by plane.)

Our early pamphlets in the late 1960s and early '70s were often gestetnered reprints, of pamphlets or articles from the US SWP or the British IMG, or interesting articles from *New Left Review*. We had access to a stencil cutting machine, and willing hands to collate and staple the printed sheets. In the 1980s, we started producing a new round of reprinted pamphlets from our large new headquarters in Melbourne. In 1980, Pathfinder Press, the publishing house of the US SWP, trusted us enough to publish a book for them, *The Balkan Wars*, Trotsky's 1912-13 war correspondence.

One of our first productions of our own, as opposed to reprints, was *The Picket*, Renfrey Clarke's account of the 1983 Tasmanian miners' struggle, published in 1984. Also in the latter year, we published two of our resolutions as books: *The Struggle for Socialism in the imperialist epoch* and *The Cuban Revolution and its extension*.

The Balkan Wars did not begin an ongoing collaboration with US Pathfinder, because we soon broke politically with the US SWP. A small pro-US split in our party in 1983 included Dave Deutschmann and Deb Shnookal. They then went to the US and became involved in Pathfinder Press US, especially the Cuban and Spanish language side of its publishing. They later had a falling out with Jack Barnes, and somehow walked off with the Spanish language rights. They became Ocean Press in Australia and were very successful, the main publisher of Cuban writings, with displays and distributions in Cuban bookshops and airports.

We also worked out a distribution arrangement with the left-wing British publisher Ink Links.

On the trams

Part of the motivation of my transfer to Melbourne was to boost the role of the leadership as part of the turn, so I got a job on the trams, which was easy to do, and we already had a growing fraction of trammies. I spent a total of two years on the trams, first as a conductor for one year, and then I qualified as a driver, driving for one year. I was based at Preston Depot in Melbourne's northern suburbs, and initially got a room at Jim McIlroy and Coral Wynter's house in Preston, which was handy, within walking distance of the depot for early morning starts.

As well as getting involved in any union activities that were happening (the Australian Tramways and Motor Omnibus Employees Association was led by Jim Harper, a semi-Maoist), our tram comrades focused a lot on *DA* sales and talking socialism on the job. It was a fraction with excellent sales experiences. Jobs on the trams were very conducive to sales. First, you had a whole week to chat up your co-worker (at that time each tram was still staffed by both a driver and a conductor). Split shifts were a bad thing for workers, with four unpaid hours in the middle of the day. But they were favoured by some workers: card players and gamblers, who wanted to spend four hours in the depot; and socialist activists and *DA* sellers who were able to find a ready audience/buyers sitting around the depot.

My sales results at Preston Depot soon got up to an average of 20, going up to 24. Our overall fraction sales were better than other fractions, in vehicle, rail, steel, or metal, in either Melbourne or other branches.

Comrades were also at Essendon, South Melbourne and Kew. The maximum number we got up to in the fraction was 14. Sol Salby, Doug Jordan and Chris Slee were long-term trammies.

After initially living in Preston near the depot, I moved to Clifton Hill, which was still OK for Preston Depot. Later I moved to Yarraville. Jim and I sold our original Sydney house in Glebe, moving to a cheaper house in the same suburb. It was old and very dilapidated, but with a spare block. And with the surplus, we were able to put a deposit on a Yarraville weatherboard house.

Standing in union elections

The question of whether or not to stand in union elections, or take up job delegates' positions, was an important difference we had with the US SWP in regard to carrying out the turn, and it was also played out in our party, in Melbourne branch. Jim presented a report on behalf of the Political Committee to a Melbourne branch meeting on September 12, 1982, on "What was wrong with our old trade union line." We firmed up our position on this at our October 9-11, 1982, NC meeting. Pat Garcia's report "Revolutionary Strategy and Tactics in the Trade Unions" pointed out that the document corrected the error of our previous political resolution, developed into an incorrect line on the question of abstaining from running for union elections and standing for delegate positions. This had been taken from the US SWP's sectarian position on union work. Pat went through four concrete possibilities that had been posed recently in our union work, each different. First, in the rubber workers union in WA, with only about 300 members, with a rotted-out weak union, we estimated we could use the position in the TLC and the ALP. Second, on the trams in Melbourne. Third, in the vehicle industry, we had been asked to run by militant stewards at Ford. Fourth, in steel, there were three national positions comrades could contest, with Robynne Murphy, Kemal Pekin and Ian Llewellyn.

We debated it out in the Melbourne branch at a meeting on December 12, 1982. In a discussion on the vehicle campaign, Dave Deutschmann defended the US SWP's abstentionist line. I outlined our document, and our Melbourne executive adopted a clear line in a report by Reihana Mohideen, who was working in vehicle. The opposing positions were published in our Discussion Bulletin.

In the Discussion Bulletin prior to our January 1983 conference, "Why we needed a change in tactics in our work in the unions" by Andrew (Jammo) Jamieson summarised and rejected the argument behind our previous position: "The picture we painted was to wait until there was a major class battle with the boss, win real leadership in the course of this victorious struggle in spite of the present officials, then translate our leadership on the job into a formal one as well when elections were held". Had we continued with that line, Jammo pointed out, it would have pushed us into the role of "critical support" to the left union bureaucrats whose leadership failures we were criticising, and into the sectarian error of telling other union militants that there was nothing they could do to get rid of the bureaucrats until conditions changed.

The HDP

In 1982 in Melbourne we recruited several socialist Croatian activists, several of whom were building workers. This was seen as suspicious by some others on the left, since all Croatian migrants were tarred by the terrorist activities of the fascist Croatian Ustasha, which carried out bombings of the Yugoslav consulate and organised groups to go back to fight inside Yugoslavia. Certainly the majority of politically active Croatian migrants were very right wing, and some were fascist, following the experience of World War II.

But Jure Lasic and others were members of the HDP, the Croatian Movement for Statehood, and considered themselves socialists. Jure and others helped renovate our big new Melbourne offices and then helped out in Sydney the following year when we bought our building at 23 Abercrombie Street. We helped print their publication. And at one stage we allocated a small room on the ground floor at the back in Anthony Street for Jure's Croatian group.

Our collaboration with the Croatian socialists was seen as an opportunity to attack us by the CPA, the US SWP and its handful of supporters in Australia, and the Fourth International.

Direct Action of June 2, 1982, carried a letter from Jure Lasic to the CPA's *Tribune* over attacks on the HDP by the CPA at the Melbourne May Day march. In it, Lasic pointed out that the HDP "stand for international socialism, we oppose US imperialism's intervention in El Salvador and attacks on the revolutionary governments of Nicaragua and Cuba … we support the Irish and Palestinian national liberation struggles and oppose the racist state of Israel, we support Argentinean sovereignty over the Malvinas and oppose British attacks on Argentina, and we generally support the peoples fighting for their freedom all around the world.

"It is a lie and a slander to identify us with the Ustasha and to call us 'fascists.'"

Jamie Doughney and Jim McIlroy wrote *DA* articles in October explaining the HDP position: "Leftward-moving Croatian organisation answers questions on its views". They explained that "Yugoslavia is defaming socialist ideals".

At the June 11-12, 1983, SWP National Committee meeting, Dave Holmes gave a thorough report on "Yugoslavia, Croatian independence and the HDP" and in *DA* 440 explained "The Croatian national struggle in history". Geoff Streeton (Renfrey Clarke) followed that up in the July 5 *DA,* and on July 19 *DA* had a four-page lift-out: "A reply to the *Australian* and *Tribune.* The truth about the Croatian national struggle" by Dave Holmes and Doug Lorimer. We also took up the Croatia debate in *Socialist Worker,* Vol. 3 No. 2.

We published Dave Holmes' NC report, the *DA* lift-out, a lengthy analysis of "The Freney School of Falsification" by Allen Myers, plus an interview with HDP member Dinko Dedic explaining the distortions and lies from Mark Aarons on an ABC broadcast, as a pamphlet, "Croatian nationalism and the fight for socialism".

A year later Doug Lorimer reported in *DA* (October 24, 1984) that the comrades were part of forming the "Croatian Socialist Party" after Jure was expelled from the HDP.

In late 1991 Jason Cheng and Dave Holmes reported on stepped-up work in Melbourne in solidarity with the Croatian independence struggle for the DSP internal bulletin, the Activist. Jure sent congratulations to *Green Left Weekly* on its 300th issue on behalf of Croatian Radio Vukovar on 3CR. Sadly, he was killed in a car crash in the '90s.

Our other buildings

It was a wise financial choice early on to buy our own headquarters. We calculated that we were better off paying off a mortgage than permanently paying rent.

We wanted security, not to be at the mercy of a capitalist landlord. One bad experience rammed this home to us. Early on in Melbourne, we thought we had an agreement to rent a new headquarters in Peel Street, but moved in and started renovating before we'd actually signed the lease. It was a disaster: the landlord refused to sign the lease and had the benefit of our renovations.

Also, the dumps we bought and renovated before the huge property market boom really took off meant we banked a huge growth in our assets. It was a wise choice (which ultimately benefited the Socialist Alliance).

In 1978, we sold the Sydney headquarters at 139 St. Johns Road, Glebe, to take a much larger first floor area in Thomas Street, Haymarket, and then also to set up a printshop in Leichhardt.

In Brisbane we bought a building in New Farm that had been an old bakery, with a four-bedroom weatherboard house out the front, where some of the more active comrades lived.

In Hobart in the '90s we bought a very impressive building in one of the main streets, with an extra large meeting room attached that could hold a meeting of 100-150 people, or our fundraising dinners.

In Newcastle we bought a two-storey building in the main street, backing on to the train line. After a while we let out the downstairs section.

In Perth, we rescued various, mostly derelict, buildings.

In the Sydney headquarters we had in George Street above the old Malaya restaurant, we were forced by the grasping landlord to buy the tacky carpet covering the floors and walls, so took it with us in 1983 when we bought the building at 23 Abercrombie Street.

Another building that we once had our eye on housed the Broadway Gym, near the corner of City Road and Parramatta Road. If we'd stretched ourselves further, we would have ended up with a great location for a bookshop and made a killing on the rising property value.

Banners

I was our early banner painter. For our more complex banners, such as the big red and black portraits we carried in Sydney and Melbourne in the '70s, I used the grid system (which I gather had also been used by Michelangelo). We developed a style with the same font for the many uniform banners we painted for May Day marches.

In Melbourne, Bob Lewis was our prolific banner painter. He was recruited from Geelong and initially studied in the art school at the Gordon Institute, before moving to Melbourne and joining the branch in 1973/74. He used acetate film and a projector to indicate the image and letters. He painted some of our most impressive banners.

Bob also did many banners for many other organisations, both when he was studying at Latrobe University (and president of the students union there) and when he was the clubs and societies officer at RMIT for 20 years. (A banner he painted for the Left Unity Conference with the CPA in 1987 was artistically very impressive, but the liberal Stalinists didn't like it and forced it to be covered up with a curtain!) Bob had an enormous library of political books, occupying nearly every wall space in his house. He also later had a huge collection of films on DVD, and a very impressive knowledge of film.

In Sydney, John Garcia did some great banners. Bob and John would have been the comrades mainly responsible for the huge impressive banners filling whole walls of our conferences, at the YWCA, or the Anthony Street top floor. It was an excellent huge space for banner painting and a great place for decorating with huge banners – they expanded to fill the available space.

Bands we have known

It is no secret that left politics and good music often go together. In May 1968, the Third World Bookshop sponsored a tour by US radical and antiwar folk singer Pete Seeger. Two concerts were staged in Sydney Town Hall.

Jean Lewis, the daughter of CPAer Sam Lewis, the Teachers Federation head, was already well established, but some of the folk singers got their start at Sydney Resistance in the '60s.

It helped that the Melbourne Anthony Street hall was a very good music venue. It helped even more that well-known percussionist Ray Pereira was touring with Jo Camileri in Jo Jo Zep when he joined the SWP in 1982. Ray then was a founding member of the band Man Friday, one of Australia's first "world music" bands. Man Friday combined rhythmic grooves with lyrics that dealt with a range of social and political issues and played several successful fundraisers for the party over the next three years.

The band Strange Tenants was known for good political lyrics. It was led by Ian Hearn, who came from an SPA family. The *DA* of December 11, 1985, carried a review of a new album by Strange Tenants. The band played for us during the 1990 Resistance conference, at North Melbourne Town Hall. Alistair Hulett, from Roaring Jack, was a member of the International Socialists but played for Resistance in Sydney at the Resistance Centre in 1989 and for a *Direct Action* harbour cruise in November 1989. Phil Monsour performed for the "Green It Up" fundraisers for *Green Left Weekly* organised by the Brisbane DSP in the early 1990s.

Printing

In Sydney, when we moved into the big new offices in Abercrombie Street, we made a major attempt to get seriously into printing. An ambitious press had been purchased, and comrades made persistent efforts to learn the trade. But it defeated us in the end; we found it cheaper to print elsewhere.

We made early printing efforts in Melbourne. We acquired an old press, which Peter Holloway kept running initially. Eventually we were able to put in a real effort, because we found a real printer. We had joined up a Turkish comrade in Hobart, who moved to Melbourne. Unal Mutercimler was a very versatile, skilful, jack of all trades, including an acrobat/juggler, as well as a printer. He ended up in the computer business, and as was his style, in all sides of it – writing software, repairing the hardware, selling computers.

He learned his printing skills in Turkey, and was involved in the underground movement, doing the printing, which I understand involved counterfeit notes, so his skills were a cut above all our previous printing efforts. He got our clapped-out machines to work. He was captured in Turkey, tortured (one of the worst aspects that he complained to us about his time in prison was that he was forced to eat without cutlery) and somehow managed to get out of the country and applied for asylum in Australia. In between he'd been to Canada, possibly other countries, and one of his other trades was circus performer; he was very skilled on the unicycle, and kept one in the downstairs printery to practice on.

Eventually it was a choice between the party ploughing more money into the printing business to get modern equipment, or Unal going it alone as a serious business. We chose the latter, and Unal put his considerable energy and talent into expanding the printing business, concentrating on the computer side of it more and eventually switching over completely to computers.

CHAPTER 5

THE HAWKE ALP GOVERNMENT

The Hawke ALP government was elected on March 5, 1983. The lead-up to the election was structured by the ALP-ACTU Prices and Incomes Accord, and the next 14 years of ALP government were dominated by it. It was probably the biggest setback for the Australian trade union movement in its history.

In 1983 we ran our biggest election campaign yet, with 48 candidates, for the Senate and House of Representatives, in all states.

January 1983 SWP conference

The SWP ninth national conference was held at Hawkesbury Agricultural College, January 5-11, 1983, with the reports: Capitalist Recession and the Fight for Socialism; Revolutionary Strategy and Tactics in the Trade Unions; The Class Struggle Road to Peace; Party Organisational Perspectives in the Economic Crisis; Youth and the Capitalist Crisis – Tasks for Resistance; The Cuban Revolution and its Extension; Poland, majority and minority; Building an International Revolutionary Leadership.

We had a number of special guests. Pedro Camejo had been scheduled to give talks on The Coming American Revolution; How to Make a Revolution; and the Central American Revolution; but he had been denied a visa, and we rescheduled his talks for a month later. Mac Warren and Nan Bailey from the US SWP attended, as did two comrades from the NZ SAL, Francis Young from Hong Kong (who was the second comrade from Hong Kong attending our school; Eva To had been the first, and years later came to stay), a Sri Lankan comrade, Ridley, from the Revolutionary Marxist Party, who was also at the school in early 1982, and a comrade from New Caledonia.

For the new National Committee, there was a change in our system. Previously, alternates were elected in a specific order, and moved on to the full NC in that order if vacancies occurred. The new procedure was that, in the event of a vacancy, the full NC could choose to elect someone from the candidate list, but was not obligated to do so.

I described it as our "best, biggest conference yet" in my report to Melbourne branch. More than 280 people registered (compared with about 250 at the 1982 education conference).

After the Poland debate, the PC majority report was adopted overwhelmingly, with one delegate against, one abstention and seven consultative delegates voting for the minority position.

It was an extremely extensive pre-conference discussion, with 12 internal discussion bulletins published before the conference.

The organisation report by Steve Painter had some ambitious projections, following our encouraging growth in 1982 of 35 percent, and in 1981 of 16 percent:
- standing 35 candidates in the federal elections (the final total was 48);
- purchasing a three-storey building for our Melbourne HQ, the deposit having already been paid;
- organising a sub and sales drive over two months, for 1,000 subs and 2,500 sales;
- setting a fund drive target of $80,000; the conference rally launched it, with $46,000 pledged to start it.

I presented an expansion slide show that documented our growth in 1982 and our ambitious plans.

Campaigning against the ACTU-ALP Accord

We began campaigning against the ACTU-ALP Accord as soon as it was mooted, pointing out that it was clearly a social contract, designed to reduce workers' wages and conditions, and limit the unions' possibilities of fighting back. There had been numerous examples of this sort of disguised attack on workers in recent decades around the world.

Unfortunately, it wasn't just the ALP reformists who were touting this betrayal. It was thought up and initiated by Laurie Carmichael, the assistant national secretary of the Amalgamated Metal Workers and Shipwrights Union, one of the strongest, and supposedly left-wing, unions. Carmichael was a leader of the CPA. The CPA and the AMWU had been preparing the ground for this "new" sort of class-collaborationist approach since they launched their People's Economic Program in 1977. We denounced it at the time and campaigned against it, and they followed it up with "increasingly conservative" justifications, with *Australia Uprooted* (1977), *Australia Ripped Off* (1979) and *Australia on the Rack* (1982).[64]

The November 4, 1981, *DA* began an ongoing polemic with the Communist Party. Throughout 1982, *DA* ran thorough analyses of the looming social contract. In the May 19, 1982, *DA,* Allen Myers wrote, "Whether it's called a 'social contract' or a 'prices and incomes policy,' the leaders of the Labor Party are looking for a deal with the trade unions to hold back wage demands".

The following week we printed a statement by the SWP Political Committee, "The Social Contract Swindle". Whether called a "social contract" or something else, the statement said, this kind of deal "amounts to the same thing: Unions give up the right to fight for wage increases". The concessions promised in return are invariably a "swindle". The experience with indexation, which was another form of social contract, proved this: indexation was often limited and always lagged behind price rises. "The only real gains for workers in 1975-81 were made when workers broke with the indexation 'guidelines' and used industrial action."

The statement pointed out why the AMWSU was central to the planned social contract: "The AMWSU is the largest union in Australia. It is also traditionally one of the most militant, a trend-setter for other parts of the workforce. Unless the AMWSU goes along, a social contract wouldn't have much chance of ever becoming real." The path for a social contract had been cleared in December 1981, when the AMWSU and other metal trades union abandoned a wage campaign short of victory and signed a "no further claims" agreement with the employers.

The June 2, 1982, *DA* reported that the social contract was launched, as ALP leader Bill Hayden, ACTU assistant secretary Bill Kelty and Laurie Carmichael publicly announced the deal and denounced their critics within the labour movement.

Over the following months *DA* editor Jon West wrote many articles analysing the Accord and the history of similar projects internationally, and we brought them together in a booklet, published in October as *Labor's Social Contract: Workers Ripped Off!*, by Jonathan West. The articles covered topics such as: "'Social contract' Bad memories for British workers", "Social Contract – a 'political' trap", "Sweden: a social contract that works?", "How incomes policies weaken unions", "Can Labor control prices?", "Tribune finds old arguments for a new social contract", "What's wrong with the ALP-ACTU 'Statement of Accord'", "CPA throws its weight behind ALP ACTU deal".

We scheduled forums in eight cities in June and July on "The Social Contract Swindle" and started a regular page 2 listing in *DA* on "The social contract swindle". Doug Lorimer also wrote many polemical articles, including "The CPA and Hayden's social contract" (*DA* August 31, 1982) and "Why wage freeze won't save jobs" (*DA* November 23, 1982).

We kept up our campaign during and after the election as well. In May 1983 we participated in and promoted an Australian Marxist Forum on "The Left and the Labor government" with speakers Pat Clancy, the national secretary of the BWIU and former national president of the SPA; Rob Durbridge, a national organiser of the CPA; Liz Fell, an activist in the women's liberation movement; Bob Debus, the

Labor MLA for the NSW state seat of the Blue Mountains; and Jim Percy. Doug Lorimer reported it in *DA:* "Sydney forum debates prices and incomes policy", and in the June 21 issue we ran Jim's remarks pointing out that the social contract was "a road to defeat." He quoted an article from *Tribune* arguing that, if the Accord collapsed, it would lead to the Liberals returning to government:

"That is, if the workers don't accept the austerity program of the government, then that government will be weakened …

"[But if] the workers accept it, *they* will be weakened. If the labor movement accepts it, *it* will be weakened. If *they're* weakened, the government will collapse anyway."

Two articles by Allen Myers in the October 18 and 25 issues sought to quantify what workers were losing. He calculated that in 1983 alone, just from the lag between price increases and the eventual indexed wage rise, Australian workers had lost a total of around $2.7 billion. Even worse, there had been no wage rise to compensate for the 9.1 percent CPI increase in the last three quarters of 1982. In the course of 1983, workers would lose a total of around $9 billion. An increase of the "social wage" through additional social welfare spending of $3 billion in the August 1983 federal budget therefore didn't begin to make up for the losses in direct wages – particularly when it was recalled that much of that increased spending came from taxes paid by working people.

SWP 1983 election campaign

In the March 1983 federal elections, we ended up fielding 38 House of Representatives candidates and 10 Senate candidates.

The February 8 *DA* had on its cover "Throw Fraser Out! Break the wage freeze! For a Labor government with socialist policies." Doug Lorimer wrote "Why Fraser went to the polls", and Allen Myers "Why we're standing". We carried interviews with railworker candidates Christine Broi and Dick Nichols in Sydney, and Sue Bolton, bus driver candidate in Brisbane. The issue had a four-page lift-out, with pictures and biographies of our 48 candidates.

The February 15 *DA* cover story was "How Labor can win". There was a two-page interview with Jim Percy, "The road to socialism", explaining our election campaign, and we began an 11-part series by Sol Salby, "Labor in power 1972-75". We had an ad for election campaign dinners in six cities, and barbecues in Perth and Newcastle.

The *DA* just before the election had a total of 28 pages, and a cover calling "For a Labor government with socialist policies. Vote 1. Socialist Workers 2. ALP." Doug Lorimer explained "The stakes for workers on March 5", and had an article on "The real meaning of Labor's prices and incomes policy". We printed the SWP election campaign statement "For a Labor government with socialist policies". Allen Myers wrote, "Who will win socialism?" Jenny O'Donnell (Rosemary McCann) wrote on "Socialist policies and women's rights", Jamie Doughney on "A new foreign policy for Labor", Roger Miles (Roger Markwick) on "State aid: what policy for Labor?" and "Socialist workers campaign for socialism" with a picture of our colourful election posters. Tony Forward wrote on "Labor's Win in WA". There were 48 candidate pictures, a four-page "How to Vote" lift-out and ads for election night parties in eight cities.

After the election, the *DA* cover was "After the victory: Labor's choice: profits or jobs", with an article by Doug Lorimer and Jenny O'Donnell (Rosemary McCann) and two pages on "Socialist Workers candidates put fighting alternative". There was a picture of huge piles of election leaflets printed by our printshop, and quotes from the press coverage we received.

One gauge of the usefulness of our election campaign was the degree to which it brought people closer. Our Melbourne dinner dance on July 2 was attended by 140 people. Speakers were Hurriyet Babican, from the Turkish community, Peter Annear, from the CISCAC National Secretariat, and a representative from the Canadian Committee in solidarity with El Salvador. Large delegations came along from the Turkish and Croatian communities.

Karl Marx Centenary Conference

The SWP initiated and built the Karl Marx Centenary Conference in Melbourne at Easter 1983, which brought together an extremely broad range of speakers and participants in a very prestigious event. The conference marked the 100th anniversary of the death of Marx. *DA* 428 in March carried an article by Jon West, "Are Marx's ideas out of date?" and a page article building the conference.

It was held at University High School in Melbourne, on April 1-4; 767 people attended, under a huge banner of Karl Marx in the main hall. Ernest Mandel got here, after his exclusion by the Australian government in 1970 (although he made it in 1974). He spoke on "The revolutionary potential of the working class" and "The capitalist world crisis, its roots and future". Other international guest speakers included Pedro Camejo, from the USA, speaking on "The achievements of the Central American revolutions" and "The coming American revolution", and Brigid Mulrennan and Russell Johnson from the NZ SAL.

We had a large number of SWP speakers, plus academics and political activists speaking on 61 panels including: Lloyd Churchward, Chris Gaffney, Charles Sowerwine, Russell Wright, a panel of HDP speakers, Joe Miller, Peter Beilharz,

Ian Ward, Patrick Wolfe, Hans Lofgren, Joan Coxsedge, Sydney Gay Solidarity group, Noel Turnbull, Theodore MacDonald, Warwick Fry, Jose Alvarez, Michael Hamel-Green, Neil Simpson, Val Noone, Ken Fry, Rajan Pathmasingham and Chris Healey.

Feature talks were given by Peta Stewart on "Karl Marx: Revolutionary Fighter" and by Jim Percy on the necessary unity of theory and practice.

"One hundred years after the death of Karl Marx, his ideas are more alive, more accepted, and more relevant than ever", began the report in the April 6 *DA* by Roger Miles (Roger Markwick) heralding the success of the conference. The same issue carried Ernest Mandel's talk, "One hundred years of Marxism since Marx".

We followed it up with a Karl Marx Centenary Conference in Perth, April 23-25, flying over some of the Melbourne speakers: Pedro Camejo, Jim Percy and Allen Myers. One hundred and nine people there registered to attend the 20 talks and panels. We also had two panel discussions on contemporary labour movement issues. The first was "Labor's prices and incomes policy – Different views from trade unionists". The speakers were Vic Williams, national committee member of the SPA; Tony Mulcahy, WA state president of the Federated Rubber Workers Union (and SWP member); Vic Slater, WA state treasurer of the Waterside Workers Federation and national committee member of the CPA; and Tony Forward, Perth branch organiser and national committee member of the SWP. The second panel was on the topic "The fight against war today", with speakers Jim Percy, Joan Williams, secretary of the WA Peace Committee, and Chuck Bonzas, Vietnam veteran and Campaign Against Nuclear Energy activist.

We also had public meetings and university meetings for Camejo in all our branches on "The Achievements of the Central American Revolutions – the Marxist View".

June 1983 SWP NC

We held an SWP NC on June 11-12, 1983, with reports: The Labor government and the response of the left, by Jim Percy; Party organisation and finance and the circulation of the party's press, Steve Painter; Turning the party to the working-class migrant communities, Pat Garcia; Yugoslavia, Croatian independence and the HDP, Dave Holmes; antiwar perspectives, Peter Annear; and World movement, Doug Lorimer.

On the HDP, Nita Keig argued strongly against our position and asked for a minority report, but in the end she declined. So did Ron Poulsen. We'd been savagely attacked by the US SWP over our position on the HDP (and also by the

Europeans in the FI). Nita and Ron had sent a three-page letter on May 21, 1983, to the National Executive "expressing our concern" about the party's position on the HDP. Dave O'Neill (Dave Riley), who was working in the NO at the time, circulated this and a number of other documents on the HDP: a letter from Ernest Mandel to us, quoting Michelle Lee as a specialist on Yugoslavia; NZ SAL National Executive minutes of April 19 criticising our line; a criticism of us in *Tribune* from Dave Davies.

In September, the NE amalgamated the Sydney and Parramatta branches. A special joint membership meeting of the two branches on September 25 voted overwhelmingly to endorse the NE decision. What were our reasons? Apart from the recession having changed the employment situation drastically, with the change to monthly branch meetings and the corresponding increased importance of the weekly fraction meetings, the importance of city-wide forms of organisation increased. There were not enough cadre to head up all the areas of work with the two branch set-up. And Sydney's political life still overwhelmingly focused on the inner city.

23 Abercrombie Street

In August 1983 we bought our four-storey National Office and Sydney branch building at 23 Abercrombie Street, just off Broadway and a short walk to Central Station. It was a big step forward for us, a big building (although not as big as our huge Melbourne building) that would house all our National Office and *Direct Action* needs, Sydney branch hall and offices, a bookshop opening onto the street and printshop behind. It cost $210,000.

The decision to buy a building for our national headquarters in Sydney was adopted at the June NC meeting, and Party Builder No. 1 launched an appeal to make this project possible. It reported that we were currently looking at a number of suitable buildings in Sydney:

> Acquiring the Anthony Street premises has put our Melbourne branch on a new plane. A similar building in Sydney will put us that much further ahead of the other left tendencies, improve our recruiting prospects, and give us a superior outlet for all our functions. Such a building would become a political centre for the whole city.
>
> This project is realisable because of the generosity of a member who has made a large donation to the party. This donation has begun the process; what we need now is a collective effort by all party members to guarantee its success …

> For this purpose we are launching the '500 Club.' We are asking
> comrades and supporters in good standing for an extraordinary effort
> above and beyond their other financial commitments to the party –
> particularly that you find a way to raise a $500 donation to the party for
> this fund. While most of us do not have such money on hand, there is
> usually a way to find it, whether through a bank loan, through family or
> friends, through a tax return, or whatever. This is not a pledge to be paid
> off over time, but a single donation made before the end of September.

At least 14 comrades had put their hands up and already raised $9,100. Peter Anderson (Peter Annear) wrote in *DA* (August 24) "Socialist Workers Party plans major expansion", with a picture of our prospective building, and announced the launch of the 500 Club. We also purchased new typesetting equipment and a printing press.

We were moving in during October, and doing renovations, estimated to be completed by early November. The biggest alteration that had to be made entailed removing the existing service lift, its housing and a surrounding metal staircase. The floor on each level was then extended, giving a lot more space, extra rooms, a kitchen for the branch and a parking bay on the ground floor. The main work was done by Jure Lasic, our Croatian building worker comrade, who came up from Melbourne to organise it.

The information newsletter/pamphlet, Party Builder, was used for motivating comrades. Party Builder No. 3 was produced in October 1983, with a photograph of our new building on the front. To meet the target of $50,000, we asked comrades "to cudgel their brains and ransack their bank accounts to find ways and means to make such a donation". Comrades had "emptied out savings accounts, deferred planned trips or special purchases, cashed insurance policies, approached parents or relatives for loans, taken out Bankcard or credit union loans, and directed their tax rebate cheques to the 500 club".

This campaign was impressive, considering that the appeal for the 500 Club was additional to the other already ambitious fundraising efforts of the party. "We are running an $80,000 Press and Education Fund Drive – the biggest in our history – and we are raising more money in weekly branch sustainers to the National Office than ever before."

With the money raised by the 500 Club, we were able to buy a big second-hand Solna 225 printing press for $13,000, plus installation costs of $1,500 for a specially hired crane and crew. The press weighed just under four tonnes, stood about two metres high, two metres wide and three metres long. It did represent a big step forward for our printshop at the time, although we never were able really to acquire all the skills necessary to make it an efficient and profitable printshop.

That issue of Party Builder also had an article about pledges being the bedrock of party finances, the overwhelming source of branch income and the foundation of the national finances of the party. We were running a campaign all year to raise the total sustainer received each week by the National Office, trying to achieve a weekly sustainer income of $2,400 – about $125,000 annually. To boost sustainer income, we had to raise the pledge income of the branches, especially from working comrades. The average pledge of working comrades was then $33.67, and we argued that we should be able to raise that to $40.

"At present we are placing a tremendous emphasis on finances", the article concluded. "This does not at all mean that the party is in a crisis. On the contrary: never before in our history have we been able to raise so much money in our various campaigns. No, what the tremendous importance we attach to finances reflects are the great opportunities facing us, opportunities we are striving to take advantage of. We are trying to achieve a great deal, we are straining ourselves to accomplish some big projects now, rather than wait for six months or a year. These projects, like the Melbourne headquarters at the beginning of the year and the national headquarters and printshop now, are enabling the party to move ahead forcefully in a very promising political situation."

The first issue of *DA* in 1984 had a new layout, new typesetting and a new masthead. It was eight pages larger and 10 cents higher in price. "Direct Action in the computer age", by Steve Painter, reported that "our new computerised typesetting system" had "replaced hours of tedious manual labour with hours of puzzling about how to make the thing work!"

International solidarity

We felt we had particular responsibility for solidarity in the Asia-Pacific region. Much of this in the 1980s focused on Vietnam. *DA* of June 7, 1983, carried an article by Rose Morley (possibly Rosemary McCann), "Australia's responsibility to aid Vietnam". The article was occasioned by Prime Minister Bob Hawke announcing that the Australian government would not restore postwar aid to Vietnam – even though the ALP 1982 federal conference had called for the resumption of aid. Australian aid had been suspended in January 1979 as part of the imperialist response to Vietnam's role in overthrowing the Khmer Rouge in Cambodia.

Morley's article defended the Vietnamese intervention in Cambodia, which came after a year and a half of escalating attacks into Vietnam by the Khmer

Rouge and which saved the lives of literally millions of Cambodians from the genocidal Pol Pot regime. It also recalled the the horrific destruction inflicted on Vietnam by the United States and its Australian ally. "The Hawke government's decision to refuse aid to Vietnam should be condemned by all sections of the labor movement in this country", Morley wrote.

In a back cover article in the July 5 issue, Roger Miles (Roger Markwick) detailed the damage done by the Australian-supported US war: 13 million tons of munitions exploded; the destruction of roads, railways, ports and nearly all industry; 26 million bomb craters preventing normal agriculture; 72 million litres of defoliants sprayed over South Vietnam; 1.5 million disabled former soldiers.

Then, after the Vietnamese victory, the US reneged on its promised US$3.2 billion in reconstruction aid, instead instituting a trade blockade; "the US even stopped the World Food Program granting [US]$5 million in credit to construct an irrigation system". The article concluded:

"Australia has been a partner in the crimes against Vietnam; for eight years Australian troops occupied its territory and committed crimes against its people. Restoring aid now could be a step towards making up for those crimes."

The *DA* of August 2 carried an advertisement for a public meeting in the Sydney Trades Hall Auditorium on "Defending the Vietnamese Revolution". Speakers were: Ken Fry; David Marr, the editor of *Vietnam Today;* Chris Rae from the CPA; Jim Percy; Jim Henderson from the SPA. There was also an ad for a Conference on Australia-Asia Relations at Sydney University, sponsored by CARPA. In the August 16 issue, Rose Morley wrote that130 people had attended a Sydney CARPA meeting urging "Restore Vietnam aid". CARPA was the vehicle for much of our Asia-Pacific solidarity activity. Another notable contribution was the magazine *Inside Indonesia,* established in November 1983, of which Max Lane was the founding editor.

Solidarity work with the Philippines was more complicated because the main left group, the Communist Party of the Philippines, led by Jose Maria Sison, was extremely sectarian towards the rest of the left – in the Philippines and internationally. We began working with Philippine activists around 1983, through contact with Francisco "Dodong" Nemenzo, the leader of a group called BISIG (Union of Filipino Socialists). Dodong was in Canberra, on an academic appointment at the ANU. Max Lane recalls:

"CARPA took up solidarity with the anti-Marcos movement because SWP members were officially excluded from the Philippines Action Support Group (PASG). I was able to be in CARPA and PASG because initially I wasn't an open SWP member, because I had been assigned to join the ALP. Our increasing

Philippines work was responded to more or less in a hostile manner by people like Denis Freney, who was one of the leading members of PASG.

"We toured Nemenzo nationally.

"In Canberra CARPA and PASG worked together with many joint events. PASG was headed up by Lynn Lee, who was non-sectarian. Later she was joined by Aida Santos, a Filipina who had been a key cadre in the Philippines underground with the CPP.

"Via Aida and through more visits to the Philippines (mainly myself I think in the '80s), as well as via Aida and Dodong, we had more communication with the CPP, although in a kind of arm's length way, except with some individual CPP leaders.

"In 1987 or 1988, after Sison was released from prison by Aquino, I met him and his wife in Manila. So it was probably in 1988 that the SWP wrote to Sison offering to tour him. Weirdly, he accepted, and all hell broke loose in Australia. PASG lobbied hard for him to withdraw the acceptance. In the end there was a compromise, that the tour would be organised by a national committee of three people: me, Lynn Lee and Bob Munz, in Melbourne. Lynn was non-sectarian; and Bob was on-and-off non-sectarian. I think Sison stayed with Jim Percy in Glebe. Sison later became hostile to us, when we wrote to him comradely taking up the issue of the CPP assassinating others on the left."[65]

Outside the Asia-Pacific, our priorities were defending and explaining the Cuban Revolution and the revolutions in Central America and the Caribbean.

When we could, we participated in the Australia-Cuba Friendship Society. The *DA* of November 1, 1983, carried an ad for ACFS's first national consultation. Some of our members also participated in solidarity brigades to Cuba. *DA* of August 29, 1984, carried a two-page feature by Greg Harris (Greg Adamson), who had been in the Eureka Brigade that spent a month in Cuba in January 1984. The article was based on a talk that he had given at the Tranby Aboriginal College in Sydney. It was titled, "How Cuba eliminated racism" ("How Cuba eliminated racial discrimination" would have been longer but more accurate). The article made clear the close ties between racism in Cuba and US imperialism; a breakout quote about conditions before 1959 stated:

"Beaches, hotels, parks and other places were off limits to a large proportion of the population. Much of this institutionalisation of racism was specifically designed to make people from the United States feel at home. Discrimination in hiring was strongest in US-owned companies."

As noted above, the resolution "The Cuban Revolution and its extension", adopted by the SWP national conference in January 1983, was one of two resolutions we considered important enough to print as a book. However, we were

still learning from these revolutionary struggles, which were important in caus-
ing us to study Lenin's approach to revolution in the underdeveloped countries.
At the National Committee meeting on October 6, 1984, the National Executive
(the body we had previously called the Political Committee) proposed some
amendments to the resolution. The report, by Doug Lorimer, explained that
the original resolution had failed to appreciate that the leaders of the Cuban
Revolution were following a Leninist strategy well before 1959; it was not forced
on them by events after they had come to power. The amendments also got
rid of the idea that the Cuban leaders had not realised the importance of in-
stitutionalising forms of socialist democracy until the failure of the 10 million
ton sugar harvest in 1970. The other major amendment deleted what were
essentially ultraleft criticisms of Cuban diplomacy.

A united front effort on Grenada

Following internal dissension in the Grenadan New Jewel Movement,
Deputy Prime Minister Bernard Coard staged a coup on October 16, 1983. Prime
Minister Maurice Bishop was placed under house arrest. Mass protests against
the action led to Bishop's escaping detention and reasserting his authority as
the head of the government, but he was eventually captured and murdered
along with several government officials loyal to him.

The US grabbed the opportunity. On October 25 it invaded, with marines
and helicopter units, the first major assertion of US military power since its defeat in Vietnam. The invasion was condemned by progressive forces around the
world as well as criticised by the governments in Canada, Trinidad and Tobago
and the United Kingdom. The United Nations General Assembly condemned
it as "a flagrant violation of international law" by a vote of 108 to 9, with 27
abstentions.

We quickly held a solidarity meeting which we organised jointly with
the SPA. With *DA* 460's cover demanding "US troops out of Grenada!", Jim
McIlroy reported on the "Strong rally for peace and solidarity" that was held
on November 6 in Sydney. Three hundred and fifty people attended. It was
sponsored by 20 organisations and co-chaired by Jim Percy and Peter Symon
of the SPA.

Speakers were: John Garcia, from CISCAC; Peter Jennings, from the
Philippines Action Support Group; Nick Papanikitas, secretary of the Original
Greek Atlas League; Maureen Watson, Aboriginal community leader; Patricia
Perez, Chile Solidarity Committee; Vijay Magan, Southern Africa Support
Campaign; Margaret Duckett, treasurer of NSW Labor Women; Suhal Farmiyan,

Arab National Federation; and Helen Jarvis, secretary of CARPA.

"Concluding the formal part of the rally – which was followed by entertainment from performers representing a number of nations – co-chair Jim Percy returned to the immediate question of Grenada …

"'The lesson for us in Australia is that we must be vigilant and seek maximum unity to defend past gains of the labor movement, and maintain the antiwar traditions of the labor movement.

"'We mustn't give an inch without a fight,' Percy said. "'We must make imperialism pay a price for Grenada. We must unite to defend Nicaragua and El Salvador.'"

Dave Holmes reported in *DA* 464 that the SWP-SPA collaboration caused a "flurry on left". It was attacked by Dave McKnight in *Tribune*, and by the SLL in *Workers News*. Holmes explained that the SWP-SPA collaboration was based on their shared opposition to the Prices and Incomes Accord and to the imperialist war drive. The SWP would like to be able to collaborate with the CPA on these issues too, Holmes wrote, but unfortunately, the CPA supported the Accord and apportioned more or less equal blame for the war drive to both Washington and Moscow.

Defending our views on these issues included discussing them with other tendencies willing to do so. *DA* for June 7, 1983, carried an ad for a Sydney debate between the International Socialists and the SWP: "Castro's Cuba – is it on the road to socialism?" The issue dated August 2, 1983, had an ad for a debate between IS and SWP in Melbourne on August 11 on the topic, "How Socialists Fight the Arms Race".

During this time we were also active in People for Nuclear Disarmament. In his October 6, 1984, NC report, Doug Lorimer explained: "We have set as our priority for antiwar work the building of a movement in solidarity with the advancing proletarian revolution in Central America …

"We should be clear that our work in the broader peace or nuclear disarmament movement that has developed in this country is subordinate to this task. That is, our work in PND groups across the country, while important in its own right[,] is[,] nevertheless, not an end in itself, but a means to help us win broader support for a movement against US intervention in Central America and for the campaign of political solidarity with the Central American revolutions organised nationally by CISCAC.

"We do this by fighting to maintain PND as a broad, non-exclusive coalition that focuses its fire on the imperialist war machine, and by raising in a transitional way the need for this movement to oppose US imperialism's war in Central America."

Split of pro-US SWP group

Peter Camejo, who had been scheduled to be here for our January 1983 conference, came several months later for the Karl Marx Centenary Conference. With our own printing press, in our new national office building, we printed the first issues of Peter Camejo's new magazine *North Star* (which no doubt didn't endear us to Jack Barnes).

We also printed *International News Service*, our replacement for *Intercontinental Press*, which was increasingly becoming an unreliable factional journal for the US SWP, a sad slide from its high status when it was founded and edited by Joe Hansen. After Joe Hansen died in 1979, his wife Reba had given our party a priceless donation of Joe's complete bound volumes of *Militant* and *International Socialist Review*. The library at our school was named the Joe Hansen Library.

Instead of the cancelled convention, the US SWP held a National Committee meeting on August 8-10, 1983, that launched an unprecedented attack on our party. Larry Seigle delivered a report on the Australian SWP. As we pointed out in a September 1 circular to our NC members, "This attack, which was based on gross misrepresentations and outright lies about our party's political positions and activities, included the following slanderous accusations:

- "that we have rejected the line and perspectives adopted by the 1979 World Congress of the Fourth International, in particular the turn to industry;
- "that we are turning our backs on the Fourth International and are on our way out of the Fourth International;
- "that we are undergoing a political degeneration similar to that of the Healy group in Britain in the 1960s;
- "that we have become apologists for a Croatian 'fascist' organisation;
- "that we have adapted to the chauvinist and racist ideology of Australian imperialism".

The attack by Seigle included the statement that the leadership of our party "is finished". In the discussion, Mac Warren, another PC member, went further, saying that our *party* was "finished".

"The only conclusion that can possibly be drawn from these positions is that the US SWP leadership advocates the splitting or destruction of our party and the construction in this country of another party in opposition to the Australian SWP.

"In view of this, the National Executive in its meeting on August 31 decided to cease all fraternal relations between our party and the US SWP, and to instruct all members of our party to cease all direct political collaboration, in any form, with the US SWP."

We were still reprinting articles in *DA* from the US SWP, from *IP* and the *Militant*, right up to this full-on attack. Our representative, Steve O'Brien, was sitting there in the hall observing as the vitriolic attack unfolded. He reported back to us by telephone.

Just after the Seigle report that wrote off our party, we bought our four-storey Sydney National Office building. The '80s was already shaping up as a decade of achievements – thinking things out for ourselves, with many important resolutions we drafted and adopted; the assets we had built up, with our buildings in Sydney, Melbourne, Brisbane and Hobart; our biggest ever election campaign; and we had made the turn to industry, without the distortions.

But we were weakened by a split in our leadership and by the cutting of our international links, certainly to the US SWP, who had been our initial teachers, but also to the FI. The international isolation probably had two sides to it. It forced us to think for ourselves and increasingly stand on our own feet, but it also led to some risky experiments: the monthly meetings; the new left party efforts. And we made some political mistakes also, for example our overblown hopes around *perestroika* (although that might have been needed), and this led to some attrition.

The US SWP declaration of war on our party was followed by them engineering a small split in 1983. We had to expel five members who were functioning as a disloyal grouping on behalf of the US SWP. An extensive information bulletin (No. 1 in 1983) containing all the material, was published in December. It was an unfortunate split. The saddest casualty was Nita Keig, who had been with us since the '60s, and had been Jim's companion in the '60s and '70s. The others were Dave Deutschmann, Deb Shnookal, Ron Poulsen and Kay McVey.

It quickly became evident that US SWP followers in other countries would join the attack on us. The New Zealand Socialist Action League held a national conference in December 1983, a month after we had expelled the five. However, all five were allowed to attend the SAL conference, and Keig and McVey were seated as "fraternal delegates". A January 16, 1984, letter to the SAL from Peter Anderson [Peter Annear] for the SWP NE protested against this and announced: "In light of your actions, which can only be interpreted as support for the split operation being carried out against our party by these five, the National Executive of the SWP at its meeting of December 30 decided to break off all fraternal relations with the SAL".

The making of a sect

At the January 3, 1984, SWP NC, a full report on the evolution of the US SWP was presented by Doug Lorimer and subsequently published as a pamphlet, *The making of a sect*. It was a thorough and pretty definitive analysis.

Doug traced the beginning of the US SWP degeneration to a misconceived approach to the turn to industry. The turn needed to be a short-lived tactic, he pointed out. This was because the concentration on building and consolidating industrial fractions necessarily diverted attention and resources from campaigns and movements that primarily involved forces *outside* the industrial unions, and "most radical political activity still occurs outside industry and the industrial unions". So, "if this tactic was made a permanent feature of party life … we would stop conducting rounded political work intervening as a vanguard political force in *all* the progressive social and political struggles and movements".

But this is precisely what the US party's leaders had done: "Today the US SWP leaders and their international faction openly argue that the turn is a permanent orientation and not a tactic … every resolution and report on the turn adopted by them since 1979 has referred to 'deepening the turn' and references to its completion have totally disappeared from their vocabulary …"

"Artificially isolating" a party from active involvement in struggles could lead to political degeneration in either of two ways. One, the party could adapt its politics to day-to-day economic struggles, becoming economist, as had happened to some Maoist groups that colonised industry in the early 1970s. The other degeneration, the sectarian course followed by the US SWP, was to justify abstention from struggles by dismissing them as "petty bourgeois".

But while claiming it was orienting purely to the working class, the US SWP had in fact turned away from real struggle in industrial unions: "From the correct general view that our strategy for transforming the unions involves winning the ranks to a class-struggle perspective, the US SWP leadership has ruled out using union elections as a tactic to help advance that strategy. Instead, they argue that socialists can only run in elections for union posts when the ranks have already attained a class-struggle perspective. In effect, this reduces the party's role in the unions to little more than abstract propaganda."

To justify this position, Doug continued, the US SWP leaders developed a theory that presented the class-collaborationist union bureaucracy as a reflection of the consciousness of better-paid workers. "This position is leading them to fetishise work among the worse-paid and most poorly organised sections of the work-force …"

The report also documented the organisational degeneration of the US party, in which the leadership had evolved into "a permanent faction or clique" that "seeks to contain all differences within itself … Maintaining the public solidarity of the grouping takes precedence over honestly presenting all political positions before the party."

Because it has been cut off from the realities of working-class politics, a sect has no objective reference by which to judge its policies, which are decided arbitrarily by the leadership. But then the leadership group requires an arbiter to rule on which policies are "correct". "A personality cult is created around this figure, who becomes the fount of political wisdom for the sect."

Other publications that have usefully analysed the sad degeneration of the US party are: "Cannonism vs Barnesism. The degeneration of the SWP", by Doug Lorimer, in *Building the Revolutionary Party. An introduction to James P. Cannon;* Pedro Camejo's pamphlet *Against Sectarianism. The Evolution of the Socialist Workers Party 1978-1993;* Barry Sheppard's *The Party: The Socialist Workers Party 1960-1988,* Vol 2.

Reassessing Trotskyism

There was an obvious link between our break with the US SWP and our reassessment of Trotskyism and break with the Fourth International, and it raises some interesting questions. For example, how much did the fact of the degeneration of the US SWP influence us to take this course? If they hadn't gone off the rails, wouldn't we have been more likely to have stayed longer in the FI, hacking away for our positions?

The degeneration of the US SWP had an impact on us in several ways. It forced us to look more closely at the problems of Trotskyism. The US SWP had a generally correct orientation to Nicaragua and the Cubans on paper, but their practice was still often sectarian, for example in their abstention from the solidarity campaign. They were able to recognise the revolutionary developments in Central America, unlike some Trotskyists, but they were still fighting for the Trotskyist mantle in the FI, fighting to establish that they had the "revolutionary continuity" from Trotsky.

Seeing their degeneration at close quarters, perhaps some of us reacted a little like "there but for the grace of God go we". We'd seen the phenomenon of other weird sects laying claim to the mantle of Trotskyism, both within the FI, Moreno of Argentina, and without – Healy, Posadas, the Spartacists. Up close to the US SWP, perhaps we didn't initially see the same phenomenon developing, just noting bits and pieces. When it struck us that here was another full-blown example of Trotskyist cultism, we were repulsed. And perhaps, if they hadn't degenerated like that, we would have been more hopeful of reforming the whole of the FI, and would have stayed in there longer – and wasted further time.

Our final decision to leave the Fourth International was made at our NC meeting in August 1985 and ratified at our 11th national conference in January 1986. In addition to the political disagreements that we had developed with the majority of the FI, and our feeling that we were unlikely to be able to convince them to change their positions, we felt the necessity to cut our links with the FI in order to make it easier to develop relations with other revolutionaries around the world.

In the 1920s, the Communist movement in many countries was given political direction and clarity by the successful Russian Revolution. The revolutions since World War II have played the same role, especially the Cuban, Nicaraguan, Vietnamese and Chinese revolutions. The key failure of the FI was its inability to respond to new revolutions, to new revolutionaries, and that was at the heart of our decision to leave the FI.

Key questions in our rethinking on Trotskyism

The main political document in which we settled our account with our Trotskyist past was our "red book", *The Struggle for Socialism in the imperialist epoch*. The draft was first adopted by our National Executive in July 1984, approved by our National Committee in October and finally adopted at our 10th national conference in January 1985. Like our Cuban resolution, we also presented this for a vote at the 1985 FI World Congress. It's a very comprehensive document. We included in it all our new thinking up to that point. In coming to grips with the mistakes of Trotskyism, the document focused on two major political errors.

First: "an underestimation of the role of national liberation struggles within the worldwide fight for socialism, in particular a programmatic error of downgrading the anti-imperialist united front and the democratic stage of revolution in the semicolonial countries, from which flow a sectarian attitude towards national liberation movements; this error was largely responsible for the delay by the majority of the FI in recognizing the creation of a workers and peasants' government in Nicaragua in July 1979".

Second: "an overestimation of the place, within the tasks confronting the workers states and within the world revolution, occupied by political revolution against the ruling castes in the bureaucratised socialist states".

On both of these key areas we became even clearer in our understanding in the intervening years, but the important thing is that we were now on the right track. (Also, the document was written to try to win support for our position within the FI, so the formulations reflected this.)

In addition to the main programmatic reorientations that the document proposed, it also began an analysis of the foundation of some of the political errors, looking at the "circle spirit" that prevailed in the Trotskyist movement, the isolation from mass struggles and the resulting fetishisation of written programmatic questions. The document looked at the history of the Trotskyist movement, recognising some of the objective difficulties in the '30s and '40s, the dominance of Stalinism and social democracy within the workers' movement. But it pointed out, "[O]bjective difficulties alone cannot account for the fact that the Fourth International remains very much a minority current after four decades of rise in the world revolution" since World War II.

Fetishising a narrow program

"Without overlooking or detracting from the many real achievements of the International and particular sections, it must be said that as a current the Fourth International has not yet overcome the vices of the 'circle spirit' against which Trotsky often warned. There is an inescapable pressure on small, isolated groups to retreat into the endless elaboration of the written program as a substitute for active involvement in the class struggle. Particular points of the program that set the group apart from other currents or the labor movement as a whole can then be elevated above their real importance – that is, they become sectarian fetishes serving to reinforce the group's isolation. The only way out of such a vicious circle appears to be the sudden junking of the program in pursuit of shortcuts. Moreover, the particular programmatic 'points of honor' are themselves likely to include mistakes of greater or lesser importance to the degree that they were developed in isolation from the class struggle; such mistakes become self-perpetuating in that they prevent the group from intervening in struggles and thereby deprive it of the possibility of checking and correcting its program in practice."

The document continued by pointing out that these pressures have been multiplied by a false conception of the way in which a revolutionary international can and should function. This conception was referred to in a resolution adopted by the FI in 1954, which described the FI as "constituted exclusively on the basis of agreement of the cadres with a precise program, strategy and tactics". Thus the isolation from the masses was converted into a virtue. This was a common theme in the Trotskyist movement. Often it was accompanied by a ritual assertion of the need to develop links with the mass movement, to end that isolation. But the fact that the international organisation was set up in this way inevitably led to political mistakes and the imposition of these generalised errors on all parties. The process of universalising the tactics to be followed all around the world began, and they were generally tactical mistakes. In the 1950s the FI made the tactic of complete immersion in the mass reformist parties a universal tactic. In the late '60s, a new universal tactic was adopted for its Latin American sections, guerrilla warfare. In 1979, another universal tactic, the "turn to industry", was adopted.

The Comintern under Stalin also had this centralist approach to an international, leading to the subordination of most of the Communist parties to the diplomatic needs of the Soviet bureaucracy. But where in the case of the Third International it led to tragedy, in the case of the Fourth International it became a farce, a centralised organisation built on nothing but small propaganda groups united around a written program.

So in the founding programmatic document of the Fourth International, the *Transitional Program*, Trotsky could state that "today there is not another revolutionary current on the face of the planet, worthy of the name". Think what it means to say that in 1938. The few thousand people in the Trotskyist movement were the only revolutionaries in the world. And in the following 10 years there were big revolutions – and they weren't led by the "only revolutionaries". We didn't really lose that sort of view of ourselves until 1979. Most Trotskyists still have it.

So the written program was elevated to our distinguishing feature. The implication was that it's a finished program. But in reality, that's not how a program is developed at all. Our *Struggle for Socialism* resolution pointed this out, and noted that among the key problems of the Fourth International had been:

- "a view of program abstracted from the practice of parties, which leads to judging other currents by their words rather than their deeds and thus to the view that the Fourth International is the only Marxist revolutionary current;
- "an attitude towards other class-struggle or revolutionary currents that downplays their achievements and seeks for programmatic differences rather than practical agreements;
- "a reluctance to put our program into practice, as seen in the failure to orient to the industrial working class and establish a base there when the conditions for doing so exist."

In addition to important lessons we learned about specific aspects of our political program and theory, we also learned some valuable lessons about the nature and role of the program itself during the 1980s. As our new program drafted in 1985 stressed at the start, a program "can never be a finished work. Marxism … is not a dogma fixed for all time and circumstance, but a guide to action. The socialist program must be constantly developed and tested in the light of the living experiences of the working-class movement, and all who are struggling for social progress."

Lenin's two-stage theory of revolution

If any programmatic position has been thoroughly tested and found correct in the light of the living experiences of the working-class movement, it must be Lenin's two-stage theory of revolution. But for decades, in spite of experience after experience to the contrary, the Trotskyist movement, and our party in its infancy and adolescence, counterposed Trotsky's theory of permanent revolution. This was the first of the two major errors that we had to overcome to break from our Trotskyist past.

As already mentioned, it was the Nicaraguan Revolution that shocked us out of this position. But the majority of the FI, desperately clinging to their unique program, wouldn't budge. A phrase you'd hear time and again in the Trotskyist movement after every revolution that took place, was, "This revolution confirms Trotsky's theory of permanent revolution". It was rather peculiar: you'd have thought it more sensible to say that, in regard to Nicaragua, for example, the revolution confirmed the Sandinista theory of revolution. And doing that would lead you to study the basic theory that guided the Sandinistas, the Cubans and the Vietnamese – Lenin's writings on the Russian Revolution. We incorporated this understanding in *The Struggle for Socialism in the imperialist epoch* (pp. 51-2):

> 1. The course of the colonial revolution continues to confirm the validity of the Marxist strategy developed by Lenin as a guide to revolution in the underdeveloped countries during the imperialist epoch. This strategy is based on four basic premises:
> 2. The national democratic revolution in the backward countries cannot be consistently led by the national bourgeoisie. If it is to carry through a thoroughgoing agrarian reform and the destruction of the old neocolonial state apparatus, it must be led by the working class, in alliance with the broad masses of the peasantry and other petty-bourgeois strata, united around a revolutionary democratic program.
> 3. On the basis of such a worker-peasant alliance, the military and political power of the bourgeoisie and large landowners must be

overthrown and replaced by a workers and peasants' government resting on the armed power of the worker-peasant masses.

4. Such a workers and peasants' government first solves the national, democratic, agrarian and anti-imperialist tasks, improving the workers' conditions and expanding their control over the economy at the expense of the capitalists.

5. As the organisation and class consciousness of the workers and their alliance with the poor peasants deepens, the revolution develops as a permanent process, growing over uninterruptedly to the specifically socialist tasks of expropriation of the bourgeoisie and establishment of a socialist state based on a nationalised, planned economy. The workers and peasants' government is thus the transitional form of the state power of the proletariat and its allies preceding the consolidation of a socialist state.

This contrasts with our previous positions, and the positions of Trotskyists (not of Trotsky from 1917 to 1924), which wouldn't contemplate the suggestion of possible stages in the revolutionary process. Trotsky's theory of permanent revolution does not give a correct formulation of the class alliances and dynamics of the revolutionary process in those countries where national democratic tasks are still to be carried through. The theory led to an ultra-left and sectarian political position. In the cruder versions of permanent revolution, it was workers revolution now, a socialist revolution immediately, or else it was a "betrayal". Our new draft program incorporated this Leninist understanding on page 17. It was a fundamental break with our Trotskyist past.

Reform in the socialist countries

The second major error central to the Trotskyist world view was also tackled in our *Struggle for Socialism* resolution. This was the Trotskyist view that correcting the errors and mistakes made in the Soviet Union in the course of constructing socialism had equal weight in the worldwide struggle for socialism with the fight against imperialist capitalism.

We recognised a real problem of Stalinophobia within the Trotskyist movement – that is, a hatred and fear of Stalinism so intense that it distorted political judgment and attitudes to the world class struggle. For example, the reason we (and the Trotskyist movement) failed to learn from the Vietnamese Revolution the lessons that we subsequently learned from the Sandinistas was our Stalinophobia: we didn't think they could teach us anything because we thought they were Stalinists.

In our red book we continued to see the need for a political revolution as "a precondition for a real reform of the state … The fight for reforms and the political revolution are transitionally linked because real and lasting improvement in the situation of the workers and peasants requires an end to the bureaucracy's material privileges and monopoly of political power." But we continued:

"The political revolutions required in the bureaucratised socialist states are qualitatively different from the social revolutions that constitute the way forward for workers and peasants in the semicolonial and imperialist countries."

In his report to the August 1985 National Committee meeting where we formally took the decision to leave the Fourth International, Doug Lorimer expanded on this question. He pointed out: "In a bureaucratised socialist state, the repressive apparatus has a dual role and character. It is used to defend the social conquests of the proletariat, the new socialist forms of property, against imperialism, and it is used by the bureaucratic oligarchy to protect its material privileges and monopoly of political power against the working class." He outlined further how the error of the Fourth International flowed from its failure to understand the anti-imperialist axis of the world revolution, including the anti-imperialist axis of the struggle to make the bureaucratised socialist states better and stronger instruments of the workers in opposing imperialism, through the radical democratisation of the institutions of these states.

(Even our characterising them as socialist states was strongly attacked by the Trotskyist movement, which still insisted that they should continue to be referred to as "workers states".)

But even in our red book, our thinking was still continuing. At the time, we were becoming increasingly sceptical about the traditional Trotskyist conception of a political revolution. In the party's new draft program reported on at our 11th national conference in January 1986, we made no mention of a call for political revolution in the bureaucratised socialist states. Even before the coming to power of Mikhail Gorbachev, we had started to leave open the possibility that the reform process in these countries might actually take place from within the Communist parties. This is something the Trotskyist movement had categorically ruled out.

We had begun to take notice of people like Soviet historian Roy Medvedev. In contrast to most Trotskyists, who had very little first-hand information about the actual situation within Soviet society and the CPSU, or who relied solely on Trotsky's writings from the 1930s, good as they were at the time, Medvedev provided very interesting information on the new educated layers rising within the Soviet party, and the different currents within the bureaucracy. We used his 1970 book *On Socialist Democracy* extensively at our party school from an early stage.

In his report on "Perestroika: The reform of the Russian Revolution," presented to our October 1987 National Committee meeting, Dave Holmes outlined the roots of the reform process in the Soviet Union, and contrasted the reality that was unfolding from within the CPSU with the rigid schema of Trotskyists like Ernest Mandel, who refused to recognise a real "political revolution" when it occurred because it didn't conform with their particular schema. Dave pointed out that Trotsky himself made a detailed, scientific analysis of Soviet reality, and never made the mistake of viewing the bureaucracy as a monolithic whole. But by adhering to an unscientific schema, Trotskyists like Mandel were backed into an impossible position. "As the Soviet reform cuts ever more deeply, Mandel has to up the ante to defend his position that it's all a bureaucratic sham. He lists 13 points which must be met before he'll recognise it as a genuine process. Most likely, as many of these conditions are met, Mandel will think of further ultimatums to make." This is what has happened as the reform process went deeper and further in the last two years.

So we were able to break out of that narrow ideological framework that would have prevented us recognising and welcoming wholeheartedly such a major development as *perestroika* and *glasnost.*

Developing our industrial tactics

Despite our criticism of prescribing the turn to industry as a universal tactic for all parties in the Fourth International irrespective of their size and the political and social situation they faced, we carried out the turn enthusiastically and thoroughly, and did succeed in getting the vast majority of our membership industrial jobs. We suffered a number of organisational and political consequences as a result. We lost a chunk of our membership for a start, which shouldn't have happened. And we disoriented the party politically, missing out on some political opportunities, since the turn was based on a prediction of a coming sharp showdown amongst the industrial working class.

But we pulled back from compounding these errors along the lines of the US SWP, which after a while decided that the turn was more than a temporary, sharp tactic, but a permanent feature of their political activity, a strategy.

At our July 1982 NC meeting, we recognised that we had completed the turn. We also recognised that political activity was not focused just on the industrial working class. We stepped up our activities in solidarity with Central America, for example, and were active in the growing anti-nuclear campaigns. In contrast, the US SWP was adopting an increasingly abstentionist position in conjunction with its turn. In May 1981 it abstained from a demonstration of 100,000 people in Washington, DC, on Central America, on the grounds that what was needed instead was a "working-class antiwar movement".

Furthermore, the US SWP had adopted a rigid and sectarian approach to tactics within the union movement, and were trying to impose this line on the rest of the Trotskyist movement, at least on their followers around the world. We had this fight out within our own party. Firstly, they insisted that comrades in industry should abstain from accepting job delegate positions. And secondly they made it a principle that we shouldn't stand in union elections for full-time positions. Although we never adopted those positions, it's worth mentioning to highlight the positions we adopted on trade union tactics, and the rich experiences we had in the unions.

We adopted a specific resolution on "Revolutionary strategy and tactics in the trade unions" at our ninth national conference, in January 1983. This was still marked by a number of schematic conceptions, and it took our continuing experience in the trade unions in the 1980s to get a more balanced, political approach to our work. A much more rounded presentation of how we thought socialists should work in the trade unions came through in Dick Nichols' report to our October 1987 NC meeting, "New right trade unionism and the crisis of the left".

Review of 1983 and perspectives for 1984

We took stock at the SWP National Executive meeting, December 18, 1983, where Jim outlined the perspectives, and they were presented in my NC report in January 1984, a review of 1983 and perspectives for 1984.

We recognised a certain quietness in the labour movement, and the need for a forced march in building ourselves and the expansion of the party apparatus in Sydney and Melbourne. This had an effect on the left – the SPA split; we split; the CPA was wracked by destructive discussions.

But we had some real growth and were able to carry out three diverse small fusions in this period: (1) with the Turkish group, Revolutionary Path; this would step up our migrant work, although we hadn't been able to get it going properly yet; (2) with the Rosebery workers on Tasmania's West Coast; (3) with Socialist Fight; uniting with this small Trotskyist group could be a pole of attraction for us, and help with our ALP work. There were lessons for the left, and it helped to refute our reputation as splitters.

What had been the negative effects of plunging organisationally and financially on growth in the previous two to three years? We pointed out it had been somewhat disorganising for the party: we had not integrated new members, there was sloppiness on recruiting, and trade union fractions were not functioning well. Youth training suffered, and we had neglected education. We had got by because of our full-time party school, with 70 comrades having gone through at that point. But other aspects of education needed attention.

The most serious consequence had been the declining sales of *DA*, going from 2,355 in 1981 to 1,866 in 1983.

A further factor was the tiredness of an older layer of cadres. There'd been a delay in replacing them. We'd done OK in keeping them, not driving them out, but the party couldn't be held back by them.

How do we lead the party today, we asked? The key, we decided, was our weekly paper, as a recruiter. So we looked at where we were going with our system of press. It had become quite diverse: *Direct Action, Labor Militant, Resistance, Socialist Worker, Venceremos, Cuba Today* and *CARPA Bulletin*. All were OK, but we were still in crisis. None of them made money. We competed with ourselves. We needed more small pamphlets, which we were preparing to produce.

The real problem was that the weekly *DA* was in a critical state. The market was there, people were willing to buy, the sales rate was still there, but the number of hours that comrades sold for had dropped. The CPA was pushing *Tribune* to be the mass paper of the left. There was some demoralisation about our paper. We were also affected by the leadership problems of the last few years. Plus cutbacks forced a reduction in page numbers; it was a smaller paper.

But the problem was deeper. Have we departed from producing a "variegated combination paper", Jim asked? We had to return to that view of the paper, the centrality of the paper. We were also miseducating the layer of new young comrades, but not just them alone, all comrades.

A turn on this could help us in all areas. For example, it would be a blow to the CPA; it could help in mass movement areas; it could help us on the job; it could help as a recruiter.

To do all this we needed a 24-page paper, to break with the lethargy, to cover all areas, with better graphics. We decided to drop the separate *Resistance* paper, so *DA* would be a joint effort. We decided to continue with *Labor Militant* as a monthly but to scrap *Socialist Worker. Intercontinental Press* was no longer useful for the education of comrades on international issues. Neither was *International Viewpoint*, published by the European FI comrades. We were not strong enough to convert *Socialist Worker* into something like that. Two sales efforts were too difficult, so *DA* would have to be the vehicle for our international views.

To finance it, we needed to push *DA* sales up to at least 3,000, which would require a different level of commitment. And the price needed to rise to 50 cents.

To lead it, Jim said we would have to change the way we'd been functioning in the NO. We needed to have the political discussion. The NO as a whole was the problem. Jim proposed to put *DA* under the control of a Political Bureau of Jim Percy, Pat Garcia, Peter Annear, Dave Holmes, Steve Painter and Janet Parker. We'd have an administration committee of Jim, Dave Holmes, Dave O'Neill (Dave Reilly) and Tony Dewberry and an international committee of Jim, John Percy, Allen Myers and Doug Lorimer.

These perspectives were presented to the SWP NC, December 31, 1983-January 2, 1984, preceding our Resistance and Socialist Educational Conference, with the following reports: Fusions, International and Antiwar, Political, Labor Party, Perspectives, World Movement. Pedro Camejo and Byron Ackerman, a comrade of Camejo's from the US, were invited to observe the NC.

We noted that we had grown well over the previous three years, from a total tendency of 212 in early 1981 to 339 in December 1983.

Resistance and educational conference

We held the Resistance and Socialist Educational Conference January 3-8, 1984, at Hawkesbury, with Resistance delegate discussion and voting on four reports: The International Situation and the Fight against War, by Margo Condoleon; The Hawke Labor Government and Perspectives for Resistance, Megan Delahunt; The Need for a Revolutionary Youth Organisation and the Role of Youth in the Class Struggle, Janet Parker; Building Resistance, Sally Low. Jim Percy gave a feature talk, "Prospects for the Socialist Movement in Australia Today", printed in four parts in *DA* in February.

Special guests were Pedro Camejo, speaking on "Can we make a revolution in advanced capitalist countries?" and "Politics in the USA in 1984"; and Frej Anderson, from Sweden, for the FI United Secretariat, speaking on "The Western European workers movement today". Other guest speakers were Raul Torchez, a representative of the World Front in Solidarity with the People of El Salvador; a Filipino guest and a comrade from Revolutionary Path.

During the conference, at least 15 participants decided to join the SWP, at least another three were seriously considering, and five joined Resistance.

Small regroupment efforts

In 1983, militant miners in Rosebery, on Tasmania's West Coast, carried out a determined struggle to defend their jobs. We sent Renfrey Clarke there to cover the campaign in *Direct Action*, which in 1984 led to publication of his book *The Picket*. The experience helped our understanding of the opportunities and problems of developing a revolutionary socialist current within the heartland of the Australian industrial working class.

We asked Andrew Jamieson to go there, where he got a job in the mines and joined some of the militants into a branch of the SWP. He built a broad base in the various mines of the area, and was elected to the local council. But eventually we were unable to continue the party branch.[66]

In January 1984 we completed a fusion with the Socialist Fight group, having merged our magazines *Socialist Fight* and *Labor Militant*. They were linked to a Trotskyist current in England (now called Workers Liberty). The fusion led to some lively pre-conference discussion in the lead-up to our January 1985 conference, but with widening differences on international and local issues, they left, preferring cosy affiliation with London to a larger, effective organisation here. They probably would have felt pleased with themselves – they left with one more member than when they joined, Richard Lane.

We also united in 1983 with a small, extremely militant group of comrades from the Turkish organisation Revolutionary Path – Dev Yol. We first met them when they were playing a key role in the big Ford strike in Melbourne in 1980. We worked with them in a united front solidarity organisation, Committee Against Repression in Turkey, in Melbourne. In October 1983, we coopted one of their leaders on to our National Committee. But cultural and language problems made it hard for the unity to be permanent.

The balance sheet of these three fusions was generally positive. They did not work out in the long run, but our openness to them, our experimental approach and our thirst to make the party grow were essentially positive.

Taft split from CPA

In the early to mid-1980s, the CPA, already in decline, haemorrhaged further. A right-wing faction headed by Bernie Taft and his son Mark split from the party in 1984. In the May 2, 1984, *DA*, Michael Peterson (Peter Boyle) reported that 23 members of the CPA's Victorian state committee, and 12 mostly young leaders of the Queensland branch, had resigned from the party. Bernie Taft told the *Australian* newspaper that there remained only 300 CPA members in Victoria, and that most of them would resign soon. The Taft group said that the CPA had declined from 25,000 members at the end of World War II to only 1,300 in 1984, and that many of those 1,300 were not active.

Headed "The continuing fragmentation of the CPA", the *DA* article outlined that process:

"The biggest decline took place with the end of the alliance between the imperialist powers and the USSR against Nazi Germany. Most members who joined in that period received little political education and were not equipped to stand up to the Cold War propaganda that began in the late 1940s. They left in their thousands.

"In 1964 a pro-Peking wing of the CPA split off to form the CPA (Marxist-Leninist). This group grew during the period of the Vietnam Moratorium movement because of its stong anti-imperialist stance, but as Peking later developed closer relations with Washington, the CPA (ML) fell apart. Recently, one of this group's best-known leaders, Clarrie O'Shea, announced his resignation.

"The CPA suffered another split in 1970 [after] the USSR invaded Czechoslovakia to crush the movement for democratic reform led by Dubcek. CPA members who objected to the party's criticism of this action left to form the Socialist Party of Australia.

"This party suffered a split of its own last year when most of its union officials, led by building union leader, Pat Clancy, resigned or were expelled. The Clancy group's political perspectives appear similar to those of the Taft group."

The Taft group intended to unite with "other genuine socialist forces" within the ALP. Peterson wrote that it would be located politically somewhere "between the Socialist Left and the Centre Unity factions of the Victorian ALP".

Social Rights Conference

We initiated the Social Rights Conference in Melbourne at Easter 1984, and built it jointly with the SPA and other forces opposed to Hawke Labor's Accord (although we did most of the organising). A manifesto, the "Charter of Social Rights", and the Social Rights Campaign flowed out of this.

The advertising leaflet stated: "The Social Rights Campaign Conference has been organised to provide an opportunity to develop an alternative strategy for the labour movement and other democratic and progressive organisations. This alternative strategy must be one that benefits the vast majority of the population and not just a tiny wealthy minority. It must also defend social and democratic rights …

"The purpose of the Conference is to aid the process of gathering together all those in the labour movement who see the imperative need to defend the working class from the attacks being made on their wages, conditions and living standards and who are concerned with the need to prevent nuclear war and discuss questions of foreign policy, solidarity and independence" – that last word being a concession to the SPA.

The conference was held at University High School, Melbourne, April 20-23, 1984, sponsored by the Social Rights Campaign. International guest speakers were Goete Kilden, a car worker from the Swedish Socialist party, a section of the FI, and Angelos Anastasiou, member of the Central Committee of the Communist Party of Greece. We had also scheduled Alain Krivine, a leader of the May-June 1968 upsurge in France and a central leader of the LCR, but unfortunately he had to cancel at the last minute because of illness.

The conference was sponsored by a very long list of union officials and shop stewards, mostly I think associated with the SWP or SPA, and some Maoists, leaders of the SWP and SPA, some academics and left-wing ALP individuals and branches (including Anthony Albanese, president of Sydney Young Labor at the time) and a range of other organisations and committees.

Over the four days, we had plenary evening sessions for the international guest speakers, plus three plenary sessions with panels of speakers that included SWP, SPA, CPA (ML) leaders and ALP lefts or militant trade unionists. Our plenary session speakers were Jim Percy, Pat Brewer and Maurice Sibelle. For the SPA there were Peter Symon, Jack McPhillips and Anna Pha. For the CPA (ML) there was at least Clarrie O'Shea. On the last day, we had a "reportbacks and perspectives" plenary to discuss "Where do we go from here?"

There were 10 other sessions, with a choice of five talks, panels or workshops covering a very broad range of topics. We were still trying to carry out an entry attitude to the ALP, so many of our union activist speakers and youth were listed as being ALP members, with the most prominent NC members being listed as SWP leaders.

For example, Jim Percy also gave a talk on "Can we make a revolution in advanced capitalist countries?" I gave a talk on "The Vietnam War and its lessons for the labour movement", and Dick Nichols, Jamie Doughney, Margo Condoleon, Brett Trenery, Tony Forward, Jim McIlroy and Janet Parker also spoke as SWP or Resistance leaders. We had a large number of speakers who had gained credentials as job delegates or union leaders.

Academics who spoke included Humphrey McQueen, Brian McKinley, Ian Ward, Ted Wheelwright, Joe Camilleri, Boris Frankel, Grant Evans, Tom Gill, Alan Roberts, Peter Beilharz and Rob Watts. Left ALP figures and union leaders who spoke included Bill Hartley, Kevin Healy and David Grove.

At the conclusion, the Social Rights Conference issued a "statement" rejecting the Accord and vowing to continue to organise further activities. Six hundred and fifty people registered for the conference. We imposed a levy on our members in other branches to facilitate the travel of Perth comrades.

We had our first real experiences of working with the Socialist Party of Australia. Our joint work in the Social Rights Campaign made us realise that changing alignments in left politics made it imperative for all possibilities of cooperation on the left to be explored fully.

We had a strong desire to break out of isolation and take advantage of the further break-up of the remaining forces that had made up the old CPA. In 1983 the SPA suffered a split of a right-wing faction of trade union officials, led by Pat Clancy of the BWIU, which had been operating increasingly independently.

The Clancy faction was based largely on layers in the trade union bureaucracy, and one of the key leaders was Bill Brown (his daughter Lee Rhiannon was later in the NSW upper house for the Greens in NSW and in 2010 elected to the Senate). This current formed the Association for Communist Unity. ("Not very Communist, and not much in favour of unity", was a frequent gibe of those who had political contact with them, including their former comrades in the SPA.)

The split of the more right wing forces in the ACU propelled the SPA partly to the left, and made our joint work, particularly on Australian issues like opposition to the Accord, more realistic.

ALP moves right

After the Social Rights Conference in Melbourne over Easter, the SWP NC met on April 24, 1984. The agenda consisted of reports on the international draft resolution, Iran, the PLO and political perspectives.

The Labor Party held its biennial national conference in July 1984. In the July 18 *DA*, John Kelly wrote that the 99 delegates included 47 federal and state parliamentarians, 19 full-time union officials, six ALP state secretaries, a "scattering" of Labor Party staff members and five lawyers. "There was not a blue-collar worker to be found." Similarly, most of the 500 observer spaces were for journalists, businesses, diplomats and party officials; fewer than 10 percent of seats were for "the public".

The conference was a solid triumph for the right faction; Bill Hayden's Centre Left faction blocked with it on most issues to defeat the left. The conference junked Labor's anti-uranium policy and endorsed access to Australian ports by the US military.

"Against the combined assault of the right and Centre Left, the left put up a fight on particular issues like uranium mining, ASIO, the US bases and abortion rights. But the left's overwhelming support for the anti-working class economic policies of the Hawke government, such as the wage cutting prices and incomes accord, effectively disarms it."

A week later, the National Committee meeting of Resistance heard a political report that noted a "delay" in workers' fight back against the real wage cuts being imposed by the Hawke ALP government. *DA* reported that the NC made an "adjustment" of Resistance's work among students. While we were still in the framework of the "working class moving to centre stage", we had enough contact with reality to recognise that there were more opportunities to win students to socialist ideas. Resistance national secretary Margo Condoleon was quoted as telling the plenum: "[W]ithin the framework of the Labor government and the accord, and the effect this has had on the working-class fightback, the possibility exists that other sections of society may come forward and play an important role.

"We have seen large numbers of students participate in peace demonstrations and the formation of antiwar groups throughout the country."

Margo also referred to the growth of anti-racist groups and the success of Resistance groups on campuses. "The conclusion", said the *DA* report, "was that Resistance should step up its work on the campuses, running regular bookstalls, forum and other activities, producing regular newssheets, and building Resistance groups".

A third report looked at the growth of an antiwar movement fuelled by "the development of the huge anti-missiles movement in Europe, the worldwide opposition to imperialist aggression against colonial countries and the widespread anger against the Hawke Labor government's warlike policies".

Setting the record straight on Vietnam

At the SWP National Committee meeting of October 6-8, 1984,[67] reports were presented by Dave Holmes, on the *Struggle for Socialism* document; Doug Lorimer, on Central America and Cuba and the Fight Against War; Allen Myers, on Vietnam; Pat Brewer, on the Australian Political Situation and Tasks in Trade Unions; Jim Percy, on the ALP and Electoral Policy, and Janet Burstall, a counter-report; Margo Condoleon, on Women's Liberation; Tony Forward, on Organisation, Party Tasks and Building Resistance; and Jim Percy, World Movement.

The report on Vietnam formalised the correction of our attitude toward the Vietnamese Communist Party, which we had earlier regarded as a Stalinist party. After being adopted by the NC, the report was published as a pamphlet, *The Vietnamese Revolution and its leadership.* This pointed out that debate about Vietnam within the Fourth International had been distorted by adherence to the Trotskyist theory of permanent revolution. One tendency, mainly the European sections, saw that a socialist revolution had occurred and concluded that the Vietnamese Communists must have followed permanent revolution, if not on a theoretical level, at least in practice. The opposing view, espoused by the US SWP and which we had shared, argued that the Vietnamese hadn't followed permanent revolution, which was certainly the case. But then, instead of concluding that the theory must be wrong, it decided that the Vietnamese CP must be a Stalinist party, which therefore didn't really want a revolution but was forced by events to go further than it intended.

Once we abandoned permanent revolution for the Leninist strategy, it was clear that we needed to take another look at our traditional analysis. This was all the more necessary because, as the report stated, we hadn't paid sufficient attention to what was actually occurring in Vietnam. When we took off the permanent revolution blinkers, we were at last able to recognise the revolutionaries who had led the Vietnamese Revolution.

Our catching up with the reality was assisted when Helen Jarvis and Allen Myers were able to spend two weeks in Vietnam, visiting both Hanoi and Ho Chi Minh City. In August and September, Allen wrote a series of four articles on their visit for *DA*.

Changing approach to ALP

Jim Percy's report on the ALP and electoral policy to the October 1984 SWP NC marked a further significant evolution in our analysis and practice regarding the Labor Party. Our rethinking on the ALP had begun early in the 1980s. It was actually a process from our beginnings in the '60s – in practice we were rejecting the inherited line of entrism, but our *Socialist Review* carried reprints of the FI's Tactics in Europe document in *SR* 1, and an argument for entrism by Ian MacDougall in *SR* 2.

Entrism into the Labor Party was a legacy of the old Australian Trotskyist group. Trotsky had proposed the "French turn" in 1935, but the Australian group didn't implement it until they were banned in 1942 during World War II and had no other choice. From then on it became not just a tactic, but was theorised into a strategy by Michel Pablo. This was the accepted wisdom of those who recruited us to Trotskyism in the 1960s.

But the campaign against the War in Vietnam, and the many other actions we were involved in outside the Labor Party, and the youth radicalisation in the '60s and '70s and the whole push by us to build an independent revolutionary party, meant that our "entrism" policy was increasingly one mainly of lip service. Successfully fighting the bureaucratic expulsion of 34 of our members and supporters from the Victorian Young Labor Association in 1974 only made us enjoy the public campaigning. Another step towards building an independent party was standing our own candidates in the federal elections in December

1975, which we'd begun discussing at the beginning of that year.

The Prices and Incomes Accord in 1982-83 dealt a further blow to the possibility of any useful work in the ALP. The rise of the Nuclear Disarmament Party and other experiences in the early 1980s clarified further that entry tactics were not where it was at.

However, we still had a theoretical assessment of the ALP as a bourgeois workers' party, a view which we finally ditched by adopting Jim's October 1984 NC report. At our January 1986 conference, we adopted a document "The ALP and the Fight for Socialism",[68] which built on our local experiences in the class struggle and our actual practice and first-hand understanding of the ALP. It also built on a thorough reading of Lenin and the Bolsheviks, which many of our comrades had been able to do intensively at our party school.

The most important programmatic change that the DSP undertook in the 1980s, after the major changes relating to our reassessing of Trotskyism (permanent revolution and political reforms in the socialist states), was in our understanding of the nature of the Australian Labor Party.

The widely held view that the ALP is the political arm of the labour movement, as distinct from the industrial arm represented by the unions, carries with it the idea that socialists are *obliged* not only to call for a vote for Labor, but to see it as the fundamental organisational framework for their political activity.

We didn't escape the influence of such misconceptions. Not only were we influenced by the prevailing view on the left, but we suffered in our early years from an inherited Trotskyist schema prescribing "entry" into the Labor Party as a universal, timeless tactic. But once we saw ourselves as outside the framework of the Fourth International, and once we developed further our habits of more independent political thinking, looking to all past lessons and overseas experiences, we developed a more Leninist analysis of the ALP.

In Jim's October 1984 report to the National Committee and our January 1986 resolution, we argued that, while it may be necessary to vote for the ALP as a lesser evil against the Liberals or Nationals, the only way really to defend working-class interests is to break politically with the ALP in every arena, including the electoral and industrial arenas. We asserted that the trade unions should disaffiliate from the Labor Party and throw their weight behind the construction of a new political party genuinely dedicated to defending working-class interests. This was a break with our previous position, which held that the ALP was a party with a dual nature, being pro-capitalist in its program and leadership but working-class in its membership and support, and that therefore it was mandatory for socialists to vote for it and to support trade union affiliation to it.

Jim's report more or less completed our coming to terms with and rejecting the policy on the ALP we'd inherited. There was a counter-report by Janet Burstall (a leader of the Socialist Fight group). Jim McIlroy reported on the NC in the October 17 *DA*, especially Jim's report:

> Jim Percy proposed some changes in the party's attitude to the ALP and electoral policy. He stressed the need to correct a number of schematic conceptions about the role of the ALP today ...
>
> Over-emphasising the importance of the union movement's "historic step forward" in forming the Labor Party at the end of last century led to underestimation of the ALP's role as the main roadblock to further advances by the labor movement today ...
>
> The Wran, Hawke and Burke experiences show that the ruling class is extremely comfortable with Labor governments. And the party's links with the ranks of the union movement are indirect, to say the least ...
>
> Setting up abstract principles about how socialists "must" relate to the Labor Party – a characteristic of the Trotskyist movement in the past, Percy said – restricted the tactics open to revolutionaries.
>
> The trade union base of the ALP affects tactics, but it doesn't determine them. The central point to consider is: What will help move the struggle forward, what will help develop workers' consciousness at any particular time?
>
> The SWP's previous understanding of the ALP, Percy said, had led to mistakes in its attitude to elections, and to how breaks with the ALP might occur.
>
> In the past the SWP had generally insisted that non-ALP opposition candidates should be linked in some way to the Labor Party, eg, "Independent Labor," before it would support them. This was an abstract "principle" with no basis in reality.
>
> The breakout from Labor partially expressed by the NDP and the Greens is a "positive development," Percy said. We should therefore call for a vote for the NDP in the senate, with preferences to Labor.
>
> Where we call for a vote for Labor, it is not because of some "principle," but because, as Lenin once pointed out, it helps socialists to get a hearing from broader layers of workers.
>
> Percy proposed dropping the SWP's previous election slogan: "For a Labor government with socialist policies." In view of the record of the Hawke government, it sounds completely unrealistic, he said.

The experience of Labor governments in later years provided overwhelming confirmation of the correctness of our new position, and our new draft program reflected this line. Our frequent use of the characterisation of Labor and the conservative parties as "Tweedledum and Tweedledee" was not invented by us. It was used by many before us, and including Manning Clark in his history, referring to Labor radical Frank Anstey's disgust and disillusionment with the ALP in 1934. "Frank Anstey has also decided to give up politics. Everything was sour in his mouth. He has decided the difference between Labor and the conservatives was the difference between Tweedledum and Tweedledee."[69]

Once we had broken with Trotskyism, and once we had corrected our analysis of the ALP, the way was open to contemplate a much wider range of political options. The possibilities emerged for seeking different types of regroupment with other political forces, and for having a much more flexible and tactical approach towards elections.

500 issues of *DA*

The 500th issue of *DA* was dated October 24, 1984. Of course, we made a fuss about it, with several articles and messages from readers. Greg Harris (Greg Adamson) wrote on *DA*'s "Beginnings" and some of the early challenges: "The first issue was produced out of the lounge-room of a run-down terrace in inner-Sydney Surry Hills. The subscription service operated out of a shoe box." The article noted that "Three of the four largest family fortunes originated in publishing … For Direct Action supporters, the money has always gone the other way …

"While out-of-touch right-wingers have been heard to mutter about rubles from Moscow, the truth is more mundane. We rely entirely on donations from our supporters to pay the bills our cover price can't meet."

An accompanying photo showed the production team for issue 500: Chris Gill, Peter Boyle, Lou Hoey, Jim McIlroy, Dawn McEwan, Liam Gash, Philippa Skinner and Steve Painter.

Like others, we were affected by inflation and rising costs. The *DA* cover price was raised from 50 to 60 cents with the March 6, 1985, issue. That wasn't enough to do away with serious financial problems and a lagging fund drive. The July 10, 1985, issue carried a two-page centrespread appeal, headlined "Direct Action Campaign for Survival".

This urged people to become "Direct Action supporters" by giving $2 a week or more – for which they would also receive a subscription. The appeal also noted what could be achieved by fairly modest donations (at least in today's terms): $15 would pay the long-distance phone charges involved in planning one issue; $50 would cover the printing of one page of the paper; $150 would pay the postage to send one issue to all our subscribers.

Three weeks later, *DA* was able to report considerable progress: In that time, $13,461 in cash and pledges had been received. "When Direct Action launched its campaign for survival, it was facing its most severe financial crisis in 14 years of publication", the report noted. With expenditure already limited to the maximum, dealing with the crisis through further savings would have meant a smaller paper or a less frequent one.

And there was still a long way to go, the article noted. We still needed $35,000 to meet the year's fund drive target of $80,000. With the August 28 issue, we raised the cover price from 60 to 80cents. A short article by Steve Painter explained why this was necessary. A year later, at the September 1986 NC, we decided to raise the price again, to $1.

Fightback Campaign

We participated in the Fightback Campaign and conferences, a continuation of the thrust of the Social Rights Campaign that tried to mobilise union and other opposition to the Accord.

Several conferences were held, the last at Easter 1987 in Melbourne. While the Fightback Campaign petered out eventually, it did allow us to do further work with the SPA, elements of the CPA and other militant groups and individuals. It gave us further experiences of united front work, but also showed the limitations of a left and union opposition while the Accord was so predominant in the labour movement.

Antiwar/peace/anti-nuke movement

While the Accord and the Hawke government were quieting the labour movement, progressive activity was occurring in other areas, particularly against war, nuclear weapons and uranium mining. The April 15, 1984 peace rallies were, as Peter Anderson (Peter Annear) wrote in the May 2 *DA*, the "biggest popular protests in Australian history". An estimated 300,000 people joined the demonstrations: Adelaide 10,000; Brisbane 10,000; Canberra 5,000; Hobart 5,000; Melbourne 100,000; Perth 25,000; Sydney 150,000. Many country towns also had demonstrations.

We sold some 3,800 *DA*s at the April 15 rallies, including 1,800 in Sydney and 900 in Melbourne. Also boosted by nearly 700 copies sold at the Social Rights Conference in Melbourne, total sales for that issue were 6,133.

The following year, we took the plunge of spending enough money to organise a massive free distribution at the rallies: 50,000 copies were given away. In 1986, another free distribution was organised. Many people decided to subscribe after getting a copy for the first time at these demonstrations.

The Nuclear Disarmament Party

We threw ourselves wholeheartedly into the Nuclear Disarmament Party campaign when that exciting opening came along in 1984. This big break in the political situation came virtually out of the blue, without any initial planning or expectation on our part. The NDP was formed from an initial small group in Canberra, largely because of disillusionment with Labor's betrayals – most immediately the sell-out on uranium mining at the July 1984 ALP national conference. The central leader and enthusiast was Dr Michael Denborough.

The emergence of the NDP was extremely timely for us, as we prepared to launch our new reach-out perspective on party building. Unburdened of our previous blinkers on the Labor Party question, we launched ourselves with gusto in support of the NDP. Jim Percy explained in a September 1984 NC report, "The NDP's three demands are a good starting point: Stop uranium mining, repudiate the contracts; US bases out; No nuclear armed ships or planes. We can unite with others in struggle around these issues. There is absolutely no contradiction between us loyally building the NDP and continuing to build the SWP." We also fielded our own candidates, seeing no contradiction in supporting both parties.

We alone on the left gave full, energetic support to the NDP in its 1984 election campaign, joining the party and working vigorously for it, even assigning a couple of comrades full time to help organise its campaign. Our comrades worked tirelessly in the election campaign, some stood as candidates, and *DA* reported its progress every week. The election issue of *DA* had a big cover headline – "Vote for Nuclear Disarmament".

December 1984 federal election

DA of August 15 and August 22, 1984, carried a two-part report that Jim Percy had given to the Melbourne SWP branch, "The Labor Party and socialist election strategy". While we had not yet completely abandoned our "dual nature" analysis, the emphasis had clearly shifted to the pro-capitalist nature of the ALP:

> The Labor Party has a dual nature. On the one hand its working class base, on the other its pro-capitalist program. In government it has

always carried out policies for the ruling class – even if granting some limited reforms for the working class at the same time.

Many Communist Party members went into the Labor Party, but in doing so most adopted the slightly left-of-centre social democratic ideology common to the Labor left. Eventually these people left the Communist Party, broke their ties with the organisation that sent them in there to do political work. Labor is not our party. Even though it is a working class party in terms of its base, even though it was built by the trade unions, it is a party that does not defend the interests of the workers of this country. In fact, it has become the main obstacle to the further development of working-class consciousness.

We'll be looking around for candidates who are taking a progressive, maybe single-issue stance. We are going to see whether we can either unite with them in a campaign, form a non-aggression pact or simply call for a vote for them. Those things we will look at case by case.

A different approach to electoral alliances may enable us … to say "Well, how can we unite?" It may help us to explain the link between the war drive and austerity – the need for a new social system.

DA of August 29 announced our plan to stand in the federal elections (which had not yet been officially called). Tony Forward reported, "SWP becomes a registered political party", which meant that the party's name would be listed on ballots.

The following issues of *DA* emphasised different parts of SWP policy: "Jobs not profits"; "For peace and jobs! Disarm the warmongers!"; "Land rights now!"; "Stop uranium mining!"

An article by Peter Anderson (Peter Annear) in the September 26 *DA* described how the rightward course of the Hawke government, and the ALP federal conference's endorsement of that course, meant that "Labor will go into this election stripped of the leftist smokescreen that usually enables it to motivate its activists and win votes". This situation had resulted in even the Australian Democrats posing to the left of Labor on anti-nuclear and pro-conservation issues.

The article pointed positively to the formation of the NDP and, in Sydney, of the Green Alliance, the latter on the initiative of "a group of people who have recently left or been expelled from the ALP, together with others such as former Leichhardt mayor Nick Origlass".

"Unlike the NDP", Anderson reported, "the Greens are developing policy on a full range of social and economic questions".

The article also noted the formation of PANEC – the Peace and Anti-Nuclear Election Commission – in NSW, which was not standing any candidates of its own or endorsing any candidates of other groups. "PANEC", Anderson explained, "represents a current in the peace movement that has consistently lined up behind the Labor government and now does not want to oppose Labor candidates".

Last but not least, the article reported on efforts we were part of in Adelaide to organise a united socialist campaign with the SPA, CPA and "independent peace activists". Describing the SWP campaign, the article pointed out that "the SWP will not run candidates in opposition to groups, such as the Sydney Greens, which are contesting the elections on consistent anti-nuclear, pro-working-class policies. The SWP will support such candidates."

In early October, the election was called for December 1. The NDP endorsed Peter Garrett in NSW and Jean Melzer in Victoria.

In the October 17 *DA*, Greg Harris (Greg Adamson) reported that a survey for the Australian Conservation Foundation found that 9.3 percent of those polled planned to vote for an anti-nuclear candidate in the Senate. An accompanying article reported that the multiparty discussions in Adelaide had borne fruit, and the United Campaign for Peace and Socialism would have Senate candidates in South Australia. The parties involved were the SWP, CPA, SPA, Italian Communist Party and the Greek party PASOK.

The November 21 *DA* cover urged: "Vote for Nuclear Disarmament". It reported that 3,000 had attended a Newcastle NDP concert, and carried an interview with NDP Senate candidate Mary-Anne Hocking. The November 28 *DA*, immediately before the election, proclaimed on the cover: "No uranium; No US war bases; No nuclear ships or bombers. Nuclear Disarmament!" Jo Vallentine was elected a senator for the NDP in Western Australia, and Peter Garrett just missed out in NSW. Immediately after the election, *DA*'s cover declared: "NDP: A new force emerges". The article, by Bill Mason (Jim McIlroy), mostly quoted Jim Percy: "The main thing to say about this election is that it is a tremendous victory for the Nuclear Disarmament Party". Jim contrasted the NDP with the earlier emergence of the Australian Democrats, which were "no challenge to the system":

"The Democrats use their anti-nuclear policies as a smokescreen, while they bloc with the coalition on anti-union legislation and tax-avoidance laws."

Jim said that the success of the NDP depended on its mobilising large numbers of people to take political action, not on whether candidates were elected. The group had come under pressure during the election to take positions on other issues, but there was no need for haste, Jim said: "Any discussion of what more needs to be done can proceed at a leisurely pace. There's time to make the most of this process, to ensure that this breakthrough by the NDP really leads to a structural change in Australian politics."

After the elections

The *DA* of December 12 carried a brief report on a Melbourne meeting to discuss left unity. Groups involved were the Italian Communist Party, the Maritime Unions Socialist Activities Association, SPA, CPA, SWP and the Union of Greek Socialists. An NDP Senate candidate in the recent election also attended "in a personal capacity". The issue also carried an interview with an SA NDP candidate, Frances Mowling.

We continued to report on and encourage the NDP and other moves towards independent politics. *DA* of January 30, 1985, carried an article, "NDP takes off in Sydney suburbs", reporting on the party's growth in Fairfield, Parramatta, Blacktown, Five Dock and North Sydney. In the lead-up to the March 1985 Victorian election, the state Labor government's broken promises regarding public transport led to dissatisfied ALP members and others setting up the Public Transport Party, which we backed. In the *DA* of February 27, Peter Green (John Percy) interviewed Janet Walk, an SWP member who was a tram driver and the PTP candidate for the seat of Melbourne. The SWP called for a first preference vote for the PTP candidates: Janet Walk in Melbourne, Tom Tyrer in Knox and Alan Parker in Prahran. In the election, Janet Walk received 6.4 percent, Tom Tyrer 3.6 percent and Alan Parker 2.3 percent.

In *DA* March 6, Peter Anderson (Peter Annear) reported, "Big meeting indicates continuing support for NDP", describing a meeting of 2,000 at Sydney Town Hall on February 25 addressed by newly elected NDP Senator Jo Vallentine, Peter Garrett and author and academic Jim Falk.

NDP conference, split

DA of March 27, 1985, was in special colour for a big distribution at the national Palm Sunday peace demonstrations. It carried an ad for the NDP first national conference, in Melbourne, April 25-28, and an interview by Ramani De Silva (Reihana Mohideen) with Jenny Cotterell, who worked in the NDP's Melbourne office.

If our joint project with the NDP had succeeded, who knows what different political landscape would exist in Australia right now? As a new force on the scene, the NDP would soon have been obliged to confront other questions.

With our participation and assistance, the policies and structures they could have adopted could have decisively broken apart the two-party deadlock at a time when the rising environmental and green movement was in its infancy, and more open to socialist ideas.

But the "star leader" element, and the anti-socialist tendency, were a strong force. They were used by the capitalist media in their (ultimately successful) campaign to smash the NDP as a potential threat to the two-party con trick, which is the bedrock of traditional Australian political stability. Peter Annear explained in a *DA* article of May 8: "Behind the NDP walkout. The NDP Split: What really happened", and we featured it on the cover. After the December 1984 election, "In mid-December, 50 NDP members from all branches met in Canberra to map out plans for a national conference". A conference was needed to take steps to develop a unified national structure, and "had to begin a much needed discussion of party policy among the members".

But "the Garrett-Vallentine group attempted a unilateral political shift in the name of the NDP". First came the attempt to conservatise the party by pushing the concept of multilateralism – that is, a call for multilateral nuclear disarmament rather than the demand for the Australian government unilaterally to cut off all ties with the nuclear arms race. Multilateralism let the Australian government off the hook by allowing it to say it agreed, but the Soviet Union and China wouldn't go along. "Vallentine also campaigned publicly for an end to the Palm Sunday peace marches."

"Along with this went an overemphasis on the NDP's parliamentary role." A red-baiting attack on the SWP was led by Ted St John, a former Liberal MP, who seemed to have Garrett's ear.

"So the campaign was carried into the conference with the demand for a national ballot – a demand that was not presented openly, but raised through a series of manoeuvres. Before the conference discussions even began, Peter Garrett and Jo Vallentine used the privilege of opening 'inspirational' addresses to argue for their views, including uncritical support for the party senator, the conscience vote, and the postal ballot."

"Right after the opening addresses, Garrett supporters surprised the conference with a list of motions which would have nullified conference decisions, instituted the national postal ballot, and set up a national executive, again prior to any democratic discussions. These moves, presented under the guise of conference 'procedures,' were rejected.

"Also rejected was a move by Vallentine to dilute the party platform …

"Finally, Vallentine forced a change in the agenda, bringing proscription and the national ballot on for discussion prior to any consideration of party structure. When she lost the ballot vote by a significant majority, her group gathered around her and left the conference."

The article explained that the proposed postal ballot "was a mechanism that would leave the leaders unfettered by participation and advice from the party membership. Despite appearances, it was a mechanism for rule from the top down." It would have cost about $10,000 per ballot!

The media seized on the issue as an opportunity to red-bait us. This included the Communist Party's *Tribune*, which included attacks on our alleged sins in Tasmania a decade and a half earlier. The *DA* of May 22 replied to some of this red-baiting, and to the actions of the Garrett-Vallentine group. Frances Collins wrote in reply to a letter and questionnaire that Peter Garrett had sent to some parts of the NDP mailing list, urging them to leave the NDP and sign up for something called "the Jo Vallentine Support Group". The questionnaire asked for yes/no answers to questions such as "I want to go on supporting Jo Vallentine as the world's first peace parliamentarian". Garrett referred to this questionnaire as a "postal ballot", indicating why the NDP conference had been wise to reject such ballots as a means of deciding policies or practices. Collins also pointed out the political reasons for the behaviour of Vallentine and Garrett: "Vallentine wanted the NDP's program made explicitly 'multilateralist' because, she said, it would enhance her credibility and enable her to work with her 'fellow parliamentarians.'"

A facing article by Kate Shannon focused on "Jo Vallentine's ballot: Machine politics in WA". This pointed out that a meeting in Perth convened supposedly to hear a report on the NDP national conference had refused to admit a representative of the Interim National Coordinating Body appointed by the national conference. The meeting had then heard a report on the conference by Vallentine, on which no questions or discussion were permitted, and then voted to establish something called the Peace and Disarmament Action Group (PANDA). The article noted: "At this stage it is not exactly clear what PANDA is. Vallentine claims it is not a political party, yet it has forbidden its members to be members of other political parties.

"The independent senator for nuclear disarmament, as Vallentine now describes herself, says PANDA will be a multi-issue organisation, but she will remain a single-issue senator, though she says she would vote against pro-abortion legislation."

The same issue also carried "How Denis Freney got into News Weekly", by Steve Painter. *News Weekly* was the publication of B.A. Santamaria and his National Civic Council. Why, Painter asked, would "one of the country's most fanatical anticommunist, antilabor organisations, reprint the work of Denis

Freney, a Communist Party journalist?" It did so because Freney's article in *Tribune* contributed to undermining the NDP.

The article also quoted Alec Kahn from the IS's *Battler:* "The real aim of Vallentine's walkout was not to counter a 'stack.' It was to use her senate seat to blackmail party activists into policies she could not win in open debate ...

"Even Reagan supports [multilateralism] since it lets the superpowers haggle endlessly while adding to their arsenals." This policy, Kahn said, was "a major concession to the pro-nuclear lobby".

The same issue of *DA* also included an article by Jim Percy, "Press violence: A reflection":

> Over the last three weeks the Socialist Workers Party has come in for a great deal of stick. The barrage has emanated mainly from the big business media. That's not surprising, malice is all we expect from such quarters.
>
> But they had to get their ammunition from somewhere, and the Garrett-Vallentine-Melzer people in the Nuclear Disarmament Party were more than willing to provide it ...
>
> Of course, the far left should know better than to do ammo runs for the press barons. The Communist Party and former members of the SWP in Tasmania, not having any grievance that could stand examination on the SWP members' conduct in the NDP, thought it would be a good time to bring up old grudges, some dating back as far as the Vietnam Moratorium Campaign of 1970-71 ... [and] ... muckraking in regard to the SWP's activities in the Hobart Unemployed People's Union ...
>
> Of course, whenever mud is thrown some will always stick. That's part of the calculation of some of the veteran mud slingers in this episode.
>
> But the recent SWP bash has provoked a new interest in our party and its ideas. That's a preliminary balance sheet, purely from the viewpoint of the SWP. Then there are the many people in the NDP who were given a crash course in these matters over the last three weeks. While they may have been cynical about the media in the past, many were able to catch it lying for the first time in their direct experience.
>
> Many of these people were prompted to begin looking for the real political issues behind the media storm.
>
> But to return to the personal effects on the individual members of the SWP. There was some anger, there may have been a certain amount of intimidation among newer members. But above all there's strengthened resolve based on an understanding that this is an overhead

price for standing up and saying you don't like things the way they are
and you want to change them.

In most countries, when you want to change things, they start
shooting at you. We can handle the paper bullets of the press, and we're
pushing on.

There was a difference within PANDA between Garrett-Vallentine followers
and former Victorian ALP Senator Jean Melzer. The former were happy with
a non-party party that left them maximum freedom from control by a membership, while Melzer was eager to establish a party as a vehicle for returning
to parliament. In October 1985, Melzer's grouping split from PANDA to form
the Nuclear-Free Australia Party. Somewhat ironically, the NFAP met with no
electoral success, but in the 1987 federal election, the NDP won a Senate place
in NSW.

CHAPTER 6

LEAVING THE FOURTH INTERNATIONAL

After our break with the US SWP, they continued to harass us. With help from the NZ SAL, they tried to build a group in Australia adhering to Barnes' thought. They eventually adopted the name "Communist League", the name for all their little sects, which were mostly in English-speaking countries.

They also attacked us in FI meetings. They refused to print or delayed printing our documents in FI discussion bulletins, for example our document on Cuba, submitted jointly by Jim Percy, Doug Lorimer and Pedro Camejo.

SWP NC meeting, October 1984

Jim Percy attended an FI United Secretariat meeting on September 6-9, 1984, and when he returned he presented a world movement report to the NE, around September 20. This became the basis for his world movement report to the October 1984 SWP NC.

We were still on a course of trying to reorient the Fourth International away from its historic sectarianism – although without great hopes of success. Jim pointed out in his report: "… for the last 25 years our movement has had a chance to break out of this trap [sectarianism], to break out of this dead end. With the victory of the Cuban Revolution, we had that chance. But the Fourth International hasn't yet seized this chance."

The relative isolation of the Trotskyist movement had encouraged a "circle spirit" and an "idealist approach", which had led to two major political errors. One derived from an attempt to apply Trotsky's theory of permanent revolution to struggles in the colonial and semicolonial countries. This we described as "an underestimation of the role of national liberations struggles within the worldwide fight for socialism, in particular a programmatic error of downgrading the anti-imperialist united front and the democratic stage of revolutions in the semicolonial countries".

The second error was "an overestimation of the place, within the tasks confronting the workers states and within the socialist revolution, occupied by political revolution against the ruling castes in the bueaucratised socialist states". The short term for this error was "Stalinophobia", Jim pointed out. We could see the effects of this in our own history: the reason we had taken so long to learn the lessons of the Vietnamese Revolution was Stalinophobia: "we didn't think they could teach us anything because we thought they were Stalinists".

"These two errors", Jim said, "meant that we have distorted the axis of the world revolutionary struggle … The revolutions in the oppressed countries of Asia, Latin America and Africa were seen as a 'long detour' – the real and decisive revolutions would come later in the imperialist countries. The analysis of Lenin and the early Comintern in regard to the axis of the world revolution as a result of the development of imperialist capitalism and its effect on the labor movement in the advanced capitalist countries – its creation of a labor bureaucracy – was downplayed or dismissed by the Trotskyist movement."

Jim added that nothing we were learning about the real process of revolutions "detracts from the pressing necessity of continuing to try to build a revolutionary vanguard party".

What should distinguish us from or unite us with other groups, Jim stressed, was primarily the class struggle in Australia: "The program of a particular revolution is primarily developed in the living class struggle in that country … our revolutionary program in this country won't include a point on Spain in 1936, for example. We want to limit the number of points of demarcation we have to make with other revolutionaries … We have to debate with the currents that are affecting the class struggle; it's correct for us to go after the CPA and the AMWU on the accord and other issues affecting the class struggle in Australia today. It's correct for us to draw those lines of demarcation, but not about other continents, other periods and so on. What makes you a revolutionist is not having a program for 20 other countries.

" … It's not a 'weakness' of the Cubans or the Sandinistas that they don't have a 'full program' for the class struggle in Iran. That's one of their strengths – their understanding that revolutionaries should unite on the tasks before them, the tasks they can affect."[70]

We presented our views at the FI's 12th World Congress in January-February 1985. Although we gained some support here and there from other sections – for example, a leader of the Mexican section supported our Cuba resolution and reported on it to the congress – the congress as a whole was disappointing, marred by factional manoeuvres and lack of clear political discussion. Doug Lorimer reported on the congress to our August 1985 SWP NC, and the conclusions that our National Executive had drawn. Our conclusion, as Doug expressed it, was: "The tendency to elevate written programmatic positions above practical activity in the class struggle continues to dominate the thinking and approach of the Fourth International leadership". Because of the supposed superiority of their written program, the FI leaders and most members "refuse to see that by continuing to keep their sights on building an international organisation on a program that is different from those of the people who have made revolutions they are blocking any real possibility of participating fully in the process of building new parties …

"This gets to the heart of the problem with the perspective of building the Fourth International: Its very existence is an *obstacle* to the revolutionaries who are in it participating fully in the process of building a new international revolutionary movement, one with mass influence …

"The continued existence of the Fourth International as an organised international current distinct from the currents that have succeeded in making revolutions and are consciously working to extend the revolutionary process, is an obstacle to its members developing" the relationships that members of the FI needed to develop with other revolutionaries. The logical conclusion, which we took, was that we should end our membership of the FI.

This did not mean cutting off relations with the FI or its members. And once the ritual period of denouncing us as bad Trotskyists had passed, we continued our collaboration with the FI on much the same basis as we did with revolutionaries from other currents.

The same NC adopted two documents for discussion leading to our 1986 conference: *Towards Socialist Renewal* and *The ALP and the Fight for Socialism*. That we were becoming a quite homogeneous party in outlook was evident in the preparation of that conference. A circular signed by Doug Lorimer from the NE to NC members on December 2, 1985, said that we were not proposing a majority platform for a vote in branches, and therefore would not call for the formation of a majority caucus to elect delegates.

"As the latest Party Organiser explains, the NE is merely calling for a registration of the membership's opinion in each branch on the general line of the resolutions and reports contained in the pamphlets 'Towards Socialist Renewal in Australia,' 'The ALP and the Fight for Socialism,' and 'The Socialist Workers Party and the Fourth International.'"

Socialist Fight resign

After our October 1984 NC, and before our January conference, the Socialist Fight comrades resigned. They had formed a tendency at the NC, but didn't wait until the conference, releasing a resignation statement signed by nine comrades, "For a new orientation to the labour movement".

"Today a group of comrades which fused with the party in late 1983 is leaving. We are defusing because:

    1. "The party's practice in the labour movement is organisationally sectarian and politically opportunist.

    2. "The party's international view is 2 campist, not proletarian internationalist.

    3. "The party is not organised as a Leninist combat party. It is bureaucratic, cliquish and increasingly operates on social democratic lines."

They probably would have been happy enough with their short entry, leaving with one more member than when they entered, but they were destined to wither, a tiny branch office of a tiny British sect. (They would also have been happy enough with their access to our Discussion Bulletin – Paul White submitting six articles to one bulletin.)

During the pre-conference discussion, John Tully and Andrew Jamieson had formed a tendency defending the theory of permanent revolution. Their discussion bulletin contribution was answered by Doug Lorimer for the NC majority, and the comrades had dissolved their tendency by the time of the following bulletin.

SWP 10th national conference, 1985

Just before our 10th national conference, the SWP NE met on December 27, 1984, and resolved to send a delegation of four to the FI's 1985 World Congress – Jim Percy, John Percy, Doug Lorimer and Pat Brewer.

The conference was held January 2-8, 1985, at the Chevron Hotel, in Kings Cross, Sydney, with the theme "Fighting war and poverty in '85". It was a departure from the comfort and familiarity of Hawkesbury, but reflected the more public approach we were adopting. We had initially projected the conference for Hawkesbury, but with the development of the NDP, and the discussions that were beginning with other left groups, we decided to open up the conference. Nine discussion bulletins had been produced before it began.

The reports presented to the conference were: Doug Lorimer: The Struggle for Socialism in the 20th Century (presenting the documents: *The Struggle for Socialism in the imperialist epoch* and *The Cuban Revolution and its extension*); Peta Stewart: The Road to Peace; Jim Percy: The New Situation in Australian politics; Jamie Doughney: Australian Trade Unions and the Accord; Lou-anne Barker: New Trends in Women's Liberation; Reihana Mohideen: Migrants and the Australian Socialist Movement; Margo Condoleon: Youth and Politics Today; John Percy: Building Socialist Unity. More than 450 people attended. We received solidarity greetings from the FSLN and the FI United Secretariat, and sent greetings to the Food Preservers Union, the Waterside Workers Federation and the Seamen's Union, and the Communist Party of Cuba. International guests were John Trinkl, from the US *Guardian*, Louis Uregei, from Kanaky, and a Filipino comrade.

Prospects for left unity

The conference guide blurb introduced my report on "Building Socialist Unity": "In Australia today the response to progressive ideas is greater than it has been for decades. Strong movements have developed in support of women, Blacks, in defence of the environment, and for peace and nuclear disarmament. Yet the socialist movement in Australia is more divided than ever before.

"In this situation there is growing concern to find ways to overcome this fragmentation. All major left groups are now discussing the question of left unity. Some have engaged in specific projects – the Social Rights Campaign, and the United Campaign for Peace and Socialism in South Australia are two examples.

"This report assesses the state of the left in Australia today, discusses the reasons for the lack of unity, and introduces some proposals from the Socialist Workers Party on the best way to achieve unity of the left."

We printed my report to the conference as a three-page feature in the February 13 *DA* headed "Prospects for left unity". Why is the left so divided? Why is there no unity on the left? I asked. "There's one clear answer to that question – politics."

"We're in a good position to show a lead: we're a growing, young and optimistic party; no other groups are as involved in mass movements as us; we're achieving greater political clarity and self-confidence; we're tied down less to political shibboleths that prevent us working out the best methods of building a revolutionary party in Australia."

I said that we saw developments towards left unity taking place on two levels. "Firstly, there's the level of discussion, and secondly, the level of action. A third level, organisational unity, organic unity, is not on the cards at the moment.

"Any group in the Australian labour movement that's serious, and has a basic level of political politeness, we should be involved with in the discussion that's opening up – all the parties resulting from the break-up of the CPA, left-wing groups and individuals in the ALP, and the many active independent left-wingers involved in the mass movements and different political campaigns.

"That's one of the reasons we threw this conference open, inviting representatives and members of other left parties to attend and observe our discussions … We wanted to set a precedent, an example, so the dialogue gets extended and the discussions get speeded up."

I outlined the number of fruitful discussions already held. "Our first main dialogue, and our most extensive to date, has been with the Socialist Party of Australia.

"Th[at] development raised the eyebrows of everyone else on the left. The fact that the SPA and the SWP, from very different origins and with some quite outstanding political differences, could sit down and discuss in a comradely fashion, set an example." The process had been set off by common opposition to the ALP's Prices and Incomes Accord.

We'd actually begun earlier discussion in Melbourne on this issue with people from the Marxist Workers Organisation, a semi-Maoist organisation that included some tramways and Telecom union officials (Jim Harper, Len Cooper).

We saw divergences in the SPA between their official line and what some of their trade union officials such as Pat Clancy and Tom McDonald were saying. The process led to the Social Rights Campaign and Social Rights Conference at Easter 1984. This led to the drafting of a joint statement in April 1984, which was attacked by Clancy, who split away and formed the Association for Communist Unity.

Also in South Australia in the lead-up to the federal elections, the United Campaign for Peace and Socialism was formed to run a joint election campaign. With the CPA there initiating it, it involved the SPA, Italian Communist Party (PCI), PASOK, SWP and individual activists. But with the CPA, the campaign couldn't have a platform explicitly rejecting the Accord.

The SA campaign provided the springboard for further developments towards left unity, I explained – "the meetings in Melbourne last month that brought together nearly all the left parties and established an ongoing mechanism for discussing and exploring the question of left unity".

The first meeting, on December 5, was initiated by comrades from the PCI, with an opening presentation by Enzo Soderini from SA. Following the report, representatives of each of the eight organisations present responded: Brian Lee, from the Maritime Unions Socialist Activities Association; George Venturini, from the NDP in a personal capacity; Trevor MacCandless, SPA; George Zengalis, CPA; Anna Kokkinos, Socialist Activities Association; Ilyas from the Union of Greek Socialists; myself for the SWP and Renato Licata from the Italian Communist Party. Also present were some comrades from different Turkish organisations.

"The following week in addition Marcus Clayton of the CPA (ML) participated, as well as a representative of the Lebanese Communist party. A process of discussion began with the CPA (ML). First with the CPA. Then with us as well. We noticed industrial articles from *DA* getting reprinted in their paper *Vanguard*."

They organised a public meeting in Melbourne, their first in 20 years, with Ted Hill, Marcus Clayton and Ted Bull. Two hundred attended; invites were sent to most left groups, including ourselves. All speakers stressed that the CPA (ML) was interested in developing united work with other left and progressive forces. There was a transition of leadership at their congress.

A more negative effort was noted in Sydney, from people associated with the Marxist Forum Group, circulating to a select list of 40, about 20 ALP lefts, the rest CPAers or Pat Clancy types. "They certainly didn't want us, or the SPA, or anyone from the BLs at this elite gathering."

"What is the way forward?" I asked. "Only by addressing the central political questions facing Australian workers and their allies today. There's no magic organisational formula. For us, the two key issues are clearly the Accord, and the NDP and the antiwar movement. Linking the two questions is an analysis of the Hawke Labor government."

I said that there were two counterposed perspectives on unity. A traditional one within the Australian labour movement looked to unity of the socialists or communists with the ALP, which had been the CPA line for the previous 50 years. This meant accepting the framework of Laborism.

Of course, we were in favour of a *united front*, unity on actions in the interests of the working class. But left unity seen in this framework was something different. It was the project of the Taft grouping, the Clancyites and fundamentally the project that the CPA leadership envisaged – from their "coalition of the left" concept in the late '60s to their "Proposal for Renewal" that resulted from their Prospects debate in the early '80s.

The CPA wanted to draw in the activists from the different movements. Its fundamental political thrust was the framework of the Accord, the framework of Laborism. But the CPA faced a fundamental contradiction. The newly radicalised layers were *breaking* from that politics, while the CPA was still tied in to it. These layers moved in their thousands to the NDP, leaving the CPA stranded, divided, embarrassed.

The second perspective on left unity was held by groups and individuals looking to the beginnings of an alternative emerging to the *left of* and *outside* the ALP. There were two main political issues: the Accord and peace and nuclear disarmament.

On the Accord, the left alternative had taken the form of the Social Rights

Campaign. On nuclear disarmament, the break took the form of the formation and success of the NDP. "It's the most important political development in Australia for years, the first big chink in Labor's armour."

Elections had been a lens that focused the key political questions. Elections led to the NDP break. In this new development in Melbourne, a crucial role was played by PCI activists: not just their organisational initiative, but their political emphasis – stressing the need for a left alternative outside the ALP, reflecting experiences and debate occurring within the Communist Party in Italy.

The third level of unity, organisational unity, could not happen without much more discussion, and many more experiences of united action. We had the *chance* to relate to new political developments; we were clearer politically, and not tied down to conceptions coming from Moscow or Beijing. "The fact we've got this far, and are in a position to move ahead, reaffirms our basic party building approach", I said.

"The task ahead of us now is to get deeply into the mass movements, into the unions, into the NDP", I concluded. "So we throw the challenge out to everyone else on the left – meet us half way. If you don't agree with us, let's talk. Where we find agreement, let's act."

We'd invited SPA national secretary Peter Symon to give a talk to the conference. We had thrown the conference open to other left groups to attend and observe. That *DA* carried an ad for the SPA's New Era bookshops.

Resistance 1985 conference

The *DA* of February 27, 1985, carried the draft resolution for Resistance's 14th national conference as a four-page lift-out, "Fighting for a future … Fighting war and poverty". The *DA* of March 27, which had special colour for a big distribution at the Palm Sunday peace marches, had an ad for the conference and an interview with Margo Condoleon. East Timorese leader Jose Ramos-Horta would be speaking at the conference, and there would be a Resistance Dance, with Man Friday and Black Coffee.

The April 17 *DA* featured a centrespread on the Resistance conference. It included mini-interviews with people attending and a description of talks to the conference by Horta, Hnalaine Uregai of New Caledonia's independence movement, the Kanak Socialist National Liberation Front, and Manni Colonzo, the Filipino secretary general of the Asian Students Association. Sally Francis (Sally Low) reported that 300 attended. Rally speakers were Bernie Hocking, Margo Condoleon, Catherine Brown, Meghan Devlin, David Grove (Food Preservers' Union), Peta Stewart, Raul Torchez and Helen Boyle.

CPA doubts about Accord

After more than two years of the Accord, continuing attacks on workers' conditions and the throttling of the unions, the CPA leadership started getting some doubts about the Accord. There were probably growing differences between their ranks and their leaders who had initiated and boosted the Accord. Perhaps some had got cold feet. Jim Percy addressed the issue in the July 10, 1985 *DA*, in an article titled "Tribune starts talking left again".

"The July 3 issue of *Tribune* … ran centre page feature articles by Brian Aarons and Brian Carey. Most immediately catching were the headlines: 'Paul Keating – demobilising the labor movement,' and 'The anti-labor path of Hawke's labor government.' This is the first time we've heard such talk in *Tribune* during the life of the Hawke government …

"This sort of language and analysis has been left to the 'dogmatists' of *Direct Action*, among other 'utopian sectarians.' Or so *Tribune* used to sneeringly imply. The very concept of social change through mobilisation of workers, of the labour movement, had been relegated to the bad old days before Laurie Carmichael and his colleagues, Bill Kelty et al, invented the accord."

But the Accord "hasn't maintained living standards. It has shackled unions. It has demoralised workers. It has not saved jobs. It has led to a decline in the social wage. It has emboldened the right wing. It has opened the way to defeat for the ALP at the next election."

How could the government could get away with the Keating tax package? "Because of the accord – the self-limiting agreement of the trade unions, which was imposed on all workers. Under this agreement, anyone who got out of line and tried to mobilise was viciously attacked."

Jim continued: "It's sufficient just to recall Laurie Carmichael's ACTU congress attack on the women Food Preservers' Union members at Heinz to figure out how the door was opened for Keating's tax adventure. The left drank the poison of a phoney deal called the accord, and *Tribune* and the CPA said, 'Drink it up. It tastes good. The label on the bottle says it's good for you.'

"It took the shock of Keating's tax rort to begin to bring the CPA to its senses …

"We welcome *Tribune*'s change but for all our sakes, please take the next step as well. Help get the shackles off the AMWU, the ARU and other unions you might influence."

Aarons had called for a broad unity in the labour movement against attacks. "But who will this broad unity be with? … We have to break with all of this rotten so-called Labor cabinet and build a unity of its victims, and of those who are struggling against it from the left."

We needed to build a genuine alternative in the labour movement, Jim wrote. "If the CPA doesn't, others will. They'll do it less effectively than if all those who use Brian Carey's language of class analysis were doing it together, but it will happen anyway. If the CPA fails to take this course, it will remain an obstacle to this necessary fight, but fortunately a declining one."

Hilton bombing frame-up

For more than a dozen years, from 1978 to 1991, there played out the framing but eventual exoneration of three young members of the Ananda Marga religious group in Sydney.

On February 13, 1978, a bomb exploded outside the Hilton Hotel in downtown Sydney, which at the time was the venue for the first Commonwealth Heads of Government Regional Meeting. The bomb, which had been placed in a rubbish bin outside the hotel, killed two garbage collectors instantly when the bin was emptied into a trash compacter; a policeman at the door of the hotel died later from injuries he received.

A few days later, an unstable former drug addict named Richard Seary offered to become an informant for the NSW Special Branch. Although this was not known until much later, Seary told the police he thought that the Hare Krishnas might have been responsible for the Hilton bombing. However, the police told him to infiltrate Ananda Marga, which he did.

However, it seems he could find no evidence of any connection to the Hilton bombing. Instead, on June 15, 1978, Seary told Special Branch that Ananda Marga intended to bomb the Yagoona home of Robert Cameron, a neo-Nazi. That night, waiting police arrested two Margis, Paul Alister and Ross Dunn. In the car with them and Seary was a bomb, which the Margis said had been brought along by Seary without their knowledge: they intended only to paint anti-Nazi graffiti. A third Margi, Tim Anderson, was arrested in Newtown; his alleged role in the supposed plot was to provide a press release after the bombing of Cameron's house – although why anyone who had just killed Cameron would want to call attention to their role is not at all clear. Alister, Dunn and Anderson were charged with conspiracy to murder Cameron. At a trial in February 1979, the jury could not reach a verdict. At a second trial, in July, they were convicted and sentenced to prison. Although no one had been charged or tried for the Hilton bombing, the prosecution strongly suggested that the three were involved with that, so making it seem more likely that they would try to blow up Cameron as well.

A coronial inquest into the Hilton bombing was held in 1982. The testimony of Seary convinced the magistrate that there was a prima facie case of murder against Alister and Dunn, and accordingly he adjourned the inquest. This finding did not lead to a trial, because Seary's testimony was soon discredited.

From the beginning, *Direct Action* reported on the doubts about the case, of which there were many. The film *Frame Up*, by Irina Dunn, was especially important in arousing public opinion. Some of the DA articles were: "Unanswered questions in Hilton bombing case", by Gordon Adler, August 17, 1978; "Bomb case frame-up?", by Gordon Adler, focusing on the testimony of police informant Seary, August 16, 1979; "Hilton Bombing case. An outrageous frame-up", by Ray Fox (Jamie Doughney), October 20, 1982; "Release Alister, Dunn, Anderson!", by Jamie Doughney, November 30, 1982.

Feeling the pressure, the NSW Labor government in 1984 ordered a judicial inquiry into the convictions over the supposed Cameron conspiracy. After a lengthy investigation, including taking testimony from Seary, Justice Wood recommended that Alister, Dunn and Anderson be pardoned.

Writing in the *DA* of May 22, 1985, after the three were released, Robyn Marshall (Coral Wynter) explained that there had been "widespread suspicion that the [Hilton] bomb had been planted by security police in order to set up a dramatic 'discovery' by a police agency", but things had gone wrong when the rubbish bin was emptied unexpectedly.

Shortly before, the Dunstan ALP government in South Australia had abolished that state's Special Branch after investigations had found it spying on Labor politicians and lying to the premier. The only other state Labor government at the time was that headed by Neville Wran in NSW. There was increasing political pressure for an investigation of the NSW Special Branch, and only four days before the Hilton bombing, Wran spoke publicly about the need for such an investigation. Marshall noted the "beneficiaries" of the bombing:

"Special Branch was never investigated. ASIO got increased funding that year and [later] … increased powers. Revealing the name of an ASIO agent was made a crime. ASIO agents were empowered to enter homes without warrants."

Alister, Dunn and Anderson were freed and given some financial compensation by the state government. But the state was not finished with the Hilton bombing. In 1989, a prison informer named Ray Denning told the NSW police that, in prison, Anderson had confessed to the bombing on four occasions. Denning's story was not very convincing; for example, it was later shown that on one of these alleged occasions, Anderson and Denning were not even in the same jail.

However, the NSW police got some extra help when a former Ananda Marga member in Queensland learned of Anderson's arrest. Evan Pederick then came forward and claimed that he had planted the bomb – on Anderson's instructions. Pederick first made this confession to a priest in Queensland, who did not believe him. He then tried to convince the Queensland police, who listened to his story and then drove him home.

But the NSW police were eager to believe Pederick, even though there were serious flaws in his story, such as the fact that Indian Prime Minister Morarji Desai, whom Pederick said the bomb was intended to kill, was not at the Hilton Hotel at the relevant time. Nevertheless, after juggling the testimony of Denning and Pederick to remove the most obvious falsehoods, the prosecution was able to convince a jury in November 1990. The NSW Court of Criminal Appeal, which ruled in the following June, was considerably more perceptive; it decided unanimously to throw out the conviction. The prosecution had persuaded the jury to "draw inferences of fact … that were in some respects contrary to the evidence".

The appeals court could have ordered a new trial, but it decided instead to acquit Anderson. Chief Justice Gleeson's ruling said that the prosecution should not "be given a further opportunity to patch up its case … It has already made one attempt too many to do that."[71]

Student unions

In early 1985 there were some moves to re-establish a new national student body after the demise of the Australian Union of Students. Caroline Petersen (Tracy Sorensen) wrote in the February 20 *DA*, "The possible reintroduction of tertiary fees has added a sense of urgency to the need to re-form a national student union. There has been no such body since the collapse of the Australian Union of Students under the weight of a sustained and heavily funded attack from National Civic Council and Liberal Party supporters."

The article reported: "The Australian Council of Tertiary Students (ACTS) was set up on January 29. It represents all factions, from the 'non-aligned' left to closet NCCers". A meeting was planned for Easter in Adelaide, and all factions were invited to send delegates with a view to establishing a formal union. There were two national left factions, the Council of ALP Students, and Left Alliance. Frances Collins reported in the following *DA:* "Right-wing students recently called a press conference to announce the birth of what they hope will be AUS's replacement, the Australian Council of Tertiary Students.

"But that bid is unlikely to win much support. Without genuine participation by the majority of students, bodies such as ACTS are doomed to be no more than factional facades."

The article also reported on the New South Wales Education Action Network, a coalition of student organisations that developed in the previous year, with Bronwyn Brown as full-time coordinator. Frances Collins followed up in the March 6 issue of *DA* with an article on "Student fees and education inequality under Labor", and on March 13 with "Labor's fees hit Asian students".

DA reported in its March 27 issue that "Students rally against reintroduction of fees", with meetings at Monash (1,000), Sydney University, Melbourne, Newcastle and UNSW. Bob Lewis wrote "Back to the Menzies Era. Labor's 'free enterprise' education".

Vietnam celebrates 10 years of liberation

DA covered the 10th anniversary of the final liberation of Vietnam, the celebrations, and also the attacks from right-wing Vietnamese. On April 30, some 250 right-wingers gathered outside a hall in the Sydney suburb of Glebe where CARPA had organised a film showing. "At first the rightists confined themselves to chanting slogans against the Vietnamese government. But as the lights were turned down for the showing of the Cuban-made film, 'The 79 Springs of Ho Chi Minh,' the right wingers began throwing rocks, bottles, and paint at the building. Several windows were smashed and several people were injured by flying glass", reported Peter Boyle in *DA* 521.

In Canberra, 1,000 right-wingers bused in from Sydney and Melbourne demonstrated outside the Vietnamese embassy on April 28. "On April 30, only 15 protesters showed up outside the Workers Club, where a large gathering, organised by CARPA and the Australia-Vietnam Society, commemorated the liberation of Vietnam.

"Present were a number of ALP and Democrat parliamentarians, trade union leaders, academics and solidarity activists." They were addressed by the Vietnamese ambassador, Hoang Boa Son. Also addressing the reception was Max Lane, president of the ACT branch of CARPA. "Many people here had their first political experiences as part of the protest movement against the Vietnam War, and in that sense we owe a big debt to the Vietnamese people", said Lane. "Vietnam needs our solidarity today."

Back to weekly meetings

At the National Executive meeting on April 8, 1985, Jim Percy gave a party-building report. We were in a difficult organisational situation, Jim said. There were several reasons for this.

"Firstly, The past – the turn, illusions associated with it, the false conjunctural analysis. Thus building the party around industrial fractions, therefore no weekly branch meetings.

"But key areas of growth remain youth; party life remains much the same. Therefore we must eradicate the last vestiges of the *workerist* aspects of the turn. We can't train new young comrades without weekly branch meetings.

"Secondly, the future – we're impatient. We see our rising status and influence and the decline of others. We say, 'We're not the vanguard yet', but drift in our projections, get impatient, for example, on left unity, the NDP. But we can't have a bigger periphery, a bigger milieu, without the cadre to hang it on.

"Thirdly, the present – we have to base it on the real level of fight back of the working class against the bourgeoisie. It was correct, what we did the last nine months, with the NDP, elections etc. But it's likely to return to normal in the labour movement." In this situation, we needed realistic plans, for *DA*, finances, cadre building. "We'll do what's necessary to save the weekly *DA*, our buildings, the school, the NO, our international work."

We proposed a new dues system, which shifted responsibility onto the branches. We decided immediately to raise *DA* bundles by 500, and to discuss increasing the paper to 28 pages and an 80 cents cover price. We also made some NO cutbacks, in the business office, printshop and writers.

Melbourne combines branches

In line with the above changes, we also decided to combine the Melbourne branches into a single branch, which was done at a meeting on September 25, 1985. A major argument for this was that we wanted to put emphasis on recruiting, which was hampered by the overheads of maintaining several branches.

"Are we chopping and changing our organisational forms too much?", I said in discussing the proposal. "No, it's what's best, most efficient for the period, the tasks we face and the objective situation. It's not a light-minded organisational change, not a change for the fun of it, or as a substitute for a political move. But we have to be flexible on organisational questions.

"In a sense, we're still working these things out for ourselves, cutting loose totally from what we took on blind faith from the US SWP, basing it now on our *own* experience. Recall that when we split branches, we immediately returned to weekly meetings; perhaps we would have thought a little more about the division if we had decided on weekly meetings first."

Party Organiser

After the blaze of publicity following the NDP conference, where we were outrageously red-baited, we started up an internal weekly organising news-sheet, Party Organiser, consisting of one or two A4 pages. We introduced it with a quote from the *Canberra Times,* April 30, 1985: "The SWP … are highly organised and very efficient at putting their policies forward".

We agreed that "we are the best organised left-wing party in the country – but not as much as we need to be. And that's what the Party Organiser is about."

The main organisational campaigns we ran were for our *DA* fund appeal and for *DA* sales. "We found that we can't go into enough detail in *Direct Action* to give the flavour of a function, or to give enough detail on the *DA* sales campaign."

"We also need a better vehicle for many of the circulars branches receive from the National Office, so that every member can receive a copy."

That first issue, No. 1, June 4, 1985, had a detailed report on how Brisbane Resistance organised a dance professionally, attracted 280 people and made $800 profit. It also explained the closure of our International News Service, which had been incorporated into *DA*. It reported that, following the mass distribution of *Direct Action* to the Palm Sunday peace marches, there had been a 22 percent increase in paid subscriptions to *Direct Action*. In addition, well over 400 people returned the trial offer cards that were inserted in the Palm Sunday issue.

The second issue had a page-long article on our success with *DA* subscriptions. "Subscription sales rose from being an average of 17% of our total circulation of *Direct Action* in the 9 weeks prior to Easter to 27% of total circulation for the issues after Easter." We also reported on a Sydney jumble sale.

The third issue reported on the campaign launched at the Easter NC meeting to raise money from outside our ranks – from our periphery and supporters. "*Direct Action* Supporters will pledge a minimum of $96 a year (or $8 a month for 12 months) to *Direct Action*. They will receive an automatic subscription to the paper as well as a special quarterly newsletter which we shall produce." We also reported on the success of Wollongong branch with a well-planned raffle.

Following issues continued to cover the fund drive and reported on money-raising ideas such as wine bottling, making use of your tax deductions, garage sales, dinners (250 attending in Sydney, 130 in Melbourne). We carried an edited version of the organisation report given by Tony Forward to the August 7 NE meeting, launching a new sales drive.

Party Organiser announced the start of pre-conference discussion, giving an explanation to new comrades of the upcoming August 16-18 NC and how the NC works, the conference agenda and how delegates were elected. It explained how we could make use of our pre-conference discussion, with our resolutions as public pamphlets and a public discussion that would be open to non-members who were moving towards us. Branches were urged to plan public forums or seminars to launch the discussion of the major documents, and special classes for provisional members on questions raised in the discussion. The NO was preparing study guides for all the major documents.

One issue carried a report that party recruiting was on the increase, describing 11 comrades who had joined Sydney branch in the past 11 weeks.

Party Organiser carried a report on building the successful Resistance conference held in Brisbane September 13-15; a report on a meeting and BBQ organised by a group of supporters in Ulladulla on the NSW South Coast; a report of a successful Melbourne forum on the Ananda Marga frame-up; and a report of a Peace and Solidarity Day held in Sydney.

DA sales

Party Organiser was especially important for motivating *DA* sales. It gave reports on a special sales campaign that Melbourne branches were organising – putting the whole weight of the party behind the campaign, forming a sales committee, leading the campaign through the executive bodies, stressing the regularity of sales spots.

"Diversity is essential. We have been attempting to distribute *Direct Action* in a number of mass movement shops, bookshops, radio stations and campus bookshops … We have *DA* posters that we put up at the shops so that people notice *DA* and actually buy it. We are in the process of building little *DA* trays with money tins that we can place in prominent positions in these shops." We carried a guide developed by Melbourne branch for approaching subscribers and potential supporters by phone, with useful questions and a readership survey.

"National *DA* sales show some improvement." Overall sales were up by about 300, from around 2,000 to around 2,300, we reported in October 1985. "But we are still not reaching the peaks established after the January 1984 conference which launched the campaign for an average 3000 national weekly sales. With the second issue of 1984 we reached 3323 sales, and an exceptional 6144 for the issue sold on Palm Sunday.

"After that sales declined for the rest of the year only to recover during the federal election, again reaching 3501 for the November 21 issue.

"During 1985, sales reached a peak of 2910 in the wake of Palm Sunday and around the NDP conference, largely due to an increase of nearly 400 in our sub base, but again fell away …

"However, the apparent improvement in DA circulation will be illusory if most comrades are simply paying for their minimum five DAs and not actually selling them. At least in some branches the effect of the new system is that less effort has been put into DA selling as comrades feel that simply paying for their papers ends their responsibilities. If we continue in this way then we will be able to finance a great paper that nearly no-one else gets to see.

"The only dramatic real improvement to DA sales has been in Melbourne where a thorough and energetic campaign began with issue 537." Overall, Melbourne sales doubled.

1985 in review

The last *DA* for 1985 (dated December 11) carried an interview with Jim Percy, "A good time to build an alternative", by Steve Painter.

"The SWP's decision to hold its11th national conference only a year after its previous conference reflects the need for thorough discussion of several important new developments in Australian and international politics, SWP national secretary Jim Percy told Direct Action this week", Painter wrote.

Following the SEQEB battle, the meatworkers' dispute, the ALP government's attacks on the BLF, "we began to realise we were starting to be in a very different framework", Jim explained.

> This year the working class has taken some severe defeats. While the SEQEB struggle is not over, for the moment it has been sold out in a vicious manner by the ACTU leadership, by the Queensland Trades and Labour Council, by the leaders of their own union, and by most other union leaderships around the country …
>
> There is a lot of discontent brewing. The problem is, for the moment people do not see any alternative to the Labor Party … The alternative to the Labor Party at the moment seems to be Howard, and that's not a very attractive alternative.
>
> Working class militants and former Labor supporters do not see an alternative, so the feeling is, 'let things go, there's not much you can do, go back to your own concerns, try to survive this period.'
>
> That mood affects us. And that's what we have to talk about: What can be done in a period like this?
>
> The paradox here, is that it's quite a good time to be building an alternative. Not that it's good in the sense that the socialist movement is

breaking out of its relative isolation with massive new growth.

That would take big struggles, like the British miners' struggle. We have not had that sort of struggle in Australia.

But there are big social protest movements. We saw this with the emergence of the Nuclear Disarmament Party ... Many people are looking leftward for an alternative.

It's not easy to build such an alternative. Working class politics in this country have been dominated for 80 years by the Labor Party. So to build a socialist movement to the left of Labor is quite difficult.

But there is quite a big debate going on about exactly these questions.

So the paradox is that even in a period of fairly general demoralisation and pessimism it is a good time to build an alternative, and this is the idea we want to discuss.

The SWP conference would also examine international developments. "Fundamentally", Jim said, "we called the conference around Australian questions, but I wouldn't be able to say that it's a good period for building an alternative if there wasn't another paradox in the world at the moment. That is, in spite of things being rather difficult for the labour movement in the advanced countries, on a world scale things are not difficult for the socialist movement. In fact they show continuous movement.

"In spite of everything, Ronald Reagan has not been able to directly intervene in Central America ...

"We want to bring the international situation to people's attention, to cut across the tendency to ignore real developments internationally, and become demoralised about the situation here."

The SWP was becoming better known and stronger, he added. "We have a bigger periphery. More people want to work with us, discuss with us, read our paper ...

"There is motion to build a new organisation, to build a new party. There'll be a lot of discussion about this next year ...

"Whether a new organisation will come out of all this is impossible to predict, but the discussion itself will be useful."

SWP 11th national conference, 1986

We held our 11th national conference January 2-7, 1986, in Canberra, at the Australian National University, using Burton and Garran Halls. Reports were given on: The Coming Revolution in South Africa, by Reihana Mohideen; World Politics Today, Margo Condoleon; Australia in the Pacific, Peter Annear;

Internationalism and the SWP, John Percy; Five Years of Hard Labor – Australia under the Hawke Government, Jim Percy; The Labor Party and the Struggle for Socialism, Steve Painter; Program of the SWP, Doug Lorimer; Recent Experiences in Party Building, Jim Percy (later produced as a pamphlet[72]); Tasks for Socialists in 1986, Tony Forward.

Talks were given on The Rural Revolt, Aboriginal land rights – the ALP's record; Gay Liberation – issues and campaigns; Unions under attack; The Philippines – a revolution on the march; and Art and Revolution. We had panels on National Liberation in Kanaky; South America Today; Revolution and Reaction in the Middle East; South-East Asia in Transition: Indonesia and Vietnam; Revolutionary Advances in Central America; Prospects for the Peace Movement; Freedom in the Lucky Country – defending civil liberties today; Sri Lanka and Civil Liberties; Immigration under Labor; Unionists Fighting Back; Positive Approaches to Women's Liberation; The Soviet Union: Views and Information.

We had introductory talks on Socialism vs. imperialism; Grey totalitarianism or workers' utopia?; Can workers make a revolution in Australia?; Useful arguments against the Accord; Did Karl Marx have a conscience? – a discussion of ethics, morality and revolution; Who is Big Brother? – an introduction to the Marxist view of the state; Humans and the environment: How relations can be improved; and Getting involved: How to join and organise with the SWP and Resistance.

We also had workshops on Privatisation and Nationalisation; The Accord Mark II; Industrial Democracy; Union Elections; The Hancock Report and Amalgamations; and Secondary Boycotts and Anti-union Legislation. We had closed workshops on the SWP's and Resistance's organisational tasks. We had a 1985 in Review slideshow presented by Janet Parker, and a cabaret, "Cults, Culture and Communism – the rave review of the SWP", and also held a dance and showed political films.

International guests attending were: Franco Turigliatto, from the Fourth International's United Secretariat (who argued against our disaffiliation from the FI), Aida Maranan, from the Philippines, and John Peu, from Kanaky.

Dave Holmes reported in the January 22 *DA* that the conference rally set a $85,000 fund drive target. The panel of rally speakers consisted of people who had joined the SWP in the recent period, chaired by Sydney SWP organiser Brett Trenery. The previous year the *DA* fund drive had comfortably exceeded its $80,000 target, reaching $84,000. The rally raised almost $45,000 in cash and pledges. Peter Lewis (possibly Steve Painter) reported that about 270 people attended the conference; 65 percent of conference participants had become involved in the socialist movement since 1980, their average age was 28 years, and 45 percent were women.

Internationalism and the SWP

My report on internationalism and the SWP pointed out that our party had been founded on internationalism, and especially on support for the struggle of Vietnam against US and Australian imperialism. But we also took to heart Lenin's injunction that real internationalism means seeking to overthrow the bourgeoisie in your own country.

I noted that, in addition to Ho Chi Minh and Che Guevara, one of our early heroes and inspirations had been Leon Trotsky and his efforts to create a movement that could carry on the world struggle for socialism abandoned and betrayed by the Stalinised Communist International. It was why we had joined the Fourth International and thrown ourselves into participating in it.

I then recalled how Jim Percy, speaking to a National Committee meeting five years earlier, had stressed that one of the four central features of our party was its independence: we were eager to learn from others, but we had to think for ourselves.

"If you look around the debris of the Communist and Trotskyist movements", I said, "you see scores of wrecks of organisations and wrecks of individuals who just functioned as branch offices or errand boys of an overseas party, until they jumped the wrong way, or too slowly, or so many jumps and kowtowing made jelly of their spines".

In addition to the centrality of independence, there was another important lesson we had had to learn. "We had to overcome the fetish that confuses a particular form of international organisation with internationalism." The victory of the Nicaraguan Sandinistas in 1979 had awakened us to the fact that we were drifting into a sectarianism towards the Cuban revolutionaries and the organisations in Central and South America that were attempting to follow their example. We began to realise the good news that there were many more revolutionaries in the world than just the few thousands grouped in the Fourth International. Hanging on to the fetish of the FI could only get in the way of collaboration with those other revolutionaries.

In addition to those broader considerations, I also pointed to immediate problems. The World Congress had shown that the FI leadership was unable to recognise the crisis it faced, let alone deal with it. In the absence of a realistic political perspective, permanent factionalism became the norm. This was a product of the idea of an international "centre" writing resolutions for countries all over the world.

The report concluded by saying that we would continue our international collaboration, among other ways, by sending Dave Holmes to Europe for a year as a *Direct Action* correspondent, and by continuing to make places in our party school for comrades from Asia and the Pacific.

Resistance conference, 1986

Two hundred and fifty people registered for the Resistance conference in Melbourne, April 25-27. The average age of new members was 19. Women made up 53 percent of Resistance members at the conference, and 48 percent of all people registered. Thirty-seven percent of the conference participants were tertiary students, 9 percent were secondary students, and 28 percent had industrial jobs.

The main report was given by Janet Parker. Caro Llewellyn reported on the history of the student movement and campus struggle, which was published in the May 21 *DA*.

There was a public meeting on the Philippines, with Francisco Nemenzo and Filipina student leader Blanche Mirandilla. Jim Percy gave a talk on the need for a broad and strong revolutionary party in Australia; Reihana Mohideen spoke on the importance of Third World struggles; Jamie Doughney talked on the need to fight for both reforms and revolutionary change.

Five hundred people attended the conference dance, with Man Friday (headed up by comrade Ray Pereira) and Swinging Sidewalks performing.

Student movement reviving

Resistance joined 157 students in university O-week 1986, and Resistance members were helping to revive the student movement. At some universities, this was reflected in elections to student bodies. At Monash University the Resistance Club candidate was Jeremy Smith; at Flinders University David Adamson was elected to the Student Association Coordinating Group. Matthew O'Halloran reported in *DA* August 27 that "Students take to the streets" in opposition to Hawke's $250 "administration fee", which was the thin end of the wedge for the restoration of university fees. By the following month, student protests had gathered steam in Melbourne, Brisbane, Newcastle and Wollongong. September 24 was set for a National Day of Action against Labor's reintroduction of fees. The *DA* of October 1 reported that 12,000 nationally marched on September 24, indicating "A new student activism". (Ironically, Joe Hockey, who was an officer in the Sydney University student union, spoke at the Sydney rally.) At the Adelaide rally, Resistance member David Adamson gave an anti-fees speech.

And Alan Edwards reported that the "OUT campaign sweeps UQ elections," winning four executive positions, plus editor of the student paper *Semper Floreat*. OUT was the result of a Resistance club initiative. Jorge Jorquera was elected as secretary, and Scott Barclay treasurer. Two weeks later Doug Hine reported in the October 16 *DA* that Resistance member Linda Mere was elected the SRC education spokesperson at the University of Tasmania.

SWP candidates

In the *DA* of January 22, 1986, Steve Painter reported on "Socialist candidates in Scullin, Fremantle". Maurice Sibelle, a 25-year-old sheet metal worker, was the SWP candidate in a by-election for the Victorian federal seat of Scullin.

"Frank Noakes, a 32-year-old bus driver, is the SWP candidate for Fremantle [in a WA state election]. A former member of the state executive of the WA Labor Party, he resigned from the ALP in late 1984 to support the campaign of the Nuclear Disarmament Party." The SWP in Fremantle received 5 percent of the vote.

In July, we announced that we were standing Val Edwards for the NSW seat of Rockdale. *DA* (July 16) described her as "until a few weeks ago a prominent activist in NSW Labor Party's Labor Women committee".

In the same issue, Steve Painter reported, "[Bill] Hartley calls for new party", and Tom Wilson wrote, "Qld Blacks to run candidates against Labor".

DA of August 27 reported that Robynne Murphy was the SWP candidate in a Heathcote, NSW, by-election. *DA* of September 3 announced that Sue Bolton and Maurice Sibelle would be standing for the SWP in the upcoming Queensland election.

Major labour struggles

In February 1985, the Queensland government headed by Joh Bjelke-Petersen provoked a major industrial dispute by allowing the South-East Queensland Electricity Board to start introducing contract labour, in preparation for eventual privatisation. The SEQEB workers, members of the Electrical Trades Union, declared an indefinite strike. Bjelke-Petersen fired 1,000 of them and also declared a state of emergency. Power station operators belonging to the Municipal Officers Association, who reduced power in solidarity with the SEQEB workers, were bludgeoned out of it with $1,000 fines for each instance of failing to follow instructions to increase power.

In the December 4 issue of *DA*, Paul Andersen summarised the process by which the workers were being defeated:

"Back in February, when the lights were out, the labour movement in this state had a real chance to defeat the Bjelke-Petersen government, and this was reflected in the willingness of the rank and file to take industrial action. Members of the Tramways union would have gone out if they had been asked. Support was reflected in collections for the sacked workers, but like the rest of the labor movement, bus drivers were not called out in support of the SEQEB workers and the lights came back on.

"That was the beginning of a process of demoralisation and confusion which only deepened when workers saw mass arrests and cop violence on the picket lines and the introduction of anti-union legislation ... which outlaws secondary boycotts and imposes massive fines on both individuals and unions – and the leadership accepting it. There was the spectacle of the secretary of the TLC, Ray Dempsey, coming out and saying that the labor movement could live with the legislation.

"The ACTU-imposed blockade in May again raised hopes that there were moves to take on the government – but again the action was called off just as it was beginning to have an effect and workers were more demoralised and confused than ever."

A more successful fight was waged by nurses in Victoria, who conducted a 50-day strike at the end of 1986. This followed on a less protracted and determined strike in 1985. The Victorian nurses had elected a new leadership under Irene Bolger, which was neither intimidated nor enticed into selling the members short. Shirley Sharma (Lalitha Chelliah) reported the outcome in *DA*, January 28, 1987: "Victorian Nurses – struggle won impressive gains".

A damaging precedent for the labour movement was established in the 1985 dispute at the Mudginberri abattoir in the Northern Territory. This was the first successful use of legal sanctions against a union since the 1969 Clarrie O'Shea events the made the penal powers a dead letter.

In 1983, the Australasian Meat Industry Employees Union served a log of claims on all abattoirs in the Northern Territory. However, the award handed down in April 1985 allowed for non-union contracts. Such a contract was in force at Mudginberri, and in May the AMIEU set up a picket line there and at several other abattoirs.

In the *DA* of July 30, 1986, Steve Painter summarised how the union had faced the combined attack of the NT Country Liberal Party government, the National Farmers' Federation and the courts, using the anti-union provisions of section 45D of the Trade Practices Act, passed by the Fraser government. The NT government gave Mudginberri proprietor Jay Pendarvis a $992,000 loan and a $180,000 grant, and guaranteed a loan to him of $2 million.

"The NFF came through with $200,000 from its 'fighting fund' to pay Pendarvis' court costs. Recognising in the NFF a potential shock force for continuing assaults on union rights, big companies around the country and internationally poured something like $11 million into the NFF's fund."

Hit with costs totalling around $190,000, the AMIEU lifted its pickets and returned to the Arbitration Commission, which in March 1986 did nothing to end non-union contracts. In July, Pendarvis was awarded $1,759,444 "damages" against the AMIEU, under section 45D.

"Through all this", Painter wrote, "the ACTU and its affiliates continued to formally support the AMIEU, but took no effective action to back its campaign.

"As in the South-East Queensland Electricity Board dispute … the ACTU's main concern was to restrict industrial action for fear of disrupting its prices-incomes accord with the federal government."

Painter quoted from a *Sydney Morning Herald* report that said unions "rarely have been subjected to civil action because employers generally have found it not worthwhile". He continued:

"Why did the bosses find it worthwhile in the Mudginberri case? Obviously, because the ACTU failed to make it not worthwhile.

"The union movement's only real defence against the bosses' court is its ability to make the bosses pay an unacceptably high price for any particular action.

"A determined, united ACTU industrial campaign in support of the AMIEU could have, as in the 1968-69 Clarrie O'Shea case, persuaded that Jay Pendarvis' sacred entrepreneurial rights came with a prohibitively expensive price tag."

Defending the BLF

While we had political differences with federal BLF leader Norm Gallagher, particularly with his 1974 campaign that succeeded in taking control over the NSW branch of the union from its democratically elected leaders, we of course came to his defence when he was attacked by the state, being brought to trial on charges of corruption for allegedly accepting free materials and labour from builders. The real reason he was targeted was his opposition to the Accord and the militancy of the BLF.

On June 13, 1985, Gallagher was convicted on 20 of 43 counts by a Melbourne court. *DA* 527, on its cover, declared "Gallagher conviction: A political trial". The article, by Steve Painter and Ramani De Silva (Reihana Mohideen), outlined both the lengths to which the state had gone in order to get Gallagher and why it had done so.

"The case against Gallagher was constructed by six cops working full-time over more than four years", Painter and De Silva pointed out. "Two other cops worked on the case part-time. To date, the cost to the [Victorian] government has been around $30 million ..."

The judge in the case went to unusual lengths to secure a verdict, the article noted:

"The jury was locked up for eight nights deliberating on the case. This is said to be the longest lockup in Victoria's legal history and the second longest in Australia.

"Twice it approached the judge, saying it could not reach a unanimous verdict. On both occasions Judge Waldron refused to discharge the jury, on the second occasion reminding the jurors that it had been a very costly trial."

The article pointed out that it was the militancy of the BLF that was the real target of the trial:

"Under Gallagher's leadership, the laborers have won improvements that have flowed through the whole industry, even benefiting more skilled building workers, such as carpenters and plumbers ...

"... no union runs campaigns like that without making powerful enemies. In the eyes of the building bosses, federal and state governments, the media, and even some less militant sectors of the labor movement, the BLF is public enemy number one."

The following issue of DA declared on its cover that Gallagher was "Jailed for the crime of militant unionism". However, the government's victory soon began to unravel. A young woman, "Kim", who was one of the jurors in Gallagher's trial, came forward saying she had favoured acquitting Gallagher on all charges but had been pressured by some of the other jurors and had finally, exhausted, given in. Her story was carried in an interview in the August 9-15, 1985, issue of the *National Times*, and in an interview by Dave Holmes and Steve Painter in the August 14 issue of *DA*.

Kim said that several jurors appeared to have made up their minds beforehand. "... some of the jurors had already decided that Gallagher had to go, and some of them had very strong personalities.

"I think it was very easy for the strong personalities to persuade the weaker ones that they were correct, and once you had made your mind up that Norm Gallagher was guilty, there was no necessity for the evidence to be weighed."

Kim said she had found the eight days of deliberation physically taxing as well as stressful. Twice the jury asked the judge to dismiss it because it couldn't reach a unanimous verdict, and twice he refused. "On the second occasion", Kim said, "he told us that a lot of money had been spent on this trial ...

"This led me to believe that since the trial had gone on for four months, it would be cheaper for the jury to be locked up for a few more weeks, even a month, two months.

"That would be cheaper than a retrial. And I just couldn't tackle the idea of being in that atmosphere for two weeks, three weeks."

The publicity surrounding Kim's disclosures created a favourable atmosphere for Gallagher's legal appeal, which was successful in October.

Mary Cassidy wrote in the October 9 *DA:* "Norm Gallagher's appeal against conviction for 20 counts of allegedly accepting bribes was upheld before a full bench of the Supreme Court in Melbourne on October 7 …

"The Chief Justice, Sir John Young, agreed with Gallagher's submission that excessive pressure on the forewoman of the trial jury had forced her to agree to convict Gallagher. The Chief Justice also stated that Justice Waldron, the trial judge, had erred in law by refusing to dismiss the jury when it was unable to reach a decision after eight days of deliberation."

However, the Victorian Labor government was determined to get Gallagher, and at a retrial nearly a year later, he was convicted and sentenced to 18 months' jail and a $60,000 fine. In "Second Gallagher show trial ends" in the September 17, 1986, *DA,* Michael Costello and Steve Painter pointed out that the developers who pleaded guilty to bribing Gallagher were sentenced to a good behaviour bond and told to contribute $5,000 to the poor box. This was part of a deal between the developers and the prosecution:

"No convictions were to be recorded, as convictions would have disqualified the developers from holding company directorships.

"When Gallagher was originally committed for trial in September 1983, 28 of the original 43 charges were dismissed for lack of evidence. But after the secret deal with the state attorney general's office, the original charges were reintroduced."

"There can be little doubt", they concluded, "that the Gallagher trial was politically motivated from start to finish.

"It was pursued by the [John] Cain [Victorian] government at a time when the Labor Party right wing was driving for total compliance with its prices-incomes accord."

By the time of the second Gallagher trial, the Cain government had already ensured that unfairly pressured jurors could not again derail a frame-up. An amendment to the Victorian Juries Act that became effective in January 1986 forbade jurors from voicing any opinions or concerns regarding a case; violations could carry a penalty of three months in prison and/or a $10,000 find (*DA* 554).

Privatisation push

The neoliberal program being implemented by Labor federal and state governments included a strong push for privatisations. Both threatened and actual sell-offs were also a weapon for reducing workforces and holding down wages.

DA of February 25, 1987, had two articles on the privatisation plans of the NSW ALP government headed by Barry Unsworth. In "Creeping privatisation. Unsworth's dockyard selloff scheme", Matthew O'Halloran interviewed workers and an AMWU delegate at the Newcastle State Dockyard, where there had already been lay-offs and more were threatened. The workers charged that the state government, and in particular Laurie Brereton, the state minister for public works, had prevented the dockyard management from tendering for work in order to close the facility and sell its equipment to several interested private companies. Only a few weeks after the article appeared, the dockyard was in fact closed.

The second article on NSW privatisations, by John Garcia and Steve Painter, was headed, "Water Board sackings reflect privatisation drive". It described sackings at the Newcastle dockyard and the Water Board, and a plan to close the Eveleigh locomotive workshops in Sydney as part of "Labor's increasing commitment to privatisation of government services that show promise of returning profits".

"The NSW developments are part of a national pattern", they wrote. "Victoria's Cain government has been particularly vigorous in running down government services – especially the railways and public hospitals – in order to open up the more profitable areas to private operators.

"In recent years, both the NSW and Victorian Labor governments have sold off millions of dollars worth of land, buildings, and other public assets.

"The Hawke government clearly supports this direction. On February 15, Treasurer Paul Keating announced that the federal government will further cut state funding at the premiers' conference next June."

"Labor plans its sale of a century" was the back cover headline on the August 19, 1987, *DA*. The article, by Steve Painter, described the Hawke government's "deliberately leaked plan to press for changes in Labor Party policy so it can hold a Thatcher-style fire sale of public assets":

"The Hawke machine plans to dump policies that have been integral to the Labor platform throughout the party's 90-year history, and it aims to sell off facilities that in some cases represent a century of slow accumulation and reform, particularly in areas such as health, education and public transport …

"Plans so far floated include selling off Australian Airlines, the

Commonwealth Bank, and Telecom."

Painter noted that some trade union figures in the ALP were opposed to these plans, but it didn't seem likely that they could defeat them.

"At the 1984 ALP national conference the Hawke machine showed that it was prepared to throw the full weight of the government behind its side in internal Labor Party discussions, and to enlist the support of the big business media for good measure.

"The fact that ALP members resigned in droves after the 1984 conference didn't matter to the Hawke machine. Its strategy is based on big business, rather than mass, support."

He added that, even in the unlikely event that Hawke's plans were officially rejected by the national conference, "creeping privatisations" by the state and federal governments were certain to continue, until the Liberals came to power and would then carry them out wholesale.

In reality, the Hawke-Keating government faced remarkably little resistance to its neoliberal plans from the union movement. Leaders of the ACTU and most of its member unions, once roped into the Accord, tended to continue to follow its class-collaborationist logic. In August-September 1986, a delegation from the ACTU and the government Trade Development Council visited Western Europe on a "fact-finding mission". On July 29, 1987, their report, a 230-page book called *Australia Reconstructed*, was launched in Melbourne at a meeting of 500 business and academic economists, union officials and ALP parliamentarians.

At the launch, employment, education and training minister John Dawkins said the report showed "a depth of commitment, at the most senior levels of the trade union movement, to maintaining Australia's international competitiveness and tackling head-on our balance of payments constraint". We didn't think that maintaining the competitiveness of Australian capitalists was a proper role for the union movement, and we said so. In *DA* issues 622-625, we ran a four-part series by Doug Lorimer explaining what was wrong with *Australia Reconstructed*. Doug began by referring to both the connection and the differences of this class-collaborationist politics with the publications like *Australia Uprooted* and *Australia Ripped Off,* which had helped to prepare the way for the Prices-Incomes Accord:

"Not so long ago, the subject of glossy booklets in the trade union movement was the need for the protection of Australian companies against international competition. But that was back when Australian companies were demanding the same thing.

"Times have changed, and so has the tune of some trade union officials.

Now, efficiency is all the go in the corporate boardroom, and some officials are hastening to help out their old mates in educating the ranks in the needs of the hour."

Over four weeks, Doug explained that the Accord had failed not only to maintain real wages – they had declined even when the ALP government's supposed improvement of the "social wage" was included – but also to increase employment:

"The accord's premise – that today's profits are tomorrow's jobs – has proven to be a mirage. Despite a substantial reduction in real wages and a consequent boost in company profits, the expected surge in productive investment and employment has not materialised.

"The decline in working people's real incomes over the last four years has simply served to fatten the bank accounts of the capitalist magnates – to make the rich richer."

The trade union leaders and the ALP government were united on "a consensus approach to policy making" – their preferred term, as Doug noted, for what others usually called "collaboration". "Consensus" was the great virtue of the Accord, they maintained. The Accord had delivered for the capitalists but not for workers, but the conclusion of *Australia Uprooted* was that everyone should try harder to get the bosses to re-invest their profits in creating jobs.

In the late 1960s and 1970s, there had been a shift in Australia in the division of national income to the advantage of workers and the disadvantage of capitalists. The accord had reversed that shift, but this did not result in the creation of more jobs. Doug explained that the union supporters of the Accord shared the view of academic economists that profit rates depended only on wages. But while the Accord had raised the amount of profit, it had not significantly raised profit rates, which depend also on the total capital invested to obtain a profit, not just on wages. So, instead of re-investing their profits productively, capitalists were using them for speculation. To the degree that they did invest productively, it was mainly investment in machinery that destroyed jobs.

'Broad Left' and other conferences

The failure of the Accord to deliver its promised improvements for workers was creating serious problems for its supporters in the labour and left movements (mostly left ALP and the right of the Communist Party). On the one hand, they could hardly deny the reality of falling real wages and high and stagnant unemployment. On the other, they were resistant, for political reasons as much as prestige, to admitting that the Accord had been a mistake in the first place.

The attempted solution was to complain that the Labor government hadn't "implemented" the Accord as it should have, and therefore to devote their attention to seeking to influence the ALP. In late August 1985, some of these supporters of the Accord circulated a letter to selected recipients calling for a "broad left" conference "to confront ... the threat from increasingly strident and militant conservatives set on destabilising the federal government", as the *Australian* newspaper put it at the time. Steve Painter wrote in the September 4 *DA* that the conference was a project "of the Labor government's favorite left wingers" – the right wing of the CPA and BWIU leader Pat Clancy. These forces were neither very broad nor very left, Painter wrote. Furthermore, they didn't show much inclination to move towards either of those characteristics. Participation in the conference was to be by invitation only, the letter proposed, in order to exclude "groups more interested in disruption and doctrinal polemics than in serious and open-minded discussion of the issues".

"Translated from Arbitration Commission unionese", Painter pointed out, "that means 'opponents of the accord need not apply.'"

The Broad Left Conference was eventually held at the Easter weekend, 1986, in Sydney. By the time it convened, political pressures had caused the organisers to make some concessions. They had now agreed to allow some opponents of the Accord to attend. At least partly, this shift may have been caused by evidence that the "broad left" was far from the only game in town: people involved in attempting to organise a Greens party had announced plans for a Getting Together Conference, also planned for Sydney at Easter.

DA intervened in both the Broad Left and the Getting Together conferences and the debates leading up to them. Two examples are articles by Steve Painter in the February 26 *DA*, "Broad Left Conference: The new right diversion", and March 12, "Broad Left Conference: Is the Accord a social contract?"

The conference drew some 1200 participants. George Petersen later wrote of it: "Bob Gould and the Socialist Workers Party and I joined together to persuade conference delegates to pass resolutions condemning the behaviour of the Hawke Labor government."[73]

Ten years after the conference, Petersen recalled:

> This conference was to be presented with a charter, widely circulated beforehand, stating broad leftist principles for consideration as the basis for the eventual formation of a new party. It was to be addressed by leading ALP and CPA figures and other left academics and activists. To combat perceived weaknesses in the Broad Left Charter, a group of people from diverse backgrounds came together to draw up an

alternative set of principles for the conference. This group consisted
of left CPA members, called by now the Rank and File Group, Socialist
Workers Party …, the Socialist Party of Australia, the Builders Labourers
Federation, Bob Gould, Frank Hardy and others. Jim McIlroy (SWP), Bob
Gould and myself drew up the alternative statement endorsed by this
group. It was agreed that the group would seek to participate in, rather
than intervene in or disrupt, the conference and that no partisan or
ideological point scoring would be engaged in, nor was the debate to
be hijacked or dominated by our group. The organisers decided to limit
the number of SWP/Gould supporters to 50, which didn't augur well
for the "broadness" aspect of the conference. Nonetheless, the group
took its arguments to the floor of the conference's various sessions. On
the major points, such as opposition to the Accord, opposition to the
deregistration of the BLF and rejection of the right-wing policies of the
Hawke government, the group won hands down. This was a serious
setback for the leadership of the CPA and created a challenge that it
eventually proved unable to meet."[74]

A workshop on the BLF attracted a record 600 delegates, overwhelmingly
opposed to deregistration. A petition opposing deregistration got 800 signa-
tures. During the conference a meeting of the militant left was also held at
Glebe Town Hall, attended by 400 independent left activists and members of
the SWP, the SPA, the CPA (ML) and International Socialists. The main speaker
was Frank Hardy, who called for a new communist party. *DA* carried papers,
talks and commentary on the conferences and meetings in subsequent issues.

Left Consultation and Fightback conferences

These conferences were followed by the Left Consultation in Melbourne in
April 1986, supported by the SWP, the SPA, the CPA-ML and some of the ALP
left. Then in July, the National Fightback Conference was held in Canberra, focusing especially on the defence of union rights. Steve Painter wrote in the May
7 *DA* that the Left Consultation on April 26, held at the Victorian Trades Hall,
agreed on united action to defend the BLF. Members of six parties and several
smaller groups participated in the consultation, attended by 160 activists. Peter
Symon from the SPA, Jim Percy from the SWP, and Ted Bull from the CPA (ML)
addressed the opening session, as did left-wing Labor MPs George Crawford
and Joan Coxsedge.

"The consultation was widely seen as another step towards establishing greater cooperation between the various parties of the left ... Further steps are likely at the National Fightback Conference, which will be held in Canberra on July 4-6."

A statement adopted by the consultation criticised the Accord: "The concepts of accord between worker and employer, class peace, tripartite discussion and other class collaborationist concepts, disarm the workers and their organisations and reduce their resolve and ability to defend gains won over many decades".

In June, Prime Minister Hawke issued a call "to the nation" for greater sacrifices to solve the country's economic problems. *DA* responded with an SWP National Executive statement, "We need a pay rise now!", and articles with the titles: "Hawke prepares the way for Thatcherism. Geniuses of '84, clowns of '86"; "Lower wages won't solve exports crisis"; "Accord has fuelled anti-union offensive"; "'Good points' of the accord. Tribune rehashes failed strategy".

On June 26, the Arbitration Commission issued its decision in the national wage case. This gave workers a rise of only 2.3 percent in compensation for inflation of 4.3 percent in the second half of 1985. In fact, the ACTU had asked for only 2.3 percent, as part of the Accord Mark II signed with the government in September 1985. The ALP government welcomed the decision, saying it expected future such discounting of rises to compensate for inflation.

The *DA* cover of July 2 was a clever reworking of the famous IWW antiwar poster in World War I ("To ARMS! Capitalists, Parsons, Politicians, Landlords, Newspaper Editors, and other Stay-at-home Patriots. Your Country needs you in the trenches! Workers, Follow your masters!"). It proclaimed: "Tighten your belts! Politicians, Judges, Bankers, Share Bludgers, Media Barons, and Other Idle Hypocrites. Sacrifice for the profit system!! Workers, Follow your masters."

The same issue contained an SWP position paper for the National Fightback Conference. This sought to move forward the initial steps towards discussion and cooperation among the various organisations and movements that were breaking with the Accord and class-collaborationist politics. It summarised both the loss in real wages and conditions and in terms of union organisation and unions' political activity on non-industrial matters (Aboriginal land rights, uranium mining, woodchipping etc.). And it pointed out that the bosses' offensive was not going to go away of its own: "The present state of affairs ... is simply the latest stage of a long-term offensive against workers' living standards, and trade union and democratic rights".

Calling for "an alternative to Laborism", the paper noted: "The experience of the Whitlam and Hawke Labor governments demonstrates for our generation that Labor has no strategy to defend working people's rights in times of capitalist crisis …

"While the ALP remains the only realistic political alternative to the Liberals, working people will remain trapped in a system that is rigged against them."

As the basis for a "fighting strategy" to "defend our democratic rights and living standards", the SWP proposed a four-point program:

1. "Campaign in every way possible for immediate wage rises to compensate for the wage cuts of the past three years …

2. "Redouble efforts to defend union and democratic rights, so that unions trying to break out of the accord are not left vulnerable to attacks such as the one against the Builders Labourers Federation.

3. "Participate in discussions towards developing a program to take real power over our lives out of the hands of the bosses, their state, and their governments …

4. "Begin the task of constructing a new party – a genuine alternative to the parties of the bosses …"

The opening rally of the conference, on the evening of July 4, was addressed by Humphrey McQueen, Helen Prendergast (from the federal government's Status of Women office), Victorian ALP left-winger Irene Robson, Filipina activist Aida Maranan and Janet Parker, Resistance national secretary.

The conference drew 550 participants. The report by Steve Painter and Peter Annear in the July 5 *DA* indicated that one major discussion was around the question of whether the left should try to work within the ALP or seek to build a new party outside it. The final declaration looked to the establishment of a rank-and-file organisation of unions and supporters of union rights, and proposed another National Fightback Conference in Melbourne at Easter 1987.

CHAPTER 7

ONGOING UNITY ATTEMPTS

In 1983-84 we had attempted fusions with the Turkish comrades from Revolutionary Path, the small group of Trotskyists in Socialist Fight, and a group of militant mineworkers in Tasmania. All of these efforts helped us develop a better understanding of the dialectics of party-building, although they didn't succeed in the short term.

We pushed again for political unity in 1986, on the political basis of opposition to Labor's class collaboration. *DA* 563 and 564 carried a two-part series by Jim Percy and Steve Painter, "Socialist renewal: Which way forward?", which was the concluding part of a position paper we had circulated at the Broad Left Conference in Sydney.

It took up the "new right" threat that was being cited by the pro-Accord left as a reason not to rock the class-collaborationist boat. The capitalists, the paper pointed out, were in a less favourable economic situation than they had been in the 1950s and '60s, and therefore they were more aggressive in pushing to make worker pay for their problems.

"But there's nothing particularly new about this 'new right.' …

"What's new about migrant bashing, opposition to Aboriginal land rights, anti-feminism, Cold War international policies, calls for privatisation of potentially profitable public services, calls for deregulation of the labor market, calls to cut back or abolish welfare services?"

What was really new in the situation was the extent to which the traditional labour movement left was retreating before the bosses' offensive, usually without even the pretence of a fight.

"As happened in the early '50s – the time of the last big capitalist ideological offensive of this nature – a section of the labor movement is ready and willing to add its weight to this attempt to push the whole political situation rightward."

At that time, this rightward push had had to split the ALP, setting up the DLP. This time, the right was in control of the ALP and the unions: "Probably never before has such a thoroughly right-wing anti-worker push controlled the ALP and the top levels of the union movement on a national scale …

"This time, important parts of the left have refused to fight. The powerful NSW Steering Committee faction of the ALP has offered no effective resistance to the right wing offensive. The Victorian CPA leadership walked out with the apparent aim of linking up with Bill Hayden's thoroughly right wing ALP Centre Left faction.

"Prominent left union officials like the CPA's Laurie Carmichael and the Association of Communist Unity's Pat Clancy have thrown their full weight behind the anti-worker accord project." Labor's increasingly brazen neoliberal politics was spurring opposition not only in the labour movement but also in social movements outside traditional union structures – such as the Nuclear Disarmament Party and the environmental movement. But some of the anti-Accord left found it difficult to relate to such movements; others thought it still possible to fight within the ALP rather than from outside it, while still others thought it a mistake to relate to the Labor Party in any fashion.

"Perhaps these political and tactical differences will wither away over time, but for the moment it's more realistic to consider alliances than organic unity."

In the September 3 *DA,* Jim wrote "Why the left needs a new party". After briefly critiquing the various reasons different people gave for opposing such a project, he concluded: "Discussion of the necessity of a new party is alone an important step. A small organisational gain on the question would be even better, though perhaps a lot more is really possible in the next few years."

I reported that "left unity" was discussed at a Melbourne conference of 250 at the Melbourne YWCA, in the lead-up to the United Left Fightback meeting planned for Easter 1987. Speakers were Bill Hartley, Neil McLean (CPA [ML]), Joan Coxsedge, Alan Miller (SPA) and Reihana Mohideen (SWP).

"What is needed is a response on the level of party politics; we need a unifying political project, a political alternative to the ALP", said Mohideen. "The tactic of staying in the ALP and fighting is futile", but the worst alternative was "to remain an individual on the sidelines of the discussion" (*DA* 584). Dawn McEwan reported from Perth that a WA Left Action Conference drew some 200 people on September 13-15. Speakers included Melbourne BLF organiser Mick Young, WA electricians union secretary Rivo Gandini and Catherine Brown from the SWP.

A September 21 Sydney meeting drew about 100 people to hear Jim Percy, CPA (ML) representative Bruce Cornwall and SPA representative Bob Hatton. The meeting was forced to close early due to disruption by Bob Gould. Steve Robson reported in *DA,* December 10, 1986, an "Important new party discussion in Canberra" on December 4, attended by 80 people, on the prospects for a new left party. Speakers were Brian Aarons, Jim Percy, Debbie McIlroy and Alex Anderson (a Getting Together Conference activist). The chair was Lynn Lee, a Philippines solidarity activist.

Mistaken hopes for perestroika, glasnost

In April 1985 the Communist Party of the Soviet Union Central Committee elected Mikhail Gorbachev as general secretary, and he embarked on his program of trying to reform the bureaucratised Soviet economy and state through *perestroika* (restructuring) and *glasnost* (openness).

DA immediately took note of the changed international situation. We welcomed perestroika and glasnost as necessary developments for the Soviet Union, and *DA*'s coverage of events there and in Eastern Europe over the last half of the 1980s was a wonderful source, invaluable to political activists and also to students and teachers of Soviet history and politics. Doug Lorimer described the developments in a two-page *DA* (March 12, 1986) article, "Gorbachev projects sweeping changes".

We noted some of the positive international consequences of perestroika, such as the lessened danger of a nuclear holocaust. We also felt that such international developments made left regroupment in Australia both more necessary and more feasible.

But unfortunately it didn't turn out as we had hoped at the start. Perhaps it was a lot of wishful thinking on our part, but the outcome was a disaster for the people of the Soviet Union and Eastern Europe. It meant a brutal return to capitalism, lowering living standards and hurting workers, who had illusions about the life of people in the "West". It gave rise to criminal oligarchs who grabbed the nationalised assets and resources for themselves. Criminals became billionaires overnight (a faster process than the normal operations of capitalism in the West).

Chernobyl

Gorbachev's reform hopes weren't helped by Chernobyl, the catastrophic nuclear accident that occurred on April 26, 1986, at the Chernobyl nuclear power plant in Ukraine (then officially the Ukrainian SSR), which was under the direct jurisdiction of the central authorities of the Soviet Union. An explosion and fire released large quantities of radioactive particles into the atmosphere, which spread over much of the western USSR and Europe. Greg Adamson covered developments for the May 7 *DA* in "Chernobyl: the threat is everywhere", also pointing out "Nuclear power's unbeatable accident record", and (May 14) "Chernobyl Danger Continues".

September 1986 SWP NC

The SWP held a National Executive meeting on August 8, 1986, at which Jim Percy gave a political report outlining the attitude of the left players towards the left unity or new party question: the CPA, the CPA (ML), the SPA, Bill Hartley. Earlier in the year, we had been having both informal and formal discussions with the SPA. For instance, on June 18 there was a joint leadership meeting on "How to Build the Communist Party Today", with presentations by Jim Percy and Jack McPhillips, followed by discussion.

At the NE meeting Jim summarised our tasks:

1. We should talk up the new party question, but clarify the axis of what we mean. Do we think it should be, for example, a Marxist-Leninist party? No, that unity of Marxist-Leninists is not possible yet. It could be a party that would unite all the social movements. Many steps would be involved in getting to such a party, perhaps going through stages of election collaboration, coordination of some of the forces, then an alliance of forces. It might be an ex-ALP party, with the focus "Fight against Labor's Liberal policies".

2. In the next federal election, we'd do better running in our own name, but *calling for* a new party. The problem is money, because we'd be selling ourselves short if it wasn't a big campaign. "Our response to Hartley's stunt [after being expelled from the ALP, Hartley had quickly set up the Industrial Labor Party to run Senate candidates in the next election], is to run with our own campaign, which poses to Hartley: are you for unity?" It would also pose that question to the CPA.

3. Youth work, which is our trump card. The only other group succeeding here is IS, which comes from our default on several levels: *DA* sales and projecting Marxism, for example through forums. So we should reorient the party to Resistance forums on Marxism and Leninism. This is the next stage of building Resistance and the other side of the SWP election campaign. We need mobilisations to counter IS.

4. Union work and mass work. Too often we do this to the exclusion of building ourselves; we can't cover every base in the mass movement.

5. Our conference. We should reach out, and also consolidate

Resistance comrades as our major effort. We can't retreat from
building a cadre party and the need to train youth. Do we need
an organised structure to bring in supporters? A change of
names? We had to think more carefully about how to compete
with the CPA, and Hartley's "party".

There was also a report on the Philippines by Max Lane, and a report
on Cuba by Jim Percy, describing the results of his recent trip, and our
expectations.

Many of these issues were elaborated on in reports to the SWP National
Committee meeting, September 4-6, 1986: international situation, Cuba,
Nicaragua, Philippines, political report youth, and organisation.

Tony Forward's organisation report pointed out: "At one stage, four
years ago, we quite deliberately loosened up membership norms: we went to
monthly branch meetings, we tried to organise the party around trade union
fractions. More recently, in the last 18 months, we tightened up membership
norms again, we returned to weekly branch meetings and made them the
major organisational focus of the party.

"At the same time, with the introduction of the dues system, we set a
minimum financial commitment necessary for membership and, with the
introduction of the *Direct Action* levy system, also established a level of activity
necessary to be in the party …

"When we saw that the idea of opening the party out, of dropping the minimum standards of membership, was having some real corrosive effects on the
norms of the party and our ability to be able to survive financially and to carry
the newspaper, we corrected that."

Tony discussed the difficult financial situation and the need for a sales
drive, and stressed the importance of cadre. "The importance of these two areas – sales and finances – is the training and education we are giving the people
joining the party. There's little point in adding to the party membership if we
inhibit our ability to act as a party. We simply add paper members or members
who really aren't as committed as we know we have to be. We need to add to,
and replace, our cadre with cadre. Anything else is fake growth." The report
concluded by projecting "returning to basic party-building norms".

Resistance also held an NC, on September 13-14. It began with a political
report by Jim Percy; we felt the need for such a report, emphasising closer collaboration between the SWP and Resistance. There was an organisation report
by Janet Parker, a mass work report by Richard Woolfe, a campus report by
Caro Llewellyn and a weekend summary by Janet Parker.

January 1987 SWP & Resistance Educational Conference

We held a SWP and Resistance Educational Conference, January 3-8, 1987, at Sydney University Union, with the theme "Towards a new party". After the CPA had started expressing some reservations about the Accord in 1985 and started talking about a "New Left Party", we had invited them to participate in the conference.

We made a group booking at a cheap downtown hotel for comrades from out of Sydney, and held an end of conference party at our Abercrombie Street centre.

The major talks were given by: Reihana Mohideen, on Labor and beyond: Challenges for the left; Jim Percy on What politics for a new party?; Margo Condoleon, on How should socialists organise today?; Pat Brewer on World politics today – and prospects for the '90s; John Percy on Independent political action from the 1890s to 1980s – Lessons for today; Peter Annear on Theory and practice – what is Marxism today?.

Two of the three CPA joint national secretaries, Laurie Aarons and Rob Durbridge, spoke. Aarons spoke on "The CPA since the sixties – the turning point and after"; Durbridge spoke on "The challenge of the new party – the hard questions". Other related talks included Claudio Crollini from tha Australian Progressive Republican Association (APRA) on "A new party for the working people" and Stan Deacon on "Some highlights from CPA history". Mahanama Gunesena, from the FI group in Sri Lanka, was an international guest, speaking on "The political crisis in Sri Lanka – an eyewitness report".

Other talks were given on After Reykjavik – prospects for the peace movement; Saving the environment – has the left done enough?; The new wages system – two tier cuts; 1968-1986: the ups and downs of student dissent; The state of the unions; The women's movement under Labor; The Australian student movement today – a new upsurge?; New challenges for the Black movement; The accord and alternative economic strategies; Nationalisation – what, why and how?; True and false roads to Australian independence; Democratic issues on the road to socialism; Parliament, the ALP and the socialist movement; The challenge of the new movements; Personal politics and revolutionary leadership; From Lenin to the Sandinistas – what lessons for us?; The experience of the German Greens; Knowing your friends – the theory of alliances; A political history of the SWP; The UK: the social crisis and the left response; The role of the USSR in world politics today; The Chinese revolution: a challenge for Marxist theory; The Philippines: what now for people's power?; Latin America:

is the fuse shortening?; South Africa: Black power, sanctions and the crisis of apartheid; Labor bureaucracy – what is it and where did it come from?; The limits of radical reform: chapters from ALP history; From Whitlam to Hawke: the evolution of Labor in government; Sexuality and socialism; From evolution to revolution – what makes history?; Culture and politics; The outcome of the 1960s radicalisation; Twenty years of Resistance.

The public meeting, "Towards a New Party", was chaired by Margo Condoleon, with speakers Lalitha Chelliah, Rob Durbridge, Reihana Mohideen, Darco Perusco (APRA) and Max Taylor, former president of the NSW Teachers' Federation. Steve Painter reported on the conference in *DA* 596 that 283 people registered for the more than 40 sessions. In his talk "A political approach to break the impasse", Jim Percy "pointed out that the Communist Party had supported the formation of a new party since 1984, but until recently hadn't made much progress as it had based its politics on the ALP-ACTU prices-incomes accord.

"That had changed after last year's Broad Left Conference, when the CPA issued an economic statement sharply disagreeing with the Labor government. Then it came out against the new, two-tier wages system that replaced the accord mark II."

Describing it as "An historic opportunity for the left", Steve Painter also reported on the January 5 public meeting during the SWP-sponsored conference. Speakers were Max Taylor; Reihana Mohideen, SWP Melbourne organiser; Lalitha Chelliah, Victorian nurses' federation organiser, CPA national executive member Rob Durbridge and Darco Perusco, APRA.

Not everyone on the left was pleased by the more civil discussions taking place between the SWP, CPA, CPA (ML) and SPA. The International Socialists appeared to have decided that the SWP was Stalinist, and that this "fact" justified them in trying to prevent us from distributing *Direct Action* and other political literature. The *DA* of October 22, 1986, carried an article by Steve Painter reporting on the IS behaviour, particularly at a "Close Pine Gap" rally in Melbourne on October 19, when IS members tried physically to prevent the SWP setting up a literature stall or selling *DA*.

"*Direct Action* sellers were surrounded by IS members, and prodded, elbowed and shoved in what appeared to be an attempt to provoke an all-in brawl. All *Direct Action* sellers were tailed by at least one IS member attempting to disrupt sales.

"Some of the more hyped-up IS members kept up a torrent of shouted abuse a few inches from *Direct Action* sellers' faces and ears.

"Melbourne branch secretary John Percy … at the end of the rally … was surrounded by three IS members, and one … punched him in the stomach, saying 'there's more where that came from.' …

"Several Asian women who are members of the SWP … received blows to the back, stomach, and breasts …

"Chris Slee, a tramway worker and member of the SWP, reports that he was repeatedly pushed and punched on the chest and back. 'They threatened that if the SWP returned to the mall next Friday we would be beaten up,' he said."

The article noted that similar if less extreme actions had been carried out by IS members in Melbourne, Sydney and Brisbane in previous months, large numbers of them surrounding individual *DA* sellers to interfere with their sales.

Solidarity with Libya

As the US government of Ronald Reagan stepped up its hostility to the nationalist regime of Muammar Gaddafi, we solidarised with Libya against US attacks. *DA* of April 16, 1986, carried an article by Sol Salby, "US prepares new aggression against Libya". On April 15, the US launched extensive air strikes on Libya. These included an attempt to kill Gaddafi by bombing his home; his adopted daughter was killed in the bombing. The following issue of *DA* had two articles by Sol, "Reagan's terror raid condemned" and "No evidence for terror charges", debunking the US pretext for the attacks, plus an article by Greg Adamson detailing "17 years of US attacks".

Quickly organised protests against the US raids drew 400 people in Canberra, 200 each in Melbourne, Hobart, Sydney and Perth and 100 in Adelaide.

A year later, *Direct Action* sent Peter Boyle to a conference of Pacific peace and national liberation organisations held in Misurata, Libya. His report in the May 13, 1987, *DA* was timely because the Hawke government tried to insinuate that the conference was some kind of terrorist planning session. "Far from being a secretive event", Boyle reported, "the entire conference was televised. A Japanese television crew was on the spot, and there were extensive local broadcasts."

In the May 27 *DA*, Peter Boyle gave an overview in "Libya: Modernisation without poverty". He described social progress and an egalitarianism based, not on "shared poverty", but on oil wealth and a small population. While Libyans called their revolution socialist, "it has not been carried out under the influence of Marxist views". Gaddafi's theory, contained in his *Green Book*, sought "to idealise a society of small producers, all of whom own their own land, machinery and plant.

"The section of the Libyan economy that appears to fit this ideal most closely is agriculture. Small private farms appear to be thriving in the narrow belt of arable land."

Over subsequent months, *DA* continued periodic coverage of Libya: "Michael Mansell: Why we're going to Libya. Aboriginal delegation", an interview by Catherine Brown, May 18, 1988; Steve Painter, "Libya. A vast construction site", March 21, 1989; Bill Mason (Jim McIlroy), "Solidarity with Libya. Third anniversary of US bombing", April 25, 1989; Steve Painter, "Libya notebook. A new type of government", May 2, 1989; Steve Painter "Libya notebook. From harem to human", June 13, 1989; Steve Painter, "Libyans celebrate anniversary of new dawn. 20 years since El Fateh Revolution", August 29, 1989; Peter Green (John Percy), "Libyan Friendship Societies celebrate", September 5, 1989.

We probably erred in the direction of giving too much credibility to Gaddafi and his "Green Revolution". We were correct to provide solidarity against the imperialist attacks, oral and especially physical. But we got caught up a bit too much in the hype, although not as badly as the SLL, which accepted large sums to buy their press, and in return were slavish boosters of the Gaddafi regime.

But we went a bit down that path, going along with the Melbourne Libyan centre organised by Robert Pash. We accepted tickets to go to events in Libya, and the reports we wrote back on Libya in *DA* probably went beyond the bounds of solidarity against imperialism, and inflated the claims of Gaddafi's Green Revolution, which was an unscientific, incomprehensible ideology, strung together to counter a Marxist analysis, which was sorely needed.

They certainly made some social progress, with attempts at major development projects, like the "Man-made River", and certainly were a better society for the Libyan people than the subsequent chaos and tribal warfare that Gaddafi's overthrow with the aid of imperialism has descended into.

Fiji coup

On May 14, 1987, Colonel Sitiveni Rabuka carried out a military coup against an elected coalition government headed by the Fiji Labour Party. Unlike the capitalist media, which generally attributed the coup to "racial divisions" between indigenous Fijians and Indian Fijians, *Direct Action* was able to point out how these divisions were created by British imperialism, and how they interacted with class and social issues. In the May 20 issue, Peter Annear wrote "Fiji. Race and Politics: What the coup revealed".

In the following issue, he followed up with two articles: "Race and class in Fiji" and "Origins of the labor movement", tracing the struggle of exploited Indian immigrants back to the 1880s.

Fightback Conference, April 1987

The Fightback Conference, held in Melbourne at the Easter 1987 weekend, drew 500 participants. Speakers at the Friday night opening public meeting included nurses leader Irene Bolger; Shane Houston, from the National Coalition of Aboriginal Organisations; and Graham Haynes from the ETU, recently involved in Robe River dispute with Peko-Wallsend.

The conference was organised by the SPA, SWP, CPA (ML), Bill Hartley, "several members" of the ALP Socialist Left and a representative from the similar conference held a year before in Canberra. The *DA* report indicated both the progress and the problems of left unity:

"The conference consisted of 13 forums covering the main issues of the day. Though no discussion was scheduled on the question of the political and organisational need for a new left party, the issue was the subject of sometimes heated discussion at most sessions.

"The conference adopted an organisational structure that emphasises local support groups. Attempts to construct a national structure were seen as premature and potentially divisive."

Resistance conference, June 1987

Resistance's 16th national conference was held at 14 Anthony Street, Melbourne, June 6-8, 1987. An enlarged SWP NC was held the day before, at which the main report was on "new party and organisation", given by Jim Percy.

In an article headed "20 years of Resistance", *DA* of June 17 reported that 270 attended the conference. Jim Percy gave a feature talk on "The long march of the left", supporting a new party of the left.

The conference noted that Resistance now had student clubs on more than 20 campuses. Janet Parker, Resistance national secretary, said, "The conference resolved to support efforts to build a new national student union capable of providing national coordination and organisation for campaigns in defence of students' rights.

"But it rejected attempts by the right-wing Council of ALP students to capture any new union in advance and render it ineffective. A peak council modelled on the ACTU's domination of the union movement would not be useful in defending students' rights."

July 1987 federal election – range of independents

The 1987 election was a double dissolution election, in which the Hawke
Labor government won four additional seats despite an overall 1.8 percent
swing against it. There were quite a few attempts to run campaigns to the left of
the ALP, and we did our best to encourage them.

DA of June 17 headlined "Alternative candidates to break the Liberal/Labor
trap". The alternatives included the Nuclear Disarmament Party, running for
the Senate in NSW, Victoria and the ACT, plus the House of Representatives in
Fraser and Canberra; the SPA and CPA running as Socialist Alliance in South
Australia; Queensland Labor Senator George Georges, forced out of the ALP,
standing as an independent; Jo Vallentine in WA, running as "independent senator for nuclear disarmament"; Industrial Labor Party of Bill Hartley, standing
Senate teams in Victoria and the NT, plus seats in the House of Representatives;
Jack Mundey, contesting the seat of Sydney as an independent; John McGlynn
in Eden Monaro, on a Peace, Environment and Social Justice platform; Greens
in SA standing a Senate ticket headed by Alli Fricker; SWP, running Jamie
Doughney for Gellibrand; Aboriginal candidate Alan Brown, standing against
Aboriginal Affairs minister Clyde Holding in the safe Labor seat of Melbourne
Ports.

A week later, *DA* promoted "Alternatives to the Labor/Liberal farce": Alan
Brown; Michael Mansell for the Senate from Tasmania; Tom Walsh, McMillan,
Victoria; Paul Keating, a vehicle worker, for Blaxland, NSW; Georgina Motion,
Curtin Guild president, against Defence Minister Kim Beazley in the seat
of Swan; Kevin O'Connell and Lisa King, Senate, Victoria, for the National
Education Coalition; George Georges; Greens Senate teams in NSW and SA; Jack
Mundey; John McGlynn; Jamie Doughney; Industrial Labor Party; CPA Senate
team in SA; SPA Senate team in Victoria, Queensland and Tasmania; and Brian
Rooney for Port Adelaide and Sophie Mavrogeorgeosis for Hindmarsh.

Doug Lorimer in *DA* 616 outlined the "SWP vote policy in the federal elections": "[T]he SWP will support a first preference vote for alternative candidates
wherever possible, and a vote for the Australian Democrats where no left alternative candidate is standing. Second preferences should be directed to the ALP
to ensure the re-election of the Hawke government." The article pointed out
that the Democrats were not part of the solution:

"The Democrats are not a genuine alternative to Labor. Like the ALP, they
are committed to the private profit system, though they would prefer to temper
it with liberal reform.

"This [is a] utopian, liberal capitalist perspective …

"While a protest vote for the Democrats is a legitimate tactic in these elections, voting for a liberal capitalist party cannot solve the longer term problems facing working people and the various progressive movements.

"The urgent need of the moment is for a genuine alternative party that can begin to challenge the entire pro-capitalist framework of parliamentary politics.

"Such a party would actively participate in and build the grassroots struggles of ordinary people, using the electoral arena to promote support for those struggles.

"In the current election campaign, the most effective way to assist the process of building such a party is to maximise support for, and encourage links between, a range of progressive alternative candidates." Steve Painter responded in the July 8 *DA* to the question, "Should the left try to bring down Labor?" (responding to people like Harry van Moorst, Albert Langer, arguing for not voting, and the Industrial Labor Party, which was calling for Labor's defeat):

"In many quarters, anger and disgust with Labor is so deep that many left-wingers want to see the Hawke government defeated, even if that means election of a Liberal government." This was short-sighted.

"There must be no room for lying claims that the left stabbed Labor in the back, or that the left prefers Liberal governments because greater hardship leads to greater militancy.

"As for hopes for revival of the Labor left, why repeat a negative experience the left has already been through?

"The Hawke government's move to the right has presented the left with a unique opportunity to break the century-long stranglehold of Laborism – left and right – over labor movement politics.

"The main problem for the left at the present time is not a lack of social ferment, or of interest in left ideas. There is anger and the will to fight, but there is no vehicle for the fight. There is no alternative party."

Some 600 people attended an election night dinner for the Charter process for a New Left Party at Balmain Town Hall.

In the August 12, 1987, *DA*, under the kicker "Disgusted ALP members reorganise", Steve Painter reported on the formation of the Illawarra Workers Party, led by George Petersen. Petersen, who held the state seat of Illawarra, had been expelled from the ALP for voting against the state Labor government's reactionary changes to workers' compensation laws.

The initial meeting of the Illawarra Workers Party drew 115 people, 93 of whom signed up as members. *DA* quoted Petersen as saying, "We simply do not want to stay in the Labor Party to provide a left cover for right-wing politicians. What we want is an alternative Labor Party."

We didn't let the election activity distract us totally from other important political activity. The *DA* of July 22, 1987, reported on CISCAC functions in several cities on the theme "Nicaragua Must Survive!" A Sydney concert drew 450 people and raised $2,000 to aid Nicaragua. In Brisbane, 250 people raised $1,000, and heard former Labor Senator George Georges toast the Nicaraguan Revolution. A meeting in Adelaide drew 100.

Opposing Labor's ID card

In the months following the 1987 election, a rapidly growing movement eventually forced the Hawke government to abandon its plans to introduce a national ID card. The government had announced the plan two years earlier, and it quickly roused sharp criticism. In the *DA* of September 18, 1985, Sally Francis (Sally Low) wrote "Labor's ID card: Opposition grows", describing the protests of civil libertarians and others.

The Labor government had presented the card as a measure against tax avoidance, but the article quoted tax experts and some ALP parliamentarians as saying it would be of little or no use for that purpose. "The ID card system will inevitably be used to restrict the rights of the poor, the unemployed, people with criminal records, and religious and political dissidents." The article was also quite far sighted for its day in noting that growing computerisation of government operations made it much easier for things like an ID card to be misused for other purposes.

By September 1987, opposition to the card was becoming overwhelming. "Growing protests against national ID card", *DA* reported on September 16. The following issue urged "Burn the ID card", and in the *DA* of September 30, Dave Holmes in Perth reported on a "Huge WA protest against ID card" that drew 20,000 to 40,000 people.

Joint Resistance and SWP NC, October 1987

Our joint SWP and Resistance National Committee meeting, held October 3-5, 1987, was an important one, to which we also invited a number of comrades as observers, making a total attendance of 79.

Reports were given by myself, on "Imperialism's Crisis and a Strategy for Socialism", and Dave Holmes on "The Reform of the Russian Revolution" (these two reports were discussed together). Steve Painter reported on "Trends and Projections in Australian Politics" and Dick Nichols on "Trade Unionism and the Crisis of the Left" (the two reports discussed together); Jim Percy on

"Building the Revolutionary Party;" Pat Brewer on "Our Tasks in the Campaign for a New Left Party" (the two reports discussed together); Linda Mere on "Building Resistance" and Jorge Jorquera on "Balance Sheet of the New Student Movement" (the two reports discussed together); and Janet Parker on "Problems and Perspectives of the Social and Political Movements". Jim Percy's report outlined our perspectives for a possible New Left Party that had opened up with the partial change in the CPA line on the Accord. At our January 1986 conference in Canberra, we had assessed the previous two years of party building, he explained. "We pointed out that 1985 had marked the end of a period of experimentation in the party. In the previous couple of years we had tried to open up the party in response to the development of the antinuclear movement and some level of fight back against the Fraser government in the early 1980s."

But with the 1983 election of the Hawke ALP government, "the party needed to regroup and assess where it was going, as the political momentum of the last years of the Fraser government abruptly died …

"For our part, in 1985 we decided to put a period of organisational experimentation behind us, and to concentrate on a process of consolidation. We saved our assets by introducing a new dues structure, and we stressed party organisation and education by going back to weekly branch meetings. We took steps to ensure that Resistance was not starved of resources, and we began explaining to people joining our movement that they should prepare for the long haul, that it was unlikely there'd be any quick breakthroughs."

We began preparing the party for a relatively difficult period, Jim said, and then in 1986, "We turned away from attempts to create a union-based fight back movement, and focused instead on the question of socialist renewal – on the need for a viable socialist alternative, a new party of the left".

But this led to a certain neglect of other areas of work, for example our anti-nuclear work, Jim said. A second problem was the tendency to neglect the immediate needs of the SWP, such as sales, finances, education and recruiting.

Then came the rise of the NDP, "which helped to change our direction quite dramatically", and we'd done all we could to promote the idea of a new party. "Our support for a new party is part of a general party-building strategy, It doesn't represent a sharp break with our past. The fact that we regard it as our main tactic indicates how much we're still in a propaganda period."

Jim was prescient about the dangers likely to challenge our party in the years (and decades) ahead. "When we talk about a new party, it can seem like a break with our past. People can think that the very act of forming a new party will make all the old party-building tactics obsolete …

"While we think that the new party represents a continuity with the past,

326 ONGOING UNITY ATTEMPTS

that's not to say there's nothing new about the new party. We mean it when we say we have learned and will continue to learn from other forces. We know that we don't have all the answers.

"At the same time, however, we should be aware that this view can weaken our resolve and our view of our own importance. If we don't have all the answers, maybe the SWP isn't so important. If we're going to dissolve into a new party, why build the old party?

"Acceptance of that attitude would be a big political error", he stressed. "Without the old party, there won't be any new party. While we might be preparing to dissolve our existing organisational forms in the context of a new party, we're not about to dissolve our program, our ideas, our individual cadre or our assets …

"It's rather inevitable that we sometimes get a little lost in this complicated new party tactic. In recent months we've probably been a party with something of an identity crisis."

Jim outlined some immediate tasks of the SWP in helping the building of a new party. He proposed going back to monthly party branch meetings (which we had tried in 1982). He also proposed we hold weekly public forums, at least in the larger branches. He stressed the importance of organising to increase *DA* sales within this framework, and addressing our financial problems, for example by raising the price of *DA* to $1.

Jim's report was fairly quickly printed as a public pamphlet (together with his report "Recent experiences in party building", presented to the SWP 11th national conference in January 1986.)[75] So everyone on the left knew exactly what we were thinking and were saying to our members.

We also printed as public pamphlets most of the other reports to that NC: My report on "Imperialism's Crisis and a Strategy for Socialism" was published as *Capitalist Crisis, Socialist Renewal. World Politics in the 1980s.* Steve Painter's "Trends and Projections in Australian Politics" was published as *Two-Tier Society. The Politics of Capitalist Decline in Australia.* Dick Nichols' "Trade Unionism and the Crisis of the Left" was published as *New-Right Trade Unionism and the Crisis of the Left.* Dave Holmes' "The Reform of the Russian Revolution" was published as *Perestroika: The Reform of the Russian Revolution.*

This plenum may have been the occasion when Jim first raised a metaphor that was frequently used in our discussions: "the psychological bullets of the bourgeoisie". This became a shorthand for the myriad capitalist propaganda lines and social pressures that seek to convince us that it's not possible, or not desirable, to replace capitalist society with socialism.

Student movement upsurge

"The last three weeks have been an exciting indicator that student radicalisation is on the rise", Resistance national secretary Janet Parker told *DA* of March 11, 1987, commenting on the experience in O-week across the country, during which Resistance joined up more than 350 students on 22 campuses. "1987 will go down as the year that really put an end to the myth the media has liked to peddle – that the '80s heralded a new conservative generation of youth", she said.

The article quoted Resistance activists in the various cities. In Sydney, the Resistance Club at Sydney University sold 200 *DA*s and joined 24 new members; at Macquarie there were a dozen new members, and at UNSW 61 new members.

In Melbourne, Resistance members sold 500 copies of *DA* on five campuses and joined up 74 members.

In Adelaide, there were 38 new members at Flinders and Adelaide universities. Perth joined 48 new members, Wollongong 23, Canberra eight. At the University of Tasmania in Hobart, there were 27 new members. At the Mitchell College of Advanced Education in Bathurst, about 40 expressed interest in the Resistance Club. At Newcastle, 13 joined. At the University of Queensland in Brisbane, 60 *DA*s were sold and 17 new members joined.

That issue of *DA* also carried a long list of events advertised for different campuses.

A major spur for student activism was the decision of the Labor government to reinstitute university tuition, initially through the not very convincing guise of a $250 "administration fee". One aspect of the opposition to this was to encourage students to boycott payment. Articles in DA regularly regularly reported on the campaign:

February 25, 1987: "Students boycott Labor's fees".

March 18, 1987: a report on the fee boycott campaigns at Curtin and Queensland universities.

March 25, 1987: "Government plans to double student fee".

April 1, 1987: Reports on March 25 demonstrations for free education. In Sydney, the rally was addressed by Sydney University Student Representative Council president Joe Hockey! Also speaking were Jack Mundey, Staff Associations president Neil Harpley and Jenny McLeod of the Australian Democrats. Two thousand marched from Belmore Park to Town Hall Square, and then on to the Education Department.

In Brisbane, an 800-strong rally was addressed by QU student union secretary Jorge Jorquera. Other rallies were in Perth and Hobart.

April 8, 1987: "Top university body opposes Labor's fee". At an April 6 meeting, as several hundred students gathered outside, the University of Queensland senate voted not to expel students failing to pay the fee. Student Union secretary Jorge Jorquera said this was the fourth time the university had delayed the final date for payment. Protests continued at Griffith and Curtin. A national meeting of the campaign was held in Brisbane, sponsored by the UQ student union, with 60 delegates from 20 campuses. It set up a National Coalition for Free Education.

April 29, 1987: "Students prepare for national fees protest", on the upcoming National Days of Action in early May.

May 13, 1987: "National actions against fees". "From May 4-8, students from around the country took to the streets, occupied Commonwealth education offices and participated in a range of other activities in a week of action against Labor's $250 'administration' fee. The week was called by the National Coalition for Free Education in support of a list of demands drawn up in Queensland at the coalition's inaugural meeting.

"The demands include the abolition of the $250 fee, the abolition of the overseas student 'visa charge,' and the provision of adequate funding for education …"

August 19, 1987: "Student occupation at UQ". An occupation by 300 students followed a rally addressed by student union secretary Jorge Jorquera.

November 25, 1987: "Queensland students protest education cuts". Five hundred students from Brisbane College of Advanced Education marched to parliament house on November 18.

The ALP soon responded to the student upsurge – by mobilising its supporters on campus to divert or undermine the free education campaign. In the May 4, 1988, *DA*, Karen Fletcher described this process at the University of Queensland, where a pro-ALP ticket won control by lying about its Labor connections and promising "free coffee, free beer and free education" while throwing mud at the activist ticket. Fletcher called it "a perfect case study in what happens when the Australian Labor Party gains power in a student union". In alliance with Liberals on the union council, the ALP not only stopped the union from organising anti-fees protests but also alienated Aboriginal and Islander students, cut off funding for the student radio station 4ZZZ and cut funding for the Women's Rights Collective.

70th anniversary of Russian Revolution

We organised a big Russian Revolution 70th anniversary dinner at our Melbourne headquarters on October 31, 1987. Jim Percy was the main speaker, and there was a guest speaker from the Soviet embassy.

We still had hopes for what perestroika and glasnost might contribute to reinvigorating the Russian Revolution. *DA* of December 2, 1987, carried an analysis by Michael Peterson (Peter Boyle): "Gorbachev's 70th anniversary speech. A critical look at Soviet history".

Rainbow Alliance

The Rainbow Alliance was a grouping responding to the need for an alternative to the ALP, mainly confined to Melbourne. It never achieved much and didn't last, although for a while many older leftists gathered around it. Steve Painter and John Percy wrote in *DA*, March 23, 1988, "The left and the search for new politics: No Gold at Rainbow Conference", which was held in Melbourne, attended by 500.

"Sections of the non-party left have also attempted to address the opportunities created by Labor's shift to the right …

"Despite having a great deal in common with the [New Left Party] Charter group, the Rainbow Alliance rejected the participation of existing parties, so the Rainbow and Charter groups proceeded separately."

We described the group as a not very promising mix of old politics. "While the Rainbow Alliance seeks to base itself at least partly on the radical constituency revealed by the emergence of the Nuclear Disarmament Party in the 1984 federal elections, the conference had little of the youthful vigor and enthusiasm of the NDP in its first flush." There was a heavy emphasis on the group's Christian wing.

"From the traditional liberal and Christian non-party left, the Rainbow's spectrum blurred quickly rightward into the crankery of the Henry George League and Shirley MacLaine-style New Age Mysticism …

"While systematically excluding rank-and-file decision-making, the organising group spared little effort in promoting views that individuals within it have traditionally supported. Alan Roberts and like-minded Melbourne peace activist Belinda Probert were billed prominently, and took the opportunity to give yet another airing to their now very mouldy speeches about the sins of left parties and the supposed failures of socialism …

"The political theme of the conference was overwhelmingly the remaking of Australian capitalism. Anti-capitalist alternatives weren't on the agenda. When socialism did get a mention, as it did, for example, in a very competent workshop talk by economist Ian Ward, there was a great deal of squirming in seats.

"On display at the Rainbow conference were some of the main obstacles to a united left approach to the present opportunities. Most of these were old problems parading in new garb:" parliamentarism, careerism and bureaucratism, liberal anti-communism, utopianism.

"Over the past 90 years, Laborism has become one of the key props of the capitalist system in this country. Indeed, the ALP and its fellow Social Democratic parties around the world are often capitalism's most reliable instruments of rule in times of crisis.

"Until the new politics in this country comes to terms with the fact that capitalism cannot be humanised, and that socialism is the only real alternative, it will remain condemned to repeat all the old errors of pro-capitalist liberalism", we wrote.

In April 1989 the Rainbow Alliance had a successful launch in Melbourne, with 600 people attending. The Rainbow Alliance was a project by a small group to put itself at the leadership of the environmental, green milieu and other movements. They had two years' preparation for the launch, and were exclusionist and undemocratic. They were holding off from the electoral arena for now. Nevertheless, they could continue to build momentum, I estimated in a report to the SWP Melbourne district in May 1989.

The CPA's New Left Party

As disillusionment with the Hawke Labor government mounted, we were actively looking for ways to channel the dissatisfaction into the construction of a larger revolutionary party. In September 1986, Jim Percy gave a report, "Towards a new party", to the SWP National Committee meeting. We reprinted it as a broadsheet in preparation for our January 1987 conference. At the conference itself, Jim gave a report on "What Politics for a New Party?" Both reports were published together in a pamphlet.[76]

When, later that year, with the further ALP sell-out on uranium, the need for socialist renewal and regroupment became even more acute, *DA* carried a big cover headline: "We need a new party of labor".

In 1986 and 1987 we explored to the fullest extent the possibility of building a New Left Party together with the Communist Party of Australia and some left independents when the leadership of the CPA started distancing themselves a little from Hawke's Accord project. This represented the biggest development of our work toward a realignment of the left in the 1980s – surprising to many, considering the longstanding rivalry, indeed hostility, between ourselves and the CPA as leading forces on the left. The CPA had been declining for decades since the height of its numbers and influence in the 1940s. The search for a New Left Party was partly a measure of desperation, but also, we judged at the time, a genuine attempt by some in the CPA to find a real path out of the dilemma felt by a divided left under a right-wing Labor government.

In "What Politics for a New Party?", Jim Percy noted: "To really take advantage of the political vacuum in Australian politics today, a new party must include new elements. One of the main points of the new party project is to find ways of involving the unorganised forces never previously in political parties."

The possible constituency for a new party, Jim said, included former ALP members, environmentalists or people identifying with the European Green parties, women, Aboriginal people, trade unionists.

But he also pointed out that regroupment was critical for the existing left, which was losing members as people became demoralised by Labor's betrayals, the defeats being suffered and the feeling that nothing could be done. This made a new party "an imperative question for every left-wing political party that wants to find a road forward.

"Without a new political party that can unite the various forces of the left and provide a framework for analysing the present situation and charting a political course, the crisis of the left will grow sharper."

NLP national conference

A complex series of regional and New Left Party Charter Group meetings took place through 1987, culminating in the NLP National Charter Conference in Melbourne, November 28-29. There were 80 delegates at the Charter conference, and Pat Brewer reported in *DA* 638 that a New Left Party was planned for 1988.

We believed at the time that good will between ourselves and the CPA leadership could have made the NLP project a success. As it turned out, the Aarons leadership got cold feet, changed their minds, succumbed to pressure from the Association for Communist Unity (which wouldn't have a bar of us). Also, after the 1987 experience, from the January conference on, they would have realised that, although they would have had the numbers in a new united party, they certainly wouldn't have had the youth or the cadres. Both were with us.

As the NLP national conference came closer, it became obvious we were being frozen out of crucial decision-making processes.

At the crunch, the conference divided on political and organisational lines. The question of a clear commitment to a "socialist objective" was one key issue.

The future role of existing parties, the continued existence of Resistance as an independent youth organisation if the SWP dissolved into an NLP, and voting methods and other organisational structures were also elements in the eventual failure of our unification process with the CPA within an NLP.

We argued that, despite the fact that neither of two Statement of Intent documents gained the necessary two-thirds majority to be adopted, the process should be sent back to the regions for further discussion.

By then, however, the die was cast. We were excluded from the NLP process from then on, and another NLP – dominated by the CPA – was founded.

Joint broadsheet

The CPA had already really decided no – not with us anyway. At the end of 1987 we jointly produced a broadsheet for inclusion in four left papers outlining the respective approaches to unity of the left.

We carried a supplement in *Direct Action* 638, also printed in the *Guardian, Vanguard* and *Tribune*. There was a page statement from each party/paper, presenting their views on left unity.

"This special four-page supplement is a project unique in Australian left politics. Each of the four pages is a statement by a different left party on political developments in 1987 and prospects for 1988. On this page are the views of the Socialist Workers Party, and on the following pages are those of the Communist Party of Australia (Marxist Leninist), the Socialist Party of Australia and the Communist Party of Australia. The same supplement will also appear this week in *Vanguard*, the *Guardian* and *Tribune*. The agreement to publish such a supplement in the journal associated with each party has been made possible by a series of party-to-party discussions in the recent past, and the improved atmosphere these discussions have created on the left. It is also a result of the will to achieve agreement and joint action on the part of the members and leaders of the parties cooperating in this project."

Our position was headed "Can the left meet the challenge? Statement of the Socialist Workers Party". *Vanguard* headed theirs "United action the people's most effective weapon". The SPA's *Guardian* wrote: "How to continue the unity process in 1988". The CPA wrote "Left needs broad approach to influence events", and to make doubly sure everyone knew about its reservations, added a box: "Broad approach needed". "In accepting the invitation to participate in this joint broadsheet, the CPA wishes to make clear at the outset that it believes the left can only influence the events in 1988 with the broadest possible unity of left and progressive forces around agreed aims. We should recognise that the organised and unorganised left goes much wider than the four parties contributing to this broadsheet, including the ALP left and the Association of Communist Unity, as well as many socialist and left activists not in any party or group. The views of all these forces must be taken account of in deciding the issues and strategies for 1988."

In my report to the SWP Melbourne district conference in May 1989, I said that the CP's NLP had an insoluble contradiction in trying to pose as an alternative – they wouldn't break from their political support to the ALP. So the CPA-ACU project should be seen as a union of their two parties, though they deny and try to hide it. It had had little response so far, with even fewer independents than in the Charter NLP. It was partly a response to the SWP-SPA unity process, and to the Rainbow Alliance. It would be politically difficult for the Rainbow and the CP-ACU to link up, though some were trying.

SWP 12th national conference, 1988

We held the SWP's 12th national conference on January 13-17, 1988, back at Hawkesbury, with the theme "Socialist Politics after the Crash: Towards Renewal". The crash, of course, was the October 1987 worldwide stock market crash. There were 252 delegates and observers, 46 percent of them women, 73 percent full or provisional members of the SWP; 9 percent Resistance members not in the SWP. The average age was 28 years.

Rather unusually for us, only two discussion bulletins were printed before the conference, one of them with documents from the NLP Charter Conference.

The delegates voted to approve four reports: Reihana Mohideen: "World politics after the crash"; Steve Painter: "Australia, the two-tier society"; Jim Percy: "Socialist renewal, a balance sheet"; Sally Low: "Social movements".

There were also a number of plenary talks and presentations: Jill Hickson on "The Peace process in Latin America"; a panel led by John Garcia on "Struggles in the Pacific"; Max Lane on political developments in the Philippines; Peter Annear and Roger Markwick on "New thinking of the Soviet leadership". And participants had the choice of four different talks from a very long list at various times during the conference.

Leadership delegations from the SPA and CPA and observers from the Cuban and Czech consulates also attended. Greetings to the conference were received from the FSLN; Workers Communist League, NZ; National Democratic Front of the Philippines; Line of March, USA; and the Maurice Bishop Patriotic Movement, Grenada.

DA 639 noted of Sally Low's report: "Commenting on how socialists should respond to this changing situation, Low noted that the decline in mass mobil-isations had 'led us, in recent years, to put more energy into the left regroup-ment, into the campaign for a new party.

"'Now, however, we know that is going to be a longer process than we had hoped. We know too that the fuel for a healthy new party is going to come out of the social movements. We need to readjust our work towards participation in these movements.'"

The conference heard that our 1987 fund appeal had fallen short, reaching $79,402 of its $85,000 target.

A change to the party's constitution abolished the category of provisional membership.

Disorientation and some exits

In early 1988, we lost several of our experienced leaders. Brett Trenery, Tony Forward, Margo Condoleon and Peta Stewart resigned. All had been on full time for the party, most until fairly recently, and had played important roles at different times. They had no clear point of political disagreement, but they were angry with the rest of the leadership, especially Jim Percy. It seemed to be general burnout, but possibly also disappointment that the link-up with the CPA and its NLP was coming to nought.

The SWP National Executive discussed the resignations on February 4, 1988. Reporting, Jim began by pointing out that comrades would have a tendency to dump on those who left, but there are no permanent enemies, so don't go overboard or engage in histrionics.

"Our political methods mean", said Jim, that if there are differences, we'll resolve them, "but we don't hold grudges". It's those "psychological bullets of the bourgeoisie" hitting home again. We saw it coming and we prepared for it as well as we could. There was a dynamic; in the last six weeks it was clear we had a clique-like formation in the party. There were no political differences, no legitimate criticisms.

The next day, a circular to branch organisers reported the results of the NE meeting and, among other things noted: "A network of former members is developing around the country which is seeking to undermine the party" and reminded members "that the internal life of the SWP is not to be discussed outside our ranks, in particular with those hostile to our party". The NE meet-ing also resolved "to urgently prepare a series of classes on party building questions, using material drawn from the history of the Bolshevik party, the Trotskyist movement and our own party and any other useful sources".

Anti-fees campaign

The student campaign against tertiary education fees continued into 1988, and *Direct Action* continued covering and encouraging it·

February 24, 1988: "Students act for free education", reporting on actions in Canberra, Brisbane, Adelaide, Tasmania, Melbourne, Newcastle, Sydney and Wollongong,

March 2, 1988: "Dawkins' Green Paper. Robotising tertiary education".

March 16, 1988: "Fees boycott continues at Macquarie".

March 23, 1988: "Macquarie sit-in. Students plan fee protests".

April 13, 1988: "Sydney students march against fees", reporting a demonstration of 4,000; and "Fees campaign takes off at Monash", where a student general meeting of 865 unanimously passed a "motion to establish an open anti-fees committee with $2000 to spend", but a motion for a demonstration was defeated after ALP students opposed it.

April 27, 1988: "Students act against fees and privatisation" – 8,000 in Melbourne met and marched on April 18.

May 18, 1988: "How can user-pays education be stopped?". Education minister John Dawkins hit by numerous demos. Protests in Sydney, Melbourne and Hobart.

July 26, 1988: "Anti-fees struggle hots up", on July 20 actions at Melbourne, Monash and La Trobe universities, including occupations at all three campuses.

August 16, 1988: "Melbourne University on strike" against fees. 1,000-strong lunchtime student-staff meeting; 500 marched to stock exchange.

August 23, 1988: "Huge Sydney rally protests education cutbacks" on August 17: 80,000 teachers, students and parents. Organised by NSW Teachers Federation, which called a one-day statewide strike to coincide with the opening of state parliament.

November 1, 1988: "Resistance wins at Flinders Uni": Tom Flanagan elected as general secretary of Students Association.

November 8, 1988: "Where to now for the Free Education movement?": Will Wroth, the acting national secretary of Resistance, wrote on how the CPA had fallen in with the ALP's strategy for demobilising the student movement: "Sensing the potential of this new wave of protest, student supporters of the ALP moved to head it off. Following the demise of the Australian Union of Students, ALP students had been instrumental in establishing a number of state-based student unions. These became a vehicle for setting up a federated national union [National Union of Students], dominated by ALP students, which could cut across the independent anti-fees campaign – or any other campaign against Labor policy."

But the Labor students needed some left cover, Wroth wrote, and they got it from the CPA: "… in exchange for a few token spots in the NUS full-time leadership [CPA strategy] has facilitated the introduction of fees and funding cuts by eliminating the only real opposition to them – the independent student protest campaign."

November 15, 1988: "What strategy for the left in higher education?": Will Wroth critiqued an article by Simon Marginson in the CPA's *Australian Left Review*, which focused on lobbying Labor rather than mobilising students.

Resistance growth

There was a good climate for socialist ideas among students at the start of the year, Resistance found. The February 24, 1988, *DA* reported on two O-week successes: "52 new Reso members in Perth" and "UQ Resistance Club off to roaring start" with 40 new members. That issue and the next both carried a full-page ad for Resistance.

The March 9 *DA* reported that 450 new members had so far joined Resistance, and the March 16 issue took the total to 540.

NSW elections

On March 19, 1988, the NSW Labor government was wiped out in a landslide (swings against it of up to 26 percent) that brought the Liberals under Nick Greiner to government. In *DA* 645, the last issue before the election, John Garcia wrote, in an article headed "NSW elections. Vote progressive independents first; Liberals/Nationals last": "One of the strongest sentiments being reflected in the polls leading up to the March 19 NSW elections is the general dissatisfaction of voters with both major parties. Some of the polls suggest that the independent candidates may get up to 16 per cent of the vote."

In fact both right-wing and "community" independents did quite well. Right-wing local business people won the seats of Wollongong, Newcastle and Swansea. Clover Moore won the Sydney seat of Bligh, and Dawn Fraser took Balmain from a Labor "left", Peter Crawford. "Labor's NSW disaster" was the headline on Dick Nichols' analysis in *DA* on March 23:

"With this vote, the working people of NSW have taken their revenge for 12 years of 'pragmatic,' 'responsible' Labor administration. For them, Labor has spelled declining living standards, greater family and personal debt, and decaying social services, especially in the area of health care."

Labor's "left" was wiped out with the right, Nichols noted. "The devastation of the Labor left was completely deserved. In 12 years of Labor administration *not one* 'left' minister resigned in protest over government policy. The only voice that was raised publicly against government policy was that of George Petersen, the now-expelled member for Illawarra."

In *DA* 648, Nichols examined the question, "Are voters becoming conservative?" His answer was that the NSW election showed an increasingly angry population searching for a political alternative, because the attacks on its living standards had been carried out by a Labor government. The voters had not yet really moved to the right, but they could well do so if the left was unable to offer them a real alternative to Labor.

Palm Sunday and peace

The *DA* (646), reporting on Labor's NSW loss, had a much larger than usual circulation. We did a special printing, in colour and 24 pages, for free distribution at the Palm Sunday peace marches. In it, Peter Annear asked, "What has happened to the peace movement?"

"At the end of 1981", he wrote, "millions across Western Europe … came out in huge demonstrations to protest US-NATO nuclear arms plans.

"A year later, and one year before the election of the Hawke Labor government, the new wave of antiwar protests hit Australia. In April 1982 100,000 people across the country staged the biggest demonstrations since the Vietnam War. A year later the figure went to 150,000 and peaked in the next two years at 300,000.

"By 1986 and 1987 the Palm Sunday marches had become traditional in the minds of hundreds of thousands Australians, but the numbers were falling …"

The article outlined a very clear history of the movement and the key issues – shutting down democratic decision making in Melbourne People for Nuclear Disarmament; pandering to anti-Soviet sentiments; the rise of the NDP; the need to go beyond parliament; the anti-bases movement; the false demand for Australian sovereignty.

"The peace movement must find political representation, but not through the existing parliamentary parties – the movement must help build a party that will genuinely express its interests …"

The article recognised the positive role of Gorbachev's new thinking on peace, the change in Soviet military and nuclear thinking.

While nothing like the marches of several years earlier, these Palm Sunday demonstrations were still substantial: Sydney 90,000; Melbourne 80,000; Adelaide 4,000; Perth 7,000; Brisbane 4,000; Canberra 2,000 (*DA* 647).

Socialist education

On the weekend following the Palm Sunday marches, we held socialist educational conferences in our Melbourne and Sydney headquarters. *DA* 647 reported that both attracted a good audience and were also financially successful. The Melbourne conference was attended by more than 70 and raised $850; Sydney drew 118 people and raised $570.

We also sought other ways to explain our ideas to a broader audience. From September to November 1988, we ran a series of articles on "What socialists stand for" by Richard Ingram (Allen Myers). Topics covered included: "Where inequality comes from"; "What is 'class'?"; "Race and sex oppression"; "Class society and the state"; "Politics and ideology"; "Where social change begins"; "The division of labor, and money"; "What determines the division of labor?"

Resistance also resumed publication of its own *Resistance* magazine, as a 12-page tabloid, after a break of five years. The Resistance 17th national conference, held in Melbourne June 11-13, included a celebration of the appeals court ruling in May which upheld a $1 million award to members of the Jobs for Women campaign, who had fought BHP for nine years.

Agent Orange betrayal

In the *DA* of June 1, 1988, Tracy Sorensen wrote "Labor clears Agent Orange. Vietnam veterans betrayed again":

"On May 19 Minister for Veterans Affairs Ben Humphreys announced that the Hawke government accepted Justice Evatt's royal commission finding that the Agent Orange herbicide was not to blame for cancer and ill-health among Australian soldiers who served in Vietnam."

CHAPTER 8

EXPLORING UNITY WITH THE SPA

In 1988 and 1989 we returned to the possibility of unity with the Socialist Party of Australia, and explored it to the full. *DA* charted the progress of our joint activities and discussions. Such unity, Jim Percy noted afterwards, would have been "an event we expected to open up opportunities to build a bigger, broader socialist party, which would have more opportunities to intervene in the political situation. We thought unity between our party and the SPA could mark a real step forward for the socialist movement."

Undoubtedly that expectation was actual. Unfortunately, the SPA leaders were not united on the prospects of unification. The factional situation within the SPA was displayed publicly at our educational conference in January 1988, when SPA leaders openly argued with one another on the unity question.

There were two main factions: one led by Peter Symon, representing the apparatus; and one by Jack McPhillips, representing the older worker militants, who respected our young activists and wanted their own earlier record of activity and militancy to be continued by a new generation. This put a dampener on things proceeding rapidly, and when the SPA publicly campaigned in favour of the Chinese CP leadership's bloody suppression of the democracy movement in Beijing in June 1989, we faced a serious political dispute which made progress on unity discussions almost impossible.

Perestroika

While our hopes for a renewal of the Russian Revolution were eventually disappointed, perestroika and glasnost contributed to an atmosphere of rethinking that provided openings for the SPA and ourselves to consider the unity question seriously. In *Direct Action*, we sought to present as much factual material and analysis as possible. For example:

February 10, 1988: a three-page feature by Renfrey Clarke, "Towards capitalism or socialism? Economic reform in the USSR".

June 8, 1988: Dick Nichols, "Behind CPSU party conference. Guaranteeing socialist democracy"; Reihana Mohideen, "Perestroika 'A dismantling of Stalinism'".

July 6, 1988: Dick Nichols, "A turning point in Soviet history", on Gorbachev's report to CPSU conference. "Making Perestroika irreversible." This was a full 10 pages!

July 13, 1988: "The economics of Perestroika. Is USSR on the capitalist road?" by Abel Aganbegyan, Soviet economist.

July 26, 1988: Dick Nichols, "Perestroika's impact on the West. Crisis of the myths, crisis of policy".

December 13, 1988: Cover: "Gorbachev's UN initiatives. New Hopes for Humanity"; Jonathan Strauss, "Soviet initiatives raise new hopes for humanity".

SWP-SPA unity statement

On May Day 1988, a "left unity contingent" of the SPA, SWP, Resistance and YSL marched in Sydney and then held a joint toast at the Resistance Centre.

The June 1 *DA* carried a short article, "Socialist parties embark on unity process". This was a statement issued by a May 24 joint meeting of the SWP and SPA national executives. "Following more than three years of discussions and joint activities", the statement began, the two parties had "begun more intense discussions to explore possibilities for greater unity in policies and activities".

It noted that, despite sometimes adopting different policies in the previous three years, the two parties had maintained friendly relations. While there were different views on the left about how to achieve greater unity, some favouring "broader left formations" – an allusion to the CPA – the SWP and SPA "have advanced the objective of bringing together into one party all who base themselves on Marxist-Leninist ideology and practice … This does not exclude working in unity with other left forces that do not presently share such a view of the party question. Both parties remain open to further discussion and activity with all others seriously interested in developing socialist unity and united left and progressive action."

The statement said that the two executives had decided on three actions: 1. "To develop a program of activities to ensure greater contact and joint experience between the members of the two parties …" 2. "To popularise the idea of left unity among the members of the two parties and in the wider left …" 3. "To set up a commission to commence work on a political program …"

The statement concluded: "The successful completion of this work will determine the next steps to further develop united action and the possibility for organisational unity of the two parties."

United election campaigns

DA of September 6, 1988, reported that the SPA and SWP would cooperate in a Socialist Alliance election campaign* in the Victorian state election set for October 1. Leesa Doughney (Wheelahan) of the SWP would stand in Footscray and Tony Pashos of the SPA in Oakleigh. The campaign launch, held at the Melbourne Resistance Centre on September 21, raised $2,000.

DA of October 4 welcomed the outcome with an article by Dawn McEwan, "Big vote for Socialist Alliance candidates". Leesa Doughney won 6.2 percent and Tony Pahos 3.5 percent. An analysis by Graham Neal in the *DA* of October 11 said that the joint campaign "gained the highest outright socialist vote in an Australian election for many years and won some of the anti-Labor protest vote which has been a feature of recent state and federal elections".

DA of November 22, 1988, announced that Janet Parker of the SWP would be the Socialist Alliance candidate for Sydney in the next federal election, whenever it occurred. As it happened, that was not until March 1990, by which time unity with the SPA was no longer a possibility.

But through 1988 and early 1989, there were many joint activities of the SPA and SWP: a joint May Day toast at the Resistance Centre in Brisbane, with Jim McIlroy from the SWP and Ray Ferguson from the SPA; a joint forum in Sydney on May 29, 1988; a socialist unity dinner in Melbourne on July 2, with speakers Jim Percy and Peter Symon; a "'New Thinking' forum" and barbecue in Brisbane in August, with speakers Jack McPhillips and Jim Percy; a Perth dinner for socialist unity in September, with speakers Robin Stevens from the SPA and Jim Percy; in October, a dinner celebrating the 10th anniversary of the SWP's presence in Wollongong, with speakers Andrew Jamieson from the SWP, SPA secretary Leon Bringholf and Fred Moore, former Miners Federation president; in November, a Brisbane dinner toasting the Russian Revolution, with speakers Jim Percy and Ray Ferguson, launching a joint election campaign of Coral Wynter for the seat of Griffith and Ray Ferguson for the seat of Forde; a dinner at South Melbourne Town Hall celebrating the Russian Revolution, with speakers Jim Percy and Victor Puhov, third secretary of the Soviet embassy; the Adelaide launch of the Socialist Alliance on April 25, 1989, attended by 200; joint May Day 1989 activities in Brisbane, Sydney and Melbourne; a Socialist Alliance launch in Melbourne with a dinner of 250 at Northcote Town Hall on May 20 and a Brisbane Socialist Alliance dinner on the same date; a May 27 Hobart Socialist Alliance fundraising cabaret.

---

*   Not to be confused with the Socialist Alliance set up in 2001.

Resistance conference June 1988

The Resistance 17th national conference was held June 11-13, 1988, at 14 Anthony Street, Melbourne, with the theme "The revolution continues". The draft resolution for the conference was printed in *DA* 651 as a four-page supplement. Tracy Sorensen reported in DA 656:

"By the end of three packed days in the Melbourne Resistance Centre over the long weekend of June 11-13, one thing was clear: Members of Australia's largest and most dynamic radical youth organisation were excited about the future" as a result of both their own political activities and "the revitalisation of social and economic life taking place in the Soviet Union … beginning to sweep aside a decades-old barrier to winning new activists to a socialist perspective.

"'What we see today is a real revival, a spirit of renewal in the student movement, and this corresponds to politics on a world scale. People are starting to get excited about politics,' Socialist Workers Party national secretary Jim Percy commented in a keynote speech on the second day of the conference."

A big red banner "was decorated with a famous graphic from the May-June 1968 students' and workers' struggle in France – a stylised hammer and sickle bearing down on the word 'Capital.'"

"Participants at the Resistance conference looked back on that time not as having a beginning and an end, but as the beginning of the political situation we face today.

"In that year, as Percy outlined in his speech, 'The beginning of a long struggle,' the Tet offensive by liberation fighters in Vietnam was an unmistakable sign that this was a fight that the most powerful imperialist country in the world, the United States, might lose."

Tracy continued, "Student struggles around the world culminated in street fighting with the police in France touching off the mass community mobilisations and crippling strikes that gave the world an image of what revolution in advanced capitalist countries might look like.

"And the 'Prague Spring' – the challenge to bureaucracy that flowered briefly in Czechoslovakia before Soviet tanks rolled in to quell it – caused many socialists around the world to rethink their old positions and come to new conclusions.

"None of this is irrelevant today …

"'The events of 1968, the period they opened up, are still with us today,' said Percy. 'In that year we saw the different forces of the world revolution coming into play. The radicalisation in the advanced capitalist countries was overwhelmingly conditioned by events in the colonial revolution.

"'The fact that people in Africa, Asia and Latin America were struggling for their liberation had a profound consciousness-raising effect on people in the West.'

"Resistance was born of that new consciousness, and the whole character of the organisation continues to the shaped by that fact."

SWP NC July 1988

The SWP National Committee met on July 10, 1988, with the main report being on party building by Jim Percy. An SWP NE on July 8 had heard a report on left unity by Jim. The NC also heard a nominations commission report, a finance and sales report and a report on security.

The nominations commission proposed, and the NC elected, Andrew Jamieson, Lalitha Chelliah and Sue Bolton to the full list, as replacements for the three comrades who had resigned on March 17 (Tony Forward, Margo Condoleon and Peta Stewart). Steve Painter reported on the expulsion of four members: Skye O'Donnell, Ruth Egg, Matthew Power and Eugene Sibelle. The report also recommended that we suspend Janet Walk. (Janet Walk later resigned; she was not able to break off relations with Brett Trenery.)

The finances report by Steve Robson reported on a large donation from John Crespin. Partly we planned to buy some much needed new equipment: a Reisa copying machine and a computer system.

Jim's party building perspectives report pointed out that with the CPA, and the Rainbow fiasco, there had been no real progress. We had felt that the dynamic of the Labor Party vacuum would move these forces in a left direction. Perhaps that might have been true when there was momentum. The momentum was much less today, so politics returns to the more traditional mould.

"We tried different tactics to achieve what we're trying to do. But we never lost sight of our revolutionary program, although some comrades did – Eugene [Sibelle?]'s letter indicated that."

Jim made an assessment of the worth of our testing it out with the CPA. He pointed out that the New Left Party possibility with other forces was closed for the foreseeable future. Alliances now had to go in the direction of the SPA. We'd agreed to do a January conference at Hawkesbury Agricultural College. The SPA was thinking it out; we discussed structures, property. (We said, let's hang on to individual property; the SPA said, let's consider the "full consequences".) On membership, the SPA was perhaps 400. We proposed equal numbers on leadership bodies. They had a very low dues structure, $20/year.

Peter Annear reported in *DA* 672 on the Socialist Party sixth national congress, September 30-October 3, in Sydney, where left unity was "adopted as a major task".

SWP NC October 1988

Our next NC meeting was held October 15-17, 1988. Reports were: "Perestroika: New Thinking about the Future of Socialism", by Jim Percy; "Labor, Big Business and the Left", by Steve Painter; "The 1988 Elections and Future Trends in US Politics", by Peter Camejo; "Socialist Unity", by Pat Brewer; "Trade Union Work Balance Sheet", by Reihana Mohideen; "Perspectives in the Social Movements", by Janet Parker; "Political Developments in Papua New Guinea", by Peter Nusa, with an introduction by Max Lane; "Party Building", by John Percy; "Resistance and Student Work – A Balance Sheet", by Will Wroth.

Peter Nusa's report described the development of Melanesian Solidarity (MelSol). University students from PNG, Vanuatu, Kanaky, Solomon Islands and other islands had formed a Melanesian Awareness Group, which held a demonstration at the French embassy over arrests in Kanaky. Brian Brunton and Peter formed MelSol at the beginning of 1988. They started as a solidarity group, then realised they needed to look at their own backyard, taking up questions of unemployment and youth. Through these campaigns, they moved to a group or a party and were now running basic classes in Marxism.

The nominations commission report recommended electing Will Wroth to the full NC to replace John Garcia, who had resigned since the previous NC, and the meeting adopted this recommendation.

We distributed a printed report from Steve Robson on the fund drive. He reported that we had received $90k from J.F. Crespin. From our normal income, we were running a deficit of $58k. Because of the money received from Crespin, and taking into account the $50k of this spent on equipment, this would lower the deficit to around $20k if we made our fund drive target.

We elected a National Executive of all full NC members resident in Sydney and referred the question of further Resistance representation to the NE itself. Steve Painter was elected assistant national secretary.

The opening night of the plenum, October 15, was also the first public meeting of a tour that we had organised for US socialist Peter Camejo, speaking on "The '88 presidential elections and the challenge of the Rainbow Coalition". The tour also included Brisbane on October 19, Adelaide on October 20 and Melbourne on October 21.

At the conclusion of the NC meeting, on the Sunday night, we held a social event and barbecue at the party school.

Party Building – returning to basics

My party-building report described the NC as a very exciting gathering, and a turning point in quite a few ways. "Our overall perspective of building a strong Marxist party with a base amongst the working class and other oppressed has not changed. *How* and *where* we can take the next steps *has* changed in response to changes in the Australian and international political scene, and objective developments within the political forces here."

I pointed out that our party had always been proud of aiming high and keeping alert for any possible political openings. At the same time, we practised "a necessary *ruthlessness* about the possibilities, discarding wishful thinking (not optimism, that's different)".

We recognised the objective situation faced by the working class in recent years, suffering blow after blow, defeat after defeat, inflicted not just by the bosses, but "even worse those dealt by federal and state Labor governments" and consolidated by the trade union officialdom. This had strangled union struggles and squeezed the life out of many of the mass movements.

We also noted that the capitalist offensive was a result of *their* crisis, the instability of their system. And unlike the dilemma of the soft left, it was not a downturn that isolated us. "In a period of capitalist crisis, ALP attacks and union betrayals, for us it remains a crucial opportunity for building an alternative. But we have to remind ourselves, again, that we're still at the propaganda stage of building the party.

"By this we don't mean we don't lead strikes, we don't lead demonstrations and so on.

"Nor does it mean that we just harp away on the question of socialism …

"It's an estimate of our relationship to the class struggle as a whole and the stage of the class struggle, which means we draw a balancing of our tasks that emphasises the patient explanation of our ideas.

"It's a preparatory period. This is all the more the case because it's a period of the remaking of the left, a period for uniting the left."

We recognised the need for a far sharper approach to the sorts of political differentiation that had to be carried through. "The prospect of a broader left regroupment has receded. The prospect for organisational unity between us and the SPA looks good."

I then briefly reviewed our political and organisational experiences in the 1980s as we tried to find a way to build a party in a difficult situation. We now had a wealth of experiences, a very rich history. I sketched the different stages:

- In the early '80s we had the perspective of a relentless offensive against Fraser, a rising mass movement, expecting campaigns in the unions. We were encouraged by some modest growth of our party.
- With the Hawke Labor victory in 1983, we entered another stage, waging a propaganda campaign against the Accord. We organised the Social Rights Campaign with the SPA. We had an illusion that the first crack in the Accord would bring it down. "We were wrong in our estimate of what the so-called 'left' unions would do to defend themselves."
- We changed our line. Others persisted with this. That was the Fightback campaign – with the CPA (ML), the SPA, some ALP lefts. We were part of it too, but we realised what was lacking. "We'd concluded that nothing would be resolved until steps were taken to resolve the *political* question. That is, until an alternative leadership to the ALP began to be developed, there'd be no fundamental breakthrough – the industrial struggle wouldn't be enough, wouldn't even happen."
- So we had the New Left Party stage, from the NDP through to the Charter process. "Having seen the development of the NDP and having jumped in quick, we realised the alternative might not focus on the socialist movement itself. We realised it might develop as a radical progressive alternative, like the Greens in Europe, for example." We gave these attempts our best shots – "opened up, pushed hard, carried the load time and again, compromised on our style, our language". "But in the end there was nothing much left – the NDP, the Charter, the Rainbow Alliance are sad little shrivelled sects or fake fronts now." So that period seemed closed as well.

I reiterated some lessons from these different periods: Firstly, without our "rethinking on Trotskyism, returning to Leninist fundamentals", we wouldn't have been able to think as flexibly on these tactical questions.

Secondly, "We were correct to try everything, to be in everything", because it "wasn't settled that there wouldn't be a major development" in these areas.

Thirdly, "The opening out of the party, the reaching out for new forces, the relaxing of some of our norms was worthwhile". Certainly it had dangers; we lost some comrades, but we also won some comrades from these milieus. "So our balance sheet of these years is certainly positive."

A fourth point was "the role of the conscious, subjective factor balanced against objective difficulties, how much *revolutionary will* can overcome problems".

"The period now is one of remaking the left", and "Our central problem, today, is to renew, maintain, preserve and build again, cadre". It was necessary to correct an error that comrades could fall into. "We shouldn't criticise our past for the wrong reasons, or reject all of our past – for example, interpreting a loosening up while we were in the NLP milieu as a rejection of our organisational norms and methods of the past in toto and in principle, ruling them out for the future.

"To have that sort of attitude to our past is to spit in our own well. In a similar way, we shouldn't sneer at the IS or SLL for the wrong reasons."

We had to redress the balance. "In the past few years it has been a bit like 'anything goes'. People can join with a very minimum commitment. And this results in giving some ground to the milieu.

"Today, what we are stressing are basics, some constants, as the way to renew and preserve our cadre."

Most of the rest of my report elaborated on our tasks with these basics – youth, Resistance work; our basic institutions – sales, finances, recruiting, forums; education and theory; our mass work; the leadership team we'd built. I also explained that we should consider locality branches, branch division, once again, especially as we got closer to unity with the SPA.

Socialist unity in Victoria

My contribution under Pat Brewer's Socialist Unity NC report was a listing of progress in Melbourne in the three months since the previous NC. We'd done much, I noted:

1. weekly coordination and collaboration;
2. a joint dinner dance on July 2, attended by 330;
3. a joint state committee/executive;
4. a joint seminar on developments in the Soviet Union;
5. attending functions together, such as Polish, Libyan, Cuban events;
6. a joint industrial committee meeting;
7. joint work, for Hiroshima Day, for the Youth Festival Committee;
8. Resistance and the YSL, joint function (they had a band);
9. having speakers at our forums – on peace, women, unions;
10. a level of enthusiasm amongst SPA members; there were a lot of good types, many of whom we'd already worked together with;

11. working for the Victorian elections, no hitch (in four weeks),
a launch and at the Lincoln Hotel for election night;
12. plans for a Melbourne Cup barbecue;
13. plans for a November 12 Russian Revolution dinner, getting
the consul general from Sydney, aiming for 400;
14. planning a joint trade union aggregate meeting.

We had to promote their attendance at our conference at Hawkesbury. How many could we get from Victoria? There was also a fear, I noted, possibly just a vagueness on the part of Alan Miller (their branch secretary), about our youth, our speed, our activity.

Campaigning for Nicaragua

Throughout this period, we continued our solidarity with Central America and with Nicaragua in particular. *DA* 673 reported that CISCAC in Sydney had opened an office/shop at 113 Arundel Street, Glebe, on October 19, 1988, with music by guitarist Ricardo Andino. In the issue of November 8, Dawn McEwan reported, "Nicaragua appeal launched at CISCAC consultation" in Melbourne.

Sydney CISCAC organised a "Nicaragua's Ten Years of Freedom Dance" at Balmain Town Hall on July 15, 1989. Nine hundred people crowded into the hall to hear Papalote, Paul Kelly and the Messengers, and the Mambologists. Several hundred people were turned away because the hall was full. The dance raised $9,000 for projects in Nicaragua and El Salvador. *DA* 703, which reported the dance, also carried a special four-page feature, "Nicaragua's Ten Years of Freedom", with four articles by Martin Mulligan (Martin Tuck) and two by Pip Hinman.

In the *DA* of June 5, 1990, Martin Mulligan reported on the CISCAC national consultation held in Canberra May 26-27. Of nine committees, Perth was the only one unable to send delegates.

CPA's NLP dead

To all intents and purposes, the CPA's New Left Party was dead in the water from day one. The CPA hung on, dying a lingering death for several more years. Because the NLP that did emerge was neither "new" nor really "left", it found no real space in the Australian political landscape. Rejecting an up-front commitment to "socialism" and refusing to set itself clearly in opposition to the ALP and the Accord, the NLP became, in reality, a left social democratic appendage to the Labor Party – i.e., it tried to fill the role the ALP Socialist Left had recently abandoned of left opposition within the labour movement. The SL under Hawke and Keating had been fully integrated into the right-controlled Labor consensus.

Just as the NLP could not succeed because there was no role for a "ginger group" in relation to the ALP, so its newspaper *Broadside* could not succeed when they published it beginning in 1991 and lasting into early 1993, because it had no activist base of sellers and distributors – unlike *Green Left Weekly*, which was launched in early 1991, a few weeks before *Broadside*.

A footnote is that a sizeable minority of CPAers opposed dissolving the CPA into a middle of the road NLP – a number of them became supporters of *Green Left Weekly*. Others joined the Democrats or the Greens, or dropped out of activity.

1989 Socialist Unity conference with SPA

A meeting of the SWP National Committee was held on January 1 to elect the National Executive. Jim reported and nominated: Peter Annear, Pat Brewer, Peter Boyle, Dave Holmes, Doug Lorimer, Jim McIlroy, Reihana Mohideen, Steve Painter, Jim Percy, John Percy. And we endorsed the proposals for three bodies: the Political Bureau, the Administration Committee and the Editorial Board.

On January 4-8, 1989, we held a joint Socialist Unity conference with the SPA, "Towards the year 2000: Socialist Reconstruction and renewal". The bulk of it was an SWP educational conference, with the main talks: "The transition to socialism", by Doug Lorimer; "The long march of the revolution", by Jim Percy; and "The politics of capitalist decline – Depression in the 1990s", by Steve Painter. Dick Nichols reported in *DA* 681 that an SWP-SPA joint seminar discussed socialist unity January 7-8. "The seminar heard accounts of the parties' joint work in 1988": the Socialist Alliance campaign in the Victorian state elections; the joint dinner dances and celebrations of the October Revolution, with 440 at the Melbourne event; and jointly sponsored forums.

"The development of perestroika and glasnost in the Soviet Union has been a major impetus to the collaboration of the two parties", Caroline Petersen (Tracy Sorensen) wrote in a two-page spread outlining the talks of the seminar speakers: for the SPA: Peter Symon, Anna Pha, Jack McPhillips, Ray Ferguson; for the SWP: Reihana Mohideen, Steve Robson, Sally Low, Jim Percy.

"Jim Percy gave an overview of the SWP's approach to the developing break with the two-party system in Australia during the Hawke years, and the SWP's involvement in the process of socialist unity and renewal.

"Essentially, the SWP had shifted its analysis away from an earlier expectation that militant trade union action would smash the Accord, opening the way for more radical political solutions.

"As it turned out, those unions that did break with Labor's enforced austerity and curbs on militancy did not 'bring the whole pack of cards tumbling down.' Instead, those unions were quickly isolated, broken and silenced.

"It became clear that the emphasis had to be on the political, not the trade union framework.

"'It was not a trade union question, fundamentally. It was a political question that had to be faced, in terms of breaking with the Accord.

"'There had to be break with the ALP, its role, its links to big business and its political and organisational domination of the working class and social movements.'"

SWP members had been involved in the various attempts to form a large, encompassing new left party. These involved many of those disillusioned with Labor, and were led by key figures in the social movements and the Communist Party of Australia. Unfortunately, these attempts had failed to create a genuine mass alternative to Laborism.

> The CPA had shown itself unable to break decisively with Labor's project, as evidenced by its support for the *Australia Reconstructed* document in mid-1987, while the various groupings around well-known figures in the social movements were suffering from a reluctance to allow their projects to bloom beyond their own organisational fetishes and controls.
>
> Because of this the key to socialist unity today was the unity of the SWP and the SPA.
>
> "We have to make a reassessment of where things are at, how the political situation has shaken out. In spite of various zig-zags and turns, the old dividing line of Lenin [that is, against opportunism] is still the relevant one."
>
> During the unity process, members of the two parties would inevitably experience doubts and hesitations. Sometimes, personal feelings would cause political differences to be exaggerated.
>
> "Well, of course, we are not identical parties, there are points of difference," said Percy. "Some of these are nuances and some may be important. But they are points of difference that can and should be contained within the one revolutionary Marxist organisation."
>
> A new spirit was beginning to prevail within and between the two parties as the unity process moved forward. It was not a question of waiting for the fruits of unity, but of enjoying the results now, as the two

parties engaged in joint work.

Unity between the two parties would put revolutionary politics back on the agenda.

But unity would not come automatically. It would be a test for the two parties, and there would be no excuses for failure.

In his summary, Percy commented that the seminar "was a chance to discuss anything we wanted to within the range of the topics without feeling in any way constrained. Comrades put forward their views and explained them, not simply in the context of SWP and SPA, but within SWP, and within SPA."

Most importantly, the discussion had been carried out with an exemplary, comradely tone.

Different currents in SPA

I reported on the conference and the stage of socialist unity to a Melbourne district conference on January 24, 1989. It was an eye-opener for our comrades, with the two opposed viewpoints in the SPA debated out before us. Our national leadership were aware of the differences in the national leadership of the SPA, but our membership as a whole weren't. Peter Symon was a minority on their CC and CC executive, supported by Anna Pha and Hannah Middleton, with the "trade unionists" Jack McPhillips, Alan Miller, Trevor McCandless, Ray Ferguson, Harry Black and Brian Rooney much more enthusiastic about unity with us. These differences were out in the open at the conference, so there were really *two* discussions – between us and the SPA, and *within* the SPA. The line of the anti-unity types was to accentuate the differences with us; the line of the pro-unity types was to stress the areas of agreement.

The Symon wing was generally supported by their "youth" (more our age), who had hopes of inheriting the apparatus. But at the cabaret that night, most of the SPA delegation got into the swing of things on the dance floor, especially the trade union wing, who were the largest part of their delegation of 35-40.

The final session of the seminar, with Ray Ferguson and Jim Percy, was the clearest. Ferguson contrasted our socialist unity, our Marxist-Leninist unity, on a class basis, with the CPA-ACU type "broadness". He gave a strong pro-unity speech. During the discussion, the differences in the SPA were right out in the open.

Jack McPhillips stated that "the seminar met in full my expectations. We are now in a position to merge the two parties. It's not a question for the dim and distant future, though we're not home and hosed yet." Peter Symon was the next speaker up, and said he had "both enthusiasm and realism, but realism was the most important", and rattled off a list of differences, some of them quite petty, and blowing up our different approaches. He preferred "not to raise the question of timing".

Ray Ferguson's summary was very strong. He said it was a successful, worthy, historical event, between two parties based on Marxism-Leninism and democratic centralism. Anyone who came along and thought the four topics of the seminar would not reveal differences is naive, he said. But they're not fundamental and can be overcome. He contrasted the processes in Melbourne and Brisbane to Sydney.

Drafting a constitution and a program must reflect the final stages, which is what we were doing at the moment. The final stage would be adopting those documents, and merging our parties. His own experience in Queensland and at the national level was that we'd reached the conclusion that there *is* the basis for unification, and there's a genuine, principled desire amongst the members to complete this process.

"If we *don't* make it", he said, "we can't go on proclaiming ourselves the vanguard. There have been too many splits in the communist movement. We have the opportunity to reverse this trend. It's a historic occasion. We should not adopt a *subjective* attitude [meaning Symon *et al.*]. The *objective* conditions are in favour."

We saw at the January conference that Peter Symon had in effect come out against unity, but the majority of the SPA were for it, the majority of the Central Committee were for it, and the majority of the CC executive were for it (we heard 7-3). They were for unity in general, for example with other parties as well, but when the ACU, the CPA and the CPA (ML) indicated they were not interested, and the ACU-CPA came out in the open with *their* unity, Symon and the minority became a bit more favourable to realising it had to be with us or nobody.

In Sydney district we now had some joint events, for example a joint May Day contingent and function. It was going well in Adelaide and Brisbane. In Adelaide they had a joint dinner of 200, and were thinking about a joint HQ.

In Melbourne in 1989 we had many joint events, for example a cadre school that was very successful and convinced some doubters. We had joint fractions, a May Day contingent and social functions. We got agreement with the SPA to set up a state election campaign coordinating committee, agreement on candidates and local and state campaign directors. Myself and Alan Miller, state secretary of the SPA, as the two state campaign directors, would liaise and in effect be a "secretariat" of the state campaign committee.

We planned a campaign dinner in May to raise funds, mail-outs and publicity. I reported that the next goal in the unity process was the drafting of a constitution and program. We tossed up three further proposals to take the process forward in Melbourne – joint meetings of the SPA state executive and the SWP administrative committee; joint country trips, to visit the SPA branches in Mildura and the border, and our Resistance contacts in the Latrobe Valley and Geelong; occasional joint local branch meetings.

Balance sheet of CPA 'unity'

Peter Annear wrote in *DA* of March 14, 1989, on "A balance sheet of socialist unity in the eighties" that described Jim's report to the joint seminar. There were basically three currents in the socialist renewal process, he stated:

1. The Green phenomenon. The Rainbow Alliance appeared to have failed, nor were other Green currents finding success, with the possible exception of Tasmania. It was "rather bureaucratic" and they were a "self-proclaimed vanguard".

2. The CPA proposals. "Labor's further turn to the right in 1986 had a big impact in the CPA, which then issued a left economic statement. It condemned Labor's retreat on Aboriginal land rights and so on. And the CPA leadership took a decision to talk to all other left groups.

"'We wondered if this was their break with the Accord at last,' said Percy. 'But the whole process was turned back again in mid-1987 when the Communist Party, not very democratically in terms of the discussion in their party, adopted the ACTU's *Australia Reconstructed* position.' …

"'Unfortunately,' said Percy, 'For a lot of people in the Communist Party the new party process did not represent a move to a new left organisation but rather a liquidationist move – they wanted to dissolve the CPA into a non-Marxist current.'

"'But in fact, the essence of the question, let alone the form, was unity between the SWP and some of the CPA. That was the best that could have come out of it. But of course several leaders of the CPA did not like that, so they aborted the process.'

"'The left members of the CPA did not like the new party process to begin with because they saw it as a proposal to liquidate the CPA. When the SWP became part of that process they could have joined in with us and created something that really did have a left-moving dynamic.'

"'There are two reasons why they didn't: their sectarianism, and their inability to break fully with left trade unionism.'

"The result was a further decline of the Communist Party."

3. SWP-SPA unity, a more direct road, "even if because of the defeat of some of those unity processes, that would not be as big a left regroupment as had been possible".

World Youth Congress

Our hopes for perestroika and glasnost encouraged us to participate to the extent we could in the World Festival of Youth and Students, held in Moscow over eight days beginning July 27, 1985. *DA* of July 10 carried a lead-up article by Meg Connelly (possibly Margo Condoleon).

In the August 28 issue, Margo Condoleon reported on her experiences as a Resistance delegate to the festival, under the heading, "Internationalism rules at World Youth Festival". Her account emphasised both the importance that the Soviet government evidently attached to the festival and the interest and enthusiasm of ordinary citizens: on the opening day, a four-kilometre march by delegates was lined the entire way by people "cheering and expressing their solidarity with the many countries and struggles represented …

"Every night, all night, Red Square would come alive as thousands of local people took to the streets together with festival participants in one big international party."

The festivals were held every four years. The next one was held in Pyongyang in July 1989. Again, Resistance had a delegate in attendance. Caroline Petersen (Tracy Sorensen) wrote in *DA* 705: "Report from Pyongyang. 15,000 out to change the world". While 15,000 delegates was an impressive figure, the Moscow event four years earlier had attracted 40,000 youth from more than 150 countries.

Petersen's report solidarised with North Koreans against imperialism without prettifying the Stalinist regime. She wrote that reports in the capitalist media wallowed in a condescension that "is all the easier for the fact that this small country, bombed flat by the United States in the '50s, has not yet experienced the renewal occurring in many other socialist countries. The DPRK is still very much pre-glasnost, with its towering monuments to Kim Il Sung and a distinctly 1950s feel to its social atmosphere.

"But it is also apparent in Pyongyang that everyone is fed and clothed and housed – something that is not true of much wealthier capitalist 'showpieces' in Asia."

Resistance grows on campus

"Radical politics alive and well on campus", Resistance national secretary Will Wroth reported in the March 14, 1989 *DA*. "Resistance, with clubs on more than 20 campuses, joined up more than 700 students nationwide during the orientation week period." This figure included Adelaide University, 36; Flinders, 41; UQ, 61; Brisbane College of Advanced Education, 37; ANU, 33; University of Tasmania, 16; Melbourne University, 69; RMIT, 31; Monash University, 28; University of WA, 51; Murdoch University, 60; Sydney University, 70; UNSW, 62; Wollongong University, 30.

"With the recent occupation and arrests at Melbourne University, the ongoing campaign against the National Party leadership of the University of Queensland Union, and the March 22 National Day of Action against the attacks on education upon us, 1989 already holds much promise for students' activity and radical politics on campus."

In the same issue of *DA*, Wroth had another article, "Education protest gears up, despite NUS". This reported on a Melbourne University sit-in in which 37 students were arrested after the university called in police. Two thousand students had joined a boycott of the government's student tax scheme. However, the Labor students running NUS pushed everything towards a High Court challenge, likely to cost $100,000, starving campuses of funds for action. Resistance had already published a pamphlet, *Free education: NUS and the left*, by Will Wroth.

DA of April 4, 1989, carried several articles on student anti-fees actions. Deb Sorensen in "Students protest Labor's policy" reported on the National Day of Action demonstrations on March 22 protesting the Labor government's White Paper on Higher Education: in Melbourne 6,000; Sydney 2,000; Adelaide 1,500, where the speaker was Flinders University Students Union secretary and Resistance member Tom Flanagan; Brisbane 450, with a march and rally chaired by UQ SRC education officer and Resistance member Roberto Jorquera; Perth a small but militant march and rally, addressed by Michelle Hovane, a member of the UWA student guild and Resistance.

"Against the wishes of students at both the University of Tasmania and Newcastle University", Deb wrote, "NUS representatives not only refused to organise any form of protest, but also prevented free education groups from organising anything themselves".

Another article, by Evan Tsaktsiras and Chris Spindler, "NUS fails to defuse Melbourne protest", described the NUS leaders' attempted sabotage: "A speaker from the Inter-Campus Coalition, which planned the demonstration, explained that while NUS representatives were included in the planning meeting, the national student union had separately organised its own public meeting in the Melbourne Town Hall, a march to Melbourne University, and a benefit concert, all to coincide with National Day of Action activities.

"The NUS events were in support of its High Court challenge to the government's education legislation …

"But the NUS scam failed – while 6000 were in the City Square on March 22 only 20 attended the NUS Melbourne Town Hall meeting."

CPA-ACU unity on pro-Accord party

Dick Nichols reported in the March 21, 1989, *DA* that the CPA and ACU had reached "unity on pro-Accord party". They produced a glossy handout, "Time to Act – For a New Left Party", which was launched at a March 14 Sydney press conference with CPA community worker Betty Hounslow; BWIU national secretary Tom McDonald; environmental activist Jack Mundey; community activist Stacey Meirs; and Sydney University academic Frank Stilwell.

"Where does this particular initiative come from? Time To Act is the result of three years of tortuous manoeuvrings by the leadership of the Communist Party of Australia to create a 'New Left Party' that preserves its own right-wing, Eurocommunist politics." Dick listed the main events in this period:

- "Easter 1986: the 1500-strong Broad Left Conference, organised by the CPA and the ACU, reveals large-scale opposition to the Accord and its by-products, such as the deregistration of the BLF.
- "Mid-1986: the CPA condemns the Hawke government for 'breaking the Accord,' issues an alternative economic statement and steps up calls for a new left party.
- "January 1987: The SWP takes up the new left party project at its annual conference and vigorously builds the New Left Party Charter process.
- "Mid-1987: The CPA leadership comes out in support of Australia Reconstructed, the grandiose ACTU corporatist scheme for a renewed Australian capitalism.
- "October 1987: CPA National Committee decides to freeze Charter process.
- "November 1987: Two clear trends emerge at first New Left Party Charter Conference, one represented by the CPA centre and right in alliance with right-wing independents, the other by the SWP, CPA left and other independents. The conference

becomes deadlocked on how to proceed democratically.
- "January 1988: CPA National Committee resolves 'not to work' further with the SWP, and renews discussions with the ACU. The CPA left protests against this decision."

Two weeks later, *DA* 689 carried an indignant letter by the ACU's Daren McDonald protesting about Dick Nichols' article, claiming that Time To Act was based on "scientific socialism" and favouring "open Marxism". Dick answered with a two-page response, "'The New Left Party' and Marxism – an exchange of views", and gave basic examples of how "Time to Act" should "apply some of the major tenets of scientific socialism to today's Australian reality".

He pointed out: "... the real political basis of Time to Act is exclusionism and support for the Labor Party's Accord ...

"Surprisingly, the two opposing fronts turn out to be the old familiar ones – reform or revolution, class struggle or class collaboration, a serious socialist organisation or a loose alliance of warring cliques ...

"In this struggle, the Time to Act initiative remains confused. Some of the language still bears the signs of its origins in Marxism. But the overall thrust is to trail behind those sections and currents which have rejected a Marxist outlook and have therefore taken up in most cases rather reactionary ideas.

"In contrast, the SWP continues to express a Marxist-Leninist approach, analysis and program as sharply, concretely and popularly as we can. Through the Socialist Alliance campaign [with the SPA] we are helping to give socialist politics their biggest public airing in decades."

Socialist unity comes unstuck

But our hopes for unity with the SPA were about to collapse. The main reason for this was our sharply differing politics regarding the democracy movement in China and its crushing by the Deng Xiaoping regime.

Tiananmen

The *DA* of May 2, 1989, carried two articles by Martin Mulligan (Martin Tuck). "Challenges for socialist democracy" reported on the massive crowd of 500,000 in Tiananmen Square on April 27, describing it as a demand for socialist democracy. "What next for China's reform process?" also indicated our support for the demonstrators.

We of course wanted to get a first-hand view of what was happening, and were fortunate to have as a member Kristian Whittaker, who was fluent in Mandarin. We sent him to Beijing to report for *Direct Action*. His articles, under the pseudonym Kui Siqin, appeared in the issue of May 30. "Eyewitness report from China" proclaimed the cover. His article on "China's glasnost" was headed "'The streets belong to the people'", and a second was "How the Beijing students organise".

The same issue of DA reported on solidarity actions in Australia: "Aust protests support Chinese students". In Adelaide, 30 Chinese students held a vigil on May 21, followed by a rally of 150 the next day. In Sydney, 150 rallied at the Chinese consulate on May 21, and 200 on May 22. In Melbourne there was an action by 500 students and supporters.

Also in that issue, Martin Mulligan (Martin Tuck) wrote "China: History of movement for socialist democracy".

On June 4, the army moved in and brutally suppressed the demonstrators in Tiananmen. The *DA* cover of June 6 headlined "Army crushes democracy protests". Martin Mulligan authored two articles: "Government orders Beijing massacre" and "Chinese students have popular support". There were three articles by Kui Siqin: "Report from China. On the eve of the army attack", "Interview with student activist" and "May 30 in Tiananmen Square".

The cover headline of the June 13 issue was "China: The struggle for socialist democracy". It carried an editorial, "The June 4 outrage and the future of socialism". Martin Mulligan (Martin Tuck) had no fewer than five articles: "Angry protests over Beijing massacre", "Dialogue the answer, says Gorbachev", "Deng clique in control", "Repression to deepen economic problems" and "Anatomy of the Deng faction. Keeping it in the family". Kui Siqin wrote "How could the People's Liberation Army do this?" and Steve Painter authored "Hawke hypocrisy", about Bob Hawke's cynical attempt to gain political traction from the events.

The June 20 issue carried more reports and analysis, again mostly by Martin: "Gorbachev opposes China crackdown", "Deng clique terror follows June 4 massacre", "Who were the democracy protesters?" and "Army, not politics, in command".

When he returned, Kristian Whittaker gave a talk on the China events to the Resistance national conference. An abridged version of the talk was printed in the July 11 *DA*, under the heading, "Students caught a glimpse of their own future". Kristian described the widespread hostility to government corruption and support for the students, including daily solidarity demonstrations by workers. He pointed out that between one in four and one in five Beijing residents "were involved in some direct way in this movement".

He concluded: "Before the massacre, the students in Tiananmen Square had caught a glimpse of their own future, and they stood at the forefront of a big movement, trying to make that future become a reality. We in Resistance can learn from those students in making a similar commitment to make our vision of the future become a reality."

Other issues

We were also very uneasy about the SPA's conservative positions on issues such as gay liberation. Did that doom the unity process even before the SPA's stand on Tiananmen? There is no way to know how much we might have been able to shift the SPA, particularly as a militant gay movement developed. But we were not about to hide or tone down our support. Jim Percy was particularly insistent that we stand firm on the issue.

Another issue that could have become a problem was that of nationalism and Australian imperialism. We had been debating this for a long time, going back to the Maoists in the 1960s and '70s. The idea that Australians are nationally oppressed by US imperialism has always found a certain hearing in the Australian labour movement. Whether or not the SPA was prepared to take a clear stand against Australian nationalism would have emerged if we had gotten further along in the writing of a joint program.

Tasmanian Green Independents

At the same time, we were reporting the beginnings of the Greens as an organised political party. The February 14, 1989, *DA* carried "Thousands protest Tasmanian pulp mill", by Ian Hopkins and Pip Hinman, reporting the Hobart demonstration of 15,000 against the $1billion Wesley Vale wood pulp and paper mill. Christine Milne was a central leader of this campaign.

The widespread opposition to the mill forced the federal Labor government to reinstate environmental guidelines for the project that had been watered down by the Tasmanian Liberal government, and this caused the investors in the mill to pull out. In the March 21 *DA,* Ian Hopkins wrote "Interview with Christine Milne: Public protest halts Wesley Vale pulp project".

A Tasmanian state election was held on May 13. Looking at the coming poll, Peter Annear wrote in the May 2 *DA,* "[Green] Independents campaign threatens Labor, Liberals". That proved accurate. In the 35-member state parliament, the Liberals went from 19 seats to 17, Labor declined from 14 to 13, and the Green Independents increased from 2 seats to 5.

The cover head on the May 16 *DA* was "Green vote cracks Liberal-Labor monopoly". Ian Hopkins wrote that the statewide swing against Liberals was 8 percent, and there was also a 1 percent swing against the ALP. "While voters deserted the Gray Liberal government in the wake of the environmental campaign centred on the proposed Wesley Vale wood pulp mill, they did not turn to Labor. They turned instead to the Green Independents."

As we had earlier in connection with the Nuclear Disarmament Party, we tried to push things in the direction of an organised political force well to the left of Labor. The August 9, 1989, *DA* carried a report by Steve Painter: "NSW. Lively forum considers formation of Green Party". Nearly 300 people had attended the forum at the University of Technology Sydney, initiated by the Sydney Greens, who had been contesting parliamentary elections since 1984.

"Representing the Sydney Greens, Hall Greenland pointed out that a Green Party would not concern itself solely with environmental issues. It should also address questions of social justice, including Aboriginal land rights and women's rights."

"The gathering resolved to convene a conference on September 9-10 ...", the article reported. Other speakers included Chris Kirkbright of the NSW Aboriginal Land Council, former NDP Senator Robert Wood, Sydney Greens member Tony Harris, Socialist Workers Party organiser Janet Parker, Milo Dunphy of the Total Environment Centre, Hayden Washington of the Nature Conservation Council, Sue Arnold of Fund for the Animals and 1987 Sydney Greens candidate Ian Cohen.

NZ New Labour Party

When MP Jim Anderton led a left-wing split from the New Zealand Labour Party to set up the New Labour Party, we reported on it enthusiastically. Norm Dixon (Terry Townsend) wrote in *DA* of May 2, 1989, "Labour leftwinger resigns, forms new party".

We immediately sent Dick Nichols to New Zealand to cover the events. In the May 9 issue, as Bruce Marlowe, he reported on the launch of the NLP at a meeting of 700 people and also interviewed Anderton.

Interviews with Anderton or others in the NLP became fairly frequent in *DA*. Anderton was interviewed again in the May 16 issue and the June 26, 1990, and July 3, 1990 issues. New Labour Party president Matt McCarten was interviewed in the May 30, 1989, issue.

That May 30 interview was part of a four-page supplement on the party by Bruce Marlowe. In the June 6 issue, he wrote "Poll lift greets founding of New Labour", reporting that a poll gave it 15 percent support, and that more than

400 delegates had attended its founding conference. Anderton also did a brief speaking tour of Australia in July, which *DA* promoted.

SWP NC June 1989

An SWP National Committee plenum was held June 22-23, 1989. On June 21, the NE met to discuss the political report that Jim Percy would give to the NC. Part of this focused on relating to the developing environmental movement and the Greens. Jim said we needed to: prepare a document on the environment; step up mass work in the area; step up agitation and propaganda on the issues, returning to a "better language" on the issues; build a left democratic current in the Greens; prepare for variants of a Red-Green Alliance.

He said we should continue the socialist unity process with the SPA. Looking only at the question of China could be deceptive, since the question had a past, namely their history of Stalinism. We should reaffirm the decision of the early '80s to become part of the process of recomposition of the international communist movement, redoubling our political and ideological work in the party. Comrades wanted a yes/no decision, but we were interested in the *process*, the direction of motion. He suggested proposing joint seminars on China and other issues. But we wouldn't put a lot of resources into Socialist Alliance (certainly not a lot of money).

At the NC, the reports were: China, New Zealand, international work, Australian political situation, building a left alternative, campaigns, and sales and finances. Jim's report on building a left alternative pointed out that, as the result of our work in the '80s, we were now the largest left faction.

On the Greens, at the end of the NLP process, we had thought a green formation would be delayed indefinitely. We now had to adjust that view: a green formation was going to emerge. The variants would be whether we were outside, or inside from the start. If we were outside, it would be harder, since the organisers were sectarian rightists. The choice was a party being run by stars, or run by the ranks. In Tasmania, it was the former, and there was a scramble on the mainland to repeat the Tasmanian experience and to grab the name. Our tasks were those outlined to the NE meeting.

Socialist unity with the SPA was the second thing we needed to do. We took a decision in the early '80s to be part of the broader revolutionary movement as we came out of the Trotskyist movement, looking towards the international communist movement, firstly towards Cuba, Vietnam and the national liberation movements. The actual developments since that decision had been beyond our wildest dreams. He looked at the good and bad points of the SPA. We had a joint commission to work on a constitution and a program. We needed discussion on the family, the gay question, two-stage revolution, Aboriginals and multiculturalism, but not on the ALP, social democracy or the trade union bureaucracy.

Jim's assessment was that we should look at it politically, not just organisationally. We were in favour of continuing the process. At certain points there would be difficult decisions. What sort of program? What sort of constitution? We should drive hard for the right ones, not compromise. But we should take risks, creating the conditions to do it properly. The work now was fundamentally political. The next steps were: using the program, presenting it at our January conference; developing political discussions with the ranks of the SPA, for example on China; continuing the Socialist Alliance election campaign since it satisfies some of our needs. (A green election alliance could satisfy more; Canberra, Perth and Hobart could experiment.) Socialist Alliance would be a loose alliance, not unity. We would do no more useless things, but political discussions, social events and specific SA activities.

The NC adopted a statement on China that was printed in *DA* 701, "Socialism has nothing to fear from democracy":

"1. The leaders of the Communist Party of China … who ordered the June 4 massacre of pro-democracy protesters in Beijing's Tiananmen Square and the present campaign of slander, arrests, show trials and executions of worker and student activists have caused immense damage to the cause of socialism in China and around the world …

"2. The Deng regime's claim that the Tiananmen protesters were a 'very small group of people' out to foment 'counter-revolution' and 'do away with the socialist system' lacks any credibility …

"3. It is particularly tragic that the Chinese regime's military crackdown takes place at a time when new forms of popular participation and democracy are being debated and experimented with in a number of socialist countries …"

The same issue carried Doug Lorimer "China's struggle for socialist democracy", an abridged version of his report to the NC. It concluded: "In the end, the June 4 massacre in Beijing was the result of the fundamental incompatibility between China's need – and the Chinese masses' desire – for socialist democracy and the Deng Xiaoping leadership's determination to maintain its bureaucratic dictatorship over the Chinese people".

The issue also carried ads for forums on China in Canberra, Melbourne and Sydney.

Resistance conference June 1989

The Resistance national conference was held June 24-26 in Melbourne. There were 71 delegates and 120 observers. The average age of delegates was 20.8 years. Women were 42 percent of the delegates. Students from 22 different campuses were 29 percent of those attending. Kristian Whittaker reported on what he had seen in China. Jim Percy gave greetings from the SWP, as did Philip Peladrinos from the Young Socialist League. Kylie Budge reported on the Australian political situation, while Anne O'Callaghan, Kath Gelber and Will Wroth reported on Resistance's role in Australian politics, "Organising against the federal Labor government's attacks on the rights of students, women and working people". The conference also adopted the political resolution by the SWP NC condemning the Chinese Communist Party's crushing of the pro-democracy protests in Tiananmen Square.

SWP NC October 1989

The SWP NC meeting on October 21-23, 1989, heard reports: international political situation, Australian political situation, building an alternative in the coming elections, building the Democratic Socialist Party, finance and sales, campaigns, youth, Socialism and Human Survival, program of the DSP.

The NC adopted the line of Doug Lorimer's report on the resolution Socialism and Human Survival, to be presented to the national conference in January. The document was adopted and printed as a book in 1990 under that title.

The NC voted to adopt the general line of the draft party program, taking account of amendments that had been proposed.

Before the NC, we had conducted a referendum on amending the party constitution to change our name to Democratic Socialist Party. This had been endorsed overwhelmingly by the members (a 6-1 margin), and the NC ratified that result.

The finance and sales report noted that the Crespin donation in 1988 meant that we were able to survive and get some new equipment for the National Office. Of our members, 54 percent participated in the Marxist Resource Fund, and we were $5,000 ahead of where we had been a year earlier. We had projected raising our total income by $60,000 over 1988, which was our deficit so far. Average *Direct Action* sales were up 150 over the street sales of 1988.

Jim Percy foreshadowed possibly expanding the full NC list at the conference to get more women into the leadership.

Smashing the pilots

After seven years of real wage cuts delivered by the Accord through partial indexation and "two-tier" wage decisions, the ALP government and the ACTU top bureaucrats realised that they needed a new gimmick with which to continue selling the Accord to workers. They came up with "award restructuring".

As had happened earlier with other aspects of the Accord, this was partly justified by claiming that it would benefit lower paid, less industrially powerful, workers. Of course, it didn't. The argument was only a pretext for attacking as "selfish" any unions that tried to break out of the Accord straitjacket.

In August 1989, the Industrial Relations Commission ruled on the ACTU wages claim. The capitalist media mostly portrayed the decision as a "victory" for unions. It could be presented in this way only because the ACTU claim was so weak that, even had it been granted 100 percent (which it wasn't), it would still have meant a further cut in real wages and in working conditions. Dick Nichols explained in the August 16 *DA* that a worker on $400 a week gross would need $446 by the end of 1990 just to keep up with inflation, but the wage decision set a maximum rise of $30 for skilled, $25 for semi-skilled and $20 for unskilled workers. And those maximums were not at all guaranteed: "There is nothing automatic about the payment of the award restructuring increase. The second payment in particular will require workers to give blood. It will also be up to the Industrial Relations Commission to decide whether the workers ... have sacrificed enough conditions to earn their increase."

Nichols' article also warned that the "award restructuring" was really more like "award dismantling". With hindsight, we can see it as paving the way for "enterprise bargaining": "Already reports are coming in of attempts by employers to negotiated local 'restructured awards' which are just another name for the type of enterprise agreements that are undercutting industry conditions in, for example, the brewing industry in Queensland."

The same issue highlighted on the cover the response of the Australian Federation of Air Pilots (AFAP): "Crash landing for the Accord? Pilots challenge wage freeze". The page 3 article, also by Dick Nichols, was headlined "Pilots show how to pull out of wages nosedive".

Six months earlier, AFAP leaders had recommended a campaign for a 30 percent wage rise, but members had decided to wait to see the result of the national wage case. Now they were ready to act. ACTU leaders, the most vociferous of whom was Bill Kelty, were strongly against the AFAP claim, which they rightly feared could sink the Accord. But, as Nichols' article pointed out, the 30 percent was simply "what the profession has lost since 1983, when the accord cemented in Fraser's wage freeze". And AFAP president Brian McCarthy, alluding to the fact that other highly skilled workers not subject to the Accord had achieved wage increases greater than inflation, was quoted as saying, "If the people who do best out of the wages system are the people who aren't in it, there wouldn't seem to be much point being in it."

DA's cover on the next issue, August 29, declared: "PILOTS. If Hawke's attacking them … They must be doing something right".

The ALP government and the bosses pulled out all the stops to defeat the pilots. Hawke brought in the RAAF and some foreign carriers to scab on the pilots. "Pilots now, who's next?" asked the cover of the September 5 *DA*, in which Dick Nichols described the attacks on the pilots, which even included a plan for the government to pay the airlines $6 million a day as "compensation" for what they were losing through the dispute, and Ansett Airlines announcing it would use common law to seize pilots' superannuation to pay for its losses.

Nichols also took to task the CPA's *Tribune*, which was trying to have two bob each way, criticising some of the Hawke government's attacks but also refusing to support the pilots' main demand, which was simply to have the right to negotiate their wages and conditions with their employers:

"Through all its [*Tribune*'s] slithery ambiguity, there is only one consistent element – nothing must be allowed to endanger the Labor government, otherwise we get the new right.

"Wake up, *Tribune!* The new right is alive and well on the federal government benches."

The Labor government soon made it clear that it intended not merely to defeat the AFAP wage claim, but to make an "example" showing that unions which tried to step outside the Accord would be destroyed. On September 13, Hawke publicly declared that the AFAP was no longer a "party to the dispute". The pilots were now being offered individual contracts. These, Dick Nichols reported in *DA* 712, "would cut take-home pay, generate huge productivity increases by increasing flying hours by 75 percent, destroy nearly all opportunities for boosting pay above the base rate, put rostering back under management control, increase the power of the companies to dismiss and stand down pilots, eliminate grievance procedures and bind pilots to have nothing to do with the AFAP".

The actions of the government and ACTU did arouse some strong protest in the union movement. On September 15, the SA United Trades and Labour Council unanimously passed a resolution condemning the Hawke government "for supporting the use of common law actions, individual or voluntary employment contracts, state of emergency legislation ... and repeal of awards to break industrial action and union organisation".

The Cockatoo Island Combined Unions Shop Committee wrote to the AFAP, congratulating the pilots on their stand: "We endorse your claim for a 30 percent wage increase and in doing so, call for a 30 percent wage increase throughout the entire workforce. In a climate where the business community and particularly the finance sector are profiteering on a grand scale, the working class cannot be expected to subsidise them through wage restraint."

The ACTU Congress, held at the end of September, endorsed the betrayal of the pilots. Kelty told the gathering: "They declared war on the wage-fixing system, the conciliation and arbitration system and ordinary working people in this country! They declared war!"

The dispute dragged on, until the courts were used to finish smashing the pilots. The airlines sued the AFAP in the Victorian Supreme Court for conspiracy to injure the airlines, procuring pilots to break their contracts, intimidation and interference with the airlines' business. On November 23, the court ruled for the airlines, exposing the AFAP to damages claims of up to $10 million. Allen Myers wrote in *DA* 721:

"The decision gives all employers a powerful legal precedent with which to attack any industrial action, taken by any union, for any reason. In ruling against the pilots, Justice Brooking wrote: 'I am satisfied the AFAP gave the directive [to impose bans] with the intention of injuring the airlines as a means to an industrial end.'

"*Any* industrial action ... can now result in workers being hauled into court if the action injures their employer – as if there were any other way of making profit-hungry bosses see reason!"

The article blamed the legal outcome on "the disgraceful behaviour of the ACTU leadership and the Labor government". "Theoretically, it has always been possible in a legal sense for employers to use common law against unions in the way the airlines did. It hasn't happened previously only because of employer fears of touching off a united fight back of the unions (like the 1969 general strike over the jailing of Clarrie O'Shea).

"But seven years of ALP corporatism, seven years of Accord politics tying the ACTU firmly into a wage-fixing system loaded against workers, have convinced more and more employers that the unions are incapable of fighting back.

"... the employers can barely conceal their glee at the prospects this has opened up for them. John Collins, president of the Australian Chamber of Commerce, put it bluntly: 'In a short-sighted attempt to preserve the sanctity of the prices and incomes accord the ACTU has, perversely, become a party to shattering one of the pillars of trade-unionism – the supposed right to strike.'"

Cockatoo Island struggle

In May 1989, workers at the Cockatoo Island naval dockyards began a heroic but ultimately unsuccessful 14-week occupation of the island in an attempt to prevent its closure and the loss of their jobs. As Norm Dixon (Terry Townsend) explained in *DA* 699, the closure was part of a Labor government strategy to step up its military resources without paying more for them, by sacking workers and privatising or corporatising government defence industries. In March 1986, defence minister Kim Beazley announced that a total of 1,544 jobs would be abolished at the Government Aircraft Factory and the Williamstown and Garden Island naval dockyards. The government said that Cockatoo would be closed in 1992, but in March 1989 the workers discovered that the island was already being advertised for sale, and they took action.

SWP members Frances Kelly and John Tognolini made a video on the struggle, *The Occupation of Cockatoo Island.*

Socialist Alliance lingers on

Collaboration with the SPA continued, at a slower pace than earlier. A jointly sponsored dinner to celebrate the anniversary of the Russian Revolution drew 80 people in November 1989. Speakers were Coral Wynter from the DSP and Ray Ferguson from the SPA.

A Socialist Alliance dinner in Adelaide celebrating the Russian Revolution was attended by 150 people, including representatives of the Chilean community and various left and progressive organisations. Speakers were Dave Holmes, the Adelaide organiser of the DSP; Brian Rooney, SPA state secretary; visiting Chilean trade unionist Juan Inostroza; SPA member Dennis White, the Socialist Alliance candidate for Spence. The event was compered by Philippa Skinner, a DSP member and the Socialist Alliance candidate for Peake. (The two candidates received 2.7 and 2.6 percent respectively in the SA state election.)

Fighting to save tram conductors

The Victorian government had announced that conductors would no longer be employed on Melbourne's trams. We had several members working on the trams, and so were involved in the campaign that sought to retain conductors. Chris Slee reported in the November 7, 1989, *DA:* "Nearly 5000 people participated in a union-community demonstration on November 2 for the retention of tram conductors. Tramways union members stopped work for four hours and took their trams and buses into the city, leaving them lined up in the streets during the rally and march from City Square to Parliament House."

In the November 21 issue, Chris Slee reported: "Tramway workers campaigning against the state Labor government's plan to abolish conductors refused to collect fares on November 14. In addition, workers from Essendon, Brunswick and Preston depots left their trams in city streets, held a stop-work meeting in the Bourke Street Mall, and marched on the Public Transport Corporation's head office."

In a Tramways Union election on November 23, Victorian secretary Jim Harper was defeated by Essendon depot delegate Luigi Di Gregorio. *DA* 721 reported: "It is widely felt that members of the Progressive Team [to which Di Gregorio belonged] have shown more commitment and activity than the Harper group in the fight to save conductors' jobs."

In the new year, Garry Walters wrote in the January 23, 1990 *DA:* "Despite being locked out without pay since January 2, tram workers have voted decisively at a January 19 mass meeting to continue their fight to retain conductors on all trams." Two thousand tram and bus members of the ATMOEA attended the meeting.

A week later, Walters wrote "Trammies still solid. Cain looks to IRC to save him", and Norrian Rundle reported: "A meeting of 200 state public sector union shop stewards on January 23 overwhelmingly supported the tram workers in their struggle to maintain all conductors' jobs".

The campaign ended with more of a whimper than a bang, however. In the *DA* of February 6, Garry Walters wrote: "A mass meeting of tramway workers voted by a three to one majority on February 2 to accept a 21-point proposal based on substantial introduction of driver-only trams. Leaders clearly unwilling to fight and the promise of pay rises were instrumental in persuading the meeting to give up the fight for conductors' jobs."

Our growth in the '80s

The "Building the DSP" report by Jim Percy to the October 1989 NC outlined the reasons for our name change from SWP to Democratic Socialist Party. We were coming to the end of a phase, Jim said. In the 1970s, we were a Trotskyist sect (but the *best* sect), and also a party under construction. Proof of how good we were was that we still existed and had been able to make so many changes in the '80s.

In the '80s we established the conditions for the push towards the Greens.

Looking at the changing relationship of forces since 1984, the CPA was more isolated in part because of the Gorbachev development. In 1987 we said that the stock market crash and Gorbachev would put off the possible formation of the Green movement, and 1987 would signal a more rapid capitalist crisis. We were wrong, not in perspective, but in timing. It wouldn't be as quick as we had hoped.

But there had been a change in the relationship of forces with the rest of the left. The CPA had been wiped out in a lot of areas and was in decline. They'd combined with the ACU and were not winning new members. The SPA didn't have 500 real members, perhaps 200. The CPA (ML) was in deep decline. The IS didn't have the same vigour it once had.

We alone on the left had grown in the '80s. In 1980, we'd possibly gone as low as 130; by March 1981 we were 157; in December 1982, 222, including provisional members; in December 1983, 256; in December 1984, 294; in December 1985 we'd dropped back to 255; in December 1986, down to 247; in December 1987, down to 235; in December 1988 we'd jumped back to 280 (a growth of 19 percent that year); and now up to 318 (a 16 percent growth so far that year.)

Jim also noted a contraction of the left as a whole. In a number of cities, we now had no competition.

How to do party building today? Jim said that had two parts: continuing the organisational form, doing the essential party building things such as sales, finances and education; and continuing the regroupment process, which was part of leaving the Trotskyist movement behind (the idea that we were "the only revolutionaries").

What frustrated us in the '80s was the gap between mass discontent and joining people. We'd experienced this gap for a long time. It had been a slow political period in advanced capitalist countries, and our errors were errors of over-projection. We had to try again: regroupment, approach to left trade unions. The '90s were going to be a different period of regroupment. The CPA and ACU would get together (just when the Greens were getting together). The SPA was in deep crisis because of persisting with a rotten line.

The name change to DSP was a good excuse to relaunch and go on a binge, with new T-shirts, posters, banners, a logo with red and green colours, and a slogan – "green, democratic and socialist" – everywhere, and a massive publicity campaign to get people to join.

The best way would have been to stand 50 candidates in the federal election, but there wasn't enough money for that. But we still had to find a means for a splash: therefore stand in a couple of seats, but build the campaign broadly. We needed forums in November and December to discuss the name change and our reasons for it.

The heart of the campaign would be basic party building things, such as the centrality of our press. How could we broaden out *DA* to be more of a tool of our regroupment process?

We were projecting a four-day Resistance conference for Easter 1990. Jim said we should counterpose it to the founding conference of the New Left Party.

He also proposed, for Sydney in September, a Socialist Scholars Conference, with Alastair Davidson helping. We were developing good relations with *New Left Review* in the UK and the US, aiming to get Robin Blackburn, Tariq Ali, Ellen Meiksins Wood. (Again, this would tread on the toes of the CPA.)

Our actual regroupment thrust was the Greens, and in the future we should be open to being part of a mass living party that is not necessarily Marxist. It's not the stage it's at at the moment. But our worst mistake would be to think the DSP is not important, and not continue to build it.

Trying to be part of the developing green parties

We had already stepped up our coverage of environmental issues and green politics in *DA*. For example, the July 25, 1989, issue cover headlined "Environment: What strategy for survival?" Articles included "A search for environmentally sound development"; "West Germany: The Greens in Parliament"; "Overcoming the effects of war: Vietnam now fights on the environmental front"; "Fight to protect Barrington Tops"; and "Brazil: Plundering rainforest for profit".

In *DA* of October 3, 1989, Tom Flanagan reported on the Ecopolitics IV conference held in Adelaide, September 21-24, which drew 400 participants and sponsored a public meeting of 1,000 to hear German Green Petra Kelly and Bob Brown. (Flanagan interviewed Kelly in the next issue of *DA*.)

In the same issue, Peter Boyle wrote on the formation of the NSW Greens at a conference in Sydney. A Green Electoral Network had been formed in April, comprising leaders of the Total Environment Centre, the Wilderness Centre, the National Conservation Council and the South East Forest Alliance. GEN was disgruntled with the NSW Greens, who wanted to campaign also on social and economic equality and justice, grassroots democracy and disarmament and non-violence.

On December 5, Jim McIlroy reported in *DA* on the "End of Joh regime" and that the Greens had received 9-10 percent in the Queensland election. Peter Gold wrote "Vic Green Alliance to stand" in next federal election, describing a seminar on November 25, at which 60 people heard a range of environmental and political speakers, including Chris Spindler of the Victorian Greens and

Reihana Mohideen from the DSP.

DA of November 21, 1989, announced "Green Democratic Alliance to stand in ACT" – our alliance there with environmentalists. The candidates in the House of Representatives were Gina Jeffrey and Sue Bolton, in the Senate, Hedley Rowe. The alliance adopted the four founding principles of the West German Greens: ecological sustainability, social and economic equality, grass roots democracy, and disarmament and non-violence.

The January 23, 1990, *DA* reported, "Socialists announce WA candidates". The DSP's branch secretary, Frank Noakes, was quoted as saying that we would have preferred an alliance, but the recently established Greens WA excluded members of other parties. We stood a ticket of three for the Senate and seven candidates for the lower house.

Socialist Worker resumes

We resumed publication of our theoretical magazine *Socialist Worker* in November 1988, edited by Doug Lorimer. Vol. 4, No. 1 contained "Perestroika and the International Socialists. A critique of the theory of 'state capitalism'", by Renfrey Clarke; "Restructuring the Soviet Economy: Its necessity, means and objectives", by Abel Aganbegyan; "Western Marxism: A critical introduction", by Steve Robson and Doug Lorimer; and reviews, by Rose McCann, of *For and Against Feminism*, and by Seymour Kramer of *Fire in the Americas*. *Socialist Worker* Vol. 4, No. 2, in March 1989, contained: "Women and Social Evolution. Part 1: The part played by women in the transition from ape to human, by Rose McCann and Doug Lorimer; "Antonio Gramsci: An introduction to his political thought", by Jonathan Strauss; and a review by Dick Nichols of *The Making of the Labor Party in New South Wales, 1880-1900.*

Vol. 4, No. 3, September 1989, contained "China's Struggle for Socialist Democracy", by Doug Lorimer (an edited version of his report to the SWP NC in June); "New Thinking and the Future of Socialism", by Jim Percy and Doug Lorimer (based on Jim's report to the October 1988 SWP NC).

After changing our name to DSP, we also changed *Socialist Worker* to *Democratic Socialism*, renumbering beginning with number 1 but also including "formerly Socialist Worker" on the cover. The first *Democratic Socialism*, December 1990-February 1991, featured "Toward a Red-Green Dialogue" and "The Collapse of Stalinism and the Future of Socialism". The second, March-May 1991, contained "The Nature and Significance of World War II", by Peter Annear; "The hidden history of World War II", by Doug Lorimer; and "The events of 1939: Interview with [Soviet historian] Alexandr Yakoviev".

Jobs for Women win

In *DA* of September 5, 1989, Tracy Sorensen reported a "Landmark ruling against discrimination" in the ongoing legal battles of the Jobs for Women campaign. The NSW Equal Opportunity Tribunal had ruled on August 18 that Robynne Murphy, as a representative of other women similarly treated, had been illegally discriminated against by BHP's Port Kembla steelworks. "This is Australia's first successful 'class action' – that is, a suit on behalf of an entire group of people, who do not, therefore, have to sue individually", the article noted.

"Tribunal Judge Graham said that the August 18 finding against Australian Iron and Steel was a landmark in Australian industrial history, as significant as the 1906 Harvester basic wage case and the equal pay cases of the 1960s and 1970s.

"Murphy told Direct Action that BHP's decision not to appeal against the latest finding was a direct outcome of the women's successful campaign, which had been waged for almost 10 years."

In the *DA* of December 12, 1989, Tracy Sorensen reported, "The celebrated Jobs for Women campaign won yet another victory on December 5, when the High Court dismissed a final appeal by BHP against a 1985 Equal Opportunity Tribunal ruling which found the company guilty of illegal discrimination against women".

Balance sheet of 1980s unity efforts

What general conclusions can we draw about the DSP's reach-out and regroupment work of the 1980s? How did it affect the development of the party and the course of the Australian left as a whole? Jim Percy summed up the process in a series of major reports at the beginning of the 1990s, which set the agenda for reorienting our work to concentrate on our own party-building for the coming decade – with regroupment and alliance work as an adjunct, not the main line. It was essentially a positive balance sheet.

At the January 1990 DSP national conference, Jim reported on "The DSP: Traditions, lessons and socialist perspectives" (printed in Party Forum No. 8, February 1990).

The Activist of November 1991 contained Jim's report to the October 1991 DSP NC, "The crisis of the left and the DSP: Party-building perspectives for the '90s". This said that the collapse of the CPA was a gain, and we played a part in it and in preventing the development of a strong New Left Party to replace it and block the road to a genuine, future socialist development.

Jim stressed that we were trying to build a Leninist party. He quoted the passage from Lenin's *What Is To Be Done?* that describes inhabitants of the "marsh" trying to entice revolutionary fighters away from their chosen path. Then Jim continued:

"... Lenin's where we begin the search for what we want to do. The relevance of our organisation, the way we build our organisation, is in the final analysis a struggle against the marsh ...

"[Lenin] said the fact we seem so far from a working-class class revolution leads to non-class popular democratic demands and struggles, i.e., to the demands to reform or improve capitalism. And of course those sorts of struggle also have an impact on working-class class demands, on working-class struggles themselves ...

"All this gives rise to non-party organisations, which we know a lot about. And these organisations are essential. But the very fact that they're struggling around immediate demands often puts off consideration of anything further, puts off consideration of any more general critique of and attack on the ills of society as a whole." Lenin, Jim said, pointed out that these struggles by themselves don't settle things: society "is divided into classes, and the struggle between them becomes a political struggle ... and the most comprehensive form of this struggle is the struggle between political parties ...

"Lenin then makes a leap ... Lenin says non-partisanship in this framework is indifference to the class struggle, and that means tacit support for those who rule.

"This is Lenin being very hard, but also very correct. He says the idea of non-partisanship is a bourgeois idea, not a socialist idea. It's a rather simple thesis of why the working class needs a party."

The regroupment and new party projects all failed to materialise. This led to some demoralisation in our ranks. On the other hand, we largely steeled our membership by explaining at each stage the political necessity for any new tactical moves. The party, at each turn, was relatively united in its approach.

Probably any demoralisation was more a result of the general retreat of the left and socialist movements than the negative results of these specific projects. The general context of a crisis of the left affected everyone. We weathered it better than any other left party, and it left our comrades experienced in reach-out politics and ready for any new tactics that might be necessary.

Our party had shown by its 1980s reach-out work that it was non-sectarian, flexible and willing to work with whoever else was moving in the direction of a progressive realignment of forces.

Upsides and downsides of unity efforts

One negative result of our 1980s ecumenicism was undoubtedly a loosening of party norms in some areas, perhaps a lessening of our ideological cohesion and "party spirit".

Could we have recruited better by ignoring the regroupment openings and continuing with our own party-building projects regardless? I doubt it. We might have done less well, in fact. Our growth in the middle to late 1980s was largely through Resistance and the student movement, but it was also a result of our broadening-out approach, our openness to new movements and ideas from the social movements – especially the burgeoning green movement.

We experimented organisationally, varying between weekly and monthly meetings in the 1980s. We went from regional branches to single branches. No organisational formula is a panacea. We must always be experimenting, trying new methods to see which work best in a particular environment.

Sales of *DA* declined drastically toward the end of the 1980s, largely a political problem of the left milieu in general. The time had arrived for a bold new paper project, *Green Left Weekly*. We recognised the reality of the red-green political project. *GLW* was a regroupment project as well as a party paper. It brilliantly answered our need simultaneously to reach out and to serve the needs of the party.

Another motivation was its role in pre-empting the dying CPA's effort at its own "broad left party".

Our attitude to regroupment projects became more cautious during the '90s. Nevertheless, we remained open to alliances, and we had greater experience to take into any new project. Our major positive gain was that we survived a hard period, while others, e.g. the CPA/NLP, collapsed. The SPA was moribund and the Greens were floundering nationally, unable to build much that was substantial despite the widespread and growing public consciousness of environmental issues.

We entered a period of political and organisational flexibility and experimentation in the early 1980s after "completing" our turn to industry. We had to reach out from our industrial orientation because we were losing members and in danger of being bypassed by the real movement of politics, which, due to the Accord and the cravenness of most union leaderships, was outside the industrial arena in the 1980s.

The political basis for our changes was set by our break from Trotskyism, our realisation of the need to link up with other forces and our change in position on the ALP.

It was also in response to real developments: the explosive development of the NDP; the changes in the old Communist movement, CPA and SPA; and the general break-up of the old left and the development of the Greens.

On the international arena, the right-wing offensive and the accelerating crisis of world Stalinism also led us to change our previous perspectives and seek to link up with progressive and revolutionary forces internationally – not confined to the FI.

These regroupment projects in Australia did not succeed in their maximum aims of creating a new, broader progressive party. But we blocked the formation (or at least domination) of a left-reformist alternative project. Our work in the 1980s gave us tremendous experience in united front tactics, in reaching out and relating to new forces and in better understanding the strengths and weaknesses of the Australian left and green movements.

We were now in a better position to deal with any new openings that might emerge, in the cold light of previous experience. While we were still too small, our relative weight on the left in Australia (and internationally) had increased substantially as a result of changes in the 1980s. The left overall was probably weaker, whereas we were stronger.

All these efforts served to illustrate our maturing as a party. They showed how we had built on our achievements in the 1970s and developed further politically. They illustrated our political and tactical flexibility, our willingness to explore many different approaches to building a political alternative. In a difficult political period, we left no opportunity unexplored. There was no really big break, such as the New Zealand New Labour Party, but we grabbed at any chance that came along to build a broad alternative to Laborism with a mass base – the NDP, the New Left Party, the Greens.

They also illustrated once again our inclusive approach to party building. We made many fusion and regroupment attempts throughout the 1980s, from small groups to larger efforts like the CPA and SPA.

And they also illustrate the seriousness with which we took our political responsibilities. We gave all these party-building projects our best shot; we threw the party into them enthusiastically and wholeheartedly. We tested the opportunities to the fullest.

Part of our ongoing reach-out efforts involved developing links with *New Left Review*. Ads for *NLR* appeared periodically in *DA* throughout 1990.

Hopes still for perestroika

While the challenges to perestroika were growing, we maintained hopes for it more or less until the coup against Gorbachev. Dick Nichols wrote in *DA*, July 18, 1989: "Poland – socialist renewal or grinding crisis? After Solidarity landslide, Bush visit". We then published a five part series (*DAs* 704-707 and

712) by him, under the general heading "'Twilight of communism'?", arguing that successful reform was possible even though not inevitable.

DA of October 31, 1989, carried Dick Nichols' "Hungary: Party takes the difficult path of reform". When the Berlin wall fell in November, *DA* 719's cover was: "The wall comes down. A new era of democratic socialism". In that issue, Dick Nichols and Tom Jordan (Max Watts) wrote "'Imagine a socialism where no-one runs away'", and Dick Nichols wrote "'Teetering on the brink' ... of socialist democracy".

In *DA* of November 21, 1989, Nichols wrote "German Democratic Republic: A new spectre haunts capitalist Europe". The cover for November 28 headlined "Czechoslovakia: Another victory for glasnost", and Peter Annear wrote "Prague protests bring down government".

The *DA* of December 5 carried Dick Nichols' "GDR: People's power sweeps all before it" and announced a *DA* fundraising raffle with the first prize being a two-week trip to the Soviet Union for two.

Collapse of the Soviet Union

Our view of where things stood in late 1989 was summarised in Dick Nichols' report for the National Executive to the October 21-23, 1989, plenum of the DSP National Committee, titled "The Crisis of Imperialism and Stalinism" and reprinted in Party Forum No. 4 for 1989.

"The main advantage that imperialism continues to enjoy over the socialist world is a higher level of productivity in every major economic sector. In the advanced capitalist countries, fed by monopoly superprofits from the Third (and First) World, this has translated into a higher standard of living for large sections of the working class."

This made democratisation and perestroika essential economically as well as politically, to unleash the creative productive power of the working class, stifled for so long by Stalinism, and allow the Soviet economy to provide working people with a greatly improved standard of living. "The main impediment to the economic advance of perestroika is the continuing inertia and sabotage of the bureaucracy and the recently exposed size of the budget deficit and the real inflation largely generated by it. This means, in turn, that the elimination of the deficit must take precedence over other priorities and that an immediate increase in the standard of living for all sections of society can't be expected ...

"This situation places a weapon in the hands of those still vast stretches of the bureaucracy that will lose from perestroika ..."

"When will the economy pull out of its nosedive?", the report asked. "That depends, in the immediate term, most of all on two interrelated factors: the speed with which new blood is injected into the party and administration at all levels … and the speed at which the remaining bureaucratic saboteurs can be weeded out."

While the report was cautiously optimistic, it made clear that the outcome of perestroika and glasnost was still to be determined by struggle. "The critical point is: a vital, if not the most vital, element in the construction of a socialist economy is the degree of commitment of the working people themselves. The more abused that commitment has been, the more alienated working people are from state property, the weaker the work ethic has become, then the more production must rely on the spur of the market and even the threat of unemployment, that is, the more it drifts back towards the methods of capitalism. It is no accident that the *worse* a nation's experience of Stalinist bureaucracy has been (Hungary, Poland), the greater the drift back towards marketisation and indebtedness to the West."

The meaning of the final defeat of perestroika and the overthrow of the Soviet government was summarised in a report by Doug Lorimer to our January 1992 national conference, which was then published as a pamphlet.[77]

"The main reason for the failure of perestroika", Doug said, "was that the Gorbachev leadership continued to rely on the Communist Party to be the driving force of the democratisation process, rather than promoting the independent self-organisation of the Soviet masses … [But] the CPSU was not only thoroughly bureaucratised, it was the linchpin of the whole system of bureaucratic rule …

"Gorbachev's course toward reform was based on holding the Communist party together. This inevitably led to a policy of compromise with the *nomenklatura* officials. One of the major compromises he made was not to challenge their special privileges, which by 1988 were not longer hidden from the Soviet masses …

"In refusing to challenge the bureaucracy's official privileges Gorbachev undermined his own credibility as an opponent of bureaucratic rule in the eyes of the Soviet masses. As the economic and social crisis deepened, he began to rely more and more on the very system of bureaucratic power he had proclaimed he sought to dismantle."

Soviet Stalinism was at a complete dead end. The report explained that the leaders of the coup against Gorbachev were not seeking to restore the old Stalinist system, but to "ensure that the spoils of privatising state property would go mainly to the central bureaucracy". Boris Yeltsin and his followers, by contrast, aimed to have the proceeds of privatisation go "to the bureaucrats controlling the republican and municipal apparatuses. as well as the technical and intellectual elites".

CHAPTER 9

1990s – SOCIALIST RENEWAL, DEMOCRATIC SOCIALIST PARTY

January 1990 DSP national conference

The 13th national conference, "For a Green, Democratic and Socialist World", was held at Hawkesbury Agricultural College January 3-8, 1990. It adopted a new party program and a major resolution on the ecological crisis, "Socialism and Human Survival". A draft of the program had been presented to the NC plenum in July. We had written the first drafts in preparation for unity discussions with the SPA. When the discussions fell through, we realised we still had a valuable product, and continued working on the document.

Reporters were: Dick Nichols, The Renewal of Socialism in Eastern Europe; Sally Low, World Politics in the '90s: Towards Capitalism or Socialism?; Steve Painter, Australian Capitalism at an Impasse; Will Wroth, Building Resistance; Jim Percy, The DSP: Traditions, Lessons and Socialist Perspectives; Pat Brewer, The Green Challenge in Australia; Peter Annear, Socialism and Human Survival (reporting on the document); Reihana Mohideen, The Program of the DSP (reporting on the document). Jim's report was published in Party Forum, and also in the book *Traditions, Lessons, and Socialist Perspectives*.

A special talk on the New Labour Party of New Zealand was given by party president Matt McCarten. The conference rally, compered by Resistance national secretary Will Wroth, launched the *DA* 1990 fund drive.

The credentials committee reported that 243 people had registered, of whom 190 were members. Women were 41 percent of members, 42 percent of attendees, and 52 percent of delegates. The average age was 31.5 for attendees, 28.7 for members and 27.4 for delegates. Eighteen percent were students, 23 percent industrial workers, 38 percent white collar workers, 12 percent professional, 8 percent unemployed or retired; 27 percent were full-timers for the party.

The nominations commission heard 51 submissions, Janet Parker reported, and the conference elected a National Committee of 32 full members and 20 candidate members.

The National Committee meeting held afterwards elected a National Executive of 15: Jim Percy, Pat Brewer, Doug Lorimer, Allen Myers, Dick Nichols, Peter Boyle, John Percy, Reihana Mohideen, Jim McIlroy, Dave Holmes, Sue

Bolton, Jane Beckman, Janet Parker, Steve Robson, Steve Painter. We also elected a Political Bureau and a Secretariat.

The NE elected a standing committee composed of the party officers: national secretary, Jim Percy; national president, John Percy; assistant national secretary, Pat Brewer; international secretary, Doug Lorimer.

1990 election campaign

Mainly because the green election campaigns were at different stages of formation, and varied in their openness to working with others, our electoral tactics in 1990 were also varied: running our own candidates but also joining green slates where we could. Chris Spindler reported in *DA*, February 13, 1990, that the Victorian Green Alliance had selected a Senate slate of Alf Bamblett, Ken McGregor and Pauline Scott, who was a member of the DSP.

In the *DA* of February 20, Steve Painter reported "Democratic Socialists to field 18 candidates" in the federal election on March 24. "The DSP will also support Green Alliance and other green and progressive candidates. In South Australia, inner-city Sydney and possibly Queensland, the party will not field its own candidates and will instead support green candidates." The DSP would "contest the Senate in Tasmania and Western Australia and House of Representative seats in WA, Tasmania, Victoria and New South Wales".

The article also reported: "By mutual agreement between the two parties, the previously announced Socialist Alliance campaign between the Democratic Socialist Party and the Socialist Party of Australia has been abandoned."

In the February 27 issue, Lisa Macdonald reported "Democratic Socialists expand election campaign" to 36 candidates. "According to national election campaign director Pat Brewer, 'The decision to run a greater number of candidates was taken with two main considerations in mind.'

"Firstly, recent polls which reveal that almost one-third of voters do not want to vote for either the Labor or Liberal parties in these elections are a strong indication that people will be looking more seriously for alternatives than they have for a long time.

"Secondly, it would appear that despite the space which is clearly opening up for alternative political parties as people become increasingly disillusioned with our current politicians, there are, in fact, very few candidates contesting these elections who present voters with a progressive alternative.

"The only significant exception to this state of affairs is in the green movement, whose candidates in South Australia, Queensland, New South Wales and Victoria will be actively supported by the DSP."

DSP member Jane Beckman, from Newcastle, was one of the six-person Green Alliance Senate ticket in NSW; DSPer Bruce Threlfo was nominated as the Greens candidate for Lowe. In Queensland, Coral Wynter, a DSP member, stood in the seat of Forde as a Green Independent. In the ACT, DSP member Sue Bolton stood for the seat of Fraser as part of the Green Democratic Alliance. In South Australia, DSP member Philippa Skinner was selected as a Senate candidate for the Green Alliance.

In the *DA* of March 6, in an article headed "Women are majority of DSP candidates", Lisa Macdonald reported, "Of the 42 DSP members standing as Greens or DSP candidates around the country, 22 are women". In another article, "Socialist challenges Democrats' leader", she reported that Tom Flanagan was standing in Kingston, where Democrat leader Janine Haines was the incumbent. Kathy Ragless stood in Hawker, Paul Petit in Port Adelaide.

The March 13 *DA* carried our election platform, "The alternative to Labor-Liberal austerity" and another major article, "For mass political action to save the environment". That issue also supported green campaigns with articles "Green tickets standing in all states", "Green campaigns challenge the old politics" and "Illawarra Greens candidate sees big impact", the last reporting that we had withdrawn our candidate for Cunningham in favour of the Illawarra Greens candidate, Steve Brigham.

DA of March 27 carried a report by Teresa Dowding on an election debate attended by 400 people in Hobart Town Hall on March 21. There were speakers from all parties, including our Senate candidate Kath Gelber. The Hobart *Mercury* conceded the DSP "won hands down".

The Democrats were enjoying something of a rise in their up-and-down career. In *DA* of March 6, Dick Nichols warned that the Democrats' turn to the left was not to be taken seriously: "An anti-working class party certainly has no hope, and as part of their leftward swing the Democrats have toned down a lot of their previous anti-union positions. Yet their industrial relations and wages policy has some revealing gaps (and some similarities to Liberal and Labor)." The following issue, March 20, reported a red-baiting attack on the DSP and the Victorian Green Alliance by the Democrat candidate for Wills.

The elections produced large votes for greens and the Democrats. Allen Myers reported in the March 27 *DA:* "The March 24 election has dealt a serious blow to the two-party domination of electoral politics, with a major swing to environmental candidates in electorates across the country.

"Complete figures are not yet available, but it appears that the total nationwide vote for Labor and the Coalition will fall below 80 per cent. For both, this is the lowest vote in post-World War II history.

"At the close of counting on Saturday night, Labor had 39 per cent of primaries – lower even than in the disastrous defeat of 1975. Labor squeaked back into office on green and Democrat preferences …

"The swing against Labor brought little comfort to the Coalition, particularly the National Party. Nationwide, the Nationals suffered a decline of more than 3 per cent from 1987, winning only about 8 per cent of primaries."

The April 3 *DA* editorial, headed "What the Green vote means", argued: "Despite attempts by sections of the Labor Party to deny it, there can be no doubt that preferences from Green and, to a lesser extent, Democrat, candidates were decisive in allowing the ALP to retain government in the March 24 election. Labor's $2 million advertising blitz seeking environmental preferences in the last week of the campaign shows how desperate the government was – and how accurately it judged the changes taking place in the electorate."

It added: "The most obvious conclusion from March 24 is that it is no longer possible for the major parties to dismiss the environment as a 'single issue' of concern only to a small sector of the electorate (whom Paul Keating would have called 'basket weavers' not very long ago). Ecology is now firmly a mainstream issue, one that cuts across traditional political alignments."

Reaffirmation of our party-building perspective

Coming out of our attempts at regroupment in the 1980s, and in face of the crisis of the Stalinist regimes in the Soviet Union and Eastern Europe, it was important to reaffirm our fundamental party-building perspectives. I stressed this in my party building report to the June 1990 NC meeting:

> The focus of this report is on the need for the party to reaffirm, re-educate in, and re-mobilise around our basic party-building norms and lessons, *at the same time as* continuing to do everything we can to reach out to, to regroup with, broader forces.
>
> These two aspects of our work are *not* in contradiction, in fact they're absolutely complementary. It's not an either/or choice for the party, but the two essential sides of our single party-building perspective.
>
> I think it's important that we all understand thoroughly what we are trying to do, and are able to put the last ten years of party-building in this context. We are *not* changing our basic party-building course when we try to break out, to link up with new forces, to explore any chance for regroupment, to get involved in new social or political movements,

when we try to link up with and recompose the vanguard as it exists and is developing.

But it's natural enough I suppose that some of the bedrock things, some of our basic party-building tasks, do seem to get a little overshadowed by the glamour or excitement of a new possibility. So we have to keep on emphasising those party building lessons time and again, and recognise that at different times during the 1980s some of our norms on these questions have slipped. In fact, rather than having any feeling that perhaps the role of the party is less important in this period when we're trying to reach out, we should be re-emphasising the essential role of our forces in bringing the real activists together and taking the struggle to the next stage.

At the same time as we are carrying through or proposing major reach-out type political initiatives – the Green work, our initiative for the Socialist Scholars Conference, our proposal for a broad new paper of the left – we are also going to be campaigning on the need to re-stress the basic party-building tasks.

The National Executive meeting on October 13, 1990, reinstituted the provisional membership category. It also passed a motion relating to the obligation of members to be active in a party branch, with the obligation to attend a certain number of branch meetings.

Part of party building was of course systematic socialist education. So, Party Forum No. 8, in February 1990, contained material on an Introduction to Marxism class series and a Program of the DSP class series. And we continued our tradition of educational camps: a Melbourne camp in May on "Main Debates in 20th Century Marxism" and a Tasmanian Resistance Camp in June near Huonville.

The Greens

Moreover, further regroupment moves with the SPA were made more difficult by the development of the Green movement and our involvement with it in the late 1980s. Then and into the early 1990s, the green movement became the focus of our regroupment work. We explored the possibilities of participating in Green Alliances in Sydney, Canberra, Melbourne and other cities at the end of the '80s.

The possibility arose in the early 1990s of our involvement in a national Green Party. This prospect was blocked by anti-socialist forces determined to restrict the breadth of a Greens formation to the "pale greens", excluding any open reds or red-greens. The development of a genuine broad Red-Green Party (on the early German model, which later went down the drain) was not on the agenda.

DA had been the paper to chart the formation and progress of Green political organisations around the country. In many cases supporters of *DA* helped to build or initiate such groups, such as the Green Alliance.

Our orientation in the 1990s shifted essentially from a new party perspective, or any untried regroupment proposal, to concentrate on building the DSP and Resistance, supporting DSP candidates in elections, while being fully prepared to support electoral alliances of broader forces.

Resistance 19th national conference

DA of April 24, 1990, reported that Resistance was "facing a decade of new challenges" as more than 250 people attended its 19th national conference in Melbourne at Easter. It was the first Resistance conference after the collapse of the Stalinist regimes in Eastern Europe. Jim Percy gave a feature talk on "The Collapse of Stalinism and the Future of Socialism". International guest speakers were the secretary of Melanesian Solidarity and Quentin Findlay from NZ New Labour's Youth Commission.

The opening report to conference by NC member Anne O'Callaghan "began the process of analysing these changes and what they will mean in the struggle for socialism", the article said. "O'Callaghan pointed out that decades of bureaucratic rule in the name of socialism had discredited the idea of socialism for millions in these countries …

"'The erosion of an explicit socialist consciousness and the suffocation of any form of political culture – of participation or democratic decision making – in the countries of Eastern Europe – is one the most criminal and far-reaching consequences of Stalinism', O'Callaghan said …

"But while the Stalinist distortion of socialism crumbles, international capitalism faces intensifying economic and environmental crises, while progressive forces are advancing, most notably in South America and southern Africa.

"The period ahead, O'Callaghan concluded, 'poses fundamental questions which have no simple solutions.' What is needed from organisations like Resistance is a politics 'prepared to ask the difficult questions, to take up the difficult challenges, to suffer setbacks but to maintain the fight' …

"The two other major reports were 'Beyond the two-party crisis: building a radical alternative', presented by Wollongong Resistance organiser Tracy Sorensen, and 'Meeting the challenge: a new decade of Resistance,' by Will Wroth, Resistance national secretary."

An international solidarity rally on the opening night of the conference was chaired by Natasha Simons; and a special panel on "Green politics after the elections: what's the next step?" was chaired by Tom Flanagan.

A DSP National Executive plenum was held April 16 at the YWCA lounge in Melbourne. We heard a report from the FMLN representative, and reports: New Developments in the Third World; Australian Political Situation after the Elections; Socialist Scholars Conference; Organisation; *DA* Distribution; International; and Eastern Europe/USSR Developments. There were also branch reports.

Green Left Weekly

The idea for *Green Left Weekly* was developed in 1990. It was seen as both a hope to boost sales, since *DA* sales had been flagging, and a political reach-out to the many independent political activists we could see out there. Proposals came up at our National Executive meeting in Melbourne immediately after the Resistance conference for investigating the possibility of launching a new, broad paper of the left. Discussions continued in the National Office. We sent a letter to all DSP NC members on May 14, 1990, raising the "Project for a new paper of the left", signed by Jim Percy, as national secretary of the DSP, and Allen Myers, editor of *Direct Action*.

None of our regroupment efforts of the 1980s had come to fruition. Our potential political partners had all backed off. They had steered themselves into oblivion, like the CPA, which finally dissolved in 1991. Or they had reaffirmed their Stalinism, like the SPA backing the Chinese CP's assault on democratic protesters in Tiananmen Square.

But we felt there were still many independent activists who could be regrouped. (In the following years, some former CPA members who felt abandoned by the CPA decision to dissolve itself in 1991 did come around us.)

So *Green Left Weekly* was envisaged as a *de facto* regroupment, after the failure of the efforts of the 1980s. We were hopeful (overly) that many of these independents and exes could be reactivated to some level of activity and commitment. My party-building report to the June 1990 DSP NC outlined the perspective:

> Obviously any new project like this will of course continue to rely on all of the resources that have been developed by the Democratic Socialist Party and the *Direct Action* staff, and all the technical resources that have been assembled over the years, but above all else, the dedication of the members of the DSP and Resistance in distributing this paper. This gives it an initial base and doesn't make it one more utopian pipe-dream of producing the perfect independent paper. But

we do want to find ways to involve others and mobilise more resources for the paper, to build on the achievements of *Direct Action*.

So our proposal is that we modify the nature and direction of our paper by a series of steps. We will act dramatically if the possibilities open up for a broader regroupment, but at least we want to take the initial steps to doing that by developing a new legal, organisational and editorial structure for the paper. We are convinced this will both improve the input and hopefully also increase the circulation of a weekly newspaper, which orients both to the constituency already developed by *Direct Action*, but also to the constituency that is increasingly opening up in the left and alternative and environmental movements. Specifically:

1. We would set up an advisory board …
2. We would change the legal structure so a partnership or co-operative was created that people could buy shares in, hopefully mobilising some more resources for the paper through this mechanism …
3. We would look for a new name for the paper, preferably something that expresses both the Red and the Green nature of our political perspectives.
4. We would thoroughly revamp the layout and look of the paper …
5. In this framework we could go on a campaign to build the paper that would have a real chance of significant success. We would have a much broader reservoir of people who we could call on to contribute to the paper, subscribe to it, and support it financially. A new exciting project like this would also have the potential to increase the effort and commitment from DSP and Resistance members in distributing and supporting the paper. We've already had some excellent responses to our proposal from people we thought might be willing to participate on our advisory board.

We drafted a letter along these lines, "Proposal for a New Broad Paper of the Left," signed by myself as DSP national president, and Allen Myers as *Direct Action* editor, and sent it out on June 21 to a wide range of potential supporters.

We projected a national teleconference of supporters of the project to decide on the name, structure and so on. It would not be a directly party paper, but we would not hide the role of the DSP and Resistance in promoting it, initiating it, supporting and distributing it. But we'd aim to get a range of movement activists, independent leftists, to come behind the paper as well. We would aim to have the paper open for debate, discussion and other contributions.

Especially in the early months of the paper, we looked closely to see how broad our range of contributors was; we kept track of the non party writers and encouraged them to do more than contribute articles. Some did get involved. But most of the money and commitment came from the DSP and Resistance. Nearly all the sales were still by DSP and Resistance members.

Collapse of Stalinism

DA Prague bureau

We established Prague and Moscow offices for the paper as the crises were unfolding, helping us to understand better what was happening, but probably not a great boost to the political morale of the comrades we sent over there to observe first hand and write back for our paper. Renfrey Clarke spoke Russian and was studying the society as part of his PhD, so had visited a number of times. We formalised his assignment and were hoping that his time in Moscow would help us also develop closer relations with *New Left Review*.

In April 1990 Steve Painter went to Prague to set up a *Direct Action* bureau covering both Eastern and Western Europe, and Tracy Sorensen followed him soon after. They provided lots of articles and interviews, reports from Czechoslovakia and Eastern Europe. They also covered political events in Western Europe – Belgium and West Germany.

The comrades rented a reasonably cheap flat in Prague, but there were financial constraints on our ability to pay for travel, and maintain comrades, especially in Western Europe. Peter Annear and Sally Low replaced Steve and Tracy after a year.

DA of April 24, 1990, carried Steve Painter's first "Report from Prague. Czechoslovakia after the 'Velvet Revolution'".

The issue of August 14, 1990 carried four articles by Steve from Ireland and Britain: "A loser in capitalist Europe", "Thatcherism in crisis", "Nuclear industry in a shambles" and "Preparing to govern for business, Labour seeks to smash left".

DA of August 21 carried "Austria's 'social partnership': A European 'accord' begins to unravel" and "Czechoslovakia: Anti-women forces raise their heads", both by Tracy, and two articles by Steve, "Czechoslovakia: New government pushes fast-track capitalism" and "Kosovans denounce Serbian reign of terror".

Around this time, Padraic McGuinness, then an *Australian* journalist after earlier working for the *Australian Financial Review* and the *Sydney Morning*

Herald, made a brief trip to Europe and returned to write: "… Australian media generally still have not realised how important Europe is going to be for the rest of this century and into the next. It is still true that there is not a single full-time Australian print journalist in post on the whole continent of Europe."

That of course became the hook for a DA fundraising ad headlined "Wrong again, McGuinness!" It pointed out, "Since April, Direct Action has had two full-time journalists based in Prague" and asked readers to help out by contributing to the *DA* fund drive.

Here is a sampling of the articles they produced for *DA:*

August 28, 1990: "Green-Socialist Network formed in Britain", "Social Democrats in crisis. The 'Swedish model' nears collapse".

September 4: "Peace conference in a city at war" (Belfast), "Europe's un-fashionable political prisoners" (Dublin).

September 11: "Birmingham Six frame-up near collapse", "Czechoslovakia: The workers who suspect 'reforms'", "East Germany collapses into unity. Free market disaster for workers, farmers".

September 18: "Poland: Activist look for a 'third way'", "Anarchists challenge Austrian yuppiedom".

October 9: "Greens convention votes to unite" (Germany).

October 23: "Czechoslovakia's 'second revolution'. Insiders, black marketeers scramble for spoils", "Netherlands. Left unites to form red-green party".

October 30: "Poland. A rapid erosion of women's rights", "The left in united Germany. Gregor Gysi: Don't replace one failed system with another" (by Tracy and Mary Merkenich).

November 6: "Czechoslovakia. Petr Uhl on prospects for the democratic left".

November 13: "Hungary. Drivers strike over petrol price", "Czechoslovakia. Right attempts to hijack Civic Forum".

November 20: "Czechoslovakia: Rapidly changing image of women".

December 4: "Tony Benn: 'War would be catastrophic'", "German left, Greens debate alliances", "Britain after Thatcher. Economic slump as Tories change horses".

It was a prodigious and quality output, providing on-the-spot and up-to-date coverage of Eastern and Western Europe. Unfortunately, they didn't last the distance in the party; perhaps the experience of the rapid return of capitalism there was too demoralising.

DA Moscow bureau

Several of Renfrey Clarke's articles on the USSR appeared in *DA* in 1987, after Renfrey had spent three months studying there. When he returned in mid-1990, he began publishing a "Moscow diary" on the conditions of life, as well as reports on events.

When the coup against Gorbachev occurred in August 1991, Renfrey was able to report for *Green Left Weekly* from inside the Russian parliament building, where the Yeltsinites organised their successful counter-coup.

Turning point for perestroika

In *DA* of July 3, 1990, Tracy Sorensen wrote from Czechoslovakia: "Any hopes that the political process begun by the Velvet Revolution of last November 17 would lead uninterruptedly in the direction of democratic socialism have by now been laid to rest: A volley of laws on the privatisation of state enterprises and restrictions on the right to strike point clearly in the other direction.

"And all this is occurring without significant resistance from the working class – demoralised, passive and confused as it is after four decades of Stalinist rule."

The 28th Congress of the Soviet CP took place in July, and *DA* of course devoted considerable coverage and analysis to it. The July 17 issue, in an article by Peter Boyle headed "Congress victory for party reformers", nevertheless noted that Gorbachev's win at the congress was far from settling what would happen:

"It's undeniable that the Communist Party of the Soviet Union (CPSU) has come a long way since Mikhail Gorbachev's reformers came to its leadership. The question, however, is whether enough change has taken place to prevent the party from being swept aside like the former ruling Communist parties of Eastern Europe."

After the coup and Yeltsin's triumph, *GLW* on September 4, 1991, carried "Why Perestroika failed", an abridged version of a talk Jim Percy gave to a Sydney forum. "The world has paid a terrible price for the fact that, since the '20s, the struggles of the oppressed have largely been represented and led by people who agreed with the policies of the Communist Party of the Soviet Union after the victory of Stalin in the '20s", Jim said. "They lead them ineffectively, they sell them out, they betray them, they set no example, they can't go forward to victory, and they ultimately lead to disasters, as we are seeing now.

"Gorbachev's election as general secretary opened up the possibility of reform of the revolutionary process, of a revival of the revolution. But it also offered the possibility of a completion of the counter-revolutionary process begun by Stalin. It is that that has now come to the fore."

Cuba: not the same

In mid-1990, we ran a three-part series (*DA* 748-750) by Colin Cleary and Doug Lorimer on how the Cuban Revolution and its leaders were responding to perestroika and the changes in Eastern Europe. At the time, opponents of socialism were vocal about their hopes that "Cuba is next" – that it would follow the path of countries like Poland and Hungary.

The series began by pointing out that "Cubans have sense to recognise themselves as Latin Americans. When Cubans assess the achievements of their revolution, the instinctive comparisons they make are not with the United States but with Latin America …

"Despite serious economic problems, Cuban gross domestic product per capita increased by 33 percent in the 1980s. In Latin America as a whole, according to United Nations figures, per capita GDP *shrank* by 8 percent. The living standards of Latin American workers, needless to say, shrank by even more." Cubans were much better off than most Latin Americans in terms of education, health care, housing and nutrition, the authors pointed out. But it was not merely "simple calculations of material advantage" that led most Cubans to reject the Eastern European course. Their support for socialism was rooted in Cuba's history and their own experience:

"As President Castro has repeatedly observed, socialism did not arrive in Cuba behind the victorious divisions of the Soviet Army. It was a home-grown product, which a large majority of Cubans came to accept and champion in the years between 1959 and 1962 as they faced off the United States in a series of battles for control of much of Cuba's productive wealth."

In addition to the issue of national self-determination, Cubans also supported their revolution because the character of the Cuban Communist Party was quite different from that of the parties in the USSR and Eastern Europe: "In Cuba the party has never suffered the divorce from the masses undergone by the Soviet Communist Party with the onset of Stalinism in the 1920s, an estrangement which marked the East European Communist Party governments from their inception."

The second article in the series looked at Cuba's economic difficulties – caused largely by the US blockade, inherited underdevelopment and objective factors such as declining terms of trade, and the government's program of "rectification of errors and negative tendencies". Rectification, like perestroika, the authors wrote, was an attempt to combat bureaucratic abuses and to make a more direct and clear connection between people's incomes and their economic contribution. But unlike perestroika, rectification did not seek to replace the command economy with markets:

"The Cubans … do not see the command economy as inherently flawed. Rectification aims at retaining Cuba's centralised planning and administrative system (which since the 1970s … has been modified by a degree of local control exercised through the Organs of People's Power) and remedying its shortcomings through systematic work to build the political understanding – and hence moral motivation – of everyone involved in the economic process."

The third and final article in the series was titled "Toward a debate on economic models". It looked at the pros and cons of the Cubans' command model and indicated some of the discussion going on in Cuba. However, the collapse of the Soviet Union a year later made this discussion outdated as Cuba was forced to enter the "special period".

DSP NC June 1990

The DSP National Committee meeting held June 9-11, 1990, heard the reports: "Perestroika in Crisis"; "Eastern Europe after the Elections"; "Capitalist Crisis and the Third World"; "Indonesia and the Revival of the Mass Movement"; "International Work"; "The Left and Australian Politics"; "Green Work after the Elections"; "Party Building/Organisation"; and "Youth Work".

My party-building report noted that we had approximately doubled our size in the 1980s. "The balance on the left has been shifting in our favor for some time now. Other groups are in crisis or disintegrating. And in area after area we're staking out more space for ourselves, taking the leading role in different movements. Among youth, of course, it's been that way for quite a while. But in recent years in many of the solidarity campaigns our role is increasingly essential.

"This year in many cities our comrades were the organisers for International Women's Day. And last weekend we capped it off with our pivotal role in organising the Environment Day rallies." Anne O'Callaghan's report on youth work recorded a certain decline in the student movement, especially as ALP student bureaucrats increasingly dominated the National Union of Students. In this situation, Resistance's priorities should be building Resistance Clubs on campus and involvement in mass movement work around environmental issues, women's liberation and international solidarity. Running in student elections should be regarded as a tactic that might or might not be useful in particular situations, not something that should automatically be attempted.

This was a shift from what Resistance had been doing in the immediately preceding period, and it led to a longer discussion on our youth work, in which Will Wroth was the main critic of the change. Unfortunately, this eventually led him to leave the party.

Range of issues

DA's coverage indicates the range of issue on which we were campaigning at this time.

Women's liberation:

February 27, 1990: Lisa Macdonald, "Women, censorship and puritanism", based on a talk to a DSP forum.

March 6, 1990: "Feminism and socialism in the 1990s", roundtable discussion with Rose McCann, Pat Brewer, Lisa Macdonald and Elizabeth Parkes.

Environment:

May 15, 1990: Jorge Jorquera, World Environment Day rallies on June 3.

June 26, 1990: Bill Mason (Jim McIlroy), "The fight for Fraser Island. Blockade takes on loggers, government".

July 10, 1990: Susan Lazlo, "Global ecological crisis. Is overpopulation to blame?"

July 24, 1990: Ben Reid, "Protests stop logging on Fraser Island".

August 21, 1990: Susan Price, "Renewed threat to Great Barrier Reef"; Susan Lazlo, "Environmental groups blast government plan"; Jill Hickson "Chemical poisons in our cities".

August 28, 1990: Maurice Sibelle, "Goss refuses to stop logging. Save Fraser Island!"

September 11, 1990: Ben Reid, "Logging blockade continues, Fraser Island's future in doubt".

Gay and lesbian liberation:

July 3, 1990: Philippa Stanford, "Gay pride week a big success" – Brisbane's first with a rally in Roma Street Forum, art show and gay film festival.

August 14, 1990: Ed Aspinall, "National Aids Conference. ACT UP exposes government stalling".

September 25, 1990: Tom Flanagan interviews Rodney Croome, "Gay law reform in Tasmania".

October 9, 1990: Ed Aspinall, "Police violence at anti-Nile demo" of 1,500 in Sydney.

International solidarity:

May 8, 1990: Max Lane, "Indonesia. New human rights coalition formed"; Max Lane, "Pro-democracy students sentenced".

May 15, 1990: Max Lane, "Suharto under pressure on elections"; Max Lane, "Farmers protest in Jakarta".

August 21, 1990: Max Lane, "Indonesia. A progressive movement begins to revive".

September 4, 1990: Helen Jarvis reported on an *Inside Indonesia*-organised Sydney seminar. "One result was the consolidation of a new activist organisation, AKSI – Action for Solidarity with Indonesia".

September 25, 1990: Max Lane, "The bloodbath that brought Suharto to power".

September 11, 1990: Helen Jarvis, "Australian groups launch campaign. Stepped up efforts for peace in Cambodia".

September 18, 1990: Norm Dixon (Terry Townsend), "Despite continued Khmer Rouge threat, Cambodia's new chance for peace".

July 3, 1990: Ad for CISLAC dance at Paddington Town Hall, with Mambologists, Papalote.

July 24, 1990: Susan Lazlo, "Nicaragua. US-backed government meets worker resistance".

July 3, 1990: Norm Dixon on South Africa, "World tour to defend sanctions. Massive outpouring of support greets Mandela".

July 31, 1990: Norm Dixon, "Africa: the other face of capitalism", centrespread feature.

September 11, 1990: Norm Dixon, "Inkatha, police massacre residents".

September 25, 1990: Norm Dixon, "'Hidden hand' aids Inkatha violence".

First Gulf War

Of course, we went all out to oppose the US invasion of Iraq. The August 14, 1990, *DA* cover headlined: "Troops out! Bush's dirty game in the Gulf". The main article, by Debra Wirth (Deb Sorensen), was "Gulf crisis: Why the US is spoiling for a fight".

The following week's cover was: "US admits: 'We want their oil'. Bring back the warships". Peter Reid wrote, "Hawke joins US in search for war", and another article described protests: "Rallies demand: Bring the ships back!" This reported initial actions: Adelaide 200; Brisbane and Melbourne 300; Perth 40; and in Lismore, Bob and Hazel Hawke were dogged by demonstrators.

The same issue also carried a statement by the DSP Political Bureau, "US troops out of the Middle East! Recall Australian warships!" It said, "The Democratic Socialist Party condemns the Iraqi occupation of Kuwait but believes that the US response poses a much greater danger. The US military build-up in the Middle East is not prompted by support for the right of self-determination of the Kuwaiti people but by a desire to maintain subservient pro-US governments in key oil-producing countries in the region …

"If it succeeds, the Bush administration will have regained much of the freedom to act as self-appointed world policeman for capitalism. It will be encouraged to use direct military force elsewhere …

"The Labor government's decision to send the warships contrasts sharply with its support for the forcible annexation of East Timor by the Indonesian Suharto dictatorship. It is not prompted by 'principle' but by support for Washington's defence of the profits of the oil monopolies."

DA of August 28 carried Peter Reid, "Why Bush blocks peace in the Middle East"; Norm Dixon (Terry Townsend), "Why Bush backs Saudi Arabia. A servant of US oil companies"; Chris Slee and Sol Salby, "Origins of the Gulf crisis. Arab nationalism versus Britain, US".

The article was accompanied by "A short list of US interventions", listing US interference in the region from the 1953 coup in Iran to the bombing of Libya in 1986 and the shooting down of the Iranian passenger airliner in 1988.

"NO GULF WAR!" was the cover headline on the September 4 issue. Articles included Peter Reid, "US prepares for long stay in Gulf" and Tracy Sorensen, "Opposition to war grows in US, Britain". "Nationwide rallies demand 'Bring frigates home!'" reported on the Nationwide Day of Action, September 1, with demonstrations in Adelaide of 400, Brisbane 500, Hobart 150, Melbourne 400, Perth 600, Sydney 2,000 and Canberra 300 a week earlier.

Related articles in the September 11 issue were: Peter Reid, "Media whip up Anti-Arab racism" and Tony Iltis, "Gulf crisis: Israeli peace group calls for negotiations".

The following week carried Peter Reid and Allen Myers, "Will Helsinki summit restrain Bush?"

In *DA* of September 25, Sally Low and Mike Trevaskis reported on a Sydney demo of 1,500 to "Bring the Frigates Home" and "No Gulf War!"

First Socialist Scholars Conference

The Socialist Scholars Conference we organised in 1990 was a big, ambitious conference that chimed in well with the developing international political situation and the need to understand what was happening in the Soviet Union and Eastern Europe. It was held September 28-October 1 at the University of Technology Sydney, with the theme "The Crisis in Europe and the Future of Socialism". It, and the second, which we organised the following year in

Melbourne, served a need for reach-out and wide-ranging discussion in a tumultuous time.

The DSP did the bulk of the organising, with the key organising role played by Pat Brewer and Lisa Macdonald, convening a secretariat for the conference on behalf of the DSP. We also set up an advisory board chaired by Professor Alastair Davidson, with other board members: Ann Curthoys, Andrew Wells, Peter Beilharz, Verity Burgmann, Joel Kahn and Wayne Cristadou, which gave the appropriate academic authority to the conference.

We cast our net wide for international guests, eventually attracting an impressive list of left academics from around the world as plenary speakers: Stanislav Menshikov, Elizabeth Wilson, Giovanni Arrighi, Robin Blackburn, Daniel Faber, Neelam Hussain, Terry Eagleton, Frigga Haug and Ralph Miliband.

The September 11 *DA* carried a Socialist Scholars Conference four-page lift-out ad/program, listing the international guest speakers and the large number of speakers and panels. Major panels involved international guests, local academics and activists, and usually a DSP speaker – Dick Nichols, Pat Brewer, Reihana Mohideen, with Jim Percy and myself chairing a major session. A large number of Australian academics and activists also spoke.[78]

There were many other panels with speakers not listed, and some film showings. As many as 16 sessions ran concurrently. The opening panel on Friday night was held at the Teachers Federation Auditorium, all the other sessions at UTS, on Broadway. A conference dinner was held on Sunday night at Glebe Town Hall.

Attendance was 1,097, of whom only 212 were DSP or Resistance members. Six hundred attended for the full three days. More than 200 presentations were fitted into the program. We organised for some of the international guests to give forums in other cities. Peter Reid wrote in the October 9 *DA* that the conference was "confident on the future of socialism".

"Conference organiser Lisa Macdonald told *Direct Action* that this was the biggest gathering of the left seen in Australia for many years …

"Despite the ongoing media hype about the 'end of socialism', the conference demonstrated that many people are still prepared to commit themselves to the socialist project. This wasn't the result of blind optimism but the result of a determination to understand today's reality and change it for the better."

There was some sabotage of the conference beforehand and sour grapes afterwards by the CPA, and considerable media attention (including from an enraged B.A. Santamaria). Norm Dixon (Terry Townsend) reported in the October 16 *DA* that the conference provided "New opportunities for left renewal" and was an "overwhelming success", with "nearly unanimous positive feedback".

Conference organiser Pat Brewer was quoted: "'We also received a lot of media interest. The media wanted to cover the international guests in a way that local socialists just aren't covered here. The stature of these guests forced the media to report the event and treat the subject with some seriousness.'

"Even the Australian's feature writer Frank Devine attended the whole conference and came out with grudging respect: 'The intelligence, vitality and idealism of the 1000 young men and women attending the Socialist Scholars Conference was inspiring.'

"Brewer pointed out that the event indicates the potential for a renewal of the socialist movement in Australia after many years of decline ...

"'Given the response – the overwhelmingly positive feedback – we are confident we could do it again.'"

Party Forum No. 13 carried an assessment by Lisa Macdonald, and in the first issue of our new internal bulletin, the Activist, Pat Brewer optimistically projected the second Socialist Scholars Conference in 1991.

End of the CPA

I wrote an article for the August 7, 1990, *DA*, "The ABC's history of the Communist Party", an assessment of *The Party's Over,* the ABC documentary aired on July 29.

"The program was billed as an attempt to unravel 'some of the reasons why the CPA died'. It fell well short of this goal ...

"Nevertheless, some of the inspiring history of the CPA did come through ...

"The overwhelming support won by Communists on the waterfront ...

"The mass support for the CPA amongst the miners in the '30s and '40s ...

"The dedication and commitment of several generations of Australian Communists shone through. The ranks of the CPA fought unstintingly for the rights and conditions of workers, the unemployed, the downtrodden, even if some of their models were flawed."

But aside from the distortions by presenter Geraldine Doogue and the program's editors, "there were a number of important gaps in the program that reflect on the CPA itself, in three areas that had some direct bearing on its decline ...

"CPA leaders were not merely slow to come to terms with Stalinism. Even when the horrific facts were public knowledge, they refused to accept the reality and continued to lie to members ...

"The second gap in explaining the CPA's decline was in regard to the ALP ...

"Writers of CPA histories often try to claim that the party was most successful when it had 'a correct united front approach to the ALP', ie, tailed it, didn't challenge it. The fact is, the CPA grew most rapidly when it took a strong stand *against* the ALP ...

"The third obvious gap was in regard to the impact of the struggle against the Vietnam War, and the youth radicalisation of the '60s and '70s, on Australian politics ...

"But this was a boat missed by the CPA, contributing to its decline and fostering the growth of other currents on the left such as Resistance and the Democratic Socialist Party ..."

"The program began with an interview with CPA National Secretary Brian Aarons", I wrote, "introduced by Doogue as 'quietly leading his party into oblivion' 73 years after the Russian Revolution. 'The period that opened with 1917 is coming to a close, it has definitely ended, and we need new forms, new ways of doing things,' said Aarons.

"Certainly communists need to explore new forms and new ways of doing things in response to changed conditions. But it's important to find the *right* responses to new situations, to be able to correct mistakes and to preserve good traditions.

"Unfortunately, the CPA has not been able to thoroughly correct its mistakes and has generally changed the *wrong* things. The CPA today, and now its New Left Party, are cynical about some of the positive aspects of CPA history, but have retained many of the negative features."

In December 1990 the CPA held its winding up conference. Although 1988 was listed by the *Sydney Morning Herald* archives as their final date, they lingered on until their final conference, setting up the Search Foundation to hold the accumulated assets, and setting up their new "broad" paper that replaced *Tribune*.

The final blow to the CPA was *Green Left Weekly:* we got it out before they were able to produce their new paper *Broadside*. Its layout was unimaginative; its political line was only slightly to the left of the ALP; and it really wasn't very "broad". It folded after about a year.

Mining and the environment

Andrew Jamieson had established himself thoroughly as both a union and community leader on Tasmania's West Coast. Jammo had transferred there in 1984 to help consolidate a group of militant miners who were interested in establishing a branch of the SWP. Although the proto-branch didn't survive for that many years, the comrades led some important struggles, and were able to establish that there was no contradiction between fighting for mine workers' jobs and community services, and also defending the growing environmental campaign.

The November 21, 1989, *DA* carried an interview by Dick Nichols with Ian (Andrew) Jamieson, "the president of the newly formed Tasmanian Mining Industry Unions Council". It was headed, "The fight for jobs, the environment and union democracy". At a time when most politicians and union officials were posing environmental protection and jobs as mutually exclusive alternatives, Jammo was insisting on our line that the labour movement had to defend both:

"… our overall approach is that the protection of the environment goes hand in hand with the protection of jobs and before the protection of profits.

"In Tasmania the mining companies have a history of ripping the place apart just to get the wealth, and they haven't worried about jobs either. So there's a real basis there for the environmental and union movements to get together."

Jammo had done a lot to encourage discussions between the Tasmanian green independents and the mining union. He was emphatic that the greens needed to focus well beyond parliament. "We supported the Independents in the campaign … I think there is an inherent danger in the way things are going at the moment. Even though they have got incredible pressure on them, no real links have been developed between them and the community. There is a real tendency for the parliamentary process to keep them in parliament."

On June 12, 1990, Jamieson, now secretary of the West Coast Combined Mining Unions Council, spoke to a Melbourne *Direct Action* forum about developments in Tasmania since the signing of the accord between Labor and the Independents. "Tasmania's green Independents are alienating much potential support in the state's mining communities", he said, and "Greens must consult with miners".

The following month Dave Andrews (Jammo), writing from Tasmania in the July 10, 1990, *DA*, analysed "A year of the Labor-Green accord" quoting himself, and in the same issue he reported on "West Coast community rallies against cuts". Tom Flanagan also wrote in the August 14 issue about "Tasmania's winter of discontent". In the same issue, Ian Hopkins and Teresa Dowding interviewed Ian Jamieson in "Why miners are fighting back". Jammo was an organiser of a rally by 1,500 West Coast residents in Hobart on August 17 to protest against state government cutbacks in social services and against threats to end mining on the West Coast.

This prompted an open letter to Ian Jamieson by Bob Burton of the Wilderness Society, "Mining and the environment: can they be compatible?" We published it in *DA* 757, with Jammo's reply, a page each. Jammo concluded:

"Society needs mining; it needs a safe and clean environment; we need jobs and a secure standard of living for ourselves and our children. Given these parameters and a democratic process, society can implement an environmentally sound and sustainable mining industry in Tasmania."

20 years of *Direct Action*

In the issue of *DA* (September 25) distributed at the 1990 Socialist Scholars Conference, we carried a four-page feature on "20 years of Direct Action". After outlining "Where we began", we carried an account of major issues we'd covered and campaigned on: "Direct Action – an inspiring tradition; 20 years of campaigning for socialism", with subheadings (and illustrations of *DA* covers) on: "Campaigning for Vietnam; The Whitlam Labor government; For a peaceful, non-nuclear world; Fighting for women's rights; A paper for young people; International solidarity; Workers' rights; Defending the environment; Regrouping the left". Our main thrust was in the article headed "Towards a new red-green paper":

> Twenty years of *Direct Action* is a tremendous achievement … But the struggle continues. We can't just rest on our laurels. And *Direct Action* can't just remain the same, no matter how good it has been over those 20 years.
>
> Socialists have to be able to respond to new openings, to new needs of the struggle. The assessment of those of us who have been producing *Direct Action* is that what's needed today is a *broader* paper that would be able to be used in all their political campaigns by a much wider and greater number of progressive movements.
>
> The current political situation demands a more united response. In the last few months, we've witnessed further betrayals by the ALP leadership, when many thought they couldn't possibly degenerate any further.
>
> Two long-standing traditions of the ALP have been unceremoniously dumped. Hawke has dispatched Australian troops in support of a US military intervention (remember Vietnam – the ALP was elected in 1972 as a result of the campaign of opposition to that military adventure). And Keating is presiding over the wholesale privatisation of our public assets and utilities – the airlines, Telecom, the Commonwealth Bank (remember the 1940s – Chifley tried to nationalise the banks!).
>
> In the 1990s, we need a response that fully encompasses the green spectrum as well as the red, as the threat to the very existence of life on this planet grows more acute each year.

> Throughout the 1980s, there have been growing consciousness and activity in defence of the environment. And more and more people are drawing the conclusion that there is a link between the struggle to save the environment and the fight for social justice on behalf of the downtrodden of the world. The link between 'green' and 'red' issues must be highlighted, and the various struggles united against the common causes of our problems.
>
> What is needed is a new paper that plays this role.
>
> The Democratic Socialist Party and *Direct Action* have initiated a process to get such a paper off the ground. An initial letter outlining such a proposal signed by *DA* editor Allen Myers and DSP president John Percy, was circulated. The response has been so favourable that a second letter supporting the project is now being sent out, supported by a much larger group of people …
>
> The goal is to make such a new paper in reality the weapon for all those in struggle, and a forum for all the movements. It's your paper. Take part in its success.

Twenty-four initial signatories supporting the proposal were listed Apart from Allen and myself, Lou-anne Barker was the only other current DSP member on the list, although there were a number of former members.[79]

Preparing for the new paper

Harry van Moorst, an activist from the 1960s who now headed up the Victorian Campaign Against Poverty and Unemployment, was interviewed by Susan Lazlo about the new paper proposal in the October 16 *DA*. He said such a paper was "both a desirable project and an important one" and there was "a real need" for it. It could help bring about greater collaboration among progressive forces.

"It is a mutual risk", he said, "a risk for the party, because the party loses its party organ … I think that is a courageous effort". For people like himself, van Moorst said, to be involved in such a project is to run the risk of "being branded a DSP member, fellow traveller or front runner for the party".

"The DSP has proposed that the new paper aim to appeal to both the 'red' and the 'green political movements. Van Moorst added that the new paper must also re-establish the legitimacy of socialist ideas within the environmental movement …

"Ultimately, Van Moorst believes that the green movement has to draw on both the theoretical foundations of the socialist movement and its practical experience at organising. This is also where the new paper can help." Rod Webb, an early leader of the SWP, and then manager of the Australian Film Institute, was one of the speakers at the September 29 dinner at the Phoenician Club in Sydney advertised as a "Dinner and Rally for a Red-Green Paper". Other speakers were Robyn Blackburn, Deborah White, Kath Gelber, Harry van Moorst and Jim Percy.

Rod's talk was excerpted in the October 9 *DA* as "Filling in the media 'blank spots'" "*Direct Action* – its 20 phenomenal years of existence – is eloquent evidence for the defence of the '60s spirit", he said. "Go back through its pages, and you'll be able fill in the blank spots in the bourgeois media that so many people want to hide …

"Celebrating 20 years of achievement is all very well, but what's more important is that history is now about to be applied to an even more significant project: to the creation of a publication which seeks to speak to a far wider audience; to an audience which is becoming more and more conscious of more and more blank spots in the bourgeois media.

"Now that's something to celebrate. So, in congratulating *Direct Action* on its 20 years, I do so doubly because of what is now proposed for the next 20."

I reported in the November 27 *DA* that the new paper would be launched in February:

> The decision to push ahead with this exciting new initiative was taken at a national phone hook-up on Sunday November 18. Six months of discussions laid the basis for this step.
>
> The paper will be produced by an unincorporated association, which people can join by buying shares. The more shares people buy, the more say they'll have in the running of the paper. A national board of management will be elected partly from an AGM and partly from regional meetings of shareholders … Shares will be sold in units of $50.
>
> Initially the *Green Left* weekly will be produced using the Democratic Socialist Party's equipment and resources. The new paper would be billed for at least some of the expenses incurred. Income from paper sales, subscriptions, advertisements, donations and shares would cover this and provide for the expansion of the paper.
>
> It is planned to begin the paper as a 24-page paper printed on good quality newsprint. It would have at least two extra colours on the front, back, and centre pages.
>
> A brochure outlining the project is being prepared for wide distribution. We are also planning other methods of publicising the *Green Left* weekly – posters, ads, videos.

There are many things you can do to help make this exciting project a success.

- Buy shares in the paper (fill in the form below).
- Publicise it among your friends, at work, in your community, during your political activity – we'll send you a bundle of leaflets and posters.
- Offer to write, take photographs, draw cartoons or help in many other ways.
- Help distribute the paper – either offer to take a bundle to sell yourself, or organise to have it sold in your local newsagent, bookshop etc.
- Take out a subscription to the new paper. (Arrangements are being made to have current subscriptions to *Direct Action* carried over to the new paper.)

The initial response to the new paper bodes well for its future. But to guarantee its success, your participation is needed. The goal is to make it a weapon for all those in struggle against injustice, and a forum for all the movements. Help it become this by joining in.

Farewell to *DA*

Jim Percy wrote in the last issue of *DA* (December 11, 1990), "An end and a beginning. Goodbye to Direct Action":

> With this issue, the second series of *Direct Action* comes to an end. In the new year, its human and financial resources will be turned to aiding the production of the new *Green Left* weekly.
>
> Resurrected in 1970, *DA* carried on the proud militant traditions of the Wobblies' *Direct Action* of World War I – against war, for union solidarity, for democratic rights.
>
> Series two, number one, appeared at the height of the Vietnam War. We have reproduced its cover on this issue, changing only the labels on the 'needles' – and not all of them. Uncle Sam then was shooting up at the rest of the world's expense. Twenty years later, he's still doing it.
>
> In spite of all the changes of the last 20 years – the defeat of the US and Australia in Vietnam, the fall of Stalinism in Eastern Europe and the USSR, the peace initiatives and limitations of nuclear weapons – things are basically as we found them 20 years ago.
>
> The world has not been transformed into the sort of place that the

young editors, writers and sellers of *DA* aspired to: a world free of want, injustice, war, racism and sexism. Those tasks remain to be tackled …

Because the world was not transformed, was the work then pointless? Not at all! Firstly, we reclaimed the lessons of the past. The Marxist tradition in this country was weak, dominated by the Stalinism of the Communist Party of Australia through much of the last 60 years.

The lessons of the past have to be won again by each new generation – especially where the continuity is weak or broken. *Direct Action* has been a necessary part of doing this, whether done well or not so well.

We may not have been able to emulate the great original thinkers of the past; that wasn't the point. Our fight was to recover what had been lost – a fight carried out in difficult circumstances. They are not better today, but the changes to us and to circumstances make the next stage in this process of recovery, rediscovery and renewal more likely to succeed. There is less in the way.

But just as we recover the lessons, we need to learn new things and say things differently. There are also change and growth, not just cyclical repetition. The world is different, and one of the lessons re-won is the importance of flexibility of language, form, style – the need to recognise real motion and not be fazed by the form and initial confusion of new developments. *Direct Action* has brought us to this point.

It has also been an inseparable part of the struggle during the past 20 years, making a modest but real contribution to progressive political activity in uncountable spheres. That alone is a source of pride, of satisfaction, and the main yardstick of measurement.

Setting up *GLW* structure

We held a national teleconference on November 18, 1990, to start the process in earnest, with participants from nine cities, both DSP members and independents.

I welcomed comrades to the teleconference (a much more pricey and complicated process than it is today) and outlined the process up to this point: the letter signed by Allen Myers and myself on June 21, the broader leaflet with signatories from all states, the first and second drafts of a structure proposal, setting up an unincorporated association, with shares, and votes proportional to the contribution of shares, and a board of management elected by both an AGM and regional meetings.

I proposed that if we had agreement on the principles of the structure, we commission a lawyer (Peter Connor, a former SWP member then practising as a lawyer in Wangaratta) to draw up a detailed constitution. We would have a further phone hook-up when the constitution was drawn up to our satisfaction to ratify it.

On the name, I proposed "Green Left". It would accurately describe what the paper would stand for. Other alternatives were not popular, or already taken, or too nondescript.

On November 26 I wrote to Peter Connor from Melbourne: "The basic principles for organising the association to produce the new paper were agreed upon at a national phone hook-up on November 18. These were the draft proposals for structure, Version 2, that I faxed to you. The discussion also agreed on a name for the paper …

"You can now put together a constitution along those lines, with the following extra details: Make provisions for the lapsing of inactive memberships. We thought it best to link it to a subscription, and for quorums for AGMs and regional meetings of shareholders, make them low."

On December 13, we received a letter from Peter Connor enclosing the first draft of the constitution (and his account for $1,560!).

The $50 per share arrangement served several purposes – supporters felt they were actively participating, it raised some money, and it meant *GL* was protected from a hostile takeover. DSP and Resistance members were the ones likely to contribute money for multiple shares; non-members rarely contributed more than the $50.

An interim executive committee was set up to coordinate production until the first AGM of the association. The governing body would be a national board of management, which would elect a national executive committee to run the association in between meetings of the board.

Green Left Weekly launched

The first issue of our new internal bulletin, the Activist, was produced in January 1991, with two articles outlining progress and plans for the new paper: "*Green Left*: Where things stand" by John Percy and "Getting going on *Green Left*" by Lisa Macdonald.

I reported on the results of the November teleconference that decided on a name for the paper and the basic principles of the association that would produce it. We'd produced a draft constitution, a brochure publicising the paper and two newsletters to sponsors, and had worked out many of the organisational details for subscriptions, advertising etc.

We produced a pilot issue of *Green Left Weekly*, number 0, during the first anti-Gulf War demos, with a limited number of pages to hand out free to publicise the paper and to campaign against the war. We printed 30,000.

The first issue, number 1, was dated February 18, 1991, and the list of sponsors had grown longer.

GL structure and sponsors

Until we had our AGM, we functioned with an interim *GL* executive, consisting of Rod Webb, Reihana Mohideen, Angela Matheson, Allen Myers, Lisa Macdonald, Dick Nichols, John Percy and Pat Gorman.

The February 18, 1991, meeting of the executive heard that the first print run would be 10,100, of which 2,800 were for complimentary mailouts, 5,500 for street sales, 1,000 for newsagent distribution and 650 for subscriptions. Newsagent distribution was being arranged in metropolitan Sydney and Melbourne, plus major rural centres in Victoria and NSW through Wrapaway. Of the $1.50 cover price, we got 50 percent, the newsagent got 25 percent and the distributor got 25 percent.

The March 6, 1991, meeting of the interim executive heard a report on finances and distribution. Income up to February 28 was $22,000 – shares, $8,000; subs, $10,2000, fund appeal, $3,500, which meant we were running on a deficit of about $2,000 per week.

Distribution was street sales, just over 4,000; newsagents in Sydney and Canberra, 1,050; complimentary mailout 1,500. We averaged street sales of 10 per hour. Subscriptions were coming in at a rate of six to 10 per day – about 700 to that point.

The list of overseas correspondents we began with was: Boris Kagarlitsky, Renfrey Clarke, Alexander Popov (Moscow); Peter Gellert (Mexico); Mike Karadjis (Athens); Tamas Krausz (Budapest); Mary Merkenich (Germany); Steve Painter, Tracy Sorensen (Prague).

By June the international correspondents were: Peter Annear (Prague), Renfrey Clarke (Moscow), Ben Cohen (London), Daniel Faber (Boston), Will Firth (Berlin), Peter Gellert (Mexico City), Boris Kagarlitsky (Moscow), Mike Karadjis (Athens), Tamas Krausz (Budapest), Keith Locke (Auckland), Sally Low (Prague), Mary Merkenich (Germany), Adam Novak (Prague), Jim O'Connor (Santa Cruz, USA), Alexander Popov (Moscow), Ian Powell (Wellington), Satendra Prasad (Fiji), David Robie (Auckland), Robert Went (Amsterdam).

Design

Philippa Skinner designed the masthead, cover and layout for the first few issues before moving to Brisbane. With the extra colour available on some pages, it had a significantly different look to the old *DA*. Susan Mackie took over and designed most of the covers in 1991, and oversaw the layout.

The quality of cartoons and the contributions of cartoonists were a huge step up from *DA*. Heinrich Hinze provided excellently drawn and politically sharp regular cartoons. (This was the pen name of David Pope, who was in the IS current, and is now the regular cartoonist for the *Canberra Times*.) Issue No. 2 used a Hinze cartoon for the front cover, "Why the US fears peace".

A more regular cartoonist was Chris Kelly, who was prolific as well as talented. We sometimes had three of his cartoons in an issue. He also produced a series of cartoons called "Banana Republic".

Other cartoonists brightening *GLW*'s pages included Jim Cane, Ange and Horacek. Very professional photographs were provided by David Brazil, who also wrote some environment articles. I created some crossword puzzles.

Green Left also had an expanded number of advertisements, some paid for at a modest price, others exchanges with other publications or organisations. In the first months there were ads for *Capitalism, Nature, Socialism;* "Night out for Nicaragua" at the Melbourne University Union; Folkways Records; New Era Bookshop, featuring Indonesian subjects; and a four-page newsletter insert, "Netnews", prepared by Visionary Media for Pegasus Networks.

There were also two *GLW* benefits: a Melbourne Workers Theatre production of *Black Cargo* and an Adelaide Junction Theatre Company performance of *Boots*.

Range of independent contributors

GLW had a regular column focusing on women's issues, "… and ain't I a woman?" written by Sally Low before she headed off to Prague, and by Tracy Sorensen after she returned. Kevin Healy, from the Melbourne ALP left, who had a regular radio program on 3CR and was a keen participant in the new paper project, had a satirical column "The week that was". There was a "Viewpoint" column, featuring a very wide range of non-DSP members who were invited to contribute. Jose Ramos-Horta wrote the column for *GLW*'s first issue.

Some ex-members, such as Rod Webb and Ken Davis, contributed articles. Dozens of other independents did so, vastly increasing our environmental coverage. Some became regular contributors. Angela Matheson became involved on the committee and a regular writer on a wide range of topics. Robin Osborne was another who wrote useful features, including an early one called "The greening of aid".

GLW of May 22 carried a review by Phil Shannon of Anita Gordon and David Suzuki's book *It's a Matter of Survival*. From then on he became a very regular reviewer for the next few decades.

DSP comrades were still overwhelmingly the backbone for the paper's sales and finances. If there was an event involving a large number of DSP members, such as a National Committee meeting over a weekend, we generally skipped an issue because the sales would drop too much. It seemed also that most of the independents had less staying power. Probably the novelty wore off, and they didn't have the understanding our members did of the importance of continuing the project.

Protests against Gulf War

Our first issue was 24 pages and had a cover headline: "Stop the War. Act Now!" Inside, "Just say no!" was a round-up of the antiwar demonstrations around Australia, and there was a centrespread of colour photos: Hobart 800 on January 14; Wollongong 1,000 on January 13; Newcastle a vigil of 250 on January 15, a church service of 600 and a peace concert of 1,000; Brisbane 3,000 on January 15; Perth a January 15 vigil of 400-500, a prayer service of 1,000 and a march of 900 when the war began. Melbourne on January 19 had 50,000; Sydney on January 19 40-50,000; Adelaide 15-20,000; Brisbane 6,000; Perth 4,000; Hobart 3-5,000; Lismore 2,000; Darwin 500. Several hundred people demonstrated outside Pine Gap, and there were actions also in Townsville, Wagga, Gosford, Albury Wodonga, Bendigo and Ballarat.

"On the following weekend, there were further large demonstrations in Melbourne, Brisbane, Sydney, Adelaide and Wollongong; on January 31 in Hobart and on February 2 in Newcastle and Perth." Tracy Sorensen reported on the "Massive opposition to war across Europe", in Germany, Britain, Greece, Italy, Netherlands, Belgium, Spain, Czechoslovakia, describing the demonstrations, opinion polls and reports of actions.

But some of the individuals who had been in the forefront of the campaign against the Vietnam War had gone off the rails. *GLW*'s second issue carried "The Gulf War and the Vietnam War. An open letter to Bernie Taft and Albert Langer", in which Dick Nichols replied to their recently expressed support for the US-led war against Iraq.

Analysing Eastern Europe

The issues of *GLW* from February 25 to March 12 carried a three-part interview with Boris Kagarlitsky that Steve Painter and Jim Percy had conducted in Rome at the end of December. A Marxist theoretician and sociologist, Kagarlitsky was a member of the Supreme Soviet and also a member of a small Marxist group, the Socialist Party of the Soviet Union.

The articles summarised Kagarlitsky as arguing "that Mikhail Gorbachev is already well advanced on a course of political self-destruction, and in fact that the Gorbachev project was doomed from the beginning because it was never anything more than a process of bureaucratic self-reform 25 years too late".

GLW of March 27, 1991, carried five articles by Peter Annear in Prague: "Czechoslovakia trades arms for oil", "Tensions rise as Albania approaches elections", "Emigres discover bitter taste of Western life" (about Albanian emigres in Italy), "Tirana, Washington resume relations" and "Eastern Europe. Can unions find a role?"

Three articles by Peter in the April 24 *GLW* were: "Hungary moves toward 'white capitalism'", "Czechoslovak economy takes a nosedive" and "Life grows hard in the world of commodities" (also about Czechoslovakia). In the same issue Renfrey Clarke, in the Soviet Union, interviewed Dmitry Solonnikov, the editor of the Leningrad youth journal *Noyaya Gazeta* on the topic: "Soviet youth: where are they going?"

GLW of May 1 carried two articles by Adam Novak, "Czech rightists stage their largest demonstration" and "Left meets in Bratislava", one by Peter Annear, "Strikers shake Serbian regime" and one by Sally Low "Young greens organise in Romania".

Laszlo Andor and Peter Annear wrote a three-part series on Hungary in the May 8-May 22 issues, "The end of 'goulash communism'".

The May 8 issue also carried "European environmentalists seek 'third way'" by Sally Low and a report by Adam Novak on a meeting of the International Union of Students that relaunched the previously Moscow-aligned organisation as an independent and decentralised organisation.

In the *GLW* of May 15, Adam Novak and Peter Annear reported "Czechoslovak privatisation hits snags", and Renfrey Clarke described "Increasing chaos in Soviet economy". Sally Low reported in the May 22 *GLW* on the first all-German convention of the Greens, and Will Firth wrote, "The Elbe: from a sewer back to a river?"

April 1991 DSP NC

Our new paper was a great success. At the April 1-3, 1991, DSP NC, in my party-building report, I was able to note that DSP branch sales of *Green Left Weekly* had increased by a factor of 2.4 compared with the average *Direct Action* sales in 1990.

That NC report also noted the final issue of *Tribune*, scheduled to appear that day, and their plan to produce their own new paper, the *Broad Left Weekly*. Another competitor of *Green Left* was *Frontline*, a monthly freebie produced in Melbourne, which had financial backing from some left unions, edited by David Spratt.

Other reports at the NC were: "The Crisis in the Soviet Union and the World Socialist Movement"; "Revolution and Counter-Revolution in Eastern Europe"; "The New Recession and Australian Politics"; "Green Politics Today"; "Women's Liberation and Socialism"; "The DSP's International Work"; "Finances and *Green Left*"; "Building Resistance".

We also decided to elect a smaller National Executive. It previously had 14 members, almost half of the NC of 30. We were now planning to have more frequent NC meetings and so did not require such a large NE. The new NE of six was Jim Percy, Pat Brewer, Doug Lorimer, Reihana Mohideen, Dick Nichols and John Percy.

We also set up several other committees to lead different areas: a Publications Committee, a Secretariat, a Finance Committee and an International Committee.

June 1991 DSP NC

The next DSP NC was held June 8-9, 1991. Reports were: "International Politics after the Gulf War"; "Economic Slump and the Working Class Movement in Australia"; "Party Perspectives"; "Party Position on Organising Exclusive Social Events"; "Balance Sheet of *Green Left Weekly*"; "Finances"; and "Our Priorities in the Social Movements".

Jim Percy's party perspectives report began by noting that it was a situation of some defeats and difficulty for the left. It was a period of shock for comrades after the Gorbachev and perestroika hopes, especially in the context of the Gulf War. This followed on the disappointments of the previous 12 years – the turn, where we had expectations of the working class moving into action, and the regroupment policies that hadn't eventuated, 1982-83 with the open party-building method, the NDP, the Charter process, the SPA and hopes for a Green party. But we were still here, so we must have been doing something right. Still, there was an ideological, political crisis, a crisis of confidence.

The lack of organisational and political alternatives was the key question. This was the first period for some time in which the party had declined (by 20 percent), so we couldn't do everything we wanted to, and we had to take stock of the '80s.

There were positive features of where the party was: We were more mature politically and tactically; we had a good national spread; we had a solid leadership team; we were younger, still with the Resistance advantage; we'd thought about organisational questions and were able to be flexible if necessary; the relationship of forces with others on the left was good.

Our problems, resulting from our course in the '80s and the retreat of the working class, included: a lack of purpose and confidence on the party question itself; a loosening of the norms of party membership, a backsliding; a political education in the party that was clearly uneven, even among leading comrades (we'd done so much in the mass movements that basic organisational questions and traditions were now the property of too few of us); a morale problem in parts of the party (we were all disappointed that the '80s roads hadn't succeeded); the limits of our weight in the mass movements, e.g. the trade unions; a financial crisis in the party. All the confusions and doubts in the movements and in the masses will find a reflection in the party, Jim said.

Thus we needed to set our goals, and the first question to answer was: do we want to remain a party or not, remain political or not? (Twenty percent of comrades had answered no!) But we remain revolutionaries; anything less than fundamental social change is a sick joke.

The second question was: *what sort* of party? Why a disciplined, democratic centralist party? Without cadre, Jim said, we couldn't achieve anything. A cadre party was necessary for training comrades. A cadre party was the only party able to resist bourgeois pressures. It needed to be fundamentally democratic, with one rule for all. If we didn't have a cadre party, we wouldn't get the party spirit that we needed in order to build. This concept was real, even if we were using new language in reaching out.

We were now making a *turn*, "moving the goalposts", Jim said, and going back to the past in some ways. Because we'd had no '80s breakthrough, our immediate perspectives were different. We had no expectation of uniting; it would be better less, but better. But that didn't mean getting any smaller; if we carried out our priorities, we could grow. But in any case, we needed this type of party.

Our central idea now was *GLW*. But if we are going back to party-building, why have a non-party paper? There were many reasons:

- It was the best tool for intervening in overlapping periods.
- From it, the DSP had gained prestige and influence.
- We'd had a big increase in DSP clip-offs coming in.
- The process of training via selling was identical with *DA*.
- It was increasing our agitation and propaganda skills.
- It related to all milieus, and could be a substitute for mass work when there weren't many opportunities for that.
- We didn't have a dogmatic prescription about what Lenin recommended.
- If we had continued with *DA*, we would have had to go monthly.
- We were taking a big part of the space for the CPA, New Left Party and its Broad Left Weekly (called *Broadside* when it appeared).
- In our competition with IS, *GLW* was hurting them badly.

The new paper was in its early days. We'd probably have to do some future adjusting, with more trade union and socialism articles. We shouldn't think that *GLW* was not us, a substitute. *GLW* events were organised by the DSP and Resistance. We were not trying to give *GLW* a separate profile, or to create an alternate party.

GLW was a winner, Jim said, one we hoped would become a central financial institution. Our central task was to get all members involved in it as their main political work. *GLW* hung in the balance; it would need the turn by the party for *GLW* to survive. This had become a criterion of leadership in the party.

GLW sales were central. But we needed a return to other party institutions also, or *GLW* would be wasted: forums, our educational program, pamphlets, our own profile, our own political culture, a return of that party building profile.

We were making a correction to our 1986 report: we were *not* making the broadest intervention in the mass struggles of the day; if we did that, we wouldn't achieve our goals, we'd decline. So *all* comrades had to prioritise; there could be no freelancing.

We were also making an adjustment in regard to the Green Alliance or a Green party. This was not a big priority, more a rearguard action, and our hope was alliances, not a Green party.

Other big things we had ahead were building the Resistance conference and the Socialist Scholars Conference.

Great response to *Green Left Weekly*

In my report on the balance sheet of *Green Left Weekly*, I outlined what a great move it had been. "Situate *Green Left Weekly* in relation to previous years, in relation to *DA*, in relation to other left papers, and in relation to the general trend of left politics in this period."

"As we've stressed this year, and as Jim's report yesterday reiterated, *Green Left Weekly* is central to all our projections in this period. It's central to our key party-building needs.

"It's essential for training new comrades in sales, in writing for the paper, in developing politically, in educating them as well as the much bigger readership.

"It's essential for increasing our political influence, and for contributing to the changing balance of forces on the left.

"It's essential for intervening in the green milieu. And in a political period like this, which will be very much a propaganda period, it's essential for getting out basic propaganda.

"It's achieved a lot for us already …

"In nearly every respect it's succeeded – the look, the content, the sales, the political impact, the reaching out to new forces, both to the green milieu and also other movement and left activists."

New sponsors kept coming in. The first public call for the paper had been signed by Allen Myers and myself and 22 independent sponsors. "Now we have listed 183 independent sponsors in Australia, and 64 DSP or Resistance members, and 13 independent international correspondents as well as five DSP international correspondents."

We had expected to distribute it mainly ourselves, but independent supporters were taking bundles that currently amounted to about 140.

"So our balance sheet so far is that *Green Left Weekly* has succeeded in becoming a broad paper that reaches out to people we would otherwise not have been able to contact … And although it's not specifically a party paper, there isn't very much that it doesn't do for us."

Our political line was coming through, and had to continue to do so. "Comrades will judge *how much* a party paper it is. And we know that comrades are responsible for more than 95 percent of the sales, and most of the fund drive organising, and the majority of the financial support. We won't get the necessary enthusiasm and support and activity from comrades if they're not 100 percent happy with the paper, if they don't feel that the party's political line comes through."

I added, "We have to continue to try to find ways of projecting some of the economic/industrial/working class/unemployment type issues, in features, news coverage, debate and on the cover.

"And we have to find a way to inject the basic educational material, educating on socialism, the fundamental questions." One suggestion was a regular column. And we still needed the extras, like our party literature on stalls and, most importantly, a recruiting leaflet.

I discussed the *GLW* structure, plans for the AGM, constitution and using the next stage of setting up the structure as an "opportunity to reach out further, as well as consolidating our current supporters".

The main section of the report was on the sales drive, and an extensive range of graphs was distributed at the NC:

- Average branch bundles and actual sales
- Total Paid Distribution during GLW Sales Drive (From issue 9 to 14, averaged over 4,000, and went below only in the first week.)
- DSP and Resistance sales compared (pretty even, but Resistance ahead in four of six weeks)
- Number of sellers each issue (DSP, Resistance and non-members)
- Print run and paid sales (print run 5,000-5,500)
- Average sales for drive in various areas
- Average sales rates for drive, by branch and nationally (8.8/hour)
- Sellers by branch
- Top sellers for sales drive, by branch (overall it was: John Percy 561 [Sydney], Jorge Jorquera 443 [Melbourne], Reihana Mohideen 428 [Sydney], Sean Healy 413 [Brisbane])
- Branch efforts compared, in average hours sold by DSP members
- DSP and non-DSP *GLW* input compared (slightly more for the DSP, but not significantly)
- Letters in *GLW* each issue (average of five, more recently up to 10)

I outlined some lessons of the drive, especially the fact that leadership is essential. "Experienced party comrades will have to lead, train, organise and set good examples for the newer comrades to follow."

I observed that the sales rate averaging nearly 9 per hour didn't vary much from issue to issue. The Resistance sales rate was generally about 2 sales an hour below the party sales rate, partly due to where comrades sell, but mostly reflecting the benefits of skills and experience.

One failure of the drive was on the number of comrades selling, with DSP averaging only 73 and Resistance 80 each week. We also needed to add the total number of hours sold as a major feature of our sales campaign. "For this drive, we averaged a total of 354.5 hours sold each issue … We know if we put in another 100 hours selling each week, we'd reach our 4,000 goal."

I stressed the important role of Resistance, and discussed other ideas and areas of sales – non-members, pub runs, cinemas, factories and the individual sellers competition.

The NC projected a 10-week subscription drive for 1,000 new subs, with a special introductory offer of $10 for 12 issues. Prizes were planned for the top three sub sellers.

We also initiated a system of *GLW* drops, in boxes at movement centres, newsagents etc., with display trays with money boxes attached.

We had a regular campaign newssheet, "Campaign 4,000". And we had a new, more comprehensive sales reporting form for branches.

"To conclude, I'd ask comrades to step back and put in perspective this wonderful achievement. It's a tremendous paper, a fantastic weapon, an opportunity we shouldn't squander.

"Step back and realise that already, branches are taking bundles of almost 4,000. Our actual sales are over 3,000. We have a paid circulation of over 4,000. Compare this with our experience with *DA*. We never really got that high. Even in the early days, *DA* was a monthly, and we were selling during the campaign against the Vietnam War. In November 1975, we hit 5,000 once. And in 1978, during the special sales weeks, we hit 6,000 twice."

Achieving the goals of 4,000 branch sales and 1,000 new subscriptions would guarantee the success of *GLW*. "But even more importantly, through this we'll consolidate the DSP, train new cadres, bolshevise the party. And we'll have a strong weapon and a strong party to take us through the fairly difficult period ahead."

Placing *GLW* in newsagents met with limited success. The financial returns weren't good enough. Most newsagents just buried *GL* under other magazines, and we weren't in a position to pay for expensive advertising. *GLW* 5 listed where it was now available from newsagents in NSW and the ACT, and *GLW* 7 listed where it was available in Victorian newsagents.

In the Activist we printed my balance sheet of the *Green Left* sales drive, largely based on my NC report. We had almost tripled our distribution compared with *DA*.

July 1991 Resistance conference

The Resistance national conference was held in Melbourne, July 13-15; more than 200 attended. The theme was: "Against their order – a new world for all".

Feature talks were given by Jim Percy and Peter Camejo. Jorge Jorquera, the Melbourne Resistance organiser, outlined the international political situation. Tracy Sorensen described the current situation in Eastern Europe. Anne O'Callaghan, Sydney Resistance organiser, discussed Resistance's response to attacks on workers and the poor in Australia.

AKSI

A movement for democracy and against the Suharto dictatorship was gradually forming in Indonesia, and we stepped up our solidarity efforts. In the March 20, 1991, *GLW,* Max Lane reported: "During the last 12 months, groups have been formed to build support for the increasingly active pro-democracy movement in Indonesia. Called AKSI (Aksi Solidaritas Indonesia – Indonesian Solidarity Action), they have been established in Sydney, Canberra and Melbourne, and it is hoped that a group may be formed soon in Perth.

"To help keep activists and other interested people informed, AKSI is publishing a 12-page bulletin of news and reports of the progressive movement in Indonesia.

"In the first issue, published this month, there are articles on the anti-Gulf War protests in Indonesia and a translation of the Indonesian Antiwar Committee's major statement opposing US interventionism – and also calling for referenda in Indonesia's own occupied areas, East Timor and West Papua."

In the May 1 *GLW,* Max Lane reported that four new political/democracy groupings had formed in Indonesia in March.

In *GLW* 12, Steve Robson reviewed *Footsteps,* the third volume in the Buru Quartet by Pramoedya Ananta Toer, translated by Max Lane.

In the October 2, 1991, issue, Greg Adamson reported: "Around 70 people attended the first national conference of the Indonesian solidarity group Aksi. Aksi committee members from Sydney, Canberra, Melbourne and Adelaide attended. Brisbane and Perth were also represented, although groups are yet to be established." The conference decided on campaigns to free imprisoned Indonesian students; to defend the island of Siberut from destruction by palm plantations and transmigration; to oppose destructive tourist development; to build ties to Indonesian trade unions; to demand that Australia admit refugees from West Papua; and to expose harmful practices by Australian businesses in Indonesia.

Environmental Youth Alliance

Issues like uranium mining and protection of forests against destructive logging were spurring the growth of environmental organisations. The idea for the Environmental Youth Alliance came from David Suzuki's visit to Australia in

1989. Resistance members were enthusiastic about EYA, and the very first issue of *GLW* carried an article by Patricia Corcoran, "Young green campers plot to save planet", about an EYA camp scheduled for the following week near Minto in NSW.

GLW 12 reported on EYA's planned national conference in Melbourne, March 29- April 1, 1991. The May 1 issue carried "Young environmentalists take on Canberra: Campaigning against resource insecurity", in which Peter Boyle interviewed activists in Melbourne EYA.

National Greens Party in formation

The cover of the April 17 *GLW* asked, "Towards a green party?" Inside, Steve Painter described "Varied views on national green party", quoting green economist Rob White, Bob Brown, Tony Harris of the Sydney Greens, Canberra environmentalist Sid Walker, Maurice Sibelle, coordinator of the Green Alliance campaign in the Brisbane city council elections (and a DSP member), Sydney environmentalist Susan Campbell and Tasmanian academic Robyn Eckersley.

Our concern was that prominent leaders of various green groups would set up a top-down Green Party structure that would exclude control by the membership and whose politics varied little from those of Labor and the Coalition except for a few pro-environment policies.

In the *GLW* of April 24, Steve Painter wrote two commentaries on what was happening. "What's intended by May meeting of greens?" explained that "Five individuals have called a national meeting in Sydney on May 18-19 to discuss setting up a national green party". The five – Bob Brown, Senator Jo Vallentine (Greens WA), Drew Hutton (Rainbow Alliance, Brisbane), Hall Greenland (Sydney Greens) and Steve Brigham (Illawarra Greens) – had planned a meeting of "between 30 and 40" people, heavily weighted towards the more conservative side of the movement. Steve Painter's other article, "Behind the rush to a national green party", extensively quoted Lisa Macdonald from the Western Suburbs Greens in Sydney. She pointed out that a major concern of the five appeared to be excluding members of existing parties from whatever new structure emerged: "This would lock out members of the Democrats, the ALP, the Democratic Socialist Party and all other parties, regardless of their commitment to green politics …

"Of even greater concern than the attempt to arbitrarily lock out members of other parties is the attempt to impose a patently top-down process on the green movement. A party declared by a hand-picked gathering organised by a self-appointed elite is unlikely to win the united support of the green movement."

"Macdonald adds", the article said, "that the timing for a national party is wrong. 'The long delay in forming a green party in Australia has placed this matter on the agenda at a rather unfortunate time, when mass political activity is at a low ebb.

"'This makes it unlikely that large numbers of people would join and actively work for the party, and that would leave it susceptible to the sort of parliamentarist degeneration that struck down the West German Greens at the last elections.'"

The calling of NSW state elections caused the national meeting to be postponed to August 3-4. The *GLW* of May 22, which reported the postponement, also printed a comment by Barrie Griffiths, the editor of the newsletter of the Green Alliance Network, "an informal network based in Singleton NSW", titled "Time for a Green Party?"

"Recent proposals for a national green party are a worry. Anticipated for some time by Graham Richardson, adept at handling peak environment groups, the proposal was put to the Ecopolitics Conference last month by imported prominent green Jonathan Porritt, in support of Bob Brown and Janet Powell", Griffiths wrote.

"Brown is talking about forming a national party and then merging with the Democrats. He didn't say what mandate he, and whoever else is involved in these discussions, feel they have to speak or act on behalf of whom.

"A very significant percentage of those who could be counted on to support a third force would be alienated by an initiative from a few prominent 'green politicians' towards a centralised structure; many others by the perceived exclusive emphasis on green issues, by the very name, by the lack even of consultation, let alone participation, in the process from the outset."

Griffiths concluded: "A move to establish a centralised party structure paying lip-service to grassroots consultation would be a disaster. Bob Brown suggests views be sent to him to be fed into these current discussions. Until we have more satisfactory mechanisms, I hope he gets lots of feedback."

A dozen or so Green candidates stood in the NSW election. *GLW* presented profiles of the candidates in its May 15 and May 22 issues.

The June 12 issue reprinted a May 24 letter from the Green Alliance of South Australia to the conveners of the proposed meeting to form a national green party: "The Green Alliance (South Australia) is interested in current moves towards forming a national green party. However we are worried that the current initiatives come apparently from a small number of 'prominent green personalities', implying a centralised and hierarchical structure, lacking the grassroots support needed for effective integration of environmental issues into the political arena ...

"A successful national green party can best be created by building on green groups with a track record in local and regional activism and political action. Decisions as to its structure and policies should be made as the result of wide consultation. A basic tenet of the green movement is commitment to diversity, inclusiveness, broad participation and non-hierarchical structures. We feel that in the formation of a national green party these principles should not be compromised in the interests of expediency."

The letter explained further: "So we are concerned not only that the South Australian Green Alliance has not been consulted about the proposed party, but that decisions are being made which appear to exclude a number of specifically 'green' and other related groups from active participation. This will limit the effectiveness of the party, not only in terms of grassroots support, but in the eyes of the still-to-be-convinced public, who will see it as 'just another party' …

"We therefore expect to be consulted about any further developments so that we can participate in the formation of a national green party. We are circulating copies of this letter to other interested groups."

In the following *GLW,* June 19, "The week in green politics" updated developments on a national green party, reporting objections from groups sidelined by the five "conveners". Under the subheading "Tasmanian second thoughts?", the same column reported: "Hall Greenland, one of the five 'conveners' of the proposed national meeting, reported to a meeting of the Sydney Greens that the Tasmanian green independents had recently decided to withdraw from the national green party process with a view to joining the Australian Democrats instead. It was reported that the Greens (WA) convinced the Tasmanians to reconsider on the proviso that the formation of a national green organisation proceed in some way as a stepping stone towards an eventual merger with the Democrats."

In the June 26 *GLW,* Steve Painter reported: "Senator Jo Vallentine has suggested cancellation of the proposed August 3-4 national meeting to discuss formation of a green party. The suggestion is contained in a June 17 letter to green groups and individuals."

"The latest change of plan", Steve wrote, "appears to be due to green groups' rejection of the conveners' proposals for decision-making and attendance at the national meeting. In response to the conveners' proposal for a 'broad-based' meeting of 30 or 40 participants, many groups responded that they would prefer a meeting open to all greens …

"It seems the August 3-4 meeting will now be replaced with a gathering open only to groups and individuals amenable to the five conveners. It is likely a criterion for participation will be non-acceptance of members of other parties in a green party.

"This in itself might be a difficult rule to enforce consistently, given that one of the conveners, Drew Hutton, belongs to the Rainbow Alliance, a party-type formation which has contested elections and whose Brisbane members at least appear to caucus before meetings …"

The "caucus" referred to a Rainbow Alliance stack of a meeting of the Queensland Green Network on June 16, reported by Maurice Sibelle and Karen Fletcher in the same issue, at which "members of the Rainbow Alliance, supported by members of the Australian Democrats and the New Left Party, split the green political movement in this city by moving to exclude all members of political parties from moves to form a national green party". Steve Painter reported in the July 3 *GLW* that the five conveners had blamed the cancellation of their planned meeting on the DSP, complaining that "most of the responses have come from registered groups where the influence of the Democratic Socialist Party (DSP) is very high (among them being Western Suburbs, Eastern Suburbs, South Sydney, NSW Green Alliance, Victorian Green Alliance, and ACT Green Democratic Alliance)".

The issue also carried a letter from Jim Percy, answering a letter from Ian Murrell in the previous issue: "Ian Murrell suggests that the DSP is in favour of a Green Alliance at this stage of building a national green movement. He is correct. The recent fiasco of an attempt to ram a national party structure on to all of the very loose and emerging movement indicates that this is the wiser course. And yes, we do see the Green Alliance experience in Brisbane as a positive example."

What we saw as the immediate way forward was indicated by the July 10 *GLW*'s report that "NSW Green Alliance activist Janet Parker is circulating a proposal for an Alternative Green Network". The proposal contained nine points:

- A provisional framework to nurture ties and dialogue between existing organisations and individuals.
- Minimal agreement around the four basic principles of the German Greens: ecological sustainability, social and economic justice, grassroots democracy and non-violence.
- A network among all existing and future green parties, movements, alliances and other organisations. This network would encourage unity and accept diversity.
- Acceptance that there can be no monopoly of green ideas or the green name.
- A national clearinghouse or newsletter "that would act as a forum for exchange of views and information".
- Encouragement of green political, social and electoral

activity.
* Regional and national conferences as necessary to exchange views, coordinate work and hopefully develop closer and more organic links among affiliates.
* Freedom of affiliates to initiate local, regional or national activities.
* Funding of AGN activities by subscription or voluntary contributions from affiliates.

The same *GLW* reported:

> The Democratic Socialist Party has replied to Senator Jo Vallentine's recent letter raking over the Nuclear Disarmament Party controversy of 1985. In a letter sent to green organisations last week, DSP national secretary Jim Percy said "it was Senator Vallentine and Peter Garrett who tried to ram their agendas through" the non-binding, consultative Melbourne conference of the NDP at which the split occurred. "They failed in spite of their high personal profiles. People were just sick of the star system of politics … The decision of Jo Vallentine and Peter Garrett to crash the NDP against the wall of a media anti-communist barrage was egotistical and destructive in the extreme."
>
> Percy is also critical of Senator Vallentine's relationship with the Greens (WA): "It's no accident that the constitution of the WA Greens offers no way of determining the activities of their parliamentary representatives. We stress here that the question is not the issue of 'wavering' of parliamentary reps … but the democratic empowerment of members …"
>
> Of recent moves for a national meeting on formation of a green party, the letter says: "What happened was a grab by part of the existing Green movement for domination and control of the agenda of any new national Green Party. That was clear from the first proposal of the five conveners."
>
> The letter adds that the latest attacks on the DSP flow from the fact that its national organisation enables it to gather and disseminate information, breaking the monopoly of parliamentarians and their staff over this process. "It's certainly not good that the emerging Green movement does not have more centres of information … But it would be much worse off if we were to rely on what we got from the parliamentary apparatuses or the five conveners only."
>
> Percy adds that the DSP's commitment to green politics is

"fundamental", and if a party similar to the German Greens in its first
decade emerged here, "we would be part of it. There would be no need
for a separate DSP … but dissolving a party before the event and after
are two different things … the sort of party controlled by politicians that
pursue the old parliamentary wheeling and dealing game doesn't turn us
on and won't solve anything." …

The letter concluded that Senator Vallentine and "all others who see it that
way" have a right to "form their own party". But "the issues of politics and
democracy inside the five conveners' sort of party will not go away, with or
without the DSP", and "those of us who see it differently won't go away either.
The issues and philosophy are too big and too important to be anyone's exclusive prerogative."

Socialist Scholars Conference 1991

We publicised the second Socialist Scholars Conference with broadsheet lift-
outs in *GLW*. The conference was held July 18-21, 1991, at Melbourne University
High with the theme "Ecology, Socialism and Human Survival". Announced
international plenary speakers were Peter Camejo, Jim Anderton, Francisco
Nemenzo, Roem Topatimasang, Tamas Krausz, Ismael Momoniat, Mary Mellor
and Ernest Mandel (who unfortunately had to withdraw because of poor health).
    In the July 31 *GLW*, Lisa Macdonald wrote that the conference attracted
around 800 activists and academics. More than 100 people presented papers.
    "The conference closed with a plenary session addressed by a panel of
speakers on the subject 'Left politics: Where to now?'. Including Joe Camilleri
from the Rainbow Alliance, Louise Connor from the New Left Party, Ken Peak
from the Australian Democrats, Reihana Mohideen from the Democratic
Socialist Party and Ted Murphy from the Socialist Left faction of the ALP, this
panel provided a forum to develop the presently limited dialogue between the
main sections of the organised left in Australia."

GLW Association AGM

The *GLW* AGM was held on July 17, 1991, at 14 Anthony Street, Melbourne,
following my letter to shareholders on June 19 with a proposed agenda, and
after being advertised in GLW. Seventy-eight people attended.
    There was a progress report by John Percy, a finance report by Reihana
Mohideen, an editorial report by Allen Myers and a constitution report by John

Percy.

For election of the board of management, I proposed that the size be 40 and that there be 50 percent regional representation. I nominated 20 people who were elected by consensus.

I also moved that the interim executive committee and editor continue until the remaining 50 percent of the board was elected from the regions and could appoint a new executive committee and editor. That is – editor: Allen Myers; executive committee: Allen Myers, Reihana Mohideen, Pat Gorman, Rod Webb, John Percy, Dick Nichols, Lisa Macdonald, Angela Matheson. That was agreed.

On August 23, as *GLW* coordinator, I wrote to shareholders, enclosing the minutes of the AGM and a copy of the constitution that was adopted:

"There is a great demand for a paper such as ours in the smaller centres. The example of our most recent distributor, on Queensland's Gold Coast, shows what is possible. Ben is a 16 year old high school student who ordered a bundle of 15 of issue 24. Selling on the main street he'd sold out in half an hour, sorely regretting the four papers he'd given free to friends. For issue 25 he's ordered a bundle of 35! He's also arranged for three of the local newsagents to take *GLW* each week."

Conservative Greens adamant on proscription

In the *GLW* of August 7, 1991, Lisa Macdonald and Karen Fletcher wrote in "Top-down agenda set for green party":

"A national teleconference initiated from WA at short notice on July 30 decided to proceed with a top-down process towards formation of a green party, incorporating a NSW proposal for a national meeting on August 17-18 …

"The July 30 hook-up was called largely because the NSW proposal, contained in a letter circulated by Sydney activist Doug Hine, was not acceptable" to the organisations of Bob Brown and Jo Vallentine.

"While the NSW proposal made acceptance of some form of proscription a precondition for participation in the national meeting, it included several options other than total proscription, including the possibility of a sunset clause … This, apparently, was not acceptable."

Only total prescription was acceptable to the parliamentarians. Brown insisted that members of existing parties should not be allowed to participate in the August meeting; otherwise he'd withdraw.

"Also apparently unacceptable was the original NSW formulation that any national party should be based on local, autonomous, parties." Also, some of the original groups had been disinvited.

"Drew Hutton, one of the five self-appointed national 'conveners', told a recent meeting of the Brisbane-based Australian Green Working Group (AGWG) that the initial invitations were issued mistakenly by Doug Hine, who had 'little idea who the legitimate green groups are'. Hutton added that Hine and Sydney-based fellow national 'convener' Hall Greenland had issued invitations to 'loonies'."

"The July 30 teleconference included representatives from Brisbane, north Queensland, WA, Tasmania, Sydney, Illawarra, Lismore and the Hunter region. There were no participants from Victoria, South Australia, the Northern Territory or the ACT.

"It seems the August meeting will now consist of six delegates from Tasmania (one from each of five local groups and one to represent the parliamentarians), 13 from branches of the Greens (WA), 15 from NSW, two each from South Australia, Victoria and the ACT, one from the Northern Territory, and six from Queensland.

"The Victorian delegates are unlikely to include members of the Rainbow Alliance because, according to prominent member Harry van Moorst, there is ambivalence in the groups towards a green party ... [I]t's clear some greens are averse to including leftist elements in a green party."

"The week in green politics" in the same issue reported:

"Hall Greenland has resigned from the Sydney Greens. He was one of the founders of the group in 1984, and has been one of the five 'conveners' of attempts to call a national meeting on formation of a green party.

"In a letter sent to some members of the Sydney Greens, he complained of the group's rejection of attempts to proscribe the Democratic Socialist Party and said discussions on this and other matters had become unbearably tense.

"The resignation follows Greenland's announcement to a recent Sydney Greens meeting that he would stand on an Open Council ticket for the inner-Sydney Leichhardt Council elections. The Greens had already decided to run their own ticket and rejected moves by Greenland to have the decision reconsidered.

"Members say Greenland had not previously informed the group that he was considering standing on another ticket and had always given the impression that he would be part of a Greens ticket."

In *GLW* of August 21, 1991, Pat Brewer reported that the "repeatedly postponed" national green meeting had taken place August 18-19. Agreement to proscription was a condition of participation. The first day was entirely concerned with proscription. "While a decision to apply proscription to the meeting was adopted fairly early in the day, on a vote of 21-8 with one abstention, lengthy discussion continued, particularly on the possibility of a sunset clause ...

"Eventually, a vote of 15-6 with 6 abstentions adopted a motion on criteria for participation in the next national meeting:

"At the national level and as the basis for participation in the next national meeting, that there be proscription of members of other parties by February 18, 1992, in each of the categories – office bearers, delegates, voting, new members, members of other political parties from now on; and that delegates at that next national meeting are proscribed …

"Bob Brown and Judy Henderson, from the Denison Greens, argued that any proposal should incorporate fusion with the Democrats so that a strong third political force could emerge as quickly as possible.

"No decisions were taken on structure … Several delegates supported moves to deregister 'unsuitable' green parties."

"The week in green politics" of the August 21 issue also reported: "Further moves towards a merger between some greens and the Australian Democrats seem likely following a report in the August 17-18 *Australian* that Democrat senators are preparing a referendum on the question, and comments by Bob Brown that supporters of the Green Independents in Tasmania will also be polled. Brown said the Tasmanian ballot would canvas the idea of a national alliance, not a merger at state level."

The column also reported: "Meeting in Brisbane on August 18, the Queensland Green Network issued a statement that six representatives from Queensland to the August 17-18 meeting of greens in Sydney 'were not representatives of the QGN. They were representatives of the Australian Green Working Group. They were never elected at a meeting of QGN and should not be considered to have represented the views of QGN.'" Pat Brewer wrote an overview of process, "Two camps in the greens", in the August 28 *GLW*. She quoted Lisa Macdonald, who had been elected the representative of the Western Suburbs Greens to the August 17-18 meeting but barred from it, on the early July teleconference of the five "conveners":

"The purpose of this teleconference was to ensure a stack of the meeting, says Macdonald. 'Participants in this teleconference, with one exception, were all from groups with total or virtually total proscription. Instead of each group having one delegate, those groups on the teleconference raised their number of delegates – in the case of the Queensland group, it was raised to five. That's how the stack was established.

"'This self-selected teleconference excluded seven NSW green parties, all of Victoria, South Australia and the ACT. It was so important to set this agenda and establish the delegate imbalance that the teleconference went on for three hours and, according to Annabel Newbury from the WA Greens, cost $1200."

"The agenda itself was a joke. Proscription was set as the unchangeable first item, regardless of many delegates' protests that it was meaningless to discuss it in isolation. The issue is related to the structure and the form of accountability to be adopted."

Pat also quoted another delegate barred from the meeting: "Proscription is no guarantee against manipulation and hidden agendas, points out Sue Bolton, a delegate from the ACT who was barred from the meeting by the proscription vote. 'Backroom cliques, secret networks and self-appointed stars can manipulate, set the agenda and block decisions, can't they? An open, democratic and accountable process is the best guarantee against such worries.'

"'What is widely rumoured although never stated openly is that those who are pushing proscription are the leaders of the peak environment councils like the Australian Conservation Foundation and the Wilderness Society who want a 'reputable' green party to run 'candidates of note'. These organisation aren't noted for their own internal democracy and accountability …'

"Bolton says that the national procedure so far has been 'a violation of the autonomy of local groups and parties which is basic to the way green parties developed in many states. Tony Harris, the registered officer of the national green name electorally, has spread access to the name to any group that would abide by the four principles of the German Greens. This invitation was extended to members of other parties, other activist groups, other social movements, and it's how every group presently registered as green got access to the name.'"

The September 11 issue carried a reply by Marit Hegge, a participant in the August 17-18 meeting who supported proscription.

However, Democrats leader Senator Janet Powell was unexpectedly challenged and replaced by the party's National Executive. Pat Brewer reported in the September 4 *GLW* that the challenge "appears to have set back plans for early electoral unity between greens and Democrats".

Another setback for the proscriptionists was the situation in WA. Frank Noakes reported in the September 18 *GLW* that a meeting of the Greens (WA) had heard differing assessments of the Sydney meeting, including "strong opposition to full proscription of members of other political parties". At the meeting, it was also revealed that the Greens (WA) could not comply with the instructions from the Sydney meeting to introduce full proscription by February 1992 because of provisions in the group's constitution when it was formed as a merger of four other groups. "It now appears that the conveners of the national meetings may have to accept the Greens (WA) grandparent clause or form a national party without them."

GLW of September 25 reported that Bruce Welch had won election to the Marrickville council, becoming the first person to be elected as a Green in

Sydney, as the ALP lost control of the council for the first time in more than 30 years. Also elected to the council was Sonia Laverty from the New Left Party, who ran as a Community Independent. Doug Hine reported in the same issue: "Balmain Green activist Nick Masterman is likely to be the last candidate elected to Leichhardt Council, contributing to a strong progressive majority of 10 on the 12-member council. Masterman was originally to have headed the Sydney Greens ticket but stood as an ungrouped independent following the collapse of the ticket due to infighting."

In a separate article, "Sydney Greens divide", Hine wrote: "A proposal that Sydney Greens adopt a form of proscription was lost with five votes for, seven against and two abstentions". Those in favour of proscription were thought unlikely to attend the next meeting.

Progress on finances

The Socialist Scholars Conference helped us with our finances. DSP Finance Campaign Notes for August 1991 reported: "From the SSC fund raising activities itself over $4000 went towards the *Green Left Weekly* fund drive. Some of the highlights being over $1000 from the SSC book stall which went towards Melbourne's fund drive, around $800 from the Melbourne DSP Open House, $1000 from the conference dinner towards the Sydney fund drive, and around $1300 profit from the catering distributed amongst Melbourne, Adelaide, Brisbane, Canberra and Perth. Meanwhile the Resistance conference catering made a profit of some $1750 for Melbourne, Adelaide and Brisbane branches, with Resistance making some money out of the conference as a whole."

The notes also reported on progress in increasing branch sustainers to the national office, which the June NC had proposed increasing by $2 per member. "The projection is that all branches aim to achieve this $2 increase per member by the beginning of September."

The Finance Campaign Notes for September concentrated on information and motivation for the *GLW* Fund Drive. One chart for the last four months showed that *GLW* bundle and subscription income ranged between $11,000 and 14,000 per month.

Cuba solidarity

Our ongoing Cuban solidarity mainly took the form of articles publicising the truth to counter the lies or the silence of the capitalist press. Some articles at this time were:

DA November 6, 1990: Susan Lazlo, "Cuba in a changing world. Economic problems and US threats"; Peter Reid, "Cuba's position on Middle East crisis"

GLW 1: Karen Wald in Havana, "Cuba goes green"

GLW 5: Greg Adamson, "Cuba faces old threats in a new world order"

GLW 20: Greg Adamson, "Tough times for revolutionary Cuba"

GLW 23: Karen Wald, "Mandela thanks Cuba for its solidarity"

GLW 29: Norm Dixon (Terry Townsend), "Cuba calls for US to close Guantanamo base"

GLW 30: Rosemary Evans, "Where the 'human face' survives"; John Mettam, "Cubans top at Pan American games"; Norm Dixon, "US troops out of Cuba. End the blockade!"

GLW 31: Inter Press International, "Washington planning aggression, says Cuba"; Pip Hinman, "Cuba solidarity conference", reporting on a planned Australia-Cuba Friendship Society conference; Norm Dixon "Growing opposition to US blockade of Cuba"

GLW 32: Norm Dixon, "US stepping up economic war against Cuba"

DSP-Resistance NC, October 1991

We held a joint National Committee meeting of the DSP and Resistance in October. Reports were: Party Building Perspectives for the 1990s; Fighting the New World Order; Australia at the Crossroads; Building the DSP; *Green Left Weekly* Progress; Building Resistance; Campuses; Ecological Work; High School Work; Indonesia; Green Movement and DSP Election Work; Decline and Fall of Stalinism; Party, Alliance and Movement.

Building the DSP report

"For the DSP and Resistance 1991 will be known as the year of *Green Left Weekly* as well as the year Stalinism was dealt a death blow", I stated in my Building the DSP report to the NC. I continued:

> Our balance sheet of the project must surely be that it's been fantastic. We'd have to record that it's been central to our success, to our very survival, this year, both politically and financially.
>
> Politically, it's been vital. Without it, we might have been tempted to beat a retreat into a small bunker, to return to a semi-sectarian existence.
>
> Having *Green Left Weekly* in this broad and ambitious form has been essential in helping us to understand the world …

> *Green Left Weekly* enabled us to reach out, in a period when the movements were even in a downturn. We've been able to influence a much wider milieu, we're talking to many new layers that we never reached before. We're in touch with many extra struggles, covering a larger number of issues.
>
> The role of *Green Left Weekly* in boosting the morale of all comrades, of making us feel excited about politics, has been invaluable.
>
> Financially, it's been a step forward. The DSP is forced to subsidise it, but not as much as we were with *Direct Action*. The branches are making money from it generally, for some it's become a positive part of their budget instead of a drain. Who would have dreamed of this sort of solution to the financial problems of a socialist party and its paper – increase the size of it by 50 percent, splash more colour on, change the name, make it broader and independent, and accessible ... Most people would have cut back, in size, or frequency, and that was the other alternative facing us. But we always were an ambitious party.
>
> In spite of the fact that it is not the paper of the DSP, *Green Left Weekly* has been a step forward in helping to build the party. It's extended the reach of the DSP – one indicator is that we're getting a greater number of clip-offs inquiring about the party than we have for years. This is to be expected, just from the increased circulation alone, but it seems to be even more than that.
>
> It's clear that *Green Left Weekly* has been partly responsible for a pleasing revival of Resistance this year.

My report outlined how we could build on this success, especially by reaffirming the role of the party. "We've been tightening up the party for at least a year and a half now, making the necessary adjustments, restoring provisional membership, making attendance at branch meetings a norm of membership, restoring the sustainers system of raising finances. They're all showing good results.

"And again at our June National Committee meeting this year the party-building report thoroughly reaffirmed our party building perspectives in the light of the developments in Eastern Europe and the impending events in the Soviet Union."

I noted that there was "a very specific central point" in that earlier report which was "still not fully implemented around the country. The report registered that party building tasks took priority over our involvement in movement/mass struggles – *Green Left Weekly*, party work, etc., first, then mass work. It was a turn from our orientation in the 1980s. It reaffirmed our turn to party-building.

"We simply must pause and put time into training and education to rebuild our cadre, our striking power." I noted our weaknesses: the inexperience of our newer cadre, the fact that we were much too small for what we'd like to do and that we were still facing a financial crisis. But probably the most important weakness was our party profile, and *GLW* couldn't go further without a strengthening of the party.

We decided to re-establish the party magazine as a quarterly; produce more posters and stickers, leaflets and pamphlets; organise more union coverage in *GLW*, and a DSP union supplement every few months, as well as other supplements; reverse our previous decision to suspend the party school for a period, and step up branch education. We needed to rewin some gains of the past, re-establishing the socialist tradition, and building up our party spirit. *GLW* had helped our finances, so there wasn't as big a deficit as in 1990; it was better this year by $70,000, but still difficult. The switch back from the Marxist Resource Fund to the sustainer system had proved extremely successful.

We looked ahead to the party's 14th national conference in January, noting that it would "mark the 20th anniversary of the founding of the party", so we wanted to use it as "a special focus for the conference, a celebration of our history, our tradition".

"All our projections and plans fit together … We need to develop a higher DSP profile, we need to raise comrades' consciousness and commitment; we need to continue to recruit and build Resistance, and educate, train, and consolidate our new comrades; we need to build on the success of *Green Left Weekly* by reaching out with it further and making our circulation targets."

Party building perspectives for the 1990s

Jim's report to the October DSP National Committee, "Party-building perspectives for the 1990s", is reprinted in *Traditions, Lessons and Socialist Perspectives*. I'd recommend the whole book, with all four important talks by Jim we printed, but especially this one.

In his report "Party, Alliance and Movement" Jim said that we needed to learn how to speak in two "languages", because our cadres, such as the NC members here, were convinced, but our newer members were not. The "party question" was the key way in which the political slide was expressed out there on the left; therefore it was the key political question.

The final defeat of the Russian Revolution affected working-class consciousness, and it shifted the labour bureaucrats towards a capitalist orientation and alliance with our rulers, as opposed to the past attempts to maintain ties with the working class.

Political leadership must be built *before*, not during a crisis. Things could get worse before they get better. But our intervention does count for something.

1992 DSP conference

Our 14th national conference was held January 2-6, 1992, at UWS Hawkesbury, with the theme, "Fighting the New World Order". Reports were: Peter Boyle, "Fighting the New World Order"; Doug Lorimer, "The Decline and Fall of Stalinism"; Dick Nichols, "Australia at the Crossroads"; Reihana Mohideen, "Political Perspectives for the DSP"; Jim Percy, "The DSP and the Crisis of the Left"; Max Lane, "Indonesian Politics 26 Years After the Coup"; John Percy, "Building the DSP in 1992"; Anne O'Callaghan, "Building Resistance in 1992"; Pat Brewer, "Women's Liberation and Socialism".

The conference rally was a celebration of the 20th anniversary of the DSP.

At the NC following the conference, I explained that some would have been aware that Jim had been ill over the last few months. He had made it through the first four days of the conference, but today he was out of it.

"It necessitates some changes in our national assignments. We're proposing Jim step back from his day-to-day role as national secretary. He'll maintain a key political role, but not stressful, not 'the buck stops here' position. We propose he becomes national president, with the assignments of an educational, political writing role, the school, and prepare documents, articles, pamphlets. (This is long overdue for us anyway, something we neglected over the last 20 years.) In some ways for the party it could be blessing in disguise, though I'm not sure Jim quite sees this very painful and debilitating illness quite like this."

So I moved that Jim become national president, I take on the assignment of national secretary, Pat Brewer be assistant national secretary, Doug Lorimer international secretary and Reihana Mohideen national finance secretary.

But Jim's illness had been misdiagnosed. It was not irritable bowel syndrome but bowel cancer, which had spread to the liver before it was properly diagnosed. Jim died in October.

Some conclusions

We had come a long way in the party's first two decades. We had survived when other currents had disintegrated. Especially, we had succeeded in relation to the CPA, the main force on the left when we began, and against whom we built first the youth organisation, and then a party.

We had also done well compared to other currents from the Trotskyist tradition, some of whom were stronger than us at different stages, especially the SLL. We learned and developed, while they succumbed to sect politics.

This volume has often focused on changes – on things we learned from experience, from our study and sometimes from mistakes. Here it's worth recapitulating those important elements of our party's program that remained the same, the basic pillars that didn't change, those features that distinguished our political theory and practice throughout the party's first two decades.

First was our basic revolutionary perspective. We carved out our political space in Australia by defending a revolutionary perspective in opposition to the reformist, class-collaborationist outlook of the Labor Party and those in the Communist movement who had been infected by this position.

Secondly, we maintained our critique of Stalinism. We continued to defend a vision of socialism as democratic and anti-bureaucratic. Although we abandoned Trotskyism, and relinquished some of the theoretical positions of Leon Trotsky, Trotsky's analysis of Stalinism still stood us in good stead.

Thirdly, we were still very much an internationalist party. We didn't belong to an international organisation, but we had an international political perspective, and put great store by the solidarity we could offer to revolutionaries around the world, and valued the lessons we could learn from them.

Fourthly, we still had a mass orientation. We knew that a successful socialist transformation of Australian society requires the active participation of the vast majority of workers, farmers, women and other oppressed layers, and that our party's role was to participate in all the struggles of the oppressed, learn from them and help lead them.

Fifthly, we had always been a serious, dedicated, activist party, and we didn't just dabble with the important goals that we set ourselves. We tried to give 100 percent commitment and effort to any task in hand. And we'd built a team and an organisation that could think independently and flexibly to carry out these tasks. This flowed from our understanding of the party question, our clear recognition of its absolute necessity, its centrality in the struggle for socialism.

Sixthly, we had always had a central orientation to young people, and we'd been successful in relating to and winning new layers of radicalising young people to socialist politics. We'd also been willing to give young revolutionaries real responsibility for leading struggles. As part of this, we had always stressed the role of a revolutionary socialist youth organisation like Resistance, remembering those lessons, continuing those struggles and joining up with a new generation of youth.

ENDNOTES

1   John Percy, *A History of the Democratic Socialist Party and Resistance. Volume 1: 1965-72, Resistance,* Chippendale NSW, Resistance Books, 2005.

2   The 1969 Fourth International World Congress discussed a document that was produced as a pamphlet that we found useful, *The Worldwide Radicalisation of Youth and the Tasks of the Fourth International.* It was written by Caroline Lund, a leader of the US SWP.

3   It lasted only six issues, but the printing business became one of the largest book publishers in Australia.

4   SWL Information Bulletin No. 5 in 1972, November.

5   Vol. 1, pp. 130-32.

6   Vol. 1, pp. 136-37.

7   Vol. 1, pp. 137-39.

8   Vol. 1, p. 281.

9   Steve Keen, "Launch of 'Political Economy Now!'", http://www.debtdeflation.com/blogs/2009/04/27/launch-of-political-economy-now/#sthash.tZtrEgio.dpuf.

10 See Denis Freney's autobiography, *A Map of Days. Life on the Left,* Heinemann, 1991.

11 An article in the US SWP journal *International Socialist Review,* June 1974, gave Gordon's history – "An Australian Communist's Political Journey; From Stalinism to Trotskyism", by Gordon Adler.

12 March 2, 1973, leaflet, presumably handed out at CP district conference.

13 Mick Armstrong, *One, Two Three, What are We Fighting For? The Australian student movement from its origins to the 1970s,* Socialist Alternative, Melbourne, 2001, p. 80.

14 Pathfinder Press, New York, 1979.

15 See Barry Sheppard, *The Party: The Socialist Workers Party 1960-1988, Volume 2: Interregnum, Decline and Collapse, 1973-1988, A Political Memoir,* London, Resistance Books, n.d., Chapter 5.

16 SWL Information Bulletins No. 3 and No. 4 in 1972.

17 Email from Chris Slee, December 11, 2015 – A.M.

18 Joe Hansen's report on the World Congress to a meeting of the New York caucus of the Leninist Trotskyist Faction on March 12, 1974, gives a thorough assessment. Hansen, *The Leninist Strategy of Party Building,* p. 442.

19 Fred Halstead, *Out Now!: A Participant's Account of the American Movement against the Vietnam War,* New York, Pathfinder Press, 1978.

20 https://www.facebook.com/personsofinteresttheasiofiles.

21 Nguyen Van Rinh, *Not only in the past,* as told to Nguyen Duy Tuong, translated by Nguyen Minh Y, Hanoi, People's Army Publishing House, 2014. Rinh later headed VAVA,

the Vietnamese Association for the Victims of Agent Orange, and toured Australia in that capacity in 2013.

22 Tiziano Terzani, *Giai Phong! The Fall and Liberation of Suigon,* New York, St. Martin's Press, 1976.

23 This article was written from the standpoint of our support for the Trotskyist theory of permanent revolution, which we had not yet abandoned. It was therefore highly critical of the Vietnamese leaders and the policies they had followed since 1945. In 2005, when the editor of *Green Left Weekly* (without having read the article carefully) sounded me out about reprinting it to mark the 30th anniversary of the Vietnamese victory, I replied that the article was "the best article I wish I had never written". – A.M.

24 This brief account is summarised from Barry Sheppard, *The Party: The Socialist Workers Party (1960-1988, Vol. 2: Interregnum, Decline and Collapse, 1973-1988,* London, Resistance Books, n.d. – A.M.

25 Lenin, "In Australia", *Collected Works,* Vol. 19, p. 216.

26 Lenin, *Collected Works,* Vol. 31, p. 257. Also in *Lenin on Britain,* Progress Publishers, Moscow, 1973, pp. 460-61.

27 *Militant,* Vol. 1, No. 1, September 1972, p. 2.

28 Tony Cliff, *The Crisis: Social Contract or Socialism,* London, Pluto Press, 1975, Chapter 9.

29 Lenin, *Collected Works,* Vol. 19, Moscow, 1964, p. 217.

30 John Percy had highlighted the reference to Anne Summers, probably indicating that he was citing this from memory and intended to check it in his files. I was not able to find the article. – A.M.

31 Jeff Sparrow and Rjurik Davidson, "A life in mirrors", Overland, Spring 2009.

32 Discussion Bulletin Vol. 7, No. 12, December 1978. Alternative organisational principles document – By John E, Chris S, Gwynn E, Iain M, Joanne T, John Ca.

33 Discussion Bulletin Vol. 7, No. 18, January 1979.

34 Resistance Books, 1998, 98 pp.

35 Lenin, *"Left-Wing" Communism: an Infantile Disorder,* https://www.marxists.org/archive/lenin/works/1920/lwc/ch07.htm.

36 Hall Greenland, *Red Hot: The Life and Times of Nick Origlass,* Wellington Lane Press, 1998.

37 John McCarthy died after a long battle with cancer in November 2008. He remained true to the socialist convictions that he'd embraced in his youth, although for the last few decades he had concentrated on his heavy responsibilities as a doctor. From 1990, he was director of intensive care at the Prince Charles Hospital, Brisbane, earning great respect for his skills, his commitment and his fiercely caring attitude to his patients. The hospital's new intensive care unit has been named after him.

38 Peter Robb became a well-reviewed author and novelist, with books *Midnight in*

Sicily; M: The Caravaggio Enigma; A Death in Brazil and *Street Fight in Naples.*
39 The "new mass vanguard" referred to the ultra-left line of the FI majority in regard to Europe.
40 Details thanks to ASIO report on Sydney I&P meeting.
41 Barney Mokgatle was one of the leaders of the 1976 Soweto student movement.
42 Bala Tampoe was the best-known leader of the Sri Lankan Trotskyists and general secretary of the Ceylon Mercantile, Industrial and General Workers Union.
43 Presumably, this was the first proposed title of the magazine eventually published as *Malaysian Socialist Review.*
44 I don't know if John recalled who this comrade was. I have not been able to discover who it was. - A.M.
45 New York, Merit Publishers, 1968.
46 https://www.marxists.org/history/etol/document/fi/1963-1985/usfi/9thWC/usfi01.htm
47 Sydney, Resistance Books, 1981.
48 Sydney, Resistance Books, 1984.
49 Graham Hastings, *It Can't Happen Here: A Political History of Australian Student Activism,* Students' Association of Flinders University, 2003, p. 323.
50 Party Organiser, Vol. 2, No. 3, June 1979. (I was not able to find this issue of the Party Organiser. The summary and quotes in the text are taken from Jim's typescript in John's files. – A.M.)
51 *The Balkan wars: 1912-13 : the war correspondence of Leon Trotsky,* Sydney, Resistance Books, 1980.
52 There were only eight names listed orginally, not nine. Thanks to Chris Slee, who tracked down the name of John Campbell in an old internal bulletin. – A.M.
53 It may be that not enough information was forthcoming in time. The printed agenda for the July 1978 National Committee meeting does not include anything on the CPA – A.M.
54 The manuscript does not indicate the subject of this circular, and I was unable to find that document in John's files. However, in separate emails dated November 2, 2015, both Udry and Sheppard indicate that the topic was probably the attempt of Argentine Trotskyist to intervene in the Nicaraguan Revolution with the so-called Simon Bolivar Brigade. – A.M.
55 Our thinking on this question was set down in Doug Lorimer, *Trotsky's theory of Permanent Revolution – A Leninist critique,* Resistance Books, Sydney, 1998.
56 Doug Lorimer, *The Making of a Sect: The evolution of the US Socialist Workers Party,* Sydney, New Course, 1984.
57 We published both of these as books. Sydney, Pathfinder Press (Australia), 1984.
58 Jim Percy and Doug Lorimer, *The Democratic Socialist Party and the Fourth*

International, Sydney, Resistance Books, 2001.

59 Sydney, Pathfinder Press, 1980.

60 Until his death, John Percy was the president of Agent Orange Justice. – A.M.

61 http://gushorowitz.wordpress.com/2012/06/24/on-the-formation-of-the-jack-barnes-cult-in-the-swp/.

62 Looking up on the internet one of John's references to an early member of the SYA and SWL, I found the person operating a blog attacking socialists on the basis that God doesn't like them. – A.M.

63 Email from Barry Sheppard, February 19, 2016. – A.M.

64 Tom Bramble, *Thirteen wasted years? Labor in power (1983-96) and its Accord with the unions,* http://sa.org.au/interventions/accord.htm.

65 Email from Max Lane, November 6, 2015. – A.M.

66 In an email (September 25, 2015), Andrew Jamieson recalled: "I shifted to Rosebery and started work in the EZ mine in February 1984. I'm not sure whether we constituted a formal branch then (there were only four of us – Jock (Finlay) Ferguson, John Rattray, Jimmy Gilleece and myself) but we certainly met to discuss political events and the industrial scene in Rosebery and beyond. Our collaboration lasted for over a year until each of the others retired and shifted to Devonport and Launceston ..." – A.M.

67 John's manuscript originally described the listed reports as being presented at both a July and an October NC meeting. From published documents, it appears that October is correct. – A.M.

68 Published in *Labor and the Fight for Socialism,* New Course, Sydney, 1988. Also included is an introduction by Steve Painter; "The ALP, the Nuclear Disarmament Party and the 1984 elections", Jim's report to the October 1984 SWP NC (incorrectly identified in the pamphlet as having occurred in September); and "SWP policy in the 1987 federal elections", a report by Doug Lorimer to the Sydney branch of the SWP on June 30, 1987.

69 Manning Clark, *A History of Australia,* Vol. 6, pp. 453-54.

70 All the remarks from Jim Percy's report, and all those below from Doug Lorimer's report, are from Jim Percy and Doug Lorimer, *The Socialist Workers Party and the Fourth International,* Pathfinder Press (Australia), 1985.

71 John Tognolini, "Hilton bombing frame-up collapses at last", *Green Left Weekly,* June 12, 1991.

72 Jim Percy, *Building the Revolutionary Party. Some recent experiences,* New Course Publications, 1988.

73 John Percy had cited this only as "Petersen p380". I do not have the book, but presume this refers to Petersen's autobiography, *George Petersen Remembers.* – A.M.

74 *Green Left Weekly,* February 28, 1996. The article was signed "John Baker", but strong internal evidence shows that this was a pseudonym for Petersen. – A.M.

75 Jim Percy, *Building the Revolutionary Party: Some recent experiences,* New Course

Publications, 1988. It was also published in Jim Percy, *Selected Writings 1980-87*, Resistance Books, 2008. pp.166-204.

76 Jim Percy, *What Politics for a New Party?*, New Course Publications, 1987.

77 Doug Lorimer, *The Collapse of 'Communism' in the USSR: Its causes & significance*, New Course Publications, 1992.

78 They included: Maria Shevtsova, Chen Ji, Sang Ye, Kate Hannan, Humphrey McQueen, Herb Thompson, Simon Marginson, Jamie Doughney, Stephen Knight, John Matthews, Peggy Trompf, John O'Brien, Tom Bramble, Stephen Wheatcroft, Dipesh Chakrabarty, Bruce Corum, Rana Roy, David McMullen, Rick Kuhn, Mervyn Hartwig, Ann Junor, Rachel Sharp, William Sutherland, David Glanz, Gerard Steele, Dennis Fitzpatrick, Bob Gould, Janet Parker, Sid Walker, Deborah White, Ian Jamieson, John Queripel, John Murphy, John Minns, Jim Falk, Pip Hinman, Kevin Parker, Dennis Altman, Helen Meekosha, Andrew Milner, Jeremy Smith, Peter Boyle, Peter Beilharz, Andrew Wells, Paul Gillen, Robyn Eckersley, Ross Gwyder, Rob White, Jim Levy, Peter Ross, Craig Everson, Ghassan Hage, Ephriam Nimni, Beverly Silver, Max Lane, Craig Browne, Matthew Stafford, Declan O'Connell, Mike Donaldson, Paul James, Phil Griffiths, Rob Gowland, Ken McKenzie Wark, Brian Martin, Mark Rix, Carole Ferrier, Rose McCann, Kathleen Weekley, Catherine Brown, Allen Myers, Gillian Fulcher, Steve Wright, Eileen Haley, Oscar Cortez, Stephen Eslake, Caroline Graham, Diane Fieldes, Jonathan Strauss, Bronwyn Levy, Ken Gelder, Jock Collins, Ken Davis, Robert Ariss, Lib Edmonds, Gerard Thomas, Diana Allen, Harry van Moorst, Coral Wynter, Nick Economou, Margo Huxley, Melba Marginson, Jack Mundey, Bruce MacFarlane, Andrew Milner, John Hinkson, Will Kenworthy, Margaret Moussa, Sue Bolton, Glenys Livingstone, David Holmes, Helen Jarvis, Joss Supraapto, Charles Sedgwick, Ed Davis, Roger Spegele, Roger Markwick, Steve Robson, Peter Lovell, Dorothy Parker, Doug Lorimer, Andrew Honey, Lisa Macdonald, Drew Hutton, Bob James, Ian Rintoul, Martin Mulligan, Mick Armstrong, Mahinda Seneviratne, Robert Bollard, Eva Cox, Julius Roe, Meredith Burgmann, Pat Gorman.

79 The others were Ian Bolas, Neville Curtis, Mark Delmege, Pat Gorman, Caroline Graham, David Groves, Kevin Healy, Marit Hegge, Clarrie Isaacs, Anne Junor, Des Lawrence, Lee Marling, Clare McNamara, Jeff Richards, Mark Taylor, Harry van Moorst, Gabrielle Walsh, Rod Webb, Sean Whelan, Deborah White, Hughie Williams.

INDEX